WORLD LITERATURE AND THOUGHT

Volume III
The Modern World to 1900

WORLD LITERATURE AND THOUGHT

Volume III
The Modern World to 1900

Donald S. Gochberg
General Editor

Surjit Singh Dulai

Aníbal González

Edward D. Graham

Kenneth W. Harrow

Priscilla Meléndez

Harcourt College Publishers

Fort Worth Philadelphia San Diego New York Orlando Austin San Antonio
Toronto Montreal London Sydney Tokyo

Publisher	Earl McPeek
Executive Editor	David Tatom
Market Strategist	Steve Drummond
Development Editor	steve Norder
Project Editor	Joyce Fink
Art Director	Burl Sloan
Production Manager	Linda McMillan

Cover credits: Left picture is Berini, *David,* Gallerai Borhese, Roma. Scala/Art Resource, NY. Right picture is *Court Official with Cross Pendant,* Court of Benin, Nigeria, Edo. Metalwork-Brass. 16–17th Century. H: 23³/4" (65.4 cm). The Metropolitan Museum of Art, Gift of Mr. & Mrs. Klaus G. Perls, 1991. (1991.17.32). Photograph © 1991 The Metropolitan Musuem of Art.

ISBN: 0-15-500921-4
Library of Congress Catalog Card Number: 97-79697

Address for Domestic Orders: Harcourt College Publishers, 6277 Sea Harbor Drive, Orlando, FL 32887-6777. 800-782-4479

Address for International Orders: International Customer Service, Harcourt, Inc., 6277 Sea Harbor Drive, Orlando, FL 32887-6777. 407-345-3800, (fax) 407-345-4060, (e-mail) hbintl@harcourt.com

Address for Editorial Correspondence: Harcourt College Publishers, 301 Commerce Street, Suite 3700, Fort Worth, TX 76102

Web Site Address: http://www.harcourtcollege.com

Printed in the United States of America

0 1 2 3 4 5 6 7 8 9   016   9 8 7 6 5 4 3 2 1

Harcourt College Publishers

Contents

World Literature and Thought
General Editor Donald S. Gochberg
Michigan State University

Volume I
The Ancient Worlds
Edited by Donald S. Gochberg, Surjit Singh Dulai,
Edward D. Graham, and Kenneth W. Harrow

Volume II
The Middle Periods
Edited by Donald S. Gochberg, Surjit Singh Dulai,
Edward D. Graham, Kenneth W. Harrow,
Priscilla Meléndez, and Aníbal González

Volume III
The Modern World to 1900
Edited by Donald S. Gochberg, Surjit Singh Dulai,
Aníbal González, Edward D. Graham,
Kenneth W. Harrow, and Priscilla Meléndez

Volume IV
The Twentieth Century
Edited by Donald S. Gochberg, Surjit Singh Dulai,
Edward D. Graham, Kenneth W. Harrow,
and Larry J. Simon

Introduction to the *World Literature and Thought* Series

The four volumes of *World Literature and Thought* offer a rich treasury of selections from many of the world's major civilizations. These books present a diverse array of genres and languages—from philosophical treatises to love lyrics, and from ancient Akkadian to modern English. The selections have been chosen for their lasting historical or intellectual significance, as well as for their readability. Because of the chronological structure of the volumes, readers can more readily understand the historical contexts of the selections. Generally, we envision these carefully edited primary documents as being of most use for college-level courses in humanities, in the history of world civilizations, and in comparative or world literature.

With such a range of possible selections available to the editors, we sought to include only works that are of interest to both the searching student and the academic specialist. We have chosen works also because they exerted a significant influence on their own and later times, frequently even well outside their original cultures. Each selection is intended to be long enough to give both a clear view of the author's ideas or narrative development and a sense of the text's literary qualities. Shorter selections—lyric poems, for example—are usually printed without any abridgment. The principles of selection and annotation are modeled after Harcourt's long-established, four-volume *Classics of Western Thought* series, 4th ed., 1988. Excellence, literary or intellectual, has remained the essential criterion of selection.

The selections appear generally in chronological order throughout the volumes: *The Ancient Worlds* (Volume I, roughly 2000 B.C. to A.D. 500), *The Middle Periods* (Volume II, 500 to 1500), *The Modern World to 1900* (Volume III, 1500 to 1900), and *The Twentieth Century* (Volume IV). Each selection is introduced by a headnote that places the work in its historical moment, gives a brief account

of the author's life (where authorship is known), and generally clarifies the significance of the particular work. Although every selection also is generously footnoted,
the astute reader will certainly want to refer occasionally to a standard college
desk dictionary since we saw no need—most of the time—to supply footnotes
for the meanings of words found there. All necessary factual information beyond
the common reader's knowledge is provided for each selection. The footnotes
clarify unusual words, as well as geographical and historical allusions. Brackets
within the texts indicate an insertion by one of the editors. Critical interpretations usually are left to the instructor and the reader. The instructor may also
wish to use the volumes in conjunction with one of the several world history narrative texts that are readily available. Each of the volumes contains sufficient depth
to function as the primary text for an academic term; all four, or any two, could
provide varied reading fare for an academic year or longer.

Scrutiny of the "Contents" for each volume will show extraordinarily varied
encounters of literature and ideas not previously seen within a single binding.
Rather than creating separate volumes for each culture or language, we have chosen
to integrate the collection. The reader, therefore, can more readily make his or
her own connections and distinctions. The choice of selections was the result of
two years of collegial discussions among the editors. Through those searching
conversations, we were also able to clarify similarities and relationships not usually noted among diverse literatures. Four of the six editors contributing to the
full series shared many years of an interdisciplinary teaching experience in the
former Department of Humanities at Michigan State University. All of the editors are both specialists in their respective fields, noted in each volume's "Preface,"
and seasoned generalists, accustomed to integrating diverse fields of knowledge.

Unique to this series is the inclusion of many documents *not* usually considered "literary." The greatest concern, in fact, when we made our choices was not
a selection's belletristic qualities but rather its intrinsic interest and readability.
We also considered whether a potential selection carried great authority in its
own time, as well as in later times and other places. Thus, for example, in
Volume I we include not only five books from Homer's adventurous epic, *The
Odyssey,* but also a generous selection from *The Laws* of the ancient Babylonian
ruler Hammurabi, which influenced the religiously-based laws of the Hebrew
Bible (also included) set down at least five centuries later. Another example of
the series' inclusiveness of genres, from the dozens of available examples, comes
from Volume II where we include not only a significant selection from the Ira-
nian (Persian) national epic *Shahnama,* but also a sampling of essential Islamic
theology that shows the interpenetration of the expanding Muslim religion with
earlier modes of literature and thought. In Volume III, illustrating the series' diversity, we include a large sampling of selections from both the Spanish conquerors of the New World and the subjugated Native Americans.

To help the reader organize his or her reading, selections from the same language and era are usually clustered together. Also, on a larger organizational scale,

each of the four volumes is divided into various parts which have both chronological and thematic significance. For example in Volume I, Part I, "Foundational Patterns," the reader can see emerging some of the basic value structures—religious, legal, societal, personal—in ancient cultures as diverse as Mesopotamia, Egypt, Israel, Greece, India, and China. These were differing cultures that were, nevertheless, struggling toward the same goal of establishing a good and stable society. Another useful feature is the part designated as "Cultural Encounters" that concludes Volumes II and III. Here is the literature of travel and exploration at the meeting points of contrasting cultures, often seen from the observation point of a non-Western traveler. Indeed, not only in the designated parts but throughout the four volumes, cultural encounters, parallels, and contrasts are revealed and pointed out to the reader.

Even with this vast library collected for the readers' instruction and delight, it was not possible to include worthy examples from all the civilizations and languages whose texts have survived to our day. Yet, though much has necessarily been omitted, much remains. It would, perhaps, not be vainly inappropriate to conclude this brief introduction with a paraphrase of Dr. Samuel Johnson to the effect that he who tires of the wealth of humanity and its works revealed in these volumes must surely be tired of life; for there is represented in *World Literature and Thought* all that life can offer.

Donald S. Gochberg
General Editor

Preface to
The Modern World to 1900

This third volume in the *World Literature and Thought* series contains an astonishing variety of texts. In the West we begin with literature by the striving new men of the Renaissance who looked back for their inspiration to what they perceived as the heroic glory of ancient Greece and Rome. We end in the West at the dawn of the twentieth century with Dostoevsky's penetration into humanity's tortured psyche and Nietzsche's yearning for a "Superman" who will rescue civilization from the mediocrity of the dominant "slave morality." In the East we begin with a fifteenth-century poem by Jami, the last major writer of classical Persian literature, and end with Vietnamese and Indian writers who exemplify the rising tides of nineteenth-century nationalism. Africa is also well represented in chronicles, epics, and tales. This is the first volume in the series to have a significant number of selections from the Americas, as those two great continents began to assume their places, first in a colonial context and then, increasingly, as independent cultures equal to long-established societies in Europe, Asia, and Africa. As we read through the volume, despite the many conflicts, we can see the prospect of a truly global society begin to emerge.

We conclude the fifty-three chapters with a series of "cultural encounters" in which travelers from one civilization or culture record their observations of other civilizations or cultures—sometimes curious and friendly, sometimes hostile and bloody. The selections are roughly in chronological order, with the earliest from the fifteenth century and the latest from the end of the nineteenth. Sometimes the chronological arrangement is disturbed a bit for the sake of linguistic, geographical, or thematic clusters. For example, Selections 42–43 are grouped together, as they each represent literary aspects of the Indian subcontinent; Selections 36–38 are widely separated in time, but their materials are all essentially African in origin. The wealth of material offered here should enable readers to pick those civilizations and topics that they find of greatest interest. Or readers may choose to read through the contents in the given order, aided by the many cross-references.

The single greatest omission from this volume is that of Shakespearian drama. Surely no education is complete without the experience of reading *Hamlet, King*

Lear, Othello, The Tempest, and other products of Shakespeare's comprehensive imagination. But those plays are so readily available in inexpensive paperback editions that the editors deemed it wiser to use their precious pages for less ubiquitous materials. Also, although a few nineteenth-century novels are excerpted in this collection, the editors believe that the instructor could select a novel for his course from among the currently available treasury of great English, French, and Russian fictional narratives to suit his own students' needs.

No rigid formula was employed in allocating the number or length of the selections for each culture, civilization, region, or language. Rather, the existing proportions resulted from the significance of particular selections within their own cultural context, as well as in the context of world history. The areas of primary editorial responsibility for this volume are the following: Donald Gochberg: General Editor, Europe, and North America (Selections 2, 3, 5, 20, 22, 27, 30, 33, 40–41, 45–48, 52); Surjit Dulai: South Asia and Islam (Selections 1, 4, 10, 12, 24–25, 42–43, 51); Aníbal González and Priscilla Meléndez: Hispanic, Portuguese, and New World (Selections 11, 16–17, 21, 23, 28–29, 32, 34-35, 39, 53); Edward Graham: East Asia (Selections 8–9, 13–15, 18–19, 44, 49–50); Kenneth Harrow: Africa and African-American (Selections 6–7, 26, 31, 36–38). Each editor is both an expert in the field appropriate to his or her individual selections and a seasoned teacher who has discussed his or her selections, as well as many others that could not be included here, with numerous university classes.

Although every selection has its own introductory headnote, there are also general introductions to each of the seven major parts of this volume: "New Vitality" (Selections 1–5), "Celebrating Past Grandeur" (Selections 6–11), "The Reality of Everyday Life" (Selections 12–19), "The Re-Examination of Tradition" (Selections 20–26), "Reason, Science, and Societal Organization" (Selections 27–34), "Gods, Human, and Nature" (Selections 35–48), and "Cultural Encounters" (Selections 49–53). The introductions to the various parts are intended to help the reader see more readily the structural scope of the volume. The editors hope that the readers of these selections will not only increase their knowledge of the varied cultures and civilizations of the early modern period, but will also better understand their own connections and debts to other continents and other times.

Donald S. Gochberg
General Editor

A Note on Pronunciation of Chinese, Japanese, Korean, and Vietnamese

Selections 8, 13, 18, and 19 are translations from Chinese; Selections 9 and 14 are from Japanese; Selection 15 from Korean; and Selection 44 from Vietnamese. The first three of these languages are written in characters whose sound values are difficult to reproduce for readers unfamiliar with these languages. In translation, therefore, they have to be Romanized, that is represented by the phonetic symbols of our Roman alphabet. With the few exceptions always needed to preserve traditional spellings, we have used the Wade-Giles system of Romanization for Chinese, the Hepburn system for Japanese, and the McCune-Reischauer system for Korean. This note is designed to help readers get a basic sense of the sounds of names and other words which appear in these selections.

Chinese

Vowel sounds (*a, e, i, o, u*) are much like those of standard English usage, with the exception of the common vowel-consonant combination *ih*, which is pronounced like the *ir* in *fir*. Vowels occurring together are pronounced as diphthongs, for instance, *ao*, which gives a combined sound like the *ow* in *now*.

The following consonants, or consonant combinations—followed by an apostrophe in the Wade-Giles system: *ch', k', p', ts',* and *tz'*—are aspirated (accompanied by a distinct exhalation of breath) and are pronounced as they would be in English. But without the apostrophe following them (unaspirated), they have these sound values: *ch* as *j, k* as a hard *g, p* as *b, ts* and *tz* as *dz*. For example, the Chin Dynasty is pronounced as if it were Jin, the twentieth-century revolutionary leader Mao Tse-tung's name is pronounced as if it were Mao dze-dung, and the capital city Peking as if it were Beijing. An initial *hs* is close to the English *sh*, and *j* has a sound closer to the English *r*.

Japanese

Vowel sounds in Japanese are much like those of English usage. Two vowel combinations, *ai* and *ei,* are sounded together as diphthongs. All other vowels are pronounced as separate syllables.

Consonants are pronounced as in English, with *g* always a hard sound.

Korean

Most vowel and consonant sounds lie reasonably close to English usage. The frequently encountered diphthong *ae* has the sound of *a* as in *and.*

Vietnamese

Under colonial rule by Europeans, the Vietnamese language came to be written in the Roman alphabet, modified by an elaborate system of diacritical marks and some arbitrary sound values. The only difficult sound encountered in Selection 44 is the initial *ng* in the name of the author, Nguyen Du. It has the sound of those letters as found buried in an English word like *linger.*

Edward D. Graham
East Asian Editor

A Note on the Cover

Throughout human history people have striven to represent the heroic ideal. In the seventeenth century, Gianlorenzo Bernini created his version of *David* (1623). This life-size marble sculpture reveals an explosion out of the classicism of Bernini's great Renaissance predecessors such as Michelangelo (Selection 5), who also created a marble David. The imperially extravagant style dominated southern Europe and was carried around the world, especially to the far—flung colonies of Spain and Portugal. The Portuguese influence is seen in the other image on the cover: a bronze sculpture (23 3/4" high) from roughly the same period as Bernini. In this depiction, a court official from the kingdom of Benin (in present-day Nigeria) is wearing a cross pendant. Cross-cultural contact affected many aspects of life throughout the world during the period covered in this volume.

Many peoples have a term for *Hero.* In Arabic script (the second line on the upper left of the cover), but written the same in Persian, Urdu, and some African languages, the term means "the greatest." The Arabs pronounced it *A'dham.* In Persian and Urdu it is *A'zam.* In the Amharic language of Ethiopia, the Ge'ez script (third line) is pronounced *Araia.* It means "exemplary leader." But no matter what term is used—*Araia, A'dham,* or *Hero*—the meaning is the same in the literature of the world. Through stories people set up the examples of the heroic ideal and lessons learned from those who fail to match the ideal.

PART I

NEW VITALITY

❦

The selections in Part I of *The Modern World to 1900* date from the late fifteenth through the mid-seventeenth centuries. Paradoxically, these examples of "new vitality" begin with a selection that provides continuity with the past, looking back to the major Persian writers represented in Volume II, *The Middle Periods*. Jami, born in 1414, is generally considered the last great classical Persian writer. Like the leading Persian writers of the three centuries preceding his time, he was an exponent of Islamic mysticism, known as Sufism. His poetic and romantic version of the famous story of Joseph and Potiphar's wife, based on narratives in the Old Testament and in the Koran, is imbued with the mystical passion of Sufism.

In contrast to Jami's religious devotion, Machiavelli's *The Prince* (Selection 2) looks forward to the often cutthroat practical politics of the modern age. Machiavelli was the first political theorist in the West to summarize honestly and accurately the realistic principles that have always guided successful rulers. He did not invent new methods of acquiring and maintaining political power; in fact, Machiavelli often used the ancient Romans as historical models of how power should be used effectively. *The Prince* remains a handbook whose principles of political leadership are still in use as you read these words.

The third selection is a representative anthology of lyric poetry written during the Renaissance. In Europe the secular lyric poem regained a power and popularity in the Renaissance that it had not achieved since the ancient Greeks and Romans. The short lyric's outpouring of an individual's private feelings suited the generally increasing sense of life on earth as something that should be pleasurable and worthy of intense focus—not merely a painful sojourn on the way to eternal salvation. The poems—from Italian, Spanish, and English sources—include lyrics by Michelangelo

Buonarroti (among the greatest of both painters and sculptors), Garcilaso de la Vega (who brought the form of the Italian sonnet into Spanish poetry), Sir Thomas Wyatt (who did the same for English poetry), William Shakespeare (whose sonnets may be worthy of being ranked alongside his massive dramatic achievement), Lope de Vega (the most popular and prolific of the great masters of poetry and drama in Spain's "Golden Age"), and, finally, Andrew Marvell (whose brilliant seduction poem reprinted here may be the finest example of the classical theme of *carpe diem*, "seize the day," in English literature).

In the *Memoirs (Baburnama)* of Babur (Selection 4) we discover an extraordinary new literary vitality. His autobiography was the first in Islamic literature fit to stand with the other well-known autobiographies in world literature, and his remarkable life was well worth recording. Babur is not only a very important figure of Turkish literature, but he was also the conquering founder of the great Mughal empire of India, establishing a dynasty that was to rule the vast subcontinent from 1526 to 1857. The first excerpt from Babur's *Memoirs* tells of the capital of modern Afghanistan, Kabul, a city he dearly loved. The second excerpt deals with his conquest of India.

The most striking examples of the "new vitality" of the European Renaissance are found in the visual arts, especially in painting and sculpture. A knowledgeable and intimate account of the lives of the most extraordinary Renaissance artists was written by Giorgio Vasari (Selection 5), a competent painter and architect, who personally knew many of the painters, sculptors, and architects whose lives he chronicled and was a close friend of the great Michelangelo. It is in Vasari's short biographies that we see clearly how the artists modeled their creations on the surviving artifacts of the golden Greco-Roman past and regarded themselves as divinely inspired—not as merely skilled craftsmen who were imitating an established tradition.

1

❧

Jami

YUSUF AND ZULAIKHA

Nur al-Din Abd al-Rahman Jami (1414–1492) is generally considered the last major writer of classical Persian literature. He was known throughout the Islamic world and held in the highest esteem by his contemporaries and successors, fellow writers, patrons, and disciples alike. Babur (Selection 4), for example, says of Jami in his Memoirs that "in . . . learning there was none equal to him in his time," that he is "too exalted for there to be any need for praising him," adding that he brings up his name only "for luck and for a blessing." Like the other leading Persian writers of the three centuries preceding his time, Jami too was a Sufi mystic. Amazingly prolific and versatile, he was the author of three Divans (collections) of lyrical poetry, seven Masnavis (long didactic poems in couplets), and a very large number of prose works covering an extremely wide range of subjects, from Koranic exegesis and evidence of the Prophet Mohammad's divine mission to prosody and music. Jami's presence was sought by all the royal courts of the Islamic lands. The Ottoman sultan honored him with an award, though the sultan's wish to have Jami come to his court in Constantinople did not materialize. As a literary authority, Jami influenced many writers of the Islamic world from India to Turkey.

Jami was born at Jam, a village near Samarkand, in present-day Uzbekistan. His pen name is derived from this biographical fact and from the word "jam" which means "wine goblet." He studied for a career in theology at Samarkand and at Herat, now in Afghanistan. During the fifteenth century Herat was the capital of Khorasan in Eastern Iran. The seat of government of a Timurid kingdom (descended from the famous Turkish conqueror Timur, or Tamerlane), it was at the time the most sumptuous center of culture and fashion in the whole Islamic world. Studying under famous teachers of his day, Jami absorbed the learning they had to impart and was soon of the opinion that he had surpassed them both in knowledge and the art of argument. He asserted that he did not owe any of his accomplishments to his academic teachers: "I have found no master

3

with whom I have read superior to myself. On the contrary, I have invariably found that in argument I could defeat them all. I acknowledge, therefore, the obligations of a pupil to his master to none of them; for if I am a pupil of anyone, it is of my own father, who taught me the language." In contrast, Jami showed the greatest respect to his spiritual teachers, the Sufis, who guided him on the mystic's path.

After completing his studies, Jami embraced the mystical life of a Sufi, becoming an adherent of the Naqshbandi order. Naqshbandi was a conservative order, its followers staying close to orthodox Islam and not straying into heterodoxy. Jami became a practitioner of Sufism and an accomplished teacher-scholar of the Sufi doctrine, Islam, and literature. Later he began to write poetry also. Proud and independent intellectually, Jami was equally proud and independent as a person. Unlike most writers of the time, he spurned the seeking of patronage. Perhaps because of his pride, however, and certainly because of his accomplishments, patronage came to him. Sultan Husayn Bayqara, the Timurid ruler of Herat (r. 1469–1506), most famous in the Islamic world for his love of art and culture, founded a college expressly for Jami and appointed him as professor there. Jami was to live in Herat for the rest of his life. Under Sultan Husayn, Herat was a brilliant center of letters, art, and culture, attracting the best artists and writers. The sultan's minister Mir Ali Shir Nawai, himself a renowned poet and a prose writer of Turkish and Persian, became Jami's close friend and patron. Nawai wrote an entire work about Jami. At the end of it he speaks about Jami's death and his funeral which, he says, was celebrated with great pomp and honor, with members of the royal family, nobles, prominent figures of the religious establishment, writers and scholars, and a vast crowd of commoners attending it.

As a writer, Jami excelled in the volume of his output and the variety of his works. In the words of E. G. Browne, the distinguished historian of Persian literature, "No other Persian poet or writer has been so successful in so many different fields, and the enthusiastic admiration of his most eminent contemporaries is justified by his prolific and many-sided genius." According to one authority, Jami authored some ninety works. Jami himself tells us that most of his writing was done during the last fifteen years or so of his life. By far the largest number of his writings are in prose. The subjects of his prose works cover the entire range of learning in religious and secular letters, from different aspects of Islam to grammar, poetry, and commentary on other writers. Most prominent among the religious subjects is Sufism, a subject on which his scholarly fame and influence rested. Some of his most ambitious works of prose are Breaths of Fellowship, *a book containing 611 biographies of Sufi saints;* Flashes, *a treatise on mysticism; and* Evidences of Prophethood, *which describes at great length the signs and evidences of prophethood throughout Muhammad's life and work.*

Jami is best known as a poet. He wrote both lyrical and didactic poetry. His *lyrical verse consists of three* Divans *(collections), their titles* — Opening of Youth, Middle of the Necklace, *and* End of Life — *covering Jami's life chronologically. In his lyrics, Jami shows the influence of the earlier Sufi poets, Rumi and Hafiz*

(Volume II, Selections 37 and 38). The pride of place in Jami's poetry, however, belongs to his long didactic work, Haft Aurang (Seven Thrones), *a collection of seven* masnavis. *Although each of them contains allegorical elements to impart moral and religious lessons, three of them are allegories based entirely on the theme of love. The most celebrated of the three is the romance of* Yusuf and Zulaikha. *The story is found in Genesis of the Hebrew Bible, where it appears as the story of Joseph and Potiphar's wife, and in the Koran (Volume II, Selection 9), which calls it "the fairest of stories." Zulaikha's love for Yusuf became one of the most popular themes of romantic poetry in Persian and Turkish literature. Poets, including eminent ones such as Ferdowsi (Volume II, Selection 12), treated it again and again. Jami's version holds the highest place among all these renderings of the tale. The poetic history of the story shows an interesting evolution. In Genesis, it is a story of the adulterous lust of Potiphar's wife and Joseph's righteous innocence. In the Koran, Zulaikha recognizes her sinful conduct but expresses her helplessness before Yusuf's beauty. Yusuf and God are both forgiving of her situation. In popular lore, the story increasingly became a story of romantic love. Jami endows it with Sufi religious meaning. Yusuf's beauty becomes a manifestation of Divine beauty, the implication being that it is inevitable for Zulaikha and other women to fall in love with Yusuf, but their love for him as a creature should serve as a bridge to the love of the Creator. Jami immensely enjoyed telling the tale. As he says, "When I withdrew the Veil from this Mystery, and prepared this strange song, / The parrot of my genius became an eater of sugar from the story of Yusuf and Zulaikha. / In this outpouring of sugar there sprang from my pen sweet verses mingled with sugar."*

The following excerpt from Yusuf and Zulaikha *contains one of the most frequently cited episodes of the poem.*

ZULAIKHA AND THE WOMEN OF MEMPHIS

Love is ill suited with peace and rest:
Scorn and reproaches become him best.
Rebuke gives strength to his tongue, and blame
Wakes the dull spark to a brighter flame.
Blame is the censor of Love's bazaar:
It suffers no rust the pure splendour to mar.

From R. T. H. Griffith, tr. *Yusuf and Zulaykha.* London: Trubner and Co., 1882.

Blame is the whip whose impending blow
Speeds the willing lover and wakes the slow;
And the weary steed who can hardly crawl
Is swift of foot when reproaches fall.
When the rose of the secret has opened and blown,
The voice of reproach was a bulbul in tone.[1]

The women of Memphis,[2] who heard the tale first,
The whispered slander received and nursed.
Then, attacking Zulaikha for right and wrong,[3]
Their uttered reproaches were loud and long:
"Heedless of honour and name she gave
The love of her heart to the Hebrew slave,
Who lies so deep in her soul enshrined
That to sense and religion her eyes are blind.
She loves her servant. 'Tis strange to think
That erring folly so low can sink;
But stranger still that the slave she woos
Should scorn her suit and her love refuse.
His cold eye to hers he never will raise;
He never will walk in the path where she strays.
He stops if before him her form he sees;
If she lingers a moment he turns and flees.
When her lifted veil leaves her cheek exposed,
With the stud of his eyelash his eye is closed.
If she weeps in her sorrow he laughs at her pain,
And closes each door that she opens in vain.
It may be that her form is not fair in his eyes,
And his cold heart refuses the proffered prize.
If once her beloved one sat with us
He would sit with us ever, not treat us thus.
Our sweet society ne'er would he leave,
But joy unending would give and receive.
But not all have this gift in their hands: to enthral
The heart they would win is not given to all.

---

[1] In Persian poetry, the rose is a standard symbol of beauty and the *bulbul* (nightingale) that of a lover. Here the voice of reproach is further compared to the bulbul and the rose to the secret held within one's heart.

[2] Memphis was the capital of ancient Egypt. It was located to the southwest of present-day Cairo. The women in the story here are from the ruling families of the time.

[3] Zulaikha, a governor's wife, has fallen in love with Yusuf, a young Hebrew bought by her husband as a slave. The other women are finding fault with her conduct.

There is many a woman, fair, good, and kind,
To whom never the heart of a man inclined;
And many a Laila with soft black eye[4]
The tears of whose heart-blood are never dry."

Zulaikha heard, and resentment woke
To punish the dames for the words they spoke.
She summoned them all from the city to share
A sumptuous feast which she bade prepare.
A delicate banquet meet for kings
Was spread with the choicest of dainty things.
Cups filled with sherbet of every hue
Shone as rifts in a cloud when the sun gleams through.
There were goblets of purest crystal filled
With wine and sweet odours with art distilled.
The golden cloth blazed like the sunlight; a whole
Cluster of stars was each silver bowl.
From goblet and charger rare odours came;
There was strength for the spirit and food for the frame.
All daintiest fare that your lip would taste,
From fish to fowl, on the cloth was placed.
It seemed that the fairest their teeth had lent
For almonds, their lips for the sugar sent.
A mimic palace rose fair to view
Of a thousand sweets of each varied hue,
Where instead of a carpet the floor was made
With bricks of candy and marmalade.
Fruit in profusion, of sorts most rare,
Piled in baskets, bloomed fresh and fair.
Those who looked on their soft transparency felt
That the delicate pulp would dissolve and melt.
Bands of boys and young maidens, fine
As mincing peacocks, were ranged in line;
And the fair dames of Memphis, like Peris eyed,[5]
In a ring on their couches sat side by side.
They tasted of all that they fancied, and each
Was courteous in manner and gentle in speech.

---

[4] Laila, famed for her beauty, is the heroine of a story of romantic love called *Laila and Majnun,* as popular as *Yusuf and Zulaykha.*

[5] The English equivalent of the Persian *peri* is "fairy." In common parlance, a peri is a graceful and beautiful woman.

The feast was ended; the cloth was raised,
And Zulaikha sweetly each lady praised.
Then she set, as she planned in her wily breast,
A knife and an orange beside each guest:
An orange, to purge the dark thoughts within
Each jaundiced heart with its golden skin.
One hand, as she bade them, the orange clasped,
The knife in the other was firmly grasped
Thus she addressed them: "Dames fair and sweet,
Most lovely of all when the fairest meet,
Why should my pleasure your hearts annoy?
Why blame me for loving my Hebrew boy?
If your eyes with the light of his eyes were filled,
Each tongue that blames me were hushed and stilled.
I will bid him forth, if you all agree,
And bring him near for your eyes to see."
"This, even this," cried each eager dame,
"Is the dearest wish that our hearts can frame.
Bid him come; let us look on the lovely face
That shall stir our hearts with its youthful grace.
Already charmed, though our eyes never fell
On the youth we long for, we love him well.
These oranges still in our hands we hold,
To sweeten the spleen with their skins of gold.
But they please us not, for he is not here:
Let not one be cut till the boy appear."

She sent the nurse to address him thus:
"Come, free-waving cypress, come forth to us.
Let us worship the ground which thy dear feet press,
And bow down at the sight of thy loveliness.
Let our love-stricken hearts be thy chosen retreat,
And our eyes a soft carpet beneath thy feet."

But he came not forth, like a lingering rose
Which the spell of the charmer has failed to unclose.
Then Zulaikha flew to the house where he dwelt,
And in fond entreaty before him knelt:
"My darling, the light of these longing eyes,
Hope of my heart," thus she spoke with sighs,
"I fed on the hope which thy words had given;
But that hope from my breast by despair is driven.
For thee have I forfeited all; my name
Through thee has been made a reproach and shame.

I have found no favour: thou wouldst not fling
One pitying look on so mean a thing.
Yet let not the women of Memphis see
That I am so hated and scorned by thee.
Come, sprinkle the salt of thy lip to cure
The wounds of my heart and the pain I endure.
Let the salt be sacred: repay the debt
Of the faithful love thou shouldst never forget."

The heart of Yusuf grew soft at the spell
Of her gentle words, for she charmed so well.
Swift as the wind from her knees she rose,
And decked him gay with the garb she chose.
Over his shoulders she drew with care,
The scented locks of his curling hair,
Like serpents of jet-black lustre seen
With their twisted coils where the grass is green.
A girdle gleaming with gold, round the waist
That itself was fine as a hair, she braced.
I marvel so dainty a waist could bear
The weight of the jewels that glittered there.
She girt his brow with bright gems; each stone
Of wondrous beauty enhanced his own.
On his shoes were rubies and many a gem,
And pearls on the latchets that fastened them.
A scarf, on whose every thread was strung
A loving heart, on his arm was hung.
A golden ewer she gave him to hold,
And a maid brow-bound with a fillet of gold
In her hand a basin of silver bore,
And shadow-like moved as he walked before.
If a damsel had looked, she at once had resigned
All joy of her life, all the peace of her mind.
Too weak were my tongue if it tried to express
The charm of his wonderful loveliness.

Like a bed of roses in perfect bloom
The secret treasure appeared in the room.[6]
The women of Memphis beheld him, and took
From that garden of glory the rose of a look.

---

[6] The "secret treasure" here is Yusuf. The secretness suggests the mystery of his being as a manifestation of Divine beauty.

One glance at his beauty o'erpowered each soul
And drew from their fingers the reins of control.
Each lady would cut through the orange she held,
As she gazed on that beauty unparalleled.
But she wounded her finger, so moved in her heart,
That she knew not her hand and the orange apart.
One made a pen of her finger, to write
On her soul his name who had ravished her sight—
A reed which, struck with the point of the knife,
Poured out a red flood from each joint in the strife.
One scored a calendar's lines in red
On the silver sheet of her palm outspread,
And each column, marked with the blood-drops, showed
Like a brook when the stream o'er the bank has flowed.

When they saw that youth in his beauty's pride:
"No mortal is he," in amaze they cried.
"No clay and water composed his frame,
But, a holy angel, from heaven he came."
"'Tis my peerless boy," cried Zulaikha, "long
For him have I suffered reproach and wrong.
I told him my love for him, called him the whole
Aim and desire of my heart and soul.
He looked on me coldly; I bent not his will
To give me his love and my hope fulfill.
He still rebelled: I was forced to send
To prison the boy whom I could not bend.
In trouble and toil, under lock and chain,
He passed long days in affliction and pain.
But his spirit was tamed by the woe he felt,
And the heart that was hardened began to melt.
Keep your wild bird in a cage and see
How soon he forgets that he once was free."

Of those who wounded their hands, a part
Lost reason and patience, and mind and heart.
Too weak the sharp sword of his love to stay,
They gave up their souls ere they moved away.
The reason of others grew dark and dim,
And madness possessed them for love of him.
Bare-headed, bare-footed, they fled amain,
And the light that had vanished ne'er kindled again.
To some their senses at length returned,
But their hearts were wounded, their bosoms burned.

They were drunk with the cup which was full to the brim.
And the birds of their hearts were ensnared by him.
Nay, Yusuf's love was a mighty bowl
With varied power to move the soul.
One drank the wine till her senses reeled;
To another, life had no joy to yield;
One offered her soul his least wish to fulfil;
One dreamed of him ever, but mute and still.
But only the woman to whom no share
Of the wine was vouchsafed could be pitied there.

2

%

Niccolò Machiavelli

THE PRINCE

Niccolò Machiavelli (1469–1527), Italian diplomat, political theorist, and historian was born in Florence and devoted much of his life to the service of that city. In 1498 he gained the office of secretary of the Republic of Florence, a post he held until he was exiled in 1512 by the Medici family who had returned to power with the fall of the republican regime. In his post as secretary of the republic, Machiavelli traveled and corresponded extensively, thereby acquiring vast experience of practical politics. The Prince, written during Machiavelli's exile, is the most famous pragmatic essay ever written on the acquisition and maintenance of political power. It begins with Machiavelli's self-serving plea to the head of the ruling Medici family to allow the author to regain a political position in his native city. Although recalled by the Medici to Florence in 1525 to assist in the development of new fortifications for the city, he never regained the trust and position he had once enjoyed. Machiavelli died soon after the Medici heirs fled Florence and the city was again proclaimed a republic. Having worked for both the republic and for the Medici, Machiavelli was suspected by the new republican rulers. He died just before the news of his dismissal from official duties reached him.

Machiavelli wrote at least five enduring literary works: The Discourses on the First Ten Books of Titus Livy (1513–1517), The Prince (1513), The Art of War (1518–1520), The History of Florence (1520–1524), and the theatrical comedies Mandragola (1520) and Clizia (1525). In his Discourses on the Roman historian Livy's History of Rome, thought by some critics to be Machiavelli's greatest analytical work, he discusses the establishment, organization, and expansion of the state. For him the ideal prince is one who seeks sole power in order to establish a principality or, preferably, a republic. Once the republic is established, the prince shares with many men the responsibility for its welfare. The men of the Roman Republic, Machiavelli strongly believed, were the most effective practitioners of politics, knowing clearly how to acquire and maintain power for the common good. Only secular—not spiritual—power can preserve the state and keep it strong. His Art of War focuses especially on his study of Roman *military tactics and their application to contemporary Italy. Those laws and actions of the state that contribute to the common good also assist in the military preparations of its citizens. Machiavelli continued his analysis of the principles of secular power in* The Prince (Il Principe), *for which he interrupted his continuing work on the* Discourses.

In 1520 Machiavelli was commissioned to write The History of Florence. *By the time it was completed five years later, his Medici patron had been elevated to the papacy as Pope Clement VII. Inspired by Livy's method, Machiavelli avoided a mere chronological catalog and instead analyzed the importance of "civil discords and internal enmities upon foreign relations," avoiding completely the medieval mode of interpreting everything in terms of God's purpose. As he said in his Preface, Machiavelli wanted the reader to "draw those practical lessons which one should seek to obtain from the study of history." Machiavelli's successful stage comedies apply the same principles of skillful intrigue to social manners and sexual liaisons, condoning the use of unscrupulous means to gain one's desired ends.*

The Prince, Machiavelli's most popular work to the present day, asserts the principle that the ruler of the state is free to use whatever means are necessary to make the state secure. Although Machiavelli simply stated a doctrine already well known to those successful political leaders whom he admired, later generations often unfairly used the term "Machiavellism" as a reference to the devil's work—as if Machiavelli had caused man's fallen nature. In fact, the nickname of "Old Nick," referring to the devil, was coined by English mockers of Machiavelli from his first name. Actually, he simply wanted the civil peace that, at least in divided Italy, only a strong—even ruthless—ruler could bring about. And the need for Italian national unity is the thesis of the concluding chapter. Given the premises of the Discourses, *Machiavelli must have intended the rule of the strong prince who establishes a centralized government to be the first step toward the establishment of a democratic republic. Nothing happens to a state except by the application of power. The wise prince knows how most effectively to use that power.*

One way of understanding Machiavelli's view of the most effective ruler is his use of the term virtù. *This word occurs fifty-nine times in* The Prince, *and it has nothing to do with the medieval passive concept of* virtù, *involving contemplation and prayer, and nothing to do with the modern usage of "virtue" meaning moral excellence. Machiavelli intended his use of* virtù *to refer to such active qualities as manly prowess (*vir *means "man" in Latin), courage, capacity for action, strategy, strength, talent, inventive power, and other such aggressively creative meanings. (Where the original text uses* virtù *in the following excerpt the word is reprinted in brackets beside its varying translation.) On seventeen occasions in the complete text* virtù *is contrasted with* fortuna, *a word that refers to those variable circumstances, like chance, over which the prince, or any individual, has no control. Machiavelli conceives human life in terms* *of a struggle between* virtù *and* fortuna. *The effective prince—active men like Philip of Macedon, Alexander the Great, and Cesare Borgia—knows how to use his* virtù *to prepare for the more destructive aspects of* fortuna. *In his bountiful examples from recorded history and personal observation, Machiavelli follows the inductive method. This contrasts with the traditional medieval deductive method of such Christian thinkers as Saint Thomas Aquinas (Volume II, Selection 34) who reasoned from a base of authority and generally received principles.*

Niccolò Machiavelli
To The
Magnificent Lorenzo, Son of Piero de' Medici[1]

Those who desire to win the favor of princes generally endeavor to do so by offering them those things which they themselves prize most, or such as they observe the prince to delight in most. Thus it is that princes have very often presented to them horses, arms, cloth of gold, precious stones, and similar ornaments worthy of their greatness. Wishing now myself to offer to your Magnificence some proof of my devotion, I have found nothing amongst all I possess that I hold more dear or esteem more highly than the knowledge of the actions of great men, which I have acquired by long experience of modern affairs, and a continued study of ancient history.

These I have meditated upon for a long time, and examined with great care and diligence; and having now written them out in a small volume, I send this to your Magnificence. And although I judge this work unworthy of you, yet I trust that your kindness of heart may induce you to accept it, considering that I cannot offer you anything better than the means of understanding in the briefest time all that which I have learnt by so many years of study, and with so much trouble and danger to myself.

From Niccolò Machiavelli, *The Prince* in *The Historical, Political, and Diplomatic Writings of Niccolò Machiavelli,* trans. Christian E. Detmold (Boston: Osgood, 1882), from the dedication and chapters XIII–XIX, XXIII–XXVI. Adapted by the editor.

[1] Lorenzo, whom Machiavelli here flatteringly calls "Magnificent," had recently been named Duke of Urbino by his uncle Giovanni de' Medici (Pope Leo X). Machiavelli had originally dedicated his book to Giuliano de' Medici, third son of Lorenzo the [genuinely] Magnificent of Florence. After Giuliano died, Machiavelli rededicated the volume to Lorenzo, the new Duke of Urbino and one of the original Lorenzo's grandsons.

I have not set off this little work with pompous phrases, nor filled it with high-sounding and magnificent words, nor with any other allurements or extrinsic embellishments with which many are accustomed to write and adorn their works; for I wished that mine should derive credit only from the truth of the matter, and that the importance of the subject should make it acceptable.

And I hope it may not be accounted presumption if a man of lowly and humble station ventures to discuss and direct the conduct of princes; for as those who wish to delineate countries place themselves low in the plain to observe the form and character of mountains and high places, and for the purpose of studying the nature of the low country place themselves high upon an eminence, so one must be a prince to know well the character of the people, and to understand well the nature of a prince one must be of the people.

May your Magnificence then accept this little gift in the same spirit in which I send it; and if you will read and consider it well, you will recognize in it my desire that you may attain that greatness which fortune and your great qualities promise. And if your Magnificence will turn your eyes from the summit of your greatness towards those low places, you will know how undeservedly I have to bear the great and continued malice of fortune.

• • •

Chapter XIII
On Auxiliary Troops and the Prince's Own Troops

• • •

A prince who does not promptly recognize evils as they arise, cannot be called wise; but unfortunately this faculty is given to but few. And if we reflect upon the beginning of the ruin of the Roman Empire, it will be found to have resulted solely from hiring the Goths for its armies; for that was the first cause of the weakening of the forces of the Empire; and the valor [*virtù*] of which the Romans divested themselves was thus transferred to the Goths.

I conclude, then, that no prince can ever be secure that has not an army of his own; and he will become wholly dependent upon fortune if in times of adversity he lacks the valor [*virtù*] to defend himself. And wise men have ever held the opinion, that nothing is more weak and unstable than the reputation of power when not founded upon forces of the prince's own; by which I mean armies composed of his own subjects or citizens, or of his own creation;—all others are either mercenaries or auxiliaries.[2]

The means for organizing such armies of his own will readily be found by the prince by studying the method in which Philip of Macedon, father of Alexander the Great, and many republics and princes, organized their armies. . . .

---

[2] By "auxiliaries" Machiavelli means allied troops that are subjects of another prince.

Chapter XIV

Of the Duties of a Prince in Relation to Military Matters

A prince, then, should have no other thought or object so much at heart, and make no other thing so much his special study, as the art of war and the organization and discipline of his army; for that is the only art that is expected of him who commands. And such is its power [*virtù*], that it not only maintains in their position those who were born princes, but it often enables men of humble origin to achieve the rank of princes. And on the other hand, we have seen that princes who thought more of indulgence in pleasure than of war have thereby lost their states.

Thus the neglect of the art of war is the principal cause of the loss of your state, while a skill in it often enables you to acquire one. Francesco Sforza, from being skilled in arms, rose from private station to be Duke of Milan; and his descendants, by shunning the labors and fatigue of arms, relapsed into the condition of private citizens.[3]

Among the other causes of evil that will befall a prince who is destitute of a proper military force is, that it will make him despised; which is one of those disgraces against which a prince ought especially to guard, as we shall demonstrate further on. For there is no sort of equality between one who is well armed and one who is not so; nor is it reasonable that he who is armed should voluntarily obey the unarmed, or that a prince who is without a military force should remain secure among his armed subjects. For when there is disdain on the one side and mistrust on the other, it is impossible that the two should work well together. A prince, then, who is not master of the art of war, besides other misfortunes, cannot be respected by his soldiers, nor can he depend upon them. And therefore the practice of arms should ever be uppermost in the prince's thoughts; he should study it in time of peace as much as in actual war, which he can do in two ways, the one by practical exercise, and the other by scientific study. As regards the former, he must not only keep his troops well disciplined and exercised, but he must also frequently follow the hunt, whereby his body will become used to hardships, and he will become familiar with the character of the country, and learn where the mountains rise and the valleys open, and how the plains lie; he will learn to know the nature of rivers and of the swamps, to all of which he should give the greatest attention. For this knowledge is valuable in many ways to the prince, who thereby learns to know his own country, and can therefore better understand its defence. Again, by the knowledge of and practical acquaintance with

---

[3] Francesco Sforza, a skilled military leader, overthrew the weak government of Milan in 1450 and became its duke. His son, Lodovico il Moro, was driven from power in 1499 by Louis XII of France.

one country, he will with greater facility comprehend the character of others, which it may be necessary for him to understand. For instance, the mountains, valleys, plains, rivers, and swamps of Tuscany [4] bear a certain resemblance to those of other provinces; so that by the knowledge of the character and formation of one country he will readily arrive at that of others. A prince who is lacking in that experience lacks the very first essentials which a commander should possess; for that knowledge teaches him where to find the enemy, to select proper places for campsites, to conduct armies, regulate marches, and order battles, and to keep the field with advantage.

Among other praises that have been accorded by different writers to Philopœmen,[5] prince of the Achaians, was, that in time of peace he devoted himself constantly to the study of the art of war; and when he walked in the country with friends, he often stopped and argued with them thus: "Suppose the enemy were on yonder mountain, and we should happen to be here with our army, which of the two would have the advantage? How could we go most safely to find the enemy, observing proper order? If we should wish to retreat, how should we proceed? and if the enemy were to retreat, which way had we best pursue him?" And thus in walking he proposed to his friends all the cases that possibly could occur with an army, hearing their opinions, and giving his own, and corroborating them with reasons; so that by these continued discussions no case could ever arise in the conduct of an army for which he had not thought of the proper answer.

As regards the exercise of the mind, the prince should read history, and therein study the actions of eminent men, observe how they bore themselves in war, and examine the causes of their victories and defeats, so that he may imitate the former and avoid the latter. But above all should he follow the example of whatever distinguished man he may have chosen for his model; assuming that some one has been specially praised and held up to him as glorious, whose actions and exploits he should ever bear in mind. Thus it is told of Alexander that he imitated Achilles, and of Cæsar that he had taken Alexander for his model, as Scipio had done with Cyrus.[6] . . .

---

[4] A region of west-central Italy that includes Florence.

[5] A Greek general and statesman (253–184 B.C.), leader of the Achaian league. His singleminded strategic training program is described by Plutarch, the second-century Greek biographer.

[6] These are examples of warriors who studied history in order to imitate the actions of eminent men. Alexander the Great (356–323 B.C.) ruled the world from Greece to India. Achilles was a legendary Greek hero of the Trojan War, the central figure of Homer's *Iliad*. Julius Caesar was a Roman general and statesman (100–44 B.C.). Scipio Africanus (236–183 B.C.) was a Roman general, conqueror of Spain and victor over Carthage. Cyrus founded the Persian Empire in the sixth century B.C.

A wise prince then should act in like manner, and should never be idle in times of peace, but should industriously lay up stores of which to avail himself in times of adversity; so that, when Fortune abandons him, he may be prepared to resist her blows.

Chapter XV

Of the Reasons Why Men, Especially Princes, Win Applause, or Incur Censure

It remains now to be seen in what manner a prince should conduct himself towards his subjects and his allies; and knowing that this matter has already been treated by many others, I apprehend that my writing upon it also may be deemed presumptuous, especially as in the discussion of the same I shall differ completely from the rules laid down by others. But as my aim is to write something that may be useful to him for whom it is intended, it seems to me proper to pursue the real truth of the matter, rather than to indulge in mere speculation on the same; for many have imagined republics and principalities such as have never been known to exist in reality. For the manner in which men live is so different from the way in which they ought to live, that he who leaves what actually occurs for that which ought to occur will find that it leads him to ruin rather than to safety. For a man who, in all respects, will carry out only his professions of good, will be apt to be ruined among so many who are evil. A prince therefore who desires to maintain himself must learn to be not always good, but to be so or not as necessity may require. Leaving aside then the imaginary things concerning princes, and confining ourselves only to the realities, I say that all men when they are spoken of, and more especially princes, from being in a more conspicuous position, are noted for some quality that brings them either praise or censure. Thus one is deemed liberal, another miserly (*misero*) to use a Tuscan expression (for avaricious is he who by rapine desires to gain, and miserly we call him who abstains too much from the enjoyment of his own). One man is esteemed generous, another rapacious; one cruel, another merciful; one faithless, and another faithful; one effeminate and cowardly, another ferocious and brave; one affable, another haughty; one lascivious, another chaste; one sincere, the other cunning; one easygoing, another harsh; one grave, another frivolous; one religious, another skeptical; and so on.

I am well aware that it would be most praiseworthy for a prince to possess all of the above-named qualities that are esteemed good; but as he cannot have them all, nor entirely observe them, because of his human nature which does not permit it, he should at least be prudent enough to know how to avoid the infamy of those vices that would rob him of his state; and if possible also to guard against such as are likely to endanger it. But if that be not possible, then he may with less hesitation follow his natural inclinations. Nor need he care about incurring a bad reputation for such vices, without which the preservation of his state may be difficult. For, all things considered, it will be found that some things that seem like virtue [*virtù*] will lead you to ruin if you follow them; while others, that apparently are vices, will, if followed, result in your safety and well-being.

Chapter XVI
Of Generosity and Stinginess

To begin with the first of the above-named qualities, I say that it is well for a prince to be deemed generous or liberal; and yet liberality, indulged in so that you will no longer be feared, will prove injurious. For liberality worthily exercised, as it should be, will not be recognized, and may bring upon you the reproach of the very opposite. For if you desire the reputation of being liberal, you must not stop at any degree of extravagance; so that a prince will in this way generally consume his entire substance, and may in the end, if he wishes to keep up his reputation for liberality, be obliged to subject his people to extraordinary burdens, and resort to taxation, and employ all sorts of measures that will enable him to procure money. This will soon make him hated by his people; and when he becomes poor, he will be condemned by everybody; so that having by his generosity injured many and benefited few, he will be the first to suffer every inconvenience, and be exposed to every danger. And when he becomes conscious of this and attempts to retrench, he will at once expose himself to the imputation of being a miser.

A prince then, being unable without injury to himself to practise the virtue [*virtù*] of liberality in such manner that it may be generally recognized, should not, when he becomes aware of this and is prudent, mind incurring the charge of stinginess. For after a while, when it is seen that by his prudence and economy he makes his revenues suffice him, and that he is able to provide for his defence in case of war, and engage in enterprises without burdening his people, he will be considered liberal enough by all those from whom he takes nothing, and these are the many; while only those to whom he does not give, and which are the few, will look upon him as stingy.

In our own times we have not seen any great things accomplished except by those who were regarded as stingy; all others have been ruined. Pope Julius II, having been helped by his reputation of liberality to attain the Pontificate, did not afterwards care to keep up that reputation to enable him to engage in war against the king of France; and he carried on ever so many wars without levying any extraordinary taxes. For his long-continued economy enabled him to supply the extraordinary expenses of his wars.

If the present king of Spain had sought the reputation of being liberal, he would not have been able to engage in so many enterprises, nor could he have carried them to a successful issue. A prince, then, who would avoid robbing his own subjects, and be able to defend himself, and who would avoid becoming poor and abject or rapacious, should not mind incurring the reputation of being parsimonious; for that is one of those vices that will enable him to maintain his state.

And should it be alleged that Julius Cæsar attained the Empire by means of his liberality, and that many others by the same reputation have achieved the highest rank, then I reply, that you are either already a prince, or are in the way of becoming one; in the first case liberality would be injurious to you, but in the second it certainly is necessary to be reputed liberal. Now Cæsar was aiming to attain the Empire of Rome; but having achieved it, had he lived and not moderated his expenditures, he would assuredly have ruined the Empire by his extravagance.

And were any one to assert that there have been many princes who have achieved great things with their armies, and who were accounted most liberal, I answer that a prince either spends his own substance and that of his subjects, or that of others. Of the first two he should be very sparing, but in spending that of others he ought not to omit any act of liberality. The prince who in person leads his armies into foreign countries, and supports them by plunder, pillage, and exactions, and thus dispenses the substance of others, should do so with the greatest liberality, as otherwise his soldiers would not follow him. For that which belongs neither to him nor to his own subjects, a prince may spend most lavishly, as was done by Cyrus, Cæsar, and Alexander. The spending of other people's substance will not diminish, but rather increase, his reputation; it is only the spending of his own that is injurious to a prince.

And there is nothing that consumes itself so quickly as liberality; for the very act of using it causes it to lose the faculty of being used, and will either impoverish and make you condemned, or it will make you rapacious and hated. And of all the things against which a prince should guard most carefully, it is the incurring the hatred and contempt of his subjects. Now, liberality will bring upon you either the one or the other; there is therefore more wisdom in submitting to be called stingy, which may bring you blame without hatred, than, by aiming to be called liberal, to incur unavoidably the reputation of rapacity, which will bring upon you infamy as well as hatred.

Chapter XVII

Of Cruelty and Mercy, and Whether It Is Better to Be Loved Than Feared

Coming down now to the other aforementioned qualities, I say that every prince ought to desire the reputation of being merciful, and not cruel; at the same time, he should be careful not to misuse that mercy. Cesare Borgia was reputed cruel, yet by his cruelty he reunited the Romagna to his states, and restored that province to order, peace, and loyalty;[7] and if we carefully examine his course, we

---

[7] Cesare Borgia, son of Pope Alexander VI, was known personally to Machiavelli, who had been sent to him by the Republic of Florence on several diplomatic missions. Borgia was well-known for his ruthless but skillful tactics. The Romagna is a region in north-central Italy, just north of Florence.

shall find it to have been really much more merciful than the course of the people of Florence, who, to escape the reputation of cruelty, allowed Pistoia to be destroyed.[8] A prince, therefore, should not mind the ill repute of cruelty, when he can thereby keep his subjects united and loyal; for a few displays of severity will really be more merciful than to allow, by an excess of leniency, disorders to occur, which are apt to result in rapine and murder; for these injure a whole community, whilst the executions ordered by the prince fall only upon a few individuals. And, above all others, the new prince will find it almost impossible to avoid the reputation of cruelty, because new states are generally exposed to many dangers. It was on this account that Virgil made Dido to excuse the severity of her government, because it was still new, saying, "Harsh necessity, and the newness of my kingdom, force me to do such things, and to guard my frontiers everywhere against foreign foes."[9]

A prince, however, should be slow to believe and to act; nor should he be too easily alarmed by his own fears, and should proceed moderately and with prudence and humanity, so that an excess of confidence may not make him incautious, nor too much mistrust make him intolerable. This, then, gives rise to the question "whether it be better to be beloved than feared, or to be feared than beloved." It will naturally be answered that it would be desirable to be both the one and the other; but as it is difficult to be both at the same time, it is much more safe to be feared than to be loved, when you have to choose between the two. For it may be said of men in general that they are ungrateful and fickle, dissemblers, avoiders of danger, and greedy of gain. So long as you shower benefits upon them, they are all yours; they offer you their blood, their substance, their lives, and their children, provided the necessity for it is far off; but when it is near at hand, then they revolt. And the prince who relies upon their words, without having otherwise provided for his security, is ruined; for friendships that are won by rewards, and not by greatness and nobility of soul, although deserved, yet are not real, and cannot be depended upon in time of adversity.

Besides, men have less hesitation in offending one who makes himself beloved than one who makes himself feared; for love holds by a bond of obligation which, as mankind is bad, is broken on every occasion whenever it is for the interest of the

---

[8] The Republic of Florence had not intervened decisively to end civil strife in the nearby city of Pistoia when it was under Florentine control. As a result Pistoia was ruined. In his *Discourses on Livy* Machiavelli says that there are only three methods of dealing with such seditious rebellions: kill the leaders, exile them, or force them to make peace. Machiavelli believes that the least effective method is the third, and Florence should have used the first.

[9] In his epic poem about the origins of Rome, the *Aeneid,* the Roman poet Virgil (70–19 B.C.) describes the effective rule of Dido, legendary queen of Carthage.

obliged party to break it. But fear holds by the apprehension of punishment, which never leaves men. A prince, however, should make himself feared in such a manner that, if he has not won the affections of his people, he shall at least not incur their hatred; for the being feared, and not hated, can go very well together, if the prince abstains from taking the property of his subjects, and leaves them their women. And if you should be obliged to inflict capital punishment upon any one, then be sure to do so only when there is manifest cause and proper justification for it; and, above all things, abstain from taking people's property, for men will sooner forget the death of their fathers than the loss of their patrimony. Besides, there will never be any lack of reasons for taking people's property; and a prince who once begins to live by rapine will ever find excuses for seizing other people's property. On the other hand, reasons for taking life are not so easily found, and are more readily exhausted. But when a prince is at the head of his army, with a multitude of soldiers under his command, then it is above all things necessary for him to disregard the reputation of cruelty; for without such severity an army cannot be kept together, nor ready for any successful feat of arms.

Among the many admirable qualities of Hannibal,[10] it is related of him that, having an immense army composed of a very great variety of races of men, which he led to war in foreign countries, no quarrels ever occurred among them, nor were there ever any dissensions between them and their chief, either in his good or in his adverse fortunes; which can only be accounted for by his extreme cruelty. This, together with his boundless courage [*virtù*], made him ever venerated and terrible in the eyes of his soldiers; and without that extreme severity all his other virtues [*virtù*] would not have sufficed to produce that result.

Inconsiderate writers have, on the one hand, admired his great deeds, and, on the other, condemned the principal cause of the same. And the proof that his other virtues [*virtù*] would not have sufficed him may be seen from the case of Scipio, who was one of the most remarkable men, not only of his own time, but in all history. His armies revolted in Spain solely in consequence of his extreme kindness, which allowed his soldiers more freedom than comports with proper military discipline. This fact was censured in the Roman Senate by Fabius Maximus, who called Scipio the corrupter of the Roman soldiers. The tribe of the Locrians having been wantonly destroyed by one of the lieutenants of Scipio, he neither punished him for that nor for his insolence, — simply because of his own easy nature; so that, when somebody wished to excuse Scipio in the Senate, he said, "that there were many men who knew better how to avoid errors themselves than to punish them in others." This easy nature of Scipio's would in time have

---

[10] Machiavelli here contrasts the effective cruelty of Hannibal, the Carthaginian general (247–183 B.C.) whose army crossed the Alps into Italy and defeated the Romans in several battles, to the kindness of Hannibal's chief antagonist, Scipio Africanus, a Roman general.

dimmed his fame and glory if he had persevered in it under the Empire; but living as he did under the government of the Senate, this dangerous quality of his was not only covered up, but actually redounded to his honor.

To come back now to the question whether it be better to be beloved than feared, I conclude that, as men love of their own free will, but are inspired with fear by the will of the prince, a wise prince should always rely upon himself, and not upon the will of others; but, above all, should he always strive to avoid being hated, as I have already said above.

Chapter XVIII

In What Manner Princes Should Keep Their Faith

It must be evident to every one that it is more praiseworthy for a prince always to keep his word and practise integrity rather than craft and deceit. And yet the experience of our own times has shown that those princes have achieved great things who made small account of honesty, and who understood by cunning to circumvent the intelligence of others; and that in the end they got the better of those whose actions were dictated by loyalty and good faith. You must know, therefore, that there are two ways of carrying on a contest; the one by law, and the other by force. The first is practised by men, and the other by animals; and as the first is often insufficient, it becomes necessary to resort to the second.

A prince then should know how to employ the nature of man, and that of the beasts as well. This was figuratively taught by ancient writers, who relate how Achilles and many other princes were given to Chiron the centaur [11] to be nurtured, and how they were trained under his tutorship; which fable means nothing else than that their teacher combined the qualities of the man and the beast; and that a prince, to succeed, will have to employ both the one and the other nature, as the one without the other cannot produce lasting results.

It being necessary then for a prince to know well how to employ the nature of the beasts, he should be able to assume both that of the fox and that of the lion; for while the latter cannot escape the traps laid for him, the former cannot defend himself against the wolves. A prince should be a fox, to know the traps and snares; and a lion, to be able to frighten the wolves; for those who simply hold to the nature of the lion do not understand their business.

A prudent prince then cannot and should not fulfil his pledges when their observance is contrary to his interest, and when the causes that induced him to pledge his faith no longer exist. If men were all good, then indeed this precept

---

[11] A creature from Greek mythology, half man and half horse, who tutored several of the most renowned Greek heroes.

would be bad; but as men are naturally bad, and will not observe their faith towards you, you must, in the same way, not observe yours to them; and no prince ever yet lacked legitimate reasons with which to color his lack of good faith. Innumerable modern examples could be given of this; and it could easily be shown how many treaties of peace, and how many engagements, have been made null and void by the faithlessness of princes; and he who has best known how to play the fox has always been the most successful.

But it is necessary that the prince should know how to color this nature well, and how to be a great hypocrite and liar. For men are so simple, and yield so much to immediate necessity, that the deceiver will never lack dupes. I will mention one of the most recent examples. Alexander VI never did nor ever thought of anything but to deceive, and always found a reason for doing so. No one ever had greater skill in declaring his assertions, or who affirmed his pledges with greater oaths and observed them less, than Pope Alexander; and yet he was always successful in his deceits, because he knew the weakness of men in that particular.

It is not necessary, however, for a prince to possess all the above-mentioned good qualities; but it is essential that he should at least seem to have them. I will even venture to say, that to have and to practise them constantly is dangerous but to seem to have them is useful. For instance, a prince should seem to be merciful, faithful, humane, religious, and upright, and should even be so in reality; but he should have his mind so trained that, when occasion requires it, he may know how to change to the opposite. And it must be understood that a prince, and especially one who has but recently acquired his state, cannot perform all those things which cause men to be esteemed as good; he being often obliged, for the sake of maintaining his state, to act contrary to humanity, charity, and religion. And therefore it is necessary that he should have a versatile mind, capable of changing readily, according as the winds and changes of fortune bid him; and, as has been said above, not to swerve from the good if possible, but to know how to resort to evil if necessity demands it.

A prince then should be very careful never to allow anything to escape his lips that does not abound in the above-named five qualities, so that to see and to hear him he may seem all charity, integrity, and humanity, all uprightness, and all piety. And more than all else is it necessary for a prince to seem to possess the last quality; for mankind in general judge more by what they see and hear than by what they feel, every one being capable of the former, and but few of the latter. Everybody sees what you seem to be, but few really feel what you are; and these few dare not oppose the opinion of the many, who are protected by the majesty of the state; for the actions of all men, and especially those of princes, are judged by the result, where there is no other judge to whom to appeal.

A prince then should look mainly to the successful maintenance of his state. The means which he employs for this will always be accounted honorable, and will be praised by everybody; for the common people are always taken by appearances and by results, and it is the vulgar mass that constitutes the world. Only a very few have rank and station, while the many have nothing to sustain them except their opinions. A certain prince of our time, whom it is well not to name, never preached anything but peace and good faith; but if he had always observed either the one or the other, it would in most instances have cost him his reputation or his state.[12]

Chapter XIX
A Prince Must Avoid Being Condemned and Hated

Having thus considered separately the most important of the qualities which a prince should possess, I will now briefly discuss the others under this general maxim: that a prince should endeavor, as has already been said, to avoid everything that would tend to make him hated and condemned. And in proportion as he avoids that will he have performed his part well, and need fear no danger from any other vices. Above all, a prince makes himself hated by rapacity, that is, by taking away from his subjects their property and their women, from which he should carefully abstain. The great mass of men will live quietly and contentedly, provided you do not rob them of their substance and their honor; so that you will have to contend only with the ambition of a few, which is easily restrained in various ways.

A prince becomes despised when he incurs by his acts the reputation of being variable, inconstant, effeminate, cowardly, and irresolute; he should therefore guard against this as against a dangerous rock, and should strive to display in all his actions grandeur, courage, seriousness, and determination. And in judging the private causes of his subjects, his decisions should be irrevocable. Thus will he maintain himself in such esteem that no one will think of deceiving or betraying him. The prince, who by his habitual conduct gives cause for such an opinion of himself, will acquire so great a reputation that it will be difficult to conspire against him, or to attack him; provided that it be generally known that he is truly excellent, and revered by his subjects. For there are two things which a prince has to fear: the one, attempts against him by his own subjects; and the other, attacks from without by powerful foreigners. Against the latter he will be able to defend himself by good armies and good allies, and whoever has the one will not lack the other. And so long as his external affairs are kept quiet, his internal security will not be disturbed, unless it should be by a conspiracy. And even if he were to be assailed from without, if he has a well-organized army and has lived as he should have done, he will always (if he stands firm) be able to withstand any such attacks, as we have related was done

---

[12] Probably a reference to Ferdinand of Spain (1452–1516), who is said to have boasted toward the end of his life that he had deceived Louis XII of France twelve times.

by Nabis, tyrant of Sparta.[13] But even when at peace externally, it nevertheless behooves the prince to be on his guard, lest his subjects conspire against him secretly. He will, however, be sufficiently secure against this, if he avoids being hated and despised, and keeps his subjects well satisfied with himself, which should ever be his aim, as I have already explained above. Not to be hated nor condemned by the mass of the people is one of the best safeguards for a prince against conspiracies; for conspirators always believe that the death of the prince will be satisfactory to the people; but when they know that it will rather offend than please the people, they will not venture upon such a course, for the difficulties that surround conspirators are infinite.

Experience proves that, although there have been many conspiracies, yet but few have come to good end; for he who conspires cannot act alone, nor can he take any associates except such as he believes to be malcontents; and so soon as you divulge your plans to a malcontent, you furnish him the means wherewith to procure satisfaction. For by denouncing it he may hope to derive great advantages for himself, seeing that such a course will insure him those advantages, while the other is full of doubts and dangers. He must indeed be a very rare friend of yours, or an inveterate enemy of the prince, to observe good faith and not to betray you.

But to reduce this matter to a few words, I say that on the side of the conspirator there is nothing but fear, jealousy, and apprehension of punishment; while the prince has on his side the majesty of sovereignty, the laws, the support of his friends and of the government, which protect him. And if to all this be added the popular good will, it seems impossible that any one should be rash enough to attempt a conspiracy against him. For ordinarily a conspirator has cause for apprehension only before the execution of his evil purpose; but in this case, having the people for his enemies, he has also to fear the consequences after the commission of the crime, and can look nowhere for a refuge.

• • •

Chapter XXIII
How to Avoid Flatterers

I will not leave unnoticed an important subject, and an evil against which princes have much difficulty in defending themselves, if they are not extremely prudent, or have not made good choice of ministers; and this relates to flatterers, who

---

[13] Nabis, ruler of Sparta, 206–192 B.C., was noted for his cruelty and was ultimately assassinated. According to the Roman historian Livy, before a battle Nabis had eighty Spartan citizens murdered.

abound in all courts. Men are generally so well pleased with themselves and their own acts, and delude themselves to such a degree, that it is with difficulty they escape from the pest of flatterers; and in their efforts to avoid them they expose themselves to the risk of being condemned. There is no other way of guarding against flattery, than to make people understand that they will not offend you by speaking the truth. On the other hand, when every one feels at liberty to tell you the truth, they will be apt to be lacking in respect for you. A prudent prince therefore should follow a middle course, choosing for ministers of his government only wise men, and to these only should he give full power to tell him the truth, and they should only be allowed to speak to him of those things which he asks of them, and of none other. But then the prince should ask them about everything, and should listen to their opinions and reflect upon them, and afterwards form his own resolutions. And he should bear himself towards all his advisers in such manner that each may know that the more freely he speaks, the more acceptable will he be. But outside of these he should not listen to any one, but follow the course agreed upon, and be firm in his resolves. Whoever acts otherwise will either be misled by his flatterers, or will vacillate in his decisions, because of the variety of opinions; and this will naturally result in his losing in public esteem. . . .

A prince nevertheless should take counsel, but only when he wants it, and not when others wish to thrust it upon him; in fact, he should rather discourage persons from tendering him advice unsolicited by him. But he should be an extensive questioner, and a patient listener to the truth respecting the things inquired about, and should even show his anger in case anyone should, for some reason, not tell him the truth.

Those who imagine that a prince who has the reputation of sagacity is not indebted for it to his own natural gifts, but to the good counsels of those who surround him, certainly deceive themselves. For it may be taken as a general and infallible rule, that a prince who is not naturally wise cannot be well advised; unless he should perchance place himself entirely in the hands of one man, who should guide him in all things, and who would have to be a man of uncommon ability. In such a case a prince might be well directed, but it would probably not last long, because his counsellor would in a short time deprive him of his state. But a prince who is not wise himself, and counsels with more than one person, will never have united counsels; for he will himself lack the ability to harmonize and combine the various counsels and suggestions. His advisers will only think of their own advantage, which the prince will neither know how to discern nor how to correct.

And things cannot well be otherwise, for men will always naturally prove bad, unless some necessity forces them to be good. Whence we conclude that good counsels, no matter whence they may come, result wholly from the prince's own wisdom; but the wisdom of the prince never results from good counsels.

Chapter XXIV

The Reason Why the Princes of Italy Have Lost Their States

A judicious observation of the above-given rules will cause a new prince to be regarded as though he were an hereditary one, and will very soon make him more firm and secure in his state than if he had grown old in its possession. For the actions of a new prince are much more closely observed and scrutinized than those of an hereditary one; and when they are known to be virtuous, they will win the confidence and affections of men much more for the new prince, and make his subjects feel under greater obligations to him, than if he were of the ancient line. For men are ever more taken with the things of the present than with those of the past; and when they find their own good in the present, then they enjoy it and seek no other, and will be ready in every way to defend the new prince, provided he is not deficient in other respects. And thus he will have the double glory of having established a new principality, and of having strengthened and adorned it with good laws, good armies, good allies, and good examples. And in the same way will it be a double shame to an hereditary prince, if through lack of prudence and ability he loses his state.

If now we examine the conduct of those princes of Italy who in our day have lost their states, such as the king of Naples, the Duke of Milan, and others, we shall note in them at once a common defect as regards their military forces, for the reasons which we have discussed at length above. And we shall also find that in some instances the people were hostile to the prince; or if he had the good will of the people, he knew not how to conciliate that of the nobles. For unless there be some such defects as these, states are not lost when the prince has energy enough to keep an army in the field.

Philip of Macedon, not the father of Alexander the Great, but he who was vanquished by Titus Quintus, had not much of a state as compared with Rome and Greece, who attacked him; yet being a military man, and at the same time knowing how to preserve the good will of the people and to assure himself of the support of the nobles, he sustained the war against the Romans and Greeks for many years; and although he finally lost some cities, yet he preserved his kingdom.[14]

Those of our princes, therefore, who have lost their dominions after having been established in them for many years, should not blame fortune, but only their own indolence and lack of energy; for in times of quiet they never thought of the possibility of a change (it being a common defect of men in fair weather to take no thought of storms), and afterwards, when adversity overtook them, their first impulse was to fly, and not to defend themselves, hoping that the people, when dis-

---

[14] Philip V of Macedon (221–179 B.C.) fought two wars against the Romans who were led by Titus Quintus Flaminius. To make his point, Machiavelli overstates the degree of Philip's success against the Romans.

gusted with the insolence of the victors, would recall them. Such a course may be very well when others fail, but it is very discreditable to neglect other means for it that might have saved you from ruin; for no one ever falls deliberately, in the expectation that some one will help him up, which either does not happen, or, if it does, will not contribute to your security; for it is a base thing to look to others for your defence instead of depending upon yourself. That defence alone is effectual, sure, and durable which depends upon yourself and your own energy [*virtù*].

Chapter XXV

Of the Influence of Fortune in Human Affairs, and How It May Be Counteracted

I am well aware that many have held and still hold the opinion, that the affairs of this world are so controlled by Fortune and by the Divine Power that human wisdom and foresight cannot modify them; that, in fact, there is no remedy against the decrees of fate, and that therefore it is not worth while to make any effort, but to yield unconditionally to the power of Fortune. This opinion has been generally accepted in our times, because of the great changes that have taken place, and are still being witnessed every day, and are beyond all human conjecture.

In reflecting upon this at times, I am myself in some measure inclined to that belief; nevertheless, as our free will is not entirely destroyed, I judge that it may be assumed as true that Fortune to the extent of one half is the arbiter of our actions, but that she permits us to direct the other half, or perhaps a little less, ourselves. I compare this to a swollen river, which in its fury overflows the plains, tears up the trees and buildings, and sweeps the earth from one place and deposits it in another. Every one flies before the flood, and yields to its fury, unable to resist it; and notwithstanding this state of things, men do not when the river is in its ordinary condition provide against its overflow by dikes and walls, so that when it rises it may flow either in the channel thus provided for it, or that at any rate its violence may not be entirely unchecked, nor its effects prove so injurious. It is the same with Fortune, who displays her power where there is no organized valor [*virtù*] to resist her, and where she knows that there are no dikes or walls to control her.

If now you examine Italy, which is the seat of the changes under consideration, and has occasioned their occurrence, you will see that she is like an open country, without dikes or any other protection against inundations; and that if she had been protected with proper valor [*virtù*] and wisdom, as is the case with Germany, Spain, and France, these inundations would either not have caused the great changes which they did, or they would not have occurred at all.

These remarks I deem sufficient as regards resisting fortune in general; but confining myself now more to particular cases, I say that we see a prince fortunate one day, and ruined the next, without his nature or any of his qualities being changed. I believe this results mainly from the causes which have been discussed at length above; namely, that the prince who relies entirely upon fortune will be ruined according as fortune varies. I believe, further, that the prince who conforms his conduct to the spirit of the times will be fortunate; and in the same way will he be unfortunate, if in his actions he disregards the spirit of the times. For we see men proceed in various ways to attain the end they aim at, such as glory and riches: the one with circumspection, the other with rashness; one with violence, another with cunning; one with patience, another with impetuosity; and all may succeed in their different ways. We also see that, of two men equally prudent, the one will accomplish his designs, while the other fails; and in the same way we see two men succeed equally well by two entirely different methods, the one being prudent and the other rash; which is due to nothing else than the character of the times, to which they either conform in their proceedings or not. Whence it comes, as I have said, that two men by entirely different modes of action will achieve the same results; while of two others, proceeding precisely in the same way, the one will accomplish his end, and the other not. This also causes the difference of success; for if one man, acting with caution and patience, is also favored by time and circumstances, he will be successful; but if these change, then will he be ruined, unless, indeed, he changes his conduct accordingly. Nor is there any man so sagacious that he will always know how to conform to such change of times and circumstances; for men do not readily deviate from the course to which their nature inclines them; and, moreover, if they have generally been prosperous by following one course, they cannot persuade themselves that it would be well to depart from it. Thus the cautious man, when the moment comes for him to strike a bold blow, will not know how to do it, and thus he will fail; while, if he could have changed his nature with the times and circumstances, his usual good fortune would not have abandoned him.

Pope Julius II was in all his actions most impetuous; and the times and circumstances happened so conformably to that mode of proceeding that he always achieved successful results. Witness the first attempt he made upon Bologna, when Messer Giovanni Bentivogli was still living. This attempt gave offense to the Venetians, and also to the kings of Spain and France, who held a conference on the subject. But Pope Julius, with his habitual boldness and impetuosity, assumed the direction of that expedition in person; which caused the Spaniards and the Venetians to remain quiet in suspense, the latter from fear, and the others from a desire to recover the entire kingdom of Naples. On the other hand, the Pope drew the king of France after him; for that king, seeing that Julius had already started on the expedition, and wishing to gain his friendship for the purpose of humbling the Venetians, judged that he could not refuse him the assistance of his army without manifest injury to himself.[15]

---

[15] Julius II, pope from 1503 to 1513, was a vigorous Church leader and military commander. Machiavelli was very conscious of Pope Julius's rashness in gambling on French support. During much of Julius's campaign Machiavelli was at the papal court as an emissary of the Republic of Florence. He could thus observe for himself the indecisiveness of the Spanish and Venetians.

Pope Julius II, then, achieved by this impetuous movement what no other pontiff could have accomplished with all possible human prudence. For had he waited to start from Rome until all his plans were definitely arranged, and everything carefully organized, as every other pontiff would have done, he would certainly never have succeeded; for the king would have found a thousand excuses, and the others would have caused him a thousand apprehensions. I will not dwell upon the other actions of Julius II, which were all of a similar character, and have all succeeded equally well. The shortness of his life saved him from experiencing any reverses; for if times had supervened that would have made it necessary for him to proceed with caution and prudence, he would assuredly have been ruined; for he could never have deviated from the course to which his nature inclined him.

I conclude, then, as long as Fortune is changeable, that men who persist obstinately in their own ways will be successful only so long as those ways coincide with those of Fortune; and whenever these differ, they fail. But, on the whole, I judge impetuosity to be better than caution; for Fortune is a woman, and if you wish to master her, you must strike and beat her, and you will see that she allows herself to be more easily vanquished by the rash and the violent than by those who proceed more slowly and coldly. And therefore, as a woman, she ever favors youth more than age, for youth is less cautious and more energetic, and commands Fortune with greater audacity.

Chapter XXVI

Exhortation to Deliver Italy from Foreign Barbarians

Reviewing now all I have said in the foregoing discourses, and thinking to myself that, if the present time should be favorable for Italy to receive and honor a new prince, and the opportunity were given to a prudent and virtuous man to establish a new form of government, that would bring honor to himself and happiness to the mass of the Italian people, so many things would combine for the advantage of such a new prince, that, so far as I know, no previous time was ever more favorable for such a change. And if, as I have said, it was necessary for the purpose of displaying the virtue [*virtù*] of Moses that the people of Israel should be held in bondage in Egypt;[16] and that the Persians should be opposed to the Medes, so as to bring to light the greatness and courage of Cyrus; [17] and that the Athenians should be dispersed for the purpose of illustrating the excellence of

---

[16] In this passage Machiavelli gives historical examples of individual ability (*virtù*). The Old Testament's Moses led the enslaved Hebrews out of Egypt toward the land that God had promised them.

[17] In the process of founding the Persian Empire, Cyrus defeated the Medes who had been a major power.

Theseus;[18] so at present, for the purpose of making manifest the power [*virtù*] of one Italian spirit, it was necessary that Italy should have been brought to her present condition of being in a worse bondage than that of the Jews, more enslaved than the Persians, more scattered than the Athenians, without a head, without order, vanquished and despoiled, lacerated, overrun by her enemies, and subjected to every kind of devastation.

And although, up to the present time, there may have been some one who may have given a gleam of hope that he was ordained by Heaven to redeem Italy, yet have we seen how, in the very zenith of his career, he was so checked by fortune that poor Italy remained as it were lifeless, and waiting to see who might be chosen to heal her wounds,—to put an end to her devastation, to the sacking of Lombardy, to the spoliation and ruinous taxation of the kingdom of Naples and of Tuscany—and who should heal her sores that have festered so long. You see how she prays God that he may send some one who shall redeem her from this cruelty and barbarous insolence. You see her eagerly disposed to follow any banner, provided there be some one to bear it aloft. But there is no one at present in whom she could place more hope than in your illustrious house,[19] O magnificent Lorenzo! which, with its virtue [*virtù*] and fortune, favored by God and the Church, of which it is now the head, could make an effectual beginning of her deliverance. And this will not be difficult for you, if you will first study carefully the lives and actions of the men whom I have named above. And although these men were rare and wonderful, they were nevertheless but men, and the opportunities which they had were far less favorable than the present; nor were their undertakings more just or more easy than this; neither were they more favored by the Almighty than what you are. Here, then, is great justice; for war is just when it is necessary, and a resort to arms is beneficent when there is no hope in anything else. The opportunity is most favorable, and when that is the case there can be no great difficulties, provided you follow the course of those whom I have held up to you as examples. Although in their case extraordinary things, without parallel, were brought about by the hand of God—the sea divided for their passage, a pillar of cloud pointed their way through the wilderness, the rock poured forth water to assuage their thirst, and it rained manna to appease their hunger[20]—yet your greatness combines all, and on your own efforts will depend the result. God will not do everything; for that would deprive us of our free will, and of that share of glory which belongs to us.

---

[18] Theseus, a hero of Greek mythology, is reputed to have brought about the union of separate villages into one state with Athens as the capital city.

[19] That is, the Medici family.

[20] Events associated with Moses's leading the Hebrews out of Egypt.

Nor should we wonder that not one of the Italians whom I have mentioned has been able to accomplish that which it is to be hoped will be done by your illustrious house; for if in so many revolutions in Italy, and in the conduct of so many wars, it would seem that military capacity [*virtù*] and valor have become extinct, it is owing to the fact that the old military system was defective, and no one has come forward capable of establishing a new one. And nothing brings a man who has newly risen so much honor as the establishing of new laws and institutions of his own creation; if they have greatness in them and become well established, they will make the prince admired and revered; and there is no lack of opportunity in Italy for the introduction of every kind of reform. The people have great courage [*virtù*], provided it be not wanting in their leaders. Look but at their single combats, and their encounters when there are but a few on either side, and see how superior the Italians have shown themselves in strength, dexterity, and ability. But when it comes to their armies, then these qualities do not appear, because of the incapacity of the chiefs, who cannot enforce obedience from those who are versed in the art of war, and every one believes himself to be so; for up to the present time there have been none so decidedly superior in valor [*virtù*] and good fortune that the others yielded him obedience. Thence it comes that in so great a length of time, and in the many wars that have occurred within the past twenty years, the armies, whenever wholly composed of Italians, have given but poor account of themselves. Witness first Taro, then Alessandria, Capua, Genoa, Vaila, Bologna, and Mestri.[21]

If, then, your illustrious house is willing to follow the examples of those distinguished men who have redeemed their countries, you will before anything else, and as the very foundation of every enterprise, have to provide yourself with a national army. And you cannot have more faithful, truer, and better soldiers than the Italians. And while each individual is good, they will become still better when they are all united, and know that they are commanded by their own prince, who will honor and support them. It is necessary, therefore, to provide troops of this kind, so as to be able successfully to oppose Italian valor [*virtù*] to the attacks of foreigners.

And although the infantry of the Swiss and of the Spaniards is looked upon as terrifying, yet both of them have a defect, which will permit a third organization not only to resist them, but confidently hope to vanquish them. For the Spaniards cannot withstand the shock of cavalry, and the Swiss dread infantry, when they encounter it in battle as obstinate as themselves. Whence we have seen, what further experience will prove more fully, that the Spaniards cannot

---

[21] Battles that occurred in Italy from 1495 to 1513, all of which ended disastrously for Italian forces. Machiavelli here clearly intends to rouse Lorenzo de' Medici with these memories of Italian disgrace.

resist the French cavalry, and that the Swiss succumb to the Spanish infantry. And although we have not yet had a full trial of the latter, yet have we had a fair specimen of it in the battle of Ravenna, where the Spanish infantry confronted the line of battle of the Germans, who have adopted the same system as the Swiss; and where the Spaniards with great agility, and protected by their bucklers, rushed under the pikes of the Germans, and were thus able to attack them securely without the Germans being able to prevent it; and had it not been for the cavalry which fell upon the Spaniards, they might have destroyed the entire German infantry.

Knowing, then, the defects of the one and the other of these systems of infantry, you can organize a new one that shall avoid these defects, and shall be able to resist cavalry as well as infantry. And this is to be done, not by a change of arms, but by an entirely different organization and discipline. This is one of the things which, if successfully introduced, will give fame and greatness to a new prince.

You must not, then, allow this opportunity to pass, so that Italy, after waiting so long, may at last see her deliverer appear. Nor can I possibly express with what affection he would be received in all those provinces that have suffered so long from this inundation of foreign foes!—with what thirst for vengeance, with what persistent faith, with what devotion, and with what tears! What door would be closed to him? Who would refuse him obedience? What envy would dare oppose him? What Italian would refuse him homage? This barbarous dominion of the foreigner offends the very nostrils of everybody!

Let your illustrious house, then, assume this task with that courage and hopefulness which every just enterprise inspires; so that under your banner our country many recover its ancient fame, and under your auspices may be verified the words of Petrarch:—

> Virtue [*virtù*] boldly against rage
> Will take up arms and make the battle short.
> For the ancient valor
> In Italian hearts is not yet dead.[22]

---

[22] Lines by Francesco Petrarca, Italian poet and scholar (1304–1374), taken from his patriotic lyrics *My Italy (Italia Mia)*, which are still well-known and loved.

3

❧

LYRIC POETRY OF THE RENAISSANCE

As a part of the outpouring of individual sentiment that was included in the European Renaissance, the lyric poem regained a potency that, except for a few medieval poets, it had not achieved since the ancient Greeks and Romans. In the modern sense, the lyric is any poem of no great length that expresses the personal feelings of a single speaker. (Although the lyric poem is always expressed in the first person, the "I" who speaks may sometimes be an invented character, not necessarily the poet.) The word lyric is derived from ancient Greek where it refers to a song intended for accompaniment on the lyre, a small harplike instrument. Thus, even in current usage, to call something "lyrical" is to suggest a songlike quality. Renaissance refers to that "rebirth" of literature, art, and learning that progressively transformed European culture from the mid-fourteenth century in Italy to the mid-seventeenth century in England. It was initiated by the rediscovery of pagan Greek and Latin literatures with their humanistic attitudes toward life, and accelerated by the invention of printing and the corresponding increase in literacy. The sixteenth-century Protestant Reformation, with its emphasis on the individual's reading of the Bible as a guide to faith, also greatly increased the impetus toward literacy. (See the introduction to Selection 5, on the lives of Leonardo and Michelangelo, for further discussion of the rise of the Renaissance.)

In the following selected lyrics, the reader can see the new emphasis on individual feelings and the greatly expanded sense of human possibilities during this life on earth. Even the recent geographical discoveries of the New World and the new sea routes to the Orient contributed to that exciting sense of the possibility of greater material and spiritual development for individuals on earth, without losing the traditional feelings about God's power. Human existence was increasingly seen as not merely a wretched transition on the way to eternity, an attitude typical of the recently past Middle Ages, but rather as an opportunity for happiness in harmony with God's will.

MICHELANGELO BUONARROTI

T*he first lyrics we shall read are Italian sonnets by Michelangelo Buonarroti (1475–1564), an impassioned poet who was also the unparalleled Renaissance master of sculpture, painting, and architecture. (For more detailed information on Michelangelo's achievements, see the excerpt from Vasari's* Life of Michelangelo *in Selection 5.) The first sonnet, quite typically irregular in its form, details Michelangelo's physical agony and psychic despair during the four years that he painted the vast interior dome of the Sistine Chapel. The others express Michelangelo's fusion of sensual and Platonic love, along with his devout Christian faith.*

To Giovanni da Pistoia[1]
On the Painting of the Sistine Chapel [2]

I've grown a goiter by dwelling in this den—
as cats from stagnant streams in Lombardy,
or in what other land they hap to be—
which drives the belly close beneath the chin:

my beard turns up to heaven; my nape falls in,
fixed on my spine: my breast-bone visibly
grows like a harp: a rich embroidery
bedews my face from brush-drops thick and thin.

My loins into my paunch like levers grind:
my buttock like a crupper[3] bears my weight;
my feet unguided wander to and fro;

Michelangelo: From *The Sonnets of Michel Angelo and Tommaso Campanella,* translated by John Addington Symonds. London: John Murray, 1878.

[1] The humanist scholar Giovanni di Benedetto da Pistoia, who wrote several sonnets to Michelangelo.

[2] Michelangelo suffered extreme physical and mental stress while painting the huge fresco that covers the interior vault of the Sistine Chapel in Rome (1508–1512) upon the command of Pope Julius II. Michelangelo painted most of it by himself while lying on a high scaffolding (see Selection 5). On the page where Michelangelo wrote this extended sonnet, he sketched himself craning his neck painfully upward while painting the ceiling.

[3] The rump or buttocks of a four-legged animal, implying inhuman distention.

in front my skin grows loose and long; behind,
by bending it becomes more taut and strait;
crosswise I strain me like a Syrian bow:[4]
    whence false and quaint, I know,
must be the fruit of squinting brain and eye;
for ill can aim the gun that bends awry.
    Come then, Giovanni, try
to succour my dead pictures and my fame;
since foul I fare and painting is my shame.[5]

To Vittoria Colonna[6]
The Model and the Statue[7]

When divine Art conceives a form and face,
she bids the craftsman for his first essay
to shape a simple model in mere clay:[8]
this is the earliest birth of Art's embrace.

From the live marble in the second place
his mallet brings into the light of day
a thing so beautiful that who can say
when time shall conquer that immortal grace?

Thus my own model I was born to be—
the model of that nobler self, whereto
schooled by your pity, lady, I shall grow.

Each overplus and each deficiency
you will make good. What penance then is due
for my fierce heat, chastened and taught by you?

---

[4] A Syrian bow was shaped into a semicircular arc.

[5] Michelangelo deeply resented the fact that Pope Julius II had ordered him to stop carving the marble figures on the pope's tomb in order to paint the fresco. He always considered himself to be, above all, a sculptor, not a painter.

[6] The most important, perhaps the only, woman in Michelangelo's adult emotional life was the learned and aristocratic Vittoria Colonna (1490–1547), with whom the artist maintained a close, adoring, and apparently chaste friendship.

[7] This is one of several sonnets hinting at Michelangelo's Christian and Neoplatonic theory of art: The artist's mental conception, which is inspired by God, is superior to the manual aspects of art.

[8] A "model" is a small-scale preliminary study for a permanent sculpture. The poet then extends the metaphor to himself as the "model" that the lady will shape into enduring maturity.

The Artist and His Work

How can that be, lady,[9] which all men learn
by long experience? Shapes that seem alive,
wrought in hard mountain marble, will survive
their maker, whom the years to dust return!

Thus to effect cause yields.[10] Art hath her turn,
and triumphs over Nature. I, who strive
with Sculpture, know this well; her wonders live
in spite of time and death, those tyrants stern.

So I can give long life to both of us
in either way, by color or by stone,
making the semblance of thy face and mine.

Centuries hence when both are buried, thus
thy beauty and my sadness shall be shown,
and men shall say, "For her 'twas wise to pine."

After the Death of Vittoria Colonna[11]

Irreparable Loss

When my rude hammer to the stubborn stone
gives human shape, now that, now this, at will,
following his hand who wields and guides it still,[12]
it moves upon another's feet alone:

but that[13] which dwells in heaven, the world doth fill
with beauty by pure motions of its own;
and since tools fashion tools which else were none,
its life makes all that lives with living skill.

---

[9] Again, Vittoria Colonna.

[10] That is, the sculptor is outlived by his creation. (The power of art to overcome nature's process of decay and death is also a frequent theme of ancient Roman literature.)

[11] The title is the translator's invention. According to some modern scholars the sonnet's theme of losing someone who has served as the artist's earthly inspiration may actually be a reference to the death of Michelangelo's brother.

[12] The "hand" of the divine sculptor, God.

[13] God's heavenly hammer. (The metaphorical analogy of God's hammer is used in Dante's *Paradiso*, 2:127–129, a source undoubtedly familiar to Michelangelo: "The motion and the power of the sacred gyres—/as the hammer's art is from the smith—/must flow/from the Blessed Movers. It is their power inspires.") The hammer image dates back to the ancient Greek philosopher Plato, known and admired by both Dante and Michelangelo.

Now, for that every stroke excels the more
the higher at the forge it doth ascend,
her soul that fashioned mine hath sought the skies:[14]

wherefore unfinished I must meet my end,
if God, the great artificer, denies
that aid[15] which was unique on earth before.

GARCILASO DE LA VEGA

*T*he second lyric poet selected for this chapter is Garcilaso de la Vega
*(1503–1536). Garcilaso was a poet of genius who succeeded in adapting the
Italian style of poetry to the Spanish language, spurred by the example of his close
friend, the poet Juan Boscán. Garcilaso's lyric production was necessarily brief and
was not published until after his heroic death in combat while leading an attack
against a French fortification. His poems, however, were enormously influential,
and upon their publication were hailed as classics by his contemporaries. During
his brief life Garcilaso distinguished himself equally in war, politics, and poetry.*

Besides his three Eclogues *(pastoral poems inspired mainly by the Roman poet
Vergil), Garcilaso's supreme poetic achievement was his thirty-eight* Sonnets. *Typical of Garcilaso is his fusion of formal elegance with a sense of amorous melancholy, derived from the Italian poet Petrarch. For Garcilaso love is always fleeting,
and tinged with a sadness that is barely consoled by muted expressions of Christian faith. Unlike some other Renaissance poets, however, melancholy seems to
have been for Garcilaso more than a mere literary topic. It had a firm biographical basis in the poet's ill-fated relationship with Isabel de Freire, an aristocratic
Portuguese lady whom Garcilaso loved deeply. He was loved by her in return,
although, unfortunately, both were already married. The six-year relationship
ended with her tragic death during childbirth. Sonnets 10, 11, and 25, reprinted
here in translation, are usually read in the biographical context of the poet's love
for Isabel. In Sonnet 10 the poet, after his beloved's death, addresses the "love tokens," gifts and tokens received from her that he now regards as foreshadowings
of her death and also of his own death. Sonnet 11 portrays the poet's sadness with
less immediacy, more aesthetically, in a scene worthy of a Renaissance painting:
the poet at the river's edge calls on the Naiads, water nymphs of Greek mythology,
to listen to his weeping and console him in his grief. Sonnet 25, like Sonnet 10,
avoids pictorial analogies in favor of a sense of immediacy. It begins by addressing
Fate, complaining of Fate's "harsh decree" in allowing the poet's lover to die like a
tree that has been cut down. The person being addressed in the concluding six*

---

[14] That is, the person who inspired my work has risen to heaven.

[15] That aid to the poet/sculptor's hammer which needs forming and inspiration from another source (formerly given by Vittoria Colonna, if the translator be correct).

lines, however, is the dead lover herself, whom the poet expects to see in the after-
life. In a totally different tone, Sonnet 23, also reprinted here, is Garcilaso's vari-
ation on a traditional theme from classical antiquity, carpe diem *("seize the*
day"), a theme we shall see again in the last poem of this chapter, Andrew Marvell's
"To His Coy Mistress."

Sonnet 10

Oh dear love tokens that did work me harm,
So dear and smiling too when heaven did smile,
Within my memory you are joined, the while
With it you plot to bring me death's alarm!
   Who would have said, when in those hours of charm
In happy state I saw myself erstwhile,
That I one day in desolation vile
Should find that thoughts of you my peace disarm?
   Since in one hour you did from me take this,
The joy, that for completion you did give,
Now take also the sorrow you did leave.
   If not, I shall suspect that to such bliss
You brought me then, that now you might achieve
My death amidst these mournful memories.

Translated by Eleanor L. Turnbull

Sonnet 11

Fair Naiads[1] of the river, that reside
Happy in grottos of rock crystal veined
With shining gems, and loftily sustained
On columns of pure glass, if now ye glide
   On duteous[2] errands, or weave side by side

From *Ten Centuries of Spanish Poetry: An Anthology in English Verse with Original Text from*
the Eleventh Century to the Generation of 1898, ed. Eleanor L. Turnbull. Baltimore: The
Johns Hopkins University Press, © 1955, pp. 163, 165. "Sonnet 10" reprinted by permission of The Johns Hopkins University Press.

[1] Greek deities of rivers, springs, fountains, and lakes.

[2] Dutiful, obedient.

Webs of fine net-work, or in groups remove
To hear and tell romantic tales of love,
Of genii, Fays and Tritons[3] of the tide,—
    Awhile remit your labours, and upraise
Your rosy heads to look on me. Not long
Will it detain you. Sweet'ners of my song,
    For pity hear me, watering as I go
With tears your borders, and for such short space,
In heavenly notes sing solace to my woe!

Translated by Jeremiah H. Wiffen

Sonnet 23

    In so much as the lily and the rose
Display their colors in thy countenance,
In so much as the burning, yet chaste, glance
Kindles the heart, then doth restraint impose;
    In that the hair, whose gold some delver[4] chose
In a deep mine, with rapid whirling dance,
The white neck's towering beauty to enhance,
The stirring winds all scattered wild dispose,
    Cull the sweet fruit of thy delightful Spring
Ere vengeful time shall come to hide with snow
The lovely summit that ariseth there,
    Frost in the wind the fading rose shall blow,
To all its glory the swift years shall bring
Change, to change not in their accustomed care.[5]

Translated by James Cleugh

Sonnet 25

    O Fate, implacable in my pursuit,
How pitiless has been thy harsh decree:
With cruel hand thou didst cut down the tree
And on the ground didst scatter flower and fruit.
    In narrow bed today my love lies mute,
And with her, all my hopes of things to be

---

[3] *Genii:* attendant spirits of a person or place; *Fays:* fairies, nature spirits; *Tritons:* in Greek myth, demigods of the sea, usually portrayed as half-men, half-fish.

[4] Digger, miner.

[5] A paradox: a quality of time that never changes is change itself.

Are but disdainful ashes, scorning me,
Deaf to my wailing, heedless of my suit.
    Accept these new-wept tears with all of those
So often shed, though naught availing thee
Where now thou dwellest in felicity,
    Until in night eternal death shall close
These eyes that saw thee, and to me be given
New eyes to see thee when I wake in heaven.

Translated by Caroline B. Bourland

SIR THOMAS WYATT

*T*he third poet selected for this chapter is that courtier who introduced the
Italian sonnet into English literature, Sir Thomas Wyatt (1503–1542), just
*as Garcilaso had done for Spanish literature. Traveling widely throughout Europe as a diplomat for King Henry VIII of England, Wyatt developed an interest
in foreign literatures, especially Italian. In addition to his many accomplished
lyrics in the English tradition, Wyatt translated and imitated the sonnets of Petrarch (Francesco Petrarca, 1304–1374), who had been an important early exponent of the Italian sonnet. In the fourteen-line Petrarchan sonnet the speaker is
often a lover in a despairing mood, enslaved by his obsessive passion, and tortured by rejection. Wyatt added greater intensity to his Italian model. The most
common rhyme scheme used in Wyatt's version of the Petrarchan sonnet is* abba
abba cddc ee; *there is often a "turn" in mood or meaning after the eighth line
(the octave). (The last three lyrics in the following selection demonstrate Wyatt's
modification of the Petrarchan sonnet.) Wyatt's adventurous life may be somewhat reflected in his poetry, since he was apparently the lover of Anne Boleyn before she became the second wife of Henry VIII. Having warned the king that he
knew her not to be suitable for the role of queen, Wyatt was apparently rewarded
for his candor with diplomatic posts when the king disregarded his advice. The
poet was, however, imprisoned twice on serious charges, including treason, and
was able from his prison window to watch the execution of Anne's postnuptial
lovers. Wyatt never published a collection of his poems, although they circulated
extensively in manuscript and were copied by hand. It was not until fifteen years
after his death that an enterprising London printer, Richard Tottel, published an
anthology of 221 poems titled* Songs and Sonnets . . . , *ninety-seven of which he
attributed to Wyatt. Since Tottel felt that Wyatt's phrasing and rhythm were crude,
he sometimes "smoothed" the poems to his own taste. Thus, the selection that follows is taken from the Egerton manuscript in Wyatt's own hand. For ease of reading the spelling has been modernized when it does not change meaning or rhythm.*

From the Egerton Manuscript in the British Museum.

They Flee from Me

They flee from me, that sometime did me seek,
With naked foot stalking in my chamber.
I have seen them, gentle, tame, and meek,
That now are wild, and do not remember
That sometime they put themselves in danger
To take bread at my hand; and now they range,
Busily seeking with a continual change.

Thankèd be fortune it hath been otherwise,
Twenty times better; but once in special,
In thin array, after a pleasant guise,
When her loose gown from her shoulders did fall,
And she me caught in her arms long and small,[1]
Therewithall sweetly did me kiss
And softly said, "Dear heart, how like you this?"

It was no dream, I lay broad waking.
But all is turned, thorough my gentleness,
Into a strange fashion of forsaking;
And I have leave to go, of her goodness,
And she also to use newfangleness.[2]
But since that I so kindely[3] am servèd,
I fain would know what she hath deservèd.

Farewell, Love

Farewell, Love, and all thy laws forever,
Thy baited hooks shall tangle me no more;
Senec and Plato call me from thy lore,
To perfect wealth my wit for to endeavor.[4]

---

[1] Long and slender.

[2] Fashionable fickleness.

[3] Appropriately; "kindely" is, of course, used here with a sarcastic tone.

[4] That is, Seneca ("Senec"), the ancient Roman Stoic philosopher, call upon the speaker to leave the distractions of physical love and to educate his mind to "perfect wealth" (spiritual and intellectual well-being).

[5] More pleasing.

In blind error when I did persever,
Thy sharp repulse, that pricketh aye so sore,
Hath taught me to set in trifles no store
And 'scape forth since liberty is lever.[5]
Therefore farewell, go trouble younger hearts,
And in me claim no more authority;
With idle youth go use thy property,
And thereon spend thy many brittle darts.
For hitherto though I have lost all my time,
Me lusteth[6] no longer rotten boughs to climb.

I Find No Peace[7]

I find no peace and all my war is done;
    I fear and hope, I burn and freeze like ice;
    I fly above the wind, yet can I not arise,
    And naught I have and all the world I seize on;
That[8] looseth nor locketh holdeth me in prison,
    And holdeth me not yet can I scape nowise;
    Nor letteth me live nor die at my devise,[9]
    And yet of death it giveth none occasion.
Without eyen[10] I see, and without tongue I plain;[11]
    I desire to perish, and yet I ask health;
    I love another, and thus I hate myself;
I feed me in sorrow, and laugh in all my pain.
    Likewise displeaseth me both death and life,
    And my delight is causer of this strife.

---

[6] I desire.

[7] This is Wyatt's version of a sonnet in Italian by Petrarch. It helped to establish in English poetry the tradition of talking about love in paradoxes.

[8] That which (love).

[9] Plan.

[10] Eyes.

[11] Complain.

[12] Wyatt's version of another sonnet in Italian by Petrarch.

[13] An allusion to the navigational terrors of Odysseus in Homer's ancient epic *The Odyssey* (see Volume I). Here, Wyatt transforms Odysseus's ship of struggling sailors into a ship of the self.

[14] Also.

My Galley Chargèd with Forgetfulness[12]

My galley chargèd with forgetfulness
    Through sharp seas, in winter night doth pass
    Tween rock and rock,[13] and eke[14] mine enemy, alas,
    That is my lord steereth with cruelness.
And every oar a thought in readiness,
    As though that death were light in such a case.[15]
    An endless wind doth tear the sail apace
    Of forcèd sighs and trusty fearfulness.[16]
A rain of tears, a cloud of dark disdain,
    Hath done the wearied cords[17] great hinderance,
    Wreathed with error and eke with ignorance.
The stars be hid that led me to this pain
    Drownèd is reason that should me consort,[18]
    And I remain despairing of the port.

WILLIAM SHAKESPEARE

The fourth lyric poet selected for this chapter is far better known for his dramas. William Shakespeare (1564–1616) may be the greatest dramatist in the history of world literature. As a result his plays are readily available in excellent inexpensive editions and were not included in this volume. Shakespeare not only wrote plays but was also an accomplished lyric poet; the publication of his Sonnets in 1609 marked the appearance of a cycle of 154 sonnets that no other poet has equaled. Neither a university graduate nor of noble birth, Shakespeare's success among his contemporaries demonstrates how the old class barriers were breaking down during the Renaissance. As Shakespeare was the foremost practitioner of the English version of the sonnet's form, that version is now often called the Shakespearean sonnet. In iambic pentameter it comprises three quatrains and a final couplet, rhyming abab cdcd efef gg. The "turn" usually comes with the ending couplet, which often achieves the neatness of an epigram. Shakespeare, however, did not limit the varied moods of his sonnets to the traditional despair of the rejected Petrarchan lover; he also includes such moods as delight, contentment, sympathy, pride (of authorship), ridicule, melancholy, shame, disgust, and fear. The sequence of Shakespeare's sonnets suggests a sort of narrative to some

---

[15] That is, as though my destruction would not matter much.

[16] Fear to trust.

[17] The rigging of the metaphorical vessel (the speaker's overwrought emotions).

[18] Accompany.

scholars (although some dispute as to whether the current order of the sonnets is actually Shakespeare's intention). Sonnets 1 to 17 celebrate the attractions of a young man and urge him to marry so as to transmit that beauty. The long sequence from 18 to 126 focuses on an ideal young man, developing the theme of the destructive power of time, balanced perhaps only by the power of love, friendship, and deathless poetry itself. The remaining sonnets, 127–154, focus especially on the "Dark Lady" as a tempting but potentially destructive object of desire. There has been much speculation about the autobiographical relevance of the sonnets, but there is not much clear factual evidence; the reader is best advised to analyze them purely as poems, not as confessions.

The selection that follows includes nine of the best known sonnets, with modernized spelling and punctuation. Sonnet 18 asserts the immortality given to the fair youth by the poet's description of him. (This boast of immortality for one's verse was a Renaissance convention that ultimately demonstrated faith in the permanence of art, not merely foolish personal pride.) Sonnet 29 shows the speaker in a lonely mood envying the prosperity and achievements of others until he remembers his friend, whose love compensates the speaker for his "outcast state." In Sonnet 30 the speaker, still lonely, takes stock of his past losses, depicted in legal and financial metaphors, and ceases to bewail his "grievances" when he thinks, consolingly, of his friend. In Sonnet 55 the speaker asserts that his "powerful rhyme" will outlast marble statues and buildings, keeping praise of the youth alive until Judgment Day. Anticipating his own death in Sonnet 71 (three score and ten sonnets now having been accomplished), the speaker implores the youth not to mourn for him, to forget him quickly, for the speaker does not wish the youth to grieve or be mocked by association with him. Through a series of images of decay the speaker points out the signs of his own aging to the youth of Sonnet 73, concluding that the brevity of time remaining should make the youth's "love more strong." In Sonnet 116 the speaker asserts the ideal of true love as unalterable. Sonnet 130 is humorously anti-Petrarchan in its denial by the male lover of the necessity for the peerless qualities usually attributed by other sonneteers to their ladies. In Shakespeare's only explicitly religious sonnet (146) the speaker addresses his own soul to question why it so richly adorns the body in which it is housed, admonishing it to prepare for death by repudiating earthly riches and accumulating spiritual wealth.

18

---

[1] That is, summer has only a brief leasehold purchased from nature.

[2] The sun is "the eye of heaven."

Shall I compare thee to a summer's day?
Thou art more lovely and more temperate:
Rough winds do shake the darling buds of May,
And summer's lease hath all too short a date:[1]
Sometime too hot the eye of heaven[2] shines,
And often is his gold complexion dimmed;
And every fair from fair sometime declines,[3]
By chance, or nature's changing course, untrimmed:
But thy eternal summer shall not fade,
Nor lose possession of that fair thou ow'st,[4]
Nor shall death brag thou wander'st in his shade
When in eternal lines to time thou grow'st:
    So long as men can breathe or eyes can see,
    So long lives this,[5] and this gives life to thee.

29

When in disgrace with fortune and men's eyes
I all alone beweep my outcast state,
And trouble deaf heaven with my bootless[6] cries,
And look upon myself, and curse my fate,
Wishing me like to one more rich in hope,
Featured like him,[7] like him with friends possessed,
Desiring this man's art[8] and that man's scope,[9]
With what I most enjoy contented least;[10]

---

[3] That is, everything that is beautiful eventually ceases to be so.

[4] "Fair thou ow'st" means "beauty you possess," but with an implication of *owing* the obligation of death as beauty's debt to nature.

[5] "This" is this sonnet; Shakespeare asserts it to be an enduring work of art that gives enduring life to its subject.

[6] Futile, hopeless.

[7] That is, with features as beautiful as some other person's (not the speaker's beloved); the speaker compares himself to five different people in lines 5–7.

[8] Skill of any kind, not necessarily literary or creative "art."

[9] Freedom, opportunity.

[10] That is, least satisfied with the things of which I have most.

[11] Perhaps; with an intimation also of "happily."

[12] Condition, state of mind; but in the final line there is also a pun on "state," meaning the chair of state, the throne.

[13] Dull, dark, shadowy.

Yet in these thoughts myself almost despising,
Haply[11] I think on thee, and then my state,[12]
Like to the lark at break of day arising,
From sullen[13] earth sings hymns at heaven's gate;
 For thy sweet love remembered such wealth brings
 That then I scorn to change my state with kings.

30

When to the sessions[14] of sweet silent thought
I summon up remembrance of things past,
I sigh the lack of many a thing I sought,
And with old woes new wail my dear time's waste;
Then can I drown an eye (unused to flow)
For precious friends hid in death's dateless[15] night,
And weep afresh love's long since cancelled woe,
And moan th'expense[16] of many a vanished sight.
Then can I grieve at grievances foregone,[17]
And heavily[18] from woe to woe tell[19] o'er
The sad account of fore-bemoaned moan,
Which I new pay, as if not paid before;
 But if the while I think on thee, dear friend,
 All losses are restored, and sorrows end.

55

Not marble, nor the gilded monuments

---

[14] The "sessions" of a law court. The extended legal and financial metaphors are expressed in such words as "summon," "dateless," "cancelled," "expense," "grievances," "account," "pay," etc. These terms suggest that the speaker is being called to account, as steward, for the estate of his life.

[15] Endless.

[16] Loss.

[17] Sorrows that belong to the past.

[18] Laboriously, sadly.

[19] Count, enumerate, the "grievances foregone."

[20] That is, more bright than the gravestone's inscription that time, portrayed as a dirty ("sluttish") housewife, has worn away and covered with grime.

[21] Battles.

[22] The sword of Mars, Roman god of war.

Of princes, shall outlive this powerful rhyme;
But you shall shine more bright in these contents
Than unswept stone, besmeared with sluttish time.[20]
When wasteful war shall statues overturn
And broils[21] root out the work of masonry,
Nor Mars his sword,[22] nor war's quick fire, shall burn
The living record of your memory:
'Gainst death, and all oblivious enmity[23]
Shall you pace forth; your praise shall still find room
Even in the eyes of all posterity
That wear this world out to the ending doom.[24]
    So till the judgment that yourself arise,[25]
    You live in this,[26] and dwell in lovers' eyes.

71

No longer mourn for me when I am dead
Than you shall hear the surly sullen bell
Give warning to the world that I am fled
From this vile world, with vilest worms to dwell:[27]
Nay, if you read this line, remember not
The hand that writ it, for I love you so
That I in your sweet thoughts would be forgot,
If thinking on me then should make you woe.
O if (I say) you look upon this verse,
When I, perhaps, compounded am with clay,
Do not so much as my poor name rehearse,

---

[23] Enmity that desires the beloved be entirely forgotten.

[24] Judgment Day, when the world (and time) will end.

[25] That is, until you rise from the dead on Judgment Day.

[26] "This powerful rhyme" (referring, perhaps, not just to this sonnet 55 but to Shakespeare's whole sequence of 154 sonnets).

[27] The speaker implores his beloved not to mourn for him longer than the deep and mournful ("surly sullen") funeral bell tolls. That bell was usually rung to announce the death of a member of the parish, one stroke for each year that had been lived.

But let your love even with my life decay;
  Lest the wise world should look into your moan,
  And mock you with me after I am gone.

73

That time of year thou mayst in me behold,
When yellow leaves, or none, or few do hang
Upon those boughs which shake against the cold,
Bare ruined choirs where late the sweet birds sang;[28]
In me thou seest the twilight of such day
As after sunset fadeth in the west,
Which by and by black night doth take away,
Death's second self that seals up all in rest;
In me thou seest the glowing of such fire
That on the ashes of his[29] youth doth lie,
As the deathbed, whereon it must expire,
Consumed with that which it was nourished by;[30]
  This thou perceiv'st, which makes thy love more strong,
  To love that well, which thou must leave ere long.

116

Let me not to the marriage of true minds
Admit impediments;[31] love is not love

---

[28] The leafless trees of winter are compared to the arching ruins of Gothic churches. The "sweet birds" had, literally, sung in the summer trees and, figuratively, sung as choirboys before the churches were destroyed. The "bare ruined choirs" thus evoke recollections of the dissolution of the English monasteries in 1539 by Henry VIII.

[29] Elizabethan English lacked the possessive "its." Therefore, "his" does not necessarily personalize "fire"; however, followed by "deathbed" it does suggest the dying embers of a person's life.

[30] That is, eaten up by that which it ate up (time or life).

[31] That is, let me not recognize objections to the union of truly loving minds. The "impediments" allude to the phrasing of the marriage service in the Anglican *Book of Common Prayer*: ". . . if any man do allege and declare any impediment why they may not be coupled together in matrimony. . . ."

[32] That is, love that changes in response to the change or departure of the beloved.

[33] A permanent beacon for ships at sea.

[34] That is, the value of the star (love) is incalculable, although its altitude has been scientifically measured.

[35] Something mocked by time.

Which alters when it alteration finds,
Or bends with the remover to remove.[32]
O no, it is an ever-fixèd mark,[33]
That looks on tempests and is never shaken;
It is the star to every wand'ring bark,
Whose worth's unknown, although his height be taken.[34]
Love's not Time's fool,[35] though rosy lips and cheeks
Within his bending sickle's[36] compass come;
Love alters not with his[37] brief hours and weeks,
But bears it out even to the edge of doom.[38]
    If this be error and upon me proved,
      I never writ, nor no man ever loved.

130

My mistress' eyes are nothing like the sun;
Coral is far more red than her lips' red;
If snow be white, why then her breasts are dun;[39]
If hairs be wires, black wires grow on her head;
I have seen roses damasked,[40] red and white,
But no such roses see I in her cheeks;
And in some perfumes is there more delight
Than in the breath that from my mistress reeks.
I love to hear her speak, yet well I know
That music hath a far more pleasing sound;
I grant I never saw a goddess go;[41]

---

[36] Time's curved sickle that cuts the growth of youthful beauty.

[37] Time's.

[38] That is, love endures even to the brink of Judgment Day.

[39] That is, if snow be white, her breasts are a dull gray-brown.

[40] Pink.

[41] Walk.

[42] That is, I think that my beloved is as extraordinary as any of those other women misrepresented by deceptively extravagent similes.

[43] The body ("sinful earth"), which is a microcosm of the world, has the soul as its center.

[44] In the original quarto publication of the sonnets (1609) the compositor apparently lost his concentration and simply repeated "my sinful earth" at the beginning of the second line. "Feeding" is, therefore, an editorial guess. The line then means that the soul has been temporarily captured by greedy, fleshly forces ("rebel powers") that decorate ("array") the soul's external surroundings, the body.

My mistress when she walks treads on the ground.
    And yet, by heaven, I think my love as rare
    As any she belied with false compare.[42]

146

Poor soul, the centre of my sinful earth,[43]
[Feeding] these rebel powers that thee array,[44]
Why dost thou pine[45] within and suffer dearth,
Painting thy outward walls so costly gay?[46]
Why so large cost, having so short a lease,
Dost thou upon thy fading mansion[47] spend?
Shall worms, inheritors of this excess,
Eat up thy charge?[48] Is this thy body's end?
Then, soul, live thou upon thy servant's loss,[49]
And let that pine to aggravate thy store;[50]
Buy terms divine in selling hours of dross;[51]
Within be fed, without be rich no more:
    So shalt thou feed on death, that feeds on men,
    And death once dead, there's no more dying then.

LOPE DE VEGA

Lope Félix de Vega Carpio (1562–1635), who was not related to Garcilaso de la Vega, was by far the most popular and prolific of the great masters of drama and poetry of Spain's Siglo de Oro ("Golden Age"). This brilliant period of Spain's literary history extended roughly from the late sixteenth century to the end of the seventeenth, coinciding with Spain's maximum imperial expansion. It produced such "golden" names as Cervantes (1547–1616; see Selection 17), Góngora (1561–1627), Quevedo (1580–1645), and Calderón (1600–1681; see Selection

---

[45] Waste away.

[46] "Gay" traditionally referred to brightly colored clothing.

[47] The aging body pictured here as a decaying house within which the soul's residence will be brief.

[48] Outlay.

[49] The rapidly approaching loss of the body which is subordinate ("servant") to the soul.

[50] That is, let the body deteriorate ("pine") in order to increase ("aggravate") the soul's riches ("store").

[51] That is, the soul should buy heavenly time without end by divesting itself of the time wasted in acquiring material rubbish ("hours of dross").

22). Numerous plays from Lope de Vega's vast number are still produced in Spain and Spanish America. Fuenteovejuna (1612), in particular, achieved international renown, and has been translated into all of the world's major languages. It tells the story of how the citizens of the small Castilian town of Fuenteovejuna collectively avenge the corrupt abuses of a military governor. The play has frequently been interpreted as Lope's exaltation of popular sovereignty over the power of the monarchy.

Spain's first great dramatist, as well as an outstanding poet, Lope de Vega was also a soldier who sailed against England with the disastrous Armada of 1588. The many love affairs in his adventurous life even included some after he became a priest in 1614, following the death of his second wife. These experiences are often reflected in the personal allusions of his plays and poems. Despite his enormous popularity and diverse experiences, Lope's life was ultimately tragic: among other misfortunes, he endured the death of his two wives, the madness of his last mistress, the death of two sons, and the abduction of a daughter by an aristocrat who was under royal protection. (Ironically, the last situation was one he had portrayed in several of his plays.) Lope de Vega was also prolific in his lyric poetry, particularly in the genre of the sonnet. The two selections, reproduced here in translation, display two very different facets of his psyche. In "Varied Effects of Love" Lope conveys, through the skillful use of antitheses, the contradictory feelings produced by love. In "Sonnet on a Sonnet" he reflects wittily on his own poetic devices.

Varied Effects of Love

To swoon, to dare, to anger yield,
Harsh, tender, ever-bold, yet shy,
In health, yet dead, alive to die,
Brave knight behind a coward's shield,

And not to find a peaceful field

From *An Anthology of Spanish Literature in English Translation,* ed. Seymour Resnick and Jeanne Pasmantier. London: John Calder Publishers, 1958, pp. 292–293.

[1] Annealing is the process of heating and cooking steel or glass to make the material less brittle.

[2] A poisonous herb, as well as the poisonous drink made from its fruit.

Apart from love; now sad, with pride
Thy mood oft times at whim will fly
Offended, haughty, glad, annealed.[1]

Forgetting gain, to court defeat,
To shun the truth that breaks the spell,
To quaff the hemlock[2] as nectar sweet:

To think that heaven fits in hell,
To give up life and soul to clear deceit:
This is love. Who tastes it knows it well.

Translated by Marguerite Gamble

Sonnet on a Sonnet

To write a sonnet doth Juana press me,
    I've never found me in such stress and pain;
    A sonnet numbers fourteen lines 'tis plain,
And three are gone ere I can say, God bless me!

I thought that spinning rhymes might sore oppress me,
    Yet here I'm midway in the last quatrain;
    And, if the foremost tercet I can gain,
The quatrains need not any more distress me.

To the first tercet I have got at last,
    And travel through it with such right good-will,
    That with this line I've finished it, I ween.[3]

I'm in the second now, and see how fast
    The thirteenth line comes tripping from my quill —
    Hurrah, 'tis done! Count if there be fourteen!

Translated by James Young Gibson

ANDREW MARVELL

*T*he last lyric poet selected for this chapter is Andrew Marvell, an Englishman
*(1621–1678). Marvell graduated from Cambridge University in 1639 and
seems to have written most of his poems during the 1650s, although they were not
published until three years after his death. He served for a time as the blind John
Milton's assistant when that Puritan epic poet was Latin Secretary for the ruling*

---

[3] I hope.

Commonwealth. *After the restoration of the monarchy in 1660, the loyal Marvell seems to have been helpful in saving Milton from an extended jail term and possible execution.*

Marvell's "To His Coy Mistress" may seem at first to be a simple poem of sexual seduction. It expresses the classical theme of carpe diem, *of seizing the pleasures of that day, for they are available to us only briefly. In a deeper sense, however, we can see that seizing the day is really a strategy for confronting the passage of time. Its iambic tetrameter couplets point out that there is no lovemaking in the afterlife. The ultimate source of the poem's argument is a poem by the ancient Greek lyric poet, Asklepiades: "You would keep your virginity? What will it profit you? It is among the living that we taste the joys of Venus. You will find no lover in Hades, girl. In Acheron, child, we shall only be bones and dust." At the heart of this argument is the desperation over growing old.*

To His Coy Mistress[1]

Had we but world enough, and time,
This coyness, lady, were no crime.
We would sit down, and think which way
To walk, and pass our long love's day.
Thou by the Indian Ganges' side
Shouldst rubies find: I by the tide
Of Humber would complain.[2] I would
Love you ten years before the flood:[3]
And you should, if you please, refuse
Till the conversion of the Jews.[4]

---

[1] "Coy Mistress" here means "shy sweetheart," since the logic of the poem necessitates that the speaker has not yet enjoyed a sexual relationship with the "mistress."

[2] The Humber is the English river that flows past Hull, Marvell's home town; its local dullness contrasts to the exotic Ganges upon whose banks rubies can be found.

[3] Almost at the beginning of earthly time, ten years before the flood described in Genesis.

[4] Almost at the end of earthly time; the final "conversion of the Jews" was supposed to be one of the events that would occur shortly before Judgment Day.

[5] Growing as slowly as vegetation.

My vegetable[5] love should grow
Vaster than empires, and more slow.
A hundred years should go to praise
Thine eyes, and on thy forehead gaze.
Two hundred to adore each breast:
But thirty thousand to the rest.
An age at least to every part,
And the last age should show your heart:[6]
For, lady, you deserve this state;[7]
Nor would I love at lower rate.
     But at my back I always hear
Time's winged chariot hurrying near:
And yonder all before us lie
Deserts of vast eternity.
Thy beauty shall no more be found;
Nor, in thy marble vault, shall sound
My echoing song: then worms shall try
That long-preserved virginity:
And your quaint honour turn to dust;[8]
And into ashes all my lust.
The grave's a fine and private place,
But none, I think, do there embrace.
     Now, therefore, while the youthful hue

---

[6] The chronological hyperbole derives from the traditional catalog of a mistress's beauties in Petrarchan sonnets and other contemporary love poetry. Here, however, the speaker realistically points out that there is no time for such leisurely adoration.

[7] Ceremonial dignity.

[8] Although the line makes sense as it stands, Marvell is clearly playing on the contemporary meaning of "quaint honor"; each of those words was a common reference to the primary female sexual organ.

[9] That is, the woman's coyness cannot prevent her passionate desire from showing immediately in her flushed face.

[10] The power of time's slowly devouring jaws.

Sits on thy skin like morning dew,
And while thy willing soul transpires
At every pore with instant fires,[9]
Now let us sport us while we may;
And now, like amorous birds of prey,
Rather at once our time devour,
Than languish in his slow-chapped power.[10]
Let us roll all our strength, and all
Our sweetness, up into one ball:
And tear our pleasures with rough strife,
Thorough[11] the iron gates of life.[12]
Thus, though we cannot make our sun
Stand still, yet we will make him run.[13]

---

[11] Through.

[12] In addition to possible historical allusions, the "iron gates" seems to be a reference to the act of defloration as the speaker tears his pleasure "with rough strife."

[13] In the final lines the speaker states that, if his argument should prove to be successful, the lovers will devour time instead of being eaten up by it, forcing the sun to keep up with them instead of hoping vainly that the sun will stop the aging process (the passing of the sunrises and sunsets).

4

❦

Babur

MEMOIRS

*Z*hiruddin Muhammad Babur (1483–1530), the founder of the magnificent Mughal empire of India and the author of the first true autobiography of the Islamic world, was a military and literary genius of the highest order. A sixth-generation descendant of the famous Turkish conqueror Amir Timur (Tamerlane) on his father's side, on his mother's he was descended from the still more famous Mongol conqueror Genghiz Khan. At the age of eleven, Babur inherited on his father's death the small kingdom of Ferghana (modern Uzbekistan and Tajikistan) in the now splintered empire of Timur. He was immediately plunged into a several years–long war with rival kinsmen and other enemies. Although he achieved some astonishing triumphs during this conflict, in the end he was ousted from Ferghana. After wandering homeless for three years, at last he gathered some troops, and by sheer daring and genius crossed the Hindu Kush Mountains and in 1504 occupied Kabul, the capital of an eastern kingdom stretching from the River Oxus to the borders of India. He was just twenty-one then. Still encountering opposition and once even driven out of Kabul, he surmounted his difficulties and, consolidating his control, ruled from Kabul for over twenty years. From there he moved into northern India and conquered it during the last five years of his life.

Spending almost his entire life in wars, Babur yet managed to record his lifelong experiences in an account of high literary merit. Circumstances and his premature death did not allow him to conclude his narrative. He even left it untitled. In course of time, the work came to be known as the Baburnama (Book of Babur) in Persian and the Memoirs in English. Babur's account comprises the first and, until recently the only, true autobiography in Islamic literature. For its frankness, honesty, intimacy of feeling, and vivid descriptions, it is considered to rank with the world's best-known autobiographies such as the Confessions of St. Augustine and the autobiographies of Rousseau and Mahatma Gandhi. In a literary context where Persian was the language of high culture in Central Asia and India, and Arabic the language of religion, Babur, although he knew these lan-

58

guages extremely well, wrote the Memoirs *in his native tongue, the Chaghatai dialect of Turkish, so named because it prevailed throughout most of the Turkish lands under Chaghatai Khan, Genghiz Khan's second son. During the century before Babur, under the influence of the Persian language, the Chaghatai dialect of Turkish had seen a literary flowering, especially in poetry. In the process, it received a strong infusion of Persian and Arabic words, but its base remained purely Turkish. The purest form of Chaghatai was spoken in Ferghana. Babur's* Memoirs *is one of the longest sustained prose narratives in that language. The natural freshness, simplicity, and directness of his medium, unlike the ornate artificiality of Persian, gave Babur's prose a clear, forceful, and unaffected style. Babur was equally a master of verse in Chaghatai Turkish and an accomplished poet of Persian as well.*

Aside from his individual talents, the foundation of Babur's achievement lay largely in the cultural sophistication typical of the Timurid princes (descended from Timur), most of whom were highly educated, well versed in the art of warfare, and possessed an intimate knowledge of their subjects. At a very young age a Timurid prince was put in the charge of a noble, designated as his ataka *(surrogate father), for upbringing and princely education. Often he lived in the ataka's territory, removed from the intrigue-ridden court. Besides the education under the ataka, a prince was entrusted to the care of an important person in the religious establishment, usually a prominent Sufi (a spiritual leader of the mystical approach to Islam), for academic, religious, and moral education. Babur speaks with great respect about a Sufi shaikh who kept him so pure in his adolescence that he would not have had a drink [of alcohol] even if he desired to. The Timurid princes lived in a world filled with love of poetry and beauty. They all read the classics of Persian poetry and acquired a taste for their appreciation. Many princes composed poetry themselves. Babur's father, Umar Shaikh Mirza, although he was not a poet, had a poetic bent of mind and a fastidious esthetic sensibility. In spite of spending most of his life on the battlefield, he regularly turned to the great Persian poets for wisdom and enjoyment. Babur was steeped in the knowledge of poetry. Often, as seen in the following excerpts, in the middle of telling a story he breaks off to quote a verse in Persian, Arabic, or Turkish. He "found leisure in the thick of his difficulties to compose an ode on his misfortunes."*

To enable a prince to learn about the ways and customs of his subjects and provide him with the experience of dealing with them, often at a very young age he was given the governorship of a province under the supervision of a noble who acted as his ataka. Babur was appointed the governor of an important province at the age of ten. A year later when his father died in an accident, he was well equipped to take over the reins of the kingdom. With the throne he inherited his father's ambition and the struggle to annex other areas of the Timurid Empire. Babur twice occupied Samarkand, the capital of the empire, claiming it as his rightful possession. However, both times he lost it. His most formidable enemies in the tussle were the Uzbeks, a rising branch of Turks from the north led by a powerful leader Shaibani Khan. After Babur's second occupation of Samarkand, when

Shaibani Khan drove him out of there, he could not even return to Ferghana, having relinquished it earlier to his brother. After he conquered Kabul, Babur immediately made plans to recover Samarkand, but because of the death of a strong ally, his plans did not materialize. Seven years later, after Shaibani Khan's death, Babur did conquer Samarkand for the third time. Within three years, however, he suffered a crushing defeat at the hands of the Uzbeks and returned to Kabul with great difficulty. Losing all hope of ever recovering his homeland and pressured by the Uzbeks even in Kabul, Babur now concentrated on the conquest of India. Having made several earlier incursions into the subcontinent, in 1526 he invaded it seriously, defeated and killed Sultan Ibrahim Lodi, and occupied Delhi and Agra, the capital cities of the sultanate. Within less than a year, Babur had to fight a far more formidable adversary in the Rajput chief Rana Sanga who had gathered, against Babur's 12,000 troops, an army of 210,000, consisting not only of Rajputs, the bravest Hindu warriors of India, but also of many Muslim feudal chiefs, all determined to expel the new foreign invader from their country. Babur was faced with the greatest crisis of his life. His army was unnerved and he himself was losing heart. Rising to the occasion, he made a momentous moral-spiritual decision. Babur possessed a highly developed moral sensibility, believing that success and happiness in the world depended on moral integrity and purity. Among the various moral weaknesses, he saw drinking of wine or hard liquor as a vice of crucial consequence. Until the age of twenty he had not touched drink. Then drinking parties with companions had become his frequent and favorite pastime. Now, he starkly realized the need to purify himself in order to come to terms with himself and the world. He forswore drinking, ordered his gold and silver drinking goblets broken, and their pieces distributed among the poor. His followers similarly vowed to abjure drinking. Since Islam forbids alcohol, the moral resolution was also a formal reaffirmation of the Muslim faith. Babur's Indian enterprise thus became a moral and a religious crusade. Infused with this spirit Babur's army routed Rana Sanga's host and Babur became the undisputed emperor of India.

Babur did not live long to enjoy the fruits of his lifelong fighting. An interesting story is told about his death. His eldest son Humayun fell desperately ill. Physicians gave up hope of his survival. Soothsayers advised Babur that if he sacrificed something most dear to his heart, the prince might recover. Babur decided that the thing dearest to him was his own life and he would give it away for his son. It is said that he walked around Humayun's bed and prayed that his life be taken in place of his son's. From that point on Babur's health declined until he died. Humayun steadily recovered.

Babur refers to his Memoirs as "history" and states his determination to be absolutely truthful, "to set down no more than the reality of every event. . . ." The book naturally tells, above all, the history of Babur's life. In the words of a translator, the Memoirs conveys "an excellent idea of Babur's policy, of his wars as well as of his manners, genius, and habits of thinking; . . . perhaps no work ever composed introduces us so completely to the court and council, the public and private life of an Eastern Sultan." However, the Memoirs is equally a history of

*the political, cultural, and geographical context of Babur's life. He describes in
minute detail the characters of the individuals he came in contact with; the conditions and circumstances of the kingdoms he knew; the customs, dress, habits,
and physique of the people of the countries he lived in or passed through; and the
climate, physical features, products, and scenery of these countries. He describes
the fauna and flora of the areas he knew in loving, encyclopedic detail. Consequently, Babur, in the* Memoirs, *is the best authority on the history of Central
Asia and India for his time.*

Babur emerges from the Memoirs *as a man with so many perfections that he
resembles a figure from* The Arabian Nights. *He was good-looking, strong, and
athletic. He swam all the rivers from the Kabul to the Ganges. He was a keen
archer and a horseman, adept in the martial arts, and a master military strategist. A brave warrior with indomitable will, he was never repressed by adversity.
A leader of men, he won the devotion of his followers by his own love of them, his
camaraderie, and his charm. He could be ruthless when necessity demanded, but
he was essentially a compassionate man, generous to friends and considerate to
defeated enemies. Though a man of action, he had a philosophic bent of mind.
Mostly busy with wars, he yet found time for reflection and appreciated tranquility. His favorite hobby was gardening. He was deeply religious but urbane and
liberal in outlook. Sensible of the tragic in life, he yet enjoyed life and beauty.
Very much a man of the world, he yet possessed an otherworldly abandon.*

*The following selection contains two excerpts. The first deals with Kabul, both
the city and the country that Babur loved. He lived there for more than twenty
years and, according to his wishes, was posthumously buried there. The second excerpt deals with the culminating point of Babur's career, his conquest of India.*

KABUL

The country of Kâbul is situated in the midst of the inhabited part of the world.
It is surrounded on all sides by hills. In winter all the roads are shut for five
months save one alone. The Kaffir robbers issue from the mountains and narrow
paths and infest this passage.[1] The country of Kâbul is very stony, and difficult of
access to foreigners or enemies. Its warm and cold districts are close to each other.

From F. G. Talbot, ed. *Memoirs of Baber Emperor of India* (London: Arthur L. Humphreys,
1909), pp. 94–96, 171–172, 181–182, 184–186, 190, 194–195, 204–206. Adapted by
the editor.

[1] Kaffirs are the inhabitants of Kaferistan, an area toward the northwest of the Indian
subcontinent.

You may go in a single day to a place where snow never falls, and in the space of two astronomical hours you may reach a place where snow lies always. To the north-west lie the meadows of Chalak, but in the summer mosquitoes greatly annoy the horses.

Kâbul is not fertile in grain — a return of four or five to one is reckoned favourable. The fruits are grapes, pomegranates, apricots, peaches, pears, apples, quinces, damsons, almonds, and walnuts. I caused the cherry-tree to be brought here and planted. It produced excellent fruit and continues thriving. It was I who planted the sugar-cane.

> Drink wine in the citadel of Kâbul, and send round the cup without
> stopping;
> For it is at once a mountain and a sea, a town and a desert.

There is a place called Kilkeneh in a retired, hidden situation. Much debauchery has gone on at that place.

> Oh, for the happy times when free and uncontrolled,
> We lived in Kilkeneh with no very good fame.

It is an excellent and profitable market. Were the merchants to carry their goods to China or Turkey they would scarcely get the same profit on them. Every year eight to ten thousand horses arrive in Kâbul. From Hindustân every year twenty thousand pieces of cloth are brought by caravan. Also slaves, white cloths, sugar candy, drugs, and spices. Merchants are not satisfied with getting three or four hundred percent.

Eleven or twelve languages are spoken in Kâbul — Arabic, Persian, Turki, Mogholi, Hindi, Afghani, [and others].

The moment you descend the hill-pass you see quite another world. Its timber, grain, animals are all different, also the manners and customs of the people.

In the mountainous country of Kaferistan is the tomb of the holy Lamech, the father of Noah.[2] On the skirts of these mountains the ground is richly diversified by various kinds of tulips. I once directed them to be counted, and they brought in thirty-three different sorts of tulips. There are large and beautiful spreading plane-trees. I planted gardens on the banks of the streams. On the side of a hill I directed a fountain to be built. Here the yellow Arghwan is very abundant, and when the flowers begin to bloom, the yellow mingling with the red, I know no place in the world to be compared to it.[3]

---

[2] The Old Testament's Noah is also frequently mentioned in the Koran, the Muslim holy scripture.

[3] The arghwan is the flower of the judas tree.

I was told that in one of the villages of Ghazni[4] there was a mausoleum, in which the tomb moved itself whenever the benediction on the Prophet was pronounced over it. I went and viewed it, and there certainly seemed to be a motion of the tomb. In the end, however, I discovered that the whole was an imposture practised by the attendants of the mausoleum. They had erected over the tomb a kind of scaffolding; contrived that it could be set in motion when any of them stood upon it, so that a looker-on imagined that it was the tomb that had moved; just as, to a person sailing in a boat, it is the bank which appears to be in motion. I directed the persons who attended the tomb to come down from the scaffolding; after which, let them pronounce as many benedictions as they would, no motion whatever took place. I ordered the scaffolding to be removed, and a dome to be erected over the tomb, and strictly enjoined the servants of the tomb not to dare to repeat this imposture.

· · ·

The Southern hills are very low, having little grass, bad water, and not a tree—an ugly and worthless country. At the same time, the mountains are worthy of the men; as the proverb says, "A narrow place is large to the narrow-minded." There are, perhaps, scarcely in the whole world such dismal-looking hill-countries as these.

In Kâbul, although the cold is intense, and much snow falls in winter, yet there is plenty of firewood, and near at hand. They can go and fetch it in one day. The fuel consists chiefly of mastick, oak, bitter almond, and the kerkend. The best of these is the mastick, which burns with a bright light, and has also a sweet perfume; it retains its heat long, and burns even when green. The oak, too, is an excellent firewood, though it burns with a duller light; yet it affords much heat and light; its embers last a long time, and it yields a pleasant smell in burning. It has one singular property: if its green branches and leaves are set fire to, they blaze up and burn from the bottom to the top briskly and with a crackling noise, and catch fire all at once. It is a fine sight to see this tree burn. The bitter almond is the most abundant and common of all, but it does not last. The kerkend is a low, prickly thorn, that burns alike whether green or dry; it constitutes the only fuel of the inhabitants of Ghazni.

THE CONQUEST OF INDIA

. . . I set out on my march to invade Hindustân. Great and small, good and bad, servants and no servants, the force numbered twelve thousand persons.

---

[4]Ghazni was a city and a region in the kingdom of Kabul during Babur's time. It is a city in present-day Afghanistan.

I halted at the Bagh-i-Vafa.[5] Here I was forced to wait some days for Hûmâiûn and the army that was with him.[6] In these Memoirs I have already repeatedly described the limits and extent of the Bagh-i-Vafa, its beauty and elegance. The garden was in great glory. No one can view it without acknowledging what a charming place it is. During the few days that we stayed there we drank a great quantity of wine at every sitting, and took regularly our morning cup. When I had no drinking parties, I had bhang parties.[7] In consequence of Hûmâiûn's delay beyond the appointed time, I wrote him sharp letters, taking him severely to task, and giving him many hard names. At last Hûmâiûn arrived. I spoke to him with considerable severity on account of his long delay. . . . [W]e marched thence, when I embarked on a raft, on which I proceeded down the river, drinking all the way till we reached Kosh-Gûmbez, where I landed and joined the camp.

A day or two after, when we halted, . . . I had fever, attended with a cough, and every time that I coughed I brought up blood. I knew whence this indisposition proceeded, and what conduct had brought on this chastisement.

Before this, whatever had come into my head, good or bad, in sport or jest, if I had turned it into verse for amusement, how bad or contemptible soever the poetry might be, I had always committed it to writing. On the present occasion, when I had composed some lines, my mind led me to reflections, and my heart was struck with regret that a tongue which could repeat the sublimest productions should bestow any trouble on such unworthy verses; that it was melancholy that a heart elevated to nobler conceptions should submit to occupy itself with these meaner and despicable fancies. From that time forward I religiously abstained from satirical or vituperative poetry. At the time of repeating this couplet I had not formed my resolution, nor considered how objectionable the practice was.

Then every one who fails and breaks his promise, that promise avenges its breach on his life; and he who adheres to his promises to God, God bestows on him boundless blessings.

What can I do with you, O my tongue!
On your account I am covered with blood within:
How long, in this strain of satire, will you delight to compose verses,
One of which is impure, and another lying?
If you say, Let me not suffer from this crime,—
Then turn your reins, and shun the field.

---

[5] The name of a "garden," which in Babur's account usually means a house or a palace with a garden around it. Bagh-i-Wafa was about a day's journey from the city of Kabul towards India.

[6] Humaiun (also spelled as Homayon) was the eldest son of Babur and the second Mughal emperor of India.

[7] Bhang is an intoxicating substance derived from marijuana.

O my Creator, I have tyrannized over my soul; and, if Thou art not bountiful unto me, of a truth I shall be of the number of the accursed.

I now once more composed myself to penitence and self-control; I resolved
to abstain from this kind of idle thoughts, and from such unsuitable amusements,
and to break my pen. Such chastenings from the throne of the Almighty, on rebellious servants, are mighty graces; and every servant who feels and benefits
from such chastisements has cause to regard them as overflowing mercies.

• • •

At this station I directed that, according to the custom of Rûm,[8] the gun-
carriages should be connected together with twisted bull-hides as with chains.
Between every two gun-carriages were six or seven breastworks. The matchlockmen stood behind these guns and breastworks, and discharged their matchlocks.
I halted five or six days in this camp, for the purpose of getting this apparatus
arranged. After every part of it was in order and ready, I called together all the
Amîrs, and men of any experience and knowledge, and held a general council. It
was settled that as Panipat was a considerable city,[9] it would cover one of our
flanks by its buildings and houses, while we might fortify our front by covered
defences, and cannon, and that the matchlockmen and infantry should be placed
in the rear of the guns and breastworks. With this resolution we moved, and in
two marches reached Panipat. On our right, were the town and suburbs. In my
front I placed the guns and breastworks which had been prepared. On the left,
and in different other points, we dug ditches and made defences of the boughs of
trees. At the distance of every bowshot, a space was left large enough for a hundred or a hundred and fifty men to issue forth. Many of the troops were in great
terror and alarm. Trepidation and fear are always unbecoming. Whatsoever
Almighty God has decreed from all eternity, cannot be reversed; though, at the
same time, I cannot greatly blame them; they had some reason; for they had come
two or three months' journey from their own country; we had to engage in arms
a strange nation, whose language we did not understand, and who did not
understand ours:

> We are all in difficulty, all in distraction,
> Surrounded by a people; by a strange people.

The army of the enemy opposed to us was estimated at one hundred thousand men; the elephants of the emperor and his officers were said to amount to

---

[8] The Ottoman Empire, called Rum because the Ottomans became the rulers of the eastern part of the ancient Roman Empire.

[9] Panipat is a town in the vast plain northwest of Delhi in India. It is the site of three decisive historical battles, the first of which was the one in 1526 between Babur and
Ibrahim Lodi the Sultan of India.

nearly a thousand. He possessed the accumulated treasures of his father and grandfather, in current coin, ready for use. It is an usage in Hindustân,[10] in situations similar to that in which the enemy now were, to expend sums of money in bringing together troops who engage to serve for hire. Had he chosen to adopt this plan, he might have engaged one or two hundred thousand more troops. But God Almighty directed everything for the best. He had not the heart to satisfy even his own army; and would not part with any of his treasure. Indeed, how was it possible that he should satisfy his troops, when he was himself miserly to the last degree, and beyond measure avaricious in accumulating pelf? He was a young man of no experience. He was negligent in all his movements; he marched without order; retired or halted without plan, and engaged in battle without foresight. . . .

By the time of early morning prayers, when the light was such that you could distinguish one object from another, notice was brought from the advanced patrols that the enemy were advancing, drawn up in order of battle. We too immediately braced on our helmets and our armour, and mounted. The right division was led by Hûmâiûn, the left division was commanded by Muhammed Sultan Mirza. The right of the centre was commanded by Chin Taimûr Sultan, the left of the centre by Khalîfeh. The advance was led by Khosrou Gokultâsh. Abdul-Azîz, master of horse, had the command of the reserve. On the flank of the right division I stationed Wali Kazîl, with their Moghuls, to act as a flanking party. On the extremity of the left division I stationed Kara-Kûzi, to form the flankers, with instructions, that as soon as the enemy approached sufficiently near, they should take a circuit and come round upon their rear.

When the enemy first came in sight, they seemed to bend their force most against the right division. I therefore detached Abdul-Azîz, who was stationed with the reserve, to reinforce the right. Sultan Ibrâhim's army, from the time it first appeared in sight, never made a halt, but advanced right upon us at a quick pace. When they came closer, and on getting a view of my troops, found them drawn up in the order and with the defences that have been mentioned, they were brought up and stood for a while, as if considering, "Shall we halt or not? Shall we advance or not?" They could not halt, and they were unable to advance with the same speed as before. I sent orders to the troops stationed as flankers on the extremes of the right and left divisions, to wheel round the enemy's flank with all possible speed, and instantly to attack them in the rear; the right and left divisions were also ordered to charge the enemy. The flankers accordingly wheeled on the rear of the enemy, and began to make discharges of arrows on them. Mehdi Khwâjeh came up before the rest of the left wing. A body of men with one elephant advanced to meet him. My troops gave them some sharp discharges of arrows, and the enemy's division was at last driven back. I dispatched from the main body Ahmedi Perwânchi to the assistance of the left division. The battle

---

[10] People to the west of India called the country Hindustan.

was likewise obstinate on the right. I ordered Muhammedi Gokultâsh to advance in front of the centre and engage. Ustâd Ali also discharged his guns many times in front of the line to good purpose. Mûstafa, the cannoneer, on the left of the centre, managed his artillery with great effect. The right and left divisions, the centre and flankers having surrounded the enemy and taken them in rear, were now engaged in hot conflict, and busy pouring in discharges of arrows on them. They made one or two very poor charges on our right and left divisions. My troops making use of their bows, plied them with arrows, and drove them in upon their centre. The troops on the right and left of their centre, being huddled together in one place, such confusion ensued, that the enemy, while totally unable to advance, found also no road by which they could flee. The sun had mounted spear-high when the onset of battle began, and the combat lasted till mid-day, when the enemy were completely broken and routed, and my friends victorious and exulting. By the grace and mercy of Almighty God, this arduous undertaking was rendered easy for me, and this mighty army, in the space of half a day, laid in the dust. Five or six thousand men were discovered lying slain, in one spot, near Ibrâhim. We reckoned that the number lying slain, in different parts of this field of battle, amounted to fifteen or sixteen thousand men. On reaching Agra,[11] we found, from the accounts of the natives of Hindustân, that forty or fifty thousand men had fallen in this field. After routing the enemy, we continued the pursuit, slaughtering, and making them prisoners. Those who were ahead, began to bring in the Amîrs and Afghâns as prisoners. They brought in a very great number of elephants with their drivers, and offered them to me as peshkesh.[12] Having pursued the enemy to some distance, and supposing that Ibrâhim had escaped from the battle, I appointed a party of my immediate adherents, to follow him in close pursuit down as far as Agra. Having passed through the middle of Ibrâhim's camp, and visited his pavilions and accommodations, we encamped on the banks of the Siâh-ab.

It was now afternoon prayers when Tahir Taberi, the younger brother of Khalîfeh, having found Ibrâhim lying dead amidst a number of slain, cut off his head, and brought it in.

• • •

Hindustân is a country that has few pleasures to recommend it. The people are not handsome. They have no idea of the charms of friendly society, of frankly mixing together, or of familiar intercourse. They have no genius, no comprehension of mind, no politeness of manner, no kindness or fellow-feeling, no ingenuity or mechanical invention in planning or executing their handicraft works, no skill

---

[11] Agra, southeast of Delhi, was the twin capital of the Muslim empire of India, the other one being Delhi.

[12] Gifts.

or knowledge in design or architecture; they have no good horses, no good flesh, no grapes or musk-melons, no good fruits, no ice or cold water, no good food or bread in their bazaars, no baths or colleges, no candles, no torches, not even a candlestick.

The chief excellency of Hindustân is that it is a large country and has abundance of gold and silver. Another convenience of Hindustân is that the workmen of every profession and trade are innumerable and without end. For any work, or any employment, there is always a set ready, to whom the same employment and trade have descended from father to son for ages. . . .

It always appears to me that one of the chief defects of Hindustân is the want of artificial water-courses. I had intended, wherever I might fix my residence, to construct water-wheels, to produce an artificial stream, and to lay out a regularly planned pleasure-ground. Shortly after coming to Agra, I passed the Jumna[13] with this object in view, and examined the country, to pitch upon a fit spot for a garden. The whole was so ugly and detestable that I repassed the river quite repulsed and disgusted. In consequence of the want of beauty, and of the disagreeable aspect of the country, I gave up my intention of making a garden; but as no better situation presented itself near Agra, I was finally compelled to make the best of this same spot. I first of all began to sink the large well which supplies the baths with water; I next fell to work on that piece of ground on which are the tamarind trees, and the octangular tank; I then proceeded to form the large tank and its inclosure; and afterwards the tank and grand hall of audience that are in front of the stone palace. I next finished the garden of the private apartments, and the apartments themselves, after which I completed the baths. In this way, going on, without neatness and without order, in the Hindu fashion, I, however, produced edifices and gardens which possessed considerable regularity. In every corner I planted suitable gardens; in every garden I sowed roses and narcissuses regularly, and in beds corresponding to each other. We were annoyed with three things in Hindustân: one was its heat, another its strong winds, the third its dust. Baths were the means of removing all three inconveniences. In the bath we could not be affected by the winds. During the hot winds, the cold can there be rendered so intense, that a person often feels as if quite powerless from it. The room of the bath, in which is the tub or cistern, is finished wholly of stone. The water-run is of white stone; all the rest of it, its floor and roof, is of a red stone. Several other people, who procured situations on the banks of the river, made regular gardens and tanks, and constructed wheels, by means of which they procured a supply of water. The men of Hind, who had never before seen places formed on such a plan, or laid out with so much beauty, gave the name of Kâbul to the side of the Jumna on which these palaces were built.

• • •

---

[13] A river in northern India.

On Monday, [February 25, 1527], I had mounted to survey my posts, and in the course of my ride, was seriously struck with the reflection that I had always resolved, one time or another, to make an effectual repentance, and that some traces of hankering after the renunciation of forbidden works had ever remained in my heart.[14] I said to myself, O, my soul!

> How long wilt thou continue to take pleasure in sin?
> Repentance is not unpalatable — Taste it.
>
> How great has been the defilement from sin! —
> How much pleasure thou didst in despair! —
> How long hast thou been the slave of thy passions! —
> How much of thy life hast thou thrown away! —
> Since thou hast set out on a Holy War,
> Thou hast seen death before thine eyes for thy salvation.
> He who resolves to sacrifice his life to save himself,
> Shall attain that exalted state which thou knowest.
> Keep thyself far away from all forbidden enjoyments;
> Cleanse thyself from all thy sins.
> Having withdrawn myself from such temptation,
> I vowed never more to drink wine.

Having sent for the gold and silver goblets and cups, with all the other utensils used for drinking parties, I directed them to be broken, and renounced the use of wine, purifying my mind. The fragments of the goblets, and other utensils of gold and silver, I directed to be divided among the poor. The first person who followed me in my repentance was Asas, who also accompanied me in my resolution of ceasing to cut the beard, and of allowing it to grow. That night and the following, numbers of Amîrs and courtiers, soldiers and persons not in the service, to the number of nearly three hundred men, made vows of reformation. The wine which we had with us we poured on the ground. I ordered that the wine should have salt thrown into it, that it might be made into vinegar. On the spot where the wine had been poured out, I directed a wâîn to be sunk and built of stone, and close by the wâîn an alms house to be erected.[15] . . .

At this time, as I have already observed, in consequence of preceding events, a general consternation and alarm prevailed among great and small. There was not a single person who uttered a manly word, nor an individual who delivered a courageous opinion. The Vazîrs, whose duty it was to give good counsel, and the

---

[14] This and the following events occur during Babur's confrontation with the powerful Rajput chief Rana Sanga.

[15] A wain is a type of water well with stairs going down to the water at an angle from one side of the well.

Amîrs who enjoyed the wealth of kingdoms, neither spoke bravely, nor was their counsel or deportment such as became men of firmness. . . . At length, observing the universal discouragement of my troops, and their total want of spirit, I formed my plan. I called an assembly of all the Amîrs and officers, and addressed them: "Noblemen and soldiers! Every man that comes into the world is subject to dissolution. When we are passed away and gone, God only survives, unchangeable. Whoever comes to the feast of life, must, before it is over, drink from the cup of death. He who arrives at the inn of mortality, must one day inevitably take his departure from that house of sorrow—the world. How much better is it to die with honour than to live with infamy!"

> With fame, even if I die, I am contented;
> Let fame be mine, since my body is Death's.

"The Most High God has been propitious to us, and has now placed us in such a crisis, that if we fall in the field, we die the death of martyrs; if we survive, we rise victorious, the avengers of the cause of God. Let us, then, with one accord, swear on God's holy word, that none of us will even think of turning his face from this warfare, nor desert from the battle and slaughter that ensues, till his soul is separated from his body."

Master and servant, small and great, all with emulation, seizing the blessed Korân in their hands, swore in the form that I had given. My plan succeeded to admiration, and its effects were instantly visible, far and near, on friend and foe.

On Saturday [March 16, 1527], having dragged forward our guns, and advanced our right, left, and centre in battle array, we reached the ground that had been prepared for us. Many tents were already pitched, and they were engaged in pitching others, when news was brought that the enemy's army was in sight. I immediately mounted, and gave orders that every man should, without delay, repair to his post, and that the guns and lines should be properly strengthened. . . . The letter announcing my subsequent victory contains a clear detailed account of it. . . .

5

❧

Giorgio Vasari

LIVES OF THE ARTISTS

There was a striking change in the artist's social role during the European period that came to be known as the Renaissance. No longer was the typical image of the artist that of an obedient craftsman working in pious anonymity for the glory of God and the adornment of his monastery or community. The major artists of the Renaissance came to be regarded as divinely inspired geniuses whose gifts allowed them to transcend the normal limits of their social origins. Beginning in Italy in the fourteenth century and continuing there until the mid-sixteenth century and in northern Europe until the seventeenth century, there was a conscious revival of the aesthetic forms and humanistic attitudes of classical Greece and Rome. The artists and writers of the Renaissance felt that they had effected a "rebirth" of the ancient civilization whose magnificent ruins, mainly Roman, they saw around them. These artists and writers looked with scorn at the recently departed Middle Ages that they eventually called the "Dark Ages"; the great spired cathedrals they labeled as "Gothic," thus comparing them to the barbarous Germanic tribes that had sacked Rome in the fifth century. No medieval scribe would have thought it appropriate to record the lives of the anonymous craftsmen who had carved the exquisite images of saints in the cathedral stones of Amiens or Chartres; but Vasari's contemporaries, including Roman Catholic popes and cardinals, applauded his biographies of the artists of his own time and their immediate predecessors. Although the period of the Middle Ages does not now seem to have been the cultural and artistic wasteland that Vasari perceived, his aesthetic and historical valuation dominated Western taste and attitudes for centuries.

Giorgio Vasari (1511–1574) was a competent painter and architect. His Lives of the Most Eminent Painters, Sculptors, and Architects (Vite dè più eccellenti pittori, scultori ed architetti), *first published in 1550, enlarged in 1568, and often referred to as simply* Lives of the Artists, *was written in Italian by Vasari so that, as he said, he might preserve the memory "of these artists . . . whose names and works should not remain prey to death and oblivion." What makes Vasari's biographies so valuable to us is that he knew personally the leading artists of his time. For a brief period as a young man he was apprenticed to Michelangelo and later became his close friend and admirer. The major theme recurring throughout Vasari's* Lives *is that the works of his divinely talented contemporaries constitute a rebirth, a "renaissance," of the forms and spirit of Greek and Roman art. Vasari's biographies thus express the essence of the Renaissance spirit. Vasari was, himself, very conscious of the comparisons he made to the great creators of the ancient world. More than mere imitation of the ancients was involved, however; for Vasari and his contemporaries believed that revival of the aesthetic forms and literature of the ancient world would also revive the humanistic creative spirit of those times, including the ability to reproduce in paint and stone the living forms of nature.*

Excerpts from two of Vasari's Lives *are included. The first is from his biography of Leonardo da Vinci (1452–1519). An extraordinarily complex personality, Leonardo still remains an enigma as historians and psychiatrists repeatedly seek explanations for the meanings of his creations, as well as for his inability to bring many of his dazzling ideas to completion. Leonardo's genius, like that of many of the other major artists of the Renaissance, expressed itself in multiple forms: drawing, painting, sculpture, architecture, as well as vast engineering projects. After describing his boyhood apprenticeship to Verrochio, where Leonardo exceeded his master at painting an angel, the excerpt notes his work in Milan on the mural of the* Last Supper. *(Some historians consider this to be the first work of the High Renaissance because of its emphasis on the psychology of the disciples and the tension of the moment when Christ announces that one of them is about to betray him, a psychological intensity quite unknown to earlier artists.) Also in Milan, demonstrating his technical skill, Leonardo began to cast the largest bronze horse ever seen. (Not until 1999, in the United States, was the great horse finally cast— as close to Leonardo's plan as modern scholarship and technology could make it.) His constant quest for further knowledge of the world is shown by his dissection of dead bodies, which he then reproduced in remarkably precise anatomical drawings, an art that had not previously been advanced since the work of Galen, the second-century Greek physician. The excerpt then goes on to describe Leonardo's portrait of the* Mona Lisa *and notes examples of Leonardo's remarkable physical strength, as well as of his beauty and grace. The mystery surrounding Leonardo, even in his own time, was accentuated by the fact that he wrote left-handed and backwards. This was assumed by many of his contemporaries to be a private code, until Vasari pointed out that Leonardo's unique script could be read with the aid of a mirror. Perhaps no greater example could be given of the newly achieved status of great artists than Vasari's description of Leonardo's death in the arms of the King of France, in a chateau given him by that king. Leonardo's work anticipated the development of modern science, which had its roots in his Renaissance spirit of relentless inquiry into the nature of the material world.*

The second excerpt is from Vasari's Life *of Michelangelo Buonarroti (1475–1564), which is by far the longest of Vasari's biographies. He saw his friend Michelangelo as "the man whose work transcends and eclipses that of every other artist, living or dead." An individualistic, highly competitive genius, Michelangelo created gigantic statues that were embodiments of power, for example, his young* David *and his mature* Moses *holding the tablets of the Law (described in the excerpt). Like Leonardo, who was twenty-three years older, Michelangelo was a master of sculpture, painting, and architecture. The excerpt describes his apprenticeship with the painter Ghirlandaio and then with the sculptor Bertoldo, and how fortunate Michelangelo was to have lived as a young man in Florence under the patronage of Lorenzo the Magnificent, its political leader. Vasari also tells how the young Michelangelo's nose was broken, marked for life by a blow from an envious sculptor. Michelangelo's first youthful* Pietà, *still exhibited at St. Peter's, has his name and hometown carved across the Virgin Mary's bosom, as Vasari tells us, because the young sculptor was angry that this early work had been attributed to someone else.*

Michelangelo came to have a close and often abrasive relationship with the dominating Pope Julius II who employed the sculptor to carve all the figures on his vast, never-to-be-finished tomb. Julius then commanded Michelangelo to interrupt his work on the tomb in order to paint the vast barrel-vaulted ceiling of the Sistine Chapel, the private chapel of the popes, named after Julius's uncle, Pope Sixtus. This great project, painted almost entirely by himself, occupied Michelangelo for four years during which he had to lie on his back on scaffolding of his own invention, with paint dripping onto his face. He never fully recovered from the strain of that creation. Vasari tells us of several violent altercations between Michelangelo and Pope Julius, who was constantly trying to view the fresco before its completion, against the painter's strong wishes. Michelangelo's poetry (included in Selection 3) makes explicit the Platonic idealism blended with Christian faith that is implicit in his sculpture and painting. In Michelangelo's works Vasari saw confirmation of the Renaissance belief that the works of certain artists were not merely the expressions of skilled craftsmen but actually creative activities like the power of God that brought form and matter out of chaos.

LEONARDO DA VINCI

The greatest gifts are often seen, in the course of nature, rained by heavenly influences on human creatures; and sometimes, in supernatural fashion, beauty, grace, and talent are united beyond measure in one single person, in a manner that to whatever such a one turns his attention, his every action is so divine, that,

From Giorgio Vasari. *Lives of the Most Eminent Painters, Sculptors, and Architects,* translated by Gaston DuC. DeVere. 10 volumes. London: The Medici Society, 1912–1915. Adapted by the editor.

surpassing all other men, it makes itself clearly known as a thing bestowed by God (as it is), and not acquired by human art. This was seen by all mankind in Leonardo da Vinci, in whom, besides a beauty of body never sufficiently extolled, there was an infinite grace in all his actions; and so great was his genius, and such its growth, that to whatever difficulties he turned his mind, he solved them with ease. In him was great bodily strength, joined to dexterity, with a spirit and courage ever royal and magnanimous; and the fame of his name so increased, that not only in his lifetime was he held in esteem, but his reputation became even greater among posterity after his death.

Truly marvelous and celestial was Leonardo, the son of Ser Piero da Vinci; and in learning and in the rudiments of letters he would have made great progress, if he had not been so variable and unstable, for he set himself to learn many things, and then, after having begun them, abandoned them. Thus, in arithmetic, during the few months that he studied it, he made so much progress, that, by continually suggesting doubts and difficulties to the master who was teaching him, he would very often bewilder him. He gave some little attention to music, and quickly resolved to learn to play the lyre, as one who had by nature a spirit most lofty and full of refinement: wherefore he sang divinely to that instrument, improvising upon it. Nevertheless, although he occupied himself with such a variety of things, he never ceased drawing and working in relief, pursuits which suited his fancy more than any other. Ser Piero, having observed this, and having considered the loftiness of his intellect, one day took some of his drawings and carried them to Andrea del Verrocchio, who was much his friend, and besought him directly to tell him whether Leonardo, by devoting himself to drawing, would make any progress. Andrea was astonished to see the extraordinary beginnings of Leonardo, and urged Ser Piero that he should make him study it; wherefore he arranged with Leonardo that he should enter the workshop of Andrea, which Leonardo did with the greatest willingness in the world. And he practiced not one branch of art only, but all those in which drawing played a part; and having an intellect so divine and marvelous that he was also an excellent geometrician, he not only worked in sculpture, making in his youth, in clay, some heads of women that are smiling, of which plaster casts are still being made, and likewise some heads of boys which appeared to have issued from the hand of a master; but in architecture, also, he made many drawings both of ground plans and of other designs of buildings; and he was the first, although a youth, who suggested the plan of reducing the river Arno to a navigable canal from Pisa to Florence. He made designs of flour mills, fulling mills, and engines, which might be driven by the force of water: and since he wished that his profession should be painting, he studied much in drawing after nature, and sometimes in making models of figures in clay, over which he would lay soft pieces of cloth dipped in clay, and then set himself patiently to draw them on a certain kind of very fine Rheims cloth, or prepared linen: and he executed them in black and white with the point of his brush, so that it was a marvel, as some of them by his hand, which

I have in our book of drawings, still bear witness; besides which, he drew on paper with such diligence and so well, that there is no one who has ever equaled him in perfection of finish; and I have one, a head drawn with the style in chiaroscuro,[1] which is divine.

And there was infused in that brain such grace from God, and a power of expression in such sublime accord with the intellect and memory that served it, and he knew so well how to express his conceptions by draftsmanship, that he vanquished with his discourse, and confuted with his reasoning, every valiant wit. And he was continually making models and designs to show men how to remove mountains with ease, and how to bore them in order to pass from one level to another; and by means of levers, windlasses, and screws, he showed the way to raise and draw great weights, together with methods for emptying harbors, and pumps for removing water from low places, things which his brain never ceased from devising; and of these ideas and labors many drawings may be seen, scattered abroad among our craftsmen; and I myself have seen not a few. He even went so far as to waste his time in drawing knots of cords, made according to an order, that from one end all the rest might follow till the other, so as to fill a round; and one of these is to be seen in the form of an engraving, most difficult and beautiful, and in the middle of it are these words, "Leonardus Vinci Accademia." And among these models and designs, there was one by which he often demonstrated to many ingenious citizens, who were then governing Florence, how he proposed to raise the Temple of S. Giovanni in Florence, and place steps under it, without damaging the building; and with such strong reasons did he urge this, that it appeared possible, although each man, after he had departed, would recognize for himself the impossibility of so vast an undertaking.

He was so pleasing in conversation, that he attracted to himself the hearts of men. And although he possessed, one might say, nothing, and worked little, he always kept servants and horses, in which the latter he took much delight, and particularly in all other animals, which he managed with the greatest love and patience; and this he showed when often passing by the places where birds were sold, for, taking them with his own hand out of their cages, and having paid to those who sold them the price that was asked, he let them fly away into the air, restoring to them their lost liberty. For which reason nature was pleased so to favor him, that, wherever he turned his thought, brain, and mind, he displayed such divine power in his works, that, in giving them their perfection, no one was ever his peer in readiness, vivacity, excellence, beauty, and grace.

---

[1] Literally, in Italian, "light-dark," referring to the gradations of light and dark within a picture, especially one in which the forms are mainly determined, not by sharp outlines, but by the hazy meeting of lighter and darker areas.

It is clear that Leonardo, through his comprehension of art, began many things and never finished one of them, since it seemed to him that the hand was not able to attain to the perfection of art in carrying out the things which he imagined; for the reason that he conceived in his ideas difficulties so subtle and so marvelous, that they could never be expressed by the hands, be they ever so excellent. And so many were his caprices, that, philosophizing of natural things, he set himself to seek out the properties of herbs, going on even to observe the motions of the heavens, the path of the moon, and the courses of the sun.

He was placed, then, as has been said, in his boyhood, at the instance of Ser Piero, to learn art with Andrea del Verrocchio, who was making a panel-picture of S. John baptizing Christ, when Leonardo painted an angel who was holding some garments; and although he was but a lad, Leonardo executed it in such a manner that his angel was much better than the figures of Andrea; which was the reason that Andrea would never again touch color, in disdain that a child should know more than he. . . .

Leonardo was so delighted when he saw certain bizarre heads of men, with the beard or hair growing naturally, that he would follow one that pleased him a whole day, and so treasured him up in idea, that afterwards, on arriving home, he drew him as if he had had him in his presence. Of this sort there are many heads to be seen, both of women and of men, and I have several of them, drawn by his hand with the pen, in our book of drawings, which I have mentioned so many times; . . .

It came to pass that Giovan Galeazzo, Duke of Milan, being dead, and Lodovico Sforza raised to the same rank, in the year 1494, Leonardo was summoned to Milan in great repute to the Duke, who took much delight in the sound of the lyre, to the end that he might play it: and Leonardo took with him that instrument which he had made with his own hands, in great part of silver, in the form of a horse's skull—a thing bizarre and new—in order that the harmony might be of greater volume and more sonorous in tone; with which he surpassed all the musicians who had come together there to play. Besides this, he was the best improviser in verse of his day. The Duke, hearing the marvelous discourse of Leonardo, became so enamored of his genius, that it was something incredible: and he prevailed upon him by entreaties to paint an altar-panel containing a Nativity, which was sent by the Duke to the Emperor.

He also painted in Milan, for the Friars of S. Dominic, at S. Maria delle Grazie, a Last Supper, a most beautiful and marvelous thing; and to the heads of the Apostles he gave such majesty and beauty, that he left the head of Christ unfinished, not believing that he was able to give it that divine air which is essential to the image of Christ. This work, remaining thus all but finished, has ever been held by the Milanese in the greatest veneration, and also by strangers as well; for Leonardo imagined and succeeded in expressing that anxiety which had seized the Apostles in wishing to know who should betray their Master. For which reason in all their faces are seen love, fear, and wrath, or rather, sorrow, at not being able to understand the meaning of Christ; which thing excites no less marvel than the sight, in contrast to it, of obstinacy, hatred, and treachery in Judas; not to mention that every least part of the work displays an incredible diligence, seeing that even in the tablecloth the texture of the stuff is counterfeited in such a manner that linen itself could not seem more real.

It is said that the Prior of that place kept pressing Leonardo, in a most hostile manner, to finish the work; for it seemed strange to him to see Leonardo sometimes stand half a day at a time, lost in contemplation, and he would have liked him to go on like the laborers hoeing in his garden, without ever stopping his brush. And not content with this, he complained of it to the Duke, and that so warmly, that he was constrained to send for Leonardo and delicately urged him to work, contriving nevertheless to show him that he was doing all this because of the importunity of the Prior. Leonardo, knowing that the intellect of that Prince was acute and discerning, was pleased to discourse at large with the Duke on the subject, a thing which he had never done with the Prior: and he reasoned much with him about art, and made him understand that men of lofty genius sometimes accomplish the most when they work the least, seeking out inventions with the mind, and forming those perfect ideas which the hands afterwards express and reproduce from the images already conceived in the brain. And he added that two heads were still to be painted; that of Christ, which he did not wish to seek on earth; and he could not think that it was possible to conceive in the imagination that beauty and heavenly grace which should be the mark of God incarnate. Next, there was lacking that of Judas, which was also troubling him, not thinking himself capable of imagining features that should represent the countenance of him who, after so many benefits received, had a mind so cruel as to resolve to betray his Lord, the Creator of the world. However, he would seek out a model for the latter; but if in the end he could not find a better, he should not lack that of the troublesome and tactless Prior. This thing moved the Duke wondrously to laughter, and he said that Leonardo had a thousand reasons on his side. And so the poor Prior, in confusion, confined himself to urging on the work in the garden, and left Leonardo in peace, who finished only the head of Judas, which seems the very embodiment of treachery and inhumanity; but that of Christ, as has been said, remained unfinished. The nobility of this picture, both because of its design, and from its having been wrought with an incomparable diligence, awoke a desire in the King of France to transport it into his kingdom; wherefore he tried by all possible means to discover whether there were architects who, with cross-stays of wood and iron, might be able to make it so secure that it might be transported safely; without considering any expense that might have been involved thereby, so much did he desire it. But the fact of its being painted on the wall robbed his Majesty of his desire; and the picture remained with the Milanese. . . .

While he was engaged on this work, he proposed to the Duke to make a horse in bronze, of a marvelous greatness, in order to place upon it, as a memorial, the image of the Duke's father. And on so vast a scale did he begin it and continue it, that it could never be completed. And there are those who have been of the opinion (so various and so often malign out of envy are the judgments of men) that he began it with no intention of finishing it, because, being of so great a size, an incredible difficulty was encountered in seeking to cast it in one piece; and it might also be believed that, from the result, many may have formed such a judgment, since many of his works have remained unfinished. But, in truth, one can believe that his vast and most excellent mind was hampered through being too full of desire, and that his wish ever to seek out excellence upon excellence, and perfection upon perfection, was the reason of it. "The work was retarded by desire," as our Petrarch has said. And, indeed, those who saw the great model that Leonardo made in clay vow that they have never seen a more beautiful thing, or a more superb; and it was preserved until the French came to Milan with King Louis of France, and broke it all to pieces. Lost, also, is a little model of it in wax, which was held to be perfect, together with a book on the anatomy of the horse made by him by way of study.

He then applied himself, but with greater care, to the anatomy of man, assisted by and in turn assisting, in this research, Messer Marc' Antonio della Torre, an excellent philosopher, who was then lecturing at Pavia, and who wrote of this matter; and he was one of the first (as I have heard tell) that began to illustrate the problems of medicine with the doctrine of Galen,[2] and to throw true light on anatomy, which up to that time had been wrapped in the thick and gross darkness of ignorance. And in this he found marvelous aid in the brain, work, and hand of Leonardo, who made a book drawn in red chalk, and annotated with the pen, of the bodies that he dissected with his own hand, and drew with the greatest diligence; wherein he showed all the frame of the bones; and then added to them, in order, all the nerves, and covered them with muscles; the first attached to the bone, the second that hold the body firm, and the third that move it; and beside them, part by part, he wrote letters of an ill-shaped character, which he made with the left hand, backwards, and whoever is not practiced in reading them cannot understand them, since they are not to be read save with a mirror. . . .

Leonardo undertook to execute, for Francesco del Giocondo, the portrait of Mona Lisa, his wife; and after toiling over it for four years, he left it unfinished; and the work is now in the collection of King Francis of France, at Fontainebleau.[3] In this head, whoever wished to see how closely art could imitate nature, was able to comprehend it with ease; for in it were counterfeited all the minutenesses that with subtlety are able to be painted, seeing that the eyes had that luster and watery sheen which are always seen in life, and around them were all those rosy and

---

[2] Ancient Greek physician, A.D. 129–199, whose scientific writings had an enduring influence on later medical works.

[3] The portrait is now in the Louvre museum in Paris.

pearly tints, as well as the lashes, which cannot be represented without the greatest subtlety. The eyebrows, through his having shown the manner in which the hairs spring from the flesh, here more close and here more scanty, and curve according to the pores of the skin, could not be more natural. The nose, with its beautiful nostrils, rosy and tender, appeared to be alive. The mouth, with its opening, and with its ends united by the red of the lips to the flesh tints of the face, seemed, in truth, to be not colors but flesh. In the pit of the throat, if one gazed upon it intently, could be seen the beating of the pulse. And, indeed, it may be said that it was painted in such a manner as to make every valiant craftsman, be he who he may, tremble and lose heart. He made use, also, of this device: Mona Lisa being very beautiful, he always employed, while he was painting her portrait, persons to play or sing, and jesters, who might make her remain merry, in order to take away that melancholy which painters often give to the portraits that they paint. And in this work of Leonardo's there was a smile so pleasing, that it was a thing more divine than human to behold; and it was held to be something marvelous, since the reality was not more alive.

• • •

. . . It is related that, a work having been allotted to him by the Pope, he straightway began to distil oils and herbs, in order to make the varnish;[4] at which Pope Leo said: "Alas! this man will never do anything, for he begins by thinking of the end of the work, before the beginning."

There was very great disdain between Michelangelo Buonarroti and him, on account of which Michelangelo departed from Florence, with the excuse of Duke Giuliano,[5] having been summoned by the Pope to the competition for the façade of S. Lorenzo. Leonardo, understanding this, departed and went into France, where the King, having had works by his hand, bore him great affection; and he desired that he should color the cartoon[6] of S. Anne, but Leonardo, according to his custom, put him off for a long time with words.

Finally, having grown old, he remained ill many months, and, feeling himself near to death, asked to have himself diligently informed of the teaching of the Catholic faith, and of the good way and holy Christian religion; and then, with many moans, he confessed and was penitent; and although he could not raise himself well on his feet, supporting himself on the arms of his friends and servants, he was pleased to take devoutly the most holy Sacrament, out of his bed. The King, who was accustomed often and lovingly to visit him, then came into

---

[4] Varnishing is the last step in the completion of an oil painting.

[5] Giovanni de' Medici (1475–1521) took the title Leo X when he became pope in 1513. Duke Giuliano was his brother.

[6] In this context, a cartoon is a full-size sketch on paper done in preparation for a painting.

the room; wherefore he, out of reverence, having raised himself to sit upon the bed, giving him an account of his sickness and the circumstances of it, showed withal how much he had offended God and mankind in not having worked at his art as he should have done. Thereupon he was seized by a paroxysm, the messenger of death; for which reason the King having risen and having taken his head, in order to assist him and show him favor, to the end that he might alleviate his pain, his spirit, which was divine, knowing that it could not have any greater honor, expired in the arms of the King.

The loss of Leonardo grieved beyond measure all those who had known him, since there was never any one who did so much honor to painting. With the splendor of his aspect, which was very beautiful, he made serene every broken spirit: and with his words he turned to yea, or nay, every obdurate intention. By his physical force he could restrain any outburst of rage: and with his right hand he twisted the iron ring of a doorbell, or a horseshoe, as if it were lead. With his liberality he would assemble together and support his every friend, poor or rich, if only he had intellect and worth. He adorned and honored, in every action, no matter what mean and bare dwelling; wherefore, in truth, Florence received a very great gift in the birth of Leonardo, and an incalculable loss in his death. In the art of painting, he added to the manner of coloring in oils a certain obscurity, whereby the moderns have given great force and relief to their figures. And in statuary, he proved his worth in the three figures of bronze that are over the door of S. Giovanni, on the side toward the north, executed by Giovan Francesco Rustici, but contrived with the advice of Leonardo; which are the most beautiful pieces of casting, the best designed, and the most perfect that have as yet been seen in modern days. By Leonardo we have the anatomy of the horse, and that of man even more complete. And so, on account of all his qualities, so many and so divine, although he worked much more by words than by deeds, his name and fame can never be extinguished.

MICHELANGELO BUONARROTI

While the most noble and industrious spirits were striving, by the light of the famous Giotto[7] and of his followers, to give to the world proof of their ability, the Ruler of Heaven in His clemency sent down to earth a spirit with universal ability in every art, who might be able, working by himself alone, to show what manner of thing is the perfection of the art of design in executing the lines, contours, shadows, and high lights, so as to give relief to works of painting, and what

---

[7]Giotto di Bondone (1276?–1337?), Florentine painter and sculptor, a leading artist of the early Renaissance and one of the founders of modern painting in his revival of the imitation of natural forms rather than the use of the customary saintly stereotypes.

it is to work with correct judgment in sculpture, and how in architecture it is possible to render habitations secure and commodius, healthy and cheerful, well-proportioned, and rich with varied ornaments. He was pleased, in addition, to endow him with the true moral philosophy and with the ornament of sweet poetry, to the end that the world might choose him and admire him as its highest exemplar in the life, works, saintliness of character, and every action of human creatures, and that he might be acclaimed by us as a being rather divine than human. And since He saw that in the practice of these rare exercises and arts—namely, in painting, in sculpture, and in architecture—the Tuscan intellects have always been exalted and raised high above all others, He chose to give him Florence for his country.

There was born a son, then, in the Casentino, in the year 1475, under a fateful and happy star, from an excellent and noble mother, to Lodovico di Leonardo Buonarroti Simoni, a descendant, so it is said, of the most noble and most ancient family of the Counts of Canossa. To that Lodovico, I say, who was in that year Podestà[8] of the township of Chiusi and Caprese, near the Sasso della Vernia, where S. Francis received the Stigmata,[9] in the Diocese of Arezzo, a son was born on the 6th of March, a Sunday, about the eighth hour of the night, to which son he gave the name Michelangelo, because he wished to suggest that he was something celestial and divine beyond the use of mortals. Having finished his office as Podestá, Lodovico returned to Florence and settled in the village of Settignano, at a distance of three miles from the city, where he had a farm that had belonged to his forefathers; which place abounds with stone and is all full of quarries of grey-stone, which is constantly being worked by stonecutters and sculptors, who for the most part are born in the place. Michelangelo was put out to nurse by Lodovico in that village with the wife of a stonecutter: wherefore the same Michelangelo, discoursing once with Vasari, said to him jestingly, "Giorgio, if I have anything of the good in my brain, it has come from my being born in the pure air of your country of Arezzo, even as I also sucked in with my nurse's milk the chisels and hammer with which I make my figures." In time Lodovico's family increased, and, being in poor circumstances, with slender revenues, he set about apprenticing his sons to the Guilds of Silk and Wool. Michelangelo, who by that time was well grown, was placed to be schooled in grammar with Maestro Francesco da Urbino; but, since his genius drew him to delight in design, all the time that he could snatch he would spend in drawing in secret, being scolded for this by his father and his other elders, and at times beaten, they perhaps considering that to give attention to that art, which was not known by them, was a mean thing and not worthy of their ancient house.

---

[8] Mayor.

[9] Marks resembling the crucifixion wounds of Christ.

At this time Michelangelo had formed a friendship with Francesco Granacci, who, likewise a lad, had placed himself with Domenico Ghirlandaio in order to learn the art of painting; wherefore Granacci, loving Michelangelo, and perceiving that he was much inclined to design, supplied him daily with drawings by Ghirlandaio, who at that time was reputed to be one of the best masters that there were not only in Florence, but throughout all Italy. Whereupon, the desire to work at art growing greater every day in Michelangelo, Lodovico, perceiving that he could not divert the boy from giving his attention to design, and that there was no help for it, and wishing to derive some advantage from it and to enable him to learn that art, resolved on the advice of friends to apprentice him with Domenico Ghirlandaio. Michelangelo, when he was placed with Domenico Ghirlandaio, was fourteen years of age. . . .

At that time the Magnificent Lorenzo de' Medici[10] kept the sculptor Bertoldo in his garden on the Piazza di S. Marco, not so much as custodian or guardian of the many beautiful antiques that he had collected and gathered together at great expense in that place, as because, desiring very earnestly to create a school of excellent painters and sculptors, he wished that these should have as their chief and guide the above-named Bertoldo, who was a disciple of Donatello.[11] Bertoldo, although he was so old that he was not able to work, was nevertheless a well-practiced master and in much repute, not only because he had polished with great diligence the pulpits cast by his master Donatello, but also on account of many castings in bronze that he had executed himself, of battles and certain other small works, in the execution of which there was no one to be found in Florence at that time who surpassed him. Now Lorenzo, who bore a very great love to painting and to sculpture, was grieved that there were not to be found in his time sculptors noble and famous enough to equal the many painters of the highest merit and reputation, and he determined, as I have said, to found a school. To this end he besought Domenico Ghirlandaio that, if he had among the young men in his workshop any that were inclined to sculpture, he might send them to his garden, where he wished to train and form them in such a manner as might do honor to himself, to Domenico, and to the whole city. Whereupon there were given him by Domenico as the best of his young men, among others, Michelangelo and Francesco Granacci; and they, going to the garden, found there that Torrigiano, a young man of the Torrigiani family, was executing in clay some figures in the round that had been given to him by Bertoldo. Michelangelo, seeing this, made some out of emulation; wherefore Lorenzo, seeing his fine spirit, always regarded him with much expectation. And he, thus encouraged, after some

---

[10] Ruler of Florence (1469–1492) and generous patron of the arts.

[11] Donatello (c. 1386–1466) was the greatest Florentine sculptor before Michelangelo.

days set himself to counterfeit from a piece of marble an antique head of a Faun that was there, old and wrinkled, which had the nose injured and the mouth laughing. Michelangelo, who had never yet touched marble or chisels, succeeded so well in counterfeiting it, that the Magnificent Lorenzo was astonished; and then, perceiving that, departing from the form of the antique head, he had opened out the mouth after his own fancy and had made a tongue, with all the teeth showing, that lord, jesting pleasantly, as was his custom, said to him, "Surely you should have known that old folks never have all their teeth, and that some are always lacking." It appeared to Michelangelo, in his simplicity, both fearing and loving that lord, that he had spoken the truth; and no sooner had Lorenzo departed than he straightway broke one of the teeth and hollowed out the gum, in such a manner, that it seemed as if the tooth had dropped out. And then he awaited with eagerness the return of the Magnificent Lorenzo, who, when he had come and had seen the simplicity and excellence of Michelangelo, laughed at it more than once, relating it as a miracle to his friends. Moreover, having made a resolve to assist and favor Michelangelo, he sent for his father Lodovico and asked for the boy from him, saying that he wished to maintain him as one of his own children; and Lodovico gave him up willingly. Thereupon the Magnificent Lorenzo granted him a chamber in his own house and had him attended, and he ate always at his table with his own children and with other persons of quality and of noble blood who lived with that lord, by whom he was much honored. This was in the year after he had been placed with Domenico, when Michelangelo was about fifteen or sixteen years of age; and he lived in that house four years, which was until the death of the Magnificent Lorenzo in 1492. During that time, then, Michelangelo had five ducats a month from that lord as an allowance and also to help his father; and for his particular gratification Lorenzo gave him a violet cloak, and to his father an office in the Customs. Truth to tell, all the young men in the garden were salaried, some little and some much, by the liberality of that magnificent and most noble citizen, and rewarded by him as long as he lived.

• • •

Now, returning to the garden of the Magnificent Lorenzo: that garden was full of antiques and richly adorned with excellent pictures, all gathered together in that place for their beauty, for study, and for pleasure. Michelangelo always had the keys, and he was much more earnest than the others in his every action, and showed himself always alert, bold, and resolute. He drew for many months from the pictures of Masaccio in the Carmine, where he copied those works with so much judgment, that the craftsmen and all other men were astonished, in such sort that envy grew against him together with his fame. It is said that Torrigiano, after contracting a friendship with him, mocked him, being moved by envy at seeing him more honored than himself and more able in art, and struck him a blow of the fist on the nose with such force, that he broke and crushed it very grievously and marked him for life; on which account Torrigiano was banished from Florence.

• • •

During his stay in Rome, Michelangelo made so much progress in the studies of art, that it was a thing incredible to see his exalted thoughts and the difficulties of the manner exercised by him with such supreme facility; to the amazement not only of those who were not accustomed to see such things, but also of those familiar with good work, for the reason that all the works executed up to that time appeared as nothing in comparison to his. These things awakened in Cardinal di San Dionigi, called Cardinal de Rohan, a Frenchman, a desire to leave in a city so famous some worthy memorial of himself by the hand of so rare a craftsman; and he caused him to make a Pietà[12] of marble in the round, which, when finished, was placed in the Chapel of the Vergine Maria della Febbre in St. Peter's. Among the lovely things to be seen in the work, to say nothing of the divinely beautiful draperies, is the body of Christ; nor let anyone think to see greater beauty of members or more mastery of art in any body, or a nude with more detail in the muscles, veins, and nerves over the framework of the bones, nor yet a corpse more similar than this to a real corpse. Here is perfect sweetness in the expression of the head, harmony in the joints and attachments of the arms, legs, and trunk, and the pulses and veins so wrought, that in truth Wonder herself must marvel that the hand of a craftsman should have been able to execute so divinely and so perfectly, in so short a time, a work so admirable; and it is certainly a miracle that a stone without any shape at the beginning should ever have been reduced to such perfection as Nature is scarcely able to create in the flesh. Such were Michelangelo's love and zeal together in this work, that he left his name — a thing he never did again in any other work — written across a sash that encircles the bosom of Our Lady. And the reason was that one day Michelangelo, entering the place where it was set up, found there a great number of strangers from Lombardy, who were praising it highly, and one of them asked one of the others who had done it, and he answered, "Our Gobbo from Milan."[13] Michelangelo stood silent, but thought it something strange that his labors should be attributed to another; and one night he shut himself in there, and, having brought a little light and his chisels, carved his name upon it. . . .

From this work he acquired very great fame, and although certain persons, rather fools than otherwise, say that he has made Our Lady too young, are these

---

[12] Literally, in Italian, "pity," a representation in painting or sculpture of the Virgin Mary mourning over the dead body of Christ taken down from the cross.

[13] Christofano Gobbo worked as a sculptor in Milan, 1490–1522. (*Gobbo* means "hunchback" in Italian.)

so ignorant as not to know that unspotted virgins maintain and preserve their freshness of countenance a long time without any mark, and that persons afflicted as Christ was do the contrary? That circumstance, therefore, won an even greater increase of glory and fame for his genius than all his previous works.

• • •

The name of Michelangelo, by reason of the Pietà that he had made, the Giant in Florence, and the cartoon, had become so famous, that in the year 1503, Pope Alexander VI having died and Julius II[14] having been elected, at which time Michelangelo was about twenty-nine years of age, he was summoned with much graciousness by Julius II, who wished to set him to make his tomb; and for the expenses of the journey a hundred crowns were paid to him by the Pope's representatives. Having made his way to Rome, he spent many months there before he was made to set his hand to any work. But finally the Pope's choice fell on a design that he had made for that tomb, and excellent testimony to the genius of Michelangelo, which in beauty and magnificence, abundance of ornamentation and richness of statuary, surpassed every ancient or imperial tomb. Whereupon Pope Julius took courage, and thus resolved to set his hand to make anew the Church of St. Peter's in Rome, in order to erect the tomb in it. And so Michelangelo set to work with high hopes; and, in order to make a beginning, he went to Carrara to excavate all the marble, with two assistants, receiving a thousand crowns on that account from Alamanno Salviati in Florence. There, in those mountains, he spent eight months without other moneys or supplies; and he had many fantastic ideas of carving great statues in those quarries, in order to leave memorials of himself, as the ancients had done before him, being invited by those masses of stone. Then, having picked out the due quantity of marbles, he caused them to be loaded on board ship at the coast and then conveyed to Rome, where they filled half the Piazza of St. Peter's, round about S. Caterina, and between the church and the corridor that goes to the Castello. In that place Michelangelo had prepared his room for executing the figures and the rest of the tomb; and, to the end that the Pope might be able to come at his convenience to see him at work, he had caused a drawbridge to be constructed between the corridor and that room, which led to a great intimacy between them. But in time these favors brought much annoyance and even persecution upon him, and stirred up much envy against him among his fellow-craftsmen.

Of this work Michelangelo executed during the lifetime and after the death of Julius four statues completely finished and eight only blocked out, as will be related in the proper place; . . .

---

[14] Pope, 1503–1513, generous and demanding patron of Michelangelo and Raphael.

He finished the Moses,[15] a statue in marble ten feet high, which no modern work will ever equal in beauty; and of the ancient statues, also, the same may be said. For, seated in an attitude of great dignity, he rests one arm on the Tablets of the Law, which he holds with one hand, and with the other he holds his beard, which is long and waving, and carved in the marble in such sort, that the hairs— in which the sculptor finds such difficulty—are wrought with the greatest delicacy, soft, feathery, and detailed in such a manner, that one cannot but believe that his chisel was changed into a pencil. To say nothing of the beauty of the face, which has all the air of a true Saint and most dread Prince, you seem, while you gaze upon it, to wish to demand from him the veil wherewith to cover that face, so resplendent and so dazzling it appears to you, and so well has Michelangelo expressed the divinity that God infused in that most holy countenance. In addition, there are draperies carved out and finished with most beautiful curves of the borders; while the arms with their muscles, and the hands with their bones and nerves, are carried to such a pitch of beauty and perfection, and the legs, knees, and feet are covered with buskins so beautifully fashioned, and every part of the work is so finished, that Moses may be called now more than ever the friend for God, seeing that He has designed to assemble together and prepare his body for the Resurrection before that of any other, by the hands of Michelangelo. Well may the Hebrews continue to go there, as they do every Sabbath, both men and women, like flocks of starlings, to visit and adore that statue; for they will be adoring a thing not human but divine.

. . . His departure from Rome is also explained in another way—namely, that the Pope became angered against Michelangelo, who would not allow any of his works to be seen; that Michelangelo suspected his own men, assuming (as happened more than once) that the Pope disguised himself and saw what he was doing on certain occasions when he himself was not at home or at work; and that on one occasion, when the Pope had bribed his assistants to admit him to see the chapel of his uncle Sixtus, which, as was related a little time back, he caused Buonarroti to paint, Michelangelo, having waited in hiding because he suspected the treachery of his assistants, threw planks down at the Pope when he entered the chapel, not considering who it might be, and drove him forth in a fury. It is enough for us to know that in the one way or the other he fell out with the Pope and then became afraid, so that he had to fly from his presence.

Now, having arrived in Bologna, he had scarcely drawn off his riding boots when he was conducted by the Pope's servants to his Holiness, who was in the Palazzo de' Medici; and he was accompanied by a Bishop sent by Cardinal Soderini, because the Cardinal, being ill, was not able to go himself. Having come into the presence of the Pope, Michelangelo knelt down, but his Holiness

---

[15] One of the statues designed to be part of Pope Julius II's tomb.

looked askance at him, as if in anger, and said to him, "Instead of coming yourself to meet us, you have waited for us to come to meet you!" meaning to infer that Bologna is nearer to Florence than Rome. Michelangelo, with a courtly gesture of the hands, but in a firm voice, humbly begged for pardon, saying in excuse that he had acted as he had done in anger, not being able to endure to be driven away so abruptly, but that, if he had erred, his Holiness should once more forgive him. The Bishop who had presented Michelangelo to his Holiness, making excuse for him, said to the Pope that such men were ignorant creatures, that they were worth nothing save in their own art, and that he should freely pardon him. The Pope, seized with anger, belabored the Bishop with a staff that he had in his hand, saying to him, "It is you that are ignorant, who level insults at him that we ourselves do not think of uttering"; and then the Bishop was driven out by the groom with fisticuffs. . . .

When the Pope had returned to Rome and Michelangelo was at work on the statue [of Moses], Bramante,[16] the friend and relative of Raphael of Urbino, and for that reason hostile to Michelangelo, perceiving that the Pope held in great favor and estimation the works that he executed in sculpture, was constantly planning with Raphael in Michelangelo's absence to remove from the mind of his Holiness the idea of causing Michelangelo, after his return, to devote himself to finishing his tomb; saying that for a man to prepare himself a tomb during his own lifetime was an evil augury and a hurrying on of his death. And they persuaded his Holiness that on the return of Michelangelo, he should cause him to paint in memory of his uncle Sixtus the vaulting of the chapel that he had built in the Palace. In this manner it seemed possible to Bramante and other rivals of Michelangelo to draw him away from sculpture, in which they saw him to be perfect, and to plunge him into despair, they thinking that if they compelled him to paint, he would do work less worthy of praise, since he had no experience of colors in fresco,[17] and that he would prove inferior to Raphael, and, even if he did succeed in the work, in any case it would make him angry against the Pope; so that in either event they would achieve their object of getting rid of him. And so, when Michelangelo returned to Rome, the Pope was not disposed at that time to finish his tomb, and requested him to paint the vaulting of the chapel. Michelangelo, who desired to finish the tomb, believing the vaulting of that chapel to be a great and difficult labor, and considering his own lack of practice in colors, sought by every means to shake such a burden from his shoulders, and proposed Raphael for the work. But the more he refused, the greater grew the

---

[16] Donato Bramante (1444–1514), architect under whose supervision the reconstruction of St. Peter's was begun in 1506. In his late years Michelangelo was placed in charge of completing the great reconstruction.

[17] Painting done on fresh, damp plaster.

desire of the Pope, who was headstrong in his undertakings, and, in addition, was being spurred on anew by the rivals of Michelangelo, and especially by Bramante; so that his Holiness, who was quick-tempered, was on the point of becoming enraged with Michelangelo. Whereupon Michelangelo, perceiving that his Holiness was determined in the matter, resolved to do it; and the Pope commanded Bramante to erect the scaffolding from which the vaulting might be painted. Bramante made it all supported by ropes, piercing the vaulting; which having perceived, Michelangelo inquired of Bramante how he was to proceed to fill up the holes when he had finished painting it, and he replied that he would think of that afterwards, and that it could not be done otherwise. Michelangelo recognized that Bramante was either not very competent for such a work or else not his friend, and he went to the Pope and said to him that the scaffolding was not satisfactory, and that Bramante had not known how to make it; and the Pope answered, in the presence of Bramante, that he should make it after his own fashion. And so he commanded that it should be erected upon props so as not to touch the walls, a method of making scaffoldings for vaults that he taught afterwards to Bramante and others, whereby many fine works have been executed. Thus he enabled a poor creature of a carpenter, who rebuilt the scaffolding, to dispense with so many of the ropes, that, after selling them (for Michelangelo gave them to him), he made up a dowry for his daughter.

He then set his hand to making the cartoons for that vaulting; and the Pope decided, also, that the walls which the masters before him in the time of Sixtus had painted should be scraped clean, and decreed that he should have fifteen thousand ducats for the whole cost of the work; which price was fixed through Giuliano da San Gallo. Thereupon, forced by the magnitude of the undertaking to resign himself to obtaining assistance, Michelangelo sent for men to Florence; and he determined to demonstrate in such a work that those who had painted there before him were destined to be vanquished by his labors, and also resolved to show to the modern craftsmen how to draw and paint. Having begun the cartoons, he finished them; and the circumstances of the work spurred him to soar to great heights, both for his own fame and for the welfare of art. And then, desiring to paint it in fresco colors, and not having any experience of them, there came from Florence to Rome certain of his friends who were painters, to the end that they might give him assistance in such a work, and also that he might learn from them the method of working in fresco, in which some of them were well-practiced; . . . but, perceiving that their efforts were very far from what he desired, and not being satisfied with them, he resolved one morning to throw to the ground everything that they had done. Then, shutting himself up in the chapel, he would never open to them, nor even allowed himself to be seen by them when he was at home. . . . Thereupon Michelangelo, having made arrangements to paint the whole work by himself, carried it well on the way to completion with the utmost solicitude, labor, and study; nor would he ever let himself be seen, lest he should give any occasion to compel him to show it, so that the desire in the minds of everyone to see it grew greater every day.

Pope Julius was always very desirous to see any undertakings that he was having carried out, and therefore became more eager than ever to see this one, which was hidden from him. And so one day he resolved to go to see it, but was not admitted, for Michelangelo would never have consented to show it to him; out of which affair arose the quarrel that has been described, when he had to depart from Rome because he would not show his work to the Pope. . . .

Now, when he had finished half of it, the Pope, who had subsequently gone to see it several times (mounting certain ladders with the assistance of Michelangelo), insisted that it should be thrown open, for he was hasty and impatient by nature, and could not wait for it to be completely finished and to receive, as the saying is, the final touch. No sooner was it thrown open than all Rome was drawn to see it, and the Pope was the first, not having the patience to wait until the dust caused by the dismantling of the scaffolding had settled. Thereupon Raphael of Urbino, who was very excellent in imitation, after seeing it straightway changed his manner, and without losing any time, in order to display his ability, painted the Prophets and Sibyls; and at the same time Bramante sought to have the other half of the chapel entrusted by the Pope to Raphael. Which hearing, Michelangelo complained of Bramante, and revealed to the Pope without any reserve many faults both in his life and in his architectural works; of which last, in the building of St. Peter's, as was seen afterwards, Michelangelo became the corrector. But the Pope, recognizing more clearly every day the ability of Michelangelo, desired that he should continue the work, judging, after he had seen it uncovered, that he could make the second half considerably better; and so in twenty months he carried that work to perfect completion by himself alone, without the assistance even of anyone to grind his colors. Michelangelo complained at times that on account of the haste that the Pope imposed on him he was not able to finish it in his own fashion, as he would have liked; for his Holiness was always asking him importunately when he would finish it. On one occasion, among others, he replied, "It will be finished when I shall have satisfied myself in the matter of art." "But it is our pleasure," answered the Pope, "that you should satisfy us in our desire to have it done quickly"; and he added, finally, that if Michelangelo did not finish the work quickly he would have him thrown down from the scaffolding. Whereupon Michelangelo, who feared and had good reason to fear the anger of the Pope, straightway finished all that was wanting, without losing any time, and, after taking down the rest of the scaffolding, threw it open to view on the morning of All Saints' Day, when the Pope went into the chapel to sing Mass, to the great satisfaction of the whole city. Michelangelo desired to retouch some parts "*a secco*,"[18] as the old masters had done on the scenes below, painting backgrounds, draperies, and skies in ultramarine, and ornaments in gold in certain places, to the end that this might produce greater richness and a more striking effect; and the Pope, having learned that this ornamentation was lacking, and

---

[18] On dry plaster.

hearing the work praised so much by all who had seen it, wished him to finish it; but, since it would have been too long a labor for Michelangelo to re-build the scaffolding, it was left as it was. His Holiness, often seeing Michelan-gelo, would say to him that the chapel should be enriched with colors and gold, since it looked poor. And Michelangelo would answer familiarly, "Holy Father, in those times men did not bedeck themselves with gold, and those that are painted there were never very rich, but rather holy men, on which account they despised riches."

For this work Michelangelo was paid by the Pope three thousand crowns on several occasions, of which he had to spend twenty-five on colors. The work was executed with very great discomfort to himself, from his having to labor with his face upwards, which so impaired his sight that for a time, which was not less than several months, he was not able to read letters or look at drawings save with his head backwards. And to this I can bear witness, having painted five vaulted cham-bers in the great apartments in the Palace of Duke Cosimo, when, if I had not made a chair on which I could rest my head and lie down at my work, I would never have finished it; even so, it has so ruined my sight and injured my head, that I still feel the effects, and I am astonished that Michelangelo endured all that discomfort so well. But in truth, becoming more and more kindled every day by his fervor in the work, and encouraged by the progress and improvement that he made, he felt no fatigue and cared nothing for discomfort.

The distribution of this work is contrived with six pendentives on either side, with one in the center of the walls at the foot and at the head, and on these he painted Sibyls and Prophets, twelve feet in height; in the center of the vault the history of the world from the Creation down to the Deluge and the Drunkenness of Noah, and in the lunettes all the Genealogy of Christ. In these compartments he used no rule of perspectives in foreshortening, nor is there any fixed point of view, but he accommodated the compartments to the figures rather than the fig-ures to the compartments, being satisfied to execute those figures, both the nude and the draped, with the perfection of design, so that another such work has never been and never can be done, and it is scarcely possible even to imitate his achievement.

• • •

When the work was thrown open, the whole world could be heard running up to see it, and, indeed, it was such as to make everyone astonished and dumb. Wherefore the Pope, having been magnified by such a result and encouraged in his heart to undertake even greater enterprises, rewarded Michelangelo liberally with money and rich gifts: and Michelangelo would say at times of the extraordi-nary favors that the Pope conferred upon him, that they showed that he fully rec-ognized his worth, and that, if by way of proving his friendliness he sometimes played him strange tricks, he would heal the wound with signal gifts and favors. As when, Michelangelo once demanding from him leave to go to Florence for the festival of S. John, and asking money for that purpose, the Pope said, "Well, but when will you have this chapel finished?" "As soon as I can, Holy Father." The Pope, who had a staff in his hand, struck Michelangelo, saying, "As soon as I can! As soon as I can! I will soon make you finish it!" Whereupon Michelangelo went back to his house to get ready to go to Florence; but the Pope straightway sent Cursio, his Chamberlain, to Michelangelo with five hundred crowns to pacify him, fearing lest he might commit one of his caprices, and Cursio made excuse for the Pope, saying that such things were favors and marks of affection. And Michelangelo, who knew the Pope's nature and, after all, loved him, laughed over it all, for he saw that in the end everything turned to his profit and advantage, and that the Pontiff would do anything to keep a man such as himself as his friend.

• • •

Michelangelo was much inclined to the labors of art, seeing that everything, however difficult, succeeded with him, he having had from nature a genius very apt and ardent in these most noble arts of design. Moreover, in order to be entirely perfect, innumerable times he made anatomical studies, dissecting men's bodies in order to see the principles of their construction and the concatenation of the bones, muscles, veins, and nerves, the various movements and all the postures of the human body; and not of men only, but also of animals, and particularly of horses, which last he much delighted to keep. Of all these he desired to learn the principles and laws in so far as touched his art, and this knowledge he so demonstrated in the works that fell to him to handle, that those who attend to no other study than this do not know more. He so executed his works, whether with the brush or with the chisel, that they are almost inimitable, and he gave to his labors, as has been said, such art and grace, and a loveliness of such a kind, that (be it said without offense to any) he surpassed and vanquished the ancients; having been able to wrest things out of the greatest difficulties with such facility, that they do not appear wrought with effort, although whoever draws his works after him finds enough in imitating them.

The genius of Michelangelo was recognized in his lifetime, and not, as happens to many, after death, for it has been seen that Julius II, Leo X, Clement VII, Paul III, Julius III, Paul IV, and Pius IV, all supreme Pontiffs, always wished to have him near them, and also, as is known, Suleiman, Emperor of the Turks, Francis of Valois, King of France, the Emperor Charles V, the Signoria of Venice, and finally, as has been related, Duke Cosimo de' Medici; all offering him honorable salaries, for no other reason but to avail themselves of his great genius. This does not happen save to men of great worth, such as he was; and it is evident and well known that all these three arts were so perfected in him, that it is not found that among persons ancient or modern, in all the many years that the sun has been whirling round, God has granted this to any other but Michelangelo. He had imagination of such a kind, and so perfect, and the things conceived by him in idea were such, that often, through not being able to express with the hands conceptions so terrible and grand, he abandoned his works—nay, destroyed many of them; and I know that a little before he died he burned a great number of designs, sketches, and cartoons made with his own hand, to the end that no one might see the labors endured by him and his methods of trying his genius, and that he might not appear less than perfect. . . .

Now, to be brief, I must record that the master's constitution was very sound, for he was lean and well knit together with nerves, and although as a boy he was delicate, and as a man he had two serious illnesses, he could always endure any fatigue and had no infirmity, save that in his old age he suffered from dysuria and from gravel, which in the end developed into the stone; wherefore for many years he was syringed by the hand of Maestro Realdo Colombo, his very dear friend, who treated him with great diligence. He was of middle stature, broad in the shoulders, but well proportioned in all the rest of the body. In his latter years he wore buskins of dogskin on the legs, next to the skin, constantly for whole months together, so that afterwards, when he sought to take them off, on drawing them off the skin often came away with them. Over the stockings he wore boots of cordwain fastened on the inside, as a protection against damp. His face was round, the brow square and spacious, with seven straight lines, and the temples projected considerably beyond the ears; which ears were somewhat on the large side, and stood out from the cheeks. The body was in proportion to the face, or rather on the large side; the nose somewhat flattened; having been broken, as was said, by Torrigiano; the eyes rather on the small side, of the color of horn, spotted with bluish and yellowish gleams; the eyebrows with few hairs, the lips thin, with the lower lip rather thicker and projecting a little, the chin well shaped and in proportion with the rest, the hair black, but mingled with white hairs, like the beard, which was not very long, forked, and not very thick.

Truly his coming was to the world, as I said at the beginning, an exemplar sent by God to the men of our arts, to the end that they might learn from his life the nature of noble character, and from his works what true and excellent craftsmen ought to be. And I, who have to praise God for infinite blessings, as is seldom wont to happen with men of our profession, count it among the greatest blessings that I was born at the time when Michelangelo was alive, that I was thought worthy to have him as my master, and that he was so much my friend and intimate, as everyone knows, and as the letters written by him to me, now in my possession, bear witness; and out of love for truth, and also from the obligation that I feel to his loving kindness, I have contrived to write many things of him, and all true, which many others have not been able to do.

PART

II

CELEBRATING PAST GRANDEUR

꿏

P art II examines texts that celebrate the glorious histories of their own
civilizations. Some of these historical accounts are based on empirical
fact and some may be based mainly on pure literary invention. Selection
6 records what was originally an epic oral account of the dynasty of Askia
Mohammed, sixteenth-century ruler of the great Sudanic empire of Songhay in West Africa. Selection 7, also an epic, is from the eastern Congo
region of Africa. It tells of Mwindo, a hero with almost superhuman powers, who, after a period of great struggle and testing, assumes his rightful
position as chief or king. Selection 8 is taken from a Chinese novel of the
fourteenth century, which is a fictionalized depiction of a crucial earlier
period in Chinese history, the late Han Dynasty of the second and third
centuries A.D. Like Shakespeare's history plays, which dramatize pivotal
events and characters in English history, the *Three Kingdoms* dramatizes
that moment when personal tragedy, based on flaws of character, becomes
a reflection of the larger tragedy of the division of China and the dissolution of the great Han Dynasty.

Japanese culture, represented in the ninth selection, derived many of
its literary forms from the larger Chinese culture nearby. The fifteenth-
century *Nō* drama of *Atsumori*, like the Chinese novel of Selection 8, tells
of the agony of a war fought centuries earlier, when opposing warriors
recognize each other's noble qualities but are compelled by their warrior
code to kill those opponents whom they most admire. Selection 10,
poems by the best-known woman poet of India, the sixteenth-century
Mirabai, celebrate the traditional ancient gods and religious values of
India, even through their unabashed sensuality. The last selection in Part

93

Two is the only Portuguese text in this volume. Selection 11 is taken from the national epic of the Portuguese nation, *The Lusiads,* written in the late sixteenth century. It looks back on the preceding century's glorious age of exploration as that nation's greatest achievement, represented in the excerpt by the voyage of Vasco da Gama to India, tying this selection to its predecessor in yet another of the global interconnections so numerous in this volume and in human history.

6

⚜

THE EPIC OF ASKIA MOHAMMED

The historical record of the rise and fall of the great Sudanic empire of Songhay (1464–1591) in West Africa is provided in various oral and written texts. Of these, The Epic of Askia Mohammed, an oral account of the dynasty of Askia Mohammed, has survived for almost five hundred years. It celebrates the reign of the second great ruler of Songhay, Askia Mohammed, who supplanted the dynasty of his predecessor and uncle, Sonni Ali Ber. The version of The Epic of Askia Mohammed reprinted here was recited in Songhay, the language of the Soninké people, by the griot, or praise singer and oral historian, Nouhou Malio; it was recorded and transcribed in 1981.

It is often the case that when one ruler supplants another, the legitimizing account of the usurpation forms the basis of a dynastic epic. Such is the case here where Askia Mohammed (1492–1528) is portrayed as the legitimate and rightful ruler, despite his having to overcome his uncle, the king, as well as other cousins, to assume his role. Like Sundiata, in the epic of Sundiata (Volume II, Selection 16), Askia Mohammed is oppressed at birth; he must prove his worth and establish his right to rule by eliminating other pretenders to the throne. This account echoes the historical facts in which Sonni Ali Ber, the previous ruler, died mysteriously on his return from a war. According to Thomas Hale, the transcriber of this version, Askia Mohammed then challenged Sonni Ali Ber's son to embrace Islam more fervently, and when he refused, Askia Mohammed attacked and assumed rule of the Songhay empire.

Historical fact and epic account meet in the broad outlines of the events that followed Askia Mohammed's ascent to power. He went on a pilgrimage to Mecca, and on his return undertook to expand his rule through a series of military expeditions. He justified these wars in the name of the expansion of Islam, while maintaining good relations with the religious authorities and scholars in the important Muslim center of Timbuktu, as well as communicating with those as far off as the countries of the Maghreb, the northwestern corner of Africa.

Although it was to be another four centuries until Islam was broadly accepted by the masses of the people in the Sahel, the region bordering the Sahara on the south, it was the name of Islam that provided the principle of legitimizing rule *on religious grounds, of spreading the rule through* jihad *(holy war), and, most of all, of constructing epics and chronicles that elevate a dynasty to a regal stature. This did not create a foreign Muslim document, however. Traditional Soninké formulations and beliefs, as seen in the presence of* sohanci *(sorcerers), in the powers of hunters, and especially in the social formulations, continued to define the world of the epic hero. The epic is textured with layers of belief and discourse that reflect not only the original historical setting but the changes brought to the Songhay community in the years that followed. The result is not an iron-bound version that passed unaltered through the centuries, but a living performance by the griot, incorporating such contemporary images as razors, and such lines as "It is not like today in the era of the Whites."*

This version of the reign of Askia Mohammed provides us with a rare glimpse into the way political power and epic expression, king and griot, collaborate in the preservation and commemoration of "words and deeds," creating the sense of greatness that informs powerful states. In this excerpt the focus is upon the birth of Askia Mohammed (also known as Mamar), his rise to power, his pilgrimage to Mecca, and finally his conquests.

❧

Mamar Kassaye, didn't the Songhay people narrate it to you?[1]
Mamar Kassaye himself whom they talk about.
Mamar himself, the son of Kassaye.
This Kassaye, it is Si who is her brother.[2]
Si and Kassaye, they have the same mother and the same father.
Kassaye is the woman.
It is Si who is the man, it is he who is on the throne, it is he who is
       the chief.
Kassaye is his sister, she is in his compound.
Any husband who marries Kassaye, and if she gives birth,

The Epic of Askia Mohamed from *Scribe, Griot, and Novelist* by Thomas Hale, copyright 1990, pp. 185, 187, 189, 191, 193, 195, 197, 199, 201, 203, 205, 207, 209, 211, and 213. Reprinted with the permission of the University Press of Florida.

[1] The griot who is performing the epic is addressing a small audience, and here is evoking the ruler, Askia Mohammed, who is also known as Mamar Kassaye.

[2] Si is Sonni Ali Ber, ruler of the Songhay empire. He is conventionally portrayed as a lukewarm Muslim, and elsewhere as an actual enemy of Islam. He is Askia Mohammed's uncle, and Askia Mohammed must usurp his rule in order to gain the throne.

The seers have said "Listen"—they told Si it is Kassaye who will give
 birth to a child[3] who will kill him and take over the throne
 of Gao.[4]
It is Kassaye who will give birth to a child.
That child will kill Si and will take the position of ruler.
Si also heard about this.
All the children that Kassaye gave birth to,
As soon as Kassaye delivered it, Si killed it.
Every child that Kassaye delivered, as soon as it was born, Si killed it.
Until she had given birth to seven children,
Which her brother Si killed.
Kassaye had enough, she said she would no longer take a husband.
She stayed like that.
Si is on his throne,
 While Kassaye remained like that.
Until, until, until, until one day, much later, in the middle of the night,
A man came who was wearing beautiful clothes.
He was a real man, he was tall, someone who looked good in white
 clothes, his clothes were really beautiful.
One could smell perfume everywhere.
He came in to sit down next to Kassaye.
They chatted with each other, they chatted, they chatted.
He said to her, "It is really true.
"Kassaye, I would like to make love with you.
"Once we make love together,
"You will give birth to a boy,
"Whom Si will not be able to kill.
"It is he who will kill Si and will become the ruler."
Kassaye said to him, "What?"
He said, "By Allah."
She said, "Good, in the name of Allah."
Each night the man came.
It is during the late hours that he came.
Each time during the coolness of the late evening.
Until Kassaye became pregnant by him.

---

[3] That is, a male child.

[4] Note how this epic pattern of the child who overthrows the brutal ruler is repeated elsewhere, as in the Greek myths, or in *The Mwindo Epic* (Selection 7). Gao is a city on the
Niger River in the eastern part of present-day Mali.

Kassaye carried her pregnancy.
Kassaye had a Bargantché captive.[5]
It is the Bargantché woman who is her captive, she lives in her house,
          and she too is pregnant.
They remained like that.
Kassaye kneeled down to give birth.
The captive kneeled down to give birth.
So Kassaye, Kassaye gave birth to a boy.
The captive gave birth to a girl.
Then Kassaye took the daughter of the captive, she took her home
          with her.
She took her son and gave it to the captive.
So the people left for the palace.
They said to Si:
"The Bargantché captive has given birth."
He said, "What did she get?"
They said, "A boy."
He said, "May Allah be praised, may our Lord give him a long life and
          may he be useful."
Then they were thoughtful for a moment.
They got up and informed him that Kassaye had given birth.
They asked, "What did she get?"
They answered, "A girl."
He said, "Have them bring it to me."
They brought it to him, he killed it.
It is the boy who remained with the captive and Kassaye.
For seven days.
His father came in the night.
He brought his animal[6] and the items necessary for the naming
          ceremony.
He gave them to Kassaye.
He said, "Go ahead and name my son.
"Let them name him Mamar."
So they named the child in the morning.
Kassaye brought the necessary items, they performed the ceremony for
          the child, and they named him Mamar.
Kassaye said to name her child Mamar.
They called him Mamar.

---

[5] The Bargantché are a neighboring people whose captives serve as personal slaves.

[6] A sheep to be sacrificed.

So, the Bargantché woman nursed him all day long.

In the evening, Kassaye took her son.

She nursed him all night.

The Bargantché captive nursed him all day, one could see him with her.

When night came, Kassaye took back her son.

She nursed him all night.

It was thus, it was thus, it was thus until the child, he began to crawl.

When he crawls, he climbs on the feet of Si.

He pulls his beard.

Si said, "Hey! This child is suspect."

Kassaye said to him, "Really?

"He is suspect, go ahead and kill your captive's son, are you going to kill him?"

"If one kills the son of his captive, one will become really famous.

"If one kills the son of one's captive, one will become really famous, go ahead and kill."[7]

"Why is he suspect? The son of your captive, do you have doubts about him too?

"I have given birth to eight children, you have killed all of them.

"The son of your captive too, you have doubts about him too.

"The one who killed the son of his captive, he is the one who loses."

Then the child walked.

Then the small child became a boy, a big, strong boy.

Then Kassaye took him by the hand to see Si, and she said,

"Si," and he said, "Yes?"

She said, "There is the son of the captive, have him care for your horse.

"I gave him to you so that he could be the groom for your horse.

"Have him go and get grass for your horse."

He said, "Good, may Allah be praised."

Si continued to have the child work.

Si continued to have the child work.

Si continued to have the child work.

Until, until, until, until the child became a young man.

He became an adolescent.

He became a young man tall and very strong, a tall young man.

The children in the compound,

They are the ones who insult him by saying that they don't know his father.

Also, they call him the little slave of Si.

---

[7] Kassaye is speaking ironically here.

"The little slave of Si, the little slave of Si."

They called him "little slave of Si," and said "We don't know your father,
you don't have a father.

"Who is your father?"

Then he came home to his mother's house and told her that the children
in the compound were really bothering him.

They say to him, "Who is your father?"

She told him, "Go sit down, you'll see your father."

He stayed there until the celebration at the end of Ramadan.

It is going to take place the next day.

Tomorrow is the celebration.[8]

Soon they will look at the moon.

The moon will appear in a short while, and they will celebrate the
next day.

It is in the night that the djin came to her,[9]

For the man is a djin.

He is also a chief of the town under the river, his land that he rules.

It is under the river that lies the country he rules.

That night he called her.

He came, the man came to Kassaye's house.

He took a ring off his middle finger.

He said to her that when daylight comes,

"Give it to your son."

He should hold it in his hand.

If he gets to the edge of the river, then he should put the ring on
his finger.

He will see his father.

She said, "So it will be."

Daylight came.

The sun was hot, I think, the sun was hot.

Then Kassaye called Mamar.

She said, "Mamar."

He said, "Yes."

She said, "Come."

He came.

She said to him, "Look, take this ring in your hand.

---

[8] The prayers and feast that accompany the end of the month of Ramadan, the month
during which Muslims must observe a fast during daylight hours.

[9] A djin is popularly believed to be a spirit capable of influencing humans for good
or evil.

"But don't put it on your finger,
"Until you get to the river.
"Then you put it on your finger.
"At that moment, you will see your father."
Mamar took the ring to the river.
Then he put the ring on his middle finger.
The water opened up.
Under the water there are so many cities, so many cities, so many cities,
        so many villages, and so many people.
It is his father too who is the chief.
They too get themselves ready, they go out to go to the prayer ground.
He said, "That's the way it is."
His father greets him with an embrace.
There is his son, there is his son.
Yes, the prince whom he fathered while away,
The chief's son whom he fathered while away has come.
He said to him, "Now go return to your home, you do not stay here.
"Go return home."
His father gave him a white stallion, really white, really, really, really,
        really, really, really, really white like, like percale.[10]
He gave him all the things necessary.
He gave him two lances.
He gave him a saber, which he wore.
He gave him a shield.
He bid him good-bye.
Si too and his people,
Si too has a daughter, two boys and one daughter that he has fathered.
He and his people go out, they went to the prayer ground.
They are at the prayer ground.
Then Mamar went around them and headed directly for them.
They were about to start the prayer.
They said, "Stop, just stop, a prince from another place is coming to
        pray with us.
"A prince from another place is coming to pray with us."
The horse gallops swiftly, swiftly, swiftly, swiftly, swiftly, swiftly he is
        approaching.
He comes into view suddenly, leaning forward on his mount.
Until, until, until, until, until, until, until he touches the prayer skin of
        his uncle, then he reins his horse there.
Those who know him say that he is like the little captive of Si.

---

[10] A cotton cloth.

Actually, he does resemble the little captive of Si, he has the same look
        as the little captive of Si.
Did you see him! When I saw him I thought that it was the little
        captive of Si.
He retraced his path only to return again.
Until he brought the horse to the same place, where he reined it again.
Now he made it gallop again.
As he approaches the prayer skin of his uncle,
He reins his horse.
He unslung his lance, and pierced his uncle with it until the lance
        touched the prayer skin.
Until the spear went all the way to the prayer skin.
At that moment, Kassaye was among the people at the prayer ground.
Kassaye is in the crowd.
Since she knew in advance what was to happen,
She is among the crowd.
All together they reach up to grab him.
She said, "Let him go!
"Let him alone, it is Mamar, son of Kassaye.
"It is Mamar, the son of Kassaye, let him go.
"Si has killed eight of my children.
"You want to catch him, someone who has taken the life of one man
        who has himself taken eight lives—leave him alone!"
They let him go.
They took away the body, and Mamar came to sit down on the prayer
        skin of his uncle.
They prayed.
They took away the body to bury it.
That is how Mamar took the chieftaincy.
When they finished praying,
He mounted his horse, and the people followed him.
Then the son of his uncle says to him, "Son of Kassaye, you did it all
        by yourself."
He did it by himself *zungudaani*.[11]
He did it himself, the people didn't do it.
Son of Kassaye, who did it himself.
He did it himself *zungudaani*.
He did it himself, the people didn't do it.

---

[11] Meaning is unclear.

Kassaye glanced in back of herself to see her nephew, the son of her
brother.

She said, "You want to shame yourself.

"You who are the son of the man, you want to beg for the son of the
woman!"

He said, "Me, I sing his praises.

"I follow him, I become a griot, I follow him."[12]

That is why we are griots.

He said, "Me, I am a griot, and I follow him.

"I put my share in his share throughout the Songhay area, and I'll take
whatever I am given."

A griot has thus been created.

There's how the profession of griot begins.

The second son, he disappeared into the sky.

He brought a handful of razors, he dumped them down.

He became a sohanci.[13]

He is at the origin of sohancis,

Who do circumcisions for people.

He became a sohanci.

The daughter cried out and jumped into the river.

She spent seven days under the water.

No one knew where she went.

It was on that day she came out as a sorko.[14]

The sorkos come from her.

Her grandchildren are the sorkos.

They are not simply hunters on water, they are called sorkos.

It is difficult to obtain a sorko, if they tell you to look for a sorko in the
countryside, now it is difficult.

The descendants of the daughter are called sorkos.

The descendants of one of the boys are called sohancis.

The descendants of the second son are we, the griots.

The descendants of the daughter are called sorkos.

Now, Mamar came to sit down.

---

[12] Though not of griot origin by birth, Sonni Ali Ber's son assumes the role of griot by becoming Askia Mohammed's praise singer. Here, the singing of praises assumes an importance that is comparable to that of the great deeds it celebrates.

[13] The second son, also the king's descendant, becomes a sorcerer, or *sohanci*. His flight
signals the end of his father's power.

[14] The daughter becomes a *sorko* or fisherman endowed with magical powers.

He ruled then, he ruled, he ruled, he ruled, he converted.[15]
Throughout Mamar's reign, what he did was to convert people.
Any village that he hears is trying to resist,
That is not going to submit,
He gets up and destroys the village.
If the village accepts, he makes them pray.
If they resist, he conquers the village, he burns the village.
Mamar made them convert, Mamar made them convert, Mamar made
      them convert.
Until, until, until, until, until, until he got up and said he would go
      to Mecca.
Thus he started off and went as far, as far, as far as the Red Sea.
He said he wants to cross.
They told him, "There is no path.
"Anyone who has killed an ancestor does not have the right to cross to
      Mecca.
"But there are two ways, three ways, so look for one you can take.
"Now you will return home.
"You must find a hen who has just produced chicks, and drive them
      from home.
"You will drive a hen who has just produced chicks and its little ones to
      the Red Sea.
"Then you can cross to go on the pilgrimage."
They said, "Either you go home,
"Or you go into the distant, uncleared bush.
"You clear it with your own hands.
"You don't let anyone help with it.
"You sow by your own hand without the help of anybody.
"You cultivate it and you recultivate it, and you leave the millet so that
      the birds and the wild animals may eat it.
"If you do that, and if you come, you can cross to go on the pilgrimage.
"Or you go home to start a holy war,
"So that you can make them submit until you reach the Red Sea.
"You will cross."
He said that he would be able to carry out the holy war.
Mamar went home to Gao.
It is at this time that he gathered together all the horses.
He took all the horses.
He began by the west.

---

[15] That is, converted people to Islam.

You have heard that among the Mossi,[16] there are descendants of
    Mamar.
They say that it is during this conquest that he continued to father them.
You have heard that they say the pure Bargantché.
In each ethnic group you hear about, people say there are descendants
    of Mamar.
Well, from that area where he started,
In each village where he stopped during the day, for example, this place,
If he arrives in midafternoon, he stops there and spends the night.
Early in the morning, they pillage and they go on to the next village, for
    example, Liboré.
The cavalier who goes there,
He traces on the ground for the people the plan for the mosque.
Once the plan for the foundation is traced,
The people build the mosque.
It is at that time,
Mamar Kassaye comes to dismount from his horse.
He makes the people—
They teach them verses from the Koran relating to prayer.
They teach them prayers from the Koran.
Any villages that refuse, he destroys the village, burns it, and moves on.
In each village where he arrives,
The village that he leaves in the morning,
The horses[17] ride ahead.
They build a mosque before his arrival.
When he arrives, he and his people,
He teaches the villagers prayers from the Koran.
He makes them pray.
They—they learn how to pray.
After that, in the morning, he continues on.
Every village that follows his orders, that accepts his wishes,
He conquers them, he moves on.
Every village that refuses his demand,
He conquers it, he burns it, he moves on.
Until the day—Mamar did that until, until, until, until the day he
    arrived at the Red Sea.
It is on that day that they gave him the right to cross.
Before arriving at the Red Sea,

---

[16] A neighboring people, here depicted as being converted to Islam by Askia Mohammed.

[17] That is, cavalry.

All the horsemen, those who died, those who were tired, returned.
Except for Modi Baja,[18] Modi Baja and the griot, his cousin, who stayed
        with him.
It is they alone who remained at his side.
He made the crossing in their company.
So they arrived in Mecca.
He made the pilgrimage and he said then that he would like to see the
        tomb of Our Lord's Messenger.[19]
In those days they had not built it yet.
He came, they told him, he said he wanted to see the tomb of Our
        Lord's Messenger.
They replied to him, "By Allah truly, the tomb, you won't see it.
"Because if you peek into this tomb,
"The thing that is in there will keep you from getting out."
He asked that they let him peek into it.
They said, "Fine, on one condition.
"Now have them go off to get large pieces of iron chain,
"To hook onto his belt.
"Some strong men should stay behind him and hold on tightly to the
        chains.
"He too should come to the edge of the hole to peek into it."
He said that he would accept that.
They brought the iron chains, they attached them to him well.
The strong men stood behind and braced themselves to hold onto the
        chains.
He came to the edge of the hole.
He peeked into it.
What he found there at the bottom of that tomb,
It resembled young onion shoots, and it looked very soft and tasty,
        very soft and tasty, very soft and tasty, very soft and tasty,
        very soft and tasty.
Now, when he stood up quickly,
He suddenly dragged the strong men with him.
He then dropped into the hole, and his two arms went into the hole
        like that.
Then he grabbed and pulled, he ate, he grabbed and pulled, he ate.
Before they pulled him up out of the hole,

---

[18] Here depicted as Askia Mohammed's companion. Eventually the name of Modi Baja
came to stand for a Fulani marabout, or Muslim holy man in the region.

[19] The prophet Muhammad.

He grabbed and pulled out two handfuls and came out with them.

His cousin was standing at his right hand, he gave that to him.

Modi Baja was standing at his left hand, he gave that to him.

Modi Baja brought his from Mecca all the way home, he sold it.

None of Modi Baja's people suffered.

From that day to the present, Our Lord did not make their lives hard.

Our ancestor ate his.

He left, and he left us in suffering.[20]

Since that day until the present, no descendant of Modi Baja has
     suffered.

They didn't tire from a hard life, they didn't seek to work hard in life.

They sup well, they lunch well, they dress well.

It is at that time that Mamar Kassaye retraced his steps.

The griots say of him,[21]

"Long live Mamar.

"Long live Kassaye *Mamadi.*"

Mamar son of Kassaye, he ran to Mecca.

He proceeded to Medina.

He prayed at Mecca, he went to visit Medina.

He [undecipherable] the Indigo Tree.[22]

He went three times around the Indigo Tree.

He repented, he repented . . . [undecipherable].

His sin and his minor sin.

He put them all together, and he put them all there.

He [undecipherable] sword of Dongo.[23]

He slung the sword of Dongo on his shoulder.

It is in these terms that griots sing his praises.

They take it from way back all the way to there.

"Long live Mamar.

"Long live Kassaye.

---

[20] At the actual performance of this epic the griot laughed at the improvidence of the
griots' ancestor who ate the holy plants, in contrast with Modi Baja whose descendants
were to benefit from his careful provisioning for them. This incident serves the function
of explaining why griots, presently considered a lower caste than the rulers, must earn
their livelihood.

[21] What follows is a praise poem of considerable antiquity about Askia Mohammed.

[22] The Indigo Tree is an ancient term for the Kaaba, the holiest of shrines at Mecca. The
indecipherable gaps occur because of difficulties in recording or transcription.

[23] Dongo is the Songhay god of lightning and thunder, a non-Islamic deity evoked here at
the crucial stage of Askia Mohammed's pilgrimage.

"Your ancestor is Mamar, Mamar son of Kassaye."

He ran to Mecca, he proceeded to Medina.

He prayed at Mecca and visited Medina.

He went around the Indigo Tree [undecipherable], he went around the
     Indigo Tree three times, that is, the Kaaba.

He [undecipherable] the Indigo Tree.

He went around the Indigo Tree three times.

[undecipherable], his sin and his minor sin.

He put them all together, and he put them all there on that day.

He . . . . [undecipherable] . . . Dongo.

He slung the sword of Dongo, which is truth.

He let go of bad ways and he took up truth on that day.

He went home.

When he arrived home, he was able to get married.

When he was in the bush, when he was conquering,

It was then that he reached the Bargantché people.

When he reached those Bargantché people,

At the time of his departure, his mother told him, "Whatever battles you
     undertake,

"When you reach the Bargantché land,

"Watch out for them, because you have the milk of a Bargantché woman
     in your stomach.

"You will not be able to conquer the Bargantché.

"You have Bargantché milk in your stomach.

"Whatever cleverness you will use, if you reach the Bargantché, watch
     out, don't quarrel with them."

He went to the land of the Bargantché people,

He arrived among the Bargantché, he said he wants to fight them.

But the Bargantché defeated him.

They said that they would injure his horse.[24]

So he withdrew, he went home to sleep.

Night came, the night became cool.

He got up suddenly and recited some holy words.

He said, among his horse, where could he find someone who could see
     his mother in a short time.

A sohanci got up quickly.

He said, "It is I who will see your mother."

He said, "What time will you come?"

He said, "Before the first cock crow.

---

[24] That is, cavalry.

"You will see me before daylight."

He said, "Good, praised be to Allah, go ahead."

He said, "If you leave, tell my mother:

"Me, I have reached the Bargantché.

"By Allah, I have fought against them but they have beaten me."

There is no longer any way of advancing.

The Bargantché man went out of the village.[25]

He went away from the crowd, and took off all his clothes.

Suddenly he took off into the sky.

The sohanci flies fast.

They fly faster than airplanes.[26]

They go faster than a hawk.

He arrived at Sikiyay, Sikiyay.[27]

It is there that he arrived, he heard them say, "Sana has given birth, Sana
      has given birth, Sana has given birth, Sana has given
      birth."[28]

So there he landed.

He hid himself as he entered into the village.

They[29] said, "What are they saying?"

They replied; "Sana has given birth."

They[30] said, "Who is Sana?"

They said, "Mamar Kassaye who went away, his wife whom he married
      before he left.

"Whom he left pregnant.

"It is that woman there who is Sana.

"It is that woman who gave birth to a boy in his absence.

"Mamar Kassaye has gone away.

"It is his wife who gave birth to a boy in his absence."

He said, "That's true."

---

[25] There appears to be a confusion in the recitation here, as the *sohanci*, or sorcerer, entrusted with the charge of telling Askia Mohammed's mother of the difficulties he is encountering, is described as a Bargantché—the enemy—unless he is a Bargantché man in the service of Askia Mohammed.

[26] A modern adaptation to an ancient text, not uncommon in oral performances.

[27] A small village on the right bank of the Niger, twenty kilometers from Niamey, the capital of present-day Niger. It was the last residence of the Songhay rulers.

[28] This is the first reference to Askia Mohammed's wife.

[29] Apparently the *sohanci* emissary of Askia Mohammed, here referred to in the plural.

[30] See footnote 29.

He said, "Now, this son,

"On the day when he was old enough to be named,[31] they gave him
a name."

He should be given the name Daouda.

Daouda Sana.

Sana Alma Daouda.

Sana Boria Alma Daouda.

Sana Boriayze Cim Daouda.

He continued on his route.[32]

He went to his mother's home.

His mother, Kassaye, had told him, "Long ago,

"I told him not to fight against the Bargantché.

"He cannot beat them, for he has in his stomach the milk of a
Bargantché."

However, she told him,

Now, she took some cotton seeds in her hand and said, "Take."

She took an egg, a chicken egg, and she said to him, "Take."

She took a stone, a river stone, she told him, "Take."

"If you go," if he goes to the Bargantché,

If the Bargantché chase him,

He should put all his horses before him and he should be the only
one behind.

He should scatter the cotton seeds behind him.

They will become a dense bushy barrier between him and them.

If they chop it down,

This dense bush will not prevent anything.

They will clear the bush in order to find him.

If the bush does not help at all,

This time, if they are still hunting him,

He should put all his cavalry in front of him.

He should throw the stone behind him.

It will become a big mountain that will be a barrier between them.

If the big mountain does not help them,

And when they chase him again,

He should put all his cavalry in front of him again,

Leaving himself in the rear.

He should throw the egg behind him.

The egg will become a river to separate them.

---

[31] That is, in the future, when he is to be named.

[32] The *sohanci* continues on to Askia Mohammed's mother, Kassaye, in Gao.

The river cannot—they will stop at the river.
That egg will become a river that will be a barrier between them.
Before the cocks crow at dawn,
When dawn has really come,
The sohanci returns, he lands on the earth.
He said, "By Allah, when I passed by Sikiyay I heard them say that
        Sana had given birth.
"Then I said that if Sana gives birth—since Sana had given birth,
"They should name the child Daouda."
He is the one who is Daouda Sana.
They continued until they . . .
He escaped from the Bargantché, the Bargantché who live along
        the river.
He never again fought against them.
Now, he just passed through their country, to go and start again
        his reign.
The day when he came back,
He came back to Gao.
The only one left with him was his griot and Modi Baja.
He came back.
He dismounted from his horse.
He brought together forty stallions.
He said that marriage should take place between him and the Songhay.[33]
It is not like today during the era of the Whites.[34]
Before, young Songhay men courting women didn't have anything.
He came back to his house.[35]

---

[33] Being of foreign origins, Askia Mohammed wishes to cement his rule over Songhay by an act of marriage. His relationship with the Songhay people is confirmed both by his marriage and by his pilgrimage to Mecca.

[34] This line is a contemporary comment by the griot who is reciting the epic.

[35] Askia Mohammed's return is followed in the full epic by accounts of his children and their deeds.

7

✿

THE MWINDO EPIC

Far from the dry savanna lands in the Sahel where the epics of the Sudanic kingdoms were sung (see, for example, Selection 6), the BaNyanga people of eastern Congo live in a mountainous rain forest in close proximity to the Pygmies. There, under the strong influence of the Pygmies, or Twa, the BaNyanga bards produced a series of epic versions during the past few centuries, sung in the Nyanga language, in praise of the hero Mwindo.

Although the BaNyanga do not have a professional caste of singers, like the griots of West Africa, a wide variety of oral narratives play an important part in their culture. Gatherings of the men provide occasions for recounting tales, quoting proverbs, solving riddles, or instructing the children. In their homes, the women narrate stories, also recite proverbs, and solve riddles of a different nature from those of the men. Expert narrators or singers are much valued and famed, and may have huge repertoires of stories, riddles, songs, prayers, eulogies, teachings, and epics.

The central hero of BaNyanga epic poetry is Mwindo, whose name signifies a male born after a succession of females. Among the many epithets accorded him, perhaps the most interesting is "the Little One Just Born He Walked." His diminutive size is not unusual: Commonly, epic heroes have some kind of disability that they overcome as proof of their superiority. For all their greatness, however, heroes like Mwindo are men, not gods, though they may possess supernatural powers and conduct battles with superhuman or divine beings. His youth consists of a period of incubation and testing, after which he invariably supplants his father, or a ruling father figure, and assumes his rightful mantle as chief or king. Like the heroes of many cultures, he is the embodiment of his people — the leader whose greatness is a metaphor for the supremacy of his people. He achieves this role by struggling on their behalf, as well as on his own. His victory is ultimately their triumph, and is often marked by a political moment of significance, as in the founding of an empire or a state.

This epic incorporates a wide range of verbal forms known to the BaNyanga, including songs with proverbs, riddles, praise songs, prayers, blessings, speeches, and improvisations. It incorporates a broad range of characters, including *humans, animals, and spiritual beings. According to Daniel Biebuyck, who tran-scribed and translated the epic of Mwindo, it provides a rich survey of the cus-toms, institutions, activities, and values found in BaNyanga culture.*

Although Mwindo is a hero, he still must undergo trials and transforma-tions to achieve his full greatness. In this version of the epic, he initially is pre-sented as an unrealistic, verbose boaster. His conquests are qualified by his ruth-lessness, and he cannot attain full glory without undergoing a catharsis. This is achieved in a celestial voyage in which he appears as a passive and suffering being. After this experience he is free of excess, a value, according to Biebuyck, that runs like a leitmotif through much BaNyanga thinking. Mwindo achieves full karamo, *or life force, and* nkuru, *or fame and force, as he adopts a moderate mode of behavior.*

Interestingly enough, Mwindo's strength does not lie in his physical force, but in his magical powers, especially in the power of his song. His generosity and hos-pitality are also marks of his stature, as are his poise and wisdom. In the end, Mwindo achieves the supreme BaNyanga virtue of karamo, *meaning, in the full sense, good health, strength, force, salvation, and good life — all the qualities sought in BaNyanga prayers and greetings. And as the BaNyanga are a people of the forest,* karamo *also means to be a successful hunter, to be free of passions, to have many children, and to have good relations with others: the good life in the fullest African sense.*

The present version was sung by Candi Rureke in the 1950s. The BaNyanga believe that the epic, called karisi, *is under the tutelage of a deity who requires certain individuals to recite it. Recitation is thus, in a sense, an act of devotion. Mr. Rureke learned the epic from a relative of his father named Mr. Kanyangara who himself had learned it from a certain Mr. Bishusha. At that point the recorded lineage of prior reciters ends, though textual evidence suggests an origin lost in the mist of time. It is highly probable that Pygmy culture and narratives had a strong influence on the epic.*

In the following excerpt we see the birth of Mwindo and the attempt of his father, Shemwindo, to kill him. Mwindo escapes, is aided by his paternal aunt, Iyangura, and ultimately defeats his father and asserts his place as ruler.

⊰⊱

MWINDO'S UNUSUAL BIRTH AND HIS BRIEF EARLY YEARS

Because of his power and virtues, *Shemwindo*,[1] together with his wives and people, became very famous not only in *Tubondo*,[2] but throughout the country. When many days had passed, his wives came into labor! They gave birth to female children only. One wife among them, the seventh and the Preferred One, lagged behind in her pregnancy. When the Preferred One saw that her companions had already given birth, whereas she was still heavy with child, she continually complained: "How terrible this is! It is only I who are still dragged down by this pregnancy. What then shall I do? My companions, with whom I became pregnant at the same time, have already gone through it all, and I alone remain with this burden. What will come out of this pregnancy?"

Just after she had finished these sad reflections, she found a bunch of firewood at her door. She did not know from where it had come. It was her child, the one that was inside her womb, who had just brought it.

After some time had passed, while looking around the house the Preferred One discovered a jar of water standing there. She did not know from whence it had come. It was as if it had brought itself into the house. And again, after some more time had passed, she found raw vegetables sitting in the house. Now, she was even more astonished. It was the child in her womb who was carrying out all these miraculous tasks for her.[3]

When the inhabitants of the village saw that the Preferred One continued to drag on with her pregnancy, they started sneering at her: "When is this one going to give birth?" they would mock. The child, dwelling in the womb of its mother, meditated to itself, saying that it could not come out from the underpart of the body of its mother, because people might make fun saying that he was the child of a woman. He did not want to emerge from the mouth of its mother, for then they might make fun, saying that he had been vomited up like a bat.[4]

The Epic of Mwindo, edited, translated, and transcribed by Daniel Biebuyck and Kahombo C. Mateene, from *African Folktales*, selected and retold by Roger D. Abrahams, copyright 1969, The Regents of the University of California. Pp. 244–260, 261–266. Reprinted by permission of the University of California Press.

[1] Shemwindo is the father of the epic's hero, Mwindo.

[2] Tubondo is the principal village where the action unfolds and over which, first, Shemwindo and, then, Mwindo rules.

[3] These tasks—gathering firewood, water, and vegetables or other food—constitute the daily chores of the women.

[4] A widespread belief of the Nyanga is that bats give birth to their young by vomiting them.

The pregnancy had gone so far beyond its term that the old midwives, the wives of counselors, came. They arrived when the Preferred One was already being troubled with labor pains. The child, dwelling in the womb, climbed to her belly, wandered through her limbs and torso, and went on and came out through her middle. The old midwives were astonished when they saw him wailing on the ground. They pointed at him, asking: "What kind of child is that?" Some among them saw that it was a male child, and were worried and wanted to shout it about the village that a male child had been born. Others refused, saying that no one should say that the child was a boy, because when *Shemwindo* heard, he would kill him. The counselors sitting with *Shemwindo,* shouted, asking: "What sort of child is born there?" But the old midwives sitting in the house kept their silence, never giving an answer. Afterwards, the midwives gave him the name *Mwindo*—first-born male—for there had only been female children born in that family before him.[5]

In the house where the birth took place that day, a cricket appeared on the wall carrying omens of great and dreadful things. After *Shemwindo* had asked what child was born and the midwives had refused to answer, the cricket had left the birthhouse and had carried the news to him: "Chief, a male child has been born to you. They call him *Mwindo,* the first boy child, and that is why those in the hut there have not answered you." When *Shemwindo* heard that his Preferred One had given birth to a boy, he took up his spear. He sharpened it on a whetstone and he carried it to the house where the child had been born. The moment he prepared to throw it into the birth hut, the child shouted from inside, saying: "Each time this spear is thrown, may it hit the bottom of the house pole, where the household spirits reside. May it never end up where these old midwives are seated here. Neither may it arrive at the place where my mother is." *Shemwindo* threw the spear into the house six times, and each time it hit nothing but the pole. When the old midwives saw those extraordinary happenings they swarmed out of the house. They fled, saying to one another that they did not want to die in that place.

When *Shemwindo* had become exhausted in his anger, for he ran back and forth with his spear but completely failed to kill *Mwindo,* he spoke to his counselors, saying that they should dig a grave to throw *Mwindo* into, for he did not want to see a male child. When the counselors had heard the order of the lord of

---

[5] It is customary for midwives to inform the men in the men's house of the birth of a child and to reveal its sex by laughing in a special way. However, it is not normal for midwives to name the child immediately after the birth, but rather for the child to receive its name from its grandfather on the third day after its birth. The name Mwindo may be linked to the verb meaning "to fell trees" or "to eradicate"; it is also the name of a spirit in the pantheon of the Nyanga people. It is given to a boy born into a family in which only girls had been born, or to a girl who follows a number of boys.

their village, they did not argue with him; rather they went ahead and dug the grave. When the grave was finished, they went to fetch the child, *Mwindo.* They carried him gently, as a baby should be handled, and went to bury him. *Mwindo* howled from within the grave, saying: "Oh, my father, this is the death that *you* will die, but first you will suffer many sorrows." When *Shemwindo* heard the remarkable curse of the little castaway,[6] he scolded his people telling them to cover the grave right away. His people went to fetch the plantain and banana trees to lay on the grave, as is the custom. They placed them on top of him and above the plantains they heaped much soil. But at that very moment, it became evident that *Mwindo* had been born with a *conga* scepter, the royal fly swatter made of the buffalo tail, which he held in his right hand.[7] He also carried an adze, which he held in his left hand. A little bag of the spirit of *Kahombo,* the carrier of good fortune, was slung across his back on the left side, and in that little bag there was a long magic rope. Most wondrously, *Mwindo* was born laughing and also speaking, already a man among men.

When the day was ending, those sitting outdoors looked to where *Mwindo* had been discarded earlier in the day, and saw that there was light coming forth, as though the sun were shining from within. They ran to tell the others in the village, and they came running. They saw the emanation, but they could not stand still there because the great heat, which was like fire, burned them. As one would pass by, he would attempt to cast his eyes on the light, but he would have to move on, it was so bright.

When everyone had fallen asleep for the night, *Mwindo* emerged from the grave and sneaked into his mother's house. There he began to wail. In his home, *Shemwindo* heard the child's wailing in the house of the Preferred One. He was totally astonished, saying: "This time what was never seen is seen for the first time. A child is crying again in that house. Has my wife given birth to another child?" *Shemwindo* was wracked with indecision, unsure whether or not he could even stand up because of his fear. But in his manliness, *Shemwindo* did stand up, going to the house of his wife, the Preferred One, slithering like a snake, without making a sound. He arrived at the hut, peeked through the open door, and cast his eye on to the child sleeping on the floor. He entered the hut and questioned his wife, saying: "Where does this child come from? Did you leave another one in the womb to whom you have given another birth?" His wife replied to him: "This is *Mwindo* here." Where *Mwindo* was sitting on the ground, he kept silent.

---

[6] The term "little castaway" signifies the child of a despised wife, implying rejection and neglect by the father.

[7] The *conga* scepter is Mwindo's single most important possession, containing magical powers and signifying ceremonial importance, as well as the hero's mental and physical force.

Shemwindo witnessing this marvelous event, his mouth itched to speak, but he left the house without being able to speak another word.

He went to wake up his counselors. Arriving there, he told them: "I was not deceived. He has returned. It is astounding." He told them also: "Tomorrow, when the sky will have become day, then you will go to cut a piece from the trunk of a tree. You will carve in it a husk for a drum. You will then put the hide of an antelope in the river to soften."

When the sky had become day, all the people called one another and assembled. Then, together they went to see *Mwindo* in his mother's house. *Mwindo* was devoured by the many longing eyes. After they had looked at him, the counselors went to the forest to cut a piece of wood for the husk of the drum. They cut it, the piece of wood, and returned with it to the village. Then they carved the wood, they hollowed it out so that it became a husk.

When the husk was finished, they went again to fetch *Mwindo*. They carried him gently and put him within the husk of the drum. *Mwindo* said: "This time, my father has no mercy. What! A small baby is being mistreated!" The people of *Shemwindo* went to get the hide for the drum. They attached it on top of the drum. They covered the drum with it. When *Shemwindo* had seen his son placed within the drum, he declared to all his people that he wanted two expert swimmers, divers, to go the next day to throw the drum into the pool where nothing moves. After the swimmers, divers, had been found, they picked up the drum. Then, all the people left the village to throw *Mwindo* into the water.

When they arrived at the pool where nothing moves, the divers dove into it with the drum, swimming in the river. When they arrived in the middle of the pool, they asked in a loud voice: "Shall we drop him here?" Those sitting on the edge of the river answered: "Yes." All said together: "Drop it there, so that you can't be accused of his return." They released the drum in the middle of the pool and it sank into the depths. The waves made rings above the place where the drum had entered.

After the swimmers had thrown him into the pool, they returned to the shore. *Shemwindo* was very pleased with them: "You have performed good work!" He awarded each swimmer a maiden. That day, when *Mwindo* was thrown away, earth and heaven joined together because of the heavy rain. It rained for seven days and that rain brought much famine in *Tubondo*.

After they had thrown *Mwindo* away, they returned to the village. When they arrived in *Tubondo*, Shemwindo threatened his wife *Nyamwindo,* the Preferred One, saying: "Don't shed tears weeping for your son. If you weep, I shall send you to the same place your son has been thrown." That very day, *Nyamwindo,* *Mwindo's* mother, turned into the Despised One.[8] Unable to weep, *Nyamwindo* went on merely sobbing—but not one little tear did she shed.

---

[8] Not a formal declaration of disgrace, but a de facto condition, based on Shemwindo's attitude.

Where *Mwindo* dwelt in the pool where he had been thrown away, when he was in the water on the sand, he moaned within the drum. He stuck his head on the side of the drum. He listened closely to its sound, and said: "I must not wash downstream in the river. I cannot leave without warning my father and all his people who have cast me away of the consequences of throwing me here. They must be able to hear the sound of my voice. If I wash away, then I am not *Mwindo*." From where the drum was beneath the water, it arose all alone to the surface of the pool—in its middle—and it remained there. It did not go down the river, neither did it go up the river.

From *Tubondo*, from the village where the people dwelt, came a row of maidens. They went to draw water from the river, at the wading place. Arriving at the river, as soon as they cast their eyes toward the middle of the pool, they saw the drum on the surface of the water, turning around and around. They inquired of each other: "Companions, we have dazzling apparitions. Lo, the drum that was thrown with *Mwindo* in it—there it is!" *Mwindo* living inside that drum in the midst of the pool, said: "If I don't sing while these maidens are still here drawing water from the river, then I shall not have anyone who will bring the news to where my father is in *Tubondo*."

While the maidens were in the act of drawing water and still had their attention fixed toward the drum, *Mwindo*, where he dwelt in the drum in the pool, threw sweet words into his mouth.[9] He sang:

> *I am saying farewell to* Shemwindo!
> *I am saying farewell to* Shemwindo!
> *I shall die, O Bira!*[10]
> *My little father threw me into the drum!*
> *I shall die,* Mwindo!
> *The counselors abandoned* Shemwindo;
> *The counselors will become dried leaves.*
> *The counselors of* Shemwindo,
> *The counselors of* Shemwindo,
> *The counselors have failed in their counseling!*
> *My little father, little* Shemwindo,
> *My little father threw me into the drum!*
> *I shall not die, while that little one survives!*

---

[9] "Sweet words," literally "sweet grains" in Nyanga, denote an oral will left by a dying father or, as in this case, a prophetic statement.

[10] Bira signifies those who are not of BaNyanga culture, particularly the lower caste, the uncircumcised Hunde. Here Mwindo is mocking and challenging his opponents.

The little one is joining Iyangura,[11]
The little one is joining Iyangura,
Iyangura, *the sister of* Shemwindo.

When the girls heard the way in which *Mwindo* was singing in the drum in the pool, they climbed up to the village, running and rushing, leaving the water jars behind them in disarray. The men, seeing them appear, running and rushing, at the outskirts of the living area, took their spears and went out believing that they were being chased by a wild beast. Seeing the spears, the maidens beseeched their fathers: "Hold it! We are going to bring the news to you of how the drum that you threw into the pool has remained there. In fact it is singing: 'The counselors of *Shemwindo*, the counselors have failed in their counseling. The counselors will become dried leaves.'" When he heard that, *Shemwindo* accused the girls of lying: "What? The drum that we threw yesterday into the depths of the pool has come to the surface again!" The maidens averred this was true: "*Mwindo* is still alive." When *Shemwindo* heard that, again he assembled his people. Everybody went down to the river carrying spears, arrows, and torches. The village remained empty.

From where *Mwindo* was floating in the river, he was able to see the way in which the maidens had run from the river toward the village. So he stopped singing for a while, saying to himself that he would sing again when the people arrived, following the girls who had just witnessed his astonishing deed. All the people of the village, children and youngsters, old men and young men, old woman and young women, when they arrived at the river, seeing the drum in the middle of the pool, were joined together in staring at it. When *Mwindo* saw them standing in a group on the shore, he threw sweet words into his mouth. He sang:

I am saying farewell to Shemwindo;
I shall die, O Bira!
The counselors abandoned Shemwindo.
The counselors will turn into dried leaves.
What will die and what will be safe[12]
Are going to encounter Iyangura.

When *Mwindo* had finished singing like that, bidding farewell to his father and to all the people of *Shemwindo*, the drum sank into the pool. The waves made rings at the surface. Where *Shemwindo* and his people were standing on the shore, they were very perplexed. They shook their heads, saying: "How terrible it

---

[11] Iyangura, Mwindo's paternal aunt, is the ritual wife of the evil water serpent–spirit Mukiti. Nevertheless, she serves as Mwindo's ally.

[12] Mwindo ascribes to himself the qualities of Life and Death in this line.

is! Will some day there be born what has never been born?" After they had witnessed this extraordinary event, they returned to the village, *Tubondo*.

Mwindo headed upstream. He went to the river's source, at *Kinkunduri's*, to begin his journey.[13] When he arrived at *Kinkunduri's*, he lodged there. He said he was going to join *Iyangura*, his paternal aunt, there where *Kahungu*[14] had told him she had gone. He met up with his aunt *Iyangura* downstream, and he sang:

> Mungai *fish, get out of my way!*
> *For* Ikukuhi, *should I go out of my way for you?*
> *You are impotent against* Mwindo,
> Mwindo *is the Little One Just Born He Walked.*
> *I am going to meet* Iyangura.
> *For* kabusa *fish, should I go out of my way for you?*
> *You are helpless against* Mwindo,
> *For* Mwindo *is the Little One Just Born He Walked.*
> Canta *fish, get out of my way!*
> Canta, *you are impotent against* Mwindo.
> *I am going to encounter* Iyangura, *my aunt.*
> *For* mutaka *fish, should I go out of my way for you?*
> *You are helpless against* Mwindo!
> *I am going to meet* Iyangura, *my aunt.*
> *For* kitoru *fish, should I go out of my way for you?*
> *You see, I am going to encounter* Iyangura, *my aunt.*
> *For crabs, should I go out of my way for you?*
> *You are impotent against* Mwindo!
> *See, I am going to encounter* Iyangura, *my aunt,*
> Iyangura, *sister of* Shemwindo.
> *For* nyarui *fish, should I go out of my way for you?*
> *Whereas* Mwindo *is the Little One Just Born He Walked.*
> *I am going to encounter* Iyangura, *my aunt,*
> *Sister of* Shemwindo.
> *For* cayo *fish, should I go out of my way for you?*
> *You see, I am going to encounter* Iyangura, *my aunt,*
> *Sister of* Shemwindo.
> *Look! You are impotent against* Mwindo.
> Mwindo, *the Little One Just Born He Walked.*
> *He who will go up against me, it is he who will die on the way.*[15]

---

[13] Kinkunduri is a species of crab. Mwindo is heading upstream, towards waters that are increasingly pure, and towards Mukiti's magical underwater realm.

[14] Kahungu is a hawk and a friendly messenger.

[15] The various species of fish and crab mentioned in this verse are personifications of ugliness and hatred, and are considered allies of Mukiti.

Each time *Mwindo* arrived in a place where there was a swimming animal, he said that it should get out of the way for him, that they were powerless against him, that he was going to his aunt, *Iyangura*. When *Mwindo* arrived at *Cayo's*, he spent the night there; in the morning he traveled on right after awakening. Again he sang:

> *For* ntsuka *fish, should I go out of my way for you?*
> *You see that I am going to encounter* Iyangura.
> *You see that you are powerless against* Mwindo.
> Mwindo *is the Little One Just Born He Walked.*
> *For* kirurumba *fish, should I get out of the way?*
> *You see that I am going to encounter Aunt* Iyangura.
> *You see that you are powerless against* Mwindo.
> *For* Mwindo *is the Little One Just Born He Walked.*
> *For* mushomwa *fish, should I go out of the way?*
> *You see I am going to encounter Aunt* Iyangura.
> *You see that you are powerless against* Mwindo.
> *For* Mwindo *is the Little One Just Born He Walked.*

Musoka,[16] the junior sister of the evil *Mukiti*, had gone to live upstream from hated *Mukiti:*

> *For* Musoka, *should I go out of my way for you?*
> *You are powerless against* Mwindo,
> Mwindo *is the Little One Just Born He Walked.*

When *Musoka* saw *Mwindo* arriving at her place, she sent an envoy to *Mukiti* to say that there was a person there where she was, at *Musoka's*, who was about to join *Iyangura*. The envoy ran quickly to *Mukiti*. Arriving, he gave the news: "There is a person back there who is joining *Iyangura*." *Mukiti* replied that the envoy should tell *Musoka* that the man must not pass beyond her place — "If not, why would I have placed her there?" That envoy arrived at *Musoka's*. He told how he had been spoken to by *Mukiti*. Then *Musoka* blocked *Mwindo's* passage, although she did not know that he was a child of *Mukiti's* wife, *Iyangura*.[17] *Musoka* spoke to *Mwindo*, saying: *Mukiti* refuses to let you by. So it is only by proving your manhood that you will be able to pass. I, *Musoka*, I am placing barriers here. You will not find a trail to pass on." *Mwindo* answered her, softening his voice: "I am *Mwindo*. Never will I be forbidden to pass on any trail. I will break through exactly at the place where you would prevent me from going by." *Mwindo*,

---

[16] A female water spirit.

[17] The closeness of Mwindo to his paternal aunt is denoted by his reference to himself as her child, and subsequently to her husband, the dreaded Mukiti, as his father.

saying this, pulled himself together. He left the water above him, he dug inside the sand, and he burrowed to a place somewhere between *Musoka* and *Mukiti.*

After *Mwindo* had passed *Musoka* in this way, having broken through *Musoka's* dam, he boasted: "Here I am, the Little One Just Born He Walked. No one ever points a finger at me." When *Musoka* saw him anew downstream, she touched her chin,[18] saying: "How then has this tough one here gotten through? If he had passed above me, I would have seen his shadow; if he had passed below me, I would have heard the sound of his feet." *Musoka* railed at his escape, saying that she would be scolded by *Mukiti.*

After *Mwindo* had passed *Musoka,* he began to journey to *Mukiti's.* He sang:

> *In* Mukiti*'s, in* Mariba*'s dwelling place!*[19]
> *For* Mukiti, *should I go out of the way for you?*
> *You see I am going to encounter* Iyangura,
> Iyangura, *sister of* Shemwindo.
> Mukiti, *you are powerless against* Mwindo.
> Mwindo *is the Little One Just Born He Walked.*

When *Mukiti* in his dwelling place heard this, he asked who was talking about his wife. He moved and shook heaven and earth. The whole pool moved. *Mwindo* on his part said: "This time we shall really get to know each other, for I, *Mwindo,* never fear one who is nothing so much as a boasting and pampered child easily angered. I won't be worried about such a one until I have myself against him."

Mwindo, organizing himself, went to appear at the spot where the monster *Mukiti* was coiled up. When *Mukiti* saw him, he said: "This time it is not the one whom I expected to see. He surpasses all expectation!" He asked: "Who are you?" *Mwindo* responded, saying that he was *Mwindo,* the Little One Just Born He Walked, child of *Iyangura. Mukiti* said to *Mwindo*: "What do you want, then?" *Mwindo* answered saying that he was going to be with his paternal aunt, *Iyangura.* Hearing that, *Mukiti* said to *Mwindo*: "You are lying. No one ever passes over these logs and dried leaves. Are you alone the man who in spite of all will be able to pass through the forbidden spot!"

While *Mukiti* and *Mwindo* were still boasting and arguing with each other, maidens went from *Iyangura's* place to draw water at *Mukiti's* place, because there is where the water hole was. As soon as the maidens heard the way in which *Mwindo* always referred to *Iyangura* as his aunt, they ran to tell her. "Over there, where your husband *Mukiti* is, a little man has come who says that *Mukiti* should let him pass, for he is *Mwindo,* that he is going to meet with *Iyangura,* his paternal aunt." When *Iyangura* heard that news, she said: "Lo! That is my child. I will go to where he is." *Iyangura* climbed up the slope. She went to the water hole.

---

[18] Expressing astonishment.

[19] That is, a pool of water.

She looked to the river that she first might see the man who was calling her his aunt. As soon as *Mwindo* saw *Iyangura* coming to him, he sang:

> *I am suffering much,* Mwindo.
> *I will die,* Mwindo.

While his aunt *Iyangura* was descending the slope, he went on singing, looking in the direction from which his aunt was coming.

> *Aunt* Iyangura,
> Mukiti *has blocked the road to me.*
> *I am going to meet Aunt* Iyangura,
> *I am going to encounter* Iyangura,
> *Sister of* Shemwindo.
> *For* Mukiti, *shall I go out of the way?*
> *I am joining* Iyangura,
> *Sister of* Shemwindo.
> *For* Mukiti, *my father, shall I go out of my way for him?*
> *You are powerless against* Mwindo.

Iyangura said: "If my sister's son, the nephew of the people of *Mitandi,*[20] is in this drum, let him come here so that I can see him before me." But though his aunt cited the people of *Mitandi* in this way, *Mwindo* refused to move in her direction. From inside the drum, *Mwindo* complained that his aunt had missed the mark. His aunt spoke again: "If you drum, if you are the nephew of the One Who Hears Secrets, come here. Draw near me." Though his aunt mentioned the One Who Hears Secrets, the drum still refused to draw near. His aunt said anew: "If you really are the nephew of the people of *Yana,*[21] come before me." When *Mwindo* heard this, he went forth from the pool singing:

> *I am going to my Aunt* Iyangura,
> Iyangura, *sister of* Shemwindo.
> Kabarebare *and* Ntabare *mountain,*
> *Where the husband of my senior sister sets fish traps.*
> *And a girl who is nice is a lady,*
> *And a nice young man is a house pole.*[22]
> *We are telling the story*

---

[20] The Mitandi are the kinship group of the spiders who in Nyanga tales are helpful creatures, makers of bridges that save the heroes.

[21] The people of Yana are the kinship group of the "hundreds," that is, those who are numerous, signifying the bats. Bats are representative of the blacksmiths who "forge" (strengthen) the heroes.

[22] The poles form the framework of house walls and symbolize straightness.

That the Babuya *have told long ago.*[23]
We are telling the story.
Kasengeri[24] *is dancing, wagging his tail;*
And you see his tail of nderema *fibers.*
Nkurongo *bird had gone to court* mususu *bird;*
Muhasha *bird has contracted asthma, is gasping for breath.*[25]
If I am at a loss for words in the great song,
If it dies out, may it not die out for me there.
They are accustomed to speak to Mukiti *with bells.*
The tunes that we are singing.
The uninitiated ones cannot know them. . . .

Mwindo was still flowing with the river, and as he floated by his aunt, she seized the drum. Her people gave her a knife and she slashed the drum open. Removing the hide, she saw the multiple rays of the rising sun and the moon—such was the beauty of the child, *Mwindo. Mwindo* rose out of the drum, still holding his *conga* scepter and his adze, together with his little bag that contained the magical rope. When Hawk saw *Mwindo* meeting with his aunt, he went to bring the news to the elder who had been sent to *Iyangura* to keep watch over her continually. He arrived there, and told him: "You, you who are here, it is not merely a little man who appears over there; he carries with him stories of his many attributes and feats. He is going to kill you." Hearing this news, *Kasiyembe*[26] said: "You bearer of news, go! When you have arrived at *Mwindo*'s, tell him he must not attempt to pass by this side, for if he tries, I will tear out his backbone. I am setting up traps here, pits and pointed sticks and razors in the ground, so that whenever he tries, I will catch him in his attempts."

Seeing all this going on, *Mukei* the Hedgehog,[27] acting as a messenger going the other way, went to *Mwindo*, and told him: "*Mwindo*, our enemies are holding secret council against you. They are even preparing pit traps against you, and pointed sticks and razors. I say this, I, *Mukei* the Hedgehog, who is a master of going underground, into the depth of the earth." *Mwindo* answered: "Yes, I always see you burrowing; it is within the earth that you live, so you must know well of such things." After warning *Mwindo, Mukei* also told him: "I am going to build a road which bypasses him, so that it goes where you are, inside

---

[23] The Babuya are a descent group in the village where the epics's narrator lived.

[24] The name of an animal designating a good dancer.

[25] The good singer is being contrasted here to the poor one. Mwindo's power and good qualities are thus associated with the epic singer's verbal and musical ability.

[26] A villain whose task is to watch over Iyangura.

[27] A messenger and ally of Mwindo.

the house of your aunt, at the base of the house pole." *Mwindo* approved of this plan gladly. *Mukei* the Hedgehog began to dig in the ground, inside it. *Mwindo* told his aunt *Iyangura*: "You, Aunt, go on ahead, get going on your way home, and I shall meet you there. *Kasiyembe,* who threatened me over there, I shall first meet up with him. If he really is powerful, I shall deal with him." He also said to his aunt: "Tell the one who is threatening me there, that he should get ready for me." Then Master Spider came out of the pit traps and began to build bridges. He built them out over the pits. Indeed, the pits became merely bridges. He said to himself that it was there that *Mwindo* was going to play. "As far as I, Master Spider, am concerned, *Mwindo* cannot be beaten as long as we are there."

After *Mwindo* had told his aunt to go along, she did not attempt to fool him—she went home. Back where *Mwindo* had stayed, he took the road made by *Mukei.* Thanks to his helpers, he came out in the house of his aunt, at *Iyangura's.* When *Kasiyembe* saw where he was, he said: "*Mwindo* is already over here. Now, from where has he come?" The people of his village said that they did not know how he had gotten there.

When *Iyangura* saw that her son *Mwindo* had already arrived, she said to him: "My boy, don't eat yet. First come to my side, so that we may dance to the rhythm of the drum." After *Mwindo* had heard his aunt's words, he came outdoors to where his aunt was. He agreed to dance with her without having eaten food, but said that he was going to faint with responding to the calls of the drum. His aunt replied to him: "Not at all! Dance away, my son. You must know I am ordered to have you do this by *Kasiyembe,* my protector, but your enemy. He says that you must dance to tire you out. What then shall we do? You must dance all the same!" Hearing the word of his aunt, *Mwindo* said: "Oh! Right you are. Let me first dance, for hunger never kills a man." *Mwindo* sang and the dance became a source of his strength. He howled, he inveighed against *Kasiyembe,* saying:

> Kasiyembe, *you are powerless against* Mwindo,
> *For* Mwindo *is the Little One Just Born He Walked.*
> Kasiyembe *said: "Let us dance together."*
> Shirungu,[28] *give us a morsel!*
> *If we die, we will die for you.*
> Kasengeri[29] *is dancing with his* conga *scepter,*
> Conga *scepter of* nderema *fibers.*
> *I am saying farewell to* Mpumba,[30]
> *My* Mpumba *with many raphia bunches.*

---

[28] Shirungu is a drummer accompanying the performance, and is here addressed by the narrator.

[29] See footnote 24.

[30] Mpumba is the name of an insect whose puniness is mocked. He is an ally of Mukiti.

Mwindo danced round about in the midst of the pits. He danced with his body bent over the pits, without being injured by the razors. He went back and forth everywhere that *Kasiyembe* had placed traps for him, without injuring himself.

Iyangura told her son to have some food, saying that since the time he arrived he had not once rinsed his mouth in preparation for eating. *Iyangura* gave her son a head of cattle as a token of hospitality. Then she killed it and prepared it for him. Those on the side, the maidens, ate from it for several days.

After *Mwindo* had received this hospitality gift (but did not eat of it), *Kasiyembe*, the man filled with hatred, persisted in trying to kill him. He said: "Is this the boy against whom I shall be impotent, whereas I heard that he came from the inside of a drum?" *Kasiyembe* implored Hedgehog, *Nkuba* the lightning hurler,[31] saying: "*Nkuba,* you must go and cut *Mwindo* in two. Come to the house where he is staying with all these young women and take care of this problem."

When *Mwindo* heard the way in which *Kasiyembe* repeatedly threatened him, he told the ladies to sit down near him because *Kasiyembe* wanted to strike him with lightning. Then *Mwindo* turned threateningly to Master *Nkuba* saying: "*Nkuba,* since you insist on attacking me, you must strike on one side of the house. You must not strike the side where *Mwindo* is sitting." Master *Nkuba,* on hearing the voice of *Kasiyembe,* ignored the warning and descended on the house. *Mwindo* pointed at him, saying: "You, too, will die the same death; you are climbing a hard tree." Master *Nkuba* then struck seven times on *Mwindo's* side of the house, but try as he might, he could not come close to the place where *Mwindo* was sitting: The fire burnt only on the side where there was no one, and that side of the house was turned into ashes.

Where *Iyangura, Mwindo's* aunt, was sitting, so many tears rolled from her eyes that they reached her legs. She feared that the boy was dying and wept that she had not even seen him well. *Mwindo* then came out of the house along with the young women. Setting himself boldly in front of the crowd of people, he announced to all that he had arrived and was well, and remained the Little One Just Born He Walked. He told his aunt to approach him so that he might speak to her. She came close and *Mwindo* spoke: "No more crying. You, my aunt, are the reason *Kasiyembe* tested me in such an evil fashion. Tomorrow, if you see me no more, it means that you are not worthy of *Mwindo*." All this he told his aunt within the twinkling of an eye. Then, by his great powers, he made *Kasiyembe's* foolish mop of hair catch on fire. Where *Kasiyembe* was, people could see, all at

---

[31] Nkuba, god of lightning, is a destructive divinity, ready to put his powers of devastation at the disposal of any solicitor, good or evil. At first he tries to aid Mwindo's enemies, and eventually allies himself with Mwindo.

once, that his foolish mop of hair was already aflame. Indeed, the tongues of flame rose into the air in such a way that all the lice and all the vermin that were nestled on his head were entirely consumed.

When they saw that *Kasiyembe*'s mop of hair was burning, the people of *Kasiyembe* went to fetch water in jars to put out the fire. But by the time they arrived with the jars, there was no water in them. All the water had dried up in the jars, there was not a drop left. They went straight to the water-carrying plantain stalks, but these, too, were already dried up. They said: "What is this? I guess we will have to spit on his head!" But even that was impossible, for their mouths, too, were so dry that no one had any spit left.

As they were going through all of this, they said: "This *Kasiyembe* is about to die. Go to his master, go to *Mukiti*'s place, and see if there is any help there, for there is a pool at *Mukiti*'s." But when they arrived, they found *Mukiti* with butterflies and flies flitting about him, for there, too, all water had evaporated. In fact the whole pool had dried up, so much so that you couldn't find a drop in it. When his aunt saw what was happening, she went to beg before the boy: "Widen your heat, you my son 'of the body,' my nephew who is such a unique creature. Did you come here just to attack us? Widen your heart for us, and take the spell off my husband. Stretch your heart that you may heal the afflicted without harboring further resentment against them." After the aunt had finished humbly imploring the boy, *Mwindo* cooled the anger of his heart. He awoke *Kasiyembe*, waving his *conga* scepter above him, and singing:

> He who went to sleep wakes up.
> You have no power against Mwindo,
> Mwindo *is the Little One Just Born He Walked.*
> He who went to sleep wakes up.
> Look, I am playing with my conga scepter.

Suddenly, *Kasiyembe* was saved. And in the storage jars water again appeared. And the green stalks of the plantains, again there was water in them. And where *Mukiti* was staying, there, too, the water came back and the river flowed on beneath. When the people saw this feat, they were much astonished, saying: "*Mwindo* must be a great man." *Kasiyembe* saluted *Mwindo*, saying "Hail! Hail! *Mwindo.*" And *Mwindo* answered, "Yes."

After he had accomplished that deed, *Mwindo* informed his aunt that he would be going to *Tubondo* the next day to fight his father, for twice his father had thrown him away, and so he would, in his turn, go to stand up against him. The aunt said to him: "O powerful one, you won't be able to overpower your father. For you are only yesterday's child, born just a little while ago. Will you be worthy of ruling *Tubondo,* village of seven meeting places? I, who had you taken out from within the drum, must strongly say no to such a question. No one should even try to go alone, for the lonely path is never a pleasant one to travel."

When *Mwindo* heard the way in which his aunt was speaking, he refused to listen; he blocked out his aunt's words by humming to himself. The aunt told him: "Do not go to fight with your father. But if you do go, then I shall go with you to watch as your father cuts you into pieces."

She instructed the maidens to pack up her household objects so she could accompany *Mwindo*, for the lonely path is never pleasant — without fail, something comes along with the power to kill. When the sky had become daylight, they breakfasted before the journey back to *Tubondo*. And *Mwindo* sang of deeds of glory to give him strength and attractiveness. *Mwindo* sang:

> *I am going with the aunt.*
> *The Little One has slept, all prepared for the journey.*
> *O my father, the Little One set out right after awakening.*
> *I warn you, we are already underway.*

The evening of this journey that *Mwindo* was making with his aunt, in spite of everything, found him at his maternal uncles, among the people of *Yana.* They had killed a goat of hospitality for him, and he rested there. After they all had eaten of the goat, *Mwindo* said to his maternal uncles: "I am going to fight *Shemwindo* in *Tubondo*. You who are the blacksmiths of large light spears, my uncles, make me strong and resistant." The people of *Yana* said that they were going to remake him by the forge. They dressed him in shoes made entirely of iron and pants all of iron too, they also made him an iron shirt and a hat of iron. They told him: "As you are going to fight your father, may the spears that they will unceasingly hurl at you stroke only this iron that is on your body." After his uncles had finished forging, they said they would no longer stay where they were, but would go with him so that they might see the battle to come. In the morning, *Mwindo* set out with his uncles, and his aunt *Iyangura*, accompanied by all of her servants. *Mwindo* sang out angrily, boasting:

> *I shall fight over there at* Shemwindo's;
> *The cattle that* Shemwindo *possesses,*
> *May they join* Mwindo.

When they had the village in sight, *Mwindo*'s aunt said to *Mwindo*: "O our leader, let's get out of here. Just looking up at your father's village makes us dizzy with fear. *Tubondo* over there is a village of seven gates. There are too many people there. They will destroy us." *Mwindo* answered his aunt: "I, *Mwindo*, I am never afraid of anyone with whom I have not yet fought, much less that overgrown child. I want to try this *Shemwindo*. He is too much spoiled by pride." *Mwindo* went on singing:

> *We are going over there to* Tubondo,
> *Where* Shemwindo *lives.*

When they arrived in the glen, he said: "Let us spend tonight in this village." His aunt howled, she said: "Where will we sleep, here there is no house, and

Kiruka-nuambura has arrived, bearer of rain that never ceases." The aunt shouted, she said: "Oh! my father,[32] where shall we sleep? The rain has just rumbled, the young woman is destitute."[33] *Mwindo* looked around, and said that he wanted to have houses—and houses assembled themselves in two rows! *Mwindo* indicated that his uncles should take one row of houses, and his aunt the other row. And *Mwindo*'s house arose by itself in the middle of them all. His aunt shouted saying: "Yes, our leader *Mwindo*, hail for these our houses. *Shemwindo* has fathered a hero. *Kahambo*,[34] my father, I shall give you some children, my father's grandchildren. Let us go with our prestigious man. May our prestigious man escape thunder and lightning! In spite of himself, *Shemwindo* brought forth a son who is never afraid. And *Mwindo* is making himself into a hero already through his great doings." There in the glen, the houses put themselves together. *Mwindo*'s aunt said to him: "O *Mwindo*, my leader, let us escape, for you are powerless in the face of this mass of people who are in *Tubondo*." *Mwindo* said that he must first test himself. *Iyangura*, *Mwindo*'s aunt, said to him: "O *Mwindo*, what shall we eat then? Look, the great number of your uncles here, and I, too, *Iyangura*, have an entourage with me, and you, *Mwindo*, you have drummers and singers with you. What will this whole group eat?" *Mwindo* saw that his aunt was telling him something important, and had to agree: "I see that the whole group that is with us is already hungry." He lifted his eyes to the sky. He said to himself that he must begin with the food that was over there in *Tubondo*, in the village of his enemies, that this must be magically captured—and so great were his powers that it happened. The food came to him, so that he might go to fight. *Mwindo* sang while carrying back the food from his father's camp. His aunt was still shouting out in hunger, "O my leader, what shall we eat today?" *Mwindo* howled back, singing:

> *The foods that are in* Tubondo,
> *May the foods come to* Mwindo,
> Mwindo, *the Little One Just Born He Walked.*
> *The animals that are in* Tubondo,
> *May the animals come to* Mwindo.
> *The meats that* Shemwindo *stores,*
> *May the meats come to* Mwindo Mboru,
> Mwindo, *the Little One Just Born He Walked.*
> *The wood that* Shemwindo *keeps,*
> *O leader, may it come to* Mwindo Mboru!
> *For* Mwindo *is the Little One Just Born He Walked.*

---

[32] "Father" used here as a term of affection and closeness, employed by parents and paternal aunts when referring to their child or nephew.

[33] "Young woman" refers ironically to Kiruka, the old woman who brings rain.

[34] The name of the spirit of good fortune.

And the fire that Shemwindo *possesses,*
May the fire also come to Mwindo.
And the water that Shemwindo *possesses,*
May the water also come to Mwindo Mboru.
The jars that are at Shemwindo's,
May the jars come to Mwindo,
Mwindo, *the Little One Just Born He Walked.*
The clothes that are at Shemwindo's,
May the clothes come to Mwindo,
Mwindo *is going to fight!*
The wooden dishes that are in Tubondo,
May the wooden dishes also come to Mwindo,
O father, Little One Just Born He Walked
Hopes to be victorious.
The beds that Shemwindo *possesses,*
May the beds come to Mwindo.
And the wicker plates that Shemwindo *possesses,*
May the wicker plates also come to Mwindo.
And the salt that Shemwindo *possesses,*
May the salt also come to Mwindo,
The Little One Just Born He Walked.

It was in this way that *Mwindo* was speaking!

• • •

And the bellows that Shemwindo *possesses,*
May the bellows also come to Mwindo;
May there be nobody left who smiths.
And the hammers that are at Shemwindo's,
May the hammers also come to Mwindo;
May there be nobody who smiths.
And the blacksmiths at Shemwindo's,
May the blacksmiths also come to Mwindo;
May there be nobody who smiths.
The nkendo *knives that are in* Tubondo,
The nkendo *knives that* Shemwindo *possesses,*
May the nkendo *knives come to* Mwindo;
May there be nobody who plaits.
The raphia palm trees that are at Shemwindo's,
May the raphia palm trees come to Mwindo;
May there be nobody who plaits
Or who traps.
And the drums that are in Tubondo,

O father the drums!
May they join Mwindo;
May there be nobody who dances.

Thus did *Mwindo* invoke and call to him magically all of his father's possessions.[35]

Mwindo and his uncles and his aunt and the servants who had arrived with them, the singers and the drummers, when the latter opened their eyes—all the things that were in *Tubondo* and at *Shemwindo*'s had come to them. When *Mwindo*'s aunt saw all these things, she said to her son *Mwindo*: "You will suffer because of those things belonging to other people that you brought together here." And it was true, for all those with *Mwindo* got sick, gorging themselves with food. They were not cold any more, they found their warmth again. They said: "Lo! *Mwindo* is a man who does not lie when he says that he is the Little One Just Born He Walked. He always has something to rely upon. The one who will try to climb over him will be the first to die alone and abandoned—he is not a man to provoke."

When *Mwindo* had seen that all the important things of his father had come to him, he said that now his father remained there, drunk and abandoned. He said to his aunt that he wanted his uncles to start the fight, and that he, *Mwindo*, would remain there with her for awhile so that he might see how his uncles handled themselves in battle. His uncles fought on the land and in the air, but the people of *Tubondo* said: "You will not win out today."

After a time, *Mwindo*'s uncles were completely wiped out. They died. The people of *Tubondo* finished them. One of *Mwindo*'s uncles escaped from the midst of the battle, but he was seriously injured. He ran to *Mwindo* to tell him the news. "The people of *Tubondo* have overcome us. All the people, all your uncles, are lying there in their own congealed blood." When *Mwindo*'s aunt saw this messenger—blood had covered his whole body—and also heard the news of how the people had completely dried up like water into the soil, she exclaimed: "O leader, *Mwindo*, I warned you of this. I said that you were going to be helpless against the people of *Shemwindo*. But you said, 'Not at all.' Now just pick up this useless tooth here, the fruit of your victory. Just look how your uncles have been wiped out." *Mwindo* said to his aunt: "First, I'm going to find out why my uncles were all defeated. And if *Shemwindo* does not meet me face to face, then I am not *Mwindo*." His aunt said to him: "Oh, *Mwindo*, don't! You will be responsible for all of us getting killed. If you enrage the people in *Tubondo*, then we are all going to die." *Mwindo* did not listen to the mouth of his aunt, and said that he was going to fight: "You, aunt, stay here with my axe and my little bag in which there is a rope. And I will carry my scepter with me."

---

[35] Mwindo's force is reflected here in the magical powers of his words rather than in physical strength.

Mwindo went climbing up to *Tubondo*. As soon as the people saw *Mwindo* arriving, they pointed to him, saying to *Shemwindo:* "See the little man who just appeared at the village entrance alone." *Shemwindo* answered his people: "What can one little man do all by himself? Even if he comes, we shall cut his throat and he will die." His people answered him: "There, from where *bisibisi* insects emerge, one day red ants will come out of it. This little man will be able to make us run away from the village and we won't be able to do anything against him." *Shemwindo* answered his people: "Let this little fool go swaggering into the garbage heap."

Mwindo came through the village entrance singing and swinging his scepter around. When *Mwindo* arrived in *Tubondo*, he came to the middle of the village. He talked to the people. He demanded to dance to the rhythm of their drums. The people of that village taunted him, seeing his size: "You are helpless against our drums here, you are a little fool." *Mwindo* answered them that this was an insult. Before he even had time to rest, they began the challenges and slanders. The people of that village told him that there was no drum there. To that *Mwindo* said that the drums would be coming. *Mwindo* went on speaking to them in that way while his father was in his compound. *Mwindo* sang his boast about himself:

> *He is climbing up here in* Tubondo,
> *He is going to fight with* Shemwindo.

While he was singing, he declaimed: "May whoever dies and whoever is saved join *Iyangura*." He raised his voice to the sky, singing:

> *What will never die but will be saved,*
> *May it, O father, join* Iyangura,
> Iyangura, *sister of* Shemwindo,
> *The most exalted mother of my cradling string.*[36]
> *O father, whoever will die and whoever will be saved,*
> *May they join their aunt,*
> *Sister of* Shemwindo!
> *My junior and my senior sisters,*
> *Be ready to join me.*
> *What will never die but will be saved,*
> *May they join* Iyangura,
> *Aunt, sister of* Shemwindo.
> *My senior brother, come,*
> *Who will die and will be saved,*
> *May they join Aunt* Iyangura.

---

[36] Highest honorific name a person can give to his or her mother or aunt.

May you, O my mothers, come!
What will not die but be saved,
May they join Aunt Iyangura.
I die, O Bira!
What has been said will be said again.
Let me fight here in Tubondo,
Even though Tubondo *has seven entrances.*
Rightly have the counselors feared to advise Shemwindo.
Whoever will die and whoever will be saved,
May they join Aunt Iyangura.
The counselors retreated before Shemwindo.
Who will die and who will be saved,
May they join Aunt Iyangura.
Hatred is in the heart.
When I have a bridge built for myself,
He who crosses it will be cut in two.
I prayed for Aunt Iyangura,
Aunt Iyangura, *may you be blessed with the favor of the spirits.*

Mwindo shouted, saying:

Hatred is in the heart,
My friend Nkuba, *god of lightning, may you be on my side*
And make me victorious.
I shall fight here in Tubondo,
Even if Tubondo *has seven entrances.*
Here, in Tubondo, *send seven lightning flashes to close them off.*
I shall fight here in Tubondo.
I send seven lightning flashes now!
Mwindo *thought back over his grievances.*
The counselors ran away leaving Shemwindo.
For the counselors were not worthy of their office.
It's you who will die, and turn into dried leaves.
My father threw me into the drum.
I shall fight here in Tubondo;
May Tubondo *turn into dried leaves, merely.*
The counselors ran away leaving Shemwindo;
The counselors were not worthy of that office.
May the counselors turn into dried leaves.
My friend Nkuba, *may you strike in victory.*
Hatred is in the heart.
I implored Aunt Iyangura,
Whoever will die or be saved,
May they join Iyangura,

Aunt, sister of Shemwindo,
My little fiery father.
My insignificant father threw me into the grave.
My insignificant father believed that I would die.

Mwindo raised his eyes into heaven and said:

My friend Nkuba,
Here in Tubondo *send seven lightning flashes!*

While *Mwindo* was looking up into the sky, he pointed his scepter there as well. From the sky where *Nkuba* dwells, seven lightning flashes came, descending on *Tubondo*, on the village. *Tubondo* turned into dust, and the dust rose up. All who lived there turned into mere dust.

Where *Shemwindo* was sitting in his compound, he exclaimed: "There is no time for lingering here." Having spoken, he went down behind the house without looking back. Where he fled, he arrived at a place in which there was a *kikoka* plant. Tearing it out, he went into the ground at the base of its root.[37]

After his victory at *Tubondo*, *Mwindo* boasted in the middle of the village. He said: "This time the one who climbs on me, the one who digs into me while fighting with me, will be wearing himself out in vain." He spoke like this when the corpses of the first of his uncles to die had already begun to decay. *Mwindo* went down to where his aunt still stayed in the glen in order that they should walk together to the crest of the hill at *Tubondo*. The aunt asked him: "Is it good news that you carry from where you are coming?" *Mwindo* answered her that *Tubondo* was ablaze. He also said to her and the others gathered: "Let's go to *Tubondo* now, for it is higher up. Let's get away from here in the lowlands." When the aunt began to gather her belongings, *Mwindo* stopped her from doing so. He said to her: "Leave all of these things, for they will bring themselves to *Tubondo*." Having spoken, he went on up the hill, and his aunt followed him, together with the group of servants who had come with them. They climbed up to *Tubondo*. When they got there, all those things they had left in the low ground came to them. *Mwindo* said he could not chase his father so long as he had not resuscitated his uncles. Then he brought them back to life, smiting them with his scepter, and singing:

He who went to sleep, awake!
My uncles, brothers of my mother, wake up.
I have been testing the people of Yana.
My uncles, brothers of my mother, forge me!

---

[37] The kikoka plant is a kind of fern used for brewing beer and for various magical purposes. In Nyanga tales, heroes and others hide in it or go underground by entering it.

You who are powerful blacksmiths and followers of Nkuba, *forge me.*
Shemwindo, *you are powerless against* Mwindo,
Mwindo *is the Little One Just Born He Walked.*
My uncles, brothers of my mother, forge me,
You who are blacksmiths of light spears. [38]

---

[38] After this point in the narrative, Mwindo chases his father in the underworld where he ultimately defeats him. Mwindo then returns to assume his position as ruler of Tubondo.

8

⁂

Lo Kuan-chung

THREE KINGDOMS

*C*hina's Ming Dynasty (A.D. 1368–1644) saw the flowering of what was to be
a great novelistic literature. The Three Kingdoms *(sometimes titled* The
Romance of the Three Kingdoms*) is one of the major works in this tradition,
and still holds its place as one of the greatest. Identifying the authors of these early
prose narratives is difficult because of the reluctance of Confucian scholars to acknowledge their authorship of popular works in everyday language, and because
all of these works underwent frequent editorial intervention over the years. As-
cription of* Three Kingdoms *to Lo Kuan-chung (1330?–1400?), a novelist and
playwright about whom little is known, is traditional but uncertain, as is his role
in the authorship of* The Water Margin *(Selection 13).*

*San kuo chih yen-i, the title in Chinese, is essentially a serious work of his-
tory whose drama is heightened by fictionalized depiction of its characters, nearly
all of whom were known actors in the crucial events of Chinese public life during
the second and third centuries A.D. Lo Kuan-chung's presentation of this history
can be compared to the "docu-dramas" of modern film and television. A truer
analogy, however, is to Shakespeare's historical plays, in that complex character
development is deftly handled and the tragic ironies of character and fate are
drawn with the skill of a master dramatist.*

*Even without fictionalized enhancement of characters, however, the historical
content of* Three Kingdoms *is dramatic. The narrative is set during the Han
Dynasty, which had been founded in 206 B.C. (See Volume I, Selection 44.) Despite a brief interruption in the imperial line early in the first century A.D., the
Han maintained its vigor and stability well into the last half of the second century. Then a series of internal disruptions—palace intrigues pitting the vast corps
of eunuchs against power-hungry generals, a popular uprising led by a group calling themselves the Yellow Scarves, and a succession of weak-willed emperors—*

began the process of decline predicted by the Chinese historical theory of the "dynastic cycle." Long before the formally acknowledged ending of the dynasty in A.D. 220, the land became divided into three regions (the Three Kingdoms of the title), each led by an able military commander ambitious to reunite all China under himself and his family. North China, the historical heartland centering on the Yellow River valley, emerged from this division as the kingdom of Wei, founded and ruled by the successors of Ts'ao Ts'ao, an able military commander but a Machiavellian (see Selection 2) schemer who is as close to a villain as Lo Kuan-chung's nuanced treatment of characters presents. The region south of the Yangtze River, that came to be known in history as the kingdom of Wu but is usually referred to in Three Kingdoms as the Southland, came under control of Sun Ch'uan, who proved difficult and untrustworthy in a series of shifting alliances. The third major figure, Liu Pei, came from a distant branch of the imperial clan and bore its patronym of Liu. Determined to restore the Liu clan to power over a reunited China, he was nevertheless forced to base his military power on the southwestern region (modern Szechwan Province) which assumed the formal name of Shu, but which is referred to in the novel as the Riverlands.

The excerpts which follow present four episodes from the long, desperate struggle among these three rivals. The first tells of the fateful meeting of Liu Pei with Kuan Yu and Chang Fei and the oath of brotherhood unto death they swear to one another in the peach garden. At this early stage of their lives these young men are patriots, enlisting to aid their emperor in putting down the uprising of the Yellow Scarves. In this work they are associated with Ts'ao Ts'ao, who as chancellor is actually their commander. But as time passes, conflicting ambitions and mutual distrust take their course and the tripartite division described above comes about. Liu Pei, personally brave and righteous, has two great warriors in his sworn brothers, but he lacks strategic wisdom. In the second excerpt Liu Pei and his companions approach and finally persuade a famous Taoist recluse, Chuko Liang, also known as K'ung-ming, to serve as their military adviser. K'ung-ming is more than a grand strategist, however, and in the third excerpt he is seen cleverly obtaining needed weapons in an unconventional way in the days leading up to the crucial Battle of Red Cliff, in which Ts'ao Ts'ao's forces are routed. The final excerpt presents Liu Pei's tragic dilemma, as he learns of Kuan Yu's execution at the hands of the Southland's ruler, Sun Ch'uan. Liu believes he must avenge his sworn brother, but his wise advisers try to persuade him that Ts'ao Ts'ao is still the real enemy, and that war against the Southland will mean an end to Liu Pei's ambition to reunite China and restore the Han Dynasty. It is in this passage of the Three Kingdoms that the personal tragedy of Liu Pei and the larger historical tragedy of China's long division become merged, and in which the greatness of the novel's human insight is firmly established.

THE OATH OF FRATERNITY IN THE PEACH GARDEN: THREE HEROES ESTABLISH THEIR NAME

The Long River passes east away,
Surge over surge,
Whiteblooming waves sweep all heroes on
As right and wrong, triumph and defeat all turn unreal.
But ever the green hills stay
To blush in the west-waning day.

The woodcutters and the fishermen,
Whiteheaded, they've seen enough
Spring air and autumn moon
To make good company over the winejars,
Where many a famed event
Provides their merriment.

They say the momentum of history was ever thus: the empire, long divided, must unite; long united, must divide. Thus the house of Chou reached its end and the empire was partitioned into seven warring kingdoms [in 403 B.C.]. Thus these seven were absorbed into the house of Ch'in, the first imperial dynasty [in 221 B.C.]. Then Han and Ch'u destroyed the Ch'in and waged war on each other until the empire was reunited under the House of Han [in 206 B.C.]. Four centuries later [in A.D. 189], the succession reached the Emperor Tributor, last of the Han, after whose generation the land was partitioned into the three kingdoms [in A.D. 220].

In the second month of the second year of his reign [A.D. 169], the Emperor Interlocutor, father of Tributor, entered the Hall of Balming Virtue. As he ascended, a violent wind sprang up from a corner of the hall. Out of it came a giant green serpent that glided down from a beam and coiled itself on a seat. The Emperor fainted and was rushed to the inner chambers. The assembly of officials bolted. In a moment the serpent was gone. Then, without warning, rain and hailstones laced through the air, pelting down for half the night and wrecking countless buildings.

Two years later earthquakes struck Lo Yang, the capital. The ocean inundated the shoreline, sweeping those who lived on the coast out to sea. Eight years later

From *Three Kingdoms: China's Epic Drama by Lo Kuan-chung,* translated and edited by Moss Roberts, English translation copyright © 1976 by Moss Roberts. New York, Pantheon Books, 1976, pp. 3–9, 122–126, 173–177, 258–260. Reprinted by permission of Moss Roberts, Professor of Chinese, New York University.

hens suddenly became transformed into roosters. And in the middle of that same year, on the first day of the sixth month, a trail of black mist one hundred feet long floated into the Hall of Balming Virtue. The next month a rainbow was observed in the Chamber of the Concubines. And there was an avalanche on the bluffs of the Wu Yuan Mountains. A variety of evil portents appeared—too many to be dismissed as isolated signs.[1]

The Emperor Interlocutor called on his officials to explain these disasters and prodigies. Some claimed that the rainbow in the Chamber of the Concubines and the transformation of the hens were a consequence of the eunuchs' interference in the government and the denial of office to men of high caliber.[2] But no reforms were made. Court administration continued to worsen until across the land men's thoughts turned to rebellion, and thieves and traitors swarmed like bees. The Court issued a call for warriors loyal to the throne.

The call was posted in Cho county, [in Yu, a northeast border province] where it was seen by a young man of the district who, though no scholar, was broad-minded and even-tempered, taciturn yet ambitious, a man of character who was himself attracted to outstanding men. His height was considerable, his ears long-lobed, his arms strikingly long, his eyes wide-set and almost able to see behind him, his face like flawless jade, his lips like dabs of rouge. A remote descendant of a son of the fourth Han Emperor, High Brilliance, he bore the dynastic patronym of Liu. His given name was Pei ("prepared"), his formal name Hsuan-te ("obscured virtue").

Many generations ago this branch of the Liu clan had held a landed estate in Cho county, but their holding had been confiscated by the Court on charges that they had evaded payments of tribute. Liu Pei's father, a government official, was cited by the Court for integrity and filial devotion. He died early, however, and Liu Pei remained with his mother, serving her with unstinting filial piety. He supported their poor household by selling sandals and weaving mats.

---

[1] Such disorders in nature were usually interpreted in China as signs that Heaven was displeased with the human order, and that the imperial line had lost "the mandate of Heaven."

[2] Eunuchs (castrated men) were a prominent feature of Chinese government from Han times down to the end of the imperial era in A.D. 1911. They were first employed as guards and administrators of the imperial harem. As they were incapable of establishing families of their own, they were regarded as more disinterested than men with potential dynastic ambitions of their own. Thus eunuchs came in some instances to be advisers to the emperor, ambassadors to foreign courts, even commanders of frontier armies. They often numbered in the thousands within the imperial household. There was always tension and sometimes outright violence between the eunuchs, an influential and often corrupt clique, and the Confucian scholar officials. As the passage excerpted here indicates, the rivalry between these powerful factions often contributed to the weakening and decline of imperial dynasties.

The family lived in a village of Cho county called Double Mulberry because of the giant mulberry tree near their home. It was over fifty feet high. Tall and proud, the tree seemed from afar like the canopy of a chariot. A fortune teller had seen in it a sign that the family would produce a man of destiny. As a youth Liu Pei had played under the mulberry, saying, "I'll be the Emperor and take my seat on this chariot." An uncle, struck by the figure of speech, had remarked, "This is no ordinary child."

Liu Pei was already twenty-eight when the provincial authorities issued the call for volunteers to fight the rebellions. The rebels were known as the Yellow Scarves. Their leader was Chang Chueh, a man who had failed the official examinations and retired to the hills to gather healing herbs. There he had met an ancient mystic, emerald-eyed and young of face, leaning on a staff of goosefoot wood. The mystic led Chang Chueh into a cavern and handed him three sacred texts.

"These are called the *Essential Arts for the Age of Equality*," the old man had said. "Now that you have them, propagate their teachings as Heaven's messenger to promote universal salvation. Use them for any other purpose and retribution will follow." With that, the old man transformed himself into a breath of crystal air and vanished.

Chang Chueh had attacked the text. He learned to summon the winds and invoke the rain and came to be called the Tao-Master for the Age of Equality. When pestilence spread through the land, he traveled far and wide curing the afflicted with charms and potions. He styled himself Great Worthy and Good Doctor, and his followers, numbering over five hundred, bound up their heads with yellow scarves. They were as mobile as the clouds, and all could write the charms and recite the spells.

As his following grew, Chang Chueh set up thirty-six commands under his chieftains and began to prepare an insurrection against the Han. He and his two brothers assumed patriarchal titles and told their people: "The Han's fated end is near. A mighty sage emerges. Let one and all, in obedience to Heaven, in true allegiance, strive for the Age of Equality." And in the four quarters of the realm the common folk bound their heads with yellow scarves and followed Chang Chueh in such numbers that the armies of the Court would flee at the rumor of their approach. The Court ordered all districts mobilized.[3]

Reading the order posted in Cho country, Liu Pei sighed with indignation that traitors would attack the throne. Someone spoke roughly behind him: "What

---

[3] This account of the Yellow Scarves rebellion is accurate in its broad outlines. It broke out in east China in A.D. 184 and its followers continued to give trouble for nearly three decades. The rebellion of the Yellow Turbans, as they were also called, suggests a pattern of popular Chinese revolts over the millenia. Nearly all of them, down to and including the devastating Taiping Rebellion in the mid-nineteenth century, centered on a charismatic religious leader.

are the long sighs for? A hardy fellow like you should be giving his all for home and country."

Liu Pei turned to see a man even taller than he, with a blunt head like a panther's, huge round eyes, a swallow's cheek, a tiger's whiskers, a thunderous voice, and a stance like a horse in stride. To Liu Pei, who asked his name, he said, "My surname is Chang, my given name Fei ('flying'), and my formal name Yi-te ('wings to virtue'). We've been in this county for generations and farm a bit of land, sell wine, and slaughter pigs. I was looking for men of adventure and, coming upon you reading the recruitment call, took the liberty of addressing you."

"Actually," Liu Pei replied, "I am an imperial relation, and I want to raise troops to destroy the Yellow Scarves and defend the people. I was reflecting on my limitations when you heard me sigh."

Chang Fei said, "I have resources that could be used to outfit some local youths. What if you were to join with me in serving this great cause?" Liu Pei was elated, and together they went to a nearby inn. As they drank, they noticed a striking fellow stop at the inn's entrance to rest.

"Some wine, and quickly," the stranger said. "I'm off to the town to volunteer." Liu Pei observed him: gleaming skin, glistening lips, eyes like the crimson phoenix, brows like nestling silkworms. His appearance was stately, his bearing awesome. Liu Pei invited him to share their table and asked who he was.

"My surname is Kuan," the man replied, "my given name Yu ('plume'), my formal name Yun-ch'ang ('cloud-lasting'). One of the notables in our district was using his position to exploit people. I killed him and had to flee. I have been on the move these past five or six years. When I heard of the mobilization I came to answer the call."

Liu Pei then told of his own ambitions, to Kuan Yu's great excitement. Together the three men went to Chang Fei's farm to talk further. Chang Fei proposed: "Behind the farm is a peach garden. The flowers are at their fullest. Tomorrow we must make offerings there to Heaven and Earth, declaring that we three join together as brothers, combining strength and purpose." To this Liu Pei and Kuan Yu agreed.

The next day they prepared their offerings, which included a black bull and a white horse. Amid burning incense the three men performed obeisance and spoke their vow:

"We three, Liu Pei, Kuan Yu, and Chang Fei, though of separate birth, now bind ourselves in brotherhood, combining our strength and purpose to relieve the present crisis. Thus we may fulfill our duty to home and country and defend the common folk of the land. We could not help our separate births, but on the self-same day we mean to die! Shining imperial Heaven, fruitful Queen Earth, witness our determination, and may god and man jointly scourge whichever of us fails his duty or forgets his obligation."

The oath sworn, Liu Pei became the eldest brother, Kuan Yu the second, and Chang Fei the youngest. When the sacrificial ceremony was concluded, they butchered the bull and spread forth the wine, gathering three hundred youths in the peach garden, where they drank themselves to sleep.

• • •

[*Editor's note:* The three sworn brothers distinguish themselves in several battles with the rebels. Imperial victories over the Yellow Scarves come at a high price. Both of the capital cities, Chang-an in the west and Loyang in the east, are destroyed; the emperor abdicates in favor of his nine-year-old heir, and a temporary capital is established. Most ominous of all, the commanders of the armies called into being to put down the rebellion now begin to contend among themselves. Foremost among these is Ts'ao Ts'ao, a man of great intelligence and ability but absolutely ruthless in this pursuit of power. By A.D. 199, Ts'ao Ts'ao, holding the office of Chancellor, comes to dominate the weak emperor.

In the early years of the story Liu Pei and his brothers fight alongside Ts'ao Ts'ao and serve him well. At one point Kuan Yu even saves Ts'ao Ts'ao from defeat at the battle of White Horse. As the saga unfolds with its many twists of alliances quickly made and treacherously broken, however, Ts'ao Ts'ao and Liu Pei become deadly enemies.

Liu Pei's position is in many ways the weakest, but in this epic struggle strategy often counts more than logistics, and Liu Pei seeks out a great sage, Chuko Liang, also known as K'ung-ming ("Sleeping dragon"). Liu Pei and his brothers twice fail to find the recluse, but on the third visit do find him asleep in his humble cottage. It is a fateful meeting.]

K'UNG-MING FIXES THE COURSE OF THE WAR

Liu Pei watched K'ung-ming sleep, face up, on a couch in the cottage; he stood below, arms folded. A while passed, but the master had not awakened. Seeing no movement, Lord Kuan and Chang Fei came in and found Liu Pei standing in attendance as before. In great anger Chang Fei said to Lord Kuan: "What insolent negligence! Our brother stands below in attendance, and he pretends to sleep peacefully on! Let me go out and torch the rear [of the cottage] and see whether that gets him up or not!" Lord Kuan calmed his junior down, and Pei sent him out to continue waiting. Soon after, K'ung-ming awoke and hummed a song:

> When all's a dream, who would first awake?
> But from our common life we learn:
> Indoors, spring's simple sleep suffices;
> But outside, summer ripens time.

K'ung-ming stopped, turned to the lad, and asked: "Any visitors from the world of men?"

The lad: "Imperial Uncle Liu is here and has been waiting."

K'ung-ming arose and said: "Why didn't you report it sooner? I still need time to change my clothes." He hurried out, and it was another while before he reappeared, clothes and cap correct, to greet Liu Pei.

K'ung-ming appeared to Liu Pei a man of medium height, face like gleaming jade, a kind of turban wound on his head, crane plumes on his body—he had the buoyant air of a spiritual transcendent.

Liu Pei made a deep gesture of reverence: "This poor unexceptional fellow, distant scion of the House of Han, has long felt your mighty name, master, reverberate in his ears like thunder. Twice before have I presented myself but, failing to gain audience, set my worthless name on a letter. I never learned whether it was brought to your discerning attention."

K'ung-ming: "This unsophisticated person of Nan Yang,[4] unresponsive and indolent by nature, is indebted to the general for the trouble he has taken to travel our way, and is overcome with compunction."

After further civilities, tea was served and the conversation continued. K'ung-ming: "I could see in the intent of your letter your deep compassion for the people and the commonwealth. But I fear that my years are too few, my talents too sparse, and that you are mistaken in seeking my help." . . .

K'ung-ming laughed. "I would learn your aspiration, general."

Liu Pei dismissed everyone who was present, moved his seat beside K'ung-ming's and declared: "The House of Han teeters on ruin. Unscrupulous subjects have stolen the mandate of rule. I failed to recognize my limitations and tried to extend the great principle of allegiance throughout the empire. But my knowledge is superficial and my methods fall short. I have made no progress so far. But if you, master, would relieve my ignorance and ease our difficulties, the blessing would be truly ten-thousand-fold!"

K'ung-ming: "Since the time of Tung Cho's sedition,[5] numerous aggressive and enterprising magnates have appeared. Ts'ao Ts'ao could overcome a Yuan Shao though his strength was inferior to Shao's, thanks to wise planning and a favorable occasion. Now Ts'ao holds sway over a population of four million. He uses his grip on the Son of Heaven [the young Han emperor] to enjoin the feudal barons. There is no way you can cross spearpoints with him. Sun Ch'uan has had a firm hold on the Southland for three generations now. Their territory is

---

[4] Nan Yang was a district of the Han Empire, roughly coterminous with modern Hupei Province.

[5] Tung Cho, a general of the imperial armies, seized the eastern capital, Loyang, in 190, replaced the emperor with one of his own followers, murdered the empress dowager and slaughtered many of the palace eunuchs. His usurpation ended with his own violent death two years later, opening the way for Ts'ao Ts'ao to assume virtual control of the young Han emperor, who had survived.

difficult of access and the people are devoted to Ch'uan. They can be used for rear support, but they are not a strategic objective.

"Chingchou commands the Han and Mien Rivers to the north.[6] It has the full benefit of the great lakes to the south. Eastward it links up with the South-land. Westward it offers access to the Riverlands. Here is the place to wage war; unless you dominate it, you will have no secure defense. And this is the very place that Heaven seems to be furnishing you with, general. Can you have second thoughts? The Riverlands are inaccessible and naturally fortified. Their fertile wildlands extend thousands of leagues—a realm that is Heaven's treasure house. Han's Supreme Ancestor based himself on them to consummate his imperial endeavor. The Riverland's governor, Liu Chang, is benighted and feeble, and though the people are loyal and the realm is rich, he does not know how to keep and care for them. Men of insight and capacity yearn for enlightened rule.

"Now, general, you are a scion of the imperial house, known across the land for allegiance in good faith, a man who keeps the contenders in hand and thirsts for men of merit. If you sit astride the two territories of Chingchou and the River-lands, guard their formidable defenses, come to terms with the various Jung tribes on the west, placate the I and Yueh to the south, form a diplomatic alliance with Sun Ch'uan, and conduct a program of reform in your own territory, then you may wait until the situation develops to the point when you can have one of your chief generals drive from Chingchou north through my home district toward the old eastern capital [Loyang]. Meanwhile you yourself can lead a Riverlands army onto the 'riverways of Ch'in' [Kuan Chung, the western heartlands, whose capital was Ch'ang An]. And won't the good common folk 'basket food and jug beverages' to welcome you, my general! Truly thus can your great endeavor be consummated and the House of Han revived! This is how I would shape strategy. It only remains for you to consider it."

K'ung-ming had a map hung up, and continued: "These are the fifty-four territories of the Riverlands region. To achieve hegemony, let Ts'ao Ts'ao assay the Heaven-sent occasions from the north; let Sun Ch'uan assay his political advantages from the south; while you, my general, assay the possibilities for political combination.

"The first step is to take Chingchou and make it your home base. Then proceed to take the Riverlands and lay the foundation for achieving your third of the triangle of power. And then you may make the high central plains to the north your objective."

---

[6] The military actions of *Three Kingdoms* take place, for the most part, in the region along and to the north of the central reaches of the Yangzte River, in modern Hupei, Hunan, and Kiangsi Provinces. K'ung-ming here displays his grasp of strategy based on knowledge of geography.

Hearing this proposition, Liu Pei came up off his mat and folded his hands in respectful gratitude. "Master, you have opened the thicket that barred my way and made me feel as if clouds and mists had parted and I had gained blue sky. The only thing is that Liu Piao of Chingchou and Liu Chang of the Riverlands are both primary kinsmen of the royal house. How could I bear to seize what is theirs?"

K'ung-ming: "At night I watch the configurations of the Heavens.[7] Liu Piao will not be long among the living. Liu Chang is not a ruler of any endeavor. In time he will transfer his allegiance to you."

Liu Pei pressed his head to the floor in respectful acknowledgment. And by this single interview K'ung-ming showed that he perceived the tripartite empire without ever having left his cottage—truly an incomparable man in any generation!

• • •

[*Editor's note:* Out of a sense of honor, Liu Pei does not move decisively enough to secure his hold on Chingchou from its dying governor and the city is lost to Ts'ao Ts'ao. The scene of warfare moves to the central Yangtze region as Liu Pei forges a shaky alliance with Sun Ch'uan, ruler of the Southlands. K'ung-ming's penetrating insight into grand strategy and his prominence as Liu Pei's adviser arouses admiration but also produces jealousy. The following episode illustrates K'ung-ming's shrewd practical intelligence, not only in solving a logistical problem but in evading a trap laid for him by the Southlands general Chou Yu, who wants him dead.]

K'UNG-MING BORROWS SOME ARROWS

The next day in the assembly of generals, Chou Yu asked K'ung-ming: "When we engage Ts'ao Ts'ao in battle, crossing arms on the river routes, what weapon should be our first choice?"

K'ung-ming: "On the Yangtze, the bow and arrow."

Chou Yu: "Precisely. But we happen to be short of arrows. Dare I trouble you, master, to take responsibility for the production of one hundred thousand shafts? This is a public service which you would favor me by not declining."

K'ung-ming: "Whatever you assign I will strive to achieve. Dare I ask by what time you will require them?"

Chou Yu: "Can you finish in ten days?"

K'ung-ming: "Ts'ao's army will arrive any moment. If we wait ten days, it will spoil everything."

---

[7] Chinese sages often foretold events by studying the constellations.

Chou Yu: "How many days do you estimate you need, master?"

K'ung-ming: "It will take only three before I can respectfully deliver the arrows."

Chou Yu: "There is no room for levity in the army."

K'ung-ming: "Dare I trifle with the chief commander? I beg to submit my oath in writing. Then if I fail to finish in three days, I deserve the maximum punishment."

This elated Chou Yu, who accepted the document. . . .

K'ung-ming [to Lu Su, another adviser to Sun Ch'uan, but less hostile toward K'ung-ming than was Chou Yu]: "I need you to lend me twenty vessels, with a crew of thirty for each. On the boats I want curtains of black cloth to conceal at least a thousand bales of straw that should be lined up on both sides. But you must not let Chou Yu know about it . . . or my plan will fail." And Lu Su obliged him, and even held his tongue.

The boats were ready, but neither on the first day nor on the second did K'ung-ming make any move. On the third day he secretly sent for Lu Su: "I called upon you especially to go with me to get the arrows." And linking the vessels with long ropes, they set out for the north shore and Ts'ao Ts'ao's fleet.

That night tremendous fogs rolled over the heavens, and the river mists were impenetrable. People could not see their companions who were directly in front of them. K'ung-ming urged his boats on.

From the ode "Great Mists Overhanging the Yangtze":

> Everywhere the fog, stock still:
> Not even a cartload can be spotted.
> All-obscuring grey vastness,
> Massive, without horizon.
> Whales hurtle over waves, and
> Dragons plunge and spew up mist.
> East they lose the shore at Chai Sang,
> South the mountains of Hsia K'ou.
> Are we returning to the state without form—
> To undivided Heaven and Earth?

At the fifth watch the boats were already nearing Ts'ao Ts'ao's river stations. K'ung-ming had the vessels lined up in single file, their prows pointed west. Then the crews began to volley with their drums and roar with their voices.

Lu Su was alarmed: "What do you propose if Ts'ao's men make a coordinated sally?"

K'ung-ming smiled: "I would be very surprised if Ts'ao Ts'ao dared plunge into this heavy a fog. Let us attend to the wine and take our pleasure. When the fog breaks we will return."

In his encampment Ts'ao Ts'ao listened to the drumming and shouting. His new naval advisers [he had executed his former naval adviser, after being tricked into believing him to be a traitor] rushed back and forth with bulletins. Ts'ao sent down an order: "The fog is so heavy it obscures the river. Enemy forces have arrived from nowhere. There must be an ambush. Our men must make absolutely no reckless movements. But let the archers fire upon the enemy at random." The naval advisers, fearing that the forces of the Southland were about to breach the camp, ordered the firing to commence. Soon over ten thousand men were concentrating their fire toward the center of the river, and the arrows came down like rain. K'ung-ming ordered the boats to reverse direction and press closer to the shore to take the arrows, while the crews continued their drumming and shouting.

When the sun rose high, dispersing the fog, K'ung-ming ordered the boats to rush homeward. The grass bales in gunny sacks bristled with arrow shafts. And K'ung-ming had each crew shout its thanks to the Chancellor [Ts'ao Ts'ao] for the arrows as it passed. By the time the reports reached Ts'ao Ts'ao, the light craft borne on swift currents were beyond overtaking, and Ts'ao Ts'ao was left with the agony of having played the fool.

K'ung-ming said to Lu Su: "Each boat has some five or six thousand arrows. So without costing the Southland the slightest effort, we have gained over one hundred thousand arrows, which tomorrow we can return to Ts'ao Ts'ao's troops—to their decided discomfort."

Lu Su: "You are supernatural! How did you know there would be such a fog today?"

K'ung-ming: "A military commander must be versed in the patterns of the Heavens, must recognize the advantages of the terrain, must appreciate the odd chance, must understand the changes of the weather, must examine the maps of the formations, must be clear about the disposition of the troops—otherwise he is a mediocrity! Three days ago I calculated today's fog. That's why I took a chance on the three-day limit. Chou Yu gave me ten days, but neither materials nor workmen, and plainly meant for my flagrant offense to kill me. But my fate is linked to Heaven. How could Chou Yu succeed?" When Chou Yu received Lu Su's report, he was amazed and resigned. "I cannot begin to approach his uncanny machinations and subtle calculations!"

• • •

[*Editor's note:* After Ts'ao Ts'ao's death in 220, the title of Prince of Wei passes to his son Ts'ao P'ei, who forces the abdication of the defenseless young emperor and usurps the throne for himself. In response, Liu Pei somewhat reluctantly makes a counter-claim and declares himself Emperor of the Han. But his accession to imperial power is overshadowed by the treacherous execution of his sworn brother Kuan Yu at the hands of the Southland's ruler, Sun Ch'uan. Liu Pei's determination to avenge this killing begins to crowd out larger considerations of state. Chao Yun, one of the so-called "tiger generals" and a longtime stalwart, tries to persuade Liu Pei to see his choices in strategic terms, as does K'ung-ming. They nearly succeed, until the arrival of the third Peach Garden brother, Chang Fei, whose passionate pleading tips the scales.]

CHAO YUN OPPOSES HIS
LORD'S CAMPAIGN

Chao Yun spoke against the expedition: "Ts'ao Ts'ao is the traitor, not Sun Ch'uan. Ts'ao P'ei has seized the Han state, to the common indignation of god and man. Let your majesty first make the land within the passes your target. Station your men along the upper Wei River to bring those noxious renegades to justice. And then the loyal scholars and officers east of the passes will bundle their grain and spur their horses to welcome the royal host. But if you neglect the Wei Dynasty to attack the Southland, once your forces are engaged they cannot be abruptly recalled. May your majesty consider this carefully."

Liu Pei, the Emperor, said: "Sun Ch'uan put our young brother to death. And many hold with me this implacably enmity. Until I gnaw his flesh and crush his clan, our humiliation is not effaced. Why would you stand in my way?"

Chao Yun: "Enmity against the Han traitors is a matter of public duty. Enmity for the sake of a brother is a personal matter. I urge you to give priority to the empire."

The Emperor replied: "If I should fail to revenge my brother, were I to come into possession of these ten thousand leagues of mountains and rivers—it would make an unworthy prize." And he ignored Chao Yun's opposition. The armies were mobilized, and Chang Fei . . . was appointed general of the chariots and cavalry.

Chang Fei was in Lang Chung when the news of Lord Kuan's fate came. Through the day he howled and wept until his shirt was damp with blood. The wine he took to ease his mind only enraged him further, so that whoever crossed him was flogged immediately. A good number died from beating.

Every day he would stare into the south, gnashing his teeth in the fury of humiliation, venting cries of anguish.

The messenger from the Emperor arrived to confer the new generalship on Chang Fei.

Chang Fei: "My will to revenge my brother's murder is deep as the sea. Why have there been no appeals for mobilization in the temple and in the Court?"

The messenger: "The majority urge that Wei be annihilated before we take up arms against the Southland."

Fei cried out, angrily. "What words! We three brothers took an oath to live and die as one. The second has passed from us before his time; shall I enjoy wealth and station without him? Take me to the Emperor himself. I shall serve in the vanguard, and under the banner of mourning take up arms against the south and bring the traitor home to sacrifice to my second brother, thus fulfilling the covenant." And Chang Fei headed back to the capital of the Riverlands with the messenger.

K'ung-ming was protesting the Emperor's decision to lead the invasion of the south: "Your majesty has mounted this treasured throne. If it is your purpose to strike out northward against the traitors to the Han, to extend throughout the empire the great principle of allegiance, then you should personally take command of the whole army. But if you merely intend to attack the south, it is sufficient to have a ranking general take command. What need is there to strain your sacred war chariot?"

In view of K'ung-ming's strenuous objections, the Emperor was developing reservations about his invasion plans, when Chang Fei's arrival was announced. The general prostrated himself before the Emperor and then, hugging his feet, began to cry. The Emperor cried also, and Chang Fei said: "Today you reign and the Peach Garden Oath is already forgotten! Why will you not revenge my brother?"

The Emperor: "My officials oppose it. I cannot act rashly."

Chang Fei: "What do others know of our past covenant? If you will not go, let me give myself to revenge our brother. Should I fail, I shall be content to die and see you no more."

The Emperor: "Then we will go together to attack the south and erase our humiliation."

Later the Emperor admonished Chang Fei, saying: "You have always turned violent after wine, beaten your yeomen, and then reassigned them in your personal guard. That is a good way to destroy yourself. Hereafter, make an effort to be tolerant and understanding."[8] Chang Fei respectfully took his leave and was gone.

• • •

[*Editor's note:* A court scholar named Ch'in Mi continues to protest the Emperor's decision whereupon, in an uncharacteristic act of tyranny, Liu Pei has him executed. K'ung-ming takes the occasion to write to Liu Pei, again urging strategic wisdom and loyalty to the Liu clan over personal vengeance.]

"The treachery of the Southland led to the disaster at Chingchou. We lost our leading star; our pillar of Heaven was broken. But however keen our grief, however unforgettable, we must also remember that the crime of displacing the sacred dynastic vessels arose through Ts'ao Ts'ao. The degradation of the holy offerings of the Liu was not Sun Ch'uan's fault. And I would presume to say that if the traitors of the Wei are removed, then the Southland will tamely submit. I implore you to accept the precious advice of Ch'in Mi and take care for the strength of our armies. There are other worthwhile strategies that will bring great good fortune to our shrines and our realm."

But the emperor threw the petition to the ground and said: "We are resolved. Let there be no further opposition." And it was decided to commence

---

[8] Chang Fei fails to heed this prudent advice, and dies shortly afterward at the hands of two of his own officers whom he had berated and who feared for their own lives.

the expedition in the seventh month of the prime year in the reign "Manifest Arms" [A.D. 221].

• • •

[*Editor's note:* Disdaining to seek further advice from K'ung-ming, Liu Pei leads his forces to near annihilation in a great battle on the banks of the Yangtze. He dies shortly afterward. China remains divided, racked by unstable governments and a prey to foreign invasion for three and a half centuries.]

9

❦

Seami Motokiyo

ATSUMORI

*J*apan's No *drama reached its maturity and its greatest artistic heights with the work of Kanami Kiyotsugu (1333–1384) and his son Seami (or Zeami) Motokiyo (1363–1443). Earlier forms of this drama, combining song, dance, and mime date from the tenth century but give no hint of the emotional, spiritual and literary power which this father and son were to achieve.*

The word "No" means "talent," implying the display of talent required to bring this formal, mannered style of theater to dramatic life. No bears many points of comparison with classical Greek drama in the West. (See Volume I, Selection 13, Antigone). Its action is concentrated in time and place; the principal actors are relatively few in number; they wear masks; there is a chorus; music and dance are interwoven with a text whose emotive power is achieved through poetry. No conventions require that the actors enter through the audience along a raised walkway to a small, square wooden stage covered by a temple-like roof. Theaters themselves are usually small, and this fact combined with the actors' tradition of speaking their opening lines as they move along the walkway, give a No performance the sort of actor/audience intimacy encountered in the West only in arena theater.

Play texts are brief. Even with the song and dance performances a No play is usually completed in an hour or so. Traditionally five plays are performed, dealing in prescribed order with the gods, a warrior, a woman, a mad person, and, finally, with a devil. Themes of the No are always serious, often tragic, but these performances are sometimes interspersed with brief comic interludes, often parodies of the serious plays which precede or follow them. Like the "comic relief" familiar to students of Shakespeare's plays, these parodies actually make a thought-provoking point about the tension of human experience between the serious and the jocular.

One important contribution of Seami and his father in refashioning the No tradition was the infusion of a Zen Buddhist attitude toward life and art. (See Volume II, Selection 28, "Japanese Buddhism.") The extreme simplicity of the No stage, the concentration of the play on a few characters and a single theme, and the reliance on the intellect and imagination of the audience, all indicate Zen in-fluence on the physical and verbal forms of the drama. Equally manifest is the Zen impact on the types of characters and on the themes of the plays. In many instances the secondary character (called the waki*) is a priest and in many, too, the theme of the play is the release of a wandering ghost from his or her ties to earth through atonement or forgiveness for some wrong committed in life, for example, an act of cruelty or of violence.*

The following selection is based on the story of the death of the young war-rior Atsumori, that would have been well known at the court of the Shogun, the military ruler of Japan, where Seami's plays were usually first performed. The classic version of the story, the primary source of the No *version, constitutes one of the most poignant passages of* The Tale of the Heiki (Heike Monogatari), *that chronicles the bitter civil war fought between 1180 and 1185, in which the Minamoto clan crushed the Taira (or Heike) and established itself as the domi-nant military power in Japan. After they were routed at the battle of Ichi no tani, fought along the shore of the Inland Sea, surviving Taira nobles tried to es-cape to their ships. The noted Minamoto warrior Kumagai no Naozane spied an elaborately armored Taira warrior riding through the surf, engaged him in com-bat, unhorsed him and ripped off his helmet only to discover that his victim was Atsumori, a mere youth the age of his own son. Kumagai would have spared the young man but they both realized that other Minamoto would soon kill him, so weeping and promising to pray for Atsumori's rebirth in paradise, Kumagai cut his head off. Stripping Atsumori's armor, Kumagai discovered a flute which even the Minamoto had heard Atsumori playing in the Taira camp on the eve of bat-tle. The flute song in the play is a haunting reminder of Atsumori's death, but it also becomes the essential accompaniment to the spiritual reconciliation between the two former enemies.*

CHARACTERS

The Priest Rensei (formerly the warrior Kumagai)
A Young Reaper, who turns out to be the ghost of Atsumori
His Companion
Chorus of Reapers

PRIEST: Life is a lying dream, he only wakes.
　　　Who casts the world aside.
　　　I am Kumagai no Naozane, a man of the country of Musashi. I have left

my home and call myself the priest Rensei; this I have done because of my grief at the death of Atsumori, who fell in battle by my hand. Hence it comes that I am dressed in priestly guise.

And now I am going down to Ichi no tani[1] to pray for the salvation of Atsumori's soul.

(*He walks slowly across the stage, singing a song descriptive of his journey.*)

I have come so fast that here I am already at Ichi no tani, in the country of Tsu.

Truly the past returns to my mind as though it were a thing of today.

But listen! I hear the sound of a flute coming from a knoll of rising ground. I will wait here till the flute-player passes, and ask him to tell me the story of this place.

REAPERS (*together*): To the music of the reaper's flute
No song is sung
But the sighing of wind in the fields.

YOUNG REAPER: They that were reaping,
Reaping on that hill,
Walk now through the fields
Homeward, for it is dusk.

REAPERS (*together*): Short is the way that leads
From the sea of Suma back to my home.
This little journey, up to the hill
And down to the shore again, and up to the hill —
This is my life, and the sum of hateful tasks.
If one should ask me
I too would answer
That on the shore of Suma
I live in sadness.
Yet if any guessed my name,
Then might I too have friends.
But now from my deep misery
Even those that were dearest
Are grown estranged. Here must I dwell abandoned
To one thought's anguish:
That I must dwell here.

PRIEST: Hey, you reapers! I have a question to ask you.

From *The No Plays of Japan*, translated by Arthur Waley, copyright © 1922 by Arthur Waley, pp 64–73. Used by permission of Grove/Atlantic, Inc.

[1] Ichi no tani, on Japan's Inland Sea, is the site of the battle in which Kumagai had slain Atsumori.

YOUNG REAPER: Is it to us you are speaking? What do you wish to know?

PRIEST: Was it one of you who was playing on the flute just now?

YOUNG REAPER: Yes, it was we who were playing.

PRIEST: It was a pleasant sound, and all the pleasanter because one
does not look for such music from men of your condition.

YOUNG REAPER: Unlooked for from men of our condition, you say!
Have you not read: —
"Do not envy what is above you
Nor despise what is below you"?
Moreover the songs of woodmen and the flute-playing of herdsmen,
Flute-playing even of reapers and songs of wood-fellers
Through poets' verses are known to all the world.
Wonder not to hear among us
The sound of a bamboo flute.

PRIEST: You are right. Indeed it is as you have told me.
Songs of woodmen and flute-playing of herdsmen . . .

REAPER: Flute-playing of reapers . . .

PRIEST: Songs of wood-fellers . . .

REAPERS: Guide us on our passage through this sad world.

PRIEST: Song . . .

REAPER: And dance . . .

PRIEST: And the flute . . .

REAPER: And music of many instruments . . .

CHORUS: These are the pastimes that each chooses to his taste.
Of floating bamboo-wood
Many are the famous flutes that have been made;
Little-Branch and Cicada-Cage,
And as for the reaper's flute,
Its name is Green-Leaf;
On the shore of Sumiyoshi
The Korean flute they play.
And here on the shore of Suma
On Stick of the Salt-kilns
The fishers blow their tune.

PRIEST: How strange it is! The other reapers have all gone home,
but you alone stay loitering here. How is that?

REAPER: How is it, you ask? I am seeking for a prayer in the voice
of the evening waves. Perhaps you will pray the Ten Prayers for me?

PRIEST: I can easily pray the Ten Prayers for you, if you will tell me who
you are.

REAPER: To tell you the truth—I am one of the family of Lord
Atsumori.

PRIEST: One of Atsumori's family? How glad I am!
Then the priest joined his hands *(he kneels down)* and prayed:

Namu Amidabu.

Praise to Amida Buddha![2]
"If I attain to Buddhahood,
In the whole world and its ten spheres
Of all that dwell here none shall call on my name
And be rejected or cast aside."

CHORUS: "Oh, reject me not!
One cry suffices for salvation,
Yet day and night
Your prayers will rise for me.
Happy am I, for though you know not my name,
Yet for my soul's deliverance
At dawn and dusk henceforward I know that you will pray."
So he spoke. Then vanished and was seen no more.

(Here follows the Interlude between the two Acts, in which a recitation concerning ATSUMORI's death takes place. These interludes are subject to variation and are not considered part of the literary text of the play.)

PRIEST: Since this is so, I will perform all night the rites of prayer for the dead, and calling upon Amida's name will pray again for the salvation of Atsumori.

(The GHOST OF ATSUMORI appears, dressed as a young warrior.)

ATSUMORI: Would you know who I am
That like the watchmen at Suma Pass
Have wakened at the cry of sea birds roaming
Upon Awaji shore?
Listen, Rensei. I am Atsumori.

PRIEST: How strange! All this while I have never stopped beating my gong and performing the rites of the Law. I cannot for a moment have dozed, yet I thought that Atsumori was standing before me. Surely it was a dream.

ATSUMORI: Why need it be a dream? It is to clear the karma[3] of my waking life that I am come here in visible form before you.

---

[2] Amida, one of the most popular Buddha manifestations in Mahanaya Buddhism, is the ruler of the western paradise. This is conceived of not as a physical place, but as a blessed state of consciousness that one who calls on Amida in the hour of death may achieve. The passage that follows within quotation marks is thought by the faithful to be Amida's pledge of universal mercy.

[3] In the Sanskrit language of the original Buddhist sutras karma meant simply "deed." It came to signify not only a deed but its consequences, the cause-result chain of the moral order.

PRIEST: Is it not written that one prayer will wipe away ten thousand sins? Ceaselessly I have performed the ritual of the Holy Name that clears all sin away. After such prayers, what evil can be left? Though you should be sunk in sin as deep . . .

ATSUMORI: As the sea by a rocky shore,
Yet should I be saved by prayer.

PRIEST: And that my prayers should save you . . .

ATSUMORI: This too must spring
From kindness of a former life.[4]

PRIEST: Once enemies . . .

ATSUMORI: But now . . .

PRIEST: In truth may we be named . . .

ATSUMORI: Friends in Buddha's Law.

CHORUS: There is a saying, "Put away from you a wicked friend; summon to your side a virtuous enemy." For you it was said, and you have proven it true.
And now come tell with us the tale of your confession, while the night is still dark.

CHORUS: He [i.e the Buddha] bids the flowers of spring
Mount the treetop that men may raise their eyes
And walk on upward paths;
He bids the moon in autumn waves be drowned
In token that he visits laggard men
And leads them out from valleys of despair.

ATSUMORI: Now the clan of Taira, building wall to wall,
Spread over the earth like the leafy branches of a great tree:

CHORUS: Yet their prosperity lasted but for a day;
It was like the flower of the convolvulus.[5]
There was none to tell them
That glory flashes like sparks from flint-stone,
And after,—darkness.
Oh wretched, the life of men!

ATSUMORI: When they were on high they afflicted the humble;
When they were rich they were reckless in pride.
And so for twenty years and more
They ruled this land.
But truly a generation passes like the space of a dream.
The leaves of the autumn of Juyei[6]

---

[4] Kumagai's remorse must spring from the fact that Atsumori had done him some kindness in an earlier incarnation.

[5] Flowering plants of the morning glory family.

[6] The year 1188.

Were tossed by the four winds;
Scattered, scattered (like leaves too) floated their ships.
And they, asleep on the heaving sea, not even in dreams
Went back to home.
Caged birds longing for the clouds—
Wild geese were they rather, whose ranks are broken
As they fly to southward on their doubtful journey.
So days and months went by; spring came again
And for a little while
Here dwelt they on the shore of Suma
At the first valley.[7]
From the mountain behind us as the winds blew down
Till the fields grew wintry again.
Our ships lay by the shore, where night and day
The sea gulls cried and salt waves washed on our sleeves.
We slept with fishers in their huts
On pillows of sand.
We knew none but the people of Suma.
And when among the pine-trees
The evening smoke was rising,
Brushwood, as they called it,
Brushwood we gathered
And spread for carpet.
Sorrowful we lived
On the wild shore of Suma,
Till the clan Taira and all its princes
Were but villagers of Suma.

ATSUMORI: But on the night of the sixth day of the second month
My father Tsunemori gathered us together.
"Tomorrow," he said, "we shall fight our last fight.
Tonight is all that is left us."
We sang songs together, and danced.

PRIEST: Yes, I remember; we in our siege-camp
Heard the sound of music
Echoing from your tents that night;
There was the music of a flute . . .

ATSUMORI: The bamboo flute! I wore it when I died.

PRIEST: We heard the singing . . .

ATSUMORI: Songs and ballads. . .

PRIEST: Many voices

---

[7] Ichi no tani translates literally as "first valley."

ATSUMORI: Singing to one measure . . . *(ATSUMORI dances.)*
> First comes the royal boat.

CHORUS: The whole clan has put its boats to sea.
> He [i.e. Atsumori] will not be left behind;
> He runs to the shore.
> But the royal boat and the soldiers' boats
> Have sailed far away.

ATSUMORI: What can he do?
> He spurs his horse into the waves.
> He is full of perplexity.
> And then

CHORUS: He looks behind him and sees
> That Kumagai pursues him;
> He cannot escape.
> Then Atsumori turns his horse
> Knee-deep in the lashing waves,
> And draws his sword.
> Twice, three times he strikes; then, still saddled,
> In close fight they twine; roll headlong together
> Among the surf of the shore.
> So Atsumori fell and was slain, but now the Wheel of Fate
> Has turned and brought him back.

(ATSUMORI rises from the ground and advances toward the PRIEST with up-lifted sword.)

> "There is my enemy," he cries, and would strike,
> But the other is grown gentle
> And calling on Buddha's name
> Has obtained salvation for his foe;
> So that they shall be reborn together
> On one lotus seat.
> "No, Rensei is not my enemy.
> Pray for me again, oh pray for me again."

10

𐰒

Mirabai

SONGS

The author of a large number of poems in Hindi called padas ("songs"), Mirabai (c.1498–c.1547) or Mira, as she is more commonly called with affection, is the best-known woman poet of India and one of the country's most popular poets. Estimates of the number of poems in Hindi attributed to her vary from 103 to several hundred. Her poems, popular in the past, are sung and heard everywhere to this day throughout India—in the Hindu temples and in secular places, in town and in the country, in homes and in the street. Her poetry set to music is almost daily fare on the All India Radio. She is particularly popular in Rajasthan, her native state, and Gujarat, the state where she lived for a considerable part of her life.

There are several reasons for her popularity. Her poems express an intensely felt personal emotional experience that has a universal human quality about it and is, therefore, readily shared by the readers, or rather listeners, for her poems are more often heard than read. Mira is one of the many medieval poets of India who first began to use the common languages of the people instead of the classical language of Sanskrit for literary expression. In this respect, they resemble their European contemporaries who adopted the vernacular languages instead of Latin for their writing. Mira not only composed in Hindi, but in the simple Hindi of everyday speech, making for an easy rapport with her audience. Her poems are also strongly musical; they are almost invariably sung to a musical accompaniment and often expressed in dance. The poems are, therefore, generally referred to as songs rather than as poems. The subject of Mira's poetry is religious, hence its sentiments are shared by all Hindus. The sentiments are couched in intensely human rather than formal religious terms, hence her poems have a universal appeal reaching far beyond Hinduism.

For the modern reader, Mira's poetry has a special appeal as the work of a woman poet. She was a practitioner of Bhakti ("the Cult of Devotion") an approach to religion which is mentioned as one of the paths to salvation by Krishna

159

in the Bhagvad Gita *of the* Mahabharata, *but which flourished most vigorously from the twelfth to the seventeenth century.* Bhakti *is a theism focusing on the love of or devotion to one or another personal god. During the late medieval and the early modern centuries, two gods, Shiva and Vishnu, both gods of the Hindu triad (which also includes Brahma), became the main foci of* Bhakti, *Shiva primarily in South India and Vishnu predominantly in North India, their worshipers known respectively as Shaivites and Vaishnavites. In the earlier stages of his worship in the Cult of Devotion, Vishnu was worshiped in the form of his incarnation as Krishna who is a character of central importance in the* Mahabharata *and in the later phase, he was worshiped in his incarnation as Rama, the hero of the ancient Sanskrit epic,* Ramayana, *as well as of Tulsi Das's* Ramcaritmanas *(Selection 24).*

Mira was a Vaishnavite and a worshiper of Vishnu as Krishna. Most important in connection with Krishna's role as the subject of Bhakti *is the legend of his growing up and his escapades as a handsome, blue-complected, flute-playing young cowherd in the pastoral community of Brindavan. All the young women of the community, known as* gopis *("cowgirls"), love him and are drawn to him by the sound of his flute. Chief among the* gopis *is Radha, his best beloved. In* Bhakti *centering on Krishna, the devotees aim to become like Radha in their love for him. In the case of male devotees, however, they can do so but symbolically. Mira, being a woman, can completely identify with Radha in her love of Krishna. That is her advantage in being a woman. However, there are also severe disadvantages. She is not as free as men in pursuing her love. Her freedom is severely curtailed by the norms and taboos of her society. Unlike men who only have to renounce the world for love of Krishna, she additionally has to rebel against social customs. Her path to divine love is thus riddled with much greater hardships and pain than that of men. However, her joy in fulfillment when it comes is also far greater and more direct. The rewards as well as the limitations of her quest are thus peculiar to her position as a woman.*

Another feminine aspect of Mira's poetry is its closeness to the tradition of women's folksongs. It is customary for women in India to sing on festive and other important occasions, such as the season of rains and the coming of spring. Their songs contain feminine sentiments, their desires, suffering, and joy. They are sung to women, even when the subject is a male. Similarly, Mira's poems are intended for recitation to other women, quite often a confidante. Though written to be shared mainly with other women, the feelings in her poetry yet appeal alike to men and women.

Except for what little can be gleaned from internal evidence in her poetry, not much is known with certainty about Mira's life. Even the information found in her poems is not always very clear. There is consensus only on the following minimal facts, although nothing in them is totally beyond dispute. Mira was the daughter of a Rajput chief, Ratan Singh, of the famous royal warrior clan, the Rathors. Her mother died when Mira was still very young. Since her warrior father was often away, she was raised by her grandfather, Rao Dudaji, the ruler of Merta, a small principality in Rajasthan in western India. She received the education usual for a Rajput princess: learning Sanskrit, studying the Vedas and other Hindu scriptures, and cultivating courtly graces, including training in music and dance. Her family were Vaishnavites and devotees of Krishna. Very early in her life, Mira consequently acquired a leaning toward the worship of Krishna. There are various versions of the story of her receiving in her childhood an image of Krishna. She became greatly attached to the image and is said to have dreamed that she was married to the god. She took the image with her when, in 1516, she was married to Bhoj Raj, the heir apparent of the formidable Rana Sanga Sisodiya, the King of Mewar and the acknowledged leader of all the Rajputs, who would about eleven years later fight against the Mughal conqueror Babur (Selection 4). The Sisodiyas were also devotees of Krishna, although they simultaneously worshiped the Mother Goddess Durga, which created some conflicts for Mira. It seems that Rana Sanga's mother encouraged Mira in her Krishna worship, initiating her into the practice of receiving Vaishnava holy men into the palace for spiritual interaction. Mira continued the practice after the old queen's death.

Mira's marriage to Bhoj Raj remained childless. Some of her poems seem to imply that the marriage was never consummated. When Bhoj Raj died about 1527, Mira became still more absorbed than before in the worship of Krishna and in receiving holy men into the women's quarters in the palace. After Rana Sanga's death in 1528, his successor sons, seeing her activities as unbecoming a respectable woman, tried to discourage them, failing which they began to persecute her. In defiance, Mira openly flouted propriety and began to go into town, mingled with the holy men there, and danced before Krishna's image in the public temple. The persecution grew worse. Vikramjit, her younger brother-in-law, tried to kill her by sending her a poisoned drink, by putting a snake in a flower basket sent to her, and other similar machinations; but she miraculously survived all attempts at her life. However, continuously harassed, she finally left Chittaur, the capital of Mewar, and returned to Merta, to take refuge with her uncle, Viramji, who now ruled there. Her stay there was short-lived, for Viramji was expelled from Merta by a neighboring king.

Leaving Merta, Mira became a wandering ascetic. She spent some time in Brindavan, the place where Krishna of the cowherd legend grew up and as a young lover sported with the gopis. After Brindavan, she wandered to other places and finally went to Dvaraka, the capital of Krishna's state in the Mahabharata. She lived there for most of the rest of her life, worshiping at the "Ranchor" temple dedicated to Krishna. The following story is told about the end of her life. Overwhelmed by its enemies, Mewar fell on evil days. The King, along with his people, feeling that this was retribution for their mistreatment of Mira, requested her to return to Chittaur. Caught in a dilemma between the desire not to leave Dvaraka and reluctance uncharitably to turn down the King's request, she sought a resolution from her deity. Going into the Ranchor temple, she began to dance before the image of Krishna and kept on dancing until she disappeared into the image, a fitting end to the legend of her quest, a legend best embodied in her poetry rather than in factual biography.

The poems in the following selection exemplify the main phases and aspects of Mira's love: her longing, her suffering in separation, and her joy in union with Krishna.

1

No, Rana,[1] I will no more submit to you, for now Giridhar is my Lord.[2]
Jewels and camphor, no matter what they say, have the same fate; the
    same end awaits the bars of gold and the clods of earth alike.
Now my refuge is the richest of the rich. I meditate on Him.
Now that I have attained communion with my God, there is no sorrow
    left. My master is my Lord.
My heart is filled with pleasure in the company of saints, but my
    relations like this not. A thousand and one times, they try
    to change my mind, but I will obey my own heart.
I have now become friends with the Dark One.[3] The crown on His head
    shines with gems and a priceless necklace dangles on his
    chest; I hear sweet music of his ankle bells.
Giving up all sense of shame and modesty, I have found shelter at His
    feet.
O Mira's Lord Giridhar, take me away, take me away, from this mean
    world.

Translated from the Hindi by Surjit S. Dulai. Copyright, Surjit S. Dulai, 1997.

[1] Rana, literally "warrior," is the title of address for a king, especially among the Rajputs, famous for their valor and martial prowess. The Rana addressed here is most probably her brother-in-law, Rana Sanga's son Vikramjit, who persistently persecuted Mira for her unconventional conduct in meeting with the holy men, going openly into town to worship at the public temple there, and mingling with the common people.

[2] Giridhar, meaning "upholder of the mountain," is Mira's most favorite name for Krishna. It is derived from a legend in which Krishna saves the people of Braj, among whom he lived as a young man, from the wrath of the god Indra who hurled the mountain Govardhan at them. Krishna caught the mountain and held it up.

[3] "Dark One" (*Shyam*) is a common epithet for Krishna because of his dark blue complexion.

2

Darling, let my life be an offering of light to you. Let your praise ring in
 my heart morn and eve. I will make of my body a lamp and
 of my mind a wick. I will burn in the lamp the oil of love; its
 light shall shine day and night.
I will lay down on the floor the carpet of knowledge and make my
 devotion a decoration for my house. For you, my beloved, I
 will give away all my wealth and my life.
My bed is filled with patterns of many rich colors; it is decked with
 many flowers; but I pass my days counting stars, my beloved
 does not come.
The month of Sravana has passed and Bhadra has begun.[4] The rainy
 season is here. Dark clouds cover the sky and showers pour
 from eyes.
My parents gave me to you and you have left. You know well that besides
 you I think of no other love. You are my only love; you alone
 can make me truly happy.
Mira is filled with anxiety; make her your own.

3

Make me your servant, my Lord, make me your servant. I will be your
 servant and tend your garden.
Daily will I see you, and through the bowers and lanes of Brindavan,[5] I
 will sing your praise.
Seeing and remembering you will be my reward for service and your love
 will be my wealth. All three are best for me.
I will lay out green plots and among them, here and there, build bowers
 and in them, dressed in flowers, I will meet my beloved.
The yogi comes to Brindavan to practice yoga and the ascetic for austerities. The devotee has come here to sing the praise of Hari.[6]
Deep and silent is Mira's Lord. O heart, do not impatient be, for your
 Lord will come to meet you at the dead of night on the
 banks of the river of love.

---

[4] In the Hindu calendar, Sravana is the first month of the rainy season. Bhadra follows
Sravana.

[5] The name of a village and its surrounding pastures where, according to one legend,
Krishna grew up in a cowherd community and as a young flute-playing cowherd lover
sported with the young maidens of the village.

[6] Hari is another name for Vishnu, hence for Krishna.

4

Now I have only Gopal[7] Giridhar and no one else.
In the company of holy men, I have abandoned all sense of shame.
Everyone knows how with tears I have watered the vine of love. It has
      flowered at last and brought me nectar as fruit.
When I came here, the *bhaktas*[8] knew, but the world shed tears.
Now I have no one with me—no servant, no friend, or relation.
I churned the curds and took out the pure butter, throwing away the
      whey.
Mira is now the servant of her beloved Giridhar, let whatever happens
      happen.

5

Forsake me not, my King!
I am a helpless poor woman, my Lord, bereft of all strength. You are the
      crown on my head.
Worthless am I, without a single virtue, while you are great and full of
      everything good.
Your slave, to whom else can I go? You are the jewel of my heart.
Mira has no other Lord but you; it is for you to redeem her honor.

6

Stand before my eyes, my dearest Lord, stand before my eyes and forget
      me not!
I am adrift on the ocean of life, hurry and pull me out to the shore.
O Mira's Lord, dear Giridhar, let this union never end.

7

For you I have forsaken all joys; why do you now keep me waiting?
The anguish of separation burns my heart; come and quench its fire.
My Lord, it does not behoove you to leave me so; come and smiling call
      me to your side.
O my beloved, Mira is your slave through ages; come to her now and
      soothe her limbs with your touch.

---

[7] Literally, "caretaker of cows," hence a name for Krishna.

[8] Devotees; practitioners of the Cult of Devotion.

8

O my friend, while the world sleeps, I alone, separated from my love,
keep awake.

Apart from their beloveds, those in *harems*[9] make garlands of pearls; but
here am I weaving a garland of tears.

My nights pass counting the stars in heaven. When will the hour of
happiness arrive?

O Mira's Lord, beloved Giridhar, leave me not after you have once come
to me.

9

I will dance before the lord of my heart and thrill Him with my abandon
and beseech His love.

Love shall be the ringing ankle bells on my flying feet and emotions the
flowing garments swaying around my frame.

I will scatter to the four winds all restraints required by noble birth and
social rank.

I will go straight into the arms of my beloved Lord.

Mira will dye herself in the color of her own dear Hari.

10

O sweet-tongued one, come to the house of your own Mira. How long
will she have to wait, wait and look expectantly at your path?
It is time that you had come.

O come to me with an easy heart, you need have no misgivings. Your
very presence will spread happiness all around. And I will
dedicate this soul and body to you, my darling Shyam.

I am in deep distress and can bear no more delay. Come; your presence
will be the consummation of my desire.

For you I have sacrificed all luxuries. Kajal, tilak, and tambol,[10] I have
given them all up.

In your absence, time hangs heavy. I wait and wait, my head lying
wearily against the palm of my hand.

Pray come! Mira, your slave for ages and ages, bares her bosom for you.

---

[9] Women's quarters in a king's palace or a nobleman's house.

[10] Some of the items of a woman's toilette. Kajal is a finely ground substance used for
darkening the eyes; tilak is the cosmetic dot, generally on the forehead; and tambol is a
kind of perfume.

11

Ah my friend, I am mad with love. No one knows how I suffer.
My bed is a bed of thorns. How can I sleep? My beloved's bed is in the
 firmament. How can we be united?
Only one who suffers, and no one who has never suffered, knows what it
 is to suffer. Only he who has tasted the poison, and no one
 else, knows its bitterness.
Maddened by suffering, I roam from forest to forest, in search of cure,
 but no physician have I found.
O Mira's Lord, only then will I find relief when Shyam is my physician.

12

My Lord, you tied the knot of love; now where have you fled?
You kindled the light of love; now you have gone away abandoning her
 who knows no one but you.
You launched the boat of love; now you have left it adrift, tossing in the
 ocean of separation.
O Mira's Lord, when will you return? Without you I can live no more.

13

The beauty of Mohan[11] has made me captive.
In the bazaar and on the street, he teases me. I have not yet learned the
 sweet desire of my beloved.
He has a handsome figure, like lotuses are his eyes. His glance is thrilling
 and enchanting are his smiles.
He is grazing cows on the bank of Jamuna,[12] playing sweet music on his
 flute.
Mira surrenders her body and soul to Giridhar and clasps his lotus-feet.

14

My beloved is angry with me, O my dear sisters, he is angry with me.
I have searched for him in the bazaars and in the village squares.
Again and again, I have looked for him in the courtyard.
Lamp in hand, I have gone in search of him in every house and searching
 I have bitterly wept.
Ah Giridhar, Mira's Lord, she sings your praise and hugs your lotus-feet.

---

[11] Literally, "charming" or "captivating," an epithet for Krishna.

[12] A well-known river, a tributary of the River Ganges. Delhi, the capital of India for centuries, is located on the banks of the Jamuna. The river also flows by Brindavan. (See footnote 5.)

15

The Sravana clouds pour forth their rain and fill my heart with solemn
    music.
My soul is filled with expectation and I hear Hari's footsteps.
Thick dark clouds gather on all sides and the lightening flashes. A storm
    is imminent. A drizzle and a halting rain come down. A cool
    breeze blows with a caressing touch.
It is Giridhar, Mira's beloved Lord, singing a joyous and holy hymn.

16

I hear Hari's footsteps. From the fortification of the palace, I look out to
    see when my King will come.
The frogs, the papia,[13] and the peacock shout in joy, and the cuckoo has
    bedecked herself for the meeting.
The clouds hanging low pour down rain and the lightning has shed her
    bashfulness.
The earth has decked herself in new clothes to meet her Lord.
O dear Giridhar, O Mira's beloved and King, quickly come and be
    united with your slave.

17

The charm of your face has me captured, my love. Once I saw your face,
    the entire world lost its charm for me, my mind no longer
    attached to it.
To pursue the pleasures of this world is to try to hold water in a sieve. I
    can now disdain those pleasures.
Lucky is Mira; her dreams have come true. Now I am the most fortunate
    of all people.

18

Outside it is raining and my beloved is with me in my hut.
As the rain gently falls, my cup of bliss overflows the brim.
It is a union coming after long ages of separation and every moment I
    am fearful of losing my beloved again.
Says Mira, "My Lord, you have quenched my vast thirst for love and
    have accepted me, my husband of former births."

---

[13]A singing bird. It sings with the approach of rain.

19

Mother dear, I have found in Rama[14] a wealth, an untold wealth indeed,
O Mother.
Any amount of spending cannot reduce this wealth; thieves cannot steal
it; it daily grows and grows.
It sinks not in water nor is by fire burned.
Compared to it, the whole earth seems much too small.
Devotion, like a boat, has carried me across the life's ocean. It is to me
the light that shows the way.
Mirabai has placed her heart at the lotus-feet of her beloved Giridhar.

20

Beloved, I have dyed myself in the color of your love.

Others' beloveds live abroad and send them letters, but my beloved lives
inside my heart and I am with him day and night.
Clothed in beautiful clothes I go out to play with my beloved. In sport I
meet him and hold him in my embrace.
Others get intoxicated by drinking wine, but I am drunk without it. I
drink the wine of love and stay intoxicated day and night.
I have lit the lamp of constant remembrance and my mind is its wick.
The oil comes from a mill beyond knowing and the lamp
burns forever and ever.
Giridhar is Mira's Lord and she is the slave at his feet.

21

Mother dear, I have purchased my beloved.
Some say, I took him by stealth, others say, I received him from begging,
but I took him openly with the beat of drums.
Some say, he is dark, some say, he is fair, but I took him with my eyes
wide open.
Some say, he is light, some say, he is heavy, but I weighed him on my
scales before I took him.
I had to take off all the ornaments from my body in order to obtain him.

---

[14] Rama, the hero of the ancient Sanskrit epic *Ramayana*, as well as of Tulsi Das's *Ramcaritmanas* (Selection 24), is, like Krishna, also an incarnation of Vishnu. Here the name
Rama is synonymous with Krishna.

22

You may undo the knot, my beloved, but I cannot. Who else will I have
    for a friend, if I tear asunder the bond of our love.
You are the tree and I a bird in it; you are the lake and I only a fish in it;
    you are the loft mountain on which I am a plant.
You are the moon and I the chakor,[15] and you, my Lord, are the pearl
    and I the thread passing through it. You are gold and I am
    the borax.[16]
O Lord of Mira, jeweler of Braj,[17] you are the Lord and I your servant.

---

[15] A mythical bird that is said to be in love with the moon. It is sometimes equated with
the lark.

[16] Borax is a substance used in the process of making jewelry from gold.

[17] The region including Brindavan where Krishna lived as a young man.

11

※

Luiz Vaz de Camões

OS LUSÍADAS

Portugal's national poet, and one of the greatest lyric poets of the sixteenth century, Luis Vaz de Camões (1524–1580) was born in Lisbon to an impoverished noble family. Portugal was at that time one of the major seafaring powers of the world, and held a vast commercial empire that stretched from West Africa to India. However, the country's best days as an imperial power were behind it; its empire, acquired during the lifetime of a single generation, was beginning to unravel just as quickly, through a combination of a small population, inept rulers at home, and corrupt viceroys in the colonies.

Three years after his birth, Camões's family moved from Lisbon to Coimbra, the site of one of Europe's oldest universities (founded in 1290). Camões was raised in that city, and eventually studied in its famed university, where he acquired an extensive knowledge of the classical Latin writers—among them Ovid, Cicero, Lucan, Horace, and Vergil. He also developed such a perfect command of Spanish that he was able to write flowing and beautiful poetry in that language. It was also at Coimbra that Camões came into contact with the Italian poets of the Renaissance and their dolce stil nuovo ("sweet new style") which Camões would master and adapt to the Portuguese language, just as his older contemporary, Garcilaso de la Vega, had done in Spanish (see Selection 3). After finishing his studies at Coimbra, Camões moved to Lisbon in 1543 in search of fortune, and at first found it, thanks to his poetic talent. He was highly admired by some at the Portuguese royal court, but envied by others, who resented the young genius from the provinces. Three years later, he was banished from the capital by the king himself, due to certain passages in his play King Seleucus which were considered insulting by the Portuguese monarch. He had also conducted an impassioned romance with a lady-in-waiting to the queen.

Camões eventually chose to exchange his exile in nearby Santarem for a commission in the Portuguese army, and service in the Portuguese-held city of Ceuta (in present-day Morocco, at the tip of Africa facing Spain), which was being *beseiged by Muslim armies. The experience in Ceuta, which was Camões's first direct contact with the Muslim world, also left him deeply embittered and physically scarred (an attack left him sightless in his right eye). Camões returned to Lisbon where, penniless and shunned by many of his former noble acquaintances, he spent his time in taverns and acquired such a reputation as a violent and dangerous swordsman that he was nicknamed "Trincafortes" (roughly, "Swashbuckler"). An incident in 1553, in which he stabbed a member of the royal court, led first to his imprisonment and later to the commutation of his sentence (thanks to his few remaining influential friends) to military service again, but this time to India, a much farther and more perilous frontier. Camões served in India until 1569. After numerous adventures and still impoverished, he returned to Portugal, where he finished and published the work that he had begun writing in the Orient and that would preserve his name for posterity, the patriotic epic* Os Lusíadas (The Lusiads), *in 1572. Always beseiged by poverty, but surrounded by a tiny circle of friends and admirers, Camões died of the plague on June 10th, 1580. At the time of his death, the fortunes of Portugal and her empire had reached their lowest ebb. Her treasury drained and her armies defeated in fruitless crusades against the Muslims of Morocco, without a clear heir to the throne after the death in battle in 1579 of King Sebastian, and racked by civil war, Portugal was annexed by Spain in 1581.*

Widely regarded as the first modern epic poem, Os Lusíadas *became a model for the genre known as the Renaissance epic. Of course, like every classically trained poet, Camões followed his models as well, chief among them Vergil and the Italian, Ludovico Ariosto. Vergil's influence is pervasive in* Os Lusíadas, *and extends to the poem's own reason for being. Like Vergil, whose* Aeneid *was, by design, the national epic of Rome,* Os Lusíadas *is the national epic of the Portuguese nation, from the beginning of its history to the poet's own time. Its title means "Sons of Lusus," the legendary progenitor of the Portuguese people and first settler of Portugal (Lusitania). Another Vergilian trait in Camões's poem is the technique of having historical events narrated by one of their participants. Similar to Aeneas's narration of the fall of Troy to queen Dido of Carthage in the* Aeneid, *in* Os Lusíadas *the great Portuguese explorer Vasco de Gama narrates the history of Portugal and his own exploits to the king of Malindi, on the east African coast in modern Kenya, while events that took place after Da Gama's great exploratory voyage around Africa to India (1497–1499) are presented as a vision and prophecy revealed to the explorer. This eastward exploration and conquest represented to Camões the triumph of the spiritual values of European Christianity.*

Ariosto's influence in Os Lusíadas *is evident in Camões's use of the* ottava rima, *an eight-line stanza in iambic pentameter with the fixed rhyme scheme* ababab cc, *a pattern retained in the following translation. This type of stanza was perfected by Ariosto in his narrative poem* Orlando Furioso *(1516), based on the legends of Charlemagne and Count Roland (Orlando). Like Ariosto's fictional knights, Camões's historical characters behave according to the code of chivalry, and experience adventures in a colorful Oriental world in which elements of Eastern geography and culture mingle with allusions to Greek and Roman deities.*

Written at the time of Portugal's imperial decline, the ten cantos (or books) of Os Lusíadas *are both a summation of that empire's history and a nostalgic epitaph to its glory. The following selection from the Seventh Book, after comparing the Portuguese with the other European nations (whom Camões judges in highly condescending ethnocentric terms), narrates Vasco da Gama's arrival in India at the port city of Calicut, and the encounter between Da Gama and a Spanish-speaking Moor (or Arab) named Monçaide, who serves as his interpreter and guide.*

1

Already they were come hard by that ground,
So long and by so many much desired,
Which by the Indus stream is girded round
And Ganges in his earthly Heaven retired.[1]
Up! Up! Strong race! To seize the palms renowned
For triumph, still in war you have aspired.
You are arrived and have the land before,
Which with abundance of all wealth flows o'er.

2

I say to you, O Lusian generation,
Yours in this world is but a little place,
Not in this world, but in His congregation.
Whose rule doth the round firmament embrace;
You, in whom risk quelled not determination
Wholly to subjugate a loathsome race,
Or greed, or an allegiance incomplete
To Her Whose Essence hath in Heaven Her seat;[2]

From *The Lusiads of Luiz de Camões,* copyright 1950. Leonard Bacon, translator. Pp. 247–259. Reprinted by permission of The Hispanic Society of America.

[1] The Indus and the Ganges are the two best-known rivers in India. According to medieval Western geographers, the Ganges was supposed to rise to the Earthly Paradise.

[2] An allusion to the Virgin Mary.

3

You Portuguese, so strong, though you are few,
Who your weak powers never stop to weigh,
Who, though you pay the price of death, ensue
The law of life that shall endure for aye,[3]
Such was the die which Heaven cast for you,
That, be your numbers little as they may,
For Christendom you act a mightly part.
So dost Thou, Christ, exalt the meek in heart!

4

Look on the proud herd of the Germans there,
Who in their vast plains find their nourishment,
And, in rebellion against Peter's heir,
Seek a new shepherd, a new sect invent.[4]
Look on the hideous wars to which they fare
(For with blind error they are not content),
Not against the Ottoman full up of pride,[5]
But the Pope's sovereign power to set aside.

5

See the hard Englishman, who King by right
Of the divine old city claims to be,[6]
Which town is ruled by the vile Ishmaelite.[7]
How far vain honor is from verity!
Amid his northern snows he seeks delight
And Christian in a novel sense is he,
Against Christ's men drawing the naked brand.
But not for the reconquest of Christ's land.

---

[3] Forever.

[4] The "new shepherd" of the Germans is Martin Luther, who began to declare the principles of the "new sect" of Protestants in 1517, attacking "Peter's heir," the pope in Rome.

[5] A reference to the Muslim Ottoman Empire of the Turks, a military threat to Christian Europe in Camões's lifetime.

[6] A supposed claim by Henry VIII of England ("the hard Englishman") to be ruler also of Jerusalem, based on conquests during the Crusades of the Middle Ages. Scholars have found no evidence to support this notion of Camões's.

[7] "Ishmaelite" is a synonym for "Arab," derived from the biblical story of Hagar and Ishmael.

6

A king unrightful has to him the sway
Of this Jerusalem on earth denied,
The while the English King will not obey
Law sacred of Jerusalem enskied.
And now of thee, vile Gaul,[8] what shall I say,
Who as "Most Christian" would be magnified,
Not to defend the Faith, or to protect,
But wholly to abhor it and reject?

7

Your claim to Christian lordships you have laid,
Though you have huge possessions of your own,
But Nile and Cinyphus[9] have not withstayed,
Of the ancient Holy name the foemen known
So men must prove the edges of the blade
On him who balks at Peter's corner-stone.
Charles! Louis! Are you their inheritor?
Their lands, their names, yet no just cause for war?

8

And what of them, who, in their luxury,
Which with vile ease must still as comrade go,
Waste all their lives, heap wealth continually,
Nor ancient courage any longer know?
Tyranny has begotten enmity,
Which makes a strong folk its own proper foe.
Italy! I speak to you, now drowning quite
In countless crimes done in your own despite.

9

Unhappy Christians, are you, as it were,
The teeth Cadméan,[10] who are sown like seed,

---

[8] An allusion to King Francis I of France. Camões accuses him of betraying the cause of Christian unity against Islam, and compares him unfavorably to his predecessors in the French throne, Charlemagne ("Charles") and Louis IX, ("Louis").

[9] Cinyphus: a river in present-day Tunisia.

[10] In Greek mythology, Cadmus, like Jason, sowed a dragon's teeth, which sprang up as armed men and killed each other, except for five survivors who helped him build Thebes.

While each becomes his brother's murderer,
Though of a single womb you are the breed?
Do you not see the Holy Sepulchre
Governed by hounds, who, being well agreed,
Still come to take your ancient lands outright,
Thus earning excellent repute in fight?

10

You see how they by custom and decree,
Which they observe with all their faith entire,
Gather their hosts stirring uneasily
Against the folk who their dear Christ desire.
But fell Alecto will not let you be,[11]
Sowing among you seeds of quarrels dire.
See if secure from danger you repose,
For they, and you yourselves, are now your foes.

11

And if the passion for a great domain
Urges you forth to conquer alien lands,
Have you not looked upon the rivers twain,
Pactolus, Hermus, rolling golden sands?[12]
Africa yet conceals the shining vein.
Assyria, Lydia, weave the aureate strands.
Such riches may perhaps your spirits spur,
Whose hearts the Holy Temple cannot stir.

12

Of those inventions terrible and new,
The mortal enginery of ordinance,
We now should make our trial stern and true
Against the walls of Turkey and Byzance.[13]
To woodland caves drive back the Turkish crew,
To Caspian heights, to Scythia's cold expanse.

---

[11] Alecto was one of the three Furies in Greek mythology. The Furies were infernal divinities whose task was to torment evildoers.

[12] Pactolus and Hermus were two rivers of Asia Minor in ancient Lydia, famous for their gold-bearing sands.

[13] Byzance is Byzantium, the ancient name for Constantinople, which had been under the rule of the Ottoman Turks since 1453.

Their progeny are waxing and grow great
Upon your wealthy Europe's pomp and state.

13

Armenia and Georgia, Greece and Thrace,
Are calling to you, for a bestial folk
Compels their dearest children to embrace
The Koran's vileness, to hard tribute broke.
Glory in this: At acts that shame the race,
Bravely and wisely, strike the avenging stroke!
Nor, proud ones, for great honors clamor longer,
Because against your friends you proved the stronger,

14

But while you are so blind and thirst so hot
For life-blood of your brothers, men insane,
Adventurous Christian courage falters not
Within our Lusitania's small domain.
Africa's ports have fallen to her lot;
In Asia more than sovereign is her reign;
In the world's new fourth part[14] she plows the field
And there will go, where more shall be revealed.

15

Now for the moment let our glance be bent
On those great sailors' fortunes once again,
After sweet Venus calmed the impotent
Opposing fury of the hurricane,
And when to them appeared the continent,
The end of all their constant strife and pain,
Whither they came Christ's law like seed to strew,
And, with a new King, brought their customs new.

16

Scarce on the coast of the strange land were they
When the light barks of fishers they beheld,
Who thereupon before them led the way
To Calicut,[15] the city where they dwelled.

---

[14] "The world's new fourth part" is the Americas. (Until the Middle Ages, cartographers believed the world was divided up into three parts: Europe, Asia, and Africa.)

[15] A city on the southwest coast of India, visited by Vasco da Gama in 1498.

And to the place the ships their courses lay,
Because it was the city that excelled
The best in Malabar,[16] where the King reigned,
Who chief dominion in the land maintained.

17

Beyond the Indus, on Ganges' hither side,
Lies an enormous region, much renowned,
Bordered upon the south by Ocean's tide,
Caverned Emodius[17] its northern bound.
There various kings impose diversified
Shapes of strange faith. Some worship vile Mahound,[18]
And some, adoring, to their idols cleave.
Others, in beasts that dwell with them, believe.

18

And in the ranges huge that cut in twain
This vast land and across all Asia lie,
Which have as various appellations ta'en
As different nations choose to call them by,
The springs are found from which the rivers drain,
Whose large floods in the Indian Ocean die,
And, circling round the cantle and the piece
Of the terra firma, form the Chersonese.[19]

19

Between the courses where the rivers stray,
A long cape thrusts afar from the main shore,
Wedge-shaped, in the sea's bosom, and alway
Looks on the island of Ceylon before.[20]
And near huge Ganges' springs, they used to say,

---

[16] The Malabar Coast is in the southwest of India and includes the port of Calicut.

[17] Emodius is the ancient Greek name for the Himalayas, the mountain range that covers Nepal, Bhutan, southern Tibet, and extreme northern India.

[18] "Mahound" was a pejorative for Muhammad, the chief prophet of Islam, thought erroneously by Christians to be the object of worship.

[19] "Chersonese" is a Greek term meaning "peninsula." Here it alludes to the fact that the Indian subcontinent juts out like a peninsula into the Indian Ocean.

[20] Ceylon is present-day Sri Lanka, a large island off the southeastern tip of India.

In keeping with old legendary lore,
That people in the neighboring regions dwelling
Lived upon odors of the flowers sweet-smelling.

20

But in customs, as in names, the populace
Of new sort and most various now is found;
It is the Delis and the Pathan race,
In numbers, as in lands, that most abound,
Deccanis, Orias, they who look for grace
Where waters of the Ganges stream resound.
There also is the country of Bengal,
So fertile that it quite outranks them all.

21

There is Cambaya's kingdom tried in fight,[21]
They say the strong King Porus held of old,[22]
And there Narsingha's realm[23] that founds her might
Not on brave men but on her gems and gold.
And from the heaving sea the vasty height
Of a very lengthy range one may behold.
For Malabar these hills are bulwark sure,
Whereby from Canará they live secure.

22

They are called Ghats by natives of the land,
And at their feet there lies, though it be strait,
Like a fringe along the coast, a stretch of strand,
Which strives against the ocean's native hate.
And here, 'mid others, no one may withstand
That Calicut enjoys such princely state
As may a fair, rich capital behove,
And Zamorin they call the lord thereof.

---

[21] Cambaya is the region of present-day Cambodia, in southeast Asia.

[22] Porus, an ancient king of Cambodia, was said to have fought against the armies of Alexander the Great with great gallantry.

[23] The term "Narsingha" translates as "Land of the Trumpet," a territory lying between the Ghat Mountains and the Bay of Bengal, on the east coast of India.

23

Scarce did the fleet that lordly coast attain
When a Portuguese went forth ambassador,
Unto the heathen monarch to make plain
Their new arrival on so far a shore.
And up a river, where it met the main,
The envoy went. The novel garb he wore,
His foreign look and color and strange air,
Brought all the people hurrying to stare.

24

Among the folk who thronged that sight to see,
There came a follower of Mahomet's law,[24]
Who had been born in the land of Barbary[25]
Where once Antaeus[26] had been held in awe.
Either he learned from such propinquity
Or from our steel might clearer knowledge draw,
But Portugal he knew at all events,
Though fate had banished him this long way thence.

25

When he saw the envoy, then with gracious cheer,
As one who well could Spanish speech construe,
He asked him: "And what was it brought you here
From Portugal to worlds so far from you?"
He answered: "We came forth the road to clear
Through the Great Deep that no man ever knew,
And find where Indus' giant stream may flow,
For thus the Faith of God will wax and grow."

26

The Moor (Monçaide called) with wonderment
Was striken, for the voyage was so great.

---

[24] That is, Muhammad's law.

[25] Barbary was the ancient name for the northwest coast of Africa bordering the Mediterranean—the region facing Spain and Portugal. It comprises the modern states of Morocco, Algeria, Tunisia, and Libya.

[26] Antaeus, in Greek mythology, was a giant of Libya whose strength was renewed by contact with the earth. He was defeated by Hercules, who held him aloft until the giant lost all strength.

He harked what woes at sea they underwent
And all the Lusitanian might narrate.
But, seeing that the message's intent
Only to the country's ruler could relate,
He told the Portuguese that the King lay
Outside the city but a little way.

27

And till the King this advent strange should know,
The Moor would well the Portuguese entreat
To rest in his own house, though it were low,
The victual of the country there to eat.
And after resting, he himself would go,
Together with the envoy, to the fleet,
For nothing is more pleasing to the mind
Than in a strange land neighbor folk to find.

28

The Portuguese well to accept was fain
The blithe Moor's offer, and with good will too.
As if old friendship were between the twain,
He ate and drank and did as bid to do.
Then from the city they went forth again
Unto such ships as well Monçaide knew.
They climbed aboard the flagship. All men there
Gave to the visitor a welcome fair.

29

The Chief [27] embraced him, for his joy was great
When he heard him speak clear language of Castile.
He set him near, and, eager yet sedate,
Begged him the country's nature to reveal.
As trees in Rhodope [28] might congregate
When the lover of Eurydice [29] made peal

---

[27] Vasco da Gama, the Portuguese leader of the expedition.

[28] Rhodope was a land in Thrace (in present-day northeastern Greece) where Orpheus, the mythological singer, charmed even the trees to follow his music.

[29] Eurydice, a nymph, was Orpheus's wife. She died from a snakebite, and Orpheus voyaged to the underworld in an attempt to rescue her.

The lyre of gold, if only they might hear,
So, but to hark the Moor, the crew drew near.

30

He spake: "All you, whom Nature has created
Near neighbors where my father's dwelling lay,
What challenge, what large destiny, has fated
That such a perilous road you should essay?
Not without cause, dark and uncontemplated,
You left hid Minho, Tagus faraway,[30]
Sailing, where no other bark has plowed the seas,
To regions as remote and lone as these.

31

"God brought you certainly, Who must intend
That you his cause should forward and maintain.
And therefore doth he guide you and defend
Against the foe, the sea, the hurricane.
You are in India, where afar extend
All sorts of peoples, who great profit gain
From shining gold, from gems of richest price,
From odorous perfume, and from burning spice.

32

"The province, in whose port you came ashore
This short while since, as Malabar is known.
Idols of an old cult, the folk adore,
And round about this faith is widely sown.
Many kings rule, though one in times before
Reigned sole, or so the ancient legends own.
Under his hand Sarama Perimal
Held last the united rule imperial.[31]

33

"However, when there came into the land
Men from beyond the Gulf of Araby,

---

[30] Minho is a region on the northern coast of Portugal. The Tagus is the longest river in the Iberian Peninsula. It flows from the Sierra de Albarracín, near Madrid, to the Bay of Lisbon in Portugal.

[31] Sarama Perimal was a ninth-century Muslim ruler of the Malabar Empire.

Who brought Mahomet's precept and command,
In which belief my parents nourished me,
Then, it befell, the wise and eloquent band
By prayer converted Perimal, and he
Forthwith turned Moslem, with belief so high
That in the faith he chose, a saint, to die.

34

"Ships he prepared, wherein he stowed with care
His offerings of richest merchandise,
That he might sail to take religion where
The prophet who first preached the doctrine lies.
But ere he left, because he had no heir,
The kingdom to his men he let devise,
And dealt so with the worthiest, indeed,
That the poor were wealthy and the subject freed.

35

"Cochin to one, to another Cananor,
Chalè to one, Pimenta's isle to one,
This man, Coulão, that other, Cranganor,
And most to him who had best service done.
But one young man to whom much love he bore
Came after all was given, whereupon
The gift of Calicut to him he made,
A noble town, grown wealthy by its trade.

36

"To him he gave the town and high estate
Of Emperor who over all holds sway.
And this done, thither he departed straight,
Where as a saint he might live out his day.
Hence the high Zamorin's style sublime and great,
Prouder than all, unto this very day
Remains unto that youth and to his heirs,
Of whom is he, the sovranty that bears.

37

"The faith of all, though rich or poor they be,
Is made of myth, so fancy must decide.
Naked they go, save that in some degree
They hide with clouts what nature bids us hide.

Two sorts there are. For the nobility
Are called the Nairs,[32] and those less dignified,
The Poleas,[33] and their law forbids these last
Ever to marry with the ancient caste.

38

"And those who always the same crafts pursue
With those outside their guild can never wed,
Nor will the sons consent a task to do
Unlike their sires' until themselves are dead.
The Nairs as horrible debasement view
A Polea's very touch, and be it said
That, if such touch unto a Nair betide,
With many rites he must be purified.

39

"The ancient Jewish stock in the same way
Would touch no person of Samaria's race,
But matters even stranger than I say
You'll note in various customs of the place.
The Nairs alone in perils of the fray
Engage and for their King a foe will face,
In the left hand still bearing in the fight
The buckler, and the good sword in the right.

40

"The Brahmins are their priests, which would appear
An ancient title of peculiar fame.
And in his famous rule they persevere,
Who, first of men, to science gave a name.[34]
They slay no living thing, such is their fear
Of all flesh, and they quite eschew the same.
And only in the sexes' intercourse
They claim more licence and less rule enforce.

---

[32] Nairs were members of the military noble caste of the Malabar Coast.

[33] "Polea" is a deformation of "pariah," which refers to the members of the lowest caste in Indian society.

[34] Following Cicero, Camões believed the ancient Greek philosopher Pythagoras to have been the first thinker to give science a name. He also thought erroneously that the Brahmins were followers of Pythagoras.

41

"Women are held in common, but they are
In this restricted to the husband's kin.
Happy that race, under a kindly star,
Who feel no pang of jealousy within.
Such practices, the men of Malabar,
Like others odder yet, esteem no sin.
And the land fattens on all trade the while,
Which the seas fetch from China to the Nile."

42

Thus spake the Moor. But now, on every hand,
Tales of the coming of a stranger race
Ran through the town, till the King gave command
That he might know the substance of the case,
While, thronging, either sex, all ages, stand
Around the princes, down the streets who pace,
And who at the King's bidding go to meet
The Captain who commands the new-come fleet.

43

He, who already had the King's consent
To disembark, with many a noble knight
Of Portugal, did not delay but went,
In his rich robes adornèd. And the bright
Constrasting colors filled with high content
The people, all enchanted at the sight.
The oar-blades, beating their due measure, thresh
First the cold sea, then river water fresh.

• • •

PART
III

THE REALITY OF EVERYDAY LIFE

⁂

Everyday life can take many forms, but the desire to record that daily life as it truly appears is in itself an assertion of the value of this world, as we can see in Part III (Selections 12–19). Chelebi's *Book of Travels,* Selection 12, is a world-famous classic of travel literature and certainly a statement of the fascinating diversity of the Muslim world in which the author lived. Written in Turkish in the seventeenth century it provides us with extensive coverage of the vastness of both Islam and of the Ottoman Empire, with its capital in Istanbul. In Selection 13 we see a Chinese novel of the Ming Dynasty, *The Water Margin,* in which the heroes are outlaws. This is not only a romanticizing of the life of outlaws, like the Robin Hood tales of medieval England, but it represents also a realistic depiction of the feelings of average peasants and city dwellers who felt helpless before the vast power of the emperor. We turn again to the literature of travel in Selection 14, Basho's *The Narrow Road to the Interior.* Here we see the poetic delicacy and preciseness typical of much Japanese literature. (The author was also the foremost master of *haiku* poetry.) Remaining in East Asia, we next read Korean Poetry of the Yi Dynasty (Selection 15). Koreans always lived a complex cultural existence between the two more powerful nations of China and Japan. With the invention of a phonetic writing system in 1443, literacy and a rich national literature, especially poetry, began to flourish in Korea. The Yi Dynasty, which began with a military coup in 1392, was to last until 1910.

We move back to Europe for an anonymous masterpiece of brutal realism. *Lazarillo de Tormes* (Selection 16) gives us a teeming sixteenth-century Spanish underworld of hungry beggars, impoverished noblemen, and immorally licentious priests. *Lazarillo* provides the basic form for all *picaresque* novels, in which the "hero" is a likable rascal like Huckleberry Finn in Mark Twain's nineteenth-century American novel. Remaining in Spain, we savor one of the most celebrated of all novels, *Don Quixote de la Mancha* (Selection 17). Its relationship to realism comes from the radical contrast between the lofty chivalric ideals of the hero and the everyday poverty and brutality endured by Sancho Panza, his faithful servant, and by most of the other characters that the deluded Don Quixote encounters.

With Selections 18 and 19 we return to the celebrated novels of the Ming Dynasty in China (1368–1644). *The Golden Lotus* (18) has long been thought of as China's most notorious pornographic novel—realistic in its depiction of the corruption and disorder that brings down a dynasty. This notoriety has obscured its qualities as social and moral satire. Finally, *The Dream of the Red Chamber* (19) is often recognized as China's greatest novel. Within a large and complex framework of multiple themes, the *Red Chamber* deals with the daily life and decline of an important aristocratic family.

12

❧

Evliya Chelebi

THE BOOK OF TRAVELS

Written in Turkish, under the Ottoman Empire, The Book of Travels (Seya-
hatname) *by Evilya Chelebi (1611–1684) is a world-famous classic in
travel literature. A massive work comprising twelve volumes, although not systematic in format, it provides a very extensive coverage of many different areas of
the vast Ottoman Empire. The approach changes from volume to volume, which
gives the book a rich variety and versatility. The first volume, for example, deals
entirely with Istanbul (formerly Constantinople), the capital of the Empire, and
the areas close to it. Volume VIII focuses on Chelebi's travels in the Balkans. In
Volume X, Chelebi describes several cities and countries of northeast Africa, including Egypt, the Sudan, and Abyssinia (Ethiopia). The book thus provides a
most interesting and informative contemporary picture of the culture and geography of the many places in the empire that he visited or lived in.*

*Chelebi was born in Istanbul. He came from a rich family, his father being
an eminent jeweler connected with the royal court and owning much real estate
in several cities as well. His mother too came from a family with royal connections. His maternal grandmother was related to Melek Ahmet Shah; he was a
high official of the imperial court and had married into the imperial family.
After primary education Chelebi spent many years at a Koranic school learning
to recite the Koran. He became such an excellent reciter that Ahmet Pasha recommended him to the sultan. The sultan being pleased with Chelebi's recitation
skill, he was admitted to the palace school for further education and training in
it. At the school he also studied Arabic language and grammar, music, and the
art of calligraphy, all related to Koranic education. The language skills he acquired here equipped him well for writing travel accounts later in his life.*

*With his superior education and his family's connections with the court, the
prospect of a secure and prestigious position in the imperial service, one of the
best in the world, lay open to Chelebi. However, the settled life of a state official
does not seem to have appealed to him. Quite early in his life he had developed a*

strong desire to travel and see the world. Gradually, the desire for travel, with all the excitement and adventure associated with it, became a passion. It is said that when he was about nineteen, the prophet Muhammad appeared to him in a dream and exhorted him to take up the life of a footloose traveler. It is most fitting that a talented young man like Chelebi living in the Istanbul of his day should dream of becoming a lifelong traveler, for the need and the opportunity to travel have always been an integral and important aspect of Islamic civilization. In its very inception Islam was conceived of as a unified and single universal community. The requirement for all adult Muslims to go on a pilgrimage to Mecca at least once in their lives reinforced this oneness by tying the far-flung parts of the community to the center like the spokes of a wheel.

So Muslims traveled over vast distances, and often. In the process, for the intellectually inclined, travel and the experience of seeing new places became a preoccupation for its own sake. No wonder, therefore, the world of Islam produced some of the greatest early geographers and world-famous travelers such as Chelebi and the fourteenth century Arab, Ibn Battutah of Morocco (see Volume II, Selection 51). The latter journeyed from the depths of West Africa through India and the Indian Ocean to the seaports of China, having traveled, according to one authority, some seventy-five thousand miles. He spent thirty years on these travels and in his memoirs left a detailed record of his observations about the places he visited. The sense of oneness of the Islamic community also contributed to the establishment of strong and very large empires such as the Abbasid Caliphate, the Mughal Empire of India, and the Ottoman Empire. These empires were generally international in character and endured for centuries. The Ottoman Empire contained several European as well as Asian countries. It was established in 1453, with the fall of Christian Constantinople, and lasted until 1916. Its vast expanse and diversity required internal territorial knowledge for political and administrative purposes and offered interesting opportunities of travel to different places in the empire as well.

His family's wealth and influence enabled Chelebi to indulge his lifelong passion for travel. He managed to travel to different places by making a variety of arrangements. Chelebi often attached himself to a high-ranking state official (pasha), such as his relative Melek Ahmet Pasha, assigned to a territory away from the capital. Sometimes he found a position as an official himself for the sake of travel. At other times he traveled as a private individual. At some places Chelebi stayed for only a short time, at others he stayed for several years. Some places he visited only once, others he went to several times. Wherever he went, Chelebi made keen observations of what he saw and recorded them in detail. His style is generally vivid and realistic. Sometimes, however, he waxes creative and has recourse to the fantastic in order to spice the narrative. Since the Ottoman Empire was still at its height, Chelebi was able to visit a wide-ranging variety of places in it, so that his Book of Travels *provides an incomparable portrait of the vast panorama of the empire.*

The following excerpt, taken from Volume VIII of The Book of Travels, *describes the city of Boudonítza, an outpost of the empire in the Peloponnesian Peninsula of Greece. The fortifications of the city and the buildings in it are old and in bad need of repair. The state of its economy is poor. The Muslims living here are outnumbered by Christians and vulnerable to pirate raids. The sad description is, however, soon relieved by miraculous stories: a Muslim saint who converts an entire community to Islam, including even the King of Spain; heavenly fire that burns Christian looters; and other such marvels. The excerpt thus expresses both imperial and Muslim concerns.*

THE CITY OF BOUDONÍTZA[1]

Description of the Powerful Towers and Mighty Walls of the Strong Castle of Boudonítza

The castle is less than two hours distance westward from the seashore. It is a strongly built circular castle, with four subdivisions, on a high place in the mountains, and it is altogether four thousand paces round in circumference. The two lower divisions of the castle, however, were destroyed after the conquest, and since that event the walls have stood in ruins in several places. But it would be an easy matter, if there were money and interest enough, to restore them. As for the third subdivision and the inner keep, they are very strong indeed.

By the will of the Lord, before arriving at this castle, your poor servant heard the noise of cannonfire and musketry on the road in front of us. Since we also heard the shouting of the Muhammedan war-cry,[2] however, we were not frightened off, but as we came up, slowly slowly, towards the city, we encountered several thousand of Muhammad's people, together with their entire households, who had fled from the place, with rags bound around their heads and feet. It appeared that the infidel[3] fleet had disembarked an army which came up from the seashore into the residential section of the castle. Together with a certain infidel named Captain Giorgio,[4] who had come from the landward side, they attacked

---

[1] A city in southern Greece (the Peloponnesus), then part of the Ottoman Turkish Empire.

[2] The phrase *Allahu Akbar*, meaning "God is great."

[3] The "infidels" are nonbelievers, in this case Christians.

[4] A notorious pirate of the region.

the city; sacked and plundered it; and after throwing everything into confusion, set fire to it and departed with two hundred prisoners, thousands of groats[5] worth of commercial goods and supplies, and the chief judge himself, whom they had taken prisoner along with his entire household.

Cause of the Assault on the Castle of Boudonítza

The judge is alleged to have been a tyrant so manifestly oppressive in his infringement of the rights of both the tributary and the exempt populace that the tributary subjects,[6] because of the judge's oppression, went off in boats to Captain Giorgio, whom they found cruising near the Venetian island of Tenos. When they got there, they complained of the judge, saying. "He has taken all our property from us so, in the name of our Lord Jesus, restore our rights to us." So saying, they gave this Captain Giorgio the pretext by which he came by land and sea, and for the sake of a single oppressive judge, the infidels destroyed and devastated this charming city, looted it, and took all those many prisoners.

We made so bold as to come into the city in the midst of this turmoil, and saw that the infidels were still busy binding and chaining their captives, poor creatures of the Lord, and sending them off. Those of Muhammad's people who were shut up in the castle opened the castle gate as soon as they saw us, and cried out to us, "Hey Heroes, what shall we do, when so many of our families, our wives and our children, are taken prisoner, and now, see, they are taking them away."

Then, making up a party together with my servants and the men of the town, we extinguished such fires as we could in some of the neighborhoods, and while we were doing so, we saw the warlike hero warriors from Zitúni,[7] horse and foot, coming to help. Then all the people of the city gathered together and attacked the low-born infidels where they had assembled their forces near the seashore, and rescued much wealth and property and many prisoners, elderly men and women of Muhammad's people. There were also forty-five infidels whose strength was exhausted from running and from carrying their heavy load of loot. These remained behind, and thanks be to the Lord, we took them prisoner. But as we went further on and arrived close to the infidels' boats at the seashore, the accursed infidels let loose at us from their galleons and six gunnery barges, with their large cannon, and we were forced to take all our prisoners and retire once again. Having liberated so many of Muhammad's people, and repossessed so

---

[5] English silver coins, widely used.

[6] Nonmuslims (Christians) who have to pay tribute under Muslim rule, as distinct from Muslims who are exempt from payment.

[7] A town to the north of Boudonítza.

much material and heavy baggage, we made them very happy when we went back to the city with our infidel prisoners and in keeping with our exploits they gave your humble servant one of the infidel prisoners. Praise be to God, we found ourselves thus in a purely fortuitous battle, but what good was there in it, since all those people of Muhammad had been taken captive? There came news too that there were infidels lying in ambush in the mountains, so all the men from Boudonítza, from Zitúni and from Molo[8] came in, several thousands of them, and gathering together they patrolled through the hills and valleys around the city, and remained on watch there.

Concluding Description of the City

One ruinous old mosque in the lower residential quarter escaped the fire, and one inn. One dirty bath, ten shops, a hundred Muslim houses and a hundred and fifty infidel houses remained, all with tile roofs, and gardens and orchards. The rest were all set afire and burned.

Later on, the warriors from Boudonítza and Zitúni who had gone out into the mountains and valleys came back with the news that there was no trace or sign of infidels to be found, but we were still too fearful to sleep in the outer city, and so went into the middle redoubt,[9] where we were hospitably entertained. It is indeed a castle which rises level with the very sky, but the hills along the road that leads to Molo give artillery command over it. In the inner redoubt there are fifty dwellings for the poor wretches of garrison personnel, supplies of produce, and stores and depositories for weapons. But the arsenal is a small one, containing only five long brass falconets.[10] There is only the one small mosque, and no other public edifices. Here and there outside the castle there are gardens and orchards.

Description of Places of Pilgrimage to the Great Saints of God in the Castle of Boudonítza

Outside the city, in the high lands to the east, there is an elevated parkland of cypresses and tall trees. Here, in a meadow from which the entire world may be observed, under a huge lead-roofed cupola, is buried that source of sacred knowledge, who is sprung from an illustrious stock, the seed of Musa Reza, the venerated offspring of Kâzim, who is buried in the heavenly paradise of Baghdad, that recourse of the righteous, entranced by the uniqueness of God, and annihilated

---

[8] A coastal village near Boudonítza.

[9] Ramparts or fortification.

[10] A type of small cannon.

in his power, that guide through the stations of sanctity and mirror of illustrious generosity, that son of the noblest of princes, the chosen servant of God, the Sheyh Sultan Veliüllah,[11] son of the Imam Ali Musa Reza, son of the Imam Kâzim, son of the Imam Ja'fer Sadik, son of the Imam Bâkir, son of the Imam Zeyn al-Abindin, son of the Imam Hüseyin, son of the Imam Ali Murteza and his wife, the glorious Lady Fatima, daughter of the excellent Muhammad, who is Ahmed, Mahmud and Mustafa, may God exalt him, and be pleased with all of them.[12]

This excellent sultan Veliüllah, being of such an illustrious line, found a final repose in this city of Boudonítza, and lies here in tranquillity, buried with all his dependents, children and friends in a brilliant shrine beneath a luminous dome.

The Eminent Glories of the Saint, Veliüllah

Because of the abuse and persecution which the family of Yezid the Umayyad visited on the Imam Hüseyin after the disaster on the plains of Kerbela,[13] this Sultan Veliüllah departed from his homeland and, desiring to become a member of the spiritual brethren in Greece, he wandered and traveled over the earth. When he came to this city of Boudonítza, which was at that time in the hands of the great King of Spain,[14] he performed the Sultani celebration of God's unity for this perverted and evil-doing king. When they had all gathered together before him to the beat of the great kettledrums, the king asked about their condition and circumstances, their origins and their quality. Once made cognizant of their secrets, this cursed king was inflamed with poisonous rage and said, "What business have you in my country? For what reason have you set your foot in this land, making your call to prayer and performing the celebration of the unity of God? Is it not because of you that the Turkish race will march into this land after you, and that you have come to show them the way?" So saying, he thrust Sultan Veliüllah into a huge cannon, but just as he was on the point of firing it, the saint, in perfect conviction and belief, began the continuous recitation of the sacred verse from the Sura "The Prophets" of the Glorious Koran, "We said, Oh

---

[11] Sheyh or Sheikh is the designation or term of address for a holy man, usually a Sufi.

[12] This attempts to trace the elaborate genealogy of the Shi'ite Imam from the prophet Muhammad. *Ahmed* (most praiseworthy), *Mahmud* (praised), and *Mustafa* (chosen by God) are different epithets used for Muhammad.

[13] Kerbela is a plain where the prophet Muhammad's grandsons, Hasan and Huseyin, were defeated and killed. This led to the schism in Islam between Shi'ites and Sunnis. The Shi'ites believe that the Caliphate should have remained in the hands of Muhammad's family. The shrine built in memory of Huseyin at Kerbala is the holiest place for the Shi'ites.

[14] Spain had taken over much of Greece during the first half of the fourteenth century.

fire, be cold and harmless to Ibrahim,"[15] While he was reciting this verse, at the very moment when the great crowd of followers at his side was totally absorbed in the celebration of the unity of God, the decision of the infidels who are consigned to Hell was no longer stayed, and the cannon was fired. By the will of God, the Imam Veliûllah blew higher and higher into the air, and as he appeared out of the sky, his voice could be heard crying, "O god, O my protector." And so, by the will of God, he floated down to land standing upright on the earth, having suffered not the slightest injury to his delicate body at impact. As soon as he had busied himself with an act of thanksgiving to All-glorious God, all the infidels ran to see the condition of the saint, and on that occasion seven thousand unbelieving infidels produced the words of witness and, having become believers and followers of the saint, stood to be led in worship. Even the king, on seeing this, produced the forefinger of attestation and on his recalling the verse that speaks the unity of God, he was honored with the welcome into Islam.[16] All his children and household too became faithful believers in God's unity, and so the first beginnings of Islam in Greece took place among those people of Boudanítza who were thus converted.

Afterwards they built a great shrine, which is still in use, on the place where the saint came down after being fired from the cannon, and gave the rations of food and drink which he established. Infidels from all the seven regions of the world used to come here and visit the saint but, for his own part, this same saint did not survive for long after he had made manifest his blessedness, but soon made the transition to the ultimate world. When he had gone to his pardon, his many thousands of followers buried him here at this palatial edifice, which is still a place of pilgrimage for men of all conditions, an immense hall full of ascetic followers and a cloister for the devotees of Haji Mehmed Bektash Veli.[17]

There are seventy Bektashis here. Wealthy in their want and poverty, rich in the skills of self-annihilation into God, brethren in the arts of self-abandonment and contemplative abstraction, they are all wonderfully kind, cultivated and wholesome spirits. Each of them is appointed to a specific task as they perform all services for the horses of every wayfarer. No matter how many horses a person may have, they do not leave it to him to deal with the blankets and nose-bags, but they bring the horses into the cloister stables and, after they have watered them, they hang a nosebag of feed on them. Then they make coffee for the traveler, and from their kitchens they offer the good things of their hospitable dining

---

[15] The Koran is arranged in *suras* (chapters). The line cited here is line 68 of sura 21.

[16] Muslims sometimes express the unity of God by raising the right forefinger while saying, "God is one." The gesture contrasts with the Orthodox Greek Christian sign for the Trinity, the raising of three fingers together in blessing.

[17] The founder of a well-known Sufi (Muslim mystic) order, the Bektashis.

halls: soups, stewed meats, pilavs and saffron rice, to rich and poor, old and young, yea even to Jew and heathen, for theirs is an immense bequest, from which they distribute their goods to all wandering travelers in accordance with the holy Sura, "There is no creature on the earth, but God has given it sustenance."[18]

All the kings of infideldom, and other infidels as well, are believers in this important sultan (Veliüllah), and every year old women come from infideldom, and traveling at the time of the new year, after the sounding of the festival kettledrum, under sacred Muhammadan sanctions, they make collections of money and provisions to provide for the sustenance of travelers.

This is a convent with a world-wide prospect which must be visited. All the buildings are roofed over with pure lead, which is one of the good works and benefactions of . . .[19] Pasha. On all sides of the sarcophagus of Saint Veliüllah, where he lies at rest under the luminous cupola, there are any number of glorious phrases written in a beautiful hand, and any number of precious incense burners, rosewater flasks, candle-holders and suspended lamps of every sort. There are rare and precious hangings too, and beautifully written inscriptions where each devout traveler by sea has left his mark. And there are articles from the apparatus of mendicant dervishes,[20] such as staffs, begging bowls, halters and gourd flasks. Besides these, there are all sorts of drums, pennants, iron clappers, banners, tambourines, kettledrums, trumpets, cymbals, . . . and whips. The Bektashis sprinkle rosewater over each pilgrim as he arrives. Beside Sultan Veliüllah is buried . . . Sultan, one of his venerable sons, and beside him, . . . Sultan, is buried. In the outer court also, there are great numbers of blessed saints buried. May God have mercy on them all.

An Account of the Verification of the Saint's Blessed Efficacy

Your lowly servitor himself and with his own eyes witnessed it, and we have ventured to recount it here that during the previous day's raid and pillaging by the many thousands of despicable and accursed infidels, there was a dull-witted, obstinate and pious detachment of several hundred infidels which came up to the sacred tomb chapel, where they saw a detachment of dervishes standing with hands clasped before them. Since all infidels are believers in this saint, they did not take his followers captive, but many of them fell upon the raw foodstuffs and set their minds to looting various articles from the cellars of the kitchen building and the dervish quarters, and stuffing them in their sacks to carry them off as booty. Now the infidels imagined that mere looting posed no danger of harm to

---

[18] Sura 11, 1. 6.

[19] Chelebi left such spaces for entering information later. He died before doing so.

[20] Muslim holy men, usually Sufis.

those who were carrying off goods and possessions, so a large number of them went in and seized the dishes, stew-pots, kettles and ladles from the kitchen, and some came out wearing the black stew-pots on their heads, on top of their black hats. On seeing this another lot of vicious infidels ventured to enter the blessed shrine itself, where they stole some items of dervish apparatus and some beautiful copies of sacred writ.[21] One infidel, however, made a particular show of defiance by laying his hands on the sacred headdress set up over the blessed head of the saint. At this moment, an aged follower named Suleyman Dede cried out distractedly, "O Saint, why do you lie there? If only you would see what is happening! Where now is the honor of Muhammad."

Glory be to God, as soon as he spoke, there came seven separate flashes and bright tongues of fire which struck each of the seven enemy infidels who were outside the luminous dome. All seven of those wretched unbelievers, condemned to eternal fire, were then destroyed within that brilliant shrine, set burning on the spot, like blackest coals. As for your humble servant, when I arrived to make my pilgrimage to the shrine, the seven human carcasses of those infidels who had been set afire, looking like skins full of black pitch, were lying like refuse under foot in the shade of the cypress trees. Your humble servant, together with my retinue and the dervishes themselves, got ropes around the feet of these stinking infidel carcasses and dragged them off away from the shrine into the open, where we left them, and when the infidels from the city saw these burned infidel cadavers they acquired the most absolute and complete belief in the Sultan Veliüllah.

Many of the other infidels, seeing that these were being burnt black as pitch, dropped the things they had just picked up and ran to tell the others, those who had earlier looted the kitchen of its dishes and pots, about these extremely depressing events. Some of the looters then dropped their booty but others dared to hold on to it and, while the latter were carrying it off, it happened by the will of God that the stew-pots on the heads of those infidels who were wearing them like black hats became suddenly hot. At once their black hair and their black heads began to ignite under their black hats from the red heat of the cooking pots. At this they dropped the pots and ran, but some remained stubbornly determined and carried their booty until their strength was at an end. They passed on their loads to other infidels, but these in turn as their bodies became powerless left the load to be taken up by others and, in the end, whatever they had taken from the shrine of Veliüllah they left strewn around the plain while they rushed onto the ships for dear life, crying out, "Let's be done with it!"

At the same time or just previously we had prevailed against the infidels . . . with what army we had and had made them drop much of their spoils, had freed many prisoners, and had captured forty-five infidel prisoners. And now, glory be to God, all the apparatus and paraphernalia came back to where it belonged.

---

[21] That is, the Koran.

Not a single thing was lost and the worthy dervishes were recently still engaged in the task of putting all the various sorts of dervish apparatus back in their proper places. The significant inference to be drawn from all these noteworthy events is that all the blessed efficacy of the saint as written about in various books of belief is absolutely true. For the soul of the eminent Sheyh Veliüllah and for the souls of his family and his sons, that God may be pleased with them, a recitation of the Fatiha.[22]

Your humble servant spent an evening being entertained by these mendicants at the gates of God and engaging in uplifting conversation. Truly these are an orthodox people here, a community of the purest law and a congregation of poor followers of the truest belief. Their spiritual leader most particularly, that Hafiz Arslan Dede who is their leader in the true way of religious adoration, is the very essence of a dervish who keeps the fast assiduously, in David's manner,[23] and utters an invocation to God in his every breath. . . . He gave us a few dervishes to take along as companions and all of our party bade farewell, but just as we were leaving, there occurred a most extraordinary spectacle as several hundred people of Boudonítza arrived with the judge from Zitúni and began to lay claim to the wealth, the apparatus and the apparel of the dervishes from this chapel.

It would seem that this lot of people from Boudonítza were all of the Greek race, a company of stubborn recusant doubters, and it was alleged that since they did not believe in Sultan Veliúllah or in any other great saints they had appropriated for their own use and enjoyment any number of gardens, orchards and cultivable fields which they treated as their own property. There doubters stated in the judge's presence that the infidel raiders had come and had robbed them and made prisoners of their entire families and households at the same time as they, the infidels, were assaulting the dervishes. They alleged further that, "As the infidels were carrying off your property, they dropped it because it was too heavy a load, but they also dropped our property as well and you, on the pretext that it was all the saint's property, gathered up all our things from the fields and brought them all to this chapel." When they made this claim, the dervishes answered, "Misguided men, the infidels went off with our dervish apparel and the pots and dishes from our kitchen, except that the infidels who came into the shrine and were taking the lamps and candle-holders and the copies of holy writ—those infidels caught fire and are left behind here burned black as cinders."

Now just as they were saying this, one man announced that, "Those Korans are mine, and just such an amount of my belongings was taken," and with that he went straight into the sacred sepulchre and in the presence of the judge and of

---

[22] The first sura of the Koran. It is often recited as an independent prayer.

[23] The Old Testament King David is known in Islam for his great piety.

my humble self, he took three large copies of the Koran from off the reading stand saying, "These are mine."

But just as he was going out the door he was struck down into a neat little heap, and his soul was burned black as hell-fire. The dervishes picked up the holy writings from the spot and put them back where they belonged. Your humble servant was left in a state of rapturous ecstasy, unable to draw breath, but then, together with my servants, we got this doubter's corpse by head and feet, and dragged it out among the above-mentioned infidels' carcasses and left it there. All the people from Boudonítza, on seeing this occurrence, took to their heels.

The poor judge was very distressed to have come from Zitúni, and he too, saying, "Glory be to God," remounted his horse and traced his steps back to Zitúni. There are any number of trustworthy witnesses to the outcome of this matter.

We ourselves, at that very time, mounted our own horses and set out once again from Boudonítza in a southeasterly direction. Taking God as our refuge, we crossed through difficult rocky hills and gulleys and over mountains and valleys and came in 4 hours to Esed Abad.

13

✥

Lo Kuan-chung

THE WATER MARGIN

M ao Tse-tung, leader of the Communist revolution in mid-twentieth-century *China, read and loved* The Water Margin *as a boy. He and many of his comrades, especially in the early 1930s when Communist forces established a besieged state-within-a-state in south central China, saw distinct parallels between their situation and tactics and those of the romanticized outlaw heroes of this Ming Dynasty novel. This is merely one example of the continuing pervasiveness and popularity of the many separate stories contained in the novel across the spectrum of Chinese society.*

As with several others of the great early novels that appeared during the Ming Dynasty (1368–1644), a good deal about The Water Margin *is disputed—its basis in historical fact, its authorship, its definitive contents, even its most apt title in translation. The action of the novel takes place during the reign of the emperor Hui-tsung (1119–1125), last ruler of the Northern Sung Dynasty (960–1126) before it was driven from north China by inner Asian barbarians. Some of the bandit heroes of* The Water Margin, *especially the central character Sung Chiang, may have been historical figures of that period, and several of the novel's episodes may have originated in near-contemporary recitations by the professional storytellers who for centuries have been a feature of Chinese teahouses and wine shops. Dramatic enactments of some of these stories were performed during the Yuan, or Mongol, Dynasty (1271–1368), and the earliest forms of the novel appeared early in the Ming. From that point onward the novel evolved over several centuries into a myriad of different versions which make it difficult to designate one version as definitive and to identify a single author. Ming Dynasty tradition gives principal credit for authorship to two fourteenth-century writers, Shih Nai-an and Lo Kuan-chung, about whose lives little is know. Modern scholars generally reject Shih Nai-an as a coauthor, and some challenge Lo Kuan-chung's authorship. Lo is also traditionally given credit as the author of the* Three Kingdoms *(Selection 8).*

The central thread of the emerging work is the gathering of a group of 108 outlaws in a mountain lair, accessible only by water, at a place called Liangshan-P'o near the juncture of the Grand Canal with the Yellow River in Shantung Province. One version, of seventy-one chapters, brings the story only to the complete gathering of the bandit heroes. Others, of lengths extending up to one hundred twenty-four chapters, carry the story forward to the heroic sacrifice of the bandit gang in a loyal, but futile, defense of the Sung dynasty against other rebels and invading barbarians. Its title in Chinese is Shui-hu chuan, *which can translate literally as* Marsh Chronicles, *but it has been variously translated into English as* The Water Margin, Outlaws of the Marsh *and, in the version excerpted here, by the Nobel laureate American novelist Pearl Buck, as* All Men Are Brothers.

It is tempting and, up to a point, useful to see The Water Margin *as a Chinese counterpart to the Robin Hood tales that originated in medieval England and that also evolved over the centuries to produce a cast of familiar folk heroes. Sung Chiang and at least some of his fellows, like Robin Hood and his "merry men" of Sherwood Forest, are decent, loyal men driven into outlawry by corrupt, vicious public officials. Both bands organize under an acknowledged natural leader, develop a bond of mutual brotherhood, live apart from civil society, rob the rich to sustain themselves and to help the downtrodden, all the while professing their loyalty to proper and righteous authority (King Richard the Lionhearted for Robin Hood, the Emperor Hui-tsung for these Chinese outlaws). The escapades of their respective stories pit the outlaws' wit and daring against the dullness and cowardice of arrogant authorities, often with a hair's breadth escape at the conclusion. Certainly the abiding popularity of these bandit sagas in both the Chinese and English traditions owes much to these shared elements.*

The differences between the two tales are marked and significant, however. As their characterizations have come down to the present age, Robin Hood and his fellows are chivalrous toward women, protective of all who are weaker then themselves, taking human life only in the extremes of combat, never for mere vengeance or the love of killing. By contrast, the portrayal of women is one of the dark sides of The Water Margin. *Although there are three women among the bandit gang, women generally get rough treatment in the novel, often portrayed as faithless schemers who lead good men into trouble. The central character Sung Chiang, for instance, first seriously breaks the law when he discovers that the slave girl he has rescued from poverty has entertained another lover in his bed and, in an uncharacteristic rage, murders her. This act of sudden and bloody violence suggests yet another contrast with the Robin Hood tradition, and points to another dark aspect of* The Water Margin. *While some characters, like Sung Chiang, renowned for his generosity and known by the epithet "The Opportune Rain," are decent men driven to crime, a good many others really are criminal types, and some — such as Li K'uei, "The Black Whirlwind" of the following excerpt — are simply killing machines who run amok from time to time. Even those who appear in the robes of Buddhist or Taoist monks are no jovial souls like Robin Hood's Friar Tuck, but turn out to be bloodthirsty louts disguised in clerical garb.*

These "dark" elements of The Water Margin *have long prompted the question of why it has remained so popular in a state and society dominated by the Confucian respect for authority and propriety. The question may, in some measure, answer itself. The Confucian demand for order has always been potentially repressive in Chinese private life and has, at times, provided a moralistic cloak for outright oppression in the life of the state. Confucius himself and his disciples through the ages have generally recognized a virtual right of revolution against unjust authority, but Chinese historical experience has made it clear that such revolution will almost inevitably be violent. Mao Tse-tung and the soldiers of the People's Liberation Army, fighting what they regarded as a corrupt and tyrannous government, could see themselves prefigured in the outlaws of* The Water Margin, *even to the extremes of vengeful violence.*

The passage excerpted here displays both the brighter and darker sides of The Water Margin, *and clearly demonstrates the dramatic suspense which these stories can generate. It is reminiscent of an episode from the Robin Hood tales in which Robin is rescued from public execution at the last minute by the daring intervention of his comrades. Here Sung Chiang, already branded and exiled for the murder of his concubine, has been further charged with fomenting rebellion because of an innocent poem he scrawled on a tavern wall in an hour of drunkenness. He is condemned to public beheading along with a former jailer, named Tai Chung, who had earlier tried to help him escape. The rescue is exciting in its careful arrangement, but becomes horribly and quite needlessly bloody as it is carried out.*

From Chapter XXXIX.

The heroes from the robbers' lair make a rescue at the execution grounds.
They gather at the Temple to the White Dragon.

It is said:

On the next day the magistrate ascended to his hall and he commanded a court scribe to come forward and he bade him write down the report of this matter [of the guilt of Sung Chiang and Tai Chung] with all speed, and he commanded that all the head jailer's confession and Sung Chiang's also should be attached to it. On the other hand the accusation against them was to be written out with the order that on the next day the pair should be beheaded in the streets. From ancient times there need be no delay in killing a revolutionist, and if these two were killed it would spare all later trouble.

Now the scribe was one named Huang and he was a close friend of Tai Chung. But he had no way to save him and he could but cry out bitterness for him. On this day, however, he said humbly to the magistrate, "Tomorrow is a memorial day for the nation. The day after is the fifteenth day of the seventh month, and it is the mid-festival. On these two days men may not be killed. On the third day is a national holiday. Only on the fifth day may men be killed."

Outside of this the scribe Huang had no other good way, except to give Tai Chung a few days longer to live. This was, moreover, a common habit with him when men were condemned to death. When the magistrate heard it he did according to these words.

But on the morning of the sixth day he sent men to the cross roads and he commanded them to sweep and put in order the execution grounds. After the early morning the magistrate appointed soldiers and armed guards and executioners, in all some five hundred men, and they all waited at the gate of the great jail. It was mid-morning. The chief warden of the jail then said that the magistrate himself would come to be the supervisor of the execution. The scribe Huang had no recourse, therefore, except to present to the magistrate the accusation he had written upon the two tablets and the magistrate set upon each the sign "Behead." The tablets were then fastened to a reed mat.

Now all the wardens and guards in the jail were friendly to Sung Chiang and to Tai Chung but there was no way by which they could now save them. They could but cry bitterness for them, and the prisoners were prepared to come forth and they were tied with ropes and bound. Their hair was pasted close to their heads and knotted upon their crowns in the shape of a horn. Into each knot was thrust a red flower. They then took the pair and brought them before the blue-faced god of the jail and there by the altar they gave to them a bowl of rice for eternal rest and the cup of wine for eternal farewell.

When they had eaten and drunk they left the altar and they were turned about and forced along. Some fifty or sixty soldiers of the jail surrounded Sung Chiang in front and Tai Chung behind and thus they pushed them to the front of the jail. Sung Chiang and Tai Chung, the pair of them, stared at each other and neither could speak a word. Sung Chiang could but stamp his foot from time to time and Tai Chung hung his head and sighed. All the people of [the town of] Chiang Chou who came to watch were pressed breast to back and shoulder to shoulder and there were many more than a thousand or two.

Thus the two were forced to the cross roads where the place of execution was and they were walled about by the weapons of the soldiers. Sung Chiang they placed with his face to the south and his back to the north, and Tai Chung they placed with his face to the north and his back to the south. Then they forced them to sit and they waited for the time after noon when the executioner was to come to kill them.

And the crowd lifted their heads to read the tablets whereon were written the accusation against the two and it said, "The revolutionist in Chiang Chou, Sung Chiang, who willfully wrote a poem to overturn the state and stirred up wild talk to make people afraid, who joined himself to the robbers in the lair at Liangshan P'o that they might all join together in revolution. According to law, he is to be beheaded."

For Tai Chung the accusation read, "The prisoner, Tai Chung, who . . . went and enticed out the robbers at Liangshan P'o that joined together they might all cause revolution. According to law he is to be beheaded. The superintendent of the execution is one surnamed Ts'ai."

And the magistrate reined in his horse and waited for one to tell him when the hour of death was come.

Now there were certain beggars who were snake charmers and with their snakes they were bent upon forcing a way through the crowd to see what was to be seen and although the soldiers beat them they would not go away. In the midst of the confusion there was to the west of the execution ground a group of wandering medicine vendors and tricksters with weapons also forcing their way in. The soldiers shouted out, "Such as you do know nothing at all! What sort of a place do you think this is that you come forcing your way in to see?"

Then those tricksters answered, "You are accursed fools yourselves! To what town and city and place have we not run? We have seen men killed everywhere. Even if the Emperor killed men in the capital we could see it! In this little small city of yours you think because you kill two men that you shake the whole earth! And if we push in to see, well, and what of it?"

Even as they were thus quarreling with the soldiers the master of the execution grounds shouted out, "Drive them away—do not let them in!"

Before the confusion was over there was seen to come from the south of the execution grounds a group of porters bearing loads and also pushing their way into the crowd. The soldiers shouted, "This is a place where men are to be killed—what are you doing here carrying loads?"

The men answered, "We are carrying things for the magistrate. How dare you stop us?"

The soldiers said, "Even though it were the men out of the court itself they must needs pass by another way than this today."

Then the men put their loads down and they freed their carrying poles[1] from the ropes and each man held his pole in his hand and they stood among the crowd and stared.

---

[1] A stout bamboo pole, four to five feet long, borne on the shoulder, from either end of which a load is suspended. Freed of the loads, the carrying pole makes a handy weapon, not unlike the quarter-stave carried by Robin Hood and his men.

Then to the north of the execution ground a party of merchants was seen to come with two carts of goods and they, too, were bent on pushing their way into the beheading place. And again the soldiers shouted out, "Whither do you men go?"

And the travelers answered, saying, "We are passing on our journey. Pray make a way for us."

But the soldiers said, "This is a place where men are to be killed. How can we let you pass? If you are on your journey, pass by another way."

The travelers laughed at this, saying, "You speak well, truly! We are men from the capital and we do not know your accursed roads and we will pass by this highway."

But how could the soldiers allow them to pass? The travelers, however, stood solidly together and did not move. The confusion on the four sides was now without bounds and the magistrate himself could not control it. Then the travelers were seen to climb up upon their carts and there they fixed themselves to see.

In a short time the people in the center of the beheading place divided and one man came forth and said in one shout, "Half after noon!"

The master of the execution said, "When they are killed, then report to me."

Then the soldiers who stood guard with their weapons and the executioners went to the prisoners to unlock their racks, and the executioners held their swords ready. To tell of it is slow. But when the travelers on the cart heard the magistrate say the word "Behead," there was one among them who took out of the bosom of this robe a small drum and he put it down upon the cart and beat it twice or thrice resonantly. On all four sides movement began, and it was swift. For there was seen in the upper storey of a tea house there at the cross roads a great black[2] tigerish fellow who was stark naked and who held in either hand a curved broadaxe. He gave a loud bellow and it was as though a crack of thunder burst from the sky. He leaped down out of midair and lifted his arms and brought the axes down and the two executioners lay dead. Then he turned toward the magistrate's horse.

When the solders rushed forward to attack him with their spears, how could they withstand him? The magistrate and those who surrounded him had already run for their lives. Then the snake charmers to the east were seen to bring knives out of their girdles and when they saw a soldier they killed him. Those who were weapon tricksters . . . ran shouting wildly, and they killed everywhere. In the shortest possible time the soldiers and the jail guards were killed.

The porters to the south lifted up their carrying poles and struck upright and crosswise blows and they knocked over soldiers and onlookers. The travelers to the north all leaped down from their carts and pushed the carts so [as] to form a

---

[2] Numbers of the outlaw heroes, including Sung Chiang himself, are described as "black," indicating merely that they were relatively dark-complexioned. Among them it seemed to be a desirable characteristic, suggesting greater ferociousness.

barricade. Two of the travelers pushed their way into the crowd and one took Sung Chiang on his back and the other took up Tai Chung. As for the others, they drew out their bows and arrows and there were some who had stones and threw them and there were some with darts. . . . Sixteen chiefs of the robber's lair were there and with the robbers they led there were more than a hundred men, and they fell to killing on all four sides.

Then that great black fellow was seen in the crowd swinging his broadaxes this way and that heedlessly. But Ch'ao Kai[3] and his comrades did not know him; only they saw he put forth more strength than any one of them and killed more than any of them. Then Ch'ao Kai suddenly thought to himself, "Tai Chung once spoke of The Black Whirlwind Li K'uei and that he was a good friend of Sung Chiang's. He is a coarse fellow, too." And Ch'ao Kai called out, "Is not that good fellow there in front The Black Whirlwind?"

But how could that fellow be willing to answer? Leaping like a flame of fire he fell upon men here and there and everywhere. Then Ch'ao Kai called to the two robbers who carried Sung Chiang and Tai Chung that they were to follow that big black fellow.

So they all left the cross roads and as they went they did not care whether they met soldiers or officials or people, they felled them all to the earth. The blood ran in a river and the ones that were speared and felled were beyond counting. The chieftains left their carts and their burdens and the whole crowd followed after the big black fellow and they slaughtered their way out of the city. . . .

And the big black fellow killed his way straight to the river's edge and his body was covered with blood. Yet even there at the river's edge he still killed on. Then Ch'ao, holding his sword, cried out, "This matter has naught to do with the people! Do not keep on killing them, therefore!"

But how could that fellow be willing to hear what Ch'ao Kai called? With every blow of an axe he struck a man down. He had gone thus some miles along the river's edge when ahead of him suddenly stretched the expanse of the river, its waters rough, and there was no further road upon the land. Ch'ao Kai, seeing it, could but cry out bitterness. Only then did the big black fellow call out, "Do not fear! Bring our elder brothers hither into the temple!"

When they all came to see, there was a great temple there beside the river and the two sides of the gate were closely fastened shut. The big black fellow struck it open with a blow of his two axes and he rushed inside. As Ch'ao Kai and the others watched they saw on both sides very ancient juniper and pine trees which cast

---

[3] Ch'ao Kai is, at this point, the leader of the Liangshan outlaws, known by the epithet "The Heavenly King." His personal bravery and leadership ability make him a major, and basically sympathetic, character. After his death in battle later in the novel, Sung Chiang succeeds him as bandit chief.

their shade over the temple, and above the gate were four great characters written in gold, and they said, "Temple To The White Dragon."

And the robbers carried Sung Chiang and Tai Chung into the temple and there put them down. Only then did Sung Chiang dare to open his eyes. He saw Ch'ao Kai and the others and he began to weep and to say, "Elder Brother,[4] are we not meeting in a dream?"

Then Ch'ao Kai exhorted him, saying, "Gracious Brother, you would not stay in our mountain and so you have met today's bitterness. Who is this strong, murderous fellow?"

Sung Chiang said, "This is The Black Whirlwind Li K'uei. Several times he would have freed me out of the jail but I was afraid I could not escape and I would not let him have his way."

Ch'ao Kai said, "It would be hard to find a man like this; he has put forth such mighty strength and he does not fear knife or axe or arrow or dart." . . .

Even as they met together here Li K'uei was seen coming out of the veranda bearing his two axes and Sung Chiang called out, saying, "Brother, whither do you go?"

Liu K'uei answered, saying, "I am seeking the priests of this temple that I may kill them all together. The cursed things, afraid of every god and devil, went and locked the temple gates in the day! I will drag them hither and sacrifice them to the gate! But I cannot find the things!"

But Sung Chiang said, "Pray come first and meet with my elder brothers the chiefs."

Now Li K'uei heard this and he dropped his two axes and came and knelt before Ch'ao Kai and he said, "Elder Brother, do not blame the coarse and stupid Iron Ox." And then he met them all. He recognized Chu Kuei as a man of his own region and the two of them were mightily pleased. Then Hua Yung said, "Elder Brother, you told us all only to follow our brother Li K'uei. Now we have come here and ahead of us a great river prevents us and there is no way to go, nor is there a ship come to meet us. What if the soldiers come out of the city to pursue and kill us? How can we then withstand them? How can we reinforce ourselves?"

Then Li K'uei said, "Do not hurry. I will go with you and kill our way into the city again and we will kill that accursed Ts'ai magistrate and all his men, and then our hearts can be happy."

---

[4] The outlaws recognize themselves as a brotherhood and often utter the Confucian phrase "All men are brothers," which gives Pearl Buck the title of this translation. But beyond this is the remarkable adherence of even the roughest of these men to traditional Chinese forms of courtesy—deeply venerating their fathers, deferring to one another as "elder brother," and performing the ritual prostrations before a respected fellow outlaw.

Now Tai Chung came to himself again and he called out, "Brother, your coarse temper will not do here. There are five or seven thousand horsemen in the city. If you slaughter your way back into the city, surely all will be lost."

Then Juan The Seventh said, "We can see several boats in the distance across the river. We three brothers [5] will swim across the water and seize these boats and bring them here and ferry you all over. How is this?"

And Ch'ao Kai answered, "This is the best way of all."

Then the three Juan brothers stripped themselves free of their clothing except their girdles and into this each man thrust a dagger and they leaped into the water. When they had swum perhaps a sixth of a mile they saw up the river three rowboats approaching them. As they came the boatmen whistled and called, and the boats flew swift as the wind. As they all watched they saw on each boat some ten-odd men and they all held weapons in their hands. They all began to be stirred in fear.

Now Sung Chiang heard this inside the temple and he said, "How can my life be so destined for such bitterness as this!" and as he hastened out of the temple to see, he saw sitting upon the foremost boat a huge fellow who held downwards a glittering five-pronged fork. About his head was wound into the knot of his hair a red cord. Upon his lower person were trousers of white silk to use in the water. He blew a whistle in his mouth. Sung Chiang, seeing this, knew he was no other than Chang Shun and in great haste Sung Chiang beckoned to him and called, "Brother, save me!"

When Chang Shun and the others with him saw it was Sung Chiang he cried out loudly, "Truly it is well!" and as though they flew they rowed to shore.

When the three Juans saw them they swam back and everyone came from the boats and went to the temple, and Sung Chiang saw Chang Shun and the ranks of good strong men with him. . . . Chang Shun saw Sung Chiang and his happiness was as though it had dropped down from Heaven, and weeping he made obeisance and he said, "Ever since my elder brother was under court arrest I have not sat or stood in peace. Yet I had no way whereby to save you. Today I heard the Tai Chung was also taken, and I did not meet Li K'uei either. I could but go and seek out my elder brother and take him to the village of the old lord Mu. There we called many such as we knew and today we were just about to fight our way to Chiang Chou and were going to force our way into the jail and rescue you. I did not dream that you, our Elder Brother, had already good fellows to save you and bring you hither. I do not dare to ask who all these braves are, but must this not be that righteous one of Liangshan P'o, The Heavenly King Ch'ao?"

---

[5] The Juan brothers are watermen from the lake which surrounds Liangshan P'o. They are prominent in a number of episodes, most notably one earlier in the novel in which a military force sent to arrest the outlaws is drawn into the marshes and annihilated.

And Sung Chiang pointed to the one standing above and said, "This one is indeed our elder brother Ch'ao Kai. All of you come hither into the temple and do him reverence." . . .

At this time these twenty-nine good fellows each performed the rites of courtesy. Then a robber was seen coming in the greatest haste to the temple to make a report, saying, "Drums are beating and gongs sounding in the city of Chiang Chou, and horses and men are prepared to come in pursuit! Far, far off we can see the great flags hiding the sun, and swords and arrows are like flax standing in the field. Before are horsemen on armored horses and behind are the soldiers with weapons and their captains. They have great knives and great axes and they are coming to do battle at The White Dragon Temple!"

Li K'uei heard this and he gave a great shout, "We will go and kill them!" And he took up his two broadaxes and rushed out of the temple.

Then Ch'ao Kai called out, "Since the first step is taken the second must follow! All of you good fellows help me who am surnamed Ch'ao! We must kill every soldier and horse of Chiang Chou! Only then can we return to our lair!"

And all the heroes rose together and answered, "We will all obey your command!"

And the hundred and forty or fifty men all shouted together and they rushed to the shore of the river.

Because of this the waves were dyed red and the dead men heaped up like mountains.

> Leaping over waves, the sky-blue dragons sent forth their fiery breath.
> Mountain-climbing tigers, the fierce ones, breathed out their windy
>   gales of death.

How, then, did Ch'ao Kai and all these good fellows leave Chiang Chou? Pray hear it told in the next chapter.[6]

---

[6] Chapters of *The Water Margin* all begin with the phrase "It is said . . ." and end with the formula seen here: a predicament, an ambivalent prophetic two-line verse, the question of how things will turn out, and the sentence, "Pray hear it told in the next chapter."

14

❧

Matsuo Basho

THE NARROW ROAD
TO THE INTERIOR

Matsuo Basho (1644–1694) can well lay claim to be the foremost master of haiku poetry, one of the world's great travel diarists, and, among Japanese, the most beloved of all writers. Basho is actually his pen name, derived from the bashoan, or plantain tree, which grew by the huts that he inhabited in the Edo area (modern Tokyo) during his mature years. He was born early in the Edo period (1603–1868), an era that took its name from the locus of real military and political power in that city. It was a period of internal peace and relative isolation that produced a rich development of Japanese culture in all its forms. Son of a minor samurai (the hereditary warrior class), at nine Basho entered the service of the local lord as a study companion to the lord's young son as they both learned the craft of poetry. After the lord's son died, Basho fled to the old capital at Kyoto, then in 1672 moved on to Edo, headquarters of the Shogun (military ruler). Edo remained Basho's home base until his death.

He soon won recognition among critics and his circle of poet friends for his skill in composing renga, or linked verse, and what in his age were called hokku, or as they are now universally known, haiku. Although modern Japanese poets sometimes say that "Haiku began and ended with Basho," that claim is more compliment than fact. The traditional brief lyric in Japan had been the tanka, a poem of thirty-one syllables, arranged in five lines of five, seven, five, seven, and seven syllables (see Volume II, Selection 21, The Manyoshu). However the popularity among circles of witty, literate men and women of spontaneously creating linked verses called for a shorter form. The linked verses of renga divided the tanka into units of seventeen and fourteen syllables, composed by different authors. It was from the opening lines of the renga that hokku, or haiku, was born, a seventeen syllable poem arranged in three lines of five, seven, and five syllables. Basho did not invent the form, but out of the depths of his knowledge of Japanese *and Chinese poetry and out of his Zen sensibility to nature and essential simplicity, he refined it to gemlike purity and brilliance.*

He saw clearly that in such a compressed form the reader has to complete the poem—find its inner truth—out of his or her own knowledge and imagination. But he also realized that the poet's task is to make the reader's leap to completion both possible and rewarding. His best known haiku *is often cited as an example of the way in which a mood is established by a clear natural image, then altered subtly but profoundly:*

furuike ya	An old pond, silent.
kawazu tobikomu	A frog leaps in.
mizu no oto	The water's splash.

(This is the editor's adaptation from several translations. The seventeen syllables of Japanese are often of varied number in translation.) The poem uses these homely images to suggest the intersection of the timeless (the still pond) with the momentary (the splash of water). Another example, from the following selection, presents a different, but no less subtle, insight inspired by a visit to a ruined castle from the age of Japan's medieval warfare:

Summer grasses:
all that remains of great soldiers'
imperial dreams.

At the age of forty Basho visited his home town of Ueno, roughly thirty miles southeast of Kyoto, a journey that gave rise to the first of what became a series of poetic travel journals. Each was based on a walking tour that included visits to places of great natural beauty, Buddhist and Shinto shrines, sites of notable events from both history and literature, the homes or haunts of great writers of the past, and sociable meetings with contemporary poets and patrons. Basho composed exquisite haiku *in response to these travel experiences. The best known and loved of these poetic rambles was based on a foot journey Basho took in 1689, accompanied by his friend and fellow poet Iwanami Sora. It was the longest and most adventurous of Basho's journeys, and its inverted U-shaped track through northern Honshu (Japan's main island) is worth tracing on a map of modern Japan. From what is now Tokyo they followed an inland route northward for almost two hundred miles, reaching the Pacific coast at Shiogama. They crossed Honshu at one of its narrowest northern passages to Kisakata (modern Sakata), then followed the coast of the Sea of Japan southward to a point west of Tokyo, finally turning inland to Ogaki. All-in-all, it had been a long, hard trek for two men no longer young and in frail health.*

Basho polished his account of the tour continuously until his death in 1694, making it as much a conscious poetic and philosophical journey as it is a traveler's tale. We know from Sora's diary, published only in modern times, that Basho invented, omitted, and rearranged some passages of the work he titled Oku no Hosomichi. *This is sometimes translated as* The Narrow Road to the North, *but the translator of this selection prefers* The Narrow Road to the Interior, *seeing a double play on the "interior" of northern Honshu and the inward journey of the poet himself.*

Basho leaves a trail of place names as well as literary and historical allusions through his account of this journey. He could be confident that Japanese readers in his own day would catch these references. No attempt has been made here to identify them all. However, in the following excerpts, the editor has sought to supply through footnotes at least a minimum of the information needed to clarify the text.

The moon and sun are eternal travelers. Even the years wander on. A lifetime adrift in a boat, or in old age leading a tired horse into the years, every day is a journey, and the journey itself is home. From the earliest times there have always been some who perished along the road. Still I have always been drawn by wind-blown clouds into dreams of a lifetime of wandering. Coming home from a year's walking tour of the coast last autumn, I swept the cobwebs from my hut on the banks of the Sumida just in time for New Year, but by the time spring mists began to rise from the fields, I longed to cross the Shirakawa Barrier[1] into the Northern Interior. Drawn by the wanderer-spirit Dōsojin, I couldn't concentrate on things. Mending my cotton pants, sewing a new strap on my bamboo hat, I daydreamed. Rubbing moxa[2] into my legs to strengthen them, I dreamed a bright moon rising over Matsushima. So I placed my house in another's hands and moved to my patron Mr. Sampū's summer house in preparation for my journey. And I left a verse by my door:

> Even this grass hut
> may be transformed
> into a doll's house

From *The Essential Basho,* translated by Sam Hamill, copyright © 1998. Reprinted by arrangement with Shambhala Publications, Inc., Boston. Pp. 3–8, 12–13, 15–20, 23, 26–33, 35–36.

[1] Various barriers are mentioned in the text. These were essentially police checkpoints through which all travelers had to pass.

[2] The leaf of the *artemisiia moxa* plant, dried and burned next to the skin, was long believed in east Asia to have curative powers.

Very early on the twenty-seventh morning of the third moon, under a predawn haze, transparent moon barely visible, Mount Fuji just a shadow, I set out under the cherry blossoms of Ueno and Yanaka. When would I see them again? A few old friends had gathered in the night and followed along far enough to see me off from the boat. Getting off at Senju, I felt three thousand miles rushing through my heart, the whole world only a dream. I saw it through farewell tears.

> Spring passes
> and the birds cry out — tears
> in the eyes of fishes

With these first words from my brush, I started. Those who remain behind watch the shadow of a traveler's back disappear.

• • •

The last night of the third moon, an inn at the foot of Mount Nikkō. The innkeeper is called Hotoke Gozaemon, "Joe Buddha." He says his honesty earned him the name and invites me to make myself at home. A merciful buddha suddenly appearing like an ordinary man to help a pilgrim along his way, his simplicity's great gift, his sincerity unaffected. A model of Confucian rectitude, my host is a bodhisattva.

• • •

Mount Kurokami still clothed in snow, faint in the mist, Sora wrote:

> Head shaven
> at Black Hair Mountain
> we change into summer clothes

Sora was named Kawai Sogoro. Sora's his nom de plume. At my old home — called Bashō-an [plantain tree hermitage] — he carried water and wood. Anticipating the pleasures of seeing Matsushima and Kisagata, we agreed to share the journey, pleasure and hardship alike. The morning we started, he put on Buddhist robes, shaved his head, and changed his name to Sogo, the Enlightened. So the "changing clothes" in his poem is pregnant with meaning.[3]

A hundred yards uphill, the waterfall plunged a hundred feet from its cavern in the ridge, falling into a basin made by a thousand stones. Crouched in the cavern behind the falls, looking out, I understood why it's called Urami-no-Taki [View-from-behind Falls].

---

[3] Basho and Sora dressed as Buddhist priests partly to symbolize the spiritual nature of their journey, but also for the very practical reasons that priests had an easier time passing the barriers and were less likely to fall prey to robbers.

Stopped awhile
inside a waterfall—
summer retreat begins

A friend lives in Kurobane on the far side of the broad Nasu Moor. Tried a short-cut running straight through, but it began to rain in the early evening, so we stopped for the night at a village farmhouse and continued again at dawn. Out in the field, a horse, and nearby a man cutting grass. I stopped to ask directions. Courteous, he thought awhile, then said, "Too many intersecting roads. It's easy to get lost. Best to take that old horse as far as he'll go. He knows the road. When he stops, get off, and he'll come back alone."

Two small children danced along behind, one with the curious name of Kasane, same as the pink flower. Sora wrote:

With this *kasane*
she's doubly pink
a fitting name

Arriving at a village, I tied a small gift to the saddle, and the horse turned back.

• • •

Not far from the temple in a mountain hermitage near Ungan Temple, my dharma master Butchō[4] wrote:

A five-foot thatched hut—
I wouldn't even put it up
but for falling rain

He inscribed the poem on a rock with charcoal—he told me long ago. Curious, several young people joined in, walking sticks pointed toward Ungan Temple. We were so caught up in talking we arrived at the temple unexpectedly. Through the long valley, under dense cedar and pine with dripping moss, below a cold spring sky—through the viewing gardens, we crossed a bridge and entered the temple gate.

I searched out back for Butchō's hermitage and found it up the hill, near a cave on a rocky ridge—like the cave where Myozenji lived for fifteen years, like Zen master Houn's retreat.

Even woodpeckers
leave it alone—hermitage
in a summer grove

---

[4] Basho studied Zen Buddhism (See Volume II, Selection 28) under Butchō between 1673 and 1684.

One small poem, quickly written, pinned to a post.

• • •

Through narrow Abumizuri Pass and on, passing Shiroishi Castle, we entered Kasashima Province. We asked for directions to the grave-mound of Lord Sanekata, Sei Shonagon's[5] exiled poet-lover, and were told to turn right on the hills near the villages of Minowa and Kasashima when we came to the shrine of Dōsojin. It lies nearly hidden in sedge grass Saigyō[6] remembered in a poem. May rains turned the trail to mud. We stopped, sick and worn out, and looked at the two aptly named villages in the distance: Straw Raincoat Village and Umbrella Island.

> Where's Kasashima?
> Lost in the rainy season
> on a muddy road

The night was spent in Iwanuma.

• • •

We stopped along the Tama River at Noda, and at the huge stone in the lake, Oki-no-ishi, both made famous in poems. On Mount Sue-no-matsu, we found a temple called Masshozan. There were graves everywhere among the pines, underscoring Po Chu-i's famous lines quoted in *The Tale of Genji,*[7] "wing and wing, branch and branch," and I thought, "Yes, what we all must come to," my sadness heavy.

At Shiogama Beach, a bell sounded evening. The summer rain-sky cleared to reveal a pale moon high over Magaki Island. I remembered the "fishing boats pulling together" in a *Kokinshū*[8] poem, and understood it clearly for the first time.

---

[5] See Volume II, Selection 26.

[6] Saigyō (1118–1190) is frequently mentioned and quoted in *Narrow Road*. He had been a samurai but at the age of twenty-three left the court to become a wandering poet. Basho took both Saigyō's nature poetry and his life as models.

[7] This is a good example of the multilayered literary allusions which came readily to Basho's mind. No educated Japanese could travel without being reminded of scenes from the great eleventh-century novel, *The Tale of Genji* (see Volume II, Selection 27), in which many of the characters, like Basho in his time, knew and could quote the T'ang Dynasty Chinese poet, Po Chu-i (See Volume II, Selection 18).

[8] The *Kokinshū*, published in the early tenth century, was one of the great poetry anthologies compiled by imperial decree.

Along the Michinoku
everyplace is wonderful,
but in Shiogama
fishing boats pulling together
are most amazing of all.

That night we were entertained by a blind singer playing a lute to boisterous back-country ballads one hears only deep inside the country, not like the *Tale of the Heike*[9] songs or the dance songs. A real earful, but pleased to hear the tradition continued.

• • •

Sun high overhead before we left the shrine, we hired a boat to cross to Matsushima, a mile or more away. We disembarked on Ojima Beach.

As many others often observed, the views of Matsushima take one's breath away. It may be—along with Lake Tung-t'ing and West Lake in China—the most beautiful place in the world. Islands in a three-mile bay, the sea to the southeast entering like flood tide on the Ch'ien-t'ang River in Chekiang. Small islands, tall islands pointing at the sky, islands on top of islands, islands like mothers with baby islands on their backs, islands cradling islands in the bay. All covered with deep green pines shaped by salty winds, trained into sea-wind bonsai. Here one is almost overcome by the sense of intense feminine beauty in a shining world. It must have been the mountain god Oyamazumi who made this place. And whose words or brush could adequately describe a world so divinely inspired?

Ojima Beach is not—as its name implies—an island, but a strand projected into the bay. Here one finds the ruins of Ungo Zenji's hermitage and the rock where he sat *zazen*.[10] And still a few tiny thatched huts under pines where religious hermits live in tranquility. Smoke of burning leaves and pine cones drew me on, touching something deep inside. Then the moon rose, shining on the sea, day turned suddenly to night. We stayed at an inn on the shore, our second-story windows opening on the bay. Drifting with winds and clouds, it was almost like a dream. Sora wrote:

In Matsushima
you'll need the wings of a crane
little cuckoo

---

[9] See the headnote to Selection 9, *Atsumori*.

[10] Sitting *zazen* is the Zen Buddhist practice of meditation designed to lead to sudden enlightenment.

I was speechless and tried to sleep, but rose to dig from my pack a Chinese-style poem my friend Sodo had written for me, something about Pine Islands. And also a *waka* by Hara Anteki, and haiku by Sampū and Jokushi.

. . .

Here [at Hiraizumi] three generations of the Fujiwara clan passed as though in a dream.[11] The great outer gates lay in ruins. Where Hidehira's manor stood, rice fields grew. Only Mount Kinkei remained. I climbed the hill where Yoshitsune died; I saw the Kitakami, a broad stream flowing down through the Nambu Plain, the Koromo River circling Izumi Castle below the hill before joining the Kitakami. The ancient ruins of Yasuhira—from the end of the Golden Era—lie out beyond the Koromo Barrier, where they stood guard against the Ainu people. The faithful elite remained bound to the castle—for all their valor, reduced to ordinary grass. To Fu[12] wrote:

> The whole country devastated
> only mountains and rivers remain
> In springtime, at the ruined castle,
> the grass is always green.

We sat a while, our hats for a seat, seeing it all through tears.

> Summer grasses:
> all that remains of great soldiers'
> imperial dreams

Sora wrote

> Kanefusa's
> own white hair
> seen in blossoming briar

. . .

The road through the Nambu Plain visible in the distance, we stayed the night in Iwate, then trudged on past Cape Oguro and Mizu Island, both along the river. Beyond Narugo Hot Springs, we crossed Shitomae Barrier and entered

---

[11] Basho and Sora are visiting the ruins of castles which date from a period in the early to mid-twelfth century, when a trio of able leaders had established a brief era of stability known thereafter as the Golden Age of the North. It ended in fratricidal violence.

[12] Tu Fu, the great Chinese poet of the T'ang Dynasty, lived, suffered through, and wrote about a terrible civil war in this own lifetime. He is another Chinese poet whom Basho greatly admired. See Volume II, Selection 18.

Dewa Province. Almost no one comes this way, and the barrier guards were suspicious, slow, and thorough. Delayed, we climbed a steep mountain in falling dark, and took refuge in a guardshack. A heavy storm pounded the shack with wind and rain for three miserable days.

> Eaten alive by
> lice and fleas — now the horse
> beside my pillow pees

> • • •

Climbed Mount Haguro on the third day of the sixth moon and, with the help of a friend who dyes cloth for mountain monks' robes, Zushi Sakichi, obtained an audience with the abbot of Gongen Shirne, Master Egaku, who greeted us warmly. He arranged for quarters at nearby South Valley Temple. The next day we met at the main temple to write haiku:

> The winds that blow
> through South Valley Temple
> are sweetened by snow

> • • •

After all the breathtaking views of rivers and mountains, lands and seas, after everything we'd seen, thoughts of seeing Kisakata's famous bay still made my heart begin to race. Twenty miles north of Sakata Harbor, as we walked the sandy shore beneath mountains where sea winds wander, a storm came up at dusk and covered Mount Chōkai in mist and rain reminiscent of Su Tung-p'o's famous poem. We made our way in the dark, hoping for a break in the weather, groping on until we found a fisherman's shack. By dawn the sky had cleared, sun dancing on the harbor. We took a boat for Kisakata, stopping by the priest Nōin's island retreat, honoring his three-year seclusion. On the opposite shore we saw the ancient cherry tree Saigyō saw reflected and immortalized, "Fishermen row over blossoms."

Near the shore, Empress Jingū's[13] tomb. And Kammanju Temple. Did the empress ever visit? Why is she buried here?

Sitting in the temple chamber with the blinds raised, we saw the whole lagoon, Mount Chōkai holding up the heavens inverted on the water. To the west the road leads to the Muyamuya Barrier; to the east it curves along a bank toward Akita; to the north, the sea comes in on tide flats at Shiogoshi. The whole lagoon, though only a mile or so across, reminds one of Matsushima, although Matsushima seems much more contented, whereas Kisakata seems bereaved. A

---

[13] Empress Jingū's dates are uncertain, but are probably late fourth century.

sadness maybe in its sense of isolation here where nature's darker spirits hide—like a strange and beautiful woman whose heart has been broken

> Kisakata rain:
> the legendary beauty Seishi
> wrapped in sleeping leaves

> At the Shallows
> the long-legged crane cool,
> stepping in the sea

Sora wrote:

> Kisakata Festival—
> at holy feasts, what specialties
> do the locals eat?

The merchant Teiji from Minō Province wrote:

> Fishermen sit
> on their shutters on the sand
> enjoying cool evening

Sora found an osprey nest in the rocks:

> May the ocean resist
> violating the vows
> of the osprey's nest

• • •

Today we came through places with names like Children-Desert-Parents, Lost Children, Send-Back-the-Dog, Turn-Back-the-Horse, some of the most fearsomely dangerous places in all the North Country. And well named. Weakened and exhausted, I went to bed early, but was roused by the voices of two young women in the room next door. Then an old man's voice joined theirs. They were prostitutes from Niigata in Echigo Province and were on their way to Ise Shrine in the south, the old man seeing them off at this barrier, Ichiburi. He would turn back to Niigata in the morning, carrying their letters home. One girl quoted the *Shinkokinshū*[14] poem, "On the beach where white waves fall, / we all wander like children into every circumstance, / carried forward every day . . ." And as they bemoaned their fate in life, I fell asleep.

In the morning, preparing to leave, they came to ask directions. "May we follow along behind?" they asked. "We're lost and not a little fearful. Your robes

---

[14] The *Shinkokinshū* was the last of the great imperial anthologies, published in 1439. For Basho it was the primary source of this knowledge of Saigyō's verse.

bring the spirit of the Buddha to our journey." They had mistaken us for priests. "Our way includes detours and retreats," I told them. "But follow anyone on this road and the gods will see you through." I hated to leave them in tears, and thought about them hard for a long time after we left. I told Sora, and he wrote down:

> Under one roof,
> courtesans and monks asleep—
> moon and bush clover

• • •

At a village called Komatsu:

> Aptly named Komatsu,
> Child Pine, a breeze blows over
> pampas and clover

Here we visited Tada Shrine to see Sanemori's[15] helmet and a piece of his brocade armor-cloth presented to him by Lord Yoshitomo when he served the Genji clan. His helmet was no common soldier's gear: engraved with chrysanthemums and ivy from eyehole to earflap, crowned with a dragon's head between two horns. After Sanemori died on the battlefield, Kiso Yoshinaka sent it with a prayer, hand-carried to the shrine by Higuchi Jirō, Sanemori's friend. The story's inscribed on the shrine.

> Pitifully—under
> a great soldier's empty helmet,
> a cricket sings

• • •

Sora, suffering from persistent stomach ailments, was forced to return to his relatives in Nagashima in Ise Province. His parting words:

> Sick to the bone
> if I should fall, I'll lie
> in fields of clover

He carries his pain as he goes, leaving me empty. Like paired geese parting in the clouds.

> Now falling autumn dew
> obliterates my hatband's
> "We are two"

---

[15] Sanemori was one of the young warriors who died heroically in the wars between the Minamoto (Genji) and Taira clans in the twelfth century.

• • •

At the Echizen Province border, at an inlet town called Yoshizaki, I hired a boat and sailed for the famous pines of Shiogoshi. Saigyō wrote:

> All the long night
> salt-winds drive
> storm-tossed waves
> and moonlight drips
> through Shiogoshi pines.

This one poem says enough. To add another would be like adding a sixth finger to a hand.

• • •

The sky cleared the morning of the sixteenth. I sailed to Iro Beach a dozen miles away and gathered several colorful shells with a Mr. Tenya, who provided a box lunch and sake and even invited his servants. Tail winds got us there in a hurry. A few fishermen's shacks dotted the beach, and the tiny Hokke temple was disheveled. We drank tea and hot sake, lost in a sweeping sense of isolation as dusk came on.

> Loneliness greater
> than *Genji's* Suma Beach:
> the shores of autumn

> Wave after wave
> mixes tiny seashells with
> bush clover flowers

Tōsai wrote a record of our afternoon and left it at the temple.

A disciple, Rotsū had come to Tsuruga to travel with me to Mino Province. We rode horses into the castle town of Ōgaki. Sora returned from Ise, joined by Etsujin, also riding a horse. We gathered at the home of Jokō, a retired samurai. Lord Zensen, the Keikou men, and other friends arrived by day and night, all to welcome me as though I'd come back from the dead. A wealth of affection!

Still exhausted and weakened from my long journey, on the sixth day of the darkest month, I felt moved to visit Ise Shrine,[16] where a twenty-one-year Rededication Ceremony was about to get underway. At the beach, in the boat, I wrote:

> Clam ripped from its shell,
> I move on to Futami Bay:
> Passing autumn

---

[16] Ise is the greatest shrine of Shinto, Japan's national religion.

15

꽃

KOREAN POETRY
OF THE YI DYNASTY

K orea's last imperial dynasty, the Yi, was established by a military coup in
1392 and lasted until the Japanese invasion and annexation of the peninsula in 1910. Like the two preceding dynasties, the Silla (57 B.C.–A.D. 935) and
Koryo (918–1392), represented in Volume II, Selection 22, the Yi lived a complex and sometimes precarious political, military, and cultural existence between
the two more powerful East Asian nations, China and Japan. Of these the Chinese cultural influence was by far the stronger. Yi Dynasty Korea was administered from the beginning by a scholar-gentry elite, the yangban, selected by an examination system, based like that in China on extensive knowledge of the
Confucian classics and adherence to neo-Confucian philosophy. Korea became, in
the words of one historian, "an almost perfect Confucian society." In Korea, however, access to the education requisite to examination success and public careers
was more limited by family considerations than it was in China's more open society. Hence the term yangban came to imply not so much a scholar-gentry aristocracy of talent as an hereditary ruling class whose power rested upon vast land-
holdings worked by semi-serf peasants or slaves.

Despite the limitations of a less than socially democratic system, the yangban
culture of the Yi showed brilliance and energy in the creation of a high culture,
especially in its first two centuries. Its most remarkable achievement was the invention under royal auspices, in 1443, of a phonetic system for writing the Korean language. Up to that point literacy among Koreans meant literacy in Chinese, with Chinese characters used to represent the sounds of spoken Korean—an
awkward business for a language whose logic was fundamentally different from
Chinese. The new writing system, known as han-gul ("Korean letters") remains
to this day perhaps the most effective phonetic writing system in the world.

It is significant that the first major work composed in han-gul was a poetic
cycle, Songs of the Dragons Flying to Heaven, commissioned by King Sejong in
1446 to establish the legitimacy of his own relatively new dynasty and to demonstrate the viability of the new writing system. It was still some years before the

yangban *poets, steeped as they were in* The Book of Songs *(see Volume I, Selection 11) and other Chinese poetry, came to be confident in the use of their own language in their own writing system. Nevertheless the* yangban *followed the example of their Chinese scholar-gentry counterparts in the composition of a large body of excellent poetry.*

Although there were several verse forms available to the scholar poets and to the kisaeng *—the highly literate women entertainers—the most attractive was the so-called* sijo. *This was a short poetic form governed, like the* haiku *in Japan (Selection 14), by certain rules of structure and syllable length. Also like the* haiku, *the essential point of the* sijo *was not so much its formal structure as the possibility for subtle, compressed expression of insight and emotion it afforded to a talented poet. The* sijo *however, was more lyrical than the* haiku *and was often intended to be sung to familiar melodies. The translations that follow, from the writing brushes of Korean poets spanning several centuries, give an indication of the great range of human concerns—politics, love, nature, reflections on the pain and absurdity of growing older—which engaged the creative imaginations of these sensitive men and women.*

HWANG CHIN-I (c. 1506–1544)[1]
Four Poems

I cut in two
A long November night, and
Place half under the coverlet,
Sweet-scented as a spring breeze.
And when he comes I shall take it out,
Unroll it inch by inch, to stretch the night.

• • •

[1] Hwang Chin-i is Korea's most highly regarded woman poet. She was a well-known *kisaeng*—one of the female entertainers trained in poetry and music, like the *geisha* in Japan. Her verse, often love poetry dealing with emotions which the Confucian scholar-officials would express only rarely, nonetheless sounds a philosophical note and reflects a keen sensitivity to the natural world.

Do not boast of your speed,
O blue-green stream running by the hills:
Once you have reached the wide ocean,
You can return no more.
Why not stay here and rest,
When moonlight stuffs the empty hills?

• • •

Mountains are steadfast but the mountain streams
Go by, go by,
And yesterdays are like the rushing streams,
They fly, they fly,
And the great heroes, famous for a day,
They die, they die.

• • •

Blue mountains speak of my desire,
Green waters reflect my Lover's love:
The mountains unchanging,
The waters flowing by.
Sometimes it seems the waters cannot forget me,
They part in tears, regretting, running away.

YI I (1536–1584)[2]
Nine Songs of Mt. Ko

Waters of Mt. Ko and their nine scenes,
They are not yet known to men.
But I weed and weave a grass hut there
And my friends come in two's and three's.
I would fancy I am on Mt. Wu-i,
And follow the steps of Master Chu.

---

[2] Yi I, after a brief flirtation with Buddhism, embarked on a study of the Chinese philosopher Chu Hsi (see Vol II, Selection 33) and in time became one of Korea's greatest neo-Confucian scholars. The "Nine Songs of Mt. Ko" actually consists of ten *sijo* poems, a prologue followed by nine descriptive pieces which follow the round of the seasons like a series of brush paintings. The Mt. Wu-i of the fifth line is in China's Fukien province and the Master Chu of the sixth line is Chu Hsi. Both are examples of the profound Chinese influence on the work of virtually all the *yangban* (scholar-gentry) poets of the Yi Dynasty.

Where shall we find the first song?
The sun lances the crown rock, and
Mist clears above the young grass.
Lo the magic views far and near—
Calling my friends I would wait
With a green goblet in a pine grove.

We shall intone the second song
By the brocaded rock in late spring.
There let the green waves bear away
The blossoms to the distant fields.
Can the dusty world fathom this joy?
I must tell men of this sunny place.

We shall hum our third song
Where leaves paint scenes of jade.
Birds alight dancing in green shade,
Sylvan friends drum and twitter.
Twisted pines tame the season's rage,
Brave the breeze, lament summer's peace.

When the sun crosses the pine cliff,
Let us sing our fourth song.
Rocks swim on the water's bosom,
They weave a rainbow of another sky.
Trees and springs are deep and good; my heart
Dances with an exalted joy.

Shall we sing our fifth song
By the screens, solemn and secret?
My humble study by the water,
O how remote, cool and free.
Here I will work to my heart's content, and make
Poems of moon and breeze.

We find the sixth song by the gorge
Where waters gurgle over silver scales.
There I and fishes delight:
Who else has a larger heart?
At twilight I walk homeward.
A rod on my shoulder and the moon above.

We sing our seventh song by the rock,
Where the scarlet leaves are autumn queens.
Traceries of frost curtain the rocks—
See the brocade on the hanging cliffs.
Alone I sit on the cold stone,
Drunk I forget to return home.

We shall hear our eighth song
When moon blesses the tinkling brook.
There I will play, play on the lute,
With jade plectrums and a gold bridge.
New tunes cannot compare with the old,
But I am happy—I am alone.

When winter crosses Mt. Mun,
There we shall sing our ninth song.
Snow falls thick and covers over
The rugged rocks and the strange stones.
Nobody comes here for pleasure now,
Fools say there is nothing to see.

IM CHE (1549–1587)[3]

On the hill where the grass grows long,
Are you sleeping, or lying at rest?
Only bones are here, weathered and silent,
Your once beautiful face, where is it,
My darling, where did it go? Alas,
To whom should I offer this cup?

YUN SON-DO (1587–1671)[4]

Expelling Gloom

Whether sad or joyful,
Whether right or wrong,
I'll order and polish

---

[3] Even in his brief and troubled lifetime Im Che earned a wide reputation: His older contemporary Yi I called him "a remarkable man." Hearing of the fame of the poetess Hwang Chin-i he made a pilgrimage to her home, only to find that she was dead. He composed this poem after visiting her tomb.

[4] Yun Son-do is still regarded as the greatest poet in the Korean language. The range of his talent is seen in the variety of subjects—from politics to praise of natural beauty—to which he could adapt the *sijo* form. His long life in and out of office at the capital also reveals the viciousness and turbulence of Korean court politics in that age: between 1635 and 1667 he was demoted and/or exiled from the capital seven different times, in each case because of intrigues by his enemies. He spent the periods of exile, however, at remote retreats which afforded him peace and the inspiration of beautiful natural surroundings, and there he wrote much of his finest verse.

Only my duty and the Way.
As for other matters,
I'll not split hairs.

I know it: sometimes I've been
Absurd, sometimes I've
Missed the mark. A
Foolish mind, you say.
Yet I desired always
Only to honor thee, great King.
Beware
The slanderous tongues of
Fools with more cunning.

O stream that runs in tears
Outside the cold Chinho Pavilion.
For what reasons, moving water,
Do you flow sobbing night and day?
My crimson heart burns still;
My faith has no restful night.

Mountain after mountain, an endless chain,
And the far-off winding of rivers.
My parents grow old far away,
In the place of my long-ago childhood.
My heart is heavy. Adrift in the sky
The wild geese float and cackle, cackle and float.

After the Rain

Has a tedious rain cleared up?
Have the livid clouds rolled away?
The deep swamps in the stream in front
You say are now still as glass.
Come then, if the water is truly clear,
Let me wash my hat strings.[5]

---

[5] The reference is to a poem attributed to the Chinese Ch'u Yuan who drowned himself in 296 B.C. after his loyalty to his king was questioned. Ch'u Yuan's lines, "When the Ts'ang-lang's waters are clear, I can wash my hat strings in them; when the Ts'ang-lang's waters are muddy, I can wash my feet in them" imply that one should seek public office in times of honorable government, avoid it in other times: a most appropriate thought for Yun Son-do.

New Songs in the Mountain

Among mountains and streams I build
A humble thatched hut.
The ignorant mock my grass roof:
Can they fathom my true intention?
Indeed this is the fittest life
To a simple but discerning mind.

Cooked barley and fresh herbs,
I have had a fair amount of them.
And by the rock in the blue stream
I play to my heart's content.
What else do I need by the water?
I long for nothing, no, nothing else.

Alone, cup in hand,
I view the calm and quiet peaks.
Love comes to this longing self,
Welcome, heart, she has come.
She neither speaks nor smiles;
But what happiness, O what joy.

Heaven, too, detected my secret
That I am by nature slow.
Hence among all things of life
It left me not a thing.
Heaven says I shall be the guardian
To keep only the hills and waters.

Sunset

Mountains are the more beautiful
After they have
Devoured the sun
And it is
Twilight.
Day closes, darkness
Settles. Boy,
Watch out for snakes, now.
Let's not
Wander about in the field.

Deep Night

Close the brushwood door; winds are neighing.
Blow out the candles; night is deepening.
Let's prop on the soft pillows
Let's sleep, sleep out the night.
Don't wake me until the sky
Is full of the dawn.

Songs of Five Friends

How many friends have I? Count them:
Water and stone, pine and bamboo—
The rising moon on the east mountain,
Welcome, it too is my friend.
What need is there, I say,
To have more friends than five?

They say clouds are fine; I mean the color.
But, alas, they often darken.
They say winds are clear; I mean the sound.
But, alas, they often cease to blow.
It is only the *water,* then,
That is perpetual and good.

Why do flowers fade so soon
Once they are in their glory?
Why do grasses yellow so soon
Once they have grown tall?
Perhaps it is the *stone,* then,
That is constant and good.

Flowers bloom when it is warm;
Leaves fall when days are cool.
But, O *pine,* how is it
That you scorn frost, ignore snow?
I know now your towering self,
Straight even among the Nine Springs.

You are not a tree, no,
Nor a plant, not even that.
Who let you shoot so straight; what
Makes you empty within?
You are green in all seasons,
Welcome, *bamboo,* my friend.

Small but floating high,
You shed light on all creation.
And what can match your brightness
In the coal dark of the night?
You look at me but with no words;
That's why, O *moon,* you are my friend.

Spring Dawn

A hard winter is over—
Where are the bitter winds now?
Distant hills are veiled in fog,
The mild air is still.
I will open the door and admire
The morning dyed by the spring mist.

To an Old Lute

I take out an abandoned lute,
Change the strings and play
An elegant tune of the past.
Yes, it makes a happy sound.
But who else knows the tune I played—
I have to put it back in the case.

YI MYONG-HAN (1595–1645)[6]

Do not draw back your sleeves and go,
My own,
With tears I beg you.
Over the long dike green with grass
Look, the sun goes down.
You will regret it, lighting the lamp
By the tavern window,
Sleepless, alone.

If my dreams
Left their footprints on the road

---

[6] Yi Myong-han was a *yangban* official with a public record of courage, a poor man who was nevertheless a generous friend, and a poet noted for the freshness and melodiousness of his verse.

The path beneath my love's window
Would be worn down, though it is stone.
Alas, in the country of dream
No roads endure, no traces remain.

ANONYMOUS *SIJO* POEMS[7]

Were you to become I, and I you
Born in each other's world,
You would have a hard time of it
And suffer a heartbreak as I have.
You would know then, taught in turn,
How I have grieved all my life.

A flickering shadow haunts the window.
I start up, open, go out.
Only clouds passing the misty moon—
No, it was not the one for whom I've been waiting.
I'm lucky, night doesn't look in to laugh;
But what if it happened in broad daylight?

A horse neighs, wants to gallop:
My love clings to me, begs me to stay.
The moving sun has crossed the hill.
I have a thousand miles to go.
My love, do not stop me:
Stop the sun from setting!

In the valley where the stream leaps,
Having built a grass hut by the rock,
I till the field under the moon,
Among the vast clouds I lie.
Heaven and earth advise me
To age together with them; what now?

---

[7] As in most great poetic traditions, in Korea anonymous poets made a powerful contribution. Roughly a third of the *sijo* which appear in the anthologies are by unknown hands. Scholars note in this anonymous verse a relatively greater concentration on love poetry and a tendency to more direct, naive language than in the poems of known authors—nearly all of whom were scholars or *kisaeng*—and speculate that some of these anonymous *sijo* may be of folk origin.

O love, round as the watermelon,
Do not use words sweet as the melon.
What you have said, this and that,
Was all wrong, you mocked me.
Enough, your empty talk
Is hollow, like a preserved melon.

Alas, they deceived me—
The autumn moon and the spring breeze.
Since they came around in every season
I believed they were sincere and sure.
But they left me graying hair,
And followed the boys and went away.

Mind, let me ask you, how is it
You're still so young?
When I am well on in years
You, too, should grow old.
Why, if I followed your lead, Mind,
People would laugh me to scorn.

16

§

LAZARILLO DE TORMES

In 1554, three editions were published of a novel titled Vida de Lazarillo de
Tormes y de sus fortunas y adversidades (Life of Lazarillo de Tormes, His
Fortunes, and His Adversities), *two in Spain (Burgos, and Alcalá), and one in
Belgium (Antwerp). The earliest of the three seems to have been the Burgos edition. No mention is made of the author's name in any of the three editions, nor
in the subsequent reprintings of the work during that century. Throughout the seventeenth and eighteenth centuries,* Lazarillo *(as the work is usually called) was often
attributed to the nobleman and humanist from Granada, Diego Hurtado de
Mendoza (1503–1575), but his authorship was decisively refuted by nineteenth-
century scholars. Today, the puzzle of* Lazarillo's *anonymity is regarded as insoluble, and research has focused more on the underlying causes its author might
have had for keeping his (or her?) identity a secret. With its brutally realistic depictions of a teeming underworld of hungry beggars, impoverished noblemen,
and licentious priests,* Lazarillo *was highly critical of the social order in Renaissance Spain, and this might be sufficient explanation for its anonymity; but it has
also been speculated that the author might have been a converted Jew* (converso),
*a group that had been cruelly persecuted in Spain since the expulsion of the Jews
in 1492.*

    The question of Lazarillo's *authorship would have been of scant interest, of
course, had the work not been so innovative for its time, and so influential in the
history of the novel in Europe. Soon after its publication, translations of* Lazarillo
*began to appear in the major European languages: French (1560), English
(1576), Dutch (1579), German (1617), and Italian (1622). Scores of imitations
and sequels were published in Spain and in other European countries, and at
least until the nineteenth century the character of Lazarus* (Lazarillo) *of Tormes
was considered as universal a prototype as Fernando de Rojas's character Celestina (Selection 45 in Volume II) or Miguel de Cervantes's Don Quixote (Selection
17 in this volume).*

    Lazarillo *is widely regarded as the germ from which the genre of the pica-
resque novel developed, and thus as the first true modern novel, totally different from the pastoral and chivalric romances that were the most popular forms*

of long narrative fiction during the late Middle Ages and the Renaissance. (The adjective "picaresque" derives from the Spanish pícaro, *a word of uncertain etymological origins meaning "rogue" or "delinquent." Curiously, the term* pícaro *is never used in* Lazarillo.*) What distinguishes the modern novel from these earlier romances is not only its realism, but its often degraded, antiheroic vision of the individual. Unlike medieval characters, Lazarus of Tormes is cast adrift in a changing society, in a world no longer dominated by spiritual values, but rather by money and social standing. Perhaps the only competitor to* Lazarillo's *title as "first modern novel" might be Rojas's* La Celestina *(1499), a lengthy dramatic work with strong novelistic elements. But* Lazarillo *is not a drama; it is a fictional prose narrative that, in most editions, runs to around a hundred pages. Its length, as well as the division of its plot into episodes, distinguishes it also from the genre of the Italian* novellini, *or short story, such as those written by Giovanni Boccaccio (1313–1375) in* The Decameron *(1349–1351), which* Lazarillo *somewhat resembles due to its use of delinquency as a theme.*

Following the structure of the relación *(a type of sworn deposition, or report, that was common in Spanish legal proceedings of the time), Lazarus addresses this first-person narrative of his origins and life to "Your Worship" (an unnamed—perhaps nonexistent—nobleman, possibly a judge). He begins by describing his illegitimate birth on the banks of the Tormes River (near Toledo), and goes on to tell of his childhood apprenticeships to a succession of masters: a blind beggar, an avaricious clergyman, an impoverished but haughty squire, a friar, a seller of indulgences, a chaplain, and a bailiff. Highly ironic throughout, Lazarus's initially self-serving discourse ends up revealing his own foolishness and misdeeds. Part of Lazarus's cynical apprenticeship is learning that, in order to "rise," however minimally, in society, he must become corrupt. Beginning with a description of events from a child's innocent point of view, the novel ends with the young man Lazarus accepting an arranged marriage with a servant woman who is, in fact, the mistress of an archpriest. Although a cuckold, Lazarus profits from this arrangement, and considers himself to be, as he says in the last line of the novel, "at the height of my good fortune."*

The following selection includes the "Prologue" and the first chapter of Lazarillo. *In the former, Lazarus parodies the erudite allusions that were common in those days, as well as the desire for individual honor and recognition typical of the Renaissance. He also sets up the narrative situation of the novel, which is that of the* relación, *or report that he gives to "Your Worship." The first chapter tells of Lazarus's dubious origins and of his apprenticeship with the blind beggar, who, despite his blindness, teaches young Lazarus a great many of the tricks necessary to survive the crushing poverty that afflicted so many in the imperial Spain of the sixteenth and seventeenth centuries.*

❧

PROLOGUE

I consider it right well that matters which are of moment should come to the attention of many persons and not be buried, unseen and unheard, in the tomb of oblivion, for it is quite possible that some readers who might chance to stumble onto such material would therein find information of great interest, and others, reading less deeply, could at least find entertainment.

In this regard Pliny tells us that there is no book, no matter how bad it may be, that has not something good about it.[1] It is obvious that not all tastes are alike, for what one person will not eat, another dies for. Certain things which are disprized by some are greatly esteemed by others. This situation fortunately allows nothing to be thrown aside or destroyed (unless it be very greatly detestable), and permits many things to be widely disseminated, especially things which are harmless and impart useful knowledge.

Few would write for a single reader, for writing is a hard job; and writers who have done their work wish to be rewarded, not with money, but with the knowledge that their works are widely known and read, and—if they merit it—praised. In this regard Cicero tells us: "The desire to be held in esteem creates all the arts."[2]

Does the first soldier who scales a wall hold his life to be less dear than any of the others do? Not at all. What impels a soldier to act dangerously is the desire to be admired. The same thing holds true for those who practice the Arts and Letters. The friar preaches very well, for he wishes to save souls; but ask him whether he is displeased when he is told: "How marvellously Your Reverence preached today!" A certain gentleman jousted very poorly—and then gave his armor to a trickster who praised him for having borne himself so well in the field. What would he have done if the compliment had been true?

It was ever thus. And I will confess I am no more saintly than my neighbors. Therefore, I shall not be disappointed if this little trifle of mine, though written in so prosaic a style, is received and enjoyed by all those readers who find pleasure in perusing the true account of a man who has had so many adventures and experienced so many dangers and adversities.

From *Lazarillo de Tormes,* copyright 1957 by Mack Hedricks Singleton, translator, and Angel Flores, editor, in *Masterpieces of the Spanish Golden Age.* Pp. 25–41.

[1] From the *Epistles* of Pliny the Younger (A.D. 61–113), Roman administrator and famous writer of letters. (The author here parodies the common usage of unnecessarily erudite quotations in prefatory dedications.)

[2] From the *Tusculan Disputations* of Marcus Tulius Cicero (106–43 B.C.), Roman orator and statesman.

I beg Your Worship[3] to receive this poor offering of one who would have made it richer had his gifts and his desires been of equal magnitude.

Since Your Worship writes me to relate these matters very fully, I have thought it best to start not in the middle but at the beginning. In this way Your Worship and others may receive a complete account of my life.

I will be clearly seen from this narrative that those who have inherited noble houses ought not to be presumptuous, since they have been favored by Fortune.

And it will likewise be seen that those to whom she has not been partial have often done much more than those who have inherited their wealth, for many times, through their own energy and pluck, the less favored have, despite ill fortune, eventually reached port.

CHAPTER 1

Lazarus tells of his life and whose son he was

I must first, sir, tell you that my name is Lazarus of Tormes, and that I am the son of Thomas Gonzáles and Antonia Pérez, native of Tejares, a village near Salamanca. I was born in the Tormes River, and so took Tormes as my surname. It happened in this manner:

My father (God forgive him!) was in charge of a watermill on the banks of that river for more than fifteen years. One night, my mother being great with child, gave birth to me there; so that in all honesty I may say I really was born in that river.

Now, when I was eight years old my father was accused of having performed various surgical operations on the bags belonging to the people who came to the mill to have their grain ground. He was arrested, confessed and denied not, and so was prosecuted.[4]

At that time an expedition was being sent against the Moors, and my father joined it, for he was in exile because of the scandal previously mentioned. He went as muleteer with a gentleman who had decided to go on the expedition; and like a faithful servant, my father ended his life at the same time as his master.

I pray to God that he is now in Paradise.

---

[3] The person, perhaps nonexistent, to whom *Lazrillo* is supposedly dedicated. Such dedications were a widespread literary device.

[4] A line has been omitted here from the Spanish original, since it makes a pun that is impossible to render into English. It is of interest to note, however, that the pun makes a sacrilegious and ironic allusion to the Christian Beatitudes, specifically to Matthew 5:10: "Blessed are those who are persecuted for righteousness' sake, for theirs is the kingdom of heaven." (Lazarus's father had been stealing grain from the bags of those who brought their grain to be ground into flour.)

My widowed mother, being then without husband and protection, decided to take up her abode among worthy people, since she was herself so, and came to live in the city. She rented a little cottage and began to prepare meals for students and to wash clothes for the horseboys of the Comendador of the parish of La Magdalena,[5] so that it was necessary for her to frequent the stables. And thus she became acquainted with a dark man who helped take care of the horses.[6] He sometimes came to our house in the evening and would leave on the following morning. On other occasions, he would come to the door on the pretext that he wished to buy eggs, and then he would enter the house.

When he first began to visit us, I did not take to him at all. I was really afraid of his black color and unprepossessing appearance. But when I saw that the quality of our food greatly improved with his visits, I began to grow fond of him, for he always brought bread and pieces of meat with him, and when winter came he would bring firewood, which kept us warm.

So it came about that as he continued to stay with us, and as he and my mother became thicker, she eventually presented me with a pretty little colored brother, whom I played with and helped keep warm.

I recall now that once when my stepfather, the negro man, was playing with the little fellow, the latter chanced to observe that my mother and I were white but that his father was not. He ran to my mother and pointing back with his little finger, said: "Mother! *Bogey-man!*" And my stepfather replied, laughing: "*You* little rascal, you! *You* little whoreson!" And, although still very young, I took note of the expression my baby brother had used, and I said to myself: "How many there must be in the world who flee from others—simply because they cannot see themselves!"

As our luck would have it, the activities of Zaide—so my stepfather was called—reached the ears of his supervisor, and when an investigation was made, it was discovered that he had stolen half of the provender bought for the horses, and, furthermore, he had pretended that many articles were lost, including bran, firewood, currycombs, aprons, and the blankets and coverings for the horses. When my stepfather could find nothing else to pilfer, he would unshoe the horses and take the horseshoes to my mother. They were later sold to a blacksmith, and the money he gave us for them helped feed and clothe my little brother.

---

[5] Originally a term used to name a knight commander of a military order, "comendador" also referred to the head of a religious establishment, such as a parish church or a monastery.

[6] By the mid-sixteenth century there were in Spain substantial numbers of enslaved and freed sub-Saharan Africans. In some cities, such as Seville, there were communities of free black artisans and laborers who formed their own Catholic religious brotherhoods and participated in the feasts of the Church. *Lazarillo*'s is an early (and not unsympathetic) literary portrayal of this new social group in Spain.

Let us not marvel that a cleric or a friar should steal from the poor or from their own houses in order to give gifts to the ladies who are their devotees, or help someone of their own sort, when we have seen how a poor slave was impelled for love's sake to do the same thing.

Zaide was convicted of all that I have mentioned, for when they asked me threateningly what *I* knew, I—in my boy's way and out of fear—revealed everything, even to the fate of those horseshoes he had had me sell to the blacksmith. My poor stepfather was whipped till the blood came, and my mother was ordered on pain of a hundred lashes not to enter the Comendador's house again or to receive the unfortunate Zaide into her own.

My poor mother exerted herself to obey the sentence, and, to avoid danger and flee from slanderous tongues, she went to work for some persons who at that time lived at the Inn of La Solana. There, undergoing a thousand hardships, she brought my little brother up to an age when he could walk, while I, at the same time grew to be a good-sized lad who could fetch wine or candles or anything else the guests required.

At this time a blind man chanced to stop at the inn. Considering that I would be a good guide, he asked my mother whether he might not take me along with him. She commended me to him saying that I was the son of a good man, who to exalt our Holy Faith, had given his life on the expedition to Gelves.[7] She said she trusted in God that I would turn out to be no worse a man than my father had been, and she besought the blind man to treat me well and care for me as properly as a fatherless child deserved. He replied that he would do so and said he accepted me not as a servant but as his son. And so I began to serve and guide my new old master.

After we had been in Salamanca for a few days, it appeared to the blind man that he could not earn there as much as he desired, so he decided to leave the place. When the time for our departure drew near, I went to see my mother, and, the two of us weeping, she gave me her blessing, saying:

"Son, well do I know I shall not see you ever again. Try hard to be good, and may the Lord direct you. I have brought you up to your present age, and I have now given you a good master. From now on, you must take care of yourself."

And so I left her and went back to my master, who was waiting for me.

We left Salamanca, and when we reached the bridge we observed there a stone animal which had almost the form of a bull, and the blind man requested me to approach the animal. When I had come near, he said to me:

---

[7]An allusion to the failed military expedition against the Moors of Gelves (in present-day Tunisia) in 1510, in which a great many Spanish noblemen died. Since the expedition was also motivated by religious fervor, many of those who died in battle were regarded as martyrs, thus making it a usefully protective allusion for Lazarus's mother.

"Lazarus, place your ear up close to the beast and you will perceive a great sound within him."

I, in my simplicity thinking it to be so, obeyed. When my master felt that I had my head alongside the stone, he knocked it with a terrific blow of his hand against the beast, so that I had a headache for three days afterwards from my butting of the bull.

And he said to me:

"Idiot! Be now aware that a blind man's boy has to know somewhat more than even the devil himself."

And he laughed heartily at his little trick.

I seemed at that instant to awaken from the naïveté in which like a little boy I had slept, and I said to myself:

"He is very right, and I must indeed have an alert eye and I must be ever watchful, since I am on my own, and I must learn to take care of myself."

We began our journey, and in a few days the blind man taught me some thieves' slang; and when he saw I was an intelligent lad, he was quite pleased and said to me:

"Gold and silver, I can give you none, but wise counsels for living, I can give you many."

And so it was indeed; for, after the Lord God, my old master took best care of me, and, although he was blind, he illuminated me, and in his own way gave me the only education I ever had.

I am happy, sir, to recount to you these childhood memories to demonstrate how virtuous it is for men to rise from low estate, and contrariwise, how vile it is to fall low from high position.

Now, to return to my excellent blind man and to proceed in the narration of matters concerning him, I would, sir, inform you that since the Creation, God has not produced a blind man who was as he so very wise and so very sagacious. In his profession he was a very eagle. He knew a hundred-odd prayers by heart. He had a deep and resonant voice which echoed throughout the church when he said his prayers. When he had finished, he would apparel his face with pious mien—but he made no faces or grimaces with eyes or mouth, as others are so often wont to do.

He had a thousand ways of getting money. He said he knew prayers for many different situations—for women who could not bear children and for those who were in travail; and for those who had made unhappy marriages he had prayers that would cause their husbands to love them dearly. To pregnant women he could predict whether the baby would be a boy or a girl. And in medical matters he said that Galen[8] knew not half so much as he when it came to teeth, faints,

---

[8] A second-century Greek physician whose medical writings were of great influence through the Middle Ages and the Renaissance.

and female ailments. In a word, no one could report any sickness to him without receiving advice of this sort: "Do this, you must do that, eat such an herb, take such a root. . . ."

And so, he was universally looked up to—especially by women, who believed everything he told them; and, because of those skills of his which I have mentioned, women greatly contributed to his income. Indeed, he could earn more in a month than a hundred other blind men could have earned in a whole year.

But, sir, you must also know that although he had acquired a great deal and kept it, there never was, I think, in all the world so miserly and niggardly a man as he—so very much so, indeed, that he almost starved me, for he never gave me the half of what my necessities required. I shall tell you in all frankness that if with my wit and tricks I had not managed to supply my wants, I should certainly have died of hunger. For despite all his craft and wisdom I so outwitted him that always—at least *almost* always—I emerged the winner. To accomplish this I was in the habit of playing upon him the most devilish tricks, some of which I shall now relate to you—although I did not always come out unscathed.

He kept his bread and other things in a canvas bag which could be fastened with an iron hoop locked with a padlock, and when he put things in it or took them out he did so with such vigilance and nice calculation that it was utterly impossible for anyone to filch anything from him, even a crumb. (I may assure you that I took every crumb I could get from him, although I could easily do away with all I got in just two mouthfuls.)

After he had closed the padlock he would relax his vigilance, thinking me occupied with other matters; and then I would often bleed the stingy bag by means of a rip which I had made in it and was careful to sew up again every time; and I took out of it good-sized hunks of bread, pieces of bacon, and some sausages. . .

What I could filch and steal I converted into half-farthings;[9] and when the blind man had been ordered to pray and was given whole farthings for that purpose, I conveniently had one of my half-farthings ready and would pop the whole one into my mouth the second it was presented, no matter how hard the blind man tried to get it first, and would then give him my own half-farthing in exchange. The wicked old fellow complained to me about it because he could *feel* the coin and tell it was not a whole farthing; and he would say:

"How in hell can this be? Ever since you have been with me I have been getting only half-farthings, though formerly I was given full farthings and very often a whole maravedí.[10] My ill luck must somehow be due to you."

---

[9] A farthing was a former British monetary unit equal to one-fourth of a penny, and a half-farthing would of course equal one-eighth of a penny. In the original Spanish, the coin alluded to is a *media blanca,* made of a mixture of silver and copper, whose value was roughly equivalent to a half-farthing's.

[10] A "maravedí" was a Spanish coin of Arab origin. Previously made of silver or gold, by the sixteenth century it was made of copper, and it was equivalent to four *medias blancas.*

He had the habit of cutting prayers short—he would, indeed, say only half a prayer if the person who had commissioned it went away—on which occasions I was instructed to give his cloak a tug. This I would do, and then he would again start calling out: "Who wishes to have a prayer said?"—which is the way the question is often put.

At our meals he usually set a little jug of wine beside him. I would then swiftly grab it and give it a couple of furtive kisses and then return it to its place. But this went on only a short while, for he know by the number of draughts left in the bottle how much was missing, and so to protect his wine he thereafter never let go of the jug but always held it tightly by the handle. But no magnet ever more successfully attracted iron to itself than I attracted that wine—this time by means of a ryestraw which I had prepared for that very occasion. I would put it in the mouth of the jug and then proceed to suck my fill of the wine within. But since the old villain was so sagacious, I am sure he caught on, for after that he changed his habit and began to place the jug between his legs, where he could cover it over with his hand; and so drank fully protected against me.

Now, being accustomed, as I was, to the drinking of wine, I was dying for it. And seeing that my little scheme of using a straw no longer produced results, I decided to make a little hole in the bottom of the jug so that the liquid would subtly drain out, and I used a little dab of wax to fill up the hole. When mealtime came I pretended to be cold and sat down between the blind man's legs to keep warm before the miserable little fire we had. When the bit of wax I had used was sufficiently warm with heat from the fire, the little hole in the jug began to let the wine drip into my mouth—and I maneuvered myself into so favorable a position that not the least drop got away. When the poor old devil started to drink he found the jug completely empty. He was amazed, he cursed himself, and, not knowing how that could be, sent the jug and the wine to the devil.

"At any rate, Uncle," I said, "you cannot accuse *me* of drinking it, for you never let it out of your hand."

He turned the jug so much about and about that he finally found the little drain and caught on to my trick; but for the time being he said nothing but pretended he still did not understand what had occurred. The next day when my jug was beginning to ooze in its usual way, I sat down according to custom, not suspecting the damage in store for me or that the blind man knew what I was doing. I sat imbibing those sweet draughts with my face upward and my eyes somewhat closed, the better to savor that delicious liqueur. The savage old blind man realized that now was the time for him to take revenge on me; so with his full strength he lifted up that—for me—bittersweet jug and with full force let it fall upon my mouth, so that your poor Lazarus, who was expecting nothing of the sort—but was, rather, carefree and joyful—really felt that the heavens and everything therein residing had fallen on top of him. The blow was such that it addled my pate and left me senseless, and the blow from the jug was so great that the pieces of it stuck in my face and tore it in several places, and it also knocked out my teeth, so that until this present day I have been toothless.

From that time on I had an aversion to that bad blind man, for although he was nice to me and treated me well and helped me recover, I knew perfectly well he was delighted with the chastisement he had given me. He bathed with wine the wounds the jug had caused me, and would often smiling say:

"How odd it is, little Lazarus! You are being healed by the very thing that hurt you." And he made further remarks in the same vein, which I did not like a bit.

When I was half recovered from my dreary punishment and my bruises, I began to consider that the cruel old man could easily put an end to me with a few more blows of the same kind, and so I decided to get away from him. But I did not leave him immediately, because I wished to put some plans into effect, carefully and to my best advantage. Although I should have liked to forget my grudge against him and forgive him for breaking the jug over my head, I was not encouraged to do so by the rough treatment he gave me from that time on, for he would strike me without cause or reason, knocking my head about and pulling my hair. And if anyone asked him why he treated me so roughly he would straightway relate the jug incident saying:

"Do you perchance think this lad of mine is some young innocent? The devil himself could hardly think up better tricks than this lad here."

And those who heard him would cross themselves, saying:

"Who would ever have thought that such a little fellow could have done such a wicked thing?"

And they would laugh over the trick, saying:

"Chastise him, Uncle, chastise him well, and heaven will reward you for it."

Which, with such encouragement, is precisely what he did.

Whereupon I began to lead him down the worst roads possible—and on purpose, in order to hurt him and endanger him. If there were stones ahead, we went that way; if there was mud we went through the deepest part of it; and although I did not emerge from it as dry-shod as I might have liked, I would have been perfectly happy to lose one of my own eyes if I could have caused him to lose both of his—if he had had any to lose.

During all this time he kept poking me in the back of my head, which was now always covered with bruises, and seemed almost bald because he had pulled so much of my hair out. And although I swore I was not doing what I did out of malice, he never believed me at all—such was the discernment and great understanding the old villain had.

Now, that you may, sir, observe how very acute the old fellow was, I shall relate to you one of the incidents that happened to me while I was with him—an incident that fully convinced me how great his astuteness really was. When we left Salamanca, his intention was to move on to Toledo, because he said the people there were better off, even though less prone to give. He gave great importance to the following proverb: "More giveth the niggard than the naked." And so we took this road, passing though the best towns. We would stop along the way wherever we found welcome and profit; and when we found neither, we made our departure the third day after our arrival.

It chanced that we came to a town by the name of Almoroz where a man who was harvesting grapes (for it was that time of year) charitably gave my blind man a bunch of grapes. Since grape baskets get rough treatment, and, too, because the grapes are very ripe at that particular season, the bunch he had received began to fall apart in his hand. If he had placed it in his pack it would certainly have turned into grape juice—it and everything with which it came in contact. So he decided to have a feast, not only because he could not take the grapes with him but also to give me some entertainment, for he had that particular day administered me a great many blows and proddings with his knees. We sat down on a fence and he said:

"Now I wish to show you how generous I am. Let us both eat this bunch of grapes, dividing it equally between us. We shall share it this way: you take one and I'll take one, but you must promise me not to take more than one at a time. I will do the very same until we have finished, and in that way no tricks will be played."

The agreement having thus been made, we began to eat. But at the very second round the old traitor changed his tactics and began to eat two grapes at a time, assuming, I suppose, that I must be doing the same. When I saw that he was breaking the contract, I determined not to be satisfied with just going along with him. I outdid him; *I* ate two at a time or three at a time, however I could. When we had finished the bunch, the blind man sat there for a while with the stem in his hand. Finally, shaking his head, he said:

"Lazarus, you were trying to deceive me. I would swear to God that you were eating three grapes at a time."

"I really wasn't," I replied. "But why do you suspect that?"

The supremely sagacious blind man answered me:

"Do you know why I was aware that you were eating them three grapes at a time? Well, when I was eating them two grapes at a time you didn't say a thing."

I laughed to myself, and although but a boy I perceived the blind man's great and discerning discretion.

To avoid prolixity, I shall not tell you all of the many amusing and profitable things which happened to me while I was with this my first master. And so I will tell you only of my leave-taking, and then bring this part of the narrative to an end.

While we were at an inn in Escalona, which is the residence of the Duke of that name, the blind man gave me a sausage to be roasted. After the juice had dripped out and had been lapped up, the blind man took a coin from his purse and told me to go and buy a maravedí's worth of wine at the tavern. The devil— the old thief-maker, they call him—placed in my imagination the trick I was to perform.

There was beside the fire a spindly little turnip which was so wretched look- ing it had no doubt been thrown there because it was not good for the cooking pot. At the moment nobody was present but the blind man and me. Since I had such a ravenous appetite because of the invasion into my very being of the sa- vory smell of that sausage—while I knew I was destined to eat—I lost all my inhibitions and putting aside all fear in the hope of achieving my desire, I grabbed the sausage while the blind man was taking the money out of his purse, and swiftly put the spindly old turnip on the spit. Then when my master had given me the money, he took up the spit and began to turn it before the fire and thus to roast something which because of its very shortcomings had previously escaped being cooked.

I went for the wine and on the way devoured the sausage. When I got back I found that the blind old sinner had lodged the turnip between two slices of bread without having caught on—since he had not touched it—that it was not his sausage. When he took up his sandwich and bit into it thinking to get a good bite of sausage, his hopes were dampened by the drab old turnip, and he became angry and said:

"What is the meaning of this, Lazarus?"

"Poor me!" I said. "And must you blame me for this too? Haven't I just returned with the wine you sent me for? Someone else was here and did this to play a trick on you."

"No, no, that cannot be," he said. "I did not let the spit out of my hands. What you say is impossible."

I began again to swear and perjure myself, saying that I was guiltless of the substitution of the turnip for the sausage; but it little availed me against the shrewdness of the accursed blind man, from whom nothing could be hidden. He got up and seized me by the head and, like a good hound, began to smell my breath to assure himself of the truth of the matter. In his great excitement he opened my mouth a little more than was bearable, and without being careful about what he was doing, stuck his nose in. Now, that part of his person was long and pointed, and, with his vexation on this particular occasion, it had expanded to a length of around nine inches. The tip of it then reached down into my throat. Because of my great fear and the recentness of my eating the sausage, that object had not yet settled in my stomach. The groping around of his very generous nose in my throat half choked me, and encouraged my unsettled stomach to reveal my guilt and greediness by returning the blind man's sausage to him. So it was that before he could get his beak out of my mouth, my stomach was so greatly moved that the nose and the poorly chewed sausage left my person at the very same instant.

O Lord! I only wished at that moment to be buried, for dead I was already. The fury of the wicked old blind man was so terrible that if people had not come to my rescue I really do think he would have killed me. They got me out of his hands, which held on to what had been the little hair remaining on my head. My face was scratched, and my neck and throat all torn. Well, the latter certainly deserved the treatment, for its sins had brought so much punishment my way. The blind man told everyone who came there of my misdeeds, and related all over again the jug incident and the grape story and also what had just happened.

The laughter of all those people was so great that everyone who came along the street approached to see the fun. And I, though weeping and so greatly maltreated, felt I did an injustice to the blind man by not laughing at his account of my wiles, for he told his tale with such skill and relish.

Meantime I was reminded of a weak and pusillanimous action I had committed, and I cursed myself for my negligence. I *should* have bitten his nose off, for, since he had himself set the stage for it, I only needed to close my teeth upon that beak of his; and since it belonged to that old scoundrel, my stomach might better have retained it than it had the sausage—and so, no evidence would have been forthcoming, and I should have been able to deny any accusation. I wished to God I had done that. It would have been wonderful.

The innkeeper's wife and others who were there patched up matters between us, and they washed my face and throat with the wine I had brought back to be drunk. The blind man's commentary on this occasion was very humorous.

"Really, this fellow makes me spend more yearly on wine to wash him with than *I* spend on wine to drink in two whole years, It may even be said, Lazarus, that you should be more grateful to wine than to your own father, for if he begot you once, wine has given you life a thousand times."

And then he would tell how many times he had beaten me about my head and bruised my face and then healed my wounds with wine. And he said:

"I do really believe that if any man is ever going to be blessed with wine it will be you."

And those who were washing me laughed greatly when they heard this, though I was cursing.

But the blind man's prediction came true; and since that time I have had many occasions to remember that man (who doubtless had the gift of prophecy), and I feel sorry because of the vexations I caused him, although I made restitution, as you shall see, sir, as my story proceeds.

Considering all this and the low tricks the blind man had played upon me, I decided to leave him for good. Since this determination was constantly on my mind, I felt that after the last trick he played on me I had better leave him now as soon as I could. And so it came about, and in the following manner.

The next day we went about the town begging alms. It had rained heavily the night before, and now because it was still pouring the blind man stood praying on an open kind of porch which there chanced to be in that town. As night came on and the downpour did not cease, the blind man said to me:

"Lazarus, this shower is interminable, and it gets worse the darker it gets. Let us seize this opportunity to reach an inn."

To get to this place we had to cross a perfect rivulet that had formed in the street.

I said to him:

"Uncle, the stream that has formed here is very wide. But, if you wish, I can find a place where we may cross quickly without getting wet. I see one spot which is quite narrow. There we shall be able to cross dry-shod."

He accepted my suggestion.

"You have a lot of good sense," he said. "That is why I am so fond of you. Take me to that place where the water is narrow. It is dangerous to get wet in winter; it is especially dangerous to get wet feet."

I, who saw that everything was set for my trick, led him from the protection of the porch straight into the square before one of several pillars that constituted the support of the projecting upper stories of several houses there, and then said to him:

"Uncle, this is the narrowest place in the stream."

It was raining hard and the poor devil was getting wet; so, because of our haste and more especially because God blinded his understanding at that moment to give me my revenge, he let himself believe me and said:

"Set me properly ready for the jump, and then you jump over the water yourself first."

I set him immediately in front of the pillar and then jumped over the water and got behind the pillar—like one awaiting the charge of a bull, and I said:

"Ready! Jump as hard as you can and you will make it!"

I had scarcely got the words out of my mouth when like a he-goat the blind man plunged forward with all his might, even taking a previous step backward to jump all the harder. He struck the pillar head-on with such force that the sound of the collision was very much as if a big pumpkin had struck the stone; and with his head split open he fell back half dead.

"So!" I cried. "So you could smell the sausage but not scent the post? Goody, goody!"

And I ran off, leaving him in the care of many people who were coming to his aid.

I reached the gates of the town in one long trot; and before nightfall I was in Torrijos.

I never learned what happened to the blind man after that; nor did I ever bother to find out.

17

❧

Miguel de Cervantes

DON QUIXOTE

W*hen the novel* El ingenioso hidalgo Don Quijote de la Mancha (The Ingenious Gentleman Don Quixote de la Mancha) *was published in Madrid in 1605, its author, Miguel de Cervantes Saavedra (1547–1616), instantly became a celebrity.* Don Quixote *had an unprecedented six printings that same year; English and French translations appeared during the following decade, and the novel enjoyed a worldwide readership thereafter. (Spanish colonists in the New World, it is known, purchased nearly three-fourths of the 1605 edition of* Don Quixote.*) In an age dominated by the prolific genius of Lope de Vega (represented in Selection 3) and the dazzling inventiveness of Luis de Góngora, the formerly obscure Cervantes became suddenly, at the then-advanced age of fifty-eight, one of the chief writers of Spain, and not long after his death, his novel was regarded as a universally revered classic. The overwhelmingly positive popular reaction to* Don Quixote *caused resentment among some of his contemporaries, who accused Cervantes of altering the established literary forms and causing a disturbance in the "republic of letters." In 1614, an author with the pseudonym of "Avellaneda" published a false sequel to* Don Quixote, *totally lacking in literary quality, which bitterly attacked Cervantes's novel. This attack prompted Cervantes to finish quickly and publish his own "second part" of* Don Quixote, *which appeared in 1615 and forms an integral part of the novel.*

Indeed, few could have foreseen Cervantes's literary greatness, despite his talent, before the publication of Don Quixote. *A veteran of the Spanish Army who served in Italy, and fought heroically at the battle of Lepanto against the Turks in 1571, Cervantes was seriously wounded in the chest and left hand, which was rendered forever useless. Captured in 1575, he was held as a slave in Algiers until 1580. After four daring escape attempts, he was eventually ransomed. Upon his return to Spain, despite his military exploits, he occupied only minor positions in government service, including the hated job of tax collector, which eventually caused him serious difficulties with the law. Falsely accused of embezzlement in his tax-collecting duties, he was imprisoned in Seville from 1597 to 1602, and was briefly imprisoned again in Valladolid, in 1603, once more under false accusations, this time of complicity in a man's death. Financial and personal difficulties also shadowed Cervantes's family life. His sole offspring, Isabel de Saavedra, was born to a mistress, Ana Franca, whom Cervantes never married; instead, in 1584 he married Catalina de Salazar y Palacios, a woman of a prosperous landowning family, who was nineteen years younger than Cervantes. His natural daughter's wayward love affairs were partly to blame for Cervantes's imprisonment in Valladolid, but so was his reputation as a gambler.*

In the midst of these troubles, Cervantes had attempted to launch his literary career by writing a pastoral romance, a popular genre of the day in which idealized shepherds and mythical nymphs courted each other in a stylized version of the countryside. Although La Galatea (1585) exhibits all the artificial conventions of its genre, it also reveals one aspect of Cervantes's dual image of reality that foreshadows a theme of Don Quixote: *an idealized vision of the world in which love is exalted to the highest degree along with the Renaissance Neoplatonic cult of beauty. His various dramas, one-act plays, and satirical poems also had only modest success at the time. A collection of his short stories,* Novelas ejemplares (Exemplary novels), *was published after* Don Quixote *in 1613. The masterly qualities of many of these earlier works began to be recognized retrospectively after the success of* Don Quixote, *although they probably would not have sufficed to ensure Cervantes's literary immortality. Shortly before his death in 1616, Cervantes finished his second and last novel,* Los trabajos de Persiles y Sigismunda (The Labors of Persiles and Sigismunda), *published posthumously in 1617. In this last work, Cervantes left aside the humorous and unconventional perspective that had served him so well in* Don Quixote, *and again tried his hand at writing a work in a conventional genre, this time a Byzantine romance (a type of novel derived from Greek narratives of late antiquity, many of which were published in Byzantium, or Constantinople). The heroes of those romances were usually a brother and a sister who suffered various misfortunes and had adventures in exotic places until they at last found their way back to their homeland. Most critics agree that, although it shows flashes of Cervantes's genius,* Persiles *is a work that was dated even in its own time—in marked contrast to* Don Quixote, *which not only belonged to its age but transcended it.*

Don Quixote, *now a classic of world literature, was initially conceived as a short story. Cervantes's avowed purpose (as he declares in his prologue to the novel's first part) was to attack by means of satire the novels of chivalry such as* Amadis of Gaul *(1508) and* Palmerín de Oliva *(1511) and their numerous sequels, which were then much in vogue in Spain and neighboring European countries, and whose reading Cervantes regarded as unhealthy. Of course, this rather limited aim was soon surpassed by the richness of* Don Quixote, *whose plot and style abound in irony, allusion, and ambiguity. In its episodic form,* Don Quixote *owes something to the picaresque novel* Lazarillo de Tormes (Selection 16).

As is well known, the novel centers around an old hidalgo *(country gentle-man) from the Castilian region of La Mancha, named Quijana or Quesada (the ambivalence is Cervantes's), who goes mad from reading too many novels of chivalry, of which he was inordinately fond. Calling himself Don Quixote, the* hidalgo *tries to become a "knight-errant" like Amadís or Palmerín (even though this practice had disappeared centuries earlier) and to go out into the world to fight injustice, battle evil wizards, and rescue damsels in distress, such as the one Don Quixote dreams up for himself, Dulcinea del Toboso. He man-ages to persuade his neighbor, Sancho Panza, an illiterate, down-to-earth peas-ant, to become his squire. Sancho's practical realism provides a corrective for his master's idealistic activism. Needless to say, Don Quixote's aspirations clash against the social and political realities of sixteenth-century Spain, where, de-spite the riches brought by Spain's imperial possessions, the nation was impover-ished by economic mismanagement and costly foreign wars. At first buffoonish and ridiculous in their misadventures, Don Quixote and Sancho slowly become more humanized, and, as critics have often remarked, Don Quixote begins to acquire some of Sancho's rough-hewn practicality, while Sancho becomes more of an idealist.*

The richness of Don Quixote *lies not only in the story itself, but in the way it is told: Not only are there "stories-within-stories" (as occur frequently in the first part, when characters tell stories about their lives to Don Quixote and San-cho), but the whole novel is playfully attributed by Cervantes to a fictional Arab historian, Cid Hamete Benengeli ("Egg-Plant"), who was said to have written it in Arabic. In this attribution, Cervantes mocked a convention of the novels of chivalry, whose text was always said to be copied or translated from an ancient historical manuscript of exotic origin. Similarly, Cervantes assigns to himself the role of mere translator, compiler, and publisher, having been aided in the trans-lation by a "morisco aljamiado" (a Castilian-speaking Arab). Thus, the story of Don Quixote is not only set in an ironic framework of multiple authorship, but also within a context of Spain's complex and problematical cultural identity, in which Christians, Muslims (Moors), and Jews interacted in multiple ways until the fifteenth century, when Spain's unification under Castile led to the persecu-tion of all non-Christian Spaniards. Recently, critics have begun to stress the many debts owed by Cervantes in* Don Quixote *to the Arabic storytelling tradi-tions (which Cervantes in all likelihood observed during his captivity in Algiers) and to Spain's own Arabic tradition, which was still alive, although secretly, in late-sixteenth-century Spain. (For over a century after the fall of Granada, Moors continued to live in southern Spain until their final expulsion, decreed by King Philip II in 1609).*

The selection that follows comes from Chapter VIII of Book I and Chapter I of Book II of the 1605 first part of Don Quixote, *in a lively English translation done in the eighteenth century by Tobias Smollett. In these two chapters we find not only the famous episode of the windmills, but also the fight between Don*

*Quixote and the Biscayan (or Basque), which allows Cervantes to create humor-
ous suspense from one book to another and to elaborate further about how he
supposedly came upon the rest of the manuscript of Don Quixote's adventures
written by Benengeli.*

BOOK I

Chapter VIII

*Of the happy success of the valiant Don Quixote, and the dreadful and
inconceivable adventure of the windmills, with other incidents worthy
to be recorded by the most able historian.*

In the midst of this their conversation, they discovered thirty or forty windmills
all together on the plain, which the knight no sooner perceived, than he said to
his squire, "Chance has conducted our affairs even better than we could either
wish or hope for; look there, friend Sancho, and behold thirty or forty outrageous giants, with whom, I intend to engage in battle, and put every soul of them
to death, so that we may begin to enrich ourselves with their spoils; for, it is a
meritorious warfare, and serviceable both to God and man, to extirpate such a
wicked race from the face of the earth." "What giants do you mean?" said Sancho
Panza in amazement. "Those you see yonder, replied his master, with vast extended arms; some of which are two leagues long." "I would your worship would
take notice, replied Sancho, that those you see yonder are no giants, but windmills; and what seem arms to you, are sails; which being turned with the wind,
make the millstone work:" "It seems very plain, said the knight, that you are but
a novice in adventures: these I affirm to be giants; and if thou art afraid, get out
of the reach of danger, and put up thy prayers for me, while I join with them in
fierce and unequal combat." So saying, he put spurs to his steed Rozinante, without paying the least regard to the cries of his squire Sancho, who assured him,
that those he was going to attack were no giants, but innocent windmills: but, he
was so much possessed with the opinion that they were giants, that he neither
heard the advice of his squire Sancho, nor would use the intelligence of his own
eyes, tho' he was very near them: on the contrary, when he approached them, he
called aloud, "Fly not, ye base and cowardly miscreants, for, he is but a single
knight who now attacks you." At that instant, a breeze of wind springing up, the
great sails began to turn; which being perceived by Don Quixote, "Tho' you

---

From *The Adventures of Don Quixote de la Mancha* by Miguel de Cervantes, translated by
Tobias Smollett (1755). Adapted by the editors.

wield," said he, "more arms than ever belonged to the giant Briareus,[1] I will make you pay for your insolence." So saying, and heartily recommending himself to his lady Dulcinea, whom he implored to succour him in this emergency, bracing on his target, and setting his lance in the rest, he put his Rozinante to full speed, and assaulting the nearest windmill, thrust it into one of the sails, which was driven about by the wind with so much fury, that the lance was shivered to pieces, and both knight and steed whirled aloft, and overthrown in very bad plight upon the plain.

Sancho Panza rode as fast as the ass could carry him to his assistance, and when he came up, found him unable to stir, by reason of the bruises which he and Rozinante had received. "Lord have mercy upon us! said the squire, did not I tell your worship to consider well what you were about? did not I assure you, they were no other than windmills? indeed no body could mistake them for any thing else, but one who has windmills in his own head!" "Prithee, hold thy peace, friend Sancho," replied Don Quixote; "the affairs of war, are more than any thing, subject to change. How much more so, as I believe, nay, am certain, that the sage Freston, who stole my closet and books, has converted those giants into mills, in order to rob me of the honour of their overthrow; such is the enmity he bears me; but, in the end, all his treacherous arts will but little avail against the vigour of my sword." "God's will be done!" replied Sancho Panza, who helped him to rise, and mount Rozinante that was almost disjointed.

While they conversed together upon what had happened, they followed the road that leads to the pass of Lapice,[2] for in that, which was a great thoroughfare, as Don Quixote observed, it was impossible but they must meet with many and diverse adventures. As he jogged along, a good deal concerned for the loss of his lance, he said to his squire, "I remember to have read of a Spanish knight, called Diego Perez de Vargas,[3] who having broken his sword in battle, tore off a mighty branch or bough from an oak, with which he performed such wonders, and felled so many Moors, that he retained the name of Machuca, or the feller, and all his descendants from that day forward, have gone by the name of Vargas and Machuca. This circumstance I mention to thee, because, from the first ash or oak that I meet with, I am resolved to rend as large and stout a bough as that, with which I expect, and intend to perform such exploits, as thou shalt think thyself extremely happy in being thought worthy to see, and give testimony to feats, otherwise credible." "By God's help, says Sancho, I believe that every thing will happen as your worship says; but pray, Sir, sit a little more upright; for you seem

---

[1] Briareus was a titan or giant of Greek and Roman mythology; he had one hundred arms and fifty heads.

[2] Place in La Mancha on the royal road from Madrid and Toledo to Andalusia.

[3] Diego Pérez de Vargas was a military hero of thirteenth-century Spain.

to lean strangely to one side, which must proceed from the bruises you received in your fall." "Thou art in the right, answered Don Quixote; and if I do not complain of the pain, it is because knights-errant are not permitted to complain of any wound they receive, even tho' their bowels should come out of their bodies." "If that be the case, I have nothing to reply, said Sancho, but God knows, I should be glad your worship would complain when any thing gives you pain: this I know, that for my own part, the smallest prick in the world would make me complain, if that law of not complaining does not reach to squires as well as the knights." Don Quixote could not help smiling at the simplicity of his squire, to whom he gave permission to complain as much and as often as he pleased, whether he had cause or no; for, as yet, he had read nothing to the contrary, in the history of knight-errantry.

Then Sancho observing that it was dinner-time, his master told him, that for the present he had no occasion for food; but, that he his squire might go to victuals when he pleased. With this permission, Sancho adjusted himself as well as he could, upon his ass, and taking out the provision with which he had stuffed his wallet, he dropped behind his master a good way, and kept his jaws agoing as he jogged along, lifting the bottle to his head from time to time, with so much satisfaction, that the most pampered vintner of Malaga might have envied his situation.

While he travelled in this manner, repeating his agreeable draughts, he never thought of the promise which his master had made to him, nor considered it as a toil, but rather as a diversion, to go in quest of adventures, how dangerous soever they might be: in fine, that night they passed under a tuft of trees, from one of which Don Quixote tore a withered branch to serve instead of a lance; and fitted to it, the iron head he had taken from that which was broken: all night long, the knight closed not an eye, but mused upon his lady Dulcinea, in order to accommodate himself to what he had read of those errants who passed many sleepless nights in woods and deserts, entertaining themselves with the remembrance of their mistresses.

This was not the case with Sancho Panza, whose belly being well replenished, and that not with plantane water, made but one nap of the whole night; and even then, would not have waked, unless his master had called to him, notwithstanding the sunbeams that played upon his face, and the singing of the birds, which in great numbers, and joyous melody, saluted the approach of the new day. The first thing he did, when he got up, was to visit his bottle, which finding considerably more empty than it was the night before, he was grievously afflicted, because in the road that they pursued he had no hopes of being able in a little time to supply its defect. Don Quixote refusing to breakfast, because, as we have already said, he regaled himself with the savoury remembrance of his mistress, they pursued their journey towards the pass, which after three days travelling, they discovered. "Here, cried Don Quixote, here, brother Sancho Panza, we shall be able to dip our hands up to the elbows, in what is called adventure; but, take notice, altho' thou seest me beset with the most extreme danger, thou must by no means, even so much as lay thy hand upon thy sword, with design to defend me, unless I am assaulted by vulgar and low-born antagonists, in which case, thou mayest come to my assistance; but, if they are knights, thou art by no means permitted or licensed, by the laws of chivalry, to give me the least succour, until thou thyself hast received the honour of knighthood." "As for that matter, replied Sancho, your worship shall be obeyed to a tittle; for, I am a very peaceable man, and not at all fond of meddling with riots and quarrels. True indeed, in the defence of my own person, I shall not pay much regard to the said laws, seeing every one that is aggrieved, is permitted to defend himself by the laws of God and man." "I say nothing to the contrary, replied Don Quixote, but, in the affair of assisting me against knights, thou must keep thy natural impetuosity under the rein." "That will I, answered Sancho, and keep your honour's command as strictly as I keep the Lord's day."

While they were engaged in this conversation, there appeared before them two Benedictine monks mounted upon dromedaries, for, their mules were not much less, with their travelling spectacles, and umbrellas; after them came a coach, accompanied by four or five people on horseback, and two mule-drivers on foot. In this carriage, it was afterwards known, a Biscayan lady was travelling to Seville to her husband, who was bound to the Indies with a rich cargo.

Don Quixote no sooner perceived the friars, (who, tho' they travelled the same road, were not of her company) than he said to his squire, "If I am not very much mistaken, this will be the most famous adventure that ever was known; for those black apparitions on the road must doubtless be enchanters, who are carrying off in that coach, some princess they have stolen; and there is a necessity for my exerting my whole power in redressing her wrongs." "This will be worse than the windmills, cried Sancho, for the love of God! Sir, consider, that there are Benedictine friars, and those who are in the coach can be no other than common travellers. Mind what I say, and consider what you do, and let not the devil deceive you." "I have told thee already, Sancho," replied Don Quixote, "that with regard to adventures, thou art utterly ignorant: what I say is true, and in a moment thou shalt be convinced."

So saying, he rode forward, and placed himself in the middle of the highway thro' which the friars were to pass, and when he thought them near enough to hear what he said, he pronounced, in a loud voice, "Monstrous and diabolical race! surrender this instant, those high-born princesses, whom you carry captives in that coach: or prepare to receive immediate death, as a just punishment for your misdeeds." The friars immediately stopped short, astonished as much at the figure, as at the discourse of Don Quixote: to which they replied, "Sir knight, we are neither diabolical nor monstrous, but innocent monks of the order of St. Benedict, who are going this way about our own affairs; neither do we know of any princesses, that are carried captives in that coach." "These fawning speeches, said Don Quixote, shall not impose upon me, who know too well what a treacherous pack you are"; and without waiting for any other reply, he put spurs to Rozinante, and couching his lance, attacked the first friar with such fury and resolution, that if he had not thrown himself from his mule, he would have come to the ground extremely ill-handled, not without some desperate wound, nay, perhaps stone dead. The second monk, who saw how his companion had been treated, clapped spurs to the flanks of his trusty mule and flew thro' the field even swifter than the wind.

Sancho Panza seeing the friar on the ground, leaped from his ass with great agility, and beginning to uncase him with the utmost dexterity, two of their servants came up, and asked for what reason he stripped their master. The squire replied, that the clothes belonged to him, as the spoils that Don Quixote his lord had won in battle: but, the others, who did not understand raillery, nor know any thing of spoils and battles, seeing Don Quixote at a good distance, talking with the people in the coach, went to loggerheads with Sancho, whom they soon overthrew, and without leaving one hair on his beard, mauled him so unmercifully, that he lay stretched upon the ground, without sense or motion. Then, with the utmost dispatch, mounted the friar, who was pale as a sheet, and almost frightened to death, and who no sooner found himself on horseback, than he galloped towards his companion, who tarried at a good distance, to see the issue of this strange adventure. However, being joined again, without waiting for the conclusion of it, they pursued their journey, making as many crosses as if the devil had been at their backs.

Don Quixote, in the mean time, as we have already observed, was engaged in conversation with the lady in the coach, to whom he expressed himself in this manner: "Beautiful lady, you may now dispose of your own person according to your pleasure, for the pride of your ravishers lies level with the ground, being overthrown by this my invincible arm; and that you may be at no difficulty in understanding the name of your deliverer, know that I am Don Quixote de la Mancha, knight-errant, adventurer and captive of the unparalleled and beautiful Donna Dulcinea del Toboso; and the only acknowledgment I expect for the benefit you have received, is, that you return to that place, and presenting yourself before my mistress, tell her what I have performed in behalf of your liberty." This whole address of the knight, was overheard by a Biscayan squire, who accompanied the coach, and who seeing, that he would not allow the carriage to pass forward but insisted upon their immediate returning to Toboso, rode up to Don Quixote, and laying hold of his lance, spoke to him thus in bad Castilian, and worse Biscayan: "Get thee gone, cavalier, go to the devil, I zay, vor, by the God that made hur, if thou wilt not let the coach alone, che will kill thee dead, as zure as che was a Biscayan."[4] The knight understanding very well what he said, replied

---

[4] *Vizcaíno* (Biscayan) was a commonly used term in Cervantes's time for the Basque people, whose homeland is in northwestern Spain and southwestern France. The Basque language is extremely ancient and totally unrelated to any other European tongue. The stereotype of the uncouth Basque who spoke broken Castilian, represented in this passage, was common in Spanish literature of the sixteenth and seventeenth centuries.

with great composure, "If thou wast a gentleman, as thou art not, I would chastise thy insolence and rashness, wretched creature." "I not a gentleman, replied the Biscayan in great choler; by God in heaven! thou liest, as I am a christian; if thou wilt throw away thy lance, and draw thy sword, che will soon zee which be the better man. Biscayan by land, gentleman by zea, gentleman by devil, and thou liest, look ye, in thy throat, if thou zayest otherwise." "Thou shalt see that presently, as Agragis said,"[5] replied Don Quixote, who throwing his lance upon the ground, unsheathing his sword, and bracing on his target, attacked the Biscayan with full resolution to put him to death.

His antagonist, who saw him approach, fain would have alighted from his mule, which being one of the worst that ever was let out for hire, could not much be depended upon: but, he scarce had time to draw his sword; however, being luckily near the coach, he snatched out of it a cushion, which served him as a shield, and then they flew upon each other as two mortal enemies. The rest of the people who were present, endeavoured, but in vain, to appease them; for the Biscayan swore, in his uncouth expressions, that if they did not leave him to fight the battle, he would certainly murder his mistress, and everybody who should pretend to oppose it. The lady in the coach, surprised and frightened at what she saw, ordered the coachman to drive a little out of the road, to a place from whence she could see at a distance this rigorous engagement. In the course of which, the Biscayan bestowed such a stroke upon the shoulder of Don Quixote, that if it had not been for the defence of his buckler, he would have been cleft down to his girdle. The knight feeling the shock of such an unconscionable blow, exclaimed aloud: "O Dulcinea! lady of my soul, thou rose of beauty, succour thy knight, who, for the satisfaction of thy excessive goodness, is now involved in this dreadful emergency." To pronounce these words, to raise his sword, to secure himself with his target, and attack the Biscayan, was the work of one instant; for, he was determined to risk his all upon a single stroke. His antagonist, who saw him advance, and by this time, was convinced of his courage by his resolution, determined to follow his example; and covering himself with his cushion, waited his assault, without being able to turn his mule either on one side or the other: for, she was already so jaded, and so little accustomed to such pastime, that she would not move one step out of the way.

Don Quixote then, as we have said, advanced against the cautious Biscayan, his sword lifted up with an intention to cleave him through the middle: the Biscayan waited his attack in the same posture, being shielded with his cushion. The frightened bystanders stood aloof, intent upon the success of those mighty strokes that threatened each of the combatants; and the lady in the coach, with the rest of her attendants, put up a thousand prayers to heaven, and vowed an offering to

---

[5] Agragis is a violent character in the chivalric romance *Amadis of Gaul.* The phrase is his opener to a fight.

every image and house of devotion in Spain, provided God would deliver the squire and them from the imminent danger in which they were: but the misfortune is, that in this very critical instant, the author of the history has left this battle in suspense, excusing himself, that he could find no other account of Don Quixote's exploits, but what has already been related. True it is, that the second author[6] of this work, could not believe that such a curious history was consigned to oblivion; nor, that there could be such a scarcity of curious scholars in la Mancha, but that some papers relating to this famous knight should be found in their archives or cabinets: and therefore, possessed of this opinion, he did not despair of finding the conclusion of this delightful history, which indeed he very providentially lighted upon, in the manner which will be related in the second book.

BOOK II

Chapter I

The conclusion and consequence of the stupendous combat between the gallant Biscayan, and the valiant knight of la Mancha.

In the first book of this history, we left the valiant Biscayan and renowned Don Quixote with their gleaming swords brandished aloft, about to discharge two such furious strokes, as must (if they had cut sheer) have cleft them both asunder, from top to toe, like a couple of pomegranates; and in this dubious and critical conjecture, the delicious history abruptly breaks off, without our being informed by the author, where or how that which is missing may be found.

I was not a little concerned at this disappointment; for, the pleasure I enjoyed in the little I had read, was changed to disgust, when I reflected on the small prospect I had of finding the greater part of this relishing story, which, in my opinion, was lost: and yet it seemed impossible, and contrary to every laudable custom, that such an excellent knight should be unprovided with some sage to undertake the history of his unheard-of exploits; a convenience which none of those knights-errant who went in quest of adventures ever lacked, each of them having been accommodated with one or two chroniclers, on purpose to record not only his achievements, but even his most hidden thoughts and amusements. Surely then such a compleat errant could not be so unlucky as to lack that, which even Platil,[7] and other such second-rate warriors enjoyed.

I could not therefore prevail upon myself to believe that such a spirited history was left so lame and unfinished, but laid the whole blame on the malignity of time, which wastes and devours all things, and by which, no doubt, this was either consumed or concealed: on the other hand, I considered, that as some

---

[6] Cervantes himself, adopting here another device found in chivalric romances in order to create suspense.

[7] Platil was a knight-errant from the Palmerín series of novels of chivalry.

books had been found in his library, so modern as the *Undeceptions of jealousy,* together with the *Nymphs and Shepherds of Henares;* [8] his own history must also be of a modern date, and the circumstances, tho' not committed to writing, still fresh in the memory of his neighbors and townsmen. This consideration perplexed and inflamed me, with the desire of knowing the true and genuine account of the life and wonderful exploits of our Spanish worthy Don Quixote de la Mancha, the sun and mirrour of Manchegan chivalry, the first who in this our age, and these degenerate times, undertook the toil and exercise of errantry and arms, to redress grievances, support the widow, and protect those damsels who stroll about with whip and palfrey, from hill to hill, and from dale to dale, on the strength of their virginity alone: for, in times past, unless some libidinous clown with hatchet and helmet, or monstrous giant, forced her to his brutal wishes, a damsel might have lived fourscore years, without ever lying under any other cover than that of heaven, and then gone to her grave as good a maiden as the mother that bore her. I say, therefore, that for these and many other considerations, our gallant Don Quixote merits incessant and immortal praise; and even I myself may claim some share, for my labour and diligence in finding the conclusion of this agreeable history; tho' I am well aware, that if I had not been favoured by fortune, chance or providence, the world would have been deprived of that pleasure and satisfaction which the attentive reader may enjoy for an hour or two, in perusing what follows:

While I was walking, one day, on the exchange of Toledo,[9] a boy coming up to a certain dealer in textiles, offered to sell him a bundle of old papers he had in his hand: now, as I have always a strong propensity to read even those scraps that sometimes fly about the streets, I was led by this my natural curiosity, to turn over some of the leaves: I found them written in Arabic, which not being able to read, tho' I knew the characters, I looked about for some Portuguese Moor[10] who should understand it; and indeed, even if the language had been both more elegant and ancient, I might easily have found an interpreter.[11] In short, I lighted upon one, to whom expressing my desire, and putting the pamphlet into his

---

[8] An ironic allusion to two mediocre pastoral romances written after Cervantes had published his own pastoral romance, *La Galatea* (1585): *Desengaño de celos (Undeceptions of Jealousy,* 1586) by Bartolomé Lopez de Enciso, and *Ninphas y pastores de Henares (Nymphs and Shepherds of Henrares,* 1587) by Bernardo González de Bobadilla.

[9] The "exchange of Toledo" is referred to in the Spanish original as the *Alcaná de Toledo,* and was a street famous for its haberdashery and spice shops. It passed through the Jewish and Moorish quarters of the city.

[10] In the Spanish original, Cervantes refers to a *morisco aljamiado,* a Castilian-speaking Moor.

[11] An ironic allusion to the Hebrew language. Cervantes implies that, despite their persecution and expulsion from Spain in 1492, there were still many Jews living in Toledo in the early 1600s.

hands, he opened it in the middle, and after having read a few lines, began to laugh; when I asked the cause of his laughter, he said it was occasioned by a whimsical annotation in the margin of the book: I begged he would tell me what it was, and he answered, still laughing. What I find written in the margin, is to this purpose: "This same Dulcinea so often mentioned in the history, is said to have had the best hand at salting pork of any woman in la Mancha."

Not a little surprised at hearing Dulcinea del Toboso mentioned, I immediately conjectured that the bundle actually contained the history of Don Quixote: possessed with this notion, I bade him, with great eagerness, read the title page, which having perused, he translated it extempore from Arabic to Spanish, in these words: "The history of Don Quixote de la Mancha, written by Cid Hamet Benengeli, an Arabian author." No small discretion was requisite to dissemble the satisfaction I felt, when my ears were saluted with the title of these papers, which, snatching from the dealer, I immediately bought all of them, for half a rial; tho', if the owner had been cunning enough to discover my eagerness to possess them, he might have laid his account with getting twelve times the sum by the bargain.

I then retired with my Moor, thro' the cloisters of the cathedral, and desired him to translate all those papers that related to Don Quixote into the Castilian tongue, without addition or diminution, offering to pay any thing he should charge for his labour: his demand was limited to two quarters of raisins, and as many bushels of wheat, for which he promised to translate them with great care, conciseness and fidelity: but, I, the more to facilitate the business, without parting with such a rich prize, conducted him to my own house, where, in little less than six weeks, he translated the whole, in the same manner as shall here be related.

In the first sheet, was painted to the life, the battle betwixt Don Quixote and the Biscayan, who were represented in the same posture as the history has already described, their swords brandished aloft, one of the antagonists covered with his shield, the other with his cushion, and the Biscayan's mule so naturally set forth, that you might have known her to have been one for hire, at the distance of a bow-shot. Under the feet of her rider, was a label, containing these words, "Don Sancho de Azpetia," which was doubtless his name; and beneath our knight was another, with the title of "Don Quixote." Rozinante was most wonderfully delineated, so long and raw-boned, so lank and meagre, so sharp in the back, and consumptive, that one might easily perceive, with what propriety and penetration the name of Rozinante had been bestowed upon him.[12] Hard by the steed was Sancho Panza, holding his ass by the halter, at whose feet was a third label, inscribed "Sancho Zancas," who, in the picture, was represented as a person of a short stature, swag belly, and long spindleshanks: for this reason, he ought to be

---

[12] The Spanish word *rocinante* refers to an old worn-out horse.

called indiscriminately by the names of Panza and Zancas; for by both these sur-names is he sometimes mentioned in history.[13]

There were divers other minute circumstances to be observed, but, all of them of small importance and concern to the truth of the history, tho' indeed nothing that is true can be irrelevant: however, if any objection can be started to the truth of this, it can be no other, but that the author was an Arabian, of a nation but too much addicted to falsehood, tho' as they are at present our enemies, it may be supposed, that he has rather failed than exceeded in the representation of our hero's exploits: for, in my opinion, when he had frequently opportunities and calls to exercise his pen in the praise of such an illustrious knight, he seems to be industriously silent on the subject; a circumstance very little to his commenda-tion, for, all historians ought to be punctual, candid and dispassionate, that nei-ther interest, rancour, fear, or affection may mislead them from the road of truth, whose mother is history, that rival of time, that depository of great actions, wit-ness of the past, example and pattern of the present, and oracle of future ages. In this, I know, will be found whatsoever can be expected in the most pleasant per-formance; and if any thing seems imperfect, I affirm it must be owing to the fault of the infidel its author, rather than to any failure of the subject itself: in short, the second book in the translation begins thus:

The flaming swords of the two valiant and incensed combatants, brandished in the air, seemed to threaten heaven, earth, and hell, such was the rage and reso-lution of those that wielded them: but, the first blow was discharged by the cho-leric Biscayan, who struck with such force and fury, that if the blade had not turned by the way, that single stroke would have been sufficient to have put an end to this dreadful conflict, and all the other adventures of our knight; but, his good genius, which preserved him for mightier things, turned the sword of his antagonist aside, so, that tho' it fell upon his left shoulder, it did no other dam-age than disarm that whole side, slicing off in its passage the greatest part of his helmet, with half of his ear, which fell to the ground, with hideous ruin, leaving him in a very uncomfortable situation. Good heavens! where is the man, who can worthily express the rage and indignation which entered into the heart of our Manchegan, when he saw himself handled in this manner? I shall only say, his fury was such, that raising himself again in his stirrups, and grasping his sword with both hands, he discharged it so full upon the cushion, and head of the Bis-cayan, which it but ill-defended, that, as if a mountain had fallen upon him, he began to spout blood from his nostrils, mouth and ears, and seemed ready to fall from his mule, which would certainly have been the case, if he had not laid hold of the mane: yet, notwithstanding this effort, his feet falling out of the stirrups,

---

[13] *Panza,* in Castilian, means "paunch," and *Zancas* means "spindly legs." (This deliberate uncertainty about the protagonists' proper names is a device used by Cervantes through-out *Don Quixote.*)

and his arms quitting their hold, the mule, which was frightened at the terrible stroke, began to run across the field, and after a few plunges, came with her master to the ground. Don Quixote, who sat observing him, with great tranquility, no sooner perceived him fall, than leaping from his horse, he ran up to him with great agility, and setting the point of his sword to his throat, bid him surrender, on pain of having his head cut off. The Biscayan was so confounded by the blow and fall he had sustained, that he could not answer one syllable, and as Don Quixote was blinded by his rage, he would have fared very ill, if the ladies of the coach, who had hitherto, in great consternation, been spectators of the battle, had not run to the place where he was, and requested, with the most fervent entreaties, that his worship would grant them the favour to spare the life of their squire.

To this petition, the knight replied, with great stateliness and gravity, "Assuredly, most beautiful ladies, I am very ready to do what you desire, but, it shall be upon condition and proviso, that this cavalier promise to go strait to Toboso, and present himself, in my behalf, before the unparalleled Donna Dulcinea, that she may use him according to her good pleasure." The timorous and disconsolate ladies, without entering into the detail of what Don Quixote desired, or inquiring who this Dulcinea was, promised that the squire should obey the knight's commands in every thing. "Upon the faith of your word, then," said Don Quixote, "I will do him no farther damage, tho' he has richly deserved it at my hand."

18

꙰

Wang Shih-chen

THE GOLDEN LOTUS

The Golden Lotus *has long been thought of as China's most notorious porno-graphic novel. This reputation hangs like a cloud over the work, has led to fanciful legends about its authorship, has distorted the understanding of genera-tions of readers about its intent as social and moral satire, and most seriously of all, has partially obscured its qualities as literature.*

Its Chinese title, Chin P'ing Mei, *translates literally as "The Plum in the Golden Vase," a title meaningless in itself but which is a composite of the names of three of the principle female characters: The Golden Lotus of the English title is the most important of these. It was probably written in the sixteenth century, to-ward the end of the Ming Dynasty (1368–1644), but not published until about 1617. Its authorship has been the subject of speculation ever since. Although the Ming produced four of China's greatest novels—the others are* Three Kingdoms *(Selection 8),* The Water Margin *(Selection 13), and* The Journey to the West—*writing popular fiction was still regarded as an inferior, if not downright disrep-utable, occupation for the Confucian scholars who aspired to careers in the impe-rial bureaucracy. Hence the authorship of such prose works was usually anonymous at the time of publication and, despite ingenious literary detective work in the intervening centuries, is still uncertain for some of these works. Attri-bution of* Chin P'ing Mei *to the Confucian scholar Wang Shih-chen (1526–1590) still has some currency, although it is disputed among a number of modern scholars who put forward a number of other possible candidates or prefer the "anonymous" label.*

Scholarly uncertainty over the authorship never stopped the legend spinners. The best known of the legends associated with The Golden Lotus *concerns a re-venge plot concocted by Wang Shih-chen against one Yen Shih-fan, who had a hand in the disgrace and death of Wang's father. Knowing Yen's corrupt nature, especially his appetite for salacious prose, Wang wrote the book as a double act of filial revenge. First, the debauched character of the novel's central figure,*

Hsi-men Ch'ing, was supposedly a thinly disguised portrait of Yen Shih-fan. But to make his revenge literally as well as morally deadly, Wang sent Yen a copy of the book on which a corner of each page was smeared with an invisible poison, and as Yen wetted his finger, eager to turn each page, he ingested enough poison to kill himself by the time he reached the end. Fanciful as it is, this legend nonetheless served its purpose, in that booksellers and readers could defend The Golden Lotus *against censorship in later times by claiming it was a work born of that admirable Confucian virtue, filial piety.*

Equally open is the question of the author's literary intent in writing The Golden Lotus. *Answers to this question over the centuries of its great popularity have ranged up and down what might be seen as a scale of moral and literary valuation. At the bottom of this scale is the answer that the work is simply a sexually explicit entertainment, perhaps the most elaborate and best written among many such works that have drifted through the substratum of Chinese literature over the centuries. More admirable, but still toward the low end of the scale, is the argument that the novel was written as an attack on the character of some specific contemporary person or persons, as in the Wang/Yen revenge story recounted above. Still higher on the scale, some scholars have stressed the novel's portrayal of contemporary bourgeois life in an extremely detailed, naturalistic way, including the facets of its moral corruption. Some have pointed to the novel's exaggerations of sexual and material corruption as the devices of a satire of manners and morals. Some have even seen* The Golden Lotus *as a Buddhist morality play. The argument for its satirical intent seems most persuasive to this editor.*

In its form, The Golden Lotus *is a novel divided into the traditional one hundred chapters. In its content, it depicts a period in the life of one Hsi-men Ch'ing, a wealthy merchant and magistrate of a large market town in what is now Shantung Province in the early twelfth century, at the end of the Northern Sung Dynasty (A.D. 960–1126). The cast of characters is immense and ranges across the social spectrum from high imperial officials with whom Hsi-men has corrupt dealings to the prostitutes he frequents and the hangers-on who leech off his generosity. However, the principal focus of character interaction is on Hsi-men's household and especially on his six concurrent wives. Chief among these are his first wife, Moon Lady, a conventional, decent woman but one not strong enough to preside over this disorderly melangé; Golden Lotus, a beautiful but vicious nymphomaniac who trails destruction in her wake until her own violent death; and Vase, Hsi-men Ch'ing's last wife and the only one toward whom he shows deep and genuine devotion.*

The Golden Lotus *is, on one level, a tale of Hsi-men Ch'ing's rising success in business and his emergence to prominence in judicial and military offices, procured through an incredible flow of presents to and favors for prominent men. The corruption, not only of the man but of the system of public maladministration which he understands and manipulates, runs parallel with the corruption of his personal life and with the disorder of his household. At its lower, sometimes comic level, this domestic disorder is seen in the squabbles over status, money, clothes, and jewelry among the servants, in their petty thievery, and in their lack of any real respect for or loyalty to the master and mistress of the establishment, Hsi-men and his first wife, Moon Lady. At another level, domestic disorder is seen in Hsi-men's careless disregard for the feelings of his first four wives, not only as he directs his considerable sexual energies almost exclusively to Golden Lotus and Vase at home, which would be fault enough, but also as he continues his career of debauchery in the town with a succession of brothel girls and with the wives of other men.*

To the critical reader, the graphic details of sexual encounters in The Golden Lotus *present a serious problem. In their explicitness, often descending to grossness, they go well beyond the demands of the naturalistic style which characterizes the novel's depiction of bourgeois life. Some critics have suggested that the salacious passages are designed as a sort of moral trap. They attract and excite the reader, but in time lead to the realization that the enjoyment of such graphic sexuality brings one down to the moral level of Hsi-men Ch'ing and his lover of the moment. At the least, one stands a bit ashamed to realize that one has been a voyeur; at best one has seen a mirror of the lustfulness of one's own heart and understands the destructive consequences of letting lust get out of control.*

In the passage excerpted here the sexuality is not as graphic as elsewhere in the novel and is not at any rate the principal substance of the passage. Rather it deals with the pervasive disorder within Hsi-men's household in the months before his death. This disorder is the result of Hsi-men's total lack of moral authority among his wives and servants, of Moon Lady's inadequate force of personality, and of Golden Lotus's unprincipled and by now largely successful attempt to control Hsi-men by sheer sexual power. While this disintegration of social and moral order focuses on a private household in the late years of the Northern Sung Dynasty, it should be seen as a metaphor for the corruption and disorder which brought down that dynasty and which was also already apparent in the late Ming Dynasty of Wang Shih-chen's own day.

On the following morning, as they lay in bed, and the conversation turned on the feast of the thirtieth day, which was to be held on the morrow, when Beggar Ying, to celebrate the birth of his child, had invited all Hsi-men's wives to his house, Golden Lotus suddenly declared, in a stubborn tone, "I'm not going."

"But why not, my dear child?"

From *Chin P'ing Mei: The Adventurous History of Hsi Men and his Six Wives.* Translated by Bernard Miall with an Introduction by Arthur Waley, copyright © 1939. Capricorn Books edition, 1960, pp. 572–573, 575–585.

"I've no furs to wear, and I don't want to catch cold on the way back, when we shall be overheated with wine. All the other wives have their fine furs, but I have none. You must give me the fur cloak which the Sixth[1] used to wear, or I shall stay home."

"We have many good furs among our pledges in the store room. You could borrow one of those."

"Thanks, I don't wear pawned articles. I want to wear the cloak I spoke of; no other. I have only to put on a white silk gown, with a dark red tunic over it, embroidered with cranes, and I look just like your Sixth."

Next moment, completely conquered by her passionate caresses, he had given the desired consent.

• • •

In the meantime Hsi-men had gone to Moon Lady in order to return the key in person.

"Why did you want it?" she asked.

"The Fifth complained that she would have no fur to wear tomorrow, when she went to the celebration of the thirtieth day at the Yings'. She was afraid of catching cold on the way home. At her request I gave her the sable cloak that the Sixth used to wear."

Moon Lady looked at him reprovingly.

"I think you are strangely inconsistent. When in accordance with the last wishes of the deceased I wanted to take the maid Apricot Blossom from the pavilion and allow her to wait on Sister Sunflower, you were angry, and reproached us bitterly, because you said we were in such a hurry to break up the household of the Sixth. And now you yourself are dispersing it and frittering it away."

Hsi-men did not know what to say to this.

That afternoon, while in the women's apartments Jade Fountain's birthday was being duly celebrated, Hsi-men was once more the host at a subscription dinner, which at the request of a number of high mandarins he was giving in honor of the Prefect of Kiu kiang, a son of the Chancellor Tsai King, then passing through the city, in the apartments which were so famed for their hospitality. Towards evening, when this official banquet was over, and the noble guests had taken their departure, he refreshed himself by an hour of jolly carousing with Beggar Ying and Master Warm.[2] At last this session also ended. Weary, and more than a little intoxicated, leaning heavily on the shoulders of his servant Lai An,

---

[1] Hsi-men's sixth wife, called Vase, had recently died and he still grieves for her. She was a beautiful and wealthy woman whom Hsi-men had seduced while she was still married to her first husband. Vase's death had been hastened by Golden Lotus's jealous scheming, a jealousy which continues even after Vase is gone.

[2] Ying and Warm are chief among a circle of spongers whom Hsi-men keeps about him for rowdy companionship. They may remind Western theater-goers of the low-life companions of Prince Hal in Shakespeare's *King Henry IV, Parts One and Two.*

he made his way, with reeling steps, to the pavilion of the Sixth. It had not occurred to him to honor his Third on her birthday with a brief hour of his society.

On hearing that he was about to go to bed Golden Lotus had hastily forsaken the feminine society assembled in Moon Lady's sitting room, and standing at the door of her pavilion, which he would be obliged to pass, she waited for him. And then he came with his escort, staggering past her with dragging feet. Without further ceremony she seized him by the hand and drew him into the pavilion, giving the servant to understand that his presence was no longer required. Lai An accordingly went to the women's apartments, where he helped wait upon the guests.

"Where is your master, then?" asked Moon Lady.

"He is with the Fifth mistress," he replied. Moon Lady was indignant.

"It's unheard-of!" she said, turning to Jade Fountain. "I expressly told him that as it was your birthday it was only proper to spend the night with you. He's forgotten it already, and now he's carrying on with the Fifth. Since he returned home it has been the same night after night. She has positively monopolized him."

"Never mind, Sister," said Jade Fountain, wearily. "You meant it kindly, but you shouldn't have spoken to her first. It looks as though I wanted to compete with her. If he doesn't come of himself. . . . To compel love . . . no, I couldn't do it."[3]

With a sigh Moon Lady changed the subject, washed her hands, and rekindled the censer. All gathered around the nun Pi, who had once more taken her place on the *kang*,[4] with her feet tucked under her. Opening the roll of the Holy Scriptures which she had brought with her, in a soporific voice she began to read the wonderful legend of the pious virgin Huang.[5]

With a few songs, contributed by Cinnamon Bud and the blind singing girl, Shen, and the consumption of enormous quantities of tea and sweetmeats, the birthday celebrations reached their close at a late hour of the night, without the assistance of Hsi-men.

Hsi-men did not remain long with Golden Lotus. When she asked him why he did not undress he confessed, with a smile, that he intended to spend the night

---

[3] Jade Fountain, Hsi-men's third wife, is a patient, long-suffering soul, seen in this excerpt as a victim of her master's neglect and also as a peace-maker within the disordered household. Her's will be a happier fate than that of many household members after Hsi-men's death. She will marry a decent widower and become a loved and respected first wife.

[4] The *kang*, common in northern Chinese houses, is a low brick or tile platform, heated from below, which provides a warm place to sit or sleep in winter.

[5] The Lady Huang is a figure of Buddhist lore, renowned for her purity, almsgiving and pious reading of scripture, and for her rebirth as a man. There is rather heavy irony in this tale of a pious virgin being solemnly recited in the sexually charged atmosphere of Hsi-men Ch'ing's household.

in the neighboring pavilion.[6] Still smiling at her reproaches, he stumbled out of the door.

Next morning Jade Flute came to Golden Lotus, faithful to the secret agreement between the two, in order to tell her what had happened the day before in Moon Lady's apartments.

"Why didn't you remain with the others last night?" Jade Flute began. "My mistress went for you sharply after you had rushed off so suddenly. She said it was unjust and tactless of you to monopolize Master Hsi-men on the Third mistress's birthday. And then the Third said you had no sense of decency, and that you were trying to play the mistress of the household, but that she refused to compete with you."

"Just wait a bit! They shall have something to complain of when I come to reckon with them!" said Golden Lotus, gnashing her teeth with rage. "But how did your mistress know that he spent last night with me?"

"Oh, well, in that connection you are the only person who counts now that the Sixth is dead."

"Really? So her empty nest has not been occupied in the meantime?"

"My mistress was annoyed, moreover, because you had taken the sable cloak of the Sixth to wear without saying a word to her first. When Master Hsi-men brought the key back to her she told him he was inconsistent, and that he himself was now squandering and frittering away the effects of his Sixth."

"Absurd. He is master in the house, and it's for him to decide what he will and won't do."

The feeling of resentment against Golden Lotus which had for some time been accumulating in Moon Lady's heart, was given further nourishment this day by two fresh incidents. While Hsi-men's five wives were being entertained in Friend Ying's house, where they were celebrating, together with a dozen wives of relatives and neighbors, the day on which Ying's offspring had safely completed his first month, another company had assembled for a joyful banquet in the pavilion of the Sixth. The nurse Ju I had invited the maids Apricot Blossom, Pear Blossom, and Spring Plum, and also Hsi-men's daughter, Sister-in-law Wu, and Golden Lotus's mother, to help her to dispose of the abundant remains of the previous night's supper. Thanks to their consumption of a very heady wine, they were soon in uproarious spirits, and little Spring Plum conceived the notion of inviting the blind singing-girl, Shen, to spice the conversation by singing a few songs. But the singer would not take orders from a maid; she proudly refused to come. And then the hot-tempered little Spring Plum made so violent a scene that

---

[6] That is, in the pavilion of his recently deceased sixth wife. With typical deviousness, Hsi-men wants this to be seen as an act of pious devotion to the dead, but he is actually looking forward to a sexual encounter with one of his dead wife's servants, the nurse Ju I.

the singer took offense, packed her things, weeping as she did so, and left the house.

In the evening, on her return from the house of Ying, Moon Lady found that the singer, who had been her guest, was gone, and learned that she had been intimidated by Spring Plum. This filled her with anger, and she felt obliged to blame Golden Lotus for the unbecoming behavior of her maid. Golden Lotus, of course, took her maid's part, and retorted with scornful personal remarks. Hsi-men refused to take the matter tragically: he thought the singer would soon be conciliated if on the morrow Spring Plum were to take her an ounce of silver and a few delicacies. Moon Lady, however, was not to be appeased; losing her temper, she retired, with Hsi-men, to her bedroom.

As a result of the uncomfortable atmosphere the rest of the women silently retired to their own apartments. Golden Lotus alone, still decked in all her splendor, and wearing the sable cloak, just as she had stepped out of her palanquin,[7] remained in the sitting room, nervously waiting for Hsi-men to appear again and accompany her to her pavilion. For this was the seven-times-seventh day of the sixty-day cycle; tonight, at all costs, she must share her couch with him and test the efficacy of Sister Pi's magic potion.[8]

But she waited in vain. Hsi-men did not appear. At last she lost patience. She simply opened the door of the adjoining room, and called out: "I can't wait for you any longer. I am going."

"Yes, you go on ahead; I shall just finish my drink and will follow you at once," he cried good-naturedly; at which she rustled away.

"You are not going to her! I won't have it!" said Moon Lady, interrupting him sternly. "For once, I must speak to you very seriously. I know, of course, that you eat out of the same platter. All the same, it is an unheard-of piece of insolence that she should actually force her way into my bedroom and call to you. She behaves as though you were her wife, and had to obey her orders, and as though the rest of us didn't exist. Since you returned from your journey we others have barely seen the edge of your shadow, she has monopolized you so completely. Not a single night have you had to spare for the rest of us. That of course, doesn't matter as far as I am concerned, but I do know of someone who is suffering

---

[7] A palanquin is a sedan chair carried on two long poles by two or more bearers.

[8] Golden Lotus, desperate to strengthen her position in the household by giving birth to a son, has obtained a "magic" medicine from a Buddhist nun, guaranteed to work only if taken before sexual intercourse on the forty-ninth day of the sixty day Chinese calendar cycle. This, like many other references to medication in the novel, is a none-too-subtle swipe at quack medical practice and at the venality of unscrupulous monks and nuns who pedal "magic" potions. Hsi-men himself will die horribly shortly after these events, when Golden Lotus administers an overdose of powerful aphrodisiac pills he had purchased from a wandering Indian monk.

greatly from this behavior of yours, even though she says nothing. Sister Jade Fountain couldn't swallow a mouthful at the party today, she was so full of suppressed emotion. Her sister-in-law Ying forced a beaker of wine on her; she drank it out of politeness, but she brought it up again immediately. You owe it to her to go to her now and ask her how she is feeling."

"I don't want any more to drink. I don't feel like it," Hsi-men declared peevishly. He rose to his feet and went off to find Jade Fountain.

She had already undressed herself and put aside her hair ornaments; she was lying face downward across the bed, dressed only in her nightgown, vomiting into a pail. Hsi-men was greatly shocked by her pitiful appearance.

"My dear, what is the matter with you? Tell me! I'll send for the doctor as soon as it's day," he said, in consternation.

She made no reply, but was sick again. He picked her up and sat down beside her.

"My stomach's upset," she said at last, speaking with difficulty, pressing her hand to the pit of her stomach. "But why do you ask? What's the use? Go away and amuse yourself!"

"My darling, I had no idea you were unwell! I have only just learned of it."

"That just shows me that for you I simply don't exist! Go away, do, go to your beloved!"

He laid his arm about her neck and kissed her. Then he called the maid Fragrant Orchid.

"Quick, some bitter tea!"

"I've just made it."

"Give it to me! And then take away the pail!"

He took the bowl of bitter, steaming tea in his hand and carefully held it to the sick woman's lips.

"Thanks, but I can manage it myself," she said, as she took the bowl from his hand. "Why do you trouble about me? For you to come here is as unnatural as though the sun were to rise in the West. I know Moon Lady persuaded you to come. I don't want you in the least."

"I really couldn't come to see you any earlier," he said in apology. "I've been so occupied all day."

"I know your heart was occupied all day!"

"You must be hungry," he said, changing the subject. "I too have had no supper. We'll have something together."

"No thanks. You have something yourself. I'm not in the mood for eating."

"Then I won't have anything. Tomorrow I'll send for Doctor Yen. And now we'll lie down and go to sleep."

• • •

As he spoke he gently drew one of her legs towards him, until it lay across his chest. How smooth and white her thigh was! And how charming the red satin slipper looked on her slender foot!

"Do you know, I think your smooth white legs are your greatest charm," he said, in a flattering tone. "In the whole world there is no one to compare with you in that respect!"

"You deceiver! Do you suppose I take any notice of your flattery? What you really mean, of course, is that there is no one in the whole world with such great legs and such a muddy skin as mine. One knows well enough that you mean right when you say left!"

"My heart, my liver, may I die here and now if I am lying!"

"Better not challenge destiny!"

He had been nestling closer and closer; and now he had found his way.

"I did beg you not to bother me with your nonsense!" she said, still feigning to resist him. But very soon her mouth was making those quivering, snapping motions which one may observe in a dog that is snapping at flies, and her lips without ceasing, uttered their tender cry of "*Ta, ta.*" With redoubled efforts Hsi-men endeavored that night to atone for the injustice with which he had treated his Third. But Golden Lotus sought her lonely couch with a heart full of bitter resentment. She had been shamefully cheated of her hope of testing the nun's magic potion on this seven-times-seventh day of the sixty day cycle.

• • •

Golden Lotus did not appear at breakfast. Moon Lady wanted to send Little Jewel for her.

"Little Jewel is in the kitchen, baking the cakes; I'll go instead," said Jade Flute; and off she went.

"I must tell you what happened last night," she said to Golden Lotus. "When you had gone my mistress said just what she thought about you. She said you were shameless, that you ruined the peace of the household, and that you and Master Hsi-men ate out of one platter. You had completely monopolized him; you ordered him about as if he had been your wife, and never let him show himself in the women's apartments. And then she sent him to the Third. He spent the night with her. What's more, she told her sister-in-law and the two nuns that you had ruined Spring Plum, and it was your fault that she had no manners. Master Hsi-men wanted to send Spring Plum to the blind singer; she was to apologize to her and take her an ounce of silver as compensation."

Golden Lotus made no reply, but what she had heard she stored up in her heart.

"Where is the Fifth?" asked Moon Lady, as Jade Flute returned.

"The Fifth mistress will be here directly."

"You see," said Moon Lady, turning to Sister-in-law Wu, "one said barely two words to her yesterday, and she's behaving as though she had been insulted. I expect there'll be another scene today."

"Who dares to say that I've monopolized him?" suddenly cried Golden Lotus's voice, from behind the curtain of the verandah door. She had crept up to the door unnoticed.

"Do you wish to deny it?" cried Moon Lady angrily. "Day after day, since his return, you have seized upon him and kept him for yourself. The rest of us barely see the edge of his shadow. You behave as if you were his only wife, as though the rest of us didn't exist. Yes, that was exactly what I said."

"And it's a pack of lies! He wasn't with me yesterday, nor the day before."

"*You* are lying! Hadn't you the insolence to come in here last night, when he was quietly sitting with me, and order him to come to you, as though it were a matter of course that he would do so? He is man enough to know what he ought to do and leave undone. How do you contrive to fetter him with cords of pig's hair and rob him of his freedom of movement? You are always running after him and trying to catch him for yourself. Is that seemly? Is it the reserve that one expects of a decent woman? Moreover, you appropriated the sable cloak of the Sixth behind my back. Couldn't you have spoken to me about it first? And what of the unmannerly way in which your maid behaved to the singing-girl, who was my guest, who frequents a hundred houses, and will of course gossip about us and bring us into disrepute? Can't you teach her better manners?"

"Well, chastise her yourself! She's as much your maid as mine. I've nothing to say to that. As for the fur, I didn't appropriate it; it was given to me. As far as that goes, on the same occasion he presented somebody else with various articles from the Sixth wife's wardrobe. Why do you blame only me for unseemly conduct?"

Moon Lady mistakenly believed that this last remark was aimed at her, although it actually referred to the nurse Ju I and her secret relations with her master. Angered beyond all control, her cheeks crimson with fury, she burst into voluble speech: "I suppose that means that I myself am guilty of unseemly behavior? No, I at all events know what is right and proper. I was decently brought up in an honorable family, and I was lawfully married to him; I am an honest and respectable wife, not a shameless harlot like yourself, who runs after every man she sees!"

"Big Sister, don't be so angry!" said Jade Fountain, seeking to appease her. "In your excitement you quite overlook the fact that you are hitting us with the same club!" And turning to Golden Lotus, "Sister Five," she said, "do let there be an end of all this controversy! Must you always have the last word?"

"This dispute is not exactly pleasant for your guests," added Sister-in-law Wu. "If it continues perhaps one had better get into one's palanquin and leave the house."

Golden Lotus, who was beside herself with rage at these rebukes, threw herself down at full length. Her hair became unfastened, tears of rage flooded her cheeks, and like a madwoman she struck herself and beat her head on the floor.

"I will endure this aimless life no longer! I would rather die!" she cried in despair. "I am supposed to have run after him when he took me into his household![9] Very well, as soon as he comes home I shall ask him for a letter of divorce, and go. Then no one can ever say again that I ran after him."

Jade Fountain could endure this squabbling no longer. She took Golden Lotus by the hand and tried to lead her away to her own pavilion.

"You really ought to control yourself better! We are making ourselves a laughing stock to our guests! Come! Stand up!" And with the help of Jade Flute she pulled the resisting woman to her feet and escorted her to her pavilion.

---

[9]She had done worse than this. She had engaged in an illicit affair with Hsi-men and murdered her husband to clear the way for Hsi-men to take her into his household. In one of the concluding chapters Golden Lotus is brutally murdered by her dead husband's brother.

19

⁂

Ts'ao Hsueh-ch'in

THE DREAM OF THE RED CHAMBER

From a time shortly after its publication in 1791, the Hung-lou-meng *or* The Dream of the Red Chamber *was acclaimed a masterpiece and has come to be universally recognized as China's greatest novel. It has been beloved by generations of Chinese readers ever since and, in translation, has found an appreciative audience the world over. A vast, complex work, it proceeds simultaneously on multiple levels of meaning — moral and spiritual symbolism, social satire, and subtle character revelation. Its psychological plausibility and its development of characters beyond the stock types of earlier Chinese fiction made the work virtually revolutionary at the time of its writing and have established it as a benchmark for Chinese fiction ever since.*

Whereas authorship of most of the great novels of the Ming Dynasty (1368–1644) remains problematic (see introductory notes to Selections 8, 13, and 18), most chapters of Red Chamber *are firmly ascribed to one Ts'ao Hsueh-ch'in (1715–1763), with probable additions and editorial revisions by one or more late-eighteenth-century literati after his death. Ts'ao came from a family of distinguished military and civil officials that had been prominent since the tenth century. Even after the Manchu invasion that established the Ch'ing Dynasty (1644–1911), the Chinese Ts'ao family held positions of influence as trusted associates of the Manchu ruling house. However, in 1728 the Ts'ao family found itself on the losing side of a power struggle within the imperial line, suffered dismissal from its lucrative office and confiscation of its property. Ts'ao Hsueh-ch'in, thus, knew affluence as boy, but for the last three and a half decades of his life tasted not only poverty but the humiliation of lost status and of dependence on the help of more fortunate relatives and friends. His knowledge of life among the wealthy and powerful, his personal experience of the cruelty of fate, and his sharp sense of moral decline within family and society — all came to inform his writing with the clear-eyed, unsentimental empathy that runs through the novel.*

The complexity of Red Chamber *is accompanied by considerable ambiguity as to its major themes and their meaning in the minds of Ts'ao Hsueh-ch'in and his later editors. An extensive body of commentary and analysis, first in China and now throughout the world, has created a scholarly discipline of its own,* Red Studies, *comparable in its way to Shakespeare Studies in the West. There is sufficiently complex material in the novel to permit arguments that it is a Confucian, or Taoist, or Buddhist morality tale. It has also been read as another in the tradition of great romantic stories. Some have seen it as a veiled depiction of the corruption of China wrought by Manchu domination. In the twentieth century, Marxist-Maoist critiques stressed the theme of degeneracy among the wealthy ruling class of what they called the "feudal society." Whatever the dominant theme or intended "message," however, few critics doubt that the work is in some measure autobiographical, with a strong identification between the author and the young hero, Pao-yu.*

In structure Red Chamber *is a frame tale whose frame is the symbolic story of a piece of magical jade and a pearl flower. The former, which gives the novel its alternative title,* The Story of the Stone (Shih-t'ou chi), *is brought to earth by an eccentric Buddhist monk and mangy Taoist priest. The precious stone is changed into a living creature, the novel's hero, Pao-yu. The flower is born into the world as Pao-yu's delicate and doomed cousin and lover, Ling Tai-yu (Black Jade). The stone/wood symbolism of these two protagonists establishes the theme of fated meeting and tragedy, while the periodic appearances of the monk and priest give them the opportunity to comment on the folly of excessive attachment to the material/sensual world. The frame is finally closed when Pao-yu renounces the world to become a Buddhist monk himself.*

Within this frame the main body of the work concerns the life and decline of a great aristocratic family, the Chias, two branches of which live in adjacent compounds, the Ningkuofu and the Yungkuofu, in the capital city. The Yungkuofu is presided over by Pao-yu's grandmother, called the Matriarch. Her two sons and their families share the compound. Phoenix, wife of one of the Matriarch's grandsons, is a beautiful, capable but ruthless woman who is effectively the stewardess of the Yungkuofu. Her unscrupulous financial dealings eventually bring ruin on the house when imperial authorities raid the compound and confiscate the Chias' property; echoes of the disaster which struck the author's family are unmistakable.

The Matriarch's younger son is a serious Confucian scholar and public official, certainly the most traditional, straightforward character among the hundreds who populate the two compounds. His daughter has been conscripted as an imperial concubine, and her brief return visit to the Chia family is a major event in the life of the clan. His son, Pao-yu, is a bright, attractive but spoiled adolescent who neglects the study his stern father urges upon him in favor of sensual relationships with his female relatives and various serving maids. Among these are two cousins, Black Jade, a beautiful but delicate and oversensitive girl whom

Pao-yu loves but can never assure of this love, and Precious Virtue, whom the family comes to favor as the more stable and sensible mate for Pao-yu. He does marry Precious Virtue, but it's an ill-fated match. On his wedding night Black Jade dies and Pao-yu has barely consummated the marriage to Precious Virtue before he renounces the world to become a monk.

The story of these "star-crossed lovers" is tragic; but the tragedy, set in the context of what is in part a novel of character analysis and social commentary, is tempered by irony. The romantic reader, for instance, may say that Black Jade dies of a broken heart; but the less tenderhearted may say she perishes of excessive self-pity. In the excerpt below, the famous dream sequence which gives the novel its popular title — the dream in and of the women's quarters or red chambers — one sees that the love story is played out in the context of an unsentimentally moral view of passion as a road to disillusionment. The irony is never far away, however, for on the evening of the day in which Pao-yu's dream presents this lesson with frightening force, he forgets the lesson and enjoys his first sexual experience with a serving girl.

Chapter 5

In which . . . the Goddess of Disillusionment fails to awaken her erstwhile attendant

Ever since Black Jade had arrived in the Yungkuofu, the Matriarch lavished on her the love and tender solicitude hitherto reserved for Pao-yu. The young girl occupied an even warmer place in the Matriarch's heart than the three Springs, her real granddaughters. She and Pao-yu had also been drawn closer together, not only because they shared the same apartment, but also because of the natural affinity which manifested itself in their first meeting. Now there suddenly appeared on the scene Precious Virtue. Though only a trifle older than Black Jade, she showed a tact and understanding far beyond her years. She was completely unspoiled, always ready to please and enter into the spirit of the occasion and always kind to the servants and bondmaids. In contrast, Black Jade was inclined to haughtiness and held herself aloof. Thus in a short time Precious Virtue won the hearts of all, and Black Jade could not help feeling a little jealous. Precious Virtue seemed wholly unaware of the situation her presence created.

As for Pao-yu, he was so simple in nature and so completely guileless that his behavior often struck people as odd if not mad. He treated everyone alike and

From *Dream of the Red Chamber* by Ts'ao Hsueh-ch'in, with a Continuation by Kao Ou, translated from the Chinese by Chi-chen Wang. Copyright © 1958 by Chi-chen Wang. Pp. 50–60.

never stopped to consider the nearness of kinship of one as compared with that of another. Often he would unwittingly offend Black Jade, sometimes in his very efforts to please her. On such occasions, it was always Pao-yu who made the conciliatory gesture.

One day when the plums in the garden of the Ningkuofu were in full bloom, Yu-shih, the wife of Chia Gen, took the occasion to invite the Matriarch, Madame Wang, Madame Hsing, and other members of the Yungkuofu to a plum-flower feast. Nothing of particular note occurred; it was simply one of these many seasonal family gatherings. After dinner, Pao-yu said he felt tired and wished to take a nap.

"We have a room ready for Uncle Pao," Chin-shih said to the Matriarch. "I'll take him there and see that he has a nice rest."

Now Chin-shih was Chias Jung's wife and the Matriarch's favorite great granddaughter-in-law. She was a very beautiful young woman, possessed of a slender figure and a most gentle and amiable disposition. The Matriarch felt safe to leave Pao-yu in her hands.

The room to which Chin-shih took Pao-yu was one of the main apartments in the Ningkuofu and was luxuriously furnished, but Pao-yu took objection to the center scroll on the wall, a painting depicting the famous Han scholar Liu Hsiang receiving divine enlightenment. He took an even more violent objection to the scrolls on either side of the painting on which was inscribed the couplet:

> To know through and through the ways of the world is Real
> Knowledge;
> To conform in every detail to the customs of society is True
> Accomplishment.

"I cannot possibly sleep in this room," he declared.

"If you do not like this room, I am afraid nothing will suit you," Chin-shih said and then added, "unless perhaps you want to use mine."

Pao-yu smiled assent, but his nurse Li Ma objected, saying, "It is hardly proper for an uncle to sleep in the bedroom of his nephew's wife.".

"Don't be ridiculous," Chin-shih said, laughing. "Uncle Pao is just a boy, if he doesn't mind my saying so. Didn't you see my younger brother when he came to visit last month? He is just Uncle Pao's age, but he is the taller of the two."

"Where is your brother?" Pao-yu asked, for he wanted to see what the brother of the beautiful Chin-shih was like. "Bring him and let me meet him."

"He is home, many miles from here," she answered. "You will meet him some other time."

Pao-yu detected a subtle and yet intoxicating fragrance as he entered Chin-shih's room. On the wall there was a painting by T'ang Yin, entitled "Lady Taking Nap under Begonia" and a couplet by a Sung poet:

> A gentle chill pervades her dreams because it is Spring,
> The fragrance intoxicates one like that of wine.

In the center of the table was a mirror once used by the Empress Wu Tse T'ien.[1] At one side there was a golden plate on which the nimble Chao Fei-yen had danced, and on the plate there was a quince that An Lu-shan had playfully thrown at the beautiful Yang Keui-fei. The carved bed once held the Princess Shou Yang and the pearl curtains were made for the Princess T'ung Chang.

"I like your room," Pao-yu exclaimed with delight.

"It is fit for the immortals, if I may say so," Chin-shih said with a smile. She spread out the silk coverlet that was once washed by Hsi Shih and put in place the embroidered pillow that was once embraced by the Red Maid. Pao-yu's nurse withdrew after helping him to bed. Only his four handmaids — Pervading Fragrance, Bright Design, Autumn Sky, and Musk Moon — remained, and they were encouraged by Chin-shih to go outside and watch the kittens play under the eaves.

Pao-yu fell asleep almost as soon as he closed his eyes. In a dream he seemed to follow Chin-shih to some wondrous place where the halls and chambers were of jade and gold and the gardens were filled with exotic blooms. Pao-yu was filled with delight. He thought to himself that he would gladly spend the rest of his life here. Suddenly he heard someone singing on the far side of the hill.

> Spring dreams vanish like ever changing clouds,
> Fallen flowers drift downstream never to return.
> And so lovers everywhere, heed my words,
> 'Tis folly to court sorrow and regret.

The song still lingered in Pao-yu's ears when there appeared before him a fairy goddess whose beauty and grace were unlike anything in the mortal world. Pao-yu greeted her and said, "Sister Immortal, where have you come from and where are you going? I have lost my way. Please help me."

She replied: "I am the Goddess of Disillusionment. I inhabit the Realm of Parting Sorrow in the Ocean of Regrets. I am in charge of the plaints of unhappy maidens and sad lovers, their debts of love and their unfulfilled desires. It is not by accident that I have encountered you. My home is not far from here. I have not much to offer you, but I have some tender tea leaves which I gathered myself and a few jars of my own wine. I have several singers trained in exotic dances and have just completed a series of twelve songs which I call 'Dream of the Red Chamber.' Why don't you come with me?"

Chin-shih having now disappeared, Pao-yu followed the Goddess and reached a place dominated by a huge stone arch across which was written the inscription "Great Void Illusion Land." On either side this couplet was inscribed:

---

[1] All of the women whose memorabilia are mentioned in this passage were famous beauties in Chinese history, most of whom exercised seductive and corrupting influence over emperors or other powerful men.

When the unreal is taken for the real, then
    the real becomes unreal;
When non-existence is taken for existence,
    then existence becomes non-existence.

Passing through the arch Pao-yu found himself standing in front of the gate of a palace above which was the inscription "Sea of Passion and Heaven of Love." The couplet read:

Enduring as heaven and earth —
    no love however ancient can ever die;
Timeless as light and shadow —
    no debt of breeze and moonlight can ever be repaid.

Pao-yu was still too young to understand the meaning of the couplet. He had a vague notion about love, but no idea at all of what breeze and moonlight might be. He was naturally curious and said to himself that he must be sure to find out before he left the place. By this innocent thought Pao-yu became inexplicably involved with the demons of passion.

Entering the second gate, Pao-yu saw long rows of chapels with inscriptions such as "Division of Perverse Sentiments, Division of Rival Jealousies, Division of Morning Weeping, Division of Evening Lament, Division of Spring Affections, and Division of Autumn Sorrows."

"Would it be possible for you to take me through these chapels?" Pao-yu asked.

"No," the Goddess answered. "They contain the past, present, and future of the maidens of the entire world. Mortal eyes may not look upon them." As they walked on, Pao-yu continued to importune the Goddess until she finally yielded, saying, "You may see this one." Pao-yu looked up and saw that the chapel was inscribed "Division of the Ill-Fated." There was also this couplet:

Sorrows of Spring and sadness of autumn are
    all one's own doing;
A face like a flower and features like the moon
    are all in vain in the end.

Inside, Pao-yu saw more than ten large cabinets all sealed and labeled with the names of different provinces. Wishing to find out about his own, he went to the cabinet marked "The Twelve Maidens of the Chinling, File No. 1."

"I have heard that Chinling is a large city. Why is it that there are only twelve maidens? Just in our family there are several hundred of them."

"We keep records of only the more important ones," the Goddess smiled indulgently.

Pao-yu looked at the next two cabinets and noted that they were marked "The Twelve Maidens of Chinling, File No. 2" and "The Twelve Maidens of

Chinling, File No. 3," respectively. He opened the last cabinet and took out a large album. The first page was completely obscured by heavy mist and dark clouds. There was no foreground whatever. Inscribed on the page were the following lines:[2]

> Clear days are rarely encountered,
> Bright clouds easily scattered.
> Her heart was proud as the sky,
> But her position was lowly on earth.
> Her beauty and accomplishments only invited jealousy,
> Her death was hastened by baseless slander.
> And in vain her faithful Prince mourns.

Pao-yu could make nothing of all this. On the next page there was a painting of a bunch of flowers and a broken mat, together with a poem.

> Gentle and gracious well she may be,
> Like cassia and orchid indeed she is.
> But what are these things to the young Prince
> When it is the mummer that destiny has favored?

This meant even less to Pao-yu. He replaced the album and took the one in cabinet 2. The first page was also a picture, this time a sprig of cassia at the top and below it a withered lotus flower on a dried-up pond. The accompanying poem read:

> Oh symbol of purity and innocence,
> Your cruel fate is least deserved.
> For in two fields one tree will grow
> And send your gentle soul to its ancient home.

Again Pao-yu failed to see the significance of the picture or poem. He tried the album in cabinet 1 and found the pictures and poems equally baffling. He was about to try again, when the Goddess, fearing that he might succeed in penetrating the secrets of Heaven if allowed to go on, took the album from him and put it back in the cabinet, saying, "Come and see the rest of the place. What is the use of puzzling over these?"

Pao-yu was led into the inner palace, which was even more splendid than what he had already seen. Several fairies come out at the call of the Goddess, but they seemed to be disappointed when they saw Pao-yu. One of them said rudely, "We thought you were going to bring Sister Crimson. Why this common creature from the mortal world?"

---

[2] In these albums Pao-yu reads poems that foretell the fates of a number of young women of the two Chia households, but he is unable to grasp their meanings.

While Pao-yu stood in awkward silence, the Goddess explained to the fairies that she had brought him in order to enlighten him, and begged them to help her in the task. The tea, the wine, and the food were all delicious beyond anything that Pao-yu had ever tasted. After the feast the Goddess bade her fairies sing "Dream of the Red Chamber." She gave Pao-yu a manuscript so that he might follow it while it was sung. "For you may not understand this as you are accustomed only to mortal music," she explained. The singing was exquisite, but Pao-yu could not understand the references and allusions in the lyrics. The Goddess sighed compassionately when she saw that Pao-yu remained unenlightened.

After a while Pao-yu began to feel sleepy and begged to be excused. The Goddess then took him to a chamber where to his astonishment he found a girl who reminded him of Precious Virtue in graciousness of manner and of Black Jade in beauty of features. He was wondering what was going to happen next when he heard the voice of the Goddess speaking to him. "In the Red Dust,"[3] she said, "the embroidered chambers are often desecrated by licentious men and loose women. What is even more deplorable are the attempts to distinguish between love of beauty and licentiousness, forgetting that one always leads to the other. The meetings at Witches' Hill and the transports of cloud and rain[4] invariably climax what is supposedly a pure and chaste love of beauty. I am now, of course, speaking of the generality of men and women. There are rare exceptions, of which you are one. Indeed, I admire you because you are the most licentious of men."

"How could you make such an accusation!" Pao-yu protested. "I have been taken to task for not applying myself to my studies and have been severely reprimanded for it by my parents, but no one has accused me of licentiousness. Besides, I am still young. I hardly know the meaning of the word."

"Do not be alarmed," the Goddess said. "Licentiousness simply means excess, and there are all kinds of excesses. The most common kind is an insatiable greed of the flesh. We are all familiar with those coarse creatures who cannot think of beautiful women except as means for gratifying their animal desires. They are a constant danger and threat to womankind. Your licentiousness, however, is of a more subtle kind, one that can only be apprehended but not described. Nevertheless, it is just as excessive and insatiable as the kind the world is familiar with, but whereas the latter constitutes a constant danger to womankind, your licentiousness makes you a most welcome companion in the maidens' chambers. But what makes you desirable in the maidens' chambers also makes you appear strange and unnatural in the eyes of the world. It is necessary for you to experience what most men experience, so that you may know its nature and limitations. I have, therefore, arranged that you should marry my sister Chien-mei. This is the night for you to consummate your union. After you have seen for

---

[3] The Red Dust, i.e., the earth.

[4] Cloud and rain are a euphemism for sexual intercourse.

yourself that the pleasures of fairyland are but thus and so, you may perhaps realize their vanity and turn your mind to the teachings of Confucius and Mencius
and devote your efforts to the welfare of mankind."[5]

She whispered in Pao-yu's ears the secrets of cloud and rain and pushed him
toward her sister Chien-mei. Then she left them, closing the door after her.
Pao-yu followed the instructions of the Goddess and disported himself with his
bride in ways that may well be imagined but may not be detailed here. The next
day Pao-yu went out for a walk with his bride. Suddenly he found himself in a
field overgrown with thorn and bramble and overrun with tigers and wolves. In
front of him an expanse of water blocked the way of escape. As he tried desperately to think of what to do, the Goddess's voice spoke to him from behind, "Stop
and turn back before it is too late!" As she spoke, a deafening roar issued from
the water, and a horde of monsters rushed toward Pao-yu. Frantically he cried
out, "Help me, Chien-mei! Help, help!" Thereupon he awoke bathed in cold
sweat, as Pervading Fragrance and the other maids rushed to his bedside, saying,
"Don't be afraid, Pao-yu. We are all here with you." Chin-shih, who had heard
Pao-yu calling Chien-mei, wondered, "How did he happen to know my childhood name?"

As Pervading Fragrance helped Pao-yu to adjust his clothes, her hand came in
contact with something cold and clammy. Quickly withdrawing her hand, she
asked Pao-yu what it was. Pao-yu did not answer, but only blushed and gave her
hand a gentle squeeze. Being a clever maid and a year or two older than Pao-yu,
she too blushed and said no more. Later that evening, when she was alone with
him in the apartment, she brought Pao-yu a change of clothing.

"Please don't tell anyone," Pao-yu said embarrassedly. Then he confided to
her his dream. When he came to what happened in the bridal chamber, the maid
blushed and laughed and covered her face with her hands. Now Pao-yu had always been very fond of the maid, so he proposed to demonstrate what the Goddess had taught him. At first Pervading Fragrance refused, but in the end she ac-
quiesced, since she knew that she would eventually be Pao-yu's concubine.
Thenceforward Pao-yu treated her with more tenderness than ever, and the maid
on her part ministered to the comforts of her young master even more faithfully
than before.

---

[5] This little Confucian lecture from the Goddess reveals something of the novel's ambivalent point of view. The main philosophical burden of the dream sequence is the
Buddhist doctrine that apparent reality is an illusion and that we suffer when we treat
illusion as reality.

PART
IV

THE REEXAMINATION
OF TRADITION

ﻉ

The reexamination of tradition in Part Four (Selections 20–26) begins with the European forms of the Christian religion. With the Protestant Reformation of the sixteenth century came a period of fierce religious wars, dividing Europe roughly between north and south, with the northern kingdoms seeking their own identities through national religions and the south, led by the Roman papacy, seeking to preserve the unity of Christianity by maintaining papal authority. (We can see some of the uncertain results of this division in Northern Ireland today.) The sparkplug of the Reformation was Martin Luther, a German, who first directly challenged the papacy in 1517. The *Address to the Christian Nobility of the German Nation*, 1520 (Selection 20), shows Luther vigorously asserting his developing Protestant doctrines, denouncing the corruptions of the papacy in distant Rome, and appealing to the national sentiments of his fellow Germans. The same militant appeal is shown in Luther's hymn reprinted here, "A Mighty Fortress Is Our God." The *Spiritual Exercises* of Saint Ignatius of Loyola (Selection 21), a Spaniard, are a direct response to what Ignatius regarded as Luther's heresy. His writings served to reaffirm Catholic doctrine, rejecting any theological compromise with the new Protestant views, while simultaneously encouraging needed reforms within the Church. As the founder of the new religious order of Jesuits, Ignatius particularly asserted the need for hierarchical authority in the Church, with the pope as its head. Yet another passionate statement of the European religious conflict is the sonnet by John Milton, "On the Late Massacre in Piedmont" (Selection 22). With vengeful anger he protests a slaughter of Italian Protestants. In his later years Milton, grown blind in his service to the Puritan Commonwealth of England, would compose perhaps the greatest Christian epic in the English language, *Paradise Lost*. In seventeenth-century Catholic Spain, religious disputation between Protestants and Catholics was not a possibility. While always confirming Catholic doctrine, the theater of Calderón in *Life Is a Dream* (Selection 23) manages to explore such questions as predestination versus free will.

Religious growth and conflict did not occur only in Europe during the period of this book. In the vastness of India the Sikh religion was born out of the interaction between Islam and Hinduism about five hundred years ago. The *Adi Granth* (*Primal Book*) is the foundation of Sikh belief and practice (Selection 24). An important group in northwestern India, the Sikhs have also emigrated to many other regions, including North America. They number about eighteen million. Composed about the same time as the Sikh *Primal Book*, the epic poem *Ramcharitmanas* (*Holy Lake of Ram's Acts*) has become the most popular scripture of Hinduism. Unlike many religious texts, it has a single author, Tulsi Das (Selection 25). We end Part Four in Africa with *The Song of Bagauda* (Selection 26), in which the Hausa people experience pressure from other Islamic groups to eliminate their traditional non-Islamic ways. Thus, we see in all the selections of Part Four the frequent reexamining and changing, as well as reconfirming, of religious traditions.

20

❧

Martin Luther

ADDRESS TO THE CHRISTIAN NOBILITY OF THE GERMAN NATION *AND* A MIGHTY FORTRESS IS OUR GOD

The supposed unity of Christianity in the West was blown apart early in the sixteenth century. The central figure in this theological and political explosion was Martin Luther (1483–1546). Luther, a German, was born in Eisleben, Saxony, the son of humble peasant parents. His father became a miner and, with considerable struggle, was able to provide the means for his son's education. At the University of Erfut the young Luther gained a general humanistic education. He initially intended to enter the field of law but in 1505 decided suddenly to devote his life to God and entered an Augustinian monastery where he lived a severely ascetic life. He was ordained a priest in 1507 and by 1511 was named Doctor of Theology and professor at the University of Wittenberg where he lectured on the New Testament.

Despite his comfortable position at Wittenberg, Luther was filled with religious questions as well as moral doubts about the corrupt church practices that he had observed, especially in Rome among those in high positions. In 1517 he directly challenged papal authority when, on the door of the castle church at Wittenberg, he posted his ninety-five theses that protested the Church's doctrine and sale of indulgences. (The posting was a customary method of demanding an open discussion of any question.) An indulgence is a remission of punishment for sin, both in this life and in the purgatorial hereafter. Luther's criticism of indulgences soon broadened to a general attack on the papally controlled Church. It stemmed from his fervent conviction that the papacy was not a divinely ordained institution but rather a creation of greedy men interested in perpetuating their own power. In 1520 Luther was excommunicated and in the following year placed under the ban of the Holy Roman Empire. The Protestant Reformation had now clearly begun and the breach with Rome would prove irreparable.

For his own safety, Luther was hidden by local members of the German nobility in his native Saxony, where, in addition to developing his ideas in numerous writings, he translated the Bible into German, thereby creating not only the Bible that is still the standard German version but really creating the basis for modern German as a literary language. By 1522, Luther was able to return to Wittenberg, having earned the support of much of the German nobility. He stayed there for some twenty years, marrying a former nun, Katherina von Bora, who bore him six children. Believing that the civil authority had the right and obligation to correct mistaken or corrupt religious beliefs and practices, Luther appealed to the German rulers to expel the "foreign tyranny of the papacy." The rulers of the northern German principalities were not only persuaded by Luther's fiery religious arguments but also found it in their national and economic interests to support him. (They had grown increasingly aggravated with seeing German wealth sent south to Rome.) In his search for followers against a hostile papacy, Luther found it practical to appeal to the entire Christian community, not just the clergy. Thus, he wrote and spoke primarily in a powerful and clear German, the language of the people, rather than in Latin, the language of scholars. The recently invented printing press became, therefore, an indispensable instrument for the spreading of Luther's ideas.

In the Address to the Christian Nobility of the German Nation *(1520) the reader can see Luther at the height of his denunciatory energies. In addition to his attacks on the papacy and on the doctrine of indulgences, it includes such fundamental points of Lutheran doctrine as the priesthood of all true believers and the supreme authority of the Bible in all religious matters. Many among the German nobility were encouraged by Luther's clear statement that members of the clergy, like all other citizens, were subject to the civil law. This had long been a point of dispute throughout Europe between civil and ecclesiastical authorities.*

Following the Address *is an English version of the lyrics for one of Luther's forty-one hymns. They have survived as living literature for common people, often inculcating Lutheran theology in ways more easily and pleasurably grasped than in a theological tract or sermon. "Ein feste Burg ist unser Gott," translated here as "A Mighty Fortress Is Our God," shows the Lutheran hymn's typically rugged strength and emotional appeal. It also shows Luther's use of the language of militant German nationalism. Luther's rhetorically powerful use of his native German was a major force in the success of the Reformation and established Lutheranism as the first major branch of Protestantism.*

To His Most Serene and Mighty Imperial Majesty[1]
and to the Christian Nobility
of the German Nation.

DR. MARTINUS LUTHER

The grace and might of God be with you, Most Serene Majesty, most gracious, well-beloved gentlemen!

It is not out of mere arrogance and perversity that I, an individual poor man, have taken upon me to address your lordships. The distress and misery that oppress all the Christian estates, more especially in Germany, have led not only myself, but every one else, to cry aloud and to ask for help, and have now forced me too to cry out and to ask if God would give His Spirit to any one to reach a hand to His wretched people. Councils have often put forward some remedy, but it has adroitly been frustrated, and the evils have become worse, through the cunning of certain men. Their malice and wickedness I will now, by the help of God, expose, so that, being known, they may henceforth cease to be so obstructive and injurious. God has given us a young and noble sovereign, and by this has roused great hopes in many hearts; now it is right that we too should do what we can, and make good use of time and grace.

The first thing that we must do is to consider the matter with great earnestness, and, whatever we attempt, not to trust in our own strength and wisdom alone, even if the power of all the world were ours; for God will not endure that a good work should be begun trusting to our own strength and wisdom. He destroys it; it is all useless, as we read in Psalm xxxiii., "There is no king saved by the multitude of a host; a mighty man is not delivered by much strength." And I fear it is for that reason that those beloved princes the Emperors Frederick, the First and the Second,[2] and many other German emperors were, in former times, so piteously spurned and oppressed by the popes, though they were feared by all the world. Perchance they trusted rather in their own strength than in God; therefore they could not but fall; and how would the sanguinary tyrant Julius II[3] have risen so high in our own days but that I fear, France, Germany, and

---

Martin Luther, *Address to the Christian Nobility of the German Nation Respecting the Reformation of the Christian Estate*, in *Luther's Primary Works*, ed. Henry Wace and C. A. Buchheim. London: Hodder and Stoughton, 1896. Pp. 161–180.

[1] Charles V, elected Holy Roman emperor in 1519.

[2] Emperors of the Holy Roman Empire, during the eleventh century and the twelfth century respectively. Frederick II, having been involved in a dispute with the Church, died under excommunication.

[3] Pope from 1503 to 1513, a major patron of Michelangelo (see Selection 5).

Venice trusted to themselves? The children of Benjamin slew forty-two thousand Israelites, for this reason: that these trusted to their own strength (Judges xx., etc.).

That such a thing may not happen to us and to our noble Emperor Charles, we must remember that in this matter we wrestle not against flesh and blood, but against the rulers of the darkness of this world (Eph. vi. 12), who may fill the world with war and bloodshed, but cannot themselves be overcome thereby. We must renounce all confidence in our natural strength, and take the matter in hand with humble trust in God; we must seek God's help with earnest prayer, and have nothing before our eyes but the misery and wretchedness of Christendom, irrespective of what punishment the wicked may deserve. If we do not act thus, we may begin the game with great pomp; but when we are well in it, the spirit of evil will make such confusion that the whole world will be immersed in blood, and yet nothing be done. Therefore let us act in the fear of God and prudently. The greater the might of the foe, the greater is the misfortune, if we do not act in the fear of God and with humility. If popes and Romanists have hitherto, with the devil's help, thrown kings into confusion, they may still do so, if we attempt things with our own strength and skill, without God's help.

THE THREE WALLS OF THE ROMANISTS

The Romanists[4] have, with great adroitness, drawn three walls round themselves, with which they have hitherto protected themselves, so that no one could reform them, whereby all Christendom has fallen terribly.

Firstly, if pressed by the temporal power, they have affirmed and maintained that the temporal power has no jurisdiction over them, but, on the contrary, that the spiritual power is above the temporal.

Secondly, if it were proposed to admonish them with the Scriptures, they objected that no one may interpret the Scriptures but the Pope.

Thirdly, if they are threatened with a council, they pretend that no one may call a council but the Pope.

Thus they have secretly stolen our three rods, so that they may be unpunished, and entrenched themselves behind these three walls, to act with all the wickedness and malice, which we now witness. And whenever they have been compelled to call a council, they have made it of no avail by binding the princes beforehand with an oath to leave them as they were, and to give moreover to the Pope full power over the procedure of the council, so that it is all one whether we

---

[4] Supporters of the Pope and advocates of papal supremacy, the traditional Roman Catholic position

have many councils or no councils, in addition to which they deceive us with false pretences and tricks. So grievously do they tremble for their skin before a true, free council; and thus they have overawed kings and princes, that these believe they would be offending God, if they were not to obey them in all such knavish, deceitful artifices.

Now may God help us, and give us one of those trumpets that overthrew the walls of Jericho, so that we may blow down these walls of straw and paper, and that we may set free our Christian rods for the chastisement of sin, and expose the craft and deceit of the devil, so that we may amend ourselves by punishment and again obtain God's favour.

THE FIRST WALL

That the Temporal Power Has No Jurisdiction over the Spirituality

Let us, in the first place, attack the first wall.

It has been devised that the Pope, bishops, priests, and monks are called the *spiritual estate,* princes, lords, artificers, and peasants are the *temporal estate.* This is an artful lie and hypocritical device, but let no one be made afraid by it, and that for this reason: that all Christians are truly of the spiritual estate, and there is no difference among them, save of office alone. As St. Paul says (1 Cor. xii.), we are all one body, though each member does its own work, to serve the others. This is because we have one baptism, one Gospel, one faith, and are all Christians alike; for baptism, Gospel, and faith, these alone make spiritual and Christian people.

As for the unction by a pope or a bishop, tonsure, ordination, consecration, and clothes differing from those of laymen — all this may make a hypocrite or an anointed puppet, but never a Christian or a spiritual man. Thus we are all consecrated as priests by baptism, as St. Peter says: "Ye are a royal priesthood, a holy nation" (1 Peter ii. 9); and in the book of Revelations: "and hast made us unto our God (by Thy blood) kings and priests" (Rev. v. 10). For, if we had not a higher consecration in us than pope or bishop can give, no priest could ever be made by the consecration of pope or bishop, nor could he say the mass, or preach, or absolve. Therefore the bishop's consecration is just as if in the name of the whole congregation he took one person out of the community, each member of which has equal power, and commanded him to exercise this power for the rest; in the same way as if ten brothers, co-heirs as king's sons, were to choose one from among them to rule over their inheritance, they would all of them still remain kings and have equal power, although one is ordered to govern.

And to put the matter even more plainly, if a little company of pious Christian laymen were taken prisoners and carried away to a desert, and had not among them a priest consecrated by a bishop, and were there to agree to elect one of them, born in wedlock or not, and were to order him to baptise, to celebrate the mass, to absolve, and to preach, this man would as truly be a priest, as if all the bishops and all the popes had consecrated him. That is why in cases of necessity every man can baptise and absolve, which would not be possible if we were not all priests. This great grace and virtue of baptism and of the Christian estate they have quite destroyed and made us forget by their ecclesiastical law. In this way the Christians used to choose their bishops and priests out of the community; these being afterwards confirmed by other bishops, without the pomp that now prevails. So was it that St. Augustine, Ambrose, Cyprian,[5] were bishops.

Since, then, the temporal power is baptised as we are, and has the same faith and Gospel, we must allow it to be priest and bishop, and account its office an office that is proper and useful to the Christian community. For whatever issues from baptism may boast that it has been consecrated priest, bishop, and pope, although it does not beseem every one to exercise these offices. For, since we are all priests alike, no man may put himself forward or take upon himself, without our consent and election, to do that which we have all alike power to do. For, if a thing is common to all, no man may take it to himself without the wish and command of the community. And if it should happen that a man were appointed to one of these offices and deposed for abuses, he would be just what he was before. Therefore a priest should be nothing in Christendom but a functionary; as long as he holds his office, he has precedence of others; if he is deprived of it, he is a peasant or a citizen like the rest. Therefore a priest is verily no longer a priest after deposition. But now they have invented *characteres indelebiles*,[6] and pretend that a priest after deprivation still differs from a simple layman. They even imagine that a priest can never be anything but a priest — that is, that he can never become a layman. All this is nothing but mere talk and ordinance of human invention.

It follows, then, that between laymen and priests, princes and bishops, or, as they call it, between spiritual and temporal persons, the only real difference is one of office and function, and not of estate; for they are all of the same spiritual estate, true priests, bishops, and popes, though their functions are not the same — just as among priests and monks every man has not the same functions. And this, as I said above, St. Paul says (Rom. xxi.; 1 Cor. xii.), and St. Peter (1 Peter ii.): "We, being many, are one body in Christ, and severally members one of another." Christ's body is not double or twofold, one temporal, the other spiritual. He is one Head, and He has one body.

---

[5] Bishops of the early Church, all elected by laymen.

[6] Indelible marks — that is, spiritual characteristics conferred by ordination that cannot be destroyed or taken away.

We see, then, that just as those that we call spiritual, or priests, bishops, or popes, do not differ from other Christians in any other or higher degree but in that they are to be concerned with the word of God and the sacraments — that being their work and office — in the same way the temporal authorities hold the sword and the rod in their hands to punish the wicked and to protect the good. A cobbler, a smith, a peasant, every man, has the office and function of his calling, and yet all alike are consecrated priests and bishops, and every man should by his office or function be useful and beneficial to the rest, so that various kinds of work may all be united for the furtherance of body and soul, just as the members of the body all serve one another.

Now see what a Christian doctrine is this: that the temporal authority is not above the clergy, and may not punish it. This is as if one were to say the hand may not help, though the eye is in grievous suffering. Is it not unnatural, not to say unchristian, that one member may not help another, or guard it against harm? Nay, the nobler the member, the more the rest are bound to help it. Therefore I say, Forasmuch as the temporal power has been ordained by God for the punishment of the bad and the protection of the good, therefore we must let it do its duty throughout the whole Christian body, without respect of persons, whether it strike popes, bishops, priests, monks, nuns, or whoever it may be. If it were sufficient reason for fettering the temporal power that it is inferior among the offices of Christianity to the offices of priest or confessor, or to the spiritual estate — if this were so, then we ought to restrain tailors, cobblers, masons, carpenters, cooks, cellarmen, peasants, and all secular workmen, from providing the Pope or bishops, priests and monks, with shoes, clothes, houses, or victuals, or from paying them tithes. But if these laymen are allowed to do their work without restraint, what do the Romanist scribes mean by their laws? They mean that they withdraw themselves from the operation of temporal Christian power, simply in order that they may be free to do evil, and thus fulfill what St. Peter said: "There shall be false teachers among you, . . . and in covetousness shall they with feigned words make merchandise of you" (2 Peter ii. 1, etc.).

Therefore the temporal Christian power must exercise its office without let or hindrance, without considering whom it may strike, whether pope, or bishop, or priest: whoever is guilty, let him suffer for it.

Whatever the ecclesiastical law has said in opposition to this is merely the invention of Romanist arrogance. For this is what St. Paul says to all Christians: "Let every soul" (I presume including the popes) "be subject unto the higher powers; for they bear not the sword in vain; they serve the Lord therewith, for vengeance on evildoers and for praise to them that do well" (Rom. xiii. 1–4). Also St. Peter: "Submit yourselves to every ordinance of man for the Lord's sake, . . . for so is the will of God" (1 Peter ii. 13, 15). He has also foretold that men would come who should despise government (2 Peter ii), as has come to pass through ecclesiastical law.

Now, I imagine, the first paper wall is overthrown, inasmuch as the temporal power has become a member of the Christian body; although its work relates to the body, yet does it belong to the spiritual estate. Therefore it must do its duty without let or hindrance upon all members of the whole body, to punish or urge, as guilt may deserve, or need may require, without respect of pope, bishops, or priests, let them threaten or excommunicate as they will. That is why a guilty priest is deprived of his priesthood before being given over to the secular arm; whereas this would not be right, if the secular sword had not authority over him already by Divine ordinance.

It is, indeed, past bearing that the spiritual law should esteem so highly the liberty, life, and property of the clergy, as if laymen were not as good spiritual Christians, or not equally members of the Church. Why should your body, life, goods, and honor be free, and not mine, seeing that we are equal as Christians, and have received alike baptism, faith, spirit, and all things? If a priest is killed, the country is laid under an interdict: why not also if a peasant is killed? Whence comes this great difference among equal Christians? Simply from human laws and inventions.

It can have been no good spirit, either, that devised these evasions and made sin to go unpunished. For if, as Christ and the Apostles bid us, it is our duty to oppose the evil one and all his works and words, and to drive him away as well as may be, how then should we remain quiet and be silent when the Pope and his followers are guilty of devilish works and words? Are we for the sake of men to allow the commandments and the truth of God to be defeated, which at our baptism we vowed to support with body and soul? Truly we should have to answer for all souls that would thus be abandoned and led astray.

Therefore it must have been the arch-devil himself who said, as we read in the ecclesiastical law, If the Pope were so perniciously wicked, as to be dragging souls in crowds to the devil, yet he could not be deposed. This is the accursed and devilish foundation on which they build at Rome, and think that the whole world is to be allowed to go to the devil rather than they should be opposed in their knavery. If a man were to escape punishment simply because he is above the rest, then no Christian might punish another, since Christ has commanded each of us to esteem himself the lowest and the humblest (Matt. xviii. 4; Luke ix. 48).

Where there is sin, there remains no avoiding the punishment, as St. Gregory[7] says, We are all equal, but guilt makes one subject to another. Now let us see how they deal with Christendom. They arrogate to themselves immunities without any warrant from the Scriptures, out of their own wickedness, whereas God and the Apostles made them subject to the secular sword; so that we must fear that it is the work of antichrist,[8] or a sign of his near approach.

---

[7] Gregory the Great, pope from 590 to 604.

[8] The incarnation of all that is hostile to Christ and His kingdom.

THE SECOND WALL
That No One May Interpret the Scriptures But the Pope

The second wall is even more tottering and weak: that they alone pretend to be considered masters of the Scriptures; although they learn nothing of them all their life. They assume authority, and juggle before us with impudent words, saying that the Pope cannot err in matters of faith, whether he be evil or good, albeit they cannot prove it by a single letter. That is why the canon law contains so many heretical and unchristian, nay unnatural, laws; but of these we need not speak now. For whereas they imagine the Holy Ghost never leaves them, however unlearned and wicked they may be, they grow bold enough to decree whatever they like. But were this true, where were the need and use of the Holy Scriptures? Let us burn them, and content ourselves with the unlearned gentlemen at Rome, in whom the Holy Ghost dwells, who, however, can dwell in pious souls only. If I had not read it, I could never have believed that the devil should have put forth such follies at Rome and find a following

But not to fight them with our own words, we will quote the Scriptures. St. Paul says, "If anything be revealed to another that sitteth by, let the first hold his peace" (1 Cor. xiv. 30). What would be the use of this commandment, if we were to believe him alone that teaches or has the highest seat? Christ Himself says, "And they shall be all taught of God" (St. John vi. 45). Thus it may come to pass that the Pope and his followers are wicked and not true Christians, and not being taught by God, have no true understanding, whereas a common man may have true understanding. Why should we then not follow him? Has not the Pope often erred? Who could help Christianity, in case the Pope errs, if we do not rather believe another who has the Scriptures for him?

Therefore it is a wickedly devised fable—and they cannot quote a single letter to confirm it—that it is for the Pope alone to interpret the Scriptures or to confirm the interpretation of them. They have assumed the authority of their own selves. And though they say that this authority was given to St. Peter when the keys were given to him, it is plain enough that the keys were not given to St. Peter alone, but to the whole community. Besides, the keys were not ordained for doctrine or authority, but for sin, to bind or loose; and what they claim besides this from the keys is mere invention. But what Christ said to St. Peter: "I have prayed for thee that thy faith fail not" (St. Luke xxii. 32), cannot relate to the Pope, inasmuch as the greater part of the Popes have been without faith, as they are themselves forced to acknowledge; nor did Christ pray for Peter alone, but for all the Apostles and all Christians, as He says, "Neither pray I for these alone, but for them also which shall believe on Me through their word" (St. John xvii.). Is not this plain enough?

Only consider the matter. They must needs acknowledge that there are pious Christians among us that have the true faith, spirit, understanding, word, and mind of Christ: why then should we reject their word and understanding, and follow a Pope who has neither understanding nor spirit? Surely this were to deny our whole faith and the Christian Church. Moreover, if the article of our faith is right, "I believe in the holy Christian Church," the Pope cannot alone be right; else we must say, "I believe in the Pope of Rome," and reduce the Christian Church to one man, which is a devilish and damnable heresy. Besides that, we are all priests, as I have said, and have all one faith, one Gospel, one Sacrament; how then should we not have the power of discerning and judging what is right or wrong in matters of faith? What becomes of St. Paul's words, "But he that is spiritual judgeth all things, yet he himself is judged of no man" (1 Cor. ii. 15), and also, "we having the same spirit of faith"? (2 Cor. iv. 13). Why then should we not perceive as well as an unbelieving Pope what agrees or disagrees with our faith?

By these and many other texts we should gain courage and freedom, and should not let the spirit of liberty (as St. Paul has it) be frightened away by the inventions of the popes; we should boldly judge what they do and what they leave undone according to our own believing understanding of the Scriptures, and force them to follow the better understanding, and not their own. Did not Abraham in old days have to obey his Sarah, who was in stricter bondage to him than we are to any one on earth? Thus, too, Balaam's ass was wiser than the prophet.[9] If God spoke by an ass against a prophet, why should He not speak by a pious man against the Pope? Besides, St. Paul withstood St. Peter as being in error (Gal. ii.). Therefore it behooves every Christian to aid the faith by understanding and defending it and by condemning all errors.

THE THIRD WALL
That No One May Call a Council But the Pope

The third wall falls of itself, as soon as the first two have fallen; for if the Pope acts contrary to the Scriptures, we are bound to stand by the Scriptures, to punish and to constrain him, according to Christ's commandment, "Moreover, if thy brother shall trespass against thee, go and tell him his fault between thee and him alone; if he shall hear thee, thou hast gained thy brother. But if he will not hear thee, then take with thee one or two more, that in the mouth of two or three witnesses every word may be established. And if he shall neglect to hear them, tell it unto the Church; but if he neglect to hear the Church, let him be unto thee as a heathen man and a publican"[10] (Matt. xviii. 15–17). Here each member is commanded to take care for the other; much more then should we do this, if it is a ruling member of the community that does evil, which by its evil-doing causes

---

[9] A reference to the biblical story of Balaam (Numbers 22: 21–35). Balaam's donkey miraculously given by God the ability to speak, saved his master's life.

[10] In the gospels a "publican" is usually a tax collector for the Roman authorities.

great harm and offence to the others. If then I am to accuse him before the Church, I must collect the Church together. Moreover, they can show nothing in the Scriptures giving the Pope sole power to call and confirm councils; they have nothing but their own laws; but these hold good only so long as they are not injurious to Christianity and the laws of God. Therefore, if the Pope deserves punishment, these laws cease to bind us, since Christendom would suffer, if he were not punished by a council. Thus we read (Acts xv.) that the council of the Apostles was not called by St. Peter, but by all the Apostles and the elders. But if the right to call it had lain with St. Peter alone, it would not have been a Christian council, but a heretical *conciliabulum*.[11] Moreover, the most celebrated council of all—that of Nicaea[12]—was neither called nor confirmed by the Bishop of Rome, but by the Emperor Constantine; and after him many other emperors have done the same, and yet the councils called by them were accounted most Christian. But if the Pope alone had the power, they must all have been heretical. Moreover, if I consider the councils that the Pope has called, I do not find that they produced any notable results.

Therefore when need requires, and the Pope is a cause of offence to Christendom, in these cases whoever can best do so, as a faithful member of the whole body, must do what he can to procure a true free council. This no one can do so well as the temporal authorities, especially since they are fellow-Christians, fellow-priests, sharing one spirit and one power in all things, and since they should exercise the office that they have received from God without hindrance, whenever it is necessary and useful that it should be exercised. Would it not be most unnatural, if a fire were to break out in a city, and every one were to keep still and let it burn on and on, whatever might be burnt, simply because they had not the mayor's authority, or because the fire perchance broke out at the mayor's house? Is not every citizen bound in this case to rouse and call in the rest? How much more should this be done in the spiritual city of Christ, if a fire of offence breaks out, either at the Pope's government or wherever it may! The like happens if an enemy attacks a town. The first to rouse up the rest earns glory and thanks. Why then should not he earn glory that descries the coming of our enemies from hell and rouses and summons all Christians?

But as for their boasts of their authority, that no one must oppose it, this is idle talk. No one in Christendom has any authority to do harm, or to forbid others to prevent harm being done. There is no authority in the Church but for reformation. Therefore if the Pope wished to use his power to prevent the calling of a free council, so as to prevent the reformation of the Church, we must not respect him or his power; and if he should begin to excommunicate and fulminate, we must despise this as the doings of a madman, and, trusting in God, excommunicate

---

[11] A mere gathering of people, whereas a *concilium* would be a proper council.

[12] In 325. Nicaea is in Asia Minor, the site of the first "universal" council of Christianity.

and repel him as best we may. For this his usurped power is nothing; he does not possess it, and he is at once overthrown by a text from the Scriptures. For St. Paul says to the Corinthians "that God has given us authority for edification, and not for destruction" (2 Cor. x. 8). Who will set this text at nought? It is the power of the devil and of antichrist that prevents what would serve for the reformation of Christendom. Therefore we must not follow it, but oppose it with our body, our goods, and all that we have. And even if a miracle were to happen in favour of the Pope against the temporal power, or if some were to be stricken by a plague, as they sometimes boast has happened, all this is to be held as having been done by the devil in order to injure our faith in God, as was foretold by Christ: "There shall arise false Christs and false prophets, and shall show great signs and wonders, insomuch that, if it were possible, they shall deceive the very elect" (Matt. xxiv. 23); and St. Paul tells the Thessalonians that the coming of antichrist shall be "after the working of Satan with all power and signs and lying wonders" (2 Thess. ii. 9).

• • •

And now I hope the false, lying spectre will be laid with which the Romanists have long terrified and stupefied our consciences. And it will be seen that, like all the rest of us, they are subject to the temporal sword; that they have no authority to interpret the Scriptures by force without skill; and that they have no power to prevent a council, or to pledge it in accordance with their pleasure, or to bind it beforehand, and deprive it of its freedom; and that if they do this, they are verily of the fellowship of antichrist and the devil, and have nothing of Christ but the name.

OF THE MATTERS TO BE CONSIDERED IN THE COUNCILS

Let us now consider the matters which should be treated in the councils, and with which Popes, cardinals, bishops, and all learned men should occupy themselves day and night, if they love Christ and His Church. But if they do not do so, the people at large and the temporal powers must do so, without considering the thunders of their excommunications. For an unjust excommunication is better than ten just absolutions, and an unjust absolution is worse than ten just excommunications. Therefore let us rouse ourselves, fellow-Germans, and fear God more than man, that we be not answerable for all the poor souls that are so miserably lost through the wicked, devilish government of the Romanists, and that the dominion of the devil should not grow day by day, if indeed this hellish government can grow any worse, which, for my part, I can neither conceive nor believe.

It is a distressing and terrible thing to see that the head of Christendom, who boasts of being the vicar of Christ and the successor of St. Peter, lives in a worldly pomp that no king or emperor can equal, so that in him that calls himself most holy and most spiritual there is more worldliness than in the world itself. He wears a triple crown, whereas the mightiest kings only wear one crown. If this resembles the poverty of Christ and St. Peter, it is a new sort of resemblance. They prate of its being heretical to object to this; nay, they will not even hear how unchristian and ungodly it is. But I think that if he should have to pray to God with tears, he would have to lay down his crowns; for God will not endure any arrogance. His office should be nothing else than to weep and pray constantly for Christendom and to be an example of all humility.

• • •

What is the use in Christendom of the people called "cardinals"? I will tell you. In Italy and Germany there are many rich convents, endowments, fiefs, and benefices,[13] and as the best way of getting these into the hands of Rome, they created cardinals, and gave them the sees, convents, and prelacies, and thus destroyed the service of God. That is why Italy is almost a desert now: the convents are destroyed, the sees consumed, the revenues of the prelacies and of all the churches drawn to Rome; towns are decayed, the country and the people ruined, because there is no more any worship of God or preaching; why? Because the cardinals must have all the wealth. No Turk could have thus desolated Italy and overthrown the worship of God.

Now that Italy is sucked dry, they come to Germany and begin very quietly; but if we look on quietly Germany will soon be brought into the same state as Italy. We have a few cardinals already. What the Romanists mean thereby the drunken Germans are not to see until they have lost everything — bishoprics, convents, benefices, fiefs, even to their last farthing. Antichrist must take the riches of the earth, as it is written (Dan. xi, 8, 39, 43). They begin by taking off the cream of the bishoprics, convents, and fiefs; and as they do not dare to destroy everything as they have done in Italy, they employ such holy cunning to join together ten or twenty prelacies, and take such a portion of each annually that the total amounts to a considerable sum. The priory of Würzburg gives one thousand guilders; those of Bamberg, Mayence, Treves, and others also contribute. In this way they collect one thousand or ten thousand guilders, in order that a cardinal may live at Rome in a state like that of a wealthy monarch.

• • •

What has brought us Germans to such a pass that we have to suffer this robbery and this destruction of our property by the Pope? If the kingdom of France has resisted it, why do we Germans suffer ourselves to be fooled and deceived? It would be more endurable if they did nothing but rob us of our property; but they destroy the Church and deprive Christ's flock of their good shepherds, and

---

[13] The property and/or income that goes with an ecclesiastical position.

overthrow the service and word of God. Even if there were no cardinals at all, the Church would not perish, for they do nothing for the good of Christendom; all they do is to traffic in and quarrel about prelacies and bishoprics, which any robber could do as well.

If we took away ninety-nine parts of the Pope's Court and only left one hundredth, it would still be large enough to answer questions on matters of belief. Now there is such a swarm of vermin at Rome, all called papal, that Babylon itself never saw the like. There are more than three thousand papal secretaries alone; but who shall count the other office-bearers, since there are so many offices that we can scarcely count them, and all waiting for German benefices, as wolves wait for a flock of sheep? I think Germany now pays more to the Pope than it formerly paid the emperors; nay, some think more than three hundred thousand guilders are sent from Germany to Rome every year, for nothing whatever; and in return we are scoffed at and put to shame. Do we still wonder why princes, noblemen, cities, foundations, convents, and people grow poor? We should rather wonder that we have anything left to eat.

Now that we have got well into our game, let us pause a while and show that the Germans are not such fools as not to perceive or understand this Romish trickery. I do not here complain that God's commandments and Christian justice are despised at Rome; for the state of things in Christendom, especially at Rome, is too bad for us to complain of such high matters. Not do I even complain that no account is taken of natural or secular justice and reason. The mischief lies still deeper. I complain that they do not observe their own fabricated canon law, though this is in itself rather mere tyranny, avarice, and worldly pomp, than a law. This we shall now show.

Long ago the emperors and princes of Germany allowed the Pope to claim the *annates* from all German benefices; that is, half of the first year's income from every benefice. The object of this concession was that the Pope should collect a fund with all this money to fight against the Turks and infidels, and to protect Christendom, so that the nobility should not have to bear the burden of the struggle alone, and that the priests should also contribute. The popes have made such use of this good simple piety of the Germans that they have taken this money for more than one hundred years, and have now made of it a regular tax and duty; and not only have they accumulated nothing, but they have founded out of it many posts and offices at Rome, which are paid by it yearly, as out of a ground-rent.

Whenever there is any pretence of fighting the Turks, they send out some commission for collecting money, and often send out indulgences[14] under the same pretext of fighting the Turks. They think we Germans will always remain

---

[14] Luther here refers to the Roman Catholic practice of that time of selling remission of punishment (indulgence) for sin—both in this world and in purgatory.

such great inveterate fools that we will go on giving money to satisfy their unspeakable greed, though we see plainly that neither *annates,* nor absolution money [indulgences], nor any other—not one farthing—goes against the Turks, but all goes into the bottomless sack. They lie and deceive, form and make covenants with us, of which they do not mean to keep one jot. And all this is done in the holy name of Christ and St. Peter.

This being so, the German nation, the bishops and princes, should remember that they are Christians, and should defend the people, who are committed to their government and protection in temporal and spiritual affairs, from these ravenous wolves in sheep's clothing, that profess to be shepherds and rulers; and since the *annates* are so shamefully abused, and the covenants concerning them not carried out, they should not suffer their lands and people to be so piteously and unrighteously flayed and ruined; but by an imperial or a national law they should either retain the *annates* in the country, or abolish them altogether. For since they do not keep to the covenants, they have no right to the *annates;* therefore bishops and princes are bound to punish this thievery and robbery, or prevent it, as justice demands. And herein should they assist and strengthen the Pope, who is perchance too weak to prevent this scandal by himself, or, if he wishes to protect or support it, restrain and oppose him as a wolf and tyrant; for he has not authority to do evil or to protect evil-doers. Even if it were proposed to collect any such treasure for use against the Turks, we should be wise in future, and remember that the German nation is more fitted to take charge of it than the Pope, seeing that the German nation by itself is able to provide men enough, if the money is forthcoming. This matter of the *annates* is like many other Romish pretexts.

Moreover, the year has been divided among the Pope and the ruling bishops and foundations in such wise that the Pope has taken every other month—six in all—to give away the benefices that fall in his month; in this way almost all the benefices are drawn into the hands of Rome, and especially the best livings and dignities. And those that once fall into the hands of Rome never come out again, even if they never again fall vacant in the Pope's month. In this way the foundations come very short of their rights, and it is a downright robbery, the object of which is not to give up anything again. Therefore it is now high time to abolish the Pope's months and to take back again all that has thereby fallen into the hands of Rome. For all the princes and nobles should insist that the stolen property shall be returned, the thieves punished, and that those who abuse their powers shall be deprived of them. If the Pope can make a law on the day after his election by which he takes our benefices and livings to which he has no right, the Emperor Charles should so much the more have a right to issue a law for all Germany on the day after his coronation that in future no livings and benefices are to fall to Rome by virtue of the Pope's month, but that those that have so fallen are to be freed and taken from the Romish robbers. This right he possesses authoritatively by virtue of his temporal sword.

A MIGHTY FORTRESS IS OUR GOD

A mighty fortress is our God.
A sword and shield victorious;
He breaks the cruel opressor's rod
And wins salvation glorious.
The old satanic foe
Has sworn to work us woe.
With craft and dreadful might
He arms himself to fight.
On earth he has no equal.

No strength of ours can match his might.
We would be lost, rejected.
But now a champion comes to fight,
Whom God himself elected.
You ask who this may be?
The Lord of hosts is he,
Christ Jesus, mighty Lord,
God's only Son, adored.
He holds the field victorious.

Though hordes of devils fill the land
All threat'ning to devour us,
We tremble not, unmoved we stand;
They cannot overpow'r us.
Let this world's tyrant rage;
In battle we'll engage.
His might is doomed to fail;
God's judgment must prevail!
One little word subdues him.

God's Word forever shall abide,
No thanks to foes, who fear it;
For God himself fights by our side
With weapons of the spirit.
Were they to take our house,
Goods, honor, child, or spouse,
Though life be wrenched away,
They cannot win the day.
The Kingdom's ours forever!

21

❧

Saint Ignatius of Loyola

SPIRITUAL EXERCISES

O n May 17 of 1521, a nobleman-soldier from the Basque region of Guipúz-
coa, Iñigo López de Loyola, was seriously wounded by a cannonball while
defending the castle of Pamplona against the French. Taken back to his family's
estate, he underwent the crude surgery of the time, and was near death. After
June 28, the vigil of Saints Peter and Paul, he began to recover, and he attributed this to Saint Peter. Early in his lengthy convalescence, Iñigo asked to read
romances of chivalry, but none were to be found in the house where he was staying, and so he was given books in Castilian Spanish to read on the life of Christ
and the lives of the saints. Partly as a result of his reading as well as of his close
brush with death, he began to reflect on the disorderly life he had been leading.
He was twenty-six years old, and had devoted much of his youth to gaining fame
in war, as well as to less honorable pursuits, such as gambling, brawling, and affairs with women. During his convalescence, he grew increasingly meditative,
and the devoutly Catholic upbringing he shared with most of his Basque countrymen returned to him in the form of a heightened spirituality. Not quite a mystic,
Iñigo nevertheless did what many Spanish mystics had done before: He wrote
about his spiritual experience. Instead of producing a confessional account of his
life, like Saint Teresa of Avila, or religious verse like Saint John of the Cross or
Fray Luis de León, however, his practicality and military penchant for discipline
and organization led him to produce a manual for spiritual development, a kind
of "how-to" book for communing with God.

By March of 1522 Iñigo had decided to dedicate his life fully to religion, and
the notes that he began taking in August of 1521 would evolve, with the passing
of time and further religious experiences in Manresa, near the shrine of Montser-
rat, into his Ejercicios espirituales (Spiritual Exercises). The definitive, printed
version of this text, which came out in 1548, also incorporated his growing experiences and university studies in Alcalá and in Paris. By then, he had been signing
his name as "Ignatius" for nearly a decade, and it was as Ignatius of Loyola that

he became the founder of a new religious order within Catholicism, the Society of Jesus (or Jesuits), in 1540. Ignatius of Loyola died in Rome in 1556. In 1622, he and his close friend Francis Xavier were canonized together.

Besides the Spiritual Exercises, *Ignatius's works comprise his nearly seven thousand collected letters, his* Spiritual Diary *(1544), the* Constitutions of the Society of Jesus *(1546), and his* Autobiography *(1553). The* Spiritual Exercises, *however, is by far the best-known of his works. In it, Ignatius offers a method for developing an individual's spirituality, with the aid of a director. The* Exercises *are divided into four groups, called "Weeks." The First Week proposes exercises devoted to the purification of the soul in order to advance toward God; the Second Week is concerned with the individual's acquisition of virtues through the imitation of Christ; the Third and Fourth Weeks offer activities to establish day-to-day, intimate communion with God, through Christ.*

A key term in Ignatius's spirituality is discernment, *which entails the individual's capacity to interpret God's will and come to a correct decision in his path to spiritual development. Roland Barthes, a twentieth-century critic, has remarked that the* Exercises' *novelty lies in turning prayer and meditation into "mantic arts," that is, into techniques for divine consultation. The* Exercises *offer a code with which to address God (a "code of demand"), but they also implicitly present a "code of response," a way to attempt the decipherment of divine messages.*

Ignatius's ideas, as represented in the Spiritual Exercises *and in his work with the Society of Jesus, blended well with the Counter-Reformation, the Catholic Church's reaction to the Protestantism of Martin Luther (see Selection 20). By focusing on the development of individual spirituality (an important concern among Protestants), although always under a hierarchical system of guidance (of equally great import to Catholics), his writings served to reaffirm Catholic doctrine while simultaneously encouraging internal reform within the Church. Ignatius also placed great emphasis on dialogue and learning, and this was reflected in the Jesuits' focus on education as a vehicle for religious conversion. Ignatius's intellectual rigor and penchant for scholarship, evident in the* Exercises *and the* Constitutions of the Society of Jesus, *became a hallmark of the Jesuits as a group, and from the sixteenth through the eighteenth centuries the Society of Jesus attracted into its membership many of the brightest intellectuals in the Catholic countries of Europe.*

THE FIRST EXERCISE IS A MEDITATION BY USING THE THREE POWERS OF THE SOUL[1] ABOUT THE FIRST, SECOND, AND THIRD SINS.

It contains, after a preparatory prayer and two preludes, three main points and a colloquy.

The Preparatory Prayer is to ask God our Lord for the grace that all my intentions, actions, and operations may be ordered purely to the service and praise of his Divine Majesty.

The First Prelude is a composition[2] made by imagining the place. Here we should take notice of the following. When a contemplation or meditation is about something that can be gazed on, for example, a contemplation of Christ our Lord, who is visible, the composition consists of seeing in imagination the physical place where that which I want to contemplate is taking place. By physical place I mean, for instance, a temple or a mountain where Jesus Christ or Our Lady happens to be, in accordance with the topic I desire to contemplate.

When a contemplation or meditation is about something abstract and invisible, as in the present case about the sins, the composition will be to see in imagination and to consider my soul as imprisoned in this corruptible body, and my whole compound self as an exile in this valley [of tears] among brute animals. I mean, my whole self as composed of soul and body.

The Second Prelude is to ask God our Lord for what I want and desire. What I ask for should be in accordance with the subject matter. For example, in a contemplation on the Resurrection, I will ask for joy with Christ in joy; in a contemplation on the Passion, I will ask for pain, tears, and suffering with Christ suffering.

In the present meditation it will be to ask for shame and confusion about myself, when I see how many people have been damned for committing a single mortal sin, and how many times I have deserved eternal damnation for my many sins.

Note. All the contemplations or meditations ought to be preceded by this same preparatory prayer, which is never changed, and also by the two preludes, which are sometimes changed in accordance with the subject matter.

The First Point will be to use my memory, by going over the first sin, that of the angels; next, to use my understanding, by reasoning about it; and then my

---

[1] The "three powers of the soul," following Scholastic doctrine, are memory, will, and intellect.

[2] "Composition" (*composición*) means for Ignatius the mental act of putting things together by means of the imagination. It also has the sense of "composing oneself," that is, preparing oneself for some other action, which in this case would be prayer.

will. My aim in remembering and reasoning about all these matters is to bring myself to greater shame and confusion, by comparing the one sin of the angels with all my own many sins. For one sin they went to hell; then how often have I deserved hell for my many sins!

In other words, I will call to memory the sin of the angels: How they were created in grace and then, not wanting to better themselves by using their freedom to reverence and obey their Creator and Lord, they fell into pride, were changed from grace to malice, and were hurled from heaven into hell. Next I will use my intellect to ruminate about this in greater detail, and then move myself to deeper affections by means of my will.

The Second Point will be meditated in the same way. That is, I will apply the three faculties to the sin of Adam and Eve. I will recall to memory how they did long penance for their sin, and the enormous corruption it brought to the human race, with so many people going to hell.

Again in other words, I will call to memory the second sin, that of our first parents: How Adam was created in the plain of Damascus and placed in the earthly paradise; and how Eve was created from his rib; how they were forbidden to eat of the tree of knowledge, but did eat, and thus sinned; and then, clothed in garments of skin and expelled from paradise, they lived out their whole lives in great hardship and penance, deprived of the original justice which they had lost. Next I will use my intellect to reason about this in greater detail, and then use the will, as is described just above.

The Third Point will likewise be to use the same method on the third sin, the particular sin of anyone who has gone to hell because of one mortal sin; and further, of innumerable other persons who went there for fewer sins than I have committed.

That is, about this third particular sin too I will follow the same procedure as above. I will call to memory the gravity and malice of the sin against my Creator and Lord; then I will use my intellect to reason about it—how by sinning and acting against the Infinite Goodness the person has been justly condemned forever. Then I will finish by using the will, as was described above.

Colloquy. Imagine Christ our Lord suspended on the cross before you, and converse with him in a colloquy: How is it that he, although he is the Creator, has come to make himself a human being? How is it that he has passed from eternal life to death here in time, and to die in this way for my sins?

In a similar way, reflect on yourself and ask: What have I done for Christ? What am I doing for Christ? What ought I to do for Christ?

In this way, too, gazing on him in so pitiful a state as he hangs on the cross, speak out whatever comes to your mind.

A colloquy is made, properly speaking, in the way one friend speaks to another, or a servant to one in authority—now begging a favor, now accusing oneself of some misdeed, now telling one's concerns and asking counsel about them. Close with an Our Father.

22

❧

John Milton

ON THE LATE MASSACRE
IN PIEDMONT

John Milton's sonnet *"On the Late Massacre in Piedmont"* (1655) *reflects the passionate religious loyalties and conflicts exemplified in the two preceding selections by Martin Luther and Saint Ignatius of Loyola. The sonnet typifies Milton's Protestant commitment to personal religious expression and his view of Roman Catholicism as a party of intolerance, hypocrisy, and repression. Such antagonism, spread generally throughout the many differing Christian religious factions, continued through the seventeenth century in Western Europe where the Protestant Reformation, sparked by the early sixteenth-century Martin Luther, led, among other bloody slaughters, to the Thirty Years War (1618–1648).*

John Milton (1608–1674) was an Englishman of remarkably strong and inflexible character. Both a Puritan and, perhaps paradoxically, a Renaissance humanist, he was one of the major poets in the entire span of English literature who devoted what would have been among the most productive years of his life to public service during the years of English Puritan rule (1649–1660). Educated at Saint Paul's School, London, and Christ's College, Cambridge, Milton was already known as a poet before he left Cambridge. Indeed, his first published poem in English, sixteen lines of skillfully rhymed couplets, appeared in nothing less than the second folio edition of Shakespeare's collected plays (1632).

After leaving Cambridge in 1632, Milton spent six years of diligent self-directed study at his father's country home, where he read widely in several languages while continuing to write and to generally prepare himself for his chosen career as poet. His best-known poem of this period is "Lycidas," an elegiac lament for Edward King, a fellow student at Cambridge who had drowned on a voyage to Ireland in 1637. The topic gave the young poet an opportunity to expound on such themes as the premature death of the gifted youth, the possibility of resurrection through God's justice, and the present corruption of the Anglican clergy

("Blind mouths!"). During this period of self-directed study he also wrote two masques, courtly staged entertainments, in which Milton's lyrics were set to music by Henry Lawes, an eminent composer. Milton himself was known as an excellent musician, especially in voice and organ, and the imagery of music recurs frequently throughout his poems.

In 1638 Milton left England for fifteen months travel on the Continent, a trip that was a customary part of an English gentleman's education. Spending most of his time in Italy, a region whose literature he already loved, he met and was befriended there by many distinguished people. He also visited one great man there, the scientist Galileo, under house arrest by the Inquisition for daring to support the heretical Copernican position that the earth was not the center of the universe. He would later refer to Galileo's situation in the Areopagitica *(1644), Milton's great call for freedom of the press. Cutting short his tour because of growing political friction in England, Milton returned home where, faced with the need to earn a living, he rented a house in London and began to take in pupils as a private schoolmaster (an occupation he always found burdensome). It was there that he first gave thought to the writing of an epic poem, but the project had to wait nearly two decades as Milton was drawn into the political and religious struggles connected to the English Civil War, fought generally between the political and military forces of the Puritan Parliament and those of the Anglican monarchy. For the next twenty years, first as a private citizen and later as Secretary for the Foreign Tongues to the Council of State, Milton served the Puritan Commonwealth by helping to formulate foreign policy and by expressing the official position of the Commonwealth in a series of controversial pamphlets. (Oliver Cromwell, eventually recognized by Parliament as Lord Protector of England, was a Puritan military commander who became the chief political force after the beheading of King Charles I in 1649.) Among Milton's official publications were several defending the right of the English people to depose and even execute their king. As a private citizen, Milton also published several pamphlets on the right to divorce. At all times his position was one that advanced the position of the individual's freedom to think, write, and act according to his own conscience. Although Milton held his important and demanding position with the ruling Council of State until the Restoration of the monarchy in 1660, his eyesight had been impaired as early as 1644, and in 1652 he became totally blind. He was thus in full darkness when he composed all of his major poetical works.*

By 1658, Milton had begun work on his massive epic poem, Paradise Lost, *having earlier rejected the concept of a national epic based on the stories of King Arthur. Basing the poem on the ancient Hebrew sources in Genesis, Milton sought to achieve a universal epic centering on the fall of Adam and Eve—and, thereby, all humankind—from their state of innocent grace in the Garden of Eden. The poem closes with their expulsion from the Garden but also with their gaining of some human wisdom and the promise of future redemption. After the Restoration relieved Milton of all public duties—even sending the official defender of regicide into hiding and then into prison for a time—he was able to devote all his time to the epic project.* Paradise Lost *was finished in 1665 and first published in 1667. It raised Milton's position from that of a well recognized poet and pamphleteer to an eminence that has, ever since, ranked him with Chaucer and Shakespeare as a shaper of English literature. His creation is still regarded as the standard of excellence for poetry in the "grand style."*

In 1671 Milton published the much shorter Paradise Regained *on the temptation of Jesus in the desert by a rather ineffectual Satan, based mainly on the account in the Gospel of Luke. Published together with that was* Samson Agonistes *("Samson the Contender"), a classical tragedy in blank verse. The figure of Samson has been perceived as a counterpart to the blind and suffering Milton after the Restoration. Supposed to be a deliverer of his people from the Philistines, Samson, instead, as a result of Dalila's treachery, is "Eyeless in Gaza at the mill with slaves, / Himself in bonds under Philistian yoke." The drama tells how Samson, guided by his sense of God's plan, pulls down the pagan theater upon himself and God's arrogantly celebrating enemies. Surely, Milton, had he been able, would have used any opportunity to destroy the recently triumphant but dissolute court of Charles II, destroying himself in the process.* Samson Agonistes *remains the finest English tragedy written on the Greek model.*

Although the sonnet reprinted here was composed in 1655, dealing with a massacre occurring in that year, it was not published until 1673, the year preceding the poet's death. In his role as Secretary for the Foreign Tongues, Milton composed an official letter of protest about a bloody slaughter of Italian Protestants in Piedmont (northern Italy). Oliver Cromwell sent Milton's letter to the Duke of Savoy (the Prince of Piedmont in whose territory the massacre had occurred), the King of France, and all of the heads of Protestant countries in Europe, suggesting that they join England in their strong protests to Savoy. We see here how far Milton has taken the form of the Petrarchan (Italian) sonnet from its origins as a poem of devotional love for a lady. (Contrast, for example, the poems of Sir Thomas Wyatt in Selection 3.) Milton's combination of vengeful anger and prayerful piety have been compared to the thunderous warnings of the Hebrew prophets in the Old Testament.

Avenge, O Lord,[1] thy slaughtered saints,[2] whose bones
Lie scattered on the Alpine mountains cold;
Even them who kept thy truth so pure of old
When all our fathers worshiped stocks and stones,[3]
Forget not: in thy book[4] record their groans
Who were thy sheep[5] and in their ancient fold
Slain by the bloody Piedmontese that rolled

---

[1] Compare the following passage from the New Testament's Book of Revelation (6:9–10): "When he opened the fifth seal, I saw under the altar the souls of those who had been slain for the word of God and for the witness they had borne; they cried out with a loud voice, 'O Sovereign Lord, holy and true, how long before thou wilt judge and avenge our blood on those who dwell upon the earth?'"

[2] The Puritans often referred to those they considered to be true believers as "saints."

[3] The "stocks and stones" are the idols made of wood and stone worshiped by pagans in ancient times. Since the slaughtered sect, the Vaudois or Waldensians, claimed their descent from apostolic times, Milton's contrast of them to idol worshipers is an apt one.

[4] The book of Life: God's record of the deeds of the righteous, referred to frequently in both Old and New Testaments.

[5] References to God's sheep and the good shepherd are standard in scripture. There is also the more ominous sense found in Psalm 44: "Nay, for thy sake we are slain all the day long, and accounted as sheep for the slaughter."

Mother with infant down the rocks.[6] Their moans
The vales redoubled to the hills, and they
    To heaven. Their martyred blood and ashes sow
    O'er all th' Italian fields, where still doth sway
The triple tyrant:[7] that from these may grow
    A hundredfold,[8] who having learnt thy way
    Early may fly the Babylonian woe.[9]

---

[6] Milton adapted specific details from the many London newsletters of his time. For weeks they gave the Piedmont massacre great prominence and reprinted gory details from each other. For example: "Women great with child frozen to death, others newly delivered, and Infants hanging upon their dry breasts, Some were led to the tops of Rocks and Precipices, and their heads being tyed down between their legs, they were tumbled down . . . . Others being naked were tyed neck and heels together, and rolled down from the tops of great Mountains. . . ."

[7] The Pope, with his three-tiered crown.

[8] The idea of the blood of the martyrs as the seed of the Church goes back at least to the writings of Tertullian in the late second century. There may also be resonance from the Gospel of Matthew (13:8). "Other seeds fell on good soil and brought forth grain, some a hundredfold. . . ." And Milton may also be alluding to the Greek myth of Cadmus who sowed in the ground the teeth of a dragon he had slain, from which armed men arose.

[9] Babylon was the place of Jewish exile after the conquest of Jerusalem in 587 B.C., hence a place of suffering that God would eventually destroy. The Puritans, and many other zealous Protestants, regarded the Church of Rome as the corrupt and doomed Babylon of Revelation (17:5): "Babylon, the great, mother of harlots, and of earth's abominations."

23

꙳

Pedro Calderón de la Barca

LIFE IS A DREAM

B orn in Madrid, the playwright Pedro Calderón de la Barca (1600–1681) is, along with Miguel de Cervantes Saavedra (Selection 17), Luis de Góngora, Lope de Vega (Selection 3), and Francisco de Quevedo, one of the leading lights in Spain's Siglo de Oro, its literary "Golden Age." Calderón was by far the youngest of the five, and he in fact belongs to a different generation of writers, one whose ideas about literature were heavily influenced by the Baroque. The Baroque style in poetry, characterized by the abundant use of antitheses, wordplay, convoluted word order, and unusual metaphors, had been first championed by Góngora and Quevedo, each in their own way: Góngora favored a more sensuous and erudite approach to poetry, using colorful images and exotic-sounding words and phrases derived from Latin and Greek, while Quevedo's poetry was more intellectual, giving greater importance to witty comparisons, complex philosophical ideas, and ingenious wordplay. Calderón, who was both playwright and poet, combined both approaches to poetry, and incorporated them into his dramatic texts. His use of this new poetic language, along with the highly elaborate stagings he helped design for his plays, made him the true initiator of Spain's Baroque theatre, perhaps one of the most influential and long-lasting literary manifestations in the Spanish language. Calderón's intense and highly stylized plays, in which music played an important part, were widely read and imitated throughout seventeenth-century Europe, and laid the groundwork for the development of opera.

Another better-known side to Calderón is the intellectualizing, philosophical qualities of his theatre. Of course, in seventeenth-century Spain, under the watchful eye of the Inquisition, philosophy in the modern sense of "critical thinking" was virtually impossible. Calderón's philosophical themes in his plays all revolve around approved tenets of Catholic doctrine, always with the intention of confirming them, never criticizing them. His theatre examines questions such as *predestination* versus *free will, the proper behavior of a Christian monarch, and the mystery of the Eucharist (communion with God).*

Calderón's background in these topics was particularly solid, since from his early youth he had been studying for the priesthood. After initial studies in the Jesuit-run Colegio Imperial, he entered the University of Alcalá in 1614, but moved in 1615 to Salamanca, where he studied canon law (the body of legal and administrative decisions by which the Church is governed). His first known play, Amor, honor y poder (Love, Honor, and Power) *was written in 1623.*

Calderón's life, however, was far from being that of a cloistered and pious scholar. In 1622, he was involved along with his two brothers in a homicide, which was resolved by paying reparations to the victim's family. Perhaps as a consequence of this affair, Calderón went off to travel in Italy and Flanders between 1623 and 1635. Back in Madrid he was again involved in a violent incident, this time on the side of the law, when he joined several police officers in pursuit of a man who had wounded one of his brothers.

By 1635, Calderón's reputation as a playwright was so high that one of his plays was performed at the opening of a royal palace, and the following year the king made him a Knight of Santiago. Following other Spanish writers' similar penchant for combining "arms and letters," Calderón enrolled in the army and fought in the civil conflicts in Catalonia in 1640, where he distinguished himself for his bravery. In 1642 he retired from military service, and in 1647 he fathered an illegitimate son, whose mother died shortly after. In 1651, he was ordained as a priest, and spent much of the rest of his long life working as a chaplain in Madrid and, of course, writing plays, until his death in 1681. Calderón's theatrical production was abundant, consisting of 120 dramas, 80 autos sacramentales (morality plays), and 20 miscellaneous pieces. Much of it was published in collections approved by Calderón himself during his lifetime.

Calderón's plays fall into two distinct types: the religious and the secular. The religious plays are the autos sacramentales, *derived from medieval morality plays, which Calderón perfected into a theatre of ideas. The secular plays are in turn divided into two thematic categories: One is more traditional and popular, derived from the theatre of Lope de Vega, and dealing with historical or legendary themes, the theme of honor, and cloak-and-dagger intrigues.* El Alcalde de Zalamea (The Mayor of Zalamea, *1636*) *is representative of this type. The other type of secular drama written by Calderón is more intellectual and philosophical, and* La vida es sueño (Life Is a Dream, *1635*) *is the outstanding example.*

Life Is a Dream *is Calderón's supreme dramatic achievement. Basing his text on such varied sources as the myth of Oedipus and the legend of the Buddha, Calderón gives them a Christian and Baroque interpretation, proposing that, although the world and material reality may be an illusion, human beings are still free either to condemn themselves or to seek redemption through faith. The play takes place in Poland (a near-mythical and remote place for seventeenth-century Spaniards). It tells the story of Prince Segismundo, son of the astrologer-king*

Basilio. The prince lives locked and chained in a tower among mountains, because his father had foreseen that he would be the cause of great catastrophes. One day, to test his prophecy, Basilio has Segismundo drugged and taken back to the palace, where, upon awakening, he is treated like a prince by those around him. Soon Segismundo displays his unrestrained temper by insulting his father, courting two women at the same time, attempting to murder his guardian Clotaldo, and throwing a servant out of a window. Persuaded that Segismundo is beyond redemption, Basilio has him drugged again and returned to the tower, where Clotaldo tries to convince him that everything that happened in the palace was just a dream. However, when Basilio's subjects learn that the king's legitimate heir, Segismundo, will not rule over them after Basilio's death, a popular revolt ensues, and Segismundo is freed by the rebels and made into their leader. Segismundo's experience of life as a dream or an illusion has made him wiser and more prudent this time, and after defeating Basilio's army he allows his father to remain on the throne. A chastened and impressed Basilio then proclaims Segismundo as his rightful successor. Even though life may be a dream, it must, nevertheless, be lived responsibly. The play also contains, in a manner typical of Calderón and much of Spanish Golden Age theatre, an intriguing and rather comical subplot in which an unfulfilled amorous relationship is presented between Segismundo and the adventurous Rosaura, who comes to Poland dressed as a man seeking Astolfo, a courtier who had fled after seducing her with promises of marriage.

The following selection consists of segments from Act One, scene 2, Rosaura and her comical servant Clarín's encounter with Segismundo in the tower; Act Two, scenes 17–19, Segismundo's return to the tower after causing havoc in the palace; and Act Three, scene 14, Segismundo's victory, in which he restores honor to Rosaura with marriage to Astolfo, and himself marries Estrella, Astolfo's fiancée. He also restores the throne to his father and order to the kingdom.

From *Life Is a Dream* by Pedro Calderón de la Barca, copyright 1958 by William E. Colford, translator. Pp. 4–8, 63–67, 96–101.

CHARACTERS

Segismundo
Rosaura
Clarín
Clotaldo
Servant
Basilio
Soldier
Astolfo
Estrella

Act One, Scene Two

[The door opens fully, revealing SEGISMUNDO *in chains, and dressed in animal skins. A light shines within the tower.]*

SEGISMUNDO: Oh, wretched me! Alas, unhappy man!
I strive, oh Heav'n, since I am treated so,
To find out what my crime against thee was
In being born; although in being born
I understand just what my crime has been.
Thy judgment harsh has had just origin:
To have been born is mankind's greatest sin.
I only seek to know, to ease my grief,
(Now setting to one side the crime of birth)
In what way greater, Heav'n, could I offend,
To merit from thee greater punishment?
Were not all others born? If so, in fine,
What dispensation theirs that was not mine?
Birds are born, rich garbed in hues that give
Them brilliant beauty; then, when scarcely more
Than feathered flow'rs or plumèd garlands, breast
The vault of air with speedy wing, and leave
The shelt'ring nest forlorn. And what of me?
Should I, with soul much greater, be less free?
Beasts are born, their skin all mottled o'er
With lovely colors; then, when scarcely more
Than starry patches, limned with learnèd brush,
The needs of man instruct them to be bold,
Cruel monsters in their lair. And what of me?

Should I, with higher instincts, be less free?
Fish are born, unbreathing spawn of ooze
And slimy seaweed; then, when scarcely more
Than tiny boats with scales upon the waves,
They swim away to measure all the vast
Cold limits of the deep. And what of me?
Should I, with greater free will, be less free?
Streams are born, and serpent-like uncoil
Among the flow'rs; then, when scarcely more
Than silv'ry snakes, they wind away and sing
In tuneful praise the rustic majesty
Stretched open to their flight. And what of me?
Should I, with life much longer, be less free?
And as I reach this angry pitch I burn
With Etna's fierce volcanic fires,[1] and want
To tear my heart in pieces from my breast.
What law, what reason can deny to man
That gift so sweet, so natural, that God
Has giv'n a stream, a fish, a beast, a bird?

ROSAURA: Fear and pity are instilled in me
By his opinions

SEGISMUNDO: Who has heard my cries?
Is that you, Clotaldo?

CLARÍN: *[Aside to his lady.]* Tell him yes.

ROSAURA: It's only one forlorn (oh, woe is me!)
Who in these frigid vaults o'erheard thy plea.

SEGISMUNDO: Then I must kill thee here in order that
[Seizing her]
Thou may'st not know—for I know thou dost know—
My weakness. Just because thou heardest me,
With these strong arms I must tear thee to bits.

CLARÍN: I am deaf, and could not overhear!

ROSAURA: If thou art human, let my prostrate form
Before thy feet suffice to set me free.

SEGISMUNDO: Thy voice has moved me, thy appearance stays
My hand, and the respect I feel for thee
Disturbs me. Who art thou? Although in here
I know so little of the world, because
This tow'r has been my cradle and my tomb;

---

[1] Mount Etna is a volcanic mountain in northeast Sicily, to which the imprisoned Segismundo compares his own pent-up rage.

And though since birth (if this is what birth is)
I only know this desert region where
I'm living like a living skeleton,
A dead man who's alive; and though I've seen
And talked to just one person here who feels
Compassion for my sorrows, and through whom
I have some notion of Heav'n and earth;
And though thou may'st be more amazed and call
Me human monster in thy stunned surprise,
I am a man among wild beasts, a wild
Beast among men; and though amid such grave
Misfortunes I have studied politics,
Informed by animals and taught by birds,
And I have traced the paths of pallid stars;
'Tis thou alone hast brought such passion to
My anger, admiration to my eyes,
And wonder to my ears. Each time I see
Thee I am more amazed, and when I look
Upon thee more, still more I want to look.
I think my eyes must have the dropsy, for
When drinking's death, they drink thee in the more;
And so, while seeing that seeing means death
To me, I am dying to see. But let
Me look at thee and die, for I know not,
Though seeing you means death, what not to see
Might mean. It would be worse than savage death,
Than fury, wrath, and deepest grief: it would
Be life; thus I have learned its bitterness,
For giving life to one importunate
Is giving death to one that's fortunate.

ROSAURA: I look at thee with wonder, and I hear
Thee with astonishment, and do not know
What I can say to thee, nor what to ask.
I'll only say that to this place today
Heaven has guided me to be consoled,
If it can be the consolation of
A wretch to see one who's more wretched still.
The tale is told about a wise man who
One day — so poor and destitute was he —
Had only lived upon some herbs he picked;
"Can there be another man," he said
Within himself, "who's poorer and unhappier
Than I?" And when he turned his head he found

The answer as he saw another sage
Was picking up the leaves he threw away.
Complaining of my lot I went along
Existing in this world, and just when I
Was saying to myself, "Is there a soul
Alive whose lot is more unfortunate?",
Thou mercifully didst the answer give
To me; for just as in the fable, I
Discover that my woes — in order to
Convert them into joys — thou hast picked up.
And if perchance my woes can be of some
Relief to thee, please pay me careful heed,
And help thyself to those I do not need.
I am . . .[2]

. . .

Act Two, Scene Seventeen

The Prince's prison in the tower. SEGISMUNDO, *as at the beginning, is wearing animal skins; he is in chains, and stretched out on the floor.*

CLOTALDO, *two servants,* CLARÍN.

CLOTALDO: Now leave him here, because today his pride
  Will end where it began.
SERVANT: I'll fasten on
  The chain again just as it was before.
CLARÍN: Do not awaken, Segismundo, to
  Behold thine own undoing; luck has changed,
  And all thy counterfeited glory was
  A shadow of this life, a flash of death.
CLOTALDO: A person who knows how to talk like that
  Should have a place provided just for him
  To argue to his heart's content; so seize
  [to the servants]
  This man and lock him in that cell.
  [pointing to the next room]
CLARÍN: Why me?
CLOTALDO: Because a trumpeter like you

---

[2] Rosaura's explanation of who she is (which readers of the play already know from scene 1) is interrupted here by the entrance of Clotaldo, Segismundo's guardian, and some soldiers.

Must be locked up in prison very tight
Where he can't blare out secrets that he knows.

CLARÍN: Do I, perchance, seek to arrange the death
Of my own father? No. Did I throw off
A balcony some little Icarus?[3]
Do I die, and come back to life again?
Am I just dreaming, or am I asleep?
What purpose is fulfilled by jailing me?

CLOTALDO: Thy name—Clarín—means trumpet.

CLARÍN: Then I say
That I shall be a horn, and will not blow,
For it is such a lowly instrument.

[They take him away; CLOTALDO *remains alone]*

Scene Eighteen

BASILIO, *disguised;* CLOTALDO; SEGISMUNDO, *asleep.*

BASILIO: Clotaldo!

CLOTALDO: Sire! Your Majesty comes here
Like that?

BASILIO: My foolish curiosity
To see how Segismundo fares (alas!)
Has brought me here like this.

CLOTALDO: Behold him there,
Reduced to his abject condition.

BASILIO: Oh,
Unhappy Prince, whose birth was under stars
Ill-fated! Go and wake him up, now that
The draught he drank has robbed him of his
strength
And violence.

CLOTALDO: He's restless, sire, and talks.

BASILIO: Now what can he be dreaming of? Well, let
Us listen.

SEGISMUNDO: *[In his sleep]* Righteous is the prince who seeks
To punish tyrants. Let Clotaldo die
At my bare hands, and let my father kiss
My feet.

CLOTALDO: He threatens me with death.

---

[3] In Greek myth, Icarus, the son of Daedalus, flew too near the sun with wings fastened on with wax, and fell to his death in the sea.

BASILIO: And me
>With violence and insult.

CLOTALDO: He intends
>To take my life.

BASILIO: And plots to humble me.

SEGISMUNDO: *[In his sleep]*
>Now let my peerless prowess enter on
>The spacious stage of this great world playhouse;
>So that my vengeance may be fitting, let
>Them see Prince Segismundo triumph o'er
>His father. *[He awakes.]* But, alas! Where am I now?

BASILIO: *[To* CLOTALDO*]*
>He must not see me here; thou knowest what
>To do; I'll listen to him from back here.
>*[He withdraws.]*

SEGISMUNDO:
>Is it I, perchance, who find myself
>In captive chains in such a state? Art thou,
>O tower, not my tomb? Indeed thou art!
>Good Heav'n above! How many things I've dreamed!

CLOTALDO: *[Aside]* And now it is my turn to make believe.

SEGISMUNDO: Now is it time to waken?

CLOTALDO: Yes, it is.
>Art thou to spend the livelong day asleep?
>And has thou not awakened since I left
>To follow that slow eagle in its flight
>Whilst thou remained behind?

SEGISMUNDO: I have not; and
>Not even now, Clotaldo, have I waked,
>For I believe that I am still asleep.
>And I am not far wrong, because if what
>Was dreamed, I saw and felt as real,
>Then what I see must be unreal; and it
>Is not surprising that I dream awake,
>Since I can see when I am fast asleep.

CLOTALDO: Now tell me what it was that thou didst dream.

SEGISMUNDO: If I thought that it all was just a dream,
>I wouldn't tell it; but, Clotaldo, I
>Shall tell thee what I really saw. I woke
>To find myself (cruel illusion) in
>A bed that could—for shades and colors—be
>Compared with springtime's bed of blooms.
>A thousand nobles, bowing at my feet,

Called me their prince and handed me rich robes
With jewels and decorations. Then thou didst
Completely change my calm to rapture when
Thou didst tell me of my good fortune: that
(Despite my present state) I was the Prince
Of Poland.

CLOTALDO: And I had, of course, a fine reward
For that.

SEGISMUNDO: Not fine at all, through treachery:
Both bold and strong, I tried to kill thee twice.

CLOTALDO: Such violence toward me?

SEGISMUNDO: I was the Lord
Of all, and took revenge on all. I loved
But one—a woman; that was true, I'm sure;
All else is gone, but that will e'er endure.
[The King withdraws.]

CLOTALDO: *[Aside]* The King has left, much moved by what
he heard.
[To SEGISMUNDO*]* Since we were talking of that
eagle when
Thou didst drop off to sleep, thy dreams were of
High power; but in dreams it would be well
To honor him who brought thee up with care;
For, Segismundo, even sleeping tight
One should not lose one's sense of what is right.
[Exit]

Act Two, Scene Nineteen

SEGISMUNDO

SEGISMUNDO: Quite so; then let us curb this temper and
This fury, this ambition, lest perchance
We are just dreaming; and indeed we will,
For we are in a world so very strange
That life is but a dream; experience
Has taught me that each man who draws a breath
Dreams what he is until he wakes in death.
The king dreams he is king; believing this
Illusion, he lives ordering, ruling,
And governing; the borrowed plaudits he
Receives are writ upon the wind, and Death
(Sad fate!) converts them all to ashes. Who
Is there would dare attempt to reign yet know

He will awake in Death's cold dream laid low?
The rich man dreams of riches, and they give
Him greater cares; the poor man dreams that he
Is suffering his wretched poverty;
The man with new-made fortune dreams; the man
Who is a social climber dreams; the man
Who is offensive dreams; and in this world,
In short, all men are dreaming what they are,
Although nobody understands, by far.
I dream that I am here, encumbered with
These chains; I dreamed that I once found myself
In yet another state more flattering.
What is life? A frenzy. What is life?
A shadow, an illusion, and a sham.
The greatest good is small; all life, it seems,
Is just a dream, and even dreams are dreams.

• • •

Act Three, Scene Fourteen

SEGISMUNDO, ESTRELLA, ROSAURA, *soldiers and retainers;*
BASILIO, ASTOLFO, CLOTALDO.

SOLDIER: Amid these winding mountain trails, among
These forest fastnesses, the king's concealed.
SEGISMUNDO: Pursue him! Have each tree upon this peak
Examined trunk by trunk and branch by branch!
CLOTALDO: Please flee, my lord!
BASILIO: What for?
ASTOLFO: What does thou have
In mind to do?
BASILIO: Astolfo, stand aside!
CLOTALDO: What dost thou wish?
BASILIO: Clotaldo, I shall try
The only remedy that's left to me.
[He addresses SEGISMUNDO, *and kneels.]*
If thou dost come, young prince, in search of me,
Behold me at thy feet, on bended knee.
Make these white hairs thy rug upon the floor;
Step down upon my neck, and trample on
My kingly crown; disgrace, degrade, drag down
My reputation and my self-esteem;
Take vengeance on my honor, and make me

A captive slave. When all these deeds are through,
Thy will be done, oh Heav'n, thy word come true!
SEGISMUNDO: Illustrious Court of Poland, you who are
All witnesses to these amazing deeds,
Give ear to me: your Prince addresses you.
What Heaven hath decreed and God hath writ
With His own hand in characters of gold
Upon a field of blue, can never be
In error, never lie; the one who lies
And is in error is the one who tries
To penetrate and understand them to
Abuse them for some other purposes.
My father, who is here, to save himself
From my true nature's wrath, made me a brute,
A human beast; and so although, through my
High birth, my noble blood, and gallant strain,
I might have been both gentle and reserved,
This way of life and strange upbringing were
Enough to make my whole behavior wild:
A fine way to prevent my being so!
If it were said to any man, "Some wild
Inhuman beast will cause thy death," then would
It be a good idea to wake the beast
When it was sleeping? If they said, "This sword
That thou art wearing round thy waist will be
What kills thee," then in order to prevent
Its happening, it would be foolish to
Unsheathe the sword and place it at thy breast.
And if they said, "Wide waters are to be
The silver monument above thy tomb,"
Thou wouldst do wrong in putting out to sea
When it was raising whitecaps angrily
And curling crystal crests of snowy foam.
The same has happened to our King as to
The man who wakes the beast that threatens him,
The man who bares the sword he fears, the man
Who dares the stormy waves. And though my wrath
(Now heed me) were just like a sleeping beast,
My fury like a sword restrained, my rage
As quiet as a calm at sea, one's fate
Does not yield to injustice and revenge:
If anything, it is incited more.
And so, if one expects to overcome

His fate, it must be done with reason and
With moderation. Even one who sees
It coming cannot stave off harm before
It comes; although he can protect himself,
Of course, with humble resignation, he
Can only do this after the event,
Which in itself cannot be warded off.
May this extraordinary spectacle,
This most amazing scene, this horror, this
Phenomenon, be an example; there
Is nothing more surprising than to see,
Despite precautions of so many kinds,
A father prostrate at my feet, a king
Trod under foot. For it was Heaven's will;
No matter how he wanted to prevent
It, he could not. How then shall I, a man
Of younger years and not so brave as he,
Nor yet so learned, counter Heaven's will?
[To the King] Rise up, my lord, and let me clasp
thy hand,
For now that Heaven has enlightened thee
About the error of thy ways in thine
Attempt to conquer it, my neck awaits
Thy vengeance humbly; I am at thy feet.

BASILIO: My son (for such a noble deed again
Engenders thee as such within my heart),
Thou art the Prince; the laurels and the palm
Belong to thee, for thou has conquered me;
Now let thy deeds crown thee with victory.

ALL: Long live Segismundo! Long live he!

SEGISMUNDO: My sword must wait to gain great victories,
So for today my greatest triumph is
The victory I've won over myself.
Astolfo, give thy hand in marriage to
Rosaura right away; it is a debt
Of honor, and I'll see that it is paid.

ASTOLFO: Although I owe her obligations, I
Admit, take note that she does not know who
She is, and it would be a stigma and
Sheer infamy to wed a woman who . . .

CLOTALDO: Do not continue! Hold! Enough! Because
Rosaura is as noble as thou art,
Astolfo, and my sword is ready to

Defend her on the field of honor; she
Is my own daughter, and that is enough!

ASTOLFO: What dost thou say?

CLOTALDO: I said that I, until
I saw her honorably married to
A nobleman, did not wish to reveal
Just who she was; her story is a long,
Involved one, but she is my child indeed.

ASTOLFO: Since that is so, I'll keep my plighted word.

SEGISMUNDO: So that the fair Estrella will not be
Disconsolate about the loss of such
A valiant and outstanding prince, I shall
Myself hand-pick for her a husband who,
If he does not exceed Astolfo in
These merits and in fortune, is at least
His equal. Take my hand.

ESTRELLA: I do indeed
Gain much in winning such great happiness.

SEGISMUNDO: As for Clotaldo, who so loyally
Did serve my father, here my open arms
Await him, with what favors he may ask.

SOLDIER: If thus thou dost grant honors to one who
Has not served thee, then what of me, who caused
Revolt within the realm, the one who freed
Thee from the tower, what wilt thou give me?

SEGISMUNDO: The tower! And so thou wilt not escape
It ever, thou shalt stay in there until
Thy death, close guarded; for the traitor is
Not needed when the need for treason's past.

BASILIO: Thy wisdom is a marvel to us all.

ASTOLFO: And what a change his nature now reveals!

ROSAURA: And how discreet and prudent he's become!

SEGISMUNDO: What is it that surprises all of you?
What startles you, if my preceptor was
A dream, and in anxiety I fear
I shall awake and find myself again
Imprisoned? Even though this were not so,
It is sufficient just to dream it is.
For this is how I learned, so it would seem,
That all our mortal bliss fades like a dream.
And now I wish to use what time remains
To ask indulgence of such noble hearts.
And pardon for all errors in our parts.

24

❧

PRIMAL BOOK

The Adi Granth (Primal Book), *written mainly in the Punjabi language, is the sacred scripture of the Sikh religion, also known as Sikhism. The religion originated in India about five hundred years ago. Its followers, the Sikhs, now number about eighteen million. Their original homeland is the Punjab, in the northwest of the Indian subcontinent, but they are also settled in significant numbers in other parts of present-day India and in many other countries across the world. The birth and evolution of Sikhism occupy an important place in the history of the world's religions. Born out of interaction between Islam and Hinduism, it naturally absorbed many elements of these two religions but emerged as a religion in its own right, with its own unique beliefs, practice, and identity. As the foundation of Sikh belief and practice, the* Adi Granth *comprises an outstanding document of religious thought and culture.*

The Adi Granth *is a voluminous work of 1,400 pages. It consists of hymns in praise of God and about human experience of the divine reality. It is entirely in verse and with the exception of one composition in it, the verse is cast in many different modes of Indian classical music. The text of the* Adi Granth *evolved over a period of two centuries, from the end of the fifteenth to about the end of the seventeenth century, corresponding to the period of the Protestant Reformation in Europe. Sikhism grew under the tutelage of ten* gurus *(spiritual teachers) who followed one another in succession from the first guru, Nanak (1469–1539), the founder of the religion, to the tenth, Gobind Singh (1666–1708), who gave Sikhism its final form and definition. Gobind Singh instituted a baptismal ritual after going through which every male Sikh acquired the second name Singh (lion) and every woman the name Kaur (princess). He introduced this ritual to turn Sikhs into saint-warriors to fight against the prevailing political oppression. The main composers of the* Adi Granth *were the Sikh gurus, hereafter referred to simply as gurus. According to the* Adi Granth, *the gurus were spiritually perfect individuals, one with God. Their verses are not to be considered literature of merely human composition. The gurus believed their compositions to be words expressing an experience of the divine reality uttered in a state of blissful communion with or anguished separation from that reality. They called the compositions of this nature* bani. *The content of the* Adi Granth, *is therefore, known as* gur-bani *(the gurus'* bani*)*.

The Adi Granth *was first compiled by the fifth guru, Arjun Dev (1563–1606). As editor, the criterion he used for the selection of compositions was both simple and exacting: The hymns included must be truly authentic* bani. *He included hymns from the first four gurus and his own hymns, the largest in number being his hymns and, next to his, those of the first guru, Nanak. In addition, he included selections from the* bani *of several* bhakti *saints and a Muslim Sufi saint of the Punjab, most probably Sheikh Farid Shakargunj (1173–1265). (For a discussion of Sufism, see Volume II, introduction to Selection 10.)* Bhakti *means "devotion to or worship of God" as a means of union with God. A main approach to God realization in classical Hinduism,* bhakti *as a religious practice increasingly gathered force in south India throughout the middle ages. In the fifteenth and sixteenth centuries,* bhakti *evolved into a powerful social-religious movement sweeping northern India in the form of numerous* bhakti *cults based on the teachings of different saintly figures who shared fundamentally common ideals and beliefs. Most* bhakti *saints were Hindu, but the movement was eclectic, at least in theory, and there were* bhakti *teachers of central importance, such as Kabir (1440–1518) who were born Muslim. The basic tenets of* bhakti *were the love of God and God's creation, the essential oneness of God despite the diversity of God's names and forms, the oneness and equality of all human beings regardless of caste and creed, and the emphasis on the inner spiritual experience instead of external forms and rituals of religion. These tenets significantly parallel the teachings of Sikhism which, like* bhakti, *draws on both Hinduism and Islam.*

Except for the hymns of the bhakti *saints who wrote in languages other than Punjabi, the language of the* Adi Granth *is Punjabi. Even in the case of these hymns in other languages, Arjun Dev selected only such hymns as are easily intelligible to the speakers of Punjabi. The* Adi Granth *is written in the script known as* gurmukhi *(from the lips of the guru). Punjabi still continues also to be written in Persian (which, since the conquest of Iran by Islam, has been written in the Arabic script) and in* devanagari *(Sanskrit) scripts. The* gurmukhi *script seems to have existed before its use by the gurus, but its regular use for writing Punjabi was certainly established by the Sikh gurus. Phonetically,* gurmukhi *is more faithful to Punjabi than the other scripts. A notable aspect of the* Adi Granth *is that its contents are arranged not according to chronology or subject matter, but according to the* ragas *(classical Indian melodic modes) in which they are composed. All the hymns in the book except the opening one are intended to be recited rhythmically or sung, often to the accompaniment of instrumental music. Their music constitutes an integral element of the hymns. When they are sung, the music of the hymns helps induce the same heightened and harmonious spiritual state as that in which they originally appeared.*

Briefly stated, the tenets of Sikhism as found in the Adi Granth *are as follows. God is one, eternal, not subject to birth or death, infinite, beyond shape or form, and the creator of all existences. God is all-knowing, omnipresent, and in an everlasting state of bliss. It is impossible to represent God in any physical form. Image worship is, therefore, sacrilegious. An essential quality of God is love of all created beings and things. In return, human beings should love God and all creation. The purpose of human life is to attain union with God and merge in the state of eternal bliss that is God. The* Adi Granth *repeatedly emphasizes the contemplation of God's Name as a means of God realization. God's Name is considered synonymous with God. The* Adi Granth *also postulates the necessity of a true guru for achieving union with God. It equates the true guru with God. The guru's grace alone can enable a person to realize God. The* Adi Granth *thus embodies a fundamentally spiritual ethic. The ethic, however, has a strong social-moral aspect. Unlike most other Indian spiritual systems, which advocate withdrawal from the world, the* Adi Granth *prescribes involvement in the world and pursuit of spiritual perfection while staying in the world. The book teaches concern for and the equality of all human beings. Socially, it preaches the abolition of all distinctions of caste, creed, and class. It also preaches morally right action in one's dealings with and responsibility towards others. Religiously, it offers a religion beyond all religions, one that would dissolve all sectarian differences in a universal oneness.*

As the following of the Sikh religion grew, it began to come into conflict with the state and Muslim religious authorities for several reasons. This was the heyday of the Mughals, the greatest Muslim emperors of India. Generally liberal in their religious policy, the Mughals were nonetheless Muslim and could occasionally be rigidly sectarian. The Muslim religious establishment saw in the rising Sikh religion an undesirable trend. Politically too, the popularity of the gurus among the masses was turning the tradition of guru leadership into an institution with growing power. Add to it the personal jealousies, rivalries, and petty-mindedness of the local authorities. The result was suspicion and hostility. Matters came to a head with the detention and subsequent brutal torture and execution of Arjun Dev, the fifth guru, in 1606. The event proved a watershed in the development of Sikhism. The sixth guru, Hargobind (1595–1644), added to the Sikh ideal of piety the need to use armed might, if necessary, in support of a just cause. He symbolized this by wearing two swords, one marking spiritual and the other temporal leadership. The conflict with the Mughal rule entered the next crucial phase with the execution of the ninth guru, Tegh Bahadur (1621–1675), by the order of the Mughal emperor. The cause was the guru's stand for religious freedom at a time when the emperor was engaged in the forcible conversion of Hindus to Islam. In response to such tyranny, the tenth and last guru, Gobind Singh, gave the Sikhs a new shape, turning them into soldier-saints committed to fighting for justice and righteousness. As a symbol of the new spirit of Sikhism, he instituted the baptismal ritual as mentioned above. Gobind Singh based the new Sikh ethic on the social commitment of the Adi Granth. *Steeled with this ethic, Sikhs became a force to reckon with and, after many vicissitudes, created the Sikh kingdom of the Punjab which lasted until its fall in 1849 to the English East India Company which by that time had already conquered most of the rest of India.*

After Arjun Dev, the sixth, seventh, or the eighth guru did not add any verses to the Adi Granth. *Arjun Dev's edition became flawed with minor changes during the process of copying. Gobind Singh had a new authoritative edition prepared, adding to it the verses of his father, the ninth guru. A prolific writer himself, he did not include any of his own works in the* Adi Granth. *Instead he compiled them in a separate volume, considering his compositions as of a different order than the* Adi Granth. *Gobind Singh also pronounced the end of guruship in human form after him and designated the* Adi Granth *as the only future guru. Sikhs, therefore, regard the book as their personal guru, venerating it with the various customary rituals of reverence due to a living guru, such as dressing the book in beautiful cloths, bowing before it in homage, closing and putting it to rest at night, opening it formally in the morning, and the like.*

The following excerpt, Japji *("Recitation"), by Nanak, the first guru, who often names himself in the work, is the most important composition of the* Adi Granth. *It is the first of the five prayers from the book that a Sikh is required to say every morning. The* Japji *is composed mainly in the verse form called the* pauri *(ladder). A* pauri *contains a number of couplets and is part of a structured long poem. Reading the* Japji, *or even the first five* pauris *of it, is considered a substitute for the whole* Adi Granth *when it is not possible to read the book in its entirety. The parenthetical number at the end of each* pauri *indicates the number of that* pauri. *Unlike the rest of the* Adi Granth, *the* Japji *is not cast in a raga. Perhaps this is because it is believed to be the epitome of the scripture and no single raga can fully encompass its spirit.*

JAPJI[1]

Seed Mantar[2]

God is One, the One whose Name is Truth, who creates, is fearless, has enmity towards none, is timeless in being, is beyond birth and death, self-existing, and found by the guru's grace.

Translated from the Punjabi by Surjit S. Dulai. Copyright 1999.

[1] *Jap* has two meanings, "recite" and "recitation," both equally applicable. *Ji* is an honorific suffix used in reference to a person or other subject, such as a work of sacred literature, worthy of reverence.

[2] *Mool* (seed) *Mantar* (formula), the opening sentence, is not strictly a part of *Japji*. It is a separate *bani* by itself and is also included at the beginning of most other *banis*. It contains the major tenets of Sikhism relating to aspects of God.

Recite:

God existed before time, existed through the ages, will always exist. Purity is not achieved by ritual cleansing, even if one does a hundred thousand ablutions. The inner calm is not attained, even if one sits forever in an endless vow of silence. The hunger of the greedy is never assuaged even when loaded with the wealth of all the worlds. A thousand feats of cleverness may increase a hundredfold; not one will go along into the hereafter.

How then to become pure, how break illusion's wall? Accept, Nanak,[3] God's ordained command and will. (1)

By divine command do creations occur; the divine command cannot be described. By divine command is one given life, by divine command is greatness granted. By divine command are some placed high, some low; by divine writ the pain and comfort in one's lot. By divine command some are granted grace, by divine command others wander from life to life.

Everyone is under God's command; exempt from it is none. Nanak, those who understand God's will never boast of I-amness. (2)

Some sing praises of Your power to the extent of their power; some sing seeing your bounties as a sign of Your nature. Some sing of Your noble attributes, Your greatness, and Your excellence; some sing through learning and arduous study. Some sing of You as One who creates the body and then reduces it to dust; some sing of You as One who takes away life and restores it again. Some sing of You as One who seems remote and distant; some sing of You as One seen face to face.

None can describe You exhaustively, though millions have tried and given as many accounts. The Giver gives on till the receivers can receive no more; they exist on Your bounty through endless ages. By divine command is the order of existence maintained. God blossoms, Nanak, in unbounded bliss. (3)

God is eternal truth, God's Name eternal truth. God speaks the language of infinite love, endlessly showering gifts on us creatures, whose prayers are a constant begging for more and more. What offering then should we make in order to be taken into the Divine presence; what words shall we utter, the sound of which will invoke God's love?

In the ambrosial morning hours, contemplate the true Name and God's greatness. By good deeds the vesture of human life is obtained and by God's grace opened salvation's door. This is the way, Nanak, to know the true One who pervades all. (4)

Neither can God be installed in an idol nor created; the pure One is self-existent. One who contemplates the Divine Being receives renown; Nanak, that treasure of virtue praise. Sing and listen to God's virtues and entertain in the heart the love of God; this will end suffering and usher one into the house of bliss.

The guru's word is divine song, the guru's word is divine knowledge, the guru's word is all-pervasive. The guru is god Shiva, the guru is Vishnu and

---

[3] The first guru, the composer of *Japji*.

Brahma, the guru is the mother-goddess, Parvati.[4] Were I to acquire knowledge of the guru's nature, it would be beyond my ability to describe, for it cannot be put into words. The guru has given me one wise insight: there is but One giver for all living beings; may I never forget the One. (5)

If I please God, that is my ablution at a sacred place; without that rituals are of no avail. In the whole created world that I see, none finds fulfillment without grace given for good deeds. The mind is filled as if with gems, jewels, and rubies, if but once one listens to the guru's word. The guru has given me one wise insight: there is but One giver for all living beings; may I never forget the One. (6)

Were the span of one's life four aeons long, and were it to become ten times longer; were one known in all the nine spheres of the created world, and were one obeyed and followed by everyone; were one, obtaining a good name, praised and renowned throughout the world; if one does not receive God's gracious glance, it is as if no one pays attention to such a person. A person like that would be considered lower than the lowest of worms and regarded sinful even by sinners.

Nanak, God endows with virtue those without virtue and fills the virtuous with virtues greater still. No such person can be conceived of who can confer virtue on God. (7)

By listening closely to God's Name, one becomes a perfect saint, a spiritual guide, a hero, and a great yogi.[5] By listening to God's Name, one learns the truth about the earth, the earth-supporting bull, and the sky.[6] By listening to God's Name, one learns about all the continents, the various worlds, and the nether regions.

Death cannot touch them who listen to God's Name. Nanak, the worshipers always wax in bliss. Listening to God's Name annihilates suffering and sin. (8)

Those who listen to God's Name become what is truly meant by Shiva, Brahma, and Indra.[7] Listening to God's Name, even the corrupt become reformed and begin to utter God's praises. By listening to the Name are found the way to union with God and the mysteries of the human self.

---

[4] Shiva, Vishnu, Brahma, and Parvati are the chief gods of Hinduism. Respectively, they are the god of fertility and destruction, the preserver and ruler of the created worlds, the creator god, and the mother goddess. The *Adi Granth* does not believe in these or in any of the multiple gods of Hinduism, but often uses allusions to Hindu mythology for comparison or illustration in presenting its own concepts. The implication here is that the guru more truly represents what the gods mentioned here are claimed to represent but actually do not.

[5] A person who practices the discipline of yoga, physical and mental exercises used to attain tranquility and — in Hindu philosophy — to unify one's self with the Supreme Being.

[6] In Hindu and in Indian mythology in general, the earth is supported by a bull on one of its horns. When the bull shifts the burden from one horn to the other, as it does from time to time, earthquakes occur.

[7] Indra is a god of Hinduism. He is conceived of as a king in the heavens.

Listening to God's Name comprises the true *Shastras, Simriti,* and *Veda.*[8] Nanak, the worshipers ever wax in bliss. Listening to God's Name annihilates suffering and sin. (9)

By listening to God's Name are found truth, contentment, and divine knowledge. Listening to the Name is the true pilgrimage to the sixty-eight holy places.[9] By listening to the Name one receives the honor sought through constant study. Listening to the Name brings spontaneous absorption in God.

Nanak, the worshipers ever wax in bliss. Listening to God's Name annihilates suffering and sin. (10)

By listening to God's Name, one fathoms the deep ocean of infinite virtue. Knowing the Name, one becomes a learned scholar and a spiritual guide and monarch.[10] By listening to the Name, even the blind find the way. By listening to the Name, the unfathomable becomes fathomable.

Nanak, the worshipers ever wax in bliss. Listening to God's Name annihilates suffering and sin. (11)

The blessed condition of the faithful believer's mind cannot be described; anyone who describes it regrets the inadequacy of the effort. There is neither the paper, nor pen, nor scribe that can record the true believer's state of mind. Such is the immaculate Name, only a true believer can experience the bliss of knowing it. (12)

Through true belief the mind and intellect attain enlightenment; through true belief is the knowledge of all the regions of the cosmos revealed. Having true belief one does not suffer the slaps of punishment.[11] Through true belief one is no more subject to death. Such is the immaculate Name, only a true believer can experience the bliss of knowing it. (13)

Having true faith one meets no obstacles on the way. Having true faith one goes through the world with honor and renown. Having true belief in God one walks the spiritual, not the worldly, path. Having true belief, one remains firmly attached to virtue. Such is the immaculate Name that only the true believer can experience the bliss of knowing it. (14)

---

[8] *Shastra* in Sanskrit means an authoritative work on a subject. There are many such works in the Hindu tradition. *Simriti* is a general term for literature of human composition as distinct from *shruti* which is believed to be received through divine revelation. The *Veda,* the most sacred scripture of Hinduism, is *shruti.* The law books of Hinduism and the Hindu epics, one of them being the *Mahabharata* (Volume I, Selection 25) are *simriti.*

[9] The popular number of the most sacred places of Hinduism.

[10] A monarch of the spirit, that is, an individual of supreme spiritual attainments.

[11] This refers to the belief, common to many Indian religions, that in the hereafter the sinners will receive blows of punishment in their faces.

Through belief one finds the door of liberation. Through belief one brings about the salvation of one's kith and kin as well. Through belief both the teacher and the disciple swim and help others to swim across the world's ocean.

Nanak, one having true belief wanders no more, begging worldly alms. Such is the immaculate Name that only the true believer can experience the bliss of knowing it. (15)

The elect are received, placed high, and honored in God's presence.[12] The elect adorn the company of the monarchs of the spirit. The elect meditate on the guru alone. However hard one tries to describe or reflect, the doings of the creator remain beyond count. The earth-supporting bull is in truth righteousness, compassion-born; it patiently sustains the balance of the world. One who understands this comes to know how heavy is the burden carried by this bull. Beyond this earth there are other earths and beyond them others still. What is the power that upholds their weight?

The names of living beings, their kinds, and their colors are all written by the divine, ever-flowing pen. Who can write an account of this writing? How large indeed such an account would be! How great is the power of God, how enchanting the divine beauty! Who is able to measure how great is God's bounty? God brought forth the vast expanse of creation with just one command; from that command flowed a hundred thousand streams of life.

What power have I to describe the marvels of Your creation? I am not worthy to constitute even one offering in Your prayer.[13] Whatever pleases You is the right pursuit; O formless One, You alone endure forever. (16)

Countless are Your worshipers, countless the ways of devotion, countless the forms of worship, and countless the ways of penance.[14] Countless are the sacred books, countless the *Vedas* for chanting, countless the yogas by which the mind becomes detached. Countless are the saints who reflect on Your virtues and on the divine knowledge, countless the practitioners of virtue, countless the philanthropists. Countless are the brave warriors who confront the steel of their enemies, countless the silent sages who sit in uninterrupted meditation.

What power have I to describe the marvels of Your creation? I who am not worthy to constitute even one offering in Your prayer. Whatever pleases You is the right pursuit; O formless One, You alone endure forever. (17)

Countless are the foolish, utterly benighted; countless are the thieves who seize what is not rightfully theirs. Countless are the rulers who go on using ruthless force; countless are the cutthroats who commit murders. Countless are the sinners who go on committing sins; countless are the liars who wander lost in the

---

[12] The elect here are the spiritually elect, who are honored in the hereafter.

[13] The word translated here as "offering" literally means "sacrifice." Its origin lies in the religious ritual of the ancient Aryans who offered animal sacrifices to their gods.

[14] Self-imposed penance as a means of spiritual development is common practice in Indian religions.

world of lies. Countless are the unclean who wallow in dirty conduct; countless the slanderers who bring on their heads the burden of maligning.

The lowly Nanak speaks about himself thus: I am not worthy to equal even one offering to God. Whatever pleases You is the right pursuit; O formless One, You alone endure forever. (18)

Countless are the names of God's creations. Countless are their locations; countless are the inscrutable realms thereof. Even the word countless cannot aptly describe their number.

By the divine word of law, we recite God's Name; by the word we express God's praise. By the word we acquire the divine knowledge and by the word sing of God's attributes. Enabled by the word we write and recite holy hymns, by the word is our destiny decided. The One who wrote this word of command is alone not bound by it, but we obtain whatever the One ordains. Whatever is created is a manifestation of God's Name; nothing exists without the Name.

What power have I to express the marvels of Your creation, I who do not amount to but one offering in Your worship? Whatever pleases You is the right pursuit; O Formless One, You alone endure forever. (19)

Hands, feet, or the entire body, if covered with dirt, can be washed clean with water. Clothes fouled with urine may be washed with soap. When the mind is filled with the dirt of sins, it is washed clean with the love of God's Name. To be virtuous or a sinner depends not on mere words; it is the result of steady deeds that goes with us. As one sows, so does one reap; Nanak, one goes the round of birth and death by this divine law. (20)

If going to a holy place, doing ritual penance, charity and giving alms bring honor, it equals but a sesame seed.[15] But one, who listens to God's Name, believes in it, and holds it dear in the heart, truly bathes in a sacred water and washes away impurities.

All virtues are Yours, I have none; without the cultivation of virtues, there can be no worship. I venerate You, the creator of maya, the word and the true Brahma; You are truth, beauty and perpetual bliss.[16]

What was the instant, what time, what day of month and week; what was the season, what month when the world was created? The learned Hindu priests could not know the time, for the *Puranas* do not record it.[17] Neither could the Muslim divines know it, for it is not written in the *Koran*.[18] Nor does the yogi know the date or the day, the season or the month. The creator alone who fashioned existence knows it all.

---

[15] That is, a very tiny amount, the size of a sesame seed.

[16] That is, God's word which produced the creation. "Maya" is an ancient Indian concept according to which the world of sensory experience is illusory.

[17] *Puranas* are a major work of Hindu tradition. They tell stories of ancient kings for didactic purposes.

[18] The scripture of Islam.

How can one capture God's greatness in words, and how can one praise God fully? How can one describe or know God? Nanak, all deliver discourses on God, each claiming to be wiser than the others, but God's greatness and the greatness of God's Name is beyond their ken. Whatever God wills, comes to pass. Nanak, whoever is self-important and vain does not receive honor in the hereafter. (21)

God created nether worlds below nether worlds, and countless other worlds beyond worlds above. Baffled in trying to fathom the limits of God's vast reality, the *Vedas* own their helplessness. The Semitic scriptures speak of eighteen thousand worlds,[19] but just One essence pervades all reality. If an account of it were possible, it would have been written, but life ends in the fruitless quest to write.

Nanak, know that God alone is great, for God alone completely knows God. (22)

Praisers praise but do not truly comprehend God's greatness, just as streams and rivers fall into the ocean but do not know its vast expanse. Shahs and sultans with ocean-wide and mountain-high piles of property and pelf will not equal an ant, if it does not let the thought of God leave its mind. (23)

Limitless is God's goodness, limitless its praise; limitless are God's doings and limitless God's bounty. There is no limit to what God sees or hears and no limit to the mysteries of God's consciousness. There is no limit to the expanse of God's creation, no limit to either its near or far end. Many vex their minds seeking to know the extent of God's reality, but they fail to find its end. No one can know this end; the more we speak of God's greatness, the more we find yet to speak about.

God is great, exalted God's place, and God's Name is higher than the most high. If one were able to attain to such a height, only then would one know the most exalted One. How great God is God alone knows; O Nanak, the compassionate One grants grace and bestows gifts on us. (24)

God's abounding bounty beggars description; the great giver holds not even a particle back. Many warriors beg boons from God; many others whose number is beyond count do the same. Many are consumed to nothing, wrecked with vice; many continuously receive God's gifts, but deny the fact; many fools keep on gluttonously consuming whatever they receive. Many are continuously punished with pain and hunger; even these are Your blessings, O great giver.

Release from bondage depends on God's will; none else can have a say in it. Fools who dare disagree with this will find out what blows of punishment will hit them in the face.

Unasked, God knows our needs and confers gifts unasked; only very few acknowledge even this. One, whom God grants the boon of praising God's goodness, is, Nanak, the king of kings. (25)

Priceless are Your virtues, priceless Your dealings in them; priceless are the traders, priceless their store of goods. Priceless is what comes from You, priceless

---

[19] The specific number simply implies a large number.

what we take from You. Priceless is Your love, priceless those absorbed in it. Price-less is Your law and priceless Your court. Priceless are Your weighing scales, priceless Your forgiving acceptance. Priceless is Your grace, priceless the sign of Your approval. Priceless is Your generosity, priceless Your command.

How priceless You are, O priceless One, cannot be told. By continually speaking of You, one stays absorbed in Your love. The books of the *Veda* and the *Puranas* speak of You; so do the learned in their discourses. The Brahmas speak in Your praise; so do the Indras; so do also the *gopis* and the cowherd Krishna.[20] Shiva utters Your praise, as do the *siddhas,* and many a created Buddha does the same.[21] The demons speak of You, as do the deities, the demi-gods, godly men, the holy sages, and Your devotees.

Many thus speak of You and many continually attempt to speak. Many have passed away, having spoken about You. Were You to create as many more people as You already have, even then they would not be able to grasp together your greatness.

You can be as great as You please to be. Says Nanak, You the true One alone knows Your greatness. If someone arrogantly claims to know You, such a person should be written down as the most ignorant of the ignorant. (26)

How magnificent would be the entrance and how splendid the mansion seated where You take care of all existence! There, countless musical instruments of many different kinds play. How large is the number of musicians! How numerous are the ragas and the harmonies set to them! How large the number of singers! Sing of You wind, water, and fire, and *Dharmaraja* serenades at Your door.[22] Sing also Chit and Gupt who record human deeds according to which *Dharmaraja* adjudicates. Ever beautiful and bedecked, Shiva, Brahma, and Devi all sing of You.[23] The Indras seated on their thrones sing along with other deities standing at Your door. Saints deep in trance sing, and other ascetics absorbed in contemplation.

The continent, the virtuous, and the contented sing; and sing as well the fierce warriors. The learned, the chanters of the *Veda,* and mighty seers in all the

---

[20] Krishna is a very important deity of Hinduism. In one of his aspects, he is envisioned as a god of the erotic impulse, playing the role of lover of a very large number of women known as *gopis*. Actually, the *gopis* are the lovers of Krishna. In response, he becomes many Krishnas to return their love individually.

[21] Siddhas are individuals who by spiritual practice have attained to semi-divine status. The reference to "many a created Buddha" alludes to the belief that there have existed many Buddhas, including the one who lived in India during the sixth and fifth centuries B.C.

[22] In Hindu mythology, Dharmaraja is the god of dharma, which means righteousness or duty.

[23] Devi is the mother goddess. She manifests herself in different forms such as the consort of Shiva.

ages sing Your praise as found in the holy texts. The enchanting celestial maids in the heavens, the middle regions, and the nether worlds sing of You.[24] The precious stones of your creation sing Your praise, along with the sixty-eight holy places of pilgrimage. Powerful warriors and the divine heroes sing; sing all four forms of life. The continents, the worlds, and the whole universe, created and upheld by You, sing. Only those sing of You whom You wish to and who are steeped in the nectar of Your love. Many others sing of You. Their number is beyond my ken. How can Nanak know them all?

God alone is ever true and true is God's Name. God is, will always be, and will never cease to exist, the One who brought forth this creation, fashioned the world, creating different species of varying colors and kinds. Having performed the act of creation, God glories in it as a manifestation of God's own greatness.

God does what pleases God, none else can order the outcome. God is the king, the king of kings; Nanak, everyone is subject to God's will. (27)

Make contentment your earrings, effort the begging bowl and pouch; smear your body with the ashes of contemplation.[25] Let the awareness of mortality be your patched robe, your conduct the purity of body, and faith in God your staff. Make universal fraternity your sect, and know that to conquer the mind is to conquer the world.

Hail, hail to the One, the primal, the pure, without beginning, the indestructible, and unchanging through all time. (28)

Make divine knowledge the stored food, compassion its despenser;[26] listen to the divine melody that resounds in every heart. God alone is the supreme controller of the entire universe; riches and miracles are useless for sustenance.[27] Union or separation from God regulate the working of the world; mortals receive their portion according to their destiny.

Hail, hail to the One, the primal, the pure, without beginning, the indestructible, and unchanging through all time. (29)

The primal mother, maya, from a mysterious union produced three offspring: one creates, another provides, and the third holds court to dispense justice.[28]

---

[24] In Indian mythology, the unearthly beautiful females, sometimes known as the *apsaras,* inhabiting the regions above and below the earth.

[25] All these and the items that follow below are the customary accoutrements of a yogi. The *pauri* lays down what qualities a person should possess. Yoga and the external requirements of a yogi are used here as metaphors for true moral and spiritual attainments.

[26] Giving away food is a common form of charity.

[27] This refers to the belief that some individuals can acquire, by esoteric practices, the power to perform miracles. The point here is that such pursuits are useless.

[28] "Maya" is the created, essentially illusory universe. Her three offspring, the Hindu gods, Brahma, Vishnu, and Shiva, are part of this transient, illusory universe.

God commands and directs the affairs of all creatures as it pleases God. God sees them all, but is not seen by them. A great marvel!

Hail, hail to the One, the primal, the pure, without beginning, the indestructible, and unchanging through all time. (30)

God's seats and provision houses are in every world. Whatever provisions were needed were put in there once for all. Having brought into being creation, the creator beholds it joyfully. True, Nanak, is the doing of the true One.

Hail, hail to the One, the primal, the pure, without beginning, the indestructible, and unchanging through all time. (31)

If one's tongue became a hundred thousand tongues, and a hundred thousand grew twentyfold, if each tongue then were to say the name of the supreme Being hundreds of thousand of times, that would be the way to the steps leading to union with God. Hearing the stories about the celestial being, even the lowly worm begins to praise God in emulation.

Nanak, by God's grace alone is God found; in vain is the bragging of the false. (32)

By ourselves, we have not the power to speak or be silent; power to ask or to give; power to live or to die; power to gain kingdoms and wealth which cause mental commotion; power to acquire divine knowledge or to contemplate; or power to find the way to release from the world. God alone holds and wields all power; none is good or bad solely by their own volition. (33)

God created nights, seasons, and the days of the months, weeks, and the air, water, fire, and the nether worlds. Amidst these, he placed the earth as the arena of righteous action, and put therein living beings of different forms and colors, their names varied and countless. They are judged according to their deeds; God is true and true is God's court of judgment. There, the elect shine in their beauty and are accepted; they bear the mark of grace and mercy. Deficiencies and perfection shall be judged there; this shall be on arrival there. (34)

In the region of righteousness, this is the moral duty.[29] Turn now to the aspects of the region of knowledge. Many are the airs, waters, and fires; many Krishnas and Shivas. There are many Brahmas fashioning creations of numerous beauties, colors, and shapes. Many are the earths as fields of action, many the mountains; many are the saints, fixed like the polar star, giving guidance. Many are the Indras, the moons, and the suns, many the universes and lands. Many are the semi-divine ascetics, the enlightened sages, and the great yogis, many the incarnations of goddesses. Many are the gods, the demons, and the holy men vowed to silence. Many are the oceans filled with precious gems. Many are the mines of rich materials, many the kinds of languages, and many the dynasties of kings. Many have divine knowledge, many are absorbed in the service of God. Nanak, God's being has no limit. (35)

---

[29] This and the following two *pauris* describe the different regions of the spiritual universe, the regions of righteousness, knowledge, and grace.

In the realm of knowledge, the light of knowledge shines unparalleled bright. There, exhilarating celestial music plays; the spirit fills with endless bliss. The language of this realm of spiritual effort is beauty. Here are formed most wondrous forms. The features of this realm defy description. One venturing to describe will only fail and regret. Here are shaped the inner consciousness, the intellect, the mind, and the understanding; here is shaped the awareness that the most pious and the semi-divine ascetics attain. (36)

The power of the spirit pervades the realm of grace; none unworthy of the place can enter there. There dwell warriors and mighty heroes of the spirit, their minds overflowing with the awareness of God. Unstirred by heat or cold, they stay absorbed in admiring God; their beauty is beyond description. They in whose hearts dwells the Name of God can neither die nor suffer fraud. Saints from many different worlds dwell there, filled with bliss, for the true One is in their heart.

In the realm of truth resides the formless God, who ceaselessly brings forth creation and constantly watches it with gracious delight. This realm embraces all the worlds and universes. Trying to tell of its extent one cannot find its end. Here are numberless creations containing worlds upon worlds, all functioning as the One commands. Watching and contemplating the created work, the Creator blossoms with joy; Nanak, it is all as hard as steel to tell. (37)

Make self-control the forge, patience the goldsmith, awakened understanding the anvil, divine knowledge the hammer, fear of God the bellows, the heat of austerities the fire, and devotion the crucible with the divine nectar culled into it. In that true mint mould the coin of the divine word. Only those on whom God casts a gracious glance are able to perform this act. (38)

Slok[30]

The air is the guru, water the father, and the vast earth the mother. Day and night are the two nurses, one male one female, and the whole world is at play. The record of good and bad deeds is reviewed before the righteous judge. Because of their own deeds, some will attain nearness to God, others will be far.

Those who meditated on the Name departed having successfully completed their task. Nanak, their faces shine and many others find release with their help.

---

[30] *Slok* is a type of verse form. Its structure often varies. Here the *slok* serves as the epilogue to *Japji.*

25

Tulsi Das

RAMCHARITMANAS

T he epic poem, Ramcharitmanas (Holy Lake of Ram's Acts) *by Tulsi Das
(1532–1623), called the* Manas *(Holy Lake) for short, has been the most
popular scripture of Hinduism for more than four hundred years. It is popular
alike among Hindus and all other Indians, regardless of their religion. A reason
for its popularity is the annual three-week long festival called* Ramlila *(the sport
of Ram) in which the entire story of the epic is acted out in a theatrical form. The
performance takes place in every town and many villages in a large open field.
Actors move around the field acting in pantomime the successive scenes from the
epic, followed by singers reciting its relevant verses to the accompaniment of musical instruments. Battle scenes involving armies take place in the middle of the
field. On one side of the field are erected gigantic effigies of some of the main evil
characters, the demon king Ravan and his chief kin. Made of paper and fabric
over bamboo frames, with explosives attached inside, the effigies are set on fire on
the last day of the festival, their burning and blowing up marking the victory of
good over evil. Over the centuries, the dramatic spectacle of the* Ramlila *has made
the story of the* Manas *an abiding part of the Indian consciousness.*

*We do not know much with certainty about the facts of Tulsi Das's life. Most
stories told about him are apocryphal. He was born a Brahmin, most probably
at Rajapur, located on the south of the River Jumna. According to a legend,
born under an inauspicious conjunction of the stars, he was abandoned by his
parents in infancy and, in childhood, had to live by begging until adopted as a
disciple by a Vaishnavite (worshiper of Vishnu) ascetic, Narahari. The boy's
name was Ram Bola (one who proclaims the name of Ram). Probably his guru
gave him the name Tulsi Das and taught him the story of Ram. Later he went
to study the Hindu scriptures at Kashi (present day Varanashi). After some fifteen years, he seems to have returned to his native place and got married. According to a story, his wife having become a devotee of Ram left him and returned to her parents' home. Tulsi Das followed her there, trying to persuade*

her to come back with him. She reproached him for being so engrossed in carnal desire and for his lack of love for Ram. Moved by her reproach, he renounced his worldly possessions and became a wandering votary of Ram. He first went to Ayodhya, the birth place and capital of Ram, according to the Ramayana. *From there he went on a pilgrimage to many sacred places. Then he returned to Ayodhya where he started writing the* Manas *in 1574. Differences with the local Vaishnavites who were too orthodox in contrast with his tendency toward liberalism, compelled him to move to Kashi where he completed the* Manas *and lived for the rest of his life. Besides the* Manas, *he wrote about a dozen other books, many of them about Ram.*

The Manas *tells in Hindi broadly the same story as the classical Sanskrit poem, the* Ramayana *of Valmiki (c. third century* B.C.*). Over the centuries many renderings of Valmiki's original* Ramayana *appeared in the different languages of the Indian subcontinent. The* Manas *became the most famous of these. The* Manas *is not exactly a translation of the Sanskrit* Ramayana. *It differs widely from Valmiki's poem in individual episodes, very significantly contracting some and expanding others, often changing their content radically, and omitting some episodes altogether while adding new ones. The two epics differ even more profoundly in spirit and purpose. The* Ramayana *tells the story of the heroic deeds of the protagonist, Ram, presenting his greatness, despite some failings, as a model of heroic conduct in strictly human terms for praise and emulation. The hero of the* Manas, *on the other hand, is God himself, both in his innate divine reality and as incarnate in the form of a perfect human being. The theme and the purpose of the* Manas *are the exposition and inculcation of devotion to God in a personal form as Ram for the attainment of liberation from the cycle of worldly existence. The* Ramcharitmanas *thus resembles the* Ramayana *only superficially. It is an independent work in its own right both in content and in message.*

In brief outline, the action of the Manas *begins with the gods, saints, and sages going to the god Vishnu to ask for his help, for the world has become overwhelmed by evil, especially in the form of demons, chief among them the powerful ten-headed demon king of Lanka, Ravan. In response to their entreaty Vishnu is born as the four sons of King Dasarath of the Raghu clan, the eldest son being the main incarnation of his deity. When the princes have grown up, a sage, Vishvamittar, comes to ask the king to send two of his sons, Ram and Lakshman, with him to cleanse the forest of demons who have been defiling his sacrifices. The princes go with the sage and rid the forest of the miscreant demons.*

At that time, Janak, the King of Videha, happens to hold the husband-choosing ceremony for his daughter, Sita. Ram and Lakshman accompany the sage Vishvamittar to Mithila, Janak's capital. Janak owns a bow given by god Shiv. The condition for the marriage is that whoever can lift and draw the bow will marry Sita. None of the multitude of suitors for Sita's hand in marriage can even move the bow. Vishvamittar tells Ram to lift and break the bow. Ram does so, and he and Sita are married.

Dasarath decides to appoint Ram as regent. The gods are worried that if Ram settles down on the throne, he would not have the occasion to conflict with the demons and achieve the purpose for which he was born. The gods plot to make Kaikeyi, Ram's stepmother, ask the king to grant two boons he had once promised her. She asks that her son, Bharat, be the regent and Ram be banished to the forests for fourteen years. The king is compelled to grant her wishes. Sita and Lakshman insist on accompanying Ram into exile and do so. As they are settled in a hermitage in the forest, one day Ravan's sister, Surpanakha, happening to see the princes, puts on a beautiful form (for the demons have the ability to change form) and harasses them with overtures of love. Annoyed by this harassment and encouraged by Ram, Lakshman cuts off her nose and ears. She goes to her brothers Khar and Dushan who come with their armies to avenge the outrage, but are defeated and killed. Surpanakha then goes to her most powerful brother, Ravan who persuades a demon, Marich, to change into a golden deer and run around the exiles' hermitage. Seeing the deer, Sita asks Ram to shoot it and bring the hide for decoration. Before going on the hunt, Ram makes Sita walk into a fire. She remains entrusted to fire until Ram's final victory over the demons. In the meantime, a likeness of Sita replaces her and even Lakshman cannot tell the difference. As the demon-deer is shot and dying, it calls out in Ram's voice for Lakshman. Sita, thinking Ram to be in trouble, compels Lakshman to go help him. Finding Sita alone, Ravan comes in the guise of an ascetic and carries her into his flying chariot. A devotee of Ram, the king of vultures, Jatayu, tries to intercept Ravan, but is cut down by the demon.

As Ram and Lakshman go in search of Sita, they meet monkeys and bears. The monkey king, Sugriv, becomes their ally and sends his lieutenants in different directions to look for Sita. His general Hanuman, who becomes the greatest devotee of Ram finds Sita in Lanka where she is kept a prisoner in a grove by Ravan. Hanuman plays havoc with the trees in the grove, is captured and brought before Ravan whom he advises to return Sita and submit to Ram. Ravan, instead, orders Hanuman's tail wrapped in rags and cotton soaked in oil and ghee and set on fire. Growing to titanic size, Hanuman leaps all over Lanka and burns it down with his tail. Then, he returns to Ram who, in the penultimate book of the epic, marches on Lanka with an army of monkeys and bears, destroys the demons, and retrieves Sita.

As mentioned above, the theme of the Manas is devotion to God, known as bhakti. The concept and practice of bhakti dates back to ancient times. In the epic, Mahabharata (c. third century B.C.) where Krishan, an incarnation of the god Vishnu, instructing Arjun, the central hero of the epic, in the means of attaining moksha (liberation from the continuing cycle of birth, death, and rebirth), tells him that one of the paths to liberation is bhakti, devotion to him, the other paths being the acquirement of the knowledge of the true reality of god or complete adherence to dharma (performance of one's social, moral, and ritual duties). In medieval and early modern times, bhakti became a movement sweeping *the length and breadth of the subcontinent in the form of numerous* bhakti *cults. Through the centuries, the dominant form of* bhakti *was the worship of the Hindu god Vishnu, in his various incarnations, the most important of these being the incarnations of Krishan and Ram. Early on, the Vaishnavites* bhakti *predominantly prevailed as Krishan* bhakti, *a late and most poignant example of it being the songs of Mirabai (Selection 10). By the late sixteenth century the focus of* bhakti *generally shifted away from Krishan, the prince of amorous dalliance, to Ram, a model of unblemished moral purity and chastity. Tulsi Das's* Manas *not only exemplifies this shift but, by its forceful impact on the masses, it permanently made Ram* bhakti *the most popular form of devotional worship in northern India.*

Bhakti being devotion to the subject of worship, emotion in varying degrees is an essential ingredient of it. Yet emotion itself does not suffice. The true basis of bhakti *is faith granted by the grace of god. All this requires that the subject of* bhakti *be conceived in a concrete personal form. Tulsi Das thus envisions Ram in the* Manas *as a person, both as Vishnu in his divine personality and as a human being. Although he often refers to Ram as also the ultimate, infinite, and formless reality — the* Brahman *of the* Upanishads — *his emphasis always remains on Ram as a person, divine or human. Tulsi Das takes great pains to underscore again and again Ram's consciousness of being actually a god. His involvement in the joys and sorrows of the world is merely a make-believe play.*

Most important characters in the Manas — *Sita, Lakshman, Hanuman, Jatayu, Vibhishan, and many others, including the evil demons who eventually also win salvation because of being killed and touched by Ram — see and know Ram as god in person. The* Manas *is the story of Ram's deeds and of the deeds of other characters in relation to him. Whether from the very beginning or at the end, because of Ram's acts and blessing, all these characters are his devotees, bhaktas. Tulsi Das shows their* bhakti *and Ram's benediction both in action as well as through his long disquisitions, thus making the* Manas *the gospel of Ram* bhakti. *To read or to listen to the words of the epic is, therefore, to be instructed in the gospel, a pilgrimage to a holy place, a bath in sacred waters. Hence the title, the* Holy Lake of Rama's Acts. *Tulsi Das composed his epic in Hindi in its colloquial form, rather than in classical Sanskrit, with the aim of spreading the benefits of Ram* bhakti *as widely as possible. Lord Ram himself is said to have appeared to Tulsi Das in a dream and instructed him to write a* Ramayana *in the language of the common people. Obeying the god, the poet met with strong opposition from the orthodox pundits for putting the sacred scripture into a vulgar tongue, but the phenomenal success of his poem within his own lifetime vindicated him. Consequently, even the most illiterate Hindus know the* Manas *far better than their Christian counterparts know the Bible. Mahatma Gandhi himself was a devotee of Ram and conceived of the ideal system of government as* Ramraj (the rule of Ram). *When he was shot by his assassin, he died with the name of Ram on his lips.*

The following excerpts are selected from some of the most important episodes of the Manas. *An attempt is made in the selection to suggest the line of the whole*

*narrative and to convey a sense of Tulsi Das's style, especially his use of similes
and metaphors.*

꒰

RAM BREAKS SHIV'S BOW[1]

There was one tier of seats, bright, spacious, and beautiful above all the rest.
Here the Raja seated the sage and the two brothers.[2] Then Janak summoned the
bards and bade them declare his condition for Sita's marriage. They announced,
"Here is the god's massy beam, and whoever in this royal assembly can bend it
shall be renowned in heaven and earth and hell, and at once without hesitation
receive in marriage the hand of the king's daughter." When they heard the condition, all the kings were full of eagerness—insolent warriors, savage of soul—
and girding up their loins they rose in haste, bowing their heads, ere they com-
menced, before their patron gods. With flushed faces and many a close look,
they assay the divine bow, but though they put forth all their strength in a thousand different ways they cannot move it. After straining at the bow, those foolish
kings, without being able to stir it, retire in confusion, as though it had gathered
strength by in turn absorbing the force of each successive warrior. Then ten
thousand princes, all at once, attempted to raise it, but it was not to be moved,
yielding as little as a virtuous wife at the words of a gallant. Then Janak said,
"Now let no warrior get wroth if I say that there are no heroes left on earth.
Give up all hope and go home; it is not God's will that Sita be married. If I break
my condition, I lose all religious merit; the girl must remain a maid; what can I
do? Had I known, I would not have made a laughing stock of myself by setting
such a harsh condition."

Vishvamittar,[3] perceiving the fitness of the occasion, spoke in gentle and affectionate tones, "Up Ram, break the bow of Shiv and relieve Janak, my son, of
his affliction." On hearing the guru's words, Ram bowed his head at his feet, and

---

Adapted—with rearrangement, emendations, and corrections—by Surjit Singh Dulai,
from F. S. Growse, tr. *The Ramayana of Tulsi Das* (Allahabad: Ram Narain Lal, Publishers
and Booksellers; 1922).

[1] Shiv is one of the three major gods of Hinduism: Brahma the creator, Vishnu the preserver, and Shiv (pronounced Shiva in Sanskrit) the destroyer. In Tulsi Das, the three
gods are not coequal. Vishnu is the supreme deity.

[2] Raja (King) Janak. The sage is the famous Vishvamittar whom Ram and Lakshman
helped with clearing the forest of evil demons. The princes now accompany him to
Sita's husband-choosing ceremony.

[3] A sage famous in Hindu lore.

without joy or sorrow in his soul,[4] rose and stood upright in all his native grace, lordly in gait as a young lion. As Raghubir ascended the stage,[5] like the sun climbing the mountains of the east, the hearts of the saints expanded like the lotus, and their eyes were glad as bees at the return of day. Sita with her eyes fixed on Ram, implored with anxious heart each god in turn, praying to them in her inward soul, "Be gracious to me and reward my service by kindly lightening the weight of the bow to a mere trifle." Oft glancing at Raghubir's form, and taking courage from her heavenward prayers, her eyes filled with tears of love and her whole body was in a tremor. As she looked now at the Lord and now at the ground, her tremulous eyes so glistened as if they were two fishes sporting in the round pond of the moon. In her lotus mouth her voice, a bee, lay bound, for modesty held it in like the night. In the corner of her eye stood a tear drop, like a miser's buried hoard. Self-conscious because of her excitement, she yet summoned enough courage to say, "If there is any truth in me and I am sincerely enamored of Raghupati's lotus feet, God who dwells in the hearts of all, will make me Ram's handmaid." As she uttered this in her heart, Ram the most merciful comprehended it all. After looking at Sita, he glanced at the bow like an eagle eyeing a little snake. He looked at the crowd of people who all stood dumb and still like painted pictures; then he turned from them to Sita, perceiving her deep concern. He perceived her to be so terribly agitated that a moment of time seemed an age in passing. If a man die of thirst for want of water, of what use to him is a lake of nectar after death? What good is the rain when the crop is already withered? Thinking thus to himself as he gazed at Janaki,[6] the lord was enraptured at the sight of her singular devotion. After making an obeisance to his guru, he took up the bow with superlative ease. As he grasped it in his hand, it gleamed like a flash of lightning. When he bent it, it seemed like the vault of heaven. Though all stood watching, before anyone could see him grasp it, he had lifted it from the ground and raised it aloft and drawn it tight and in an instant broken it into two halves. A deafening crash resounded through the worlds.

The crash so shook the worlds that the horses of the Sun left their course and strayed, the elephants of the four quarters groaned, the earth shivered, the great serpent, the boar, and the tortoise tottered. Gods, demons, and sages put their hands to their ears and all wondered about the cause, but when they learnt that Ram had broken Shiv's bow, all uttered shouts of victory. The Lord tossed upon the ground the two halves of the bow and at the sight the multitude rejoiced. Vishmamittar's love, like the clear unfathomed depth of the ocean, swelled to the

---

[4] A spiritually perfect person is above joys and sorrows which are part of one's being bound by the world.

[5] Raghubir or other epithets beginning with the prefix Raghu refer to Ram as the scion of the Raghu clan.

[6] That is, Sita, the daughter of King Janak.

highest tide of ecstasy under the pull of the full moon of Ram's presence. There was jubilant music in the sky; heavenly nymphs danced and sang; Brahma and all the other gods and saints and sages praised and blessed the hero and rained down wreaths of many-colored flowers. Sita drew near to Ram. Graceful in motion as a swan and of infinite beauty in every limb, she came with her companions singing auspicious songs. Resplendent in their midst as the Queen of grace, she held in her lotus hand the fair wreath of victory. As she drew near and beheld Ram's beauty, she stood motionless like a painted picture until a watchful attendant roused her, saying, "Invest him with the ennobling wreath!" At the word she raised the wreath with both hands, but was too overcome by feelings to garland him till as the lotus flower and stalk shrink under the moonlight, her hand and arm drooped in the glory of Ram's moon-like face. At the sight of his beauty her maiden friends broke into song, while she let fall the wreath upon his breast.

· · ·

RAM'S EXILE TO THE FOREST

The envious gods prayed that difficulties might arise; the rejoicing at Avadh pleased them as little as a moonlit night pleases a thief. The gods called in Sarasvati and again and again threw themselves at her feet:[7] "O Mother, regard our great distress and make haste to relieve it! If Ram refuses the throne and retires to the forest, all will be well with us." On hearing the gods' petition, she stood still thinking sadly: "I am like a winter's night to a bed of lotuses." The gods seeing her hesitate cried yet once more: "O Mother, not the least blame will attach to you; for Raghurai—you know his nature well—is free from sorrow as from joy; and as for his people, like all other creatures, they have their share in pain or pleasure, under the law of necessity. Go, therefore, to Avadh and befriend us gods." She yielded, though still thinking to herself: "The gods are a mean-spirited crew; though they dwell on high, their acts are low; they cannot endure to see another's prosperity." . . . Kaikeyi had a wicked maid,[8] named Manthara. Sarasvati distorted her mind, making her a very storehouse of meanness. Then she went her way.

When Manthara heard of Ram's inauguration, her soul was on fire. The wicked wretch that she was, like a crafty hill-woman who sees a honeycomb hanging in a tree and schemes to pluck it, she plotted to undo the plans that very night. So she went crying to Bharat's mother.[9] "What is wrong?" the queen asked

---

[7] Sarasvati, the consort of Brahma, is the goddess of speech and learning, the inventor of the Sanskrit and Devanagari (Hindi) script, and the patroness of the arts and sciences. The task assigned to her of poisoning the wicked maid Manthara's mind is below her dignity and arises from the gods' desperation and pettiness.

[8] Kaikeyi is Ram's step-mother and apparently his father's favorite queen at the time.

[9] Bharat is Kaikeyi's son.

smiling. She answered not, but drew a deep sigh and, like a woman, began to shed a flood of tears. Laughing, the queen said, "You were always an impudent girl, and I suspect Lakshman has been giving you lessons." Still the wicked maid remained wordless, breathing hard like a serpent full of venom. "Is Ram not well, or the king, or Bharat, or Lakshman, or Satrughan?"[10] the queen pursued. The words tortured the heart of the humpbacked girl.[11] . . . "Who could be as well today as Ram whom the king is going to install on the throne? Why don't you go and see the magnificent celebrations the sight of which has so agitated me? Your son is away and you pay no heed to using your influence with the king, and not seeing his treachery and cunning, so drowsy you are and concerned only for your bed and pillow!" Hearing these affectionate but too forward words, the queen burst out, "Stop! If you ever speak to me like this again, I will have your tongue pulled out from the root. . . . Ram is dearer to me than life; why then should you be troubled at his being crowned King? I command you in Bharat's name to tell me the truth without any fraud or concealment; declare to me the reason why you are distressed in a time of such gladness." "I have spoken once and I am satisfied; yet I will have a second tongue and speak a little more. The wretch that I am, I deserve to have my head smashed on a funeral pile, since I cause you such pain by my well-meant words. Those who make the false appear true please you, my queen, while I offend you. From now on I too will speak only as it pleases my mistress or else remain silent day and night. Whoever is king, what do I lose? Shall I cease to be a maid and become a queen? It is just my worthless character that I cannot bear to see you disgraced and hence gave utterance to a word or two; but forgive me, mistress, it was a great mistake on my part." On hearing these subtle and affectionate words, so deep and crafty, the queen being only a weak-minded woman and under the influence of divine delusion, really believed her enemy to be her friend. Again and again in kindly terms she questioned Manthara, like a fawn bewitched by the song of a huntress. Her reason went astray as fate would have it so. The slave-girl rejoiced at the success of her scheme, "Thinking yourself the king's favorite and that he is quite in your power, you notice nothing; but however fair his words, his heart is black; but you are so good-natured. Ram's mother, on the contrary, is deep and crafty; and having found the means has furthered her own purpose. The king has greater love for you than for anyone else and like a rival, she cannot bear to see it. For her own ends she has worked upon the king and got him to fix the day for Ram's coronation. Now Ram's promotion is a good thing for the family; all are pleased with it, and I too like it well. But I am alarmed when I consider the consequences. Heaven make them recoil on her own head. Should Ram be crowned tomorrow, God will have sown for you a seed of woe. I draw this line on the ground, O lady, and most

---

[10] Satrughan is Lakshman's real brother.

[11] Manthara's being humpbacked is seen as an indication of her being an evil person.

emphatically say that you will be like a fly in a milk-bowl. If you and your son will submit to be servants, you will be able to stay; but on no other condition."

When she heard these cutting words, Kekaya's daughter could say nothing;[12] she was all in a fever for fear. Her limbs were bathed in perspiration and she trembled like a plantain stalk. "Hearken, Manthara, your words are true; my right eye is always throbbing, and every night I have some evil dreams; but in my folly I did not tell you. What can I do, friend?" Bringing Kaikeyi as a victim for the slaughter, the humpback sharpened the knife of treachery on the whetstone of her heart, and the queen, like a sacrificial beast that nibbles the green sward, saw not the approaching danger. Pleasant to hear, but deadly in their results, her words were like honey mingled with fatal poison. She said, "Do you or do you not, my lady, remember the tale you once told me of the two boons promised you by the king? Ask for them now and relieve your soul: the kingdom for your son, banishment to the woods for Ram. Thus shall you triumph over all your rivals. But ask not till the king has sworn by Ram, so that he may not go back on his word."

At eventide the happy king repaired to Kaikeyi's apartments, as if it were Love incarnate visiting Obduracy. He was dismayed when he heard of the chamber of wrath and could scarcely put his feet on the ground for fear.[13] Anxiously, he approached the queen and was terribly distressed to see her condition, she lying on the ground in old and coarse clothing with all personal adornments cast away, her wretched appearance matching her wretched design, as if in mourning for her imminent widowhood. The king drew near and asked in gentle tones, "Why are you angry, my heart's delight?" She put away her lord and flashed upon him a furious glance like an enraged serpent, with her two wishes for its double tongue, and the boons for fangs, spying for a vulnerable spot to sting. Under the influence of fate, says Tulsi, the king took it all as one of love's devices. "O my beloved, my life, my sons, and everything that I own, my palace, my subjects are at your disposal. If I tell you a word of untruth, a hundred curses fall on Ram's life. Ask with a smile whatever you desire; adorn your lovely person with jewels; consider within yourself what an hour of torture this is for me, and at once, my darling, put away this unseemly attire."

On hearing this and considering the greatness of the oath, the wicked queen arose with a smile and resumed her royal attire, like a huntress who sets the snare on marking the chase. Thinking her reconciled, the king spoke again in soft and winning accents, his body quivering with love, "Your heart's desire, lady, has come to pass; there is joy and gladness in every house in the city; tomorrow I give Ram the rank of Regent; so, my love, make ready for the festival." At the sound of these untoward words she sprang up with a bound, like an over-ripe gourd

---

[12] Kaikeyi derives her name from her father, Kekaya.

[13] It was customary for women, particularly queens, to have a room to which they consigned themselves when angry or unhappy.

that bursts at touch. With a smile on her lips, but with such a secret pain at heart as a thief's wife who dares not cry openly. "You say, 'Ask, Ask,' indeed; but tell me, dear husband, when has it come to giving and taking? You once promised me two boons, and yet I doubt my getting them. Hear, my beloved, and grant me the boon my heart desires. Install Bharat as regent. Second, I beg with folded hands, may Ram be banished to the woods for fourteen years to dwell there as a hermit." Hearing this the king's heart grew faint. He trembled all over, nor could he, like a quail at the swoop of a falcon, utter a sound. The mighty monarch was as crestfallen as a palm tree struck by lightning. Hands to his forehead and eyes closed, a picture of grief, he moaned, "My desire that had blossomed like the tree of paradise has been struck and uprooted as it were by an elephant at the time of its bearing fruit." The wicked woman, seeing the king's response, taunted thus, "What, then, is Bharat not your son too, and am I a slave bought for a price? If my words pierce your heart thus like arrows, why did you not think before you spoke? Answer now yes or no, most truthful lord of Raghu's truthful line! Refuse me the boon you promised, break your word, and be publicly disgraced!" The righteous king took courage and opening his eyes, he saw Kaikeyi standing before him, burning with wrath. Her fury was like a naked sword out of the sheath, with ill counsel for its hilt, and cruelty for its sharp edge whetted on the humpback grindstone. He cried in suppliant tones, "Bharat and Ram are my two eyes. Shiv is my witness, I tell you the truth. At daybreak, I will call the two brothers here and fixing an auspicious day, solemnly confer the kingdom on Bharat. There is only one thing that pains me, your second demand, really an unreasonable request. Your bosom burns with unwonted fire; is it anger, or do you jest, or is it all really true? Rather might a fish live out of water, I tell you the simple truth that there is no life for me without Ram. My very existence depends upon my seeing him."

Hearing this soft speech, the wicked queen blazed up like a fire on which has fallen an oblation of *ghee*,[14] "You may devise any number of plans, your subterfuges will not work. Grant my request, or refuse and be disgraced. I do not want any long discussions." So saying the evil queen arose like a swollen flood of wrath bursting out of the mountains of sin, turgid with streams of passion, terrible to behold, with the two boons for banks, her obduracy for its current, her voluble speech for its whirling eddies, overthrowing the king like a tree torn up by its roots, as it rushed on the ocean of disasters. The king perceived that what he saw was all true; death in the shape of a woman was dancing over his head. Realizing that his disease was incurable, he fell on the ground, beat his head, and sobbed, "Ram! O Ram!"

The treacherous queen sent the king's chief minister to fetch Ram. The jewel of Raghu's race came and saw the king's miserable condition, like an aged pain-stricken

---

[14] *Ghee* is clarified butter. It is an important ingredient poured on fire as oblation in Hindu religious rituals. It can be also used as a fuel in oil lamps or for lighting a fire.

elephant in the grip of a tigress. He asked, "Tell me, mother, the cause of my father's distress so that I may endeavor to relieve it." "Listen Ram," she answered, "the sole cause is the king's love of you. He had promised to grant me two requests and I asked for what I wanted, but he is disturbed on hearing it, because he cannot get rid of a scruple on your account. On the one side is his promise, on the other his love for you; he is in a strait. If you can, be obedient to his command and terminate his misery." She sat and spoke bitter words so composedly that Cruelty itself was disturbed to hear her. From the bow of her tongue she shot the arrows of her speech against the king as on some yielding target, as though Obduracy itself had taken form and become a bold and accomplished archer. Sitting like the very incarnation of heartlessness, she narrated to Raghupati the whole story. Ram, the sun of the solar race, the fountain of every joy, smiled inwardly and replied in guileless terms, so soft and gracious that they seemed the very jewels of the goddess of speech, "Mother, blessed is the son who obeys his parents' commands. A son who cherishes his father and mother is not often found in the world. I have a particular wish to join the hermits in the woods, and now there is also my father's command and your approval, mother."

• • •

THE ABDUCTION OF SITA

One day Ravan's sister, Surpanakha, foul-hearted and venomous like a serpent came to Panchavati and was excited when she saw the two princes.[15] Like the sunstone,[16] in her excitement she could not contain herself. Assuming a beautiful shape, she approached Ram with many smiles and addressed him thus, "There is not another man like you, nor a woman like me; this is a match that God has taken pains to make. I have searched the three spheres,[17] but have not found anywhere another man with beauty equal to mine. For this reason I have remained a virgin, but now that I have seen you I am satisfied." Ram glanced at Sita and said, "My younger brother is a bachelor." Surpanakha went to Lakshman. He looked toward Ram and said in gentle tones, "Fair lady, I am his servant. It is not right that you should be in subjection to anyone." Again she turned to Ram, but he sent her back once more to Lakshman. Annoyed, Lakshman said to her, "The bridegroom for you must be a man lost to all sense of shame!" In a fury she returned to Ram, revealing herself in a shape of terror. Raghurai, seeing

---

[15] Panchvati is one of the places where Ram, Lakshman, and Sita live during the exile. Ravan is the ten-headed demon king of Lanka.

[16] A type of precious stone.

[17] Hindu cosmology sees the universe as divided into three regions, upper, middle, and lower.

Sita frightened, made a sign to Lakshman who with the utmost speed struck off her nose and ears.

[*Editor's note:* Surpanakha goes wailing to her brothers, Khar and Dushan who attack Ram and Lakshman, but they are defeated and slain along with their vast army. So Surpanakha goes to her most powerful brother, Ravan, the Ten-Headed king of Lanka, beseeching him to wreak vengeance on Ram and Lakshman for the outrage. Ravan goes to a demon relative, Marich, with a scheme to abduct Sita. In the meantime, Ram has Sita enter fire and stay absorbed in it until he has completed the destruction of the demons. Only an image of Sita of exactly the same appearance and disposition as her remains behind.]

Ravan mounted his flying chariot and drove off unattended to where Marich lived by the seashore. The Ten-Headed laid the whole matter before him and added, "For the purpose of deception, you assume the form of a deer; by this means, I will be able to carry off the princess." "Listen, O Ten-Headed, though in form of man, Prince Ram is the Lord of all creation. There is no fighting against him, Sire. If he kills, you die; if you live, it is he who gives you life. Wherever I look, I see the two brothers and my senses are bewildered like a fly hypnotized by a spider. Even if he is only a man, he is a mighty hero; opposition to him will do no good. Think, then, of the welfare of your family and go home." Ravan was furious and abused Marich soundly, "You fool, you take upon yourself to teach me as if you were my master! Tell me where in the world there is another warrior to equal me?" Marich thought to himself, "There are nine whom it is not wise to make enemies: an armed man, an accomplice, a king, a man without principle, a rich man, a physician, a panegyrist, poet or any person of special ability." He saw that either way, he must die, but reflected that Ram would be his sanctuary. With these thoughts, staunch in devotion to Ram's feet, and with an exceeding gladness of heart, he accompanied the Ten-Headed. "Today," he said to himself, "I shall behold my beloved."

When the Ten-Headed drew near, Marich took the form of a deer, so beautifully spotted as to beggar description, with a body of gold, all bespangled with jewels. When Sita saw the wondrously beautiful creature clothed with loveliness in every limb, she cried, "O Raghubir, kind Lord, this deer has a most charming skin. I pray you, shoot it, my most admirable Lord, and bring me the hide." Thereupon Ram, who understood the reason behind it all, arose with joy to accomplish the purpose of the gods. Having marked the deer, he girded up his loins, took bow in hand and trimmed his shapely arrows. Then the Lord cautioned Lakshman, "Many demons, brother, roam the forest. Take care of Sita with all thought and consideration and with force too, if need be." The deer, seeing Ram, took to flight, but he pursued it with ready bow; even he, to whom the *Veda* cannot attain,[18] not Shiv able to contemplate, hastened in pursuit of a

---

[18] Hindus consider *Veda*, literally meaning knowledge, as their holiest scripture.

mimic deer. Now close at hand, now fleeing at a distance, at one time in sight, at another hid, alternately showing and concealing itself and practicing many a trick, it took the Lord far away. At last Ram aimed and let fly the fatal shaft. The deer fell to the ground with a terrible cry, first calling aloud to Lakshman, then mentally invoking Ram. As his life ebbed, Marich resumed his natural form and devoutly repeated the name of Ram, who in his wisdom recognized his inward love and granted him that liberation which even sages can scarcely attain.

When Sita heard Marich's agonizing cry, she called to Lakshman in great alarm, "Hurry to help, your brother seems to be in some strait!" Lakshman replied with a smile, "Mother, he by the play of whose eyebrows the world is annihilated, cannot be imagined to have fallen into difficulty." But when Sita urged him with taunting words, Lakshman's resolution—for such was Hari's will[19]—was shaken. He made over charge of everything to the forest and its gods, and went to look for Ram. When the Ten-Headed saw Sita alone, he drew near in the guise of an ascetic. He, for fear of whom gods and demons trembled and could neither sleep by night nor eat by day, even that Ravan came looking to this side and that as furtively as a dog bent on thieving. After he had turned his steps to this vile course, not a particle of his majesty, or intellect, or strength of body was left in him. After repeating a variety of legends and moral sentiments, he took recourse to threats and blandishments. Sita said to him, "Hear, reverend Father, what you say is hateful to me." At this Ravan revealed his proper form and she was terror-struck when he declared his name. But plucking all her resolute courage, she warned, "Stay as you are, wretch, my Lord is at hand. As a hare might desire to wed a lioness, so have you wooed your own destruction, O demon king." On hearing these defiant words, the Ten-Headed was furious, though in his heart he delighted to adore her feet. Then in a frenzy, he seized and lifted her into his chariot. As he took his way through the air, he was so agitated with fear that he could scarcely drive.

Sita wailed, "Ah, brave Raghurai, sovereign of the universe, for what fault of mine have you forgotten mercy? Ah, reliever of distress, health-giving sanctuary, sun of the lotuses of the Raghu race! Ah, Lakshman, this is no fault of yours. I have reaped the fruit of the temper I showed." Many were the lamentations she thus uttered. "My affectionate and loving Lord is far away. Who will tell him of my calamity? That an ass should devour the oblation for the gods! Hearing Sita's grievous cries all created beings, living or inanimate, were sad. The king of the vultures too heard her piteous cry and recognized the wife of the glory of Raghu's line, whom the vile demon was carrying away, like the famous dun cow that had fallen into the hands of some savage. "Fear not Sita, my daughter, I will annihilate this monster." In fury, the bird darted forth like a thunderbolt hurled upon a mountain. "Stop, you villain! How dare you go on thus and pay no heed to me?" Seeing him bearing down on him like the angel of death, Ravan paused and

---

[19] Hari is another name of Vishnu.

thought, "Is it mount Mainaka or the king of the birds?[20] Anyhow, they both know my might, as also do their lords." When he knew that it was poor old Jatayu, he cried, "He shall leave his body at the shrine of my hands." At this, the vulture rushed in a fury and yelled, "Hearken Ravan, to my advice. Surrender Janaki and go home in peace! If not, despite your many arms, it will turn out thus: Ram's wrath is like a fierce flame; your whole house will be consumed in it like a moth." The demon warrior gave no answer. The vulture flew at him in a rage and clutching him by the hair, hurled him out of the chariot, so that he fell to the ground. Having sheltered Sita, the vulture turned again and with his beak tore and rent Ravan's body. For nearly half an hour the demon lay in a swoon. Then gnashing his teeth and drawing his monstrous sword, he cut off Jatayu's wings. The bird fell to the ground, calling on Ram and doing marvelous feats of courage. The demon put Sita in the chariot again and drove off in a hurry in no little alarm. Sita was borne through the air wailing like a fawn captured by a hunter. Seeing some monkeys sitting on the rocks, she cried out Hari's name and dropped down her scarf. In this manner, Ravan carried away Sita and put her in his Grove of Ashok trees.

• • •

HANUMAN[21] GOES TO LANKA[22]

There was a majestic rock by the seashore. He lightly sprang on to its top. Then, again and again invoking Raghubir, the Son of the God of Wind leaped with all his might. The mountain he had planted his feet on sank down instantly into the depths of hell. As Ram's unerrring arrow flies, so sped Hanuman on his way. The Ocean having regard for Ram's envoy told Mainaka to make his leap easier, but Hanuman merely touched the mountain and saluted him, saying, "I can stop nowhere until I have performed my mission."

Alighting on the other shore, he marked the beauty of the woods, with the bees buzzing in their search for honey, the diverse trees resplendent with different kinds of flowers and fruits, and multitudes of birds and deer delightful to behold. Seeing a lofty hill, he fearlessly sprang to its top. Standing on the hill, he surveyed

---

[20] Mainaka is a winged mountain. According to a Hindu myth all mountains had wings at one time. The god Indra shot their wings off, except for Mainaka who escaped with the help of the Wind god and hid in the depth of the ocean where he guards demons in a prison. When Hanuman leaped over the ocean on his way to Lanka, Mainaka arose out of the sea to offer him a place to step on in his jump. Here Ravan compares Jatayu, the king of the vultures, with or mistakes him for Mainaka.

[21] The general of the monkey king, Sugriv. He becomes the greatest devotee of Ram.

[22] Lanka seems to be based on the island country, Sri Lanka, to the south of India. In the epic, it is Ravan's city.

Lanka, a magnificent fortress defying description, with the deep all around its golden walls of dazzling splendor, studded with all kinds of jewels. A marvelous sight, with market places, bazaars, quays, streets, and all the other parts of a fine city. Who could count the multitude of elephants, horses, and mules, the crowds of footmen and chariots, and the troops of demons of every size, a formidable army beyond all description. The woods, gardens, groves, and pastures, ponds, wells and water reservoirs were all superb. There were girls—the daughters of men, Nagas, gods, and Gandharvas[23]—so beautiful that they would ravish a sage's soul. Wrestlers of gigantic stature, grappling with one another in numerous courts, roared like thunder with shouts of mutual defiance. Myriads of soldiers of huge size sedulously guarded the city on all sides. Elsewhere, horrid demons banqueted in the shape of buffaloes, oxen, asses, and goats. Tulsi Das devotes a few words to mentioning them for the reason that they lost their lives by Ram's hallowed shafts and were, therefore, assured of entrance into heaven.

Seeing the large number of guards, the monkey thought to himself, "I must make myself very small and slip into the city at night." Thereupon he assumed the form of a gnat and after invoking Vishnu entered Lanka. [Advised and directed by Vibhishan][24] the Son of the Wind arrived at the Ashok Grove where Sita was kept. As soon as he saw her, he mentally prostrated himself before her. She had spent the first watch of the night sitting awake, haggard in appearance, her hair knotted in a single braid on her head,[25] repeating to herself Raghupati's perfections. Her eyes fixed on her own feet, her soul was absorbed in the contemplation of the feet of her Lord. Hidden behind the leaves of a tree, Hanuman communed with himself, "Come, sir, what ought you to do?"

Just at this time Ravan came with a troop of females in various attires. The villain tried in every way—by blandishments, offers of bribes, threats, and misrepresentations—to attract Sita. "Hear, fair lady," he beseeched, "I swear, I will make Mandodari and all my other queens your handmaids,[26] if you vouchsafe but one glance at me." Sita plucked a blade of grass and with averted face, fondly remembering her dear Lord, replied, "Listen, Ten-Headed! Will the lotus expand at the sight of a glow-worm? Ponder this well. Wretch, have you no fear of Ram's shafts? Even though absent, Hari will rescue me. O shameless monster, have some shame. I tell you, you are but a firefly, while even the sun is only a shadow of Ram." Hearing this defiant retort, Ravan drew his sword and yelled in utmost fury, "Sita, you have humiliated me. I will strike off your head with this sharp

---

[23] In Indian mythology the Nagas, literally snakes, are seen as a people. The Gandharvas are semi-celestial beings who dwell mainly in Amravati, the kingdom of the god Inder. They are singers and musicians who attend the banquets of Inder and other gods. However, they can go to other places as in the present case.

[24] A brother of Ravan. He is a devotee of Ram.

[25] Hair knotted in a single braid indicates mourning.

[26] Mandodari is Ravan's primary queen.

blade. If you do not obey my words at once, you will forfeit your life, my lady."
"My Lord's arms, Ravan, are beautiful like a string of dark lotuses and mighty as
an elephant's trunk," retorted Sita. "Either they shall have my neck; if not, your
sword will. Listen, O villian, to this my solemn vow. With your gleaming sword
put an end to my distress, and let the fire of anguish in which I burn in separation from Ram be quenched in death with the sharp edge of your sword. Rid me,
O demon, of the burden of my pain!" Hearing these words, Ravan again rushed
forward to slay her, but the daughter of Maya,[27] Mandodari, checked him with
words of admonition. He then summoned all the female demons and ordered
them to go terrorize Sita. "If she does not pay heed to my wishes within a month,"
he exclaimed, "I will pull out my sword and slay her."

A single moment seemed like an age to the monkey as he beheld Sita's piteous
condition. After pondering a while, he threw down Ram's signet ring. It fell like a
spark from the ashok tree. Sita started with joy and clasped it in her hand. When
she looked at the lovely ring, beautifully engraved with Ram's name, she was all
amazement. She recognized it and her heart fluttered with mingled joy and sorrow. All sorts of fancies passed through her mind until Hanuman spoke in honeyed accents recounting Ramchander's praises.[28] As soon as she heard him, her
grief took flight. Intently she listened with all her soul as well as her ears, while
he told the whole story from the very beginning. "The tale you tell is like am-
brosia to my ears; why do you not show yourself, friend?" [Hanuman tells Sita
that Ram and Lakshman are well. As Sita asks whether Ram ever remembers her,
Hanuman continues as follows.]

"Take courage now and listen to Ram's message." So saying, the monkey's
voice failed him and his eyes filled with tears. Then he told her of Ram's forlorn
condition. "Everything," says he, "is changed into its opposite. The fresh buds on
the trees burn like fire; night seems as the night of death; and the moon scorches
like the sun. A bed of lotuses hurts like a prickly brake and the rain-clouds rain
boiling oil. The trees only add to my pain and the winds—soft, gentle, and fragrant—are like a serpent's hissing. Nothing relieves my torment and there is no
one to whom I may tell about it. The meaning of such love as yours and mine,
my beloved, only my soul can comprehend, and my soul is always with you. Know
such to be the depth of my love." As the Videhan princess listened to Ram's message, she became so absorbed in love that she lost all consciousness of self. Said
the monkey, "Compose yourself, Mother, remembering that Ram is the benefactor of all who serve him. Reflect upon his might and, as you listen to my words,
put away all anxiety. The demon troops are like moths and Raghupati's shafts are
flames. Be strong of heart, Mother, and rest assured that they will be consumed. I
have the strength to take you with me to Ram at once myself, but I swear to you

---

[27] The father of Mandodari, Maya is an architect and artificer of the demons.

[28] Ramchander is the full name of Ram.

by Ram, I do not have his order for that. Wait patiently, Mother, a few more days and he will arrive with his monkeys, slay the demons, and take you with him."

[Sita gives Hanuman her blessings.] Hearing her words, Hanuman became utterly overwhelmed with emotion. Again and again he bowed his head at her feet, and with folded hands said, "Now, Mother, I am fully rewarded. But please, Mother, I am frightfully hungry and I see the trees laden with delicious fruit." "Know, my son, this grove is guarded by most valiant and ferocious demons." "They do not scare me, Mother, if only you keep your mind easy." Seeing the monkey so mighty and wise, Janaki said, "Go, my son, eat of this luscious fruit, with your heart fixed on Hari's feet." He bowed his head and went and entered the garden. After having eaten the fruit, he began to break down the trees. Many strong watchmen were posted there. Some he killed and others ran away, calling for help.

[Hearing about the damage, Ravan sent warriors to the grove. Hanuman put them to rout, killing many, including Ravan's young son.] When he heard of his son's death, the king of Lanka was furious and sent the valiant Meghnad.[29] "Do not kill him, my son, but capture him. I would like to see this monkey and know where he has come from." Inderjit sallied forth,[30] a peerless champion, full of fury at the news of his brother's death. When the monkey saw the formidable warrior draw near, he gnashed his teeth and with a roar rushed forward to meet him. He tore up a tree of enormous size with which he swept the prince of Lanka from his car. As for the other champions who accompanied him, he seized them one by one and crushed them under his weight. Having thus disposed of them, he closed with the leader. It was like the encounter of two majestic elephants. After striking Meghnad a blow with his fist, Hanuman climbed up a tree, while his enemy lay in a swoon. The demon soon arose and practiced many enchantments, but the Son of Wind was not deterred. The demon prepared to shoot the magic weapon given him by Brahma. The monkey thought to himself, "If I do not submit to Brahma's shaft, its divine virtue will be proved false." So hit by the magic dart he fell, crushing a host beneath him as he fell. Seeing that he had swooned, the demon bound him in a noose and carried him off.

[Brought before him, Hanuman advises Ravan to know Ram's power and submit to him. Instead, Ravan orders Hanuman's tail burnt.]

"The poor tailless monkey can then go home and fetch his master, and I shall have an opportunity to see the might of one whom he has so extravagantly exalted." The monkey smiled to himself to hear these threats. The demons made their foolish preparations. Not a rag was left in the city nor a drop of *ghee* or oil, to such a length the tail grew. Then they made sport of him. The citizens thronged to see the sight, kicked him with their feet and greatly jeered at him.

---

[29] Ravan's most valiant son.

[30] Meghnad is known as Inderjit, because he once fought against and defeated the god Inder.

With the beating of drums and clapping of hands, they took him through the city and set fire to his tail. When Hanuman saw the fire blazing, he instantly reduced himself to a minuscule size, and slipping out of his bonds sprang on to the top storey of the gilded royal palace, to the dismay of the giant's wives. At that very moment, the forty-nine winds, whom Hari had sent, began to blow. The monkey shouted and roared with laughter, swelling himself at the same time to such a large size that his head touched the sky. Enormous in size yet possessing marvelous agility, he leaped and ran from palace to palace.

As the city was set ablaze, all its people were at their wits' end, for the terrible flames engulfed countless millions of places. They screamed in terror, "Ah, Father, Mother, hearken to my cry. Who will save us now? As I said, this is no monkey, but some god in that form. This comes of not taking good advice. Our city is burnt down as though it had no protector." The city was razed to the ground except for Vibhishan's house. Having turned Lanka upside down, Hanuman threw himself into the middle of the sea. Having extinguished his tail and recovered from fatigue, he assumed his usual form and went and stood before Janaki with folded hands. "Be pleased, Mother, to give me some token to take to Ram." Sita unfastened the jewel in her hair and gave it to him. "Salute him respectfully for me, my son, and give him this message: 'my Lord, you never fail to fulfil and are renowned as the suppliant's friend; relieve me then from my distress'."

26

❧

THE SONG OF BAGAUDA

The northern cities and kingdoms of Nigeria have been home to the Hausa people for more than one and a half millennia. As Islam expanded into Africa, the Hausa were exposed to Muslim traders and religious practitioners, and gradually they converted to Islam. As this was a long and slow process, the Islamic practices and doctrines that were adopted were often altered by local custom and belief, leading to a syncretic form of Islam often subject to the criticisms of those who wished to purify the religion. In the late eighteenth and nineteenth centuries a series of jihads, or religious wars, led by the Fulani, a people who were more stringently doctrinal in their beliefs, brought pressure on the Hausa, and their Habe ruling dynasty, to eliminate the presence of traditional, non-Islamic Hausa ways. It is this historical pressure for purification that is reflected in the Song of Bagauda.

In a sense the Song of Bagauda is itself both a product of historical change and a record of that change. Those who have transmitted it believe it to be a chronicle of all the kings of Kano, a major Hausa city of northern Nigeria, dating back to the first such king, Bagauda, legendary founder of the Hausa people. After the death of each king, the song was subject to additions and revisions, continuing to grow in this way until the death of the ruler Abdullahi Bayero in 1953. The present Hausa version was collected, transcribed, and translated by Mervyn Hiskett who obtained two written versions and one oral version. Hiskett recorded the latter from a performance in 1960 by Hawwa, an old Hausa woman. Hawwa, who claimed to be one hundred years old, stated that she had learned the poem as a young girl, before the arrival of the Europeans, from the grandfather of a contemporary malam, or religious teacher. She reported that the song was always sung by beggars, and that with the death of Abdullahi Bayero the tradition had come to an end.

Although the song contains a chronicle of kings, perhaps the most important cultural quality of the song is its testimony to the issue of syncretism. It contains a call to purify and remove "pagan" practices from Islam; yet, we see the ways in which traditional beliefs, images and discursive systems continue to express Hausa culture. The entire Song itself resembles the classical Arabic ode called the qasida,

which opens with a eulogy on the prophet Muhammad, and which then contin-
ues with a series of separate movements. The Islamic components may be seen in
the opening prayer in which conventional Islamic praise of Muhammad is ex-
pressed. Even in this section, however, we witness traditional Hausa images, as in
the relationship between Allah and Muhammad: When Allah wishes to confide in
Muhammad, He has him approach, admitting Muhammad into his presence onto
his carpet without having the prophet even remove his sandals—a custom reflec-
tive of Hausa kings and their retainers or confidants.

After the opening prayer, there is a lengthy homily on the futility of the
worldly path, on the necessity to forego the attractions of the material world, de-
picted here as a seductive woman—an image imbued with the Qur'anic doctrine
of the end of the world. This admonition is based upon an ascetic approach to
Islam and an otherworldliness often associated with Sufi Islam practiced by
Hausa and Fulani Muslims after the sixteenth century.

Traditional Hausa values can be seen in part in the mockery of the village
malams, unrefined Muslim teachers likened to country bumpkins with their
cockroach-infested satchels. In various parts of the poem, changes in pure Islamic
practice are dubbed "innovation," and the warning against this is couched in
terms of the opposition between innovation and Islamic traditions or Sunna:
*"*Sunna *and innovation are not compatible," we are warned. Despite the warn-*
ings, traditional Hausa imagery persists: Invalid worship or "pagan" practice is
likened to guinea-corn sown on dry ground. Greedy materialism is represented by
a hyena. Haughty and impatient malams, *conventionally associated by the Hausa*
with sedentary Fulani scholars, are set in contrast with the narrator's point of
view that is both deferential and down to earth. Most importantly, correct reli-
gious practice is presented not as a foreign incursion, but as a normal path to
righteousness taught by the knowledgeable Hausa and Fulani malams *of old. The*
poem ends with an appeal to the virtue of this way and to the power of correct
teachings to lead the believers to salvation.

In the name of God the Merciful, the Compassionate. May God bless our Lord
Muhammad and his family, and his Companions, and his wives, and his offspring, and grant them peace.

> Let us thank our Lord Who has created all,
> > Who has sent down the paragon of Prophets.
> We invoke blessing and peace

The Song of Bagauda, edited and translated by Mervyn Hiskett, copyright 1965, vol. XXVIII,
pt. 1, pp. 112–116; 120–123; 128; 132–135. Reprinted from the Bulletin of the School of
Oriental and African Studies (London) by permission of Oxford University Press.

Upon the fine, the noble Arabian;
To the sea of light his heart was taken;
　　You split it open, and you took out that which causes anger;
It was washed thoroughly and impurities were removed.[1]
　　He does not grow angry, but is munificent to all.
His heart was emptied; there was nothing in it
　　Except the light of knowledge and righteous action.
Muhammadu,[2] the leader of all the Apostles,
　　With him You completed the number of the Prophets;
From the beginning there has been none like him, neither at the end.
　　When he and the Almighty spoke together,
They made their secret covenant, they two, there was no third;
　　Only he and the Almighty alone.
The Almighty said to those near at hand:
　　I am calling the Beloved and he comes;
Keep your distance! Even Gabriel,[3] he also
　　Withdrew far from the place where he had been standing.
Save only he, he will descend here because of the trust
　　And the acceptance and the honour which we accord him.
He worshipped when he saw the throne of majesty;
　　He showed reverence, bending his head lower and lower.
When He had welcomed him, the Almighty king
　　Said: You are distant; come nearer.
He rose and moved a little closer. God said:
　　Stand upon the carpet, for you are greater than all.
With his sandals he stepped upon it; he was not told to take them off![4]
　　Know you well, there is not his like among the Prophets.
He and the Almighty spoke together in love and trust;
　　Between them there was no keeping of distance.
God said to him: I have called you to a trust,
　　The trust of Islam; go to Mecca explaining
The creed of the Unity,[5] and prayer,[6] these I give you in trust.

---

[1] A popular legend about Muhammad's early infancy.

[2] An alternate version of Muhammad's name, found throughout much of West Africa, including Hausaland.

[3] The angel and divine messenger.

[4] Muhammad's privileged and honored position is indicated by this gift of God in allowing him to approach. In West Africa kings are kept isolated and distant from the common people.

[5] That there is only one God.

[6] In the obligation to prayer five times a day.

And then the obligatory Fast,[7] which completes the tenets of Islam.
Say to them that I tell them to put aside *zakā*[8]
And he who refuses shall descend into Hell-fire.
Let them perform the Pilgrimage,[9] if they can,
    For it is an obligatory duty if there is sufficient provision for the journey.
Let them help their brethren by giving wealth
    And clothing; let them give them food.
Let them cease being angry and impatient with their kindred.
    Verily I have sent you to them with a stern admonition saying:
Give your kindred of your goods when they come to you.
    Cease the implied slander of refusing to seek charity from anyone.[10]
Always imitate the Prophet and his relatives;
    He is cheerful; moreover he is munificent towards them.
Cease to despise them because they have nothing;
    It is the Almighty alone who makes a man rich.
If you have anything to pray for, pray to God
    The Almighty; He alone gives to everyone.
Abandon pride in the greatness of kingship,
    And in transitory worldly possessions.
Be it kingship and wealth that the world has given you,
    Then refrain from lifting up your head and being constantly puffed up;
Gather up your good sense, that it may come to you.
    The promise of the world is untrustworthy.
Let there be less of your haughty arrogance: this world is but transitory.
    That which she gives does not abide.
Look behind you; then look before.
    If you have good sense, and much prudent reflection,
Look at the kings who have flourished in the past,
    Their story is near to being obliterated.
Bagauda made the first clearing in the Kano[11] bush.
    It was then uninhabited jungle;
A vast forest with nothing save idols,
    Waterbuck, buffalo, and elephant.
Bagauda had his home back at Gaya;[12]

---

[7] The monthlong fast of Ramadan during daylight hours.

[8] That is, alms.

[9] The pilgrimage to Mecca, an obligation every Muslim is expected to fulfill, if possible, once in his or her lifetime.

[10] Possibly an admonition against looking down on beggars, and therefore on begging.

[11] Kano is a Hausa city in northern Nigeria.

[12] Another city in northern Nigeria.

He was a mighty hunter, a slayer of wild beasts.
He came foraging in the dry season, and made himself a grass hut at
    Madatai.[13]
He remained there, and his relations came after him,
Hunters all of them, they continued to come and camp
    Around him, slaying lion and elephant.
Of meat there was plenty, fresh and dried.
    There were no women; indeed it was men who cooked.
The encampment became extensive, grass hut upon grass hut.
    Then they sent for the women, and they started coming.
Now Gwale together with Yakasa, Sheshe
    And Guguwa;[14] the mighty men of the Maguzawa,
It is said of them that they were farmer
    Chieftains coming to explore the bush.
Whilst surveying the bush they took up farms
    And then sent for their families to come.
From Malam Nuhu I heard this; he does not fabricate.[15]
    In this story there is no falsification.
Kanau were the ancestors of the Kutunbawa:[16]
    Malam Nuhu is well informed about this, and reflects much.
It was from him that I heard it; I have passed it on without addition,
    For the character of men is to dispute!
Come here my good friend, and I will recite to you.
    It is this story of our ancestors that I am establishing.
These farmers, when they first came
    They cut down the forest and chopped it up.
Then the rain of the hot season came down,
    And they sowed their seed and it sprouted and did not dry up.
Know you that bulrush millet will thrive in newly cleared bush,
    And guinea-corn, not one plant is stunted.
They cultivated guinea-corn and bulrush millet such as had not been
    seen before.
    Then came a killing famine
And there was no corn to be had; only by coming to them
    Could it be had, and they doled it out in small quantities.
They became well off in slaves and horses too;
    They were the great traders.

---

[13] A district in Kano.

[14] Names of pre-Islamic Hausa ancestors after whom districts in Kano are named.

[15] In Hausaland, a *malam* is an Islamic teacher. The narrator refers to several religious authorities in the course of the poem, all of whom lend authority to the narration.

[16] The ancestors of the Habe dynasty, until recently the ruling Hausa dynasty in Kano.

From the east they came; from the west, even unto the north;
> From the south the pagan Hausa forced their way in,

The Bornu people and the Katsina people, (people) from Daura,
> And from Zanfara of the Habe and the men of Gobir;

They began to come and establish habitations.
> Kaba people, Kambarawa, and people from Adar.[17]

When the famine was at its height it extended to Asben.[18]
> They fled to Kano where there was relief.

At the river of Kura they pitched their camp,
> Until the famine began to abate

And better conditions and abundance prevailed.
> One night people looked and there was no one.

Now the Tokarci are the slaves of the Asben people.
> They refused to follow them; they saw a place where they could live in ease.

The Bugaje,[19] those who play the game of the blacksmiths,
> They have no master other than the Asben people.

Now even from as far off as Lambu a clearing in the bush was established,
> By way of Kanwa and Kunkuso up to Tanburawa,

And even as far afield as Yankatsare the settlement extended,
> By way of Mariri it reached Gunduwawa.

Compounds were many even as far as Gungun and other places,
> And Jirima, so many as to be beyond counting.[20]

The people were living widely dispersed over the open country, not subject to any authority.
> There was no chief, no protecting town wall.

Tunbi together with Washa[21] saw an easy prey
> And they joined forces, conquering the people of Kano.

The elders said: let a chieftaincy be established.
> They appointed Bagauda the protector.[22]

Bagauda reigned for fifty years.
> He was chief of Kano with power to summon all.

He died and Warsa succeeded.

---

[17] The names of regions or states in or near northern Nigeria.

[18] Asben is a Saharan oasis.

[19] Slaves from the Tuareg people of the Sahara and Sahel.

[20] All sites in or near northern Nigeria.

[21] Pre-Islamic forebears of the Hausa.

[22] Here the list of Hausa rulers of Kano begins with Bagauda, and continues down to the time of the recitation of the *Song.*

When he had reigned for forty years he went to the pit of the grave.
Nawatau reigned for seventy years.
   In the very month that he cleared a site to build a walled town, it was
      built.
Gawata reigned for thirty years
   And then his appointed time came to him, killing him.
What of Ajimasu, he too was chief of Kano!
   He had forty years of prohibiting and commanding.
Makankari was first Galadima;
   Then he reigned for a long time.
When he had reigned for seventy years and seven more, he passed on.
   The unseen prowler came upon him unexpectedly.[23]
Guguwa reigned for seventy years;
   When he rode forth there was no one in Kano dared loiter.
Know you that the chief Wada ruled;
   He reigned for seven years, no more, no less.
Gakin-Gakuma reigned for sixty years;
   When he prayed this became the cause of his death.
Bagaji when he had reigned for twelve years, he reigned no more;
   It was a reign which did not last long.
Know you that Shekarau reigned for ten years
   And seven; then (came death) the snatcher away.
Kunajiji, when he had reigned for twenty years, he died.
   These were the chiefs of the pagan Hausa.
Now Umaru was one learned in Islam; he it was who escaped (Hell-fire);
   He lit a fire which defied extinction.
He drove out the pagan Hausa and they fled to the bush.
   He reigned a full twelve years.
Muhamman Rumfa was a generous chief;
   The reign of Rumfa was of benefit to all.
He reigned for thirty years. When he set out to give alms

• • •

Uthmanu reigned for six years;
   The people of Kano had no power to dispute (his will).
Then death came to him, and snatched him away.[24]
   That which you have done, nothing is left of it except the telling!
Pay attention to the world; her character is to go back on her word.
   Meanness is not a trait to be honoured!

---

[23] That is, death as the "unseen prowler."

[24] Uthmanu is the king who preceded Abdullahi Bayero, who reigned until 1953, during
the narrator's lifetime.

She likes to make sport (of you); she is plausible
    In her talk, (but) there is not a word of truth in it.
You will not find another who talks as vainly as the world does
    In your longest memory and searching.
When she says 'Yes' to you, you should understand 'No';
    When she lifts you up, it is only to let you fall!
When she throws you down with a bang your head will split,
    And you will lack the means to buy antimony to salve it.
Cease your clamouring after her; there is bane in the world
    In full measure; when she has afflicted you with it, there is nothing
    for you but death.
She leaves you alone with your sickness, madly
    Seeking sorcerers and spell-binders.[25]
You are eager for her to return, thinking this will be the cure.
    In travail she takes you to the brink of death.
You who woo the world, act circumspectly;
    It is her nature to turn and butt you aside.
You have your life, and your health;
    She lashes out with a kicking foot,
And when she kicks you, you fall flat.
    You faint, and they all come and pour water over you.
The water which they pour on you is the water of 'God prolong your life'
    And 'respects to you, Malam' and you become increasingly puffed up.
They are laughing at you, abusing you, and making grimaces;
    Your insight is obscured, and you do not realize what is happening.
In his lust such a one has converse with the world,
    And she causes him to suffer pox—a deadly disease
Which gives him ulceration of the scrotum; faith peels away like diseased
    skin;
    It leaves him with itching in the throat.
Such is his state that, if he but stirs,
    The itch will prevent the heart from carrying out the humblest task.
A penny, nay a halfpenny, is more than all your estate is worth.
    In the measure of your arrogance you are too proud for humble work.
She causes piles which protrude at the anus,
    And a man cannot sit down, let alone stand up,
And he chatters garrulously as if he had shot a hyena;[26]

---

[25] Non-Islamic traditional healers or religious specialists, often termed "bori," and denigrated by the Muslim narrator.

[26] The hyena is said to have the power to strike a person speechless, and paralyze him or her with fear. If the hyena is shot, this power is destroyed, and consequently the shooter will babble like a madman.

Or as if a rosary had snapped and the beads were tumbling down.
During the time that we were at Gungurke it was I whom they wanted
    To watch out riding, mounted so impressively.[27]
It was the chief who gave me a chestnut horse, and a cream dun.
    He bought a black horse from the Asben people, which he gave me.
You mount the chestnut as though you were mounting your throne.
    You hold your head high and ride at a swaggering gait.
He who is captivated by the world is like a dun ass
    When he lusts after the she-ass, and pays no attention to her kicking.
He who loves the world is likewise a dog;
    The world bites like a bitch, but he comes ever nearer.
Remember that this world is old,
    And an old man carries no load except he lets it fall.
When she takes you up into a high tree she then cuts it down
    At the root and you topple over.
Observe what has happened in recent times;
    To see with your own eye is better than being told about it.
The master's compound in which the great ones lived
    Has become empty, and there are none in it.
For they had made friends with the lovers of the world,
    And with madmen—an undiscriminating friendship.
Of the wife of a labourer none but a greenhorn,
    And an outcast of war take notice.
Do not turn your heads when she calls you; pretend to be deaf,
    For to answer her call bodes no good.
Know you that if her character were good,
    She would not be constantly marrying and deserting her husband.
Know you that Nimrod[28] married the world;
    They had their brief hour of joy, but it did not last.
They married frivolously; inevitably they parted.
    The foolhardy says *he* can marry the world.
Buhtu[29] married her during the three months divorce period;
    A profligate marriage which did not last.
Dhu'l-Qarnain[30] and the world married;

---

[27] The sudden appearance of the first-person point of view is intended to be the direct speech of one infatuated by sudden good fortune and the favors of the chief, and is meant to be read mockingly.

[28] Proverbially wealthy biblical ruler, mentioned as such in the Qur'an.

[29] Nebuchadnezzar—like Nimrod, a wealthy biblical ruler.

[30] Alexander the Great.

He held her to be of no account, and did not support her properly.
She saw that there was no opportunity to deceive him;
   She said that she could not remain there with him.
He drove her out. Then Sulaiman[31] married her.
   She behaved with the submissiveness of a bride, but he heeded not.
Who will make the world his favourite wife,
   Except a fool and one who is in a frenzy to die?
When she gives you dominion or wealth,
   Refrain from being proud, considering yourself better than all others.
Refrain also from slighting the dignity of the Muslims,
   Abusing them and treating them as slaves,
Consider Bawa jan Gwarzo and Yunfa;
   Dan Soba and Yakubu, the men of Gobir.[32]
They flaunted themselves in the world and ruled as kings;
   Whatever they wished to do, they accomplished.
Verily they have gone to where they are as nothing;
   A dog is more than they. They have gone to the place of failure.

· · ·

The opposite of worship is indiscriminate eating.
Through her greed the hyena gets herself killed,
   And (because of) lack of discrimination as to what she puts in her throat.
Lacking discrimination, she eats everything, stuffing it down
   Into her stomach; how can it fail to cause distension of the belly?
A belly that is distended is prone to flatulence;
   It is not healthy, but suffers from diarrhoea.
Food which is lawful, food which is disapproved of, and food which is forbidden,
   Being an Imām,[33] you should repent of mixing them together.
Eschew the filthy food of the heron
   When you eat and drink; that is the proper thing to do.
Lack of piety causes your good works to disperse;
   They become but ones and twos and cannot be collected together.
You should build a wall to enclose your good works;
   A fence of corn stalks, its effectiveness lasts only for a year!
Because of desiring a little, much is lost;
   For a little dough and a little millet gruel!

---

[31] Solomon, greatest of biblical rulers according to the Qur'an.

[32] All four were Nigerian rulers.

[33] Muslim figure of authority.

Be less greedy to be given money and threshed corn;
    The consuming of these things reduces the reward in the next world.

• • •

If a Muslim desires to be united with
    Our Saviour,[34] the chief of the Prophets,
Then it is God's intention that all impurities should be taken away
    From us, and He has said (in the Qur'an) that one's women-folk
    must remain in purdah.[35]
In Lahzabi, there you read the verse;[36]
    It is the word of God; is there any who is slow to obey it
Save only perhaps the rustic *malams* of the village
    With their satchels that contain only cockroaches,
And their fez hats crowned with turbans?
    At the naming ceremony and the funeral assembly
Their zeal is all for a little grain and dough;
    On a ball of dough their attention is fixed.
The blind man comes to seek one to guide him,
    And finds a guide whose own eyes are failing.
Malam Dadumau,[37] I have come to you (to inquire about)
    The going out and about of women, which the Shehu[38] forbade.
I attended the instruction of Malam Dubai;[39]
    He does not guard against the going out of women;
(Those who follow his teaching) have followed the one who leads
    along the way of the errant,
    And who then plunges them into the uninhabited bush.
He who loves God and the Prophet, if he wishes
    To be saved, let him leave the way of transgression.
And Malam Gungama[40] and Malam Adama,[41]
    What they say is apostate; cease hankering to follow it.

---

[34] Muhammad.

[35] That is, in seclusion, and veiled when in public.

[36] A verse in the Qur'an.

[37] Malam "Rapacious."

[38] Probably Shehu (Sheikh) Usman Dan Fodio, a major nineteenth-century Hausa Islamic leader and conqueror, whose authority is here cited.

[39] A common name indicating one not worthy of respect.

[40] Malam "Cock Pigeon."

[41] One who is said to be unreliable.

Their talk is of a sheep with black rings round its eyes;[42]
> Of a red (copper) ring and white fowls.[43]

They practise divination that they may discern the hidden mysteries of God
> In their drawings on the ground,[44] because of their apostasy.

Both the fortune-teller and he who believes him,
> The Angel of Hell-fire will they meet with!

Stop seeking counsel of a magician
> And (keep away from) Malam Gagarau[45] if you heed my advice.

They entice the ignorant and the blind,
> And lead them into water which engulfs them;

They spread out the leaves of a book and say: Take hold of a sheet;[46]
> They open it and come out with lying words;

They tell you that it's a black hen you should look for
> Saying: Know you, it will ward off the evil spirits of the bush.

I give you a warning my brothers:
> Cease going to the place of perdition.

And Malam Mance,[47] he has forgotten the meeting
> With the Glorious King who has the power over all.

He has a red ring on his thumb;
> A black ring[48] which he always presses down firmly on his middle finger.

The damned, they are the ones who gather around him!
> He speaks with them in his crookedness;

He has a charm made of the horn of a duiker,[49]
> And he has cowrie shells[50] of the sort used in the necromancy of the Nupe people.

All his talk is of a queen,[51]

---

[42] Certain organs of sheep are eaten after slaughter, and are said to have magical properties —an indication of pre-Islamic beliefs here being mocked.

[43] Copper is said to be efficacious in protecting against curses. The white fowls are a reference to the all-white attire of the pilgrims at Mecca.

[44] Sand divination, widespread throughout North Africa.

[45] Another mocking name.

[46] A means of fortune-telling found widely throughout the Muslim world, a synthesis of Muslim and pre-Islamic practices.

[47] Malam "Forgetful."

[48] An iron ring, serving as a charm against the "bori."

[49] An antelope horn used as a container for charms against evil spirits.

[50] Small shells also commonly used in divination.

[51] Apparently a woman possessed of magical powers, from the neighboring Nupe people.

And of fetishism. O Muslim, have no truck with him.
He is always urging his associates to do magic to counteract
    The spirits of the bush. Verily you should desist from acquiescing
In medicine men and *bori* practitioners, and cease
    To pay heed to their talk, for there is no good in it.
If you do not abandon it before you come to the Day of Resurrection
    You will weep tears without respite.
Avoid taking money to the tombs of *walīs*[52]
    For it is Shehu Sa'idu[53] who has forbidden this.
Preserve me O Lord, from following the talk of such as these
    Who have turned aside from the path of the Prophets,
And Malam Dangirau,[54] who seek to reveal the hidden mysteries.
    With forty cowrie shells he casts horoscopes.
Each one of these forty has something to be said about it
    Which is different; there is not one of which he says the same thing
    as of another!
He will go through all his mumbo-jumbo without having any success;
    His clients depart, grumbling, the ignorant ones!
I told you before, and I tell you again, repent, cease sinning.
    Only God can make known the hidden mysteries to anyone.
I am making an announcement to you, O people; hear it
    With your ears; it is the heart that retains it.
When a person leaves you, refrain from following him
    With your carping tongue.
He who makes a practice of spiteful backbiting,
    Jahannam[55] will assuredly be his abode,
For when the time comes to die it is difficult
    To recite the words of the *Shāhada*[56] over one who has slandered
    everyone.
The fire of the Seventh Hell waits for him who retails tittle-tattle,
    The slanderer, the shameless one, the instigator of strife.
It is he who stirs up enmity between kinsfolk,
    And discord, preventing the civil exchange of greetings.
The Muslim who desires to be saved on the Day of Resurrection,
    Let him repent lest it bring him to perdition.

---

[52] Muslim holy men.

[53] Said to have been a member of Shehu Usman Dan Fodio's family.

[54] A term of contempt.

[55] One of the stages of Hell, according to Islamic belief.

[56] The basic Muslim credo that asserts the unity of God and the prophetic mission of
Muhammad.

A characteristic which is bad, said the Shehu,
> Is apt to hinder the happy conclusion of one's days.

I laugh at the worshipper
> Who goes before a crowd of people, making great show

Of much supererogatory prayer and pious devotion,
> And almsgiving. Avoid making a public display.

Know you that much talking mars good works,
> And excessive verbosity reduces the eternal reward.

I pray the Almighty that he who hears
> This song will desire to pass it on.

With praise to God my song is ended,
> And with praise to the Prophet Ahmadu,[57] scion of the Hashimites.

---

[57] That is, Muhammad.

PART
V

REASON, SCIENCE, AND SOCIETAL ORGANIZATION

⅏

We begin Part Five (Selections 27–34) with selections that represent their authors' desire to establish new methods of scientific inquiry and, thereby, discover new truths about the universe. In Selection 27, Francis Bacon in his *Novum Organum* (*New Instrument of Knowledge*) reveals his passion for experimental science. Bacon, reacting against the deductive thought of the Middle Ages, wished to establish a clear method of acquiring new and useful knowledge of the world through empirical observation and experience. Man, Bacon asserted, can thereby learn to control nature and advance human welfare. That is certainly an attitude that Americans, who pride themselves on their practicality, can readily understand, appreciate, and utilize. Bacon, thus, shows himself a modern man in his view of knowledge as material power. A contrasting method in the search for truth is illustrated by the rationalist René Descartes (Selection 28), who proposed that we doubt everything except the fact that we are doubting (or thinking about doubting). Thus, the existence of thought (and, by implication, a thinker) becomes the basis of a whole system of reliable knowledge, according to Descartes.

Another aspect of the modern age is the rise of women in the arts and professions. This is certainly true of the Mexican nun, Sister Juana Inés de la Cruz. Of mixed racial parentage she entered the Church as one of the few ways a precocious intellectual young woman could pursue her passion for learning. Paradoxically, her poems (Selection 29) also reveal genuine religious passion. In contrast to that Mexican nun, the French satirist

Voltaire (Selection 30) was distinctly anticlerical. In his humorous philosophical tale *Candide* he reveals human folly in its many institutional and personal forms. Voltaire's antipathy to organized religions, as well as to many other societal institutions that he regarded as irrationally repressive, is clear in *Candide*. His desire to see religious institutions divorced from political power corresponds to another aspect of the secular modern world. Contrast, for example, the Middle Ages, a period in which, at least in Europe, the Church dominated human life.

Another way in which reason and the rise of science affected societal organization is in the changing attitudes toward slavery. The legalized treatment of humans as property goes back as far as the beginnings of recorded history. In Selection 31, *The Interesting Narrative* of Olaudah Equiano (1789), we read the first-person account of a boy who was captured by African slave traders, then transported across West Africa, sold into the transatlantic slave trade, sent to Barbados, then to Virginia, and finally to England. Eventually, he was able to buy his own freedom, become a prosperous British citizen, write his autobiographical account, and speak eloquently against the institution of slavery. Such a life would not have been possible in an earlier century and, thus, shows the changing attitudes of humanity during the progress of the eighteenth-century Enlightenment, changing attitudes which were also foundational to America's revolutionary and constitutional history. Similarly, one of the greatest Spanish American novels of the nineteenth century, Villaverde's *Cecilia Valdés* (Selection 32), deals with the question of slavery, as well as with racial and class relations, within the steaming, potentially incestuous, intimacy of Cuban society.

There is no more systematic application of reason and the scientific method to societal organization than the political and economic theories of Karl Marx. In fact, Marx, a German, described his type of communism as "scientific socialism." In *The Communist Manifesto* of 1848 (Selection 33) Marx spells out his radical economic and political platform, and issues a call to arms. Although communism as an economic system for large societies seems to have worn out its usefulness at the end of the twentieth century, it should be noted that many of Marx's perceptive criticisms of mid-nineteenth-century capitalism have been incorporated into the capitalistic system as it exists today. Thus, the abuses of labor and the vast cycles of overproduction and depression that he described have entered into the planning of today's political economists who, warned by Marx, have taken preventive measures. Certainly, for much of the twentieth century, Marxism seemed for many millions of people to be the wave of the future, and it thus cannot be ignored in our overview of influential nineteenth-century thought. We end Part Five with a realistic Spanish novel, Galdós's *Fortunata and Jacinta* (Selection 34), published near the end of the nineteenth century. In its depictions of the irreconcilable gaps that divide Madrid's rich and poor, we can see the reflection of Marx's dictum that, ultimately, economic class structures shape human perceptions and human history.

27

❦

Francis Bacon

THE NEW INSTRUMENT
OF KNOWLEDGE

*I*n one of his letters Francis Bacon (1561–1626) wrote that "I have taken all
knowledge to be my province." In the magnitude of that assertion Bacon exemplifies the bold spirit of the European Renaissance. His passion for experimental
science exceeded the conventions of his times just as notably as Leonardo and
Michelangelo did earlier in their titanic artistic endeavors (see Selection 5).

    *Born to an aristocratic English family, Francis Bacon was the son of Sir
Nicholas Bacon, Lord Keeper of the Great Seal and a fervent Protestant. Through
his mother he was related to the Cecil family, who were politically powerful through
the reigns of Elizabeth I (1558–1603) and James I (1603–1625). Bacon studied
at Cambridge University (1573–1575) and then, after a diplomatic assignment
at the British Embassy in Paris, studied law at Grays Inn, London. Admitted to the
bar in 1582, he entered Parliament in 1584. Rising rapidly in the legal profession,
Bacon was commissioned by the queen to examine the conspirators in the charge of
treason brought against his earlier friend and benefactor, the Earl of Essex, a former favorite of Elizabeth who, in 1601, had attempted a rebellion against her.
Bacon's efforts were instrumental in winning a prompt execution for the ill-advised
Essex. At Elizabeth's command, Bacon also wrote an account of the conspiracy.
Later, becoming a close adviser to Elizabeth's successor, James I, Bacon guided the
monarch in his ceaseless struggles with Parliament. James awarded him with high
offices, for example, appointing him as Solicitor General in 1607, Attorney General in 1613, Baron Verulam and Lord Chancellor in 1618.

    In 1621, Bacon's numerous enemies in Parliament accused him of accepting
bribes in office. Perhaps naively, Bacon admitted accepting the bribes, a common
practice of those times, but he claimed that his judicial decisions had not been influenced by the gifts. He was convicted, fined, and stripped of all his public offices.
Quickly pardoned by James I and released from confinement in the Tower of Lon-*

don, Bacon continued his writing and scientific research in his retirement. Ironically, he died after catching a chill when he left his coach to gather snow in order to test its preservative effects on chicken flesh. In a sense, therefore, Francis Bacon was the first martyr to experimental science.

Bacon's fame in English literature is based mainly on his Essays (published as a collection of ten essays in 1597, thirty-eight in 1612, fifty-eight in 1625). Beginning as jottings in his commonplace book, based on his own experiences and reflections, Bacon expanded his thoughts into distinctive essays, mostly on how to get ahead in life. In pithy sentences, without a word wasted, Bacon expressed some of the most memorable and penetrating aphorisms ever penned in English: "He that hath wife and children hath given hostages to fortune, for they are impediments to great enterprises, either of virtue or mischief"; "Men fear death, as children fear to go in the dark; and as that natural fear in children is increased with tales, so is the other"; "Reading maketh a full man; conference a ready man; and writing an exact man." Such lucid and eloquent phrases have provoked certain "Baconians," up to the present day, to advance the startling thesis that the true author of Shakespeare's plays was Francis Bacon — not that country boy from Stratford, Bacon's contemporary, who never went to university.

It is, however, as a philosopher of science that Bacon has had the greatest influence on world thought. He rejected the deductive thought of the Middle Ages (exemplified in the works of Saint Thomas Aquinas, Volume II, Selection 34) and looked forward to the general acceptance of the new science, based on observation of nature, which would give men power over their environment. Bacon articulated the principles of acquiring new and useful knowledge of the world through empirical observation and experience. Only direct observation of nature followed by experiment could lead to the discovery of truth. The purpose of such discovery was the gaining of the power to control nature and thereby advance the welfare of mankind. Through the new inductive science — based on observations of particulars, not the general axioms of deductive logic — humanity could become the master of its own destiny.

In 1620, Bacon published his Novum Organum, the work excerpted here, the most complete and influential statement of his philosophy. Bacon intended the work to represent a rejection of the old Organon (Method or Instrument) of Aristotle, the ancient Greek philosopher. Aristotle's text had over the centuries become the authoritative textbook for logical method in the acquisition of knowledge. Bacon wrote his Novum Organum in Latin, as he did most of his works. Latin was then the international language for all European intellectuals, and Bacon wished his scientific philosophy to gain the greatest readership. (For clarity, the title is here translated as The New Instrument of Knowledge.) Bacon regarded the medieval intellectuals, the scholastics of the preceding centuries who cited Aristotle as their methodological master, as those who had studied only words instead of real matter, ignored nature, and developed an abstract and useless rationalism that provided no material benefit to humanity.

The deductive method, favored by the Aristoteleans, starts with accepted general premises and deduces specific instances from them. For example, the syllogism: All men are mortal; the King of England is a man; therefore, the King of England is mortal. Such a method can produce particular insights but cannot achieve new truths. The inductive method advanced by Bacon, on the other hand, accumulates large numbers of specific instances and only then arrives at a general statement of new truth. Bacon did not invent the inductive method. (Ironically, in fact, the Novum Organum *is not an example of induction but is really a series of aphorisms—short, witty observations—rather than a systematic accumulation of evidence.) Bacon's role was rather to be the literary champion of inductive reasoning. Although, if he were to return alive, he might be bewildered by today's highly theoretical and mathematical sciences, which often start with hypotheses, nevertheless, Bacon's magnificent plea in the* Novum Organum *for studying facts without prejudicial preconceptions makes him, in the opinion of many scholars, "the Father of Modern Science."*

AUTHOR'S PREFACE
• • •

Moreover, I have one request to make. I have on my own part made it my care and study that the things which I shall propound should not only be true, but should also be presented to men's minds, how strangely soever preoccupied and obstructed, in a manner not harsh or unpleasant. It is but reasonable, however (especially in so great a restoration of learning and knowledge), that I should claim of men one favor in return, which is this: if anyone would form an opinion or judgment either out of his own observation, or out of the crowd of authorities, or out of the forms of demonstration (which have now acquired a sanction like that of judicial laws), concerning these speculations of mine, let him not hope that he can do it in passage or by the by; but let him examine the thing thoroughly; let him make some little trial for himself of the way which I describe and lay out; let him familiarize his thoughts with that subtlety of nature to which experience bears witness; let him correct by seasonable patience and due delay the depraved and deep-rooted habits of his mind; and when all this is done and he has begun to be his own master, let him (if he will) use his own judgment.

From *The Works of Francis Bacon, Baron of Verulam, Viscount St. Albans, and Lord High Chancellor of England,* eds. James Spedding, Robert Leslie Ellis, and Douglas Denon Heath. Boston: Houghton, Mifflin and Company, 1900. Vol. VIII, *Translations of the Philosophical Works,* pp. 64 ff.

APHORISMS CONCERNING THE INTERPRETATION OF NATURE AND THE KINGDOM OF MAN
[Book One]
1

Man, being the servant and interpretor of Nature, can do and understand so much and so much only as he has observed in fact or in thought[1] of the course of nature. Beyond this he neither knows anything nor can do anything.

• • •

3

Human knowledge and human power meet in one; for where the cause is not known the effect cannot be produced. Nature to be commanded must be obeyed;[2] and that which in contemplation is as the cause is in operation as the rule.

• • •

8

Moreover, the works already known are due to chance and experiment rather than to sciences; for the sciences we now possess are merely systems for the nice ordering and setting forth of things already invented, not methods of invention or directions for new works.

• • •

11

As the sciences which we now have do not help us in finding out new works, so neither does the logic[3] which we now have help us in finding out new sciences.

12

The logic now in use serves rather to fix and give stability to the errors which have their foundation in commonly received notions than to help the search after truth. So it does more harm than good.

• • •

---

[1] That is, either by observation only or by reflection after observation.

[2] That is, followed.

[3] The logic referred to here is deductive or syllogistic logic, which depends upon the truth of its preestablished major premises. Since many of the established principles in the science of Bacon's time were false, this deductive logic only continued the errors.

14

The syllogism consists of propositions, propositions consist of words, words are symbols of notions. Therefore if the notions themselves (which is the root of the matter) are confused and overhastily abstracted from the facts, there can be no firmness in the superstructure. Our only hope therefore lies in a true induction.

• • •

18

The discoveries which have hitherto been made in the sciences are such as lie close to vulgar notions,[4] scarcely beneath the surface. In order to penetrate into the inner and further recesses of nature, it is necessary that both notions and axioms[5] be derived from things by a more sure and guarded way, and that a method of intellectual operation be introduced altogether better and more certain.

19

There are and can be only two ways of searching into and discovering truth. The one flies from the senses and particulars to the most general axioms, and from these principles, the truth of which it takes for settled and immovable, proceeds to judgment and to the discovery of middle axioms. And this way is now in fashion. The other derives axioms from the senses and particulars, rising by a gradual and unbroken ascent, so that it arrives at the most general axioms last of all. This is the true way, but as yet untried.

• • •

23

There is a great difference between the Idols of the human mind and the Ideas of the divine. That is to say, between certain empty dogmas, and the true signatures and marks set upon the works of creation as they are found in nature.

24

It cannot be that axioms established by argumentation should avail for the discovery of new works, since the subtlety of nature is greater many times over than the subtlety of argument. But axioms duly and orderly formed from particulars easily discover the way to new particulars, and thus render sciences active.[6]

• • •

---

[4] Popular ideas unsupported by science or reason.

[5] Established principles generally recognized as true.

[6] That is, principles formed from observation of particulars may be applied in a practical way, and science, thereby, made more useful.

26

The conclusions of human reason as ordinarily applied in matters of nature, I call for the sake of distinction *Anticipations of Nature* (as a thing rash or premature). That reason which is elicited from facts by a just and methodical process, I call *Interpretation of Nature.*

• • •

28

For the winning of assent, indeed, anticipations are far more powerful than interpretations, because being collected from a few instances, and those for the most part of familiar occurrence, they straightway touch the understanding and fill the imagination; whereas interpretations, on the other hand, being gathered here and there from very various and widely dispersed facts, cannot suddenly strike the understanding; and therefore they must needs, in respect of the opinions of the time, seem harsh and out of tune, much as the mysteries of faith do.

29

In sciences founded on opinions and dogmas, the use of anticipations and logic is good; for in them the object is to command assent to the proposition, not to master the thing.

30

Though all the wits of all the ages should meet together and combine and transmit their labors, yet will no great progress ever be made in science by means of anticipations; because radical errors in the first concoction of the mind are not to be cured by the excellence of functions and subsequent remedies.

31

It is idle to expect any great advancement in science from the superinducing and engrafting of new things upon old. We must begin anew from the very foundations, unless we would revolve forever in a circle with mean and contemptible progress.

• • •

36

One method of delivery alone remains to us which is simply this: we must lead men to the particulars themselves, and their series and order; while men on their side must force themselves for a while to lay their notions by and begin to familiarize themselves with facts.

37

The doctrine of those who have denied that certainty could be attained at all has some agreement with my way of proceeding at the first setting out; but they end in being infinitely separated and opposed. For the holders of that doctrine assert simply that nothing can be known. I also assert that not much can be known in nature by the way which is now in use. But then they go on to destroy the authority of the senses and understanding; whereas I proceed to devise and supply helps for the same.

38

The idols and false notions which are now in possession of the human understanding, and have taken deep root therein, not only so beset men's minds that truth can hardly find entrance, but even after entrance is obtained, they will again in the very instauration[7] of the sciences meet and trouble us, unless men being forewarned of the danger fortify themselves as far as may be against their assaults.

39

There are four classes of Idols[8] which beset men's minds. To these for distinction's sake I have assigned names, calling the first class *Idols of the Tribe*; the second, *Idols of the Cave*; the third, *Idols of the Market Place*; the fourth, *Idols of the Theater*.

40

The formulation of ideas and axioms by true induction is no doubt the proper remedy to be applied for the keeping off and clearing away of idols. To point them out, however, is of great use; for the doctrine of Idols is to the interpretation of nature what the doctrine of the refutation of sophisms[9] is to common logic.

41

The Idols of the Tribe have their foundation in human nature itself, and in the tribe or race of men. For it is a false assertion that the sense of man is the measure of things. On the contrary, all perceptions as well of the sense as of the mind are according to the measure of the individual and not according to the measure of the universe. And the human understanding is like a false mirror, which, receiving rays irregularly, distorts and discolors the nature of things by mingling its own nature with it.

42

The Idols of the Cave are the idols of the individual man. For everyone (besides the errors common to human nature in general) has a cave or den of his own, which refracts and discolors the light of nature, owing either to his own proper

---

[7] Renewal; the entire *Novum Organum* was part of a grand scheme that Bacon titled *Magna Instauratio* (*The Great Instauration*).

[8] False beliefs; not the carved images of false gods condemned in the Bible.

[9] False arguments.

and peculiar nature; or to his education and conversation with others; or to the reading of books, and the authority of those whom he esteems and admires; or to the differences of impressions, accordingly as they take place in a mind preoccupied and predisposed or in a mind indifferent and settled; or the like. So that the spirit of man (according as it is meted out to different individuals) is in fact a thing variable and full of perturbation, and governed as it were by chance. . . .

43

There are also Idols formed by the intercourse and association of men with each other, which I call Idols of the Market Place, on account of the commerce and consort of men there. For it is by discourse that men associate, and words are imposed according to the apprehension of the vulgar. And therefore the ill and unfit choice of words wonderfully obstructs the understanding. Nor do the definitions or explanations wherewith in some things learned men are wont to guard and defend themselves, by any means set the matter right. But words plainly force and overrule the understanding, and throw all into confusion, and lead men away into numberless empty controversies and idle fancies.

44

Lastly, there are Idols which have immigrated into men's minds from the various dogmas of philosophies, and also from wrong laws of demonstration. These I call Idols of the Theater, because in my judgment all the received systems are but so many stage plays, representing worlds of their own creation after an unreal and scenic fashion. Nor is it only of the systems now in vogue, or only of the ancient sects and philosophies, that I speak; for many more plays of the same kind may yet be composed and in like artificial manner set forth; seeing that errors the most widely different have nevertheless causes for the most part alike. Neither again do I mean this only of entire systems, but also of many principles and axioms in science, which by tradition, credulity, and negligence have come to be received.

But of these several kinds of Idols I must speak more largely and exactly, that the understanding may be duly cautioned.

45

The human understanding is of its own nature prone to suppose the existence of more order and regularity in the world than it finds. And though there be many things in nature which are singular and unmatched, yet it devises for them parallels and conjugates and relatives which do not exist. Hence the fiction that all celestial bodies move in perfect circles. . . .

46

The human understanding when it has once adopted an opinion (either as being the received opinion or as being agreeable to itself) draws all things else to support and agree with it. And though there be a greater number and weight of instances to be found on the other side, yet these it either neglects and despises, or else by some distinction sets aside and rejects, in order that by this great and pernicious predetermination the authority of its former conclusions may remain inviolate. And therefore it was a good answer that was made by one[10] who, when they showed him hanging in a temple a picture of those who had paid their vows as having escaped shipwreck, and would have him say whether he did not now acknowledge the power of the gods — "Aye," asked he again, "but where are they painted that were drowned after their vows?" And such is the way of all superstition, whether in astrology, dreams, omens, divine judgments, or the like; wherein men, having a delight in such vanities, mark the events where they are fulfilled, but where they fail, though this happen much oftener, neglect and pass them by. But with far more subtlety does this mischief insinuate itself into philosophy and the sciences; in which the first conclusion colors and brings into conformity with itself all that come after, though far sounder and better. Besides, independently of that delight and vanity which I have described, it is the peculiar and perpetual error of the human intellect to be more moved and excited by affirmatives than by negatives; whereas it ought properly to hold itself indifferently disposed toward both alike. Indeed, in the establishment of any true axiom, the negative instance is the more forcible of the two.

· · ·

59

But the *Idols of the Market Place* are the most troublesome of all — idols which have crept into the understanding through the alliances of words and names. For men believe that their reason governs words; but it is also true that words react on the understanding; and this it is that has rendered philosophy and the sciences sophistical and inactive. Now words, being commonly framed and applied according to the capacity of the vulgar, follow those lines of divisions which are most obvious to the vulgar understanding. And whenever an understanding of greater acuteness or a more diligent observation would alter those lines to suit the true divisions of nature, words stand in the way and resist the change. Whence it comes to pass that the high and formal discussions of learned men end oftentimes in disputes about words and names; with which (according to the use[11] and wisdom of mathematicians) it would be more prudent to begin, and so by means of definitions reduce them to order. Yet even definitions cannot cure this evil in dealing with natural and material things, since the definitions themselves consist of words, and those words beget others. So that it is necessary to recur to individual instances, and those in due series and order, as I shall say presently when I come to the method and scheme for the formation of notions and axioms.

· · ·

---

[10] Diagorus, an ancient Athenian philosopher of the fifth century B.C. who became well known as an atheist.

[11] Custom.

62

Idols of the Theater, or of Systems, are many, and there can be and perhaps will be yet many more. For were it not that now for many ages men's minds have been busied with religion and theology; and were it not that civil governments, especially monarchies, have been averse to such novelties, even in matters speculative; so that men labor therein to the peril and harming of their fortunes—not only unrewarded, but exposed also to contempt and envy—doubtless there would have arisen many other philosophical sects like those which in great variety flourished once among the Greeks. For as on the phenomena of the heavens many hypotheses may be constructed, so likewise (and more also) many various dogmas may be set up and established on the phenomena of philosophy.[12] And in the plays of this philosophical theater you may observe the same thing which is found in the theater of the poets, that stories invented for the stage are more compact and elegant, and more as one would wish them to be, than true stories out of history.

In general, however, there is taken for the material of philosophy either a great deal out of a few things, or a very little out of many things; so that on both sides philosophy is based on too narrow a foundation of experiment and natural history, and decides on the authority of too few cases. . . .

• • •

68

So much concerning the several classes of Idols and their equipage;[13] all of which must be renounced and put away with a fixed and solemn determination, and the understanding thoroughly freed and cleansed; the entrance into the kingdom of man, founded on the sciences, being not much other than the entrance into the kingdom of heaven, whereinto none may enter except as a little child.

• • •

81

Again there is another great and powerful cause why the sciences have made but little progress, which is this. It is not possible to run a course aright when the goal itself has not been rightly placed. Now the true and lawful goal of the sciences is none other than this: that human life be endowed with new discoveries and powers. But of this the great majority have no feeling, but are merely hireling and professorial; except when it occasionally happens that some workman of acuter wit and covetous of honor applies himself to a new invention, which he mostly does at the expense of his fortunes. But in general, so far are men from

---

[12] "Philosophy" usually means science in Bacon's discussion, where "science" (Latin: *scientia*) retains its Latin meaning of "knowledge."

[13] Accompanying "baggage."

proposing to themselves to augment the mass of arts and sciences, that from the mass already at hand they neither take nor look for anything more than what they may turn to use in their lectures, or to gain, or to reputation, or to some similar advantage. And if any one out of all the multitude court science with honest affection and for her own sake, yet even with him the object will be found to be rather the variety of contemplations and doctrines than the severe and rigid search after truth. And if by chance there be one who seeks after truth in earnest, yet even he will propose to himself such a kind of truth as shall yield satisfaction to the mind and understanding in rendering causes for things long since discovered, and not the truth which shall lead to new assurance of works and new light of axioms. If then the end of the sciences has not as yet been well placed, it is not strange that men have erred as to the means.

82

And as men have misplaced the end and goal of the sciences, so again, even if they had placed it right, yet they have chosen a way to which it is altogether erroneous and impassible. And an astonishing thing it is to one who rightly considers the matter, that no mortal should have seriously applied himself to the opening and laying out of a road for the human understanding direct from the sense, by a course of experiment orderly conducted and well built up, but that all has been left either to the mist of tradition, or the whirl and eddy of argument, or the fluctuations and mazes of chance and of vague and ill-digested experience. Now let any man soberly and diligently consider what the way is by which men have been accustomed to proceed in the investigation and discovery of things, and in the first place he will no doubt remark a method of discovery very simple and inartificial, which is the most ordinary method, and is no more than this. When a man addresses himself to discover something, he first seeks out and sets before him all that has been said about it by others; then he begins to meditate for himself; and so by much agitation and working of the wit solicits and as it were evokes his own spirit to give him oracles; which method has no foundation at all, but rests only upon opinions and is carried about with them.

Another may perhaps call in logic to discover it for him, but that has no relation to the matter except in name. For logical invention does not discover principles and chief axioms, of which arts are composed, but only such things as appear to be consistent with them. For if you grow more curious and importunate and busy, and question her of probations and invention of principles or primary axioms, her answer is well known; she refers you to the faith you are bound to give to the principles of each separate art.

There remains simple experience which, if taken as it comes, is called accident; if sought for, experiment. But this kind of experience is no better than a broom without its band, as the saying is — a mere groping, as of men in the dark, that feel all around them for the chance of finding their way, when they had much better wait for daylight, or light a candle, and then go. But the true method of experience, on the contrary, first lights the candle, and then by means of the candle shows the way; commencing as it does with experience duly ordered and digested, not bungling or erratic, and from it educing axioms, and from established axioms again new experiments; even as it was not without order and method that the divine word operated on the created mass. Let men therefore cease to wonder that the course of science is not yet wholly run, seeing that they have gone altogether astray, either leaving and abandoning experience entirely, or losing their way in it and wandering round and round as in a labyrinth. Whereas a method rightly ordered leads by an unbroken route through the woods of experience to the open ground of axioms.

83

This evil, however, has been strangely increased by an opinion or conceit, which though of long standing is vain and hurtful, namely, that the dignity of the human mind is impaired by long and close intercourse with experiments and particulars, subject to sense and bound in matter; especially as they are laborious to search, ignoble to meditate, harsh to deliver, illiberal to practice, infinite in number, and minute in subtlety. So that it has come at length to this, that the true way is not merely deserted, but shut out and stopped up; experience being, I do not say abandoned or badly managed, but rejected with disdain.

$$\bullet \quad \bullet \quad \bullet$$

89

Neither is it to be forgotten that in every age natural philosophy has had a troublesome and hard to deal with adversary—namely, superstition, and the blind and immoderate zeal of religion. For we see among the Greeks that those who first proposed to men's then uninitiated ears the natural causes for thunder and for storms were thereupon found guilty of impiety. Nor was much more forbearance shown by some of the ancient fathers of the Christian church to those who on most convincing grounds (such as no one in his senses would now think of contradicting) maintained that the earth was round, and of consequence asserted the existence of the antipodes.[14]

Moreover, as things now are, to discourse of nature is made harder and more perilous by the summaries and systems of the schoolmen[15] who, having reduced theology into regular order as well as they were able, and fashioned it into the shape of an art, ended in incorporating the contentious and thorny philosophy of Aristotle, more than was fit, with the body of religion.

To the same result, though in a different way, tend the speculations of those who have taken upon them to deduce the truth of the Christian religion from

---

[14] Any two places on the globe (earth) that are diametrically opposite each other.

[15] Medieval "scholastic" philosophers who derived their system of logic from the works of Aristotle, the ancient Greek philosopher.

the principles of philosophers, and to confirm it by their authority, pompously solemnizing this union of the sense and faith as a lawful marriage, and entertaining men's minds with a pleasing variety of matter, but all the while disparaging things divine by mingling them with things human. Now in such mixtures of theology with philosophy only the received doctrines of philosophy are included; while new ones, albeit changes for the better, are all but expelled and exterminated.

Lastly, you will find that by the simpleness of certain divines,[16] access to any philosophy, however pure, is well-nigh closed. Some are weakly afraid lest a deeper search into nature should transgress the permitted limits of sober-mindedness, wrongfully wresting and transferring what is said in Holy Writ against those who pry into sacred mysteries, to the hidden things of nature, which are barred by no prohibition. Others with more subtlety surmise and reflect that if second causes are unknown everything can more readily be referred to the divine hand and rod, a point in which they think religion greatly concerned—which is in fact nothing else but to seek to gratify God with a lie. Others fear from past example that movements and changes in philosophy will end in assaults on religion. And others again appear apprehensive that in the investigation of nature something may be found to subvert or at least shake the authority of religion, especially with the unlearned. But these two last fears seem to me to savor utterly of carnal wisdom; as if men in the recesses and secret thought of their hearts doubted and distrusted the strength of religion and the empire of faith over the sense, and therefore feared that the investigation of truth in nature might be dangerous to them. But if the matter be truly considered, natural philosophy is, after the word of God, at once the surest medicine against superstition and the most approved nourishment for faith, and therefore she is rightly given to religion as her most faithful handmaid, since the one displays the will of God, the other his power. For he did not err who said, "Ye err in that ye know not the Scriptures and the power of God," thus coupling and blending in an indissoluble bond information concerning his will and meditation concerning his power. Meanwhile it is not surprising if the growth of natural philosophy is checked when religion, the thing which has most power over men's minds, has by the simpleness and incautious zeal of certain persons been drawn to take part against her.

90

Again, in the customs and institutions of schools, academies, colleges, and similar bodies destined for the abode of learned men and the cultivation of learning, everything is found adverse to the progress of science. For the lectures and exercises there are so ordered that to think or speculate on anything out of the common way can hardly occur to any man. And if one or two have the boldness to use any liberty of judgment, they must undertake the task all by themselves; they

---

[16] Christian clergy, especially theologians.

can have no advantage from the company of others. And if they can endure this also, they will find their industry and largeness of mind no slight hindrance to their fortune. For the studies of men in these places are confined and as it were imprisoned in the writings of certain authors, from whom if any man dissent he is straightway arraigned as a turbulent person and an innovator. But surely there is a great distinction between matters of state and the arts; for the danger from new motion and from new light is not the same. In matters of state a change even for the better is distrusted, because it unsettles what is established; these things resting on authority, consent, fame and opinion, not on demonstration. But arts and sciences should be like mines, where the noise of new works and further advances is heard on every side. But though the matter be so according to right reason, it is not so acted on in practice; and the points above mentioned in the administration and government of learning put a severe restraint upon the advancement of the sciences.

• • •

95

Those who have handled sciences have been either men of experiment or men of dogmas. The men of experiment are like the ant, they only collect and use; the reasoners resemble spiders, who make cobwebs out of their own substance. But the bee takes a middle course: it gathers its material from the flowers of the garden and of the field, but transforms and digests it by a power of its own. Not unlike this is the true business of philosophy; for it neither relies solely or chiefly on the powers of the mind, nor does it take the matter which it gathers from natural history and mechanical experiments and lay it up in the memory whole, as it finds it, but lays it up in the understanding altered and digested. Therefore from a closer and purer league between these two faculties, the experimental and the rational (such as has never yet been made), much may be hoped.

28

⅊

René Descartes

DISCOURSE ON METHOD

*I*n *1637, the French philosopher, mathematician, and naturalist René Descartes (1596–1650) published anonymously, and in the French vernacular, three sample essays of his work:* Geometry, Optics, *and* Meteorology. *But it was the preface to these essays that was to become one of the great classics in philosophy:* Discourse on the Method of Rightly Conducting Reason and Reaching the Truth in the Sciences. *The anonymity and the use of the French language (rather than the Latin, normally used in scholarly or scientific writings at the time), were due to Descartes's caution after hearing of the Italian physicist Galileo Galilei's troubles with the Catholic Church. (Galileo's scientific works, which supported the heliocentric system, were deemed contrary to church tenets and banned in 1633.) Descartes, like Galileo, remained throughout his life a practicing Roman Catholic, and in his work he sought to provide the basis for a new theology based on both philosophy and science. Nevertheless, Descartes's writings proved to be as controversial as Galileo's among Protestants as well as Catholics, and they were eventually officially banned and placed on Rome's* Index *of prohibited books. Despite this prohibition, Descartes's philosophy continued to be studied and debated from the seventeenth century to our time. His work, which laid the foundations for rationalism, was enormously popular among scientists in the seventeenth and eighteenth centuries, and it directly influenced three other great philosophers of his age: Baruch Spinoza (1632–1677), John Locke (1632–1704), and Gottfried Wilhelm Leibniz (1646–1716). Descartes is generally regarded today as the originator of modern philosophy, by virtue of his attempts to show how the world described by physics and mathematics can be understood independently of the often misleading perceptions of our sensory organs.*

Born in 1596 near the city of Tours, in a small town formerly known as La Haye, but which now bears his name, Descartes was educated by the Jesuits in the college of La Flèche in Anjou. After taking a law degree at the University of Poitiers, he traveled to Holland, where he joined the army of Prince Maurice of

Nassau. While traveling in Germany, on November 10, 1619, he had a dream vision of a new mathematical and scientific system which would unify all the sciences. After returning to France in 1622, he again moved in 1628 to Holland, where he would write all of his major philosophical works, including the Meditations on First Philosophy, *in Latin, which also included a collection of seven sets of objections to the arguments of the* Meditations *along with replies by Descartes. The objections came from friends and acquaintances of Descartes who were themselves important thinkers, such as Thomas Hobbes (1588–1679), Pierre Gassendi (1592–1655), and Antoine Arnauld (1612–1694).*

Despite the controversies elicited by his philosophy, Descartes was highly respected in his lifetime; he corresponded with important members of the European nobility, such as Princess Elizabeth of Bohemia, was awarded a pension by the king of France in 1647, and traveled to Sweden on the invitation of Queen Christina in 1649 to take a position as her tutor. It was in Sweden that he published his last philosophical treatise, The Passions of the Soul *(1649). The Swedish climate and the job's demands proved too much for Descartes, and he died in Stockholm the following year, of pneumonia.*

In the following "Fourth Part" of his Discourse on Method *(as this work is commonly known) and, in a more detailed manner, in the first "Meditation" of his* Meditations on First Philosophy *(1641), Descartes presents his arguments in favor of a fundamental principle that would guarantee the certainty of knowledge. If the senses frequently deceive us, if our reasoning is fallible, and if our dream thoughts are indistinguishable from our waking thoughts, how can we tell if something is true? Is there anything that can be said to be absolutely true and certain? Descartes's reply, embodied in his famous principle,* Cogito, ergo sum *(in Latin: "I am thinking, therefore I exist"), was that the act of thinking was unquestionably true in itself, since one cannot deny thought without thinking about such a denial and thus reaffirming the existence of thought. From this starting point, Descartes proposed, a whole system of reliable knowledge could be constructed. He asserts a radically different method of gaining knowledge from that of Francis Bacon (Selection 27) who assumes the reality of the material world and proposes a purely inductive method, based on direct observation of nature.*

Despite his desire to unify philosophy with the sciences in a single system of knowledge, Descartes believed that the mind was totally distinct from matter. In this view, which has become known as "Cartesian dualism," the workings of the mind (or the soul, which for Descartes amounts to the same thing) are fundamentally independent of the body—despite the obvious existence of corporeal sensations in human beings, which suggest that the mind and the body are somehow fused. Partly, Descartes's emphasis on the independence of the mind is due to his preference for ideas and principles that are independent of the senses (such as mathematics) and his belief that humans are born with a generous endowment of innate knowledge. Descartes was never able to resolve this so-called "mind-body problem," other than to assert that a perfect God would not allow us to be constantly deceived, but his compelling formulation of this problem has influenced all subsequent thinking about it.

�֎

PART IV

I am in doubt as to the propriety of making my first meditations, in the place above mentioned, matter of discourse; for these are so metaphysical, and so uncommon, as not, perhaps, to be acceptable to everyone. And yet, that it may be determined whether the foundations that I have laid are sufficiently secure, I find myself in a measure constrained to advert to them. I had long before remarked that, in relation to practice, it is sometimes necessary to adopt, as if above doubt, opinions which we discern to be highly uncertain, as has been already said; but as I then desired to give my attention solely to the search after truth, I thought that a procedure exactly the opposite was called for, and that I ought to reject as absolutely false all opinions in regard to which I could suppose the least ground for doubt, in order to ascertain whether after that there remained anything in my belief that was wholly indubitable. Accordingly, seeing that our senses sometimes deceive us, I was willing to suppose that there existed nothing really such as they presented to us; and because some men err in reasoning, and fall into paralogisms,[1] even on the simplest matters of Geometry, I, convinced that I was as open to error as any other, rejected as false all the reasonings I had hitherto taken for demonstrations; and finally, when I considered that the very same thoughts (presentations) which we experience when awake may also be experienced when we are asleep, while there is at that time not one of them true, I supposed that all the objects (presentations) that had ever entered into my mind when awake, had in them no more truth than the illusions of my dreams. But immediately upon this I observed that, while I thus wished to think that all was false, it was absolutely necessary that I, who thus thought, should be somewhat; and as I observed that this truth, I THINK, HENCE I AM, was so certain and of such evidence, that no ground of doubt, however extravagant, could be alleged by the Sceptics[2] capable

---

From *The Method, Meditations, and Philosophy of Descartes,* translated by John Veitch (1901). Adapted by the editors.

[1] Fallacious reasoning or invalid argument.

[2] Those who assert the doctrine that true knowledge is uncertain. Scepticism first arose in Hellenistic Greece, and made a forceful return to European culture from the fifteenth to the seventeenth centuries, when theological conflicts and religious schisms, as well as the new scientific and geographic discoveries, raised doubts about traditional concepts of the universe.

of shaking it, I concluded that I might, without scruple, accept it as the first principle of the Philosophy of which I was in search.

In the next place, I attentively examined what I was, and as I observed that I could suppose that I had no body, and that there was no world nor any place in which I might be; but that I could not therefore suppose that I was not; and that, on the contrary, from the very circumstance that I thought to doubt of the truth of all things, it most clearly and certainly followed that I was; while, on the other hand, if I had only ceased to think, although all the other objects which I had ever imagined had been in reality existent, I would have had no reason to believe that I existed; I thence concluded that I was a substance whose whole essence or nature consists only in thinking, and which, that it may exist, has need of no place, nor is dependent on any material thing; so that "I," that is to say, the mind by which I am what I am, is wholly distinct from the body, and is even more easily known than the latter, and is such, that although the latter were not, it would still continue to be all that it is.

After this I inquired in general into what is essential to the truth and certainty of a proposition; for since I had discovered one which I knew to be true, I thought that I must likewise be able to discover the ground of this certitude. And as I observed that in the words I THINK, HENCE I AM, there is nothing at all which gives me assurance of their truth beyond this, that I see very clearly that in order to think it is necessary to exist, I concluded that I might take, as a general rule, the principle, that all the things which we very clearly and distinctly conceive are true, only observing, however, that there is some difficulty in rightly determining the objects which we distinctly conceive.

In the next place, from reflecting on the circumstance that I doubted, and that consequently my being was not wholly perfect (for I clearly saw that it was a greater perfection to know than to doubt), I was led to inquire whence I had learned to think of something more perfect than myself; and I clearly recognized that I must hold this notion from some Nature which in reality was more perfect. As for the thoughts of many other objects external to me, as of the sky, the earth, light, heat, and a thousand more, I was less at a loss to know whence these came; for since I remarked in them nothing which seemed to render them superior to myself, I could believe that, if these were true, they were dependencies on my own nature, in so far as it possessed a certain perfection, and, if they were false, that I held them from nothing, that is to say, that they were in me because of a certain imperfection of my nature. But this could not be the case with the idea of a Nature more perfect than myself; for to receive it from nothing was a thing manifestly impossible; and, because it is not less repugnant that the more perfect should be an effect of, and dependence on the less perfect, than that something should proceed from nothing, it was equally impossible that I could hold it from myself: accordingly, it but remained that it had been placed in me by a Nature which was in reality more perfect than mine, and which even possessed within itself all the perfections of which I could form any idea: that is to say, in a single word, which was God. And to this I added that, since I knew some perfections which I did not possess, I was not the only being in existence, (I will here, with your permission, freely use the terms of the Schools);[3] but on the contrary, that there was of necessity some other more perfect Being upon whom I was dependent, and from whom I had received all that I possessed; for if I had existed alone, and independently of every other being, so as to have had from myself all the perfection, however little, which I actually possessed, I should have been able, for the same reason, to have had from myself the whole remainder of perfection, of the want of which I was conscious, and thus could of myself have become infinite, eternal, immutable, omniscient, all-powerful, and, in fine, have possessed all the perfections which I could recognize in God. For in order to know the nature of God (whose existence has been established by the preceding reasonings), as far as my own nature permitted, I had only to consider in reference to all the properties of which I found in my mind some idea, whether their possession was a mark of perfection; and I was assured that no one which indicated any imperfection was in him, and that none of the rest was awanting. Thus I perceived that doubt, inconstancy, sadness, and such like, could not be found in God, since I myself would have been happy to be free from them. Besides, I had ideas of many sensible and corporeal things; for although I might suppose that I was dreaming, and that all which I saw or imagined was false, I could not, nevertheless, deny that the ideas were in reality in my thoughts. But because I had already very clearly recognized in myself that the intelligent nature is distinct from the corporeal, and as I observed that all composition is an evidence of dependency, and that a state of dependency is manifestly a state of imperfection, I therefore determined that it could not be a perfection in God to be compounded of these two natures, and that consequently he was not so compounded; but that if there were any bodies in the world, or even any intelligences, or other natures that were not wholly perfect, their existence depended on his power in such a way that they could not subsist without him for a single moment.

I was disposed straightway to search for other truths; and when I had represented to myself the object of the geometers, which I conceived to be a continuous body, or a space indefinitely extended in length, breadth, and height or depth, divisible into divers parts which admit of different figures and sizes, and of being moved or transposed in all manner of ways (for all this the geometers suppose to be in the object they contemplate), I went over some of their simplest demonstrations. And, in the first place, I observed, that the great certitude which by common consent is accorded to these demonstrations, is founded solely upon this, that they are clearly conceived in accordance with the rules I have already

---

[3] Another name for "scholasticism," the tradition of medieval philosophy that arose in the universities and is associated with philosophers of the thirteenth to the fourteenth centuries such as St. Thomas Aquinas, Duns Scotus, and William of Ockham. Broadly stated, scholasticism was concerned with the question of the compatibility between Christianity and reason.

laid down. In the next place, I perceived that there was nothing at all in these demonstrations which could assure me of the existence of their object; thus, for example, supposing a triangle to be given, I distinctly perceived that its three angles were necessarily equal to two right angles, but I did not on that account perceive anything which could assure me that any triangle existed; while, on the contrary, recurring to the examination of the idea of a Perfect Being, I found that the existence of the Being was comprised in the idea in the same way that the equality of its three angles to two right angles is comprised in the idea of a triangle, or as in the idea of a sphere, the equidistance of all points on its surface from the center, or even still more clearly; and that consequently it is at least as certain that God, who is this Perfect Being, is, or exists, as any demonstration of Geometry can be.

But the reason which leads many to persuade themselves that there is a difficulty in knowing this truth, and even also in knowing what their mind really is, is that they never raise their thoughts above sensible objects, and are so accustomed to consider nothing except by way of imagination, which is a mode of thinking limited to material objects, that all that is not imaginable seems to them not intelligible. The truth of this is sufficiently manifest from the single circumstance, that the philosophers of the Schools accept as a maxim that there is nothing in the Understanding which was not previously in the Senses, in which however it is certain that the ideas of God and of the soul have never been; and it appears to me that they who make use of their imagination to comprehend these ideas do exactly the same thing as if, in order to hear sounds or smell odors, they strove to avail themselves of their eyes; unless indeed that there is this difference, that the sense of sight does not afford us an inferior assurance to those of smell or hearing; in place of which, neither our imagination nor our senses can give us assurance of anything unless our Understanding intervene.

Finally, if there be still persons who are not sufficiently persuaded of the existence of God and of the soul, by the reasons I have adduced, I am desirous that they should know that all the other propositions, of the truth of which they deem themselves perhaps more assured, as that we have a body, and that there exist stars and an earth, and such like, are less certain; for, although we have a moral assurance of these things, which is so strong that there is an appearance of extravagance in doubting of their existence, yet at the same time no one, unless his intellect is impaired, can deny, when the question relates to a metaphysical certitude, that there is sufficient reason to exclude entire assurance, in the observation that when asleep we can in the same way imagine ourselves possessed of another body and that we see other stars and another earth, when there is nothing of the kind. For how do we know that the thoughts which occur in dreaming are false rather than those other which we experience when awake, since the former are often not less vivid and distinct than the latter? And though men of the highest genius study this question as long as they please, I do not believe that they will be able to give any reason which can be sufficient to remove this doubt, unless they presuppose the existence of God. For, in the first place, even the principle which

I have already taken as a rule, that is, that all the things which we clearly and distinctly conceive are true, is certain only because God is or exists, and because he is a Perfect Being, and because all that we possess is derived from him: whence it follows that our ideas or notions, which to the extent of their clearness and distinctness are real, and proceed from God, must to that extent be true. Accordingly, whereas we not unfrequently have ideas or notions in which some falsity is contained, this can only be the case with such as are to some extent confused and obscure, and in this proceed from nothing, (participate of negation), that is, exist in us thus confused because we are not wholly perfect. And it is evident that it is not less repugnant that falsity or imperfection, in so far as it is imperfection, should proceed from God, than that truth or perfection should proceed from nothing. But if we did not know that all which we possess of real and true proceeds from a Perfect and Infinite Being, however clear and distinct our ideas might be, we should have no ground on that account for the assurance that they possessed the perfection of being true.

But after the knowledge of God and of the soul has rendered us certain of this rule, we can easily understand that the truth of the thoughts we experience when awake, ought not in the slightest degree to be called in question on account of the illusions of our dreams. For if it happened that an individual, even when asleep, had some very distinct idea, as, for example, if a geometer should discover some new demonstration, the circumstance of his being asleep would not militate against its truth; and as for the most ordinary error of our dreams, which consists in their representing to us various objects in the same way as our external senses, this is not prejudicial, since it leads us very properly to suspect the truth of the ideas of sense; for we are not unfrequently deceived in the same manner when awake; as when persons in the jaundice see all objects yellow, or when the stars or bodies at a great distance appear to us much smaller than they are. For, in brief, whether awake or asleep, we ought never to allow ourselves to be persuaded of the truth of anything unless on the evidence of our Reason. And it must be noted that I say of our REASON, and not of our imagination or of our senses: thus, for example, although we very clearly see the sun, we ought not therefore to determine that it is only of the size which our sense of sight presents; and we may very distinctly imagine the head of a lion joined to the body of a goat, without being therefore shut up to the conclusion that such a monster exists; for it is not a dictate of Reason that what we thus see or imagine is in reality existent; but it plainly tells us that all our ideas or notions contain in them some truth; for otherwise it could not be that God, who is wholly perfect and veracious, should have placed them in us. And because our reasonings are never so clear or so complete during sleep as when we are awake, although sometimes the acts of our imagination are then as lively and distinct, if not more so than in our waking moments, Reason further dictates that, since all our thoughts cannot be true because of our partial imperfection, those possessing truth must infallibly be found in the experience of our waking moments rather than in that of our dreams.

29

༅

Sor Juana Inés de la Cruz

POEMS

The woman who was to be hailed by her contemporaries as "the Tenth Muse," and who today is regarded as one of the greatest Latin American writers, the Mexican nun Sor [Sister] Juana Inés de la Cruz (1651–1695), was born Juana Ramírez de Asbaje in a small farm called San Miguel de Nepantla. Mexico was then part of the Viceroyalty of New Spain, one of the administrative subdivisions of the vast Spanish Empire in the New World. Like her mother, who was also born in New Spain, Sor Juana was a criolla, or Creole, a term coined by the Spanish colonists to refer to anyone who had been born in the Americas. In the Spanish Empire, Creoles, although they could own land and amass great wealth, were barred from occupying high governmental and ecclesiastical positions. Furthermore, Sor Juana was an illegitimate child. Her father had been a military man from Spain, Pedro de Asbaje. As if being a Creole and illegitimate were not enough, being a woman also put Sor Juana at a disadvantage in a society where men held all the power and women were confined to the household and forbidden from intellectual pursuits.

Perhaps Sor Juana inherited (or learned) her independence and strength of character from her mother, who not only ran the family farm but also bore her other five children out of wedlock and by two different fathers. In any case, as Sor Juana herself relates in her partly autobiographical letter, Respuesta a Sor Filotea de la Cruz ("Reply to Sister Philotea of the Cross," 1691), several lucky circumstances allowed her talents to develop and to be recognized. Having a precocious intellect, she learned to read when she was three or four years old, and was able to satisfy in part her obsessive inclination to study by reading all of the books in her maternal grandfather's library at the nearby Hacienda de Panoayan. Around the age of eight, she was sent by her mother to live with relatives in the capital. There she studied Latin with a tutor, and was able to learn that language in a mere twenty lessons.

Her unusual intelligence and aptitude for poetry came to be noticed by the viceroy himself, the Marquis of Mancera, and his wife. They soon invited Juana to their court, where she won everyone's admiration not only for her wit and beauty, but also for her literary talents. At one point, as a peculiar sort of "graduation exercise," as well as a recognition of her unusual achievements, the viceroy organized a public oral examination of Juana by forty scholarly specialists, which she passed with flying colors. No doubt the young Juana, although a personal friend of the Manceras, also functioned at court as something of an entertainment; she was, after all, a great oddity in seventeenth-century Hispanic society: a female intellectual. At the request of her sponsors, but also following her own literary inclinations, she wrote abundant poetry, as well as theatre pieces.

In 1667, however, she left behind the splendor of the viceregal court and, with the sponsorship of the Manceras, entered the aristocratic Carmelite convent of Mexico City. The following year, at the age of seventeen, perhaps finding the Carmelite order too rigorous, or perhaps irked by the snobbishness of the many Spanish-born ladies cloistered in that particular convent, Juana Ramírez entered the convent of St. Jerome, and took the religious name of Sor Juana Inés de la Cruz. She would remain a Jeronymite nun until her death. Scholars (and Sor Juana herself) have proposed a variety of reasons for her choice of the convent life, but they essentially center on the fact that only life as a nun would allow her to pursue her studies relatively unmolested. For her, as she declares in her Respuesta, *marriage was out of the question, and she could not remain in the viceroyal court after reaching a marriageable age. On the other hand, cloistered convents in seventeenth-century New Spain were for the most part places where women could enjoy together a certain measure of freedom from the conventions of the outside world. Well-to-do nuns (such as Sor Juana) had comfortable living quarters with libraries, and they even owned slaves. Screened parlors allowed nuns to converse with visitors without being seen by them. Sor Juana was thus able to continue reading and writing, and to receive visits by some of the most distinguished Mexican intellectuals of the time.*

She also continued to fulfill requests by the viceregal court, the cathedral, and the city hall for verses and prose writings to be used in pageants and festivities. After the Manceras returned to Spain (viceroys were periodically recalled to the home country), Sor Juana enjoyed the friendship of their successors, the marquis of La Laguna and his wife the countess of Paredes, to whom she dedicated a large number of poems. It was the countess of Paredes who, on her return to Madrid, sponsored the publication of the first edition of Sor Juana's collected works, Inundación castálida (The Muses' Flood, *1689).*

As Sor Juana's international renown grew, so did her conflicts with various church authorities, who began to pressure her to abandon her studies and writing. She persevered, however. In poems such as her famous satire that begins: "Hombres necios que acusáis . . ." ("Misguided men, who will chastise . . .") and in plays such as Los empeños de una casa (The Trials of a Noble House), *she vindicated her sex and denounced some of the injustices committed against women. In 1692 she composed what is undoubtedly her masterwork, a lengthy philosophical poem in the complex Baroque style of Luis de Góngora and Pedro Calderón de la Barca (Selection 23), titled* El sueño (The Dream), *in which she implicitly challenges the notion that only men could engage in scientific or philosophical pursuits.*

But, as a person, Sor Juana was not wholly an anachronism in the seventeenth century; she also belonged to her age, and shared many of its prejudices and attitudes. Like many Baroque writers, she was prone to feelings of profound disillusionment and uncertainty. A few years before her death from the plague in 1695, she discarded all her books and scientific instruments, did penance, and renewed her religious vows, signing them literally in her own blood.

The selections that follow are but a small sample of Sor Juana's abundant poetry: they include the previously mentioned satirical quatrains beginning "Misguided men, who will chastise . . . ," and four sonnets. They are among the best-known and most beloved poems for readers in the Hispanic world. Characterized by Baroque wordplay and brilliant displays of irony and wit, these poems, particularly the sonnets, also hint at deep emotions beneath their elegant surfaces.

A PHILOSOPHICAL SATIRE

She Proves the Inconsistency of the Caprice and Criticism of Men Who Accuse Women of What They Cause

Misguided men, who will chastise
a woman when no blame is due,
oblivious that it is you
who prompted what you criticize;
    if your passions are so strong
that you elicit their disdain,
how can you wish that they refrain
when you incite them to their wrong?
    You strive to topple their defense,
and then, with utmost gravity,
you credit sensuality
for what was won with diligence.
    Your daring must be qualified,
your sense is no less senseless than

From *Poems, Protest, and a Dream* by Sor Juana Inés de la Cruz. Translated by Margaret Sayers Peden, 1997. Pp. 149, 151, 169, 171, 181, 183. Reprinted by permission of Bilingual Press/Editorial Bilingüe, Arizona State University, Tempe.

the child who calls the boogeyman,
then weeps when he is terrified.
    Your mad presumption knows no bounds,
though for a wife you want Lucrece,[1]
in lovers you prefer Thaïs,[2]
thus seeking blessings to compound.

    If knowingly one clouds a mirror
—was ever humor so absurd
or good counsel so obscured?—
can he lament that it's not clearer?

    From either favor or disdain
the selfsame purpose you achieve,
if they love, they are deceived,
if they love not, hear you complain.

    There is no woman suits your taste,
though circumspection be her virtue:
ungrateful, she who does not love you,
yet she who does, you judge unchaste.

    You men are such a foolish breed,
appraising with a faulty rule,
the first you charge with being cruel,
the second, easy, you decree.

    So how can she be temperate,
the one who would her love expend?
if not willing, she offends,
but willing, she infuriates.

    Amid the anger and torment
your whimsy causes you to bear,
one may be found who does not care:
how quickly then is grievance vent.

    So lovingly you inflict pain
that inhibitions fly away;
how, after leading them astray,
can you wish them without stain?

    Who does the greater guilt incur
when a passion is misleading?
She who errs and heeds his pleading,

---

[1] Lucrece (or Lucretia) was the wife of the ancient Etruscan patrician Tarquin. Her suicide after having been raped by the son of the King of Rome became a symbol of honor; it drove her husband to lead the rebellion that finally overthrew the Roman monarchy (c. 509 B.C.).

[2] Thaïs was a famous Greek courtesan of the fourth century B.C. She was the lover of Alexander the Great.

or he who pleads with her to err?
    Whose is the greater guilt therein
when either's conduct may dismay:
she who sins and takes the pay,
or he who pays her for the sin?
    Why, for sins you're guilty of,
do you, amazed, your blame debate?
Either love what you create
or else create what you can love.
    Were not it better to forbear,
and thus, with finer motivation,
obtain the unforced admiration
of her you plotted to ensnare?
    But no, I deem you still will revel
in your arms and arrogance,
and in promise and persistence
adjoin flesh and world and devil.

She Attempts to Minimize the Praise Occasioned by a Portrait of Herself Inscribed by Truth — Which She Calls Ardor

    This that you gaze on, colorful deceit,
that so immodestly displays art's favors,
with its fallacious arguments of colors
is to the senses cunning counterfeit,
    this on which kindness practiced to delete
from cruel years accumulated horrors,
constraining time to mitigate its rigors,
and thus oblivion and age defeat,
    is but an artifice, a sop to vanity,
is but a flower by the breezes bowed,
is but a ploy to counter destiny,
    is but a foolish labor, ill-employed,
is but a fancy, and, as all may see,
is but cadaver, ashes, shadow, void.

She Laments Her Fortune, She Hints of Her Aversion to All Vice, and Justifies Her Diversion with the Muses

    In my pursuit, World, why such diligence?
What my offense, when I am thus inclined,
insuring elegance affect my mind,
not that my mind affect an elegance?
    I have no love of riches or finánce,

and thus do I most happily, I find,
expend finances to enrich my mind
and not mind expend upon finánce.

    I worship beauty not, but vilify
that spoil of time that mocks eternity,
nor less, deceitful treasures glorify,

    but hold foremost, with greatest constancy,
consuming all the vanity in life,
and not consuming life in vanity.

She Answers Suspicions In the Rhetoric of Tears

    My love, this evening when I spoke with you,
and in your face and actions I could read
that arguments of words you would not heed,
my heart I longed to open to your view.

    In this intention, Love my wishes knew
and, though they seemed impossible, achieved:
pouring in tears that sorrow had conceived,
with every beat my heart dissolved anew.

    Enough of suffering, my love, enough:
let jealousy's vile tyranny be banned,
let no suspicious thought your calm corrupt

    with foolish gloom by futile doubt enhanced,
for now, this afternoon, you saw and touched
my heart, dissolved and liquid in your hands.

Which Recounts How Fantasy Contents Itself with Honorable Love

    Stay, shadow of contentment too short-lived,
illusion of enchantment I most prize,
fair image for whom happily I die,
sweet fiction for whom painfully I live.

    If answering your charms' imperative,
compliant, I like steel to magnet fly,
by what logic do you flatter and entice,
only to flee, a taunting fugitive?

    'Tis no triumph that you so smugly boast
that I fell victim to your tyranny;
though from encircling bonds that held you fast

    your elusive form too readily slipped free,
and though to my arms you are forever lost,
you are a prisoner in my fantasy.

30

꒰

Voltaire

CANDIDE

*I*n 1759 a book appeared that created a publishing sensation throughout Europe, reprinted some forty times in its first year alone. Its full title was Candide or Optimism, Translated from the German of Doctor Ralph with the Additions found in the Doctor's Pocket When he Died at Minden in the Year of our Lord 1759. *Of course, everyone in intellectual and literary circles knew that "Doctor Ralph" was really the* nom de plume *of Voltaire, the most influential satirist of his age, who typically protected himself by denying or disguising the authorship of his many dangerous writings.* Candide *was soon translated into several European languages and proved to be one of those widely read tales, masquerading as entertainment, that illustrated the irrationality of the contemporary structures of secular and ecclesiastical authority and helped to create an intellectual climate that would, in 1789, bring down the powerful French monarchy and send revolutionary tremors throughout the world.*

François-Marie Arouet (1694–1778), better known by his pen name of Voltaire, was probably the most famous figure of the eighteenth-century European Enlightenment. Born the son of a middle-class Parisian lawyer, during his long life he flooded Europe with works of history, philosophy, drama, poetry, fiction, and biography. All of Voltaire's works, in one way or another, reflect his belief in science, reason, and freedom; they also reflect his hatred of superstition, intolerance, and the privilege of power as the sources of most of the evil in society. Often, in an impatient reaction to the Catholic Church's reaction to his writings, he broadened his habitual criticism of established institutions into a general hostility toward organized religion. Although he started as a law student, as a young man he turned toward the writing of satire as a more effective entry into aristocratic Parisian society. However, as the result of several periods of imprisonment and exile, he came to realize the irrational unfairness of French society and his permanent position as an outsider to the people of inherited power. Voltaire, thus, turned from an opportunistic society wit into a crusader against what he saw as

*the accumulated rubbish that filled people's minds and prevented them from liv-
ing a happier, more reasonable and productive existence. Unwelcome in France,
Voltaire eventually bought homes in Geneva and Ferney, a village on French soil
but prudently near the Swiss border. His great estate at Ferney became a major
stop for young men taking the grand tour of Europe and eager to hear the new
ideas of the Enlightenment, exalting the rule of reason, from their most famous
exponent. With such works as his* Treatise on Tolerance *and the* Philosophical
Dictionary, *Voltaire illustrated his motto of "Écrasez l'infâme!" ("Wipe out the
infamy!"). Increasingly, for Voltaire, the infamy became identified with the per-
secuting power of organized religion, as well as many of the other traditional societal institutions; he vigorously (and with great publicity) defended Protestants
in Catholic countries and Catholics in Protestant countries.*

*By the last year of his life, Voltaire, now generally regarded as the grand pa-
triarch of Ferney, was welcomed back into Paris to the great acclaim of both commoners and at least the more intellectual aristocrats. He saw the successful opening of his new play, addressed the French Academy, even met Benjamin Franklin;
but the constant activity was too stressful for his aging heart, and he died in Paris.
Refused Christian burial by the Archbishop of Paris, Voltaire's body was disguised
and secretly transported out of the city to the grounds of an abbey in Troyes, not
far from Paris. (His beloved Ferney, where he had wished to be buried, was too
distant for safe transportation.) After the Revolution, however, the remains of
Voltaire were exhumed and brought in great ceremony to the Pantheon in Paris,
the resting place of French national heroes.*

*Voltaire was not, as many labeled him, an atheist, but rather a deist, a be-
liever in the religion of reason and a rational god, free of "superstitious" obser-
vances, self-interested priests, and false traditions. He believed in a natural
morality, based on reason, which all humanity, beneath the surface differences,
ultimately shares. To make that natural morality operative would be to create a
world in which persecutions would cease and all men would work harmoniously,
"cultivating their gardens" without the conflicts created by irrational institutions.
Above all, Voltaire was a humanist who wished to better the human condition
and improve nature's usefulness through the use of reason.*

Written when its author was sixty-five years old, Candide *is still the most
widely read of all Voltaire's works. It is even the basis for a very successful Broad-
way musical comedy. Like the* Adventures of Huckleberry Finn *in American literature,* Candide *tells of a young innocent learning about the wickedness of the
world. The hero's adventures, concurrently comical and horrifying, ultimately
show him to be a man of good sense, who has learned to apply his own power of
reason to the problems of daily living. In its literary form* Candide *is a parody of
the popular romances of the day with their characters constantly surviving cata-
strophic occurrences, only to be reunited again and again in absurd recognition
scenes. The characters and events not only entertain but also function as symbols
of ideas and institutions, which are subjected to withering satire. One such idea,
mentioned in the tale's full title, is the doctrine of philosophical optimism. It is at*

the center of Voltaire's satire and is represented in the tale by the character of Doctor Pangloss. A fashionable philosophy of the time, optimism was developed by the German philosopher Leibnitz with his "pre-established harmony" and popularized by the English poet Alexander Pope in his Essay on Man *(1733) who wrote that "All Nature is but Art, unknown to thee; / All Chance, Direction, which thou canst not see; / All Discord, Harmony not understood; / All partial Evil, universal Good; / and, spite of Pride, in erring Reason's spite, / One truth is clear, WHATEVER IS, IS RIGHT." Voltaire found such optimism to be absurd and ultimately a philosophy of despair, for it tended to accept the suffering that clearly existed as necessary in "this best of all possible worlds." As a practical reformer, Voltaire believed that much human suffering was avoidable, especially that caused by ignorance and by ideological dogmatism. At the tale's conclusion Candide speaks for Voltaire when he concludes that the world is mad and that people should direct their labors toward tasks that are within their power to accomplish and that sustain and improve their lives.*

CHAPTER I

How Candide was Brought Up in a Noble Castle and How He was Expelled From the Same

In the castle of Baron Thunder-ten-tronckh in Westphalia[1] there lived a youth, endowed by Nature with the most gentle character. His face was the expression of his soul. His judgment was quite honest and he was extremely simple-minded; and this was the reason, I think, that he was named Candide.[2] Old servants in the house suspected that he was the son of the Baron's sister and a decent honest gentleman of the neighborhood, whom this young lady would never marry because he could only prove seventy-one quarterings,[3] and the rest of his genealogical tree was lost, owing to the injuries of time.

From Voltaire, *Candide and other Romances,* trans. Richard Aldington. London: George Routledge and Sons Ltd, New York: E. P. Dutton & Co., 1927. Chapters I–XII, XXIX–XXX.

[1] Westphalia is a region of Germany just east of Holland. In 1750, when Voltaire passed through it on his way to the court of Frederick the Great in Berlin, he was shocked by Westphalia's poverty.

[2] In French, an adjective meaning "open, frank, candid, sincere."

[3] Voltaire enjoyed mocking pride of ancestry. Since each quartering represents one generation, seventy-one quarterings would have made the family older than Christianity. Actually, sixty-four quarterings were considered the maximum possible.

The Baron was one of the most powerful lords in Westphalia, for his castle possessed a door and windows. His Great Hall was even decorated with a piece of tapestry. The dogs in his stable-yards formed a pack of hounds when necessary; his grooms were his huntsmen; the village curate was his Grand Almoner. They all called him "My Lord," and laughed heartily at his stories.

The Baroness weighed about three hundred and fifty pounds, was therefore greatly respected, and did the honors of the house with a dignity which rendered her still more respectable. Her daughter Cunegonde, aged seventeen, was rosy-cheeked, fresh, plump and tempting. The Baron's son appeared in every respect worthy of his father. The tutor Pangloss[4] was the oracle of the house, and little Candide followed his lessons with all the candor of his age and character.

Pangloss taught metaphysico-theologo-cosmolonigology.[5] He proved admirably that there is no effect without a cause and that in this best of all possible worlds,[6] My Lord the Baron's castle was the best of castles and his wife the best of all possible Baronesses.

"'Tis demonstrated," said he, "that things cannot be otherwise; for, since everything is made for an end, everything is necessarily for the best end. Observe that noses were made to wear spectacles; and so we have spectacles. Legs were visibly instituted to be breeched, and we have breeches.[7] Stones were formed to be quarried and to build castles; and My Lord has a very noble castle; the greatest Baron in the province should have the best house; and as pigs were made to be eaten, we eat pork all the year round; consequently, those who have asserted that all is well talk nonsense; they ought to have said that all is for the best."

Candide listened attentively and believed innocently; for he thought Mademoiselle Cunegonde extremely beautiful, although he was never bold enough to tell her so. He decided that after the happiness of being born Baron of Thunder-ten-tronckh, the second degree of happiness was to be Mademoiselle Cunegonde; the third, to see her every day; and the fourth to listen to Doctor Pangloss, the greatest philosopher of the province and therefore of the whole world.

One day when Cunegonde was walking near the castle, in a little wood which was called The Park, she observed Doctor Pangloss in the bushes, giving a lesson in experimental physics to her mother's waiting maid, a very pretty and docile brunette. Mademoiselle Cunegonde had a great inclination for science and

---

[4] In Greek: "all tongue."

[5] The suggestion here is that "all tongue" is teaching abstract nonsense, words with no relationship to reality.

[6] Throughout *Candide* Voltaire ridicules the philosophy of optimism, which states that all things are necessarily for the best. Pangloss's optimism is a caricature of the position of the German philosopher Leibnitz (1646–1716), popularized by the English poet Alexander Pope in his *Essay on Man* (1733).

[7] Comical examples of what Pangloss, in his dogmatic optimism, intends as serious proofs of philosophical final causes, that is, the ends or purposes for which things are made.

watched breathlessly the reiterated experiments she witnessed; she observed clearly the Doctor's sufficient reason, the effects and the causes, and returned home very much excited, pensive, filled with the desire of learning, reflecting that she might be the sufficient reason of young Candide and that he might be hers.

On her way back to the castle she met Candide and blushed; Candide also blushed. She bade him good-morning in a hesitating voice; Candide replied without knowing what he was saying. Next day, when they left the table after dinner, Cunegonde and Candide found themselves behind a screen; Cunegonde dropped her handkerchief, Candide picked it up; she innocently held his hand; the young man innocently kissed the young lady's hand with remarkable vivacity, tenderness and grace; their lips met, their eyes sparkled, their knees trembled, their hands wandered. Baron Thunder-ten-tronckh passed near the screen, and, observing this cause and effect, expelled Candide from the castle by kicking him in the backside frequently and hard. Cunegonde swooned; when she recovered her senses, the Baroness slapped her in the face; and all was in consternation in the noblest and most agreeable of all possible castles.

CHAPTER II

What Happened to Candide Among the Bulgarians[8]

Candide, expelled from the earthly paradise, wandered for a long time without knowing where he was going, weeping, turning up his eyes to Heaven, gazing back frequently at the noblest of castles which held the most beautiful of young Baronesses; he lay down to sleep supperless between two furrows in the open fields; it snowed heavily in large flakes. The next morning the shivering Candide, penniless, dying of cold and exhaustion, dragged himself towards the neighboring town, which was called Waldberghoff-trarbk-dikdorff.[9] He halted sadly at the door of an inn. Two men dressed in blue noticed him.

"Comrade," said one, "there's a well-built young man of the right height."[10] They went up to Candide and very civilly invited him to dinner.

---

[8] In an intentionally insulting personal reference Voltaire represented the Prussians of his time, ruled by Frederick II ("the Great"), as "Bulgarians." Voltaire wished to insinuate that Frederick was a pederast: the French *bougre*, like the English "bugger," comes from *Bulgare* (Bulgarian). Note, for example, the victimizing of the Baron's son by Bulgarian soldiers in Chapter 4.

[9] An example of how Voltaire liked to caricature what he regarded as the harsh dissonance of German names.

[10] Frederick the Great's recruiting officers, dressed in blue uniforms, were much feared in eighteenth-century Europe. Frederick had a passion for sorting out his regiments by the height of his soldiers. It was a common practice for all sides throughout Europe to "press" young men into military service in a fashion not very different from what the unfortunate Candide endures.

"Gentlemen," said Candide with charming modesty, "you do me a great honor, but I have no money to pay my share."

"Ah, sir," said one of the men in blue, "persons of your figure and merit never pay anything; are you not five feet five tall?"

"Yes, gentlemen," said he, bowing, "that is my height."

"Ah, sir, come to table; we will not only pay your expenses, we will never allow a man like you to be short of money; men were only made to help each other."

"You are in the right," said Candide, "that is what Doctor Pangloss was always telling me, and I see that everything is for the best."

They begged him to accept a few crowns, he took them and wished to give them an I O U; they refused to take it and all sat down to table. "Do you not love tenderly . . ."

"Oh, yes," said he. "I love Mademoiselle Cunegonde tenderly."

"No," said one of the gentlemen. "We were asking if you do not tenderly love the King of the Bulgarians."

"Not a bit," said he, "for I have never seen him."

"What! He is the most charming of Kings, and you must drink his health."

"Oh, gladly, gentlemen." And he drank.

"That is sufficient," he was told. "You are now the support, the aid, the defender, the hero of the Bulgarians; your fortune is made and your glory assured."

They immediately put irons on his legs and took him to a regiment. He was made to turn to the right and left, to raise the ramrod and return the ramrod, to take aim, to fire, to double time, and he was given thirty strokes with a stick; the next day he drilled not quite so badly, and received only twenty strokes; the day after, he only had ten, and was looked on as a prodigy by his comrades.

Candide was completely mystified and could not make out how he was a hero. One fine spring day he thought he would take a walk, going straight ahead, in the belief that to use his legs as he pleased was a privilege of the human species as well as of animals. He had not gone two leagues when four other heroes, each six feet tall, fell upon him, bound him and dragged him back to a cell. He was asked by his judges whether he would rather be thrashed thirty-six times by the whole regiment or receive a dozen lead bullets at once in his brain.[11] Although he protested that men's wills are free and that he wanted neither one nor the other, he had to make a choice; by virtue of that gift of God which is called *liberty*, he determined to run the gauntlet thirty-six times and actually did so twice. There were two thousand men in the regiment. That made four thousand strokes which laid bare the muscles and nerves from his neck to his backside. As they were about to proceed to a third turn, Candide, utterly exhausted, begged as a favor that

---

[11] This episode was suggested by the experience of a Frenchman who had deserted from the Prussian Army and been severely beaten for it. Voltaire intervened with Frederick to gain the man's release into a hospital.

they would be so kind as to smash his head; he obtained this favor; they bound his eyes and he was made to kneel down. At that moment the King of Bulgarians came by and inquired the victim's crime; and as this King was possessed of a vast genius, he perceived from what he learned about Candide that he was a young metaphysician very ignorant in worldly matters, and therefore pardoned him with a clemency which will be praised in all newspapers and all ages. An honest surgeon healed Candide in three weeks with the ointments recommended by Dioscorides.[12] He had already regained a little skin and could walk when the King of the Bulgarians went to war with the King of the Abares.[13]

CHAPTER III

How Candide Escaped From the Bulgarians and What Became of Him

Nothing could be smarter, more splendid, more brilliant, better drawn up than the two armies. Trumpets, fifes, oboes, drums, cannons, formed a harmony such as has never been heard even in hell. The cannons first of all laid flat about six thousand men on each side; then the musketry removed from the best of worlds some nine or ten thousand blackguards who infested its surface. The bayonet also was the sufficient reason for the death of some thousands of men. The whole might amount to thirty thousand souls. Candide, who trembled like a philosopher, hid himself as well as he could during this heroic butchery.

At last, while the two Kings each commanded a *Te Deum*[14] in his camp, Candide decided to go elsewhere to reason about effects and causes. He clambered over heaps of dead and dying men and reached a neighboring village, which was in ashes; it was an Abare village which the Bulgarians had burned in accordance with international law. Here, old men dazed with blows watched the dying agonies of their murdered wives who clutched their children to their bleeding breasts; there, disembowelled girls who had been made to satisfy the natural appetites of heroes gasped their last sighs; others, half-burned, begged to be put to death. Brains were scattered on the ground among dismembered arms and legs.

Candide fled to another village as fast as he could; it belonged to the Bulgarians, and Abarian heroes had treated it in the same way. Candide, stumbling over quivering limbs or across ruins, at last escaped from the theatre of war, carrying a little food in his knapsack, and never forgetting Mademoiselle Cunegonde. His

---

[12] A famous ancient Greek physician who wrote a pharmacy text riddled with errors that, nevertheless, became the standard for many centuries.

[13] In Voltaire's allegorical satire the Abares are actually the French, who sided with the Austrians against the Prussians in the conflict later known as the Seven Years War (1756–1763).

[14] *Te Deum laudamus* ("We praise thee, O God"), a Latin hymn of thanks to God for victory.

provisions were all gone when he reached Holland; but, having heard that everyone in that country was rich and a Christian, he had no doubt at all but that he would be as well treated as he had been in the Baron's castle before he had been expelled on account of Mademoiselle Cunegonde's pretty eyes.

He asked an alms of several grave persons, who all replied that if he continued in that way he would be shut up in a house of correction to teach him how to live. He then addressed himself to a man who had been discoursing on charity in a large assembly for an hour on end. This orator, glancing at him askance, said: "What are you doing here? Are you for the good cause?"

"There is no effect without a cause," said Candide modestly. "Everything is necessarily linked up and arranged for the best. It was necessary that I should be expelled from the company of Mademoiselle Cunegonde, that I ran the gauntlet, and that I beg my bread until I can earn it; all this could not have happened differently."

"My friend," said the orator, "do you believe that the Pope is Anti-Christ?"[15]

"I had never heard so before," said Candide, "but whether he is or isn't, I am starving."

"You don't deserve to eat," said the other. "Hence, rascal; hence, you wretch; and never come near me again."

The orator's wife thrust her head out of the window and seeing a man who did not believe that the Pope was Anti-Christ, she poured on his head a full . . . O Heavens! To what excess religious zeal is carried by ladies!

A man who had not been baptized, an honest Anabaptist[16] named Jacques, saw the cruel and ignominious treatment of one of his brothers, a featherless two-legged creature with a soul;[17] he took him home, cleaned him up, gave him bread and beer, presented him with two florins, and even offered to teach him to work at the manufacture of Persian rugs which are made in Holland. Candide threw himself at the man's feet, exclaiming: "Doctor Pangloss was right in telling me that all is for the best in this world, for I am vastly more touched by your extreme generosity than by the harshness of the gentleman in the black cloak and his good lady."

The next day when he walked out he met a beggar covered with sores, dull-eyed, with the end of his nose fallen away, his mouth awry, his teeth black, who talked huskily, was tormented with a violent cough and spat out a tooth at every cough.

---

[15] Voltaire here mocks those Protestant zealots whose entire creed consisted of the belief that every pope was really the Antichrist. In this episode the orator's anti-Catholicism becomes his excuse for not practicing charity.

[16] A religious group, barely tolerated in Protestant Holland, that refused military service and believed in adult baptism and strict church-state separation.

[17] An allusion to Plato's famous minimal definition of a human. The point is that the "heretical" Anabaptist sympathizes with the plight of Candide simply because he is human.

CHAPTER IV

How Candide Met His Old Master in Philosophy, Doctor Pangloss, and What Happened

Candide, moved even more by compassion than by horror, gave this horrible beggar the two florins he had received from the honest Anabaptist, Jacques. The phantom gazed fixedly at him, shed tears and threw its arms round his neck. Candide recoiled in terror.

"Alas!" said the wretch to the other wretch, "don't you recognize your dear Pangloss?"

"What do I hear? You, my dear master! You, in this horrible state! What misfortune has happened to you? Why are you no longer in the noblest of castles? What has become of Mademoiselle Cunegonde, the pearl of young ladies, the masterpiece of Nature?"

"I am exhausted," said Pangloss. Candide immediately took him to the Anabaptist's stable where he gave him a little bread to eat; and when Pangloss had recovered: "Well!" said he, "Cunegonde?"

"Dead," replied the other.

At this word Candide swooned; his friend restored him to his senses with a little bad vinegar which happened to be in the stable. Candide opened his eyes. "Cunegonde dead! Ah! best of worlds, where are you? But what illness did she die of? Was it because she saw me kicked out of her father's noble castle?"

"No," said Pangloss. "She was disembowelled by Bulgarian soldiers, after having been raped to the limit of possibility; they broke the Baron's head when he tried to defend her; the Baroness was cut to pieces; my poor pupil was treated exactly like his sister; and as to the castle, there is not one stone standing on another, not a barn, not a sheep, not a duck, not a tree; but we were well avenged, for the Abares did exactly the same to a neighboring barony which belonged to a Bulgarian Lord." At this, Candide swooned again; but, having recovered and having said all that he ought to say, he inquired the cause and effect, the sufficient reason which had reduced Pangloss to so piteous a state.

"Alas!" said Pangloss, "'tis love; love, the consoler of the human race, the preserver of the universe, the soul of all tender creatures, gentle love."

"Alas!" said Candide, "I am acquainted with this love, this sovereign of hearts, this soul of our soul; it has never brought me anything but one kiss and twenty kicks in the backside. How could this beautiful cause produce in you so abominable an effect?"

Pangloss replied as follows: "My dear Candide! You remember Paquette, the maidservant of our august Baroness; in her arms I enjoyed the delights of Paradise which have produced the tortures of Hell by which you see I am devoured; she was infected and perhaps is dead. Paquette received this present from a most learned monk, who had it from the source; for he received it from an old countess, who had it from a cavalry captain, who owed it to a marchioness, who derived it from a page, who had received it from a Jesuit, who, when a novice, had it in a direct line from one of the companions of Christopher Columbus.[18] For my part, I shall not give it to anyone, for I am dying."

"O Pangloss!" exclaimed Candide, "this is a strange genealogy! Wasn't the devil at the root of it?"

"Not at all," replied that great man. "It was something indispensable in this best of worlds, a necessary ingredient; for, if Columbus in an island of America had not caught this disease, which poisons the source of generation, and often indeed prevents generation, we should not have chocolate and cochineal;[19] it must also be noticed that hitherto in our continent this disease is peculiar to us, like theological disputes. The Turks, the Indians, the Persians, the Chinese, the Siamese and the Japanese are not yet familiar with it; but there is a sufficient reason why they in their turn should become familiar with it in a few centuries. Meanwhile, it has made marvelous progress among us, and especially in those large armies composed of honest, well-bred mercenaries who decide the destiny of States; it may be asserted that when thirty thousand men fight a pitched battle against an equal number of troops, there are about twenty thousand with the pox[20] on either side."

"Admirable!" said Candide. "But you must get cured."

"How can I?" said Pangloss. "I haven't a sou, my friend, and in the whole extent of this globe, you cannot be bled or receive an enema without paying or without someone paying for you."

This last speech determined Candide; he went and threw himself at the feet of his charitable Anabaptist, Jacques, and drew so touching a picture of the state to which his friend was reduced that the good easy man did not hesitate to succor Pangloss; he had him cured at his own expense. In this cure Pangloss only lost one eye and one ear. He could write well and knew arithmetic perfectly. The Anabaptist made him his bookkeeper. At the end of two months he was compelled to go to Lisbon[21] on business and took his two philosophers on the boat with him. Pangloss explained to him how everything was for the best. Jacques was not of this opinion.

"Men," said he, "must have corrupted nature a little, for they were not born wolves, and they have become wolves. God did not give them twenty-four-pounder cannons or bayonets, and they have made bayonets and cannons to destroy each other. I might bring bankruptcies into the account and Justice which seizes the goods of bankrupts in order to deprive the creditors of them."[22]

---

[18] According to the medical authorities of Voltaire's time, along with the various goods and slaves that Columbus and his crew carried back from the New World, they also carried the syphilitic infection that soon spread rapidly throughout Europe.

[19] A red dye originating in Central and South America, highly valued in Europe.

[20] A common term for syphilis—which was also known as "the French disease" and "the Spanish disorder."

[21] The capital city and major port of Portugal.

"It was all indispensable," replied the one-eyed doctor, "and private misfortunes make the public good, so that the more private misfortunes there are, the more everything is well."[23]

While he was reasoning, the air grew dark, the winds blew from the four quarters of the globe and the ship was attacked by the most horrible tempest in sight of the port of Lisbon.

CHAPTER V

Storm, Shipwreck, Earthquake, and What Happened to Dr. Pangloss, to Candide and the Anabaptist Jacques

Half the enfeebled passengers, suffering from that inconceivable anguish which the rolling of a ship causes in the nerves and in all the humors of bodies shaken in contrary directions,[24] did not retain strength enough even to trouble about the danger. The other half screamed and prayed; the sails were torn, the masts broken, the vessel leaking. Those worked who could, no one cooperated, no one commanded. The Anabaptist tried to help the crew a little; he was on the main deck; a furious sailor struck him violently and stretched him on the deck; but the blow he delivered gave him so violent a shock that he fell head-first out of the ship. He remained hanging and clinging to part of the broken mast. The good Jacques ran to his aid, helped him to climb back, and from the effort he made was flung into the sea in full view of the sailor, who allowed him to drown without condescending even to look at him. Candide came up, saw his benefactor reappear for a moment and then be engulfed for ever. He tried to throw himself after him into the sea; he was prevented by the philosopher Pangloss, who proved to him that the Lisbon roads had been expressly created for the Anabaptist to be drowned in them.[25] While he was proving this *a priori*,[26] the vessel sank, and every one perished except Pangloss, Candide and the brutal sailor who had drowned the virtuous Anabaptist; the blackguard swam successfully to the shore and Pangloss and Candide were carried there on a plank.

---

[22] Voltaire had suffered financial losses due to the bankruptcies of others, so his satire here has a bitter personal edge.

[23] A further step in Voltaire's reduction of Pangloss's philosophical optimism to total absurdity.

[24] The bodily "humors," according to the medical theories of that time, were the four fluids—blood, phlegm, black bile, and yellow bile—that determined a person's temperament and general health.

[25] "Roads," used here as part of another mocking reference to Pangloss's philosophy, are a sheltered area of water in which ships may ride at anchor.

[26] Reasoning from preestablished principles, rather than from experience.

When they had recovered a little, they walked toward Lisbon; they had a little money by the help of which they hoped to be saved from hunger after having escaped the storm. Weeping the death of their benefactor, they had scarcely set foot in the town when they felt the earth tremble under their feet; the sea rose in foaming masses in the port and smashed the ships which rode at anchor. Whirlwinds of flame and ashes covered the streets and squares; the houses collapsed, the roofs were thrown upon the foundations, and the foundations were scattered; thirty thousand inhabitants of every age and both sexes were crushed under the ruins.[27] Whistling and swearing, the sailor said: "There'll be something to pick up here."

"What can be the sufficient reason for this phenomenon?" said Pangloss.

"It is the last day!" cried Candide.

The sailor immediately ran among the debris, dared death to find money, found it, seized it, got drunk, and having slept off his wine, purchased the favors of the first woman of good will he met on the ruins of the houses and among the dead and dying. Pangloss, however, pulled him by the sleeve. "My friend," said he, "this is not well, you are disregarding universal reason, you choose the wrong time."

"Blood and 'ounds!" he retorted, "I am a sailor and I was born in Batavia;[28] four times have I stamped on the crucifix during four voyages to Japan;[29] you have found the right man for your universal reason!"

Candide had been hurt by some falling stones; he lay in the street covered with debris. He said to Pangloss: "Alas! Get me a little wine and oil; I am dying."

"This earthquake is not a new thing," replied Pangloss. "The town of Lima felt the same shocks in America last year; similar causes produce similar effects; there must certainly be a train of sulphur underground from Lima to Lisbon."

"Nothing is more probable," replied Candide; "but, for God's sake, a little oil and wine."

"What do you mean, probable?" replied the philosopher; "I maintain that it is proved."

Candide lost consciousness, and Pangloss brought him a little water from a neighboring fountain.

Next day they found a little food as they wandered among the ruins and regained a little strength. Afterwards they worked like others to help the inhabitants who had escaped death. Some citizens they had assisted gave them as good

---

[27] The actual Lisbon earthquake and ensuing fire occurred on November 1, 1755. Its destructiveness, including the loss of over 30,000 lives, confirmed Voltaire in his rejection of philosophical optimism and motivated him to write immediately his poem on *The Lisbon Disaster. Candide* followed in 1759.

[28] A city in the former Dutch East Indies, now Jakarta, capital of Indonesia.

[29] Fearful of Catholic missionaries, the Japanese expelled the Spanish and Portuguese in the early seventeenth century. Only the Dutch traders were allowed to retain a small foothold in Japan under humiliating conditions (stamping on a crucifix) to ensure they were not proselytizing for Christianity.

a dinner as could be expected in such a disaster; true, it was a dreary meal; the hosts watered their bread with their tears, but Pangloss consoled them by assuring them that things could not be otherwise. "For," said he, "all this is for the best; for, if there is a volcano at Lisbon, it cannot be anywhere else; for it is impossible that things should not be where they are; for all is well."

A little, dark man, a familiar of the Inquisition,[30] who sat beside him, politely took up the conversation, and said: "Apparently, you do not believe in original sin; for, if everything is for the best, there was neither fall nor punishment."

"I most humbly beg your excellency's pardon," replied Pangloss still more politely, "for the fall of man and the curse necessarily entered into the best of all possible worlds."

"Then you do not believe in free will?" said the familiar.

"Your excellency will pardon me," said Pangloss; "free will can exist with absolute necessity; for it was necessary that we should be free; for in short, limited will . . ."

Pangloss was in the middle of his phrase when the familiar nodded to his armed attendant who was pouring out port or Oporto wine for him.

CHAPTER VI

How a Splendid Auto-da-fé Was Held to Prevent Earthquakes, and How Candide Was Flogged

After the earthquake which destroyed three-quarters of Lisbon, the wise men of that country could discover no more efficacious way of preventing a total ruin than by giving the people a splendid *auto-da-fé*.[31] It was decided by the university of Coimbre that the sight of several persons being slowly burned in great ceremony is an infallible secret for preventing earthquakes. Consequently they had arrested a Biscayan convicted of having married his fellow-godmother, and two Portuguese who, when eating a chicken, had thrown away the bacon;[32] after dinner they came and bound Dr. Pangloss and his disciple Candide, one because

---

[30] The Inquisition (the Congregation of the Holy Office) employed such "familiars" or undercover agents. A Roman Catholic tribunal, the Inquisition sought out heretics and punished them, often by burning at the stake. Most active in Spain, Portugal, and Italy, it lasted from the fifteenth to the early nineteenth century.

[31] Literally, "act of faith" in Portuguese: the term used by the Inquisition for the ceremony of burning convicted heretics at the stake. There was, in fact, such a ceremony in Lisbon following the 1755 earthquake.

[32] The Biscayan had married someone to whom he was somehow related, a form of spiritual incest (continuing Voltaire's ridicule of the Church's complex prohibitions). The men who threw away the bacon were convicted of being secret Jews or Muslims—followers of those religions having been long since expelled from Spain and Portugal.

he had spoken and the other because he had listened with an air of approbation; they were both carried separately to extremely cool apartments,[33] where there was never any discomfort from the sun; a week afterwards each was dressed in a sanbenito[34] and their heads were ornamented with paper mitres;[35] Candide's mitre and sanbenito were painted with flames upside down and with devils who had neither tails nor claws; but Pangloss's devils had claws and tails, and his flames were upright.[36]

Dressed in this manner they marched in procession and listened to a most pathetic sermon, followed by lovely plain song music. Candide was flogged in time to the music, while the singing went on; the Biscayan and the two men who had not wanted to eat the bacon were burned, and Pangloss was hanged, although this is not the custom. The very same day, the earth shook again with a terrible clamor.[37]

Candide, terrified, dumbfounded, bewildered, covered with blood, quivering from head to foot, said to himself: "If this is the best of all possible worlds, what are the others? Let it pass that I was flogged, for I was flogged by the Bulgarians, but, O my dear Pangloss! The greatest of philosophers! Must I see you hanged without knowing why! O my dear Anabaptist! The best of men! Was it necessary that you should be drowned in port! O Mademoiselle Cunegonde! The pearl of women! Was it necessary that your belly should be slit!"

He was returning, scarcely able to support himself, preached at, flogged, absolved and blessed, when an old woman accosted him and said: "Courage, my son, follow me."

CHAPTER VII

How an Old Woman Took Care of Candide and How He Regained That Which He Loved

Candide did not take courage, but he followed the old woman to a hovel; she gave him a pot of ointment to rub on, and left him food and drink; she pointed out a fairly clean bed; near the bed there was a suit of clothes. "Eat, drink, sleep," said she, "and may our Lady of Atocha, my Lord Saint Anthony of Padua and my Lord Saint James of Compostella take care of you; I shall come back tomorrow."

---

[33] That is, prison cells underground.

[34] A cape worn by those punished at the *auto-da-fé*. A yellow sanbenito decorated with flames pointed downward indicated that the heretic's life had been spared; a person to be burned wore a black sanbenito with flames pointing upward.

[35] A cone-shaped paper cap, resembling a bishop's miter.

[36] Candide, apparently, escaped death by confessing his crime; while Pangloss was condemned as a stubborn (optimistic) heretic.

[37] Lisbon actually suffered a second earthquake about seven weeks after the first. (The *auto-da-fé*, apparently, had not accomplished its purpose.)

Candide, still amazed by all he had seen, by all he had suffered, and still more by the old woman's charity, tried to kiss her hand. "'Tis not my hand you should kiss," said the old woman, "I shall come back tomorrow. Rub on the ointment, eat and sleep."

In spite of all his misfortune, Candide ate and went to sleep. Next day the old woman brought him breakfast, examined his back and smeared him with another ointment; later she brought him dinner, and returned in the evening with supper. The next day she went through the same ceremony.

"Who are you?" Candide kept asking her. "Who has inspired you with so much kindness? How can I thank you?"

The good woman never made any reply; she returned in the evening without any supper. "Come with me," said she, "and do not speak a word."

She took him by the arm and walked into the country with him for about a quarter of a mile; they came to an isolated house, surrounded with gardens and canals. The old woman knocked at a little door. It was opened; she led Candide up a back stairway into a gilded apartment, left him on a brocaded sofa, shut the door and went away. Candide thought he was dreaming, and felt that his whole life was a bad dream and the present moment an agreeable dream. The old woman soon reappeared; she was supporting with some difficulty a trembling woman of majestic stature, glittering with precious stones and covered with a veil.

"Remove the veil," said the old woman to Candide. The young man advanced and lifted the veil with a timid hand. What a moment! What a surprise! He thought he saw Mademoiselle Cunegonde, in fact he was looking at her, it was she herself. His strength failed him, he could not utter a word and fell at her feet. Cunegonde fell on the sofa. The old woman dosed them with distilled waters; they recovered their senses and began to speak: at first they uttered only broken words, questions and answers at cross purposes, sighs, tears, exclamations. The old woman advised them to make less noise and left them alone.

"What! Is it you?" said Candide. "You are alive, and I find you here in Portugal! Then you were not raped? Your belly was not slit, as the philosopher Pangloss assured me?"

"Yes, indeed," said the fair Cunegonde; "but those two accidents are not always fatal."

"But your father and mother were killed?"

"'Tis only too true," said Cunegonde, weeping.

"And your brother?"

"My brother was killed too."[38]

---

[38] As Candide will later discover, contrary to Cunegonde's belief, her brother also had recovered from his Bulgarian abuse and become commander of the Jesuit army in Paraguay. (Very few characters fail to survive in this satire of man's cruelty to man. Pangloss too will reappear in the plot's parody of the adventures in popular romances.)

"And why are you in Portugal? And how did you know I was here? And by what strange adventure have you brought me to this house?"

"I will tell you everything," replied the lady, "but first of all you must tell me everything that has happened to you since the innocent kiss you gave me and the kicks you received."

Candide obeyed with profound respect; and, although he was bewildered, although his voice was weak and trembling, although his back was still a little painful, he related in the most natural manner all he had endured since the moment of their separation. Cunegonde raised her eyes to heaven; she shed tears at the death of the good Anabaptist and Pangloss, after which she spoke as follows to Candide, who did not miss a word and devoured her with his eyes.

CHAPTER VIII
Cunegonde's Story

"I was fast asleep in bed when it pleased Heaven to send the Bulgarians to our noble castle of Thunder-ten-tronckh; they murdered my father and brother and cut my mother to pieces. A large Bulgarian six feet tall, seeing that I had swooned at the spectacle, began to rape me; this brought me to, I recovered my senses, I screamed, I struggled, I bit, I scratched, I tried to tear out the big Bulgarian's eyes, not knowing that what was happening in my father's castle was a matter of custom; the brute stabbed me with a knife in the left side where I still have a scar."

"Alas! I hope I shall see it," said the naive Candide.

"You shall see it," said Cunegonde, "but let me go on."

"Go on," said Candide.

She took up the thread of her story as follows: "A Bulgarian captain came in, saw me covered with blood, and the soldier did not disturb himself. The captain was angry at the brute's lack of respect to him, and killed him on my body. Afterwards, he had me bandaged and took me to his billet as a prisoner of war. I washed the few shirts he had and did the cooking; I must admit he thought me very pretty; and I will not deny that he was very well built and that his skin was white and soft; otherwise he had little wit and little philosophy; it was plain that he had not been brought up by Dr. Pangloss. At the end of three months he lost all his money and got tired of me; he sold me to a Jew named Don Issachar,[39] who traded in Holland and Portugal and had a passion for women. This Jew devoted himself to my person but he could not triumph over it; I resisted him better than the Bulgarian soldier; a lady of honor may be raped once, but it strengthens her virtue. In order to subdue me, the Jew brought me to this country house.

---

[39] Although Voltaire, a religious skeptic, deplored the long persecution of Jews in the Christian world, he was quick to blame his own bad investments on Jewish financiers—satirized here as Don Issachar. (In reality, a Jew could not have flourished in a country dominated by the Inquisition.)

Up till then I believed that there was nothing on earth so splendid as the castle of Thunder-ten-tronckh; I was undeceived.

"One day the Grand Inquisitor noticed me at Mass; he ogled me continually and sent a message that he wished to speak to me on secret affairs. I was taken to his palace; I informed him of my birth; he pointed out how much it was beneath my rank to belong to an Israelite. A proposition was made on his behalf to Don Issachar to give me up to His Lordship. Don Issachar, who is the court banker and a man of influence, would not agree. The Inquisitor threatened him with an *auto-da-fé*. At last the Jew was frightened and made a bargain whereby the house and I belong to both in common. The Jew has Mondays, Wednesdays and the Sabbath day, and the Inquisitor has the other days of the week. This arrangement has lasted for six months. It has not been without quarrels; for it has often been debated whether the night between Saturday and Sunday belonged to the old law or the new.[40] For my part, I have hitherto resisted them both; and I think that is the reason why they still love me.

"At last My Lord the Inquisitor was pleased to arrange an *auto-da-fé* to remove the scourge of earthquakes and to intimidate Don Issachar. He honored me with an invitation. I had an excellent seat; and refreshments were served to the ladies between the Mass and the execution. I was indeed horror stricken when I saw the burning of the two Jews and the honest Biscayan who had married his fellow-godmother; but what was my surprise, my terror, my anguish, when I saw in a sanbenito and under a mitre a face which resembled Pangloss's! I rubbed my eyes, I looked carefully, I saw him hanged; and I fainted. I had scarcely recovered my senses when I saw you stripped naked; that was the height of horror, of consternation, of grief and despair. I will frankly tell you that your skin is even whiter and of a more perfect tint than that of my Bulgarian captain. This spectacle redoubled all the feelings which crushed and devoured me. I exclaimed, I tried to say: 'Stop, Barbarians!' but my voice failed and my cries would have been useless. When you had been well flogged, I said to myself: 'How does it happen that the charming Candide and the wise Pangloss are in Lisbon, the one to receive a hundred lashes, and the other to be hanged, by order of My Lord the Inquisitor, whose darling I am? Pangloss deceived me cruelly when he said that all is for the best in the world.'

"I was agitated, distracted, sometimes beside myself and sometimes ready to die of faintness, and my head was filled with the massacre of my father, of my mother, of my brother, the insolence of my horrid Bulgarian soldier, the gash he gave me, my slavery, my life as a kitchen wench, my Bulgarian captain, my horrid Don Issachar, my abominable Inquisitor, the hanging of Dr. Pangloss, that long plain song *miserere*[41] during which you were flogged, and above all the kiss I gave you behind the screen that day when I saw you for the last time. I praised

---

[40] That is, the Old Testament or the New Testament.

[41] The Latin chant, "Have mercy Upon me, O God."

God for bringing you back to me through so many trials, I ordered my old woman to take care of you and to bring you here as soon as she could. She has carried out my commission very well; I have enjoyed the inexpressible pleasure of seeing you again, of listening to you, and of speaking to you. You must be very hungry; I have a good appetite; let us begin by having supper."

Both sat down to supper; and after supper they returned to the handsome sofa we have already mentioned; they were still there when Signor Don Issachar, one of the masters of the house, arrived. It was the day of the Sabbath. He came to enjoy his rights and to express his tender love.

CHAPTER IX

What Happened to Cunegonde, to Candide, to the Grand Inquisitor and to a Jew

This Issachar was the most choleric Hebrew who had been seen in Israel since the Babylonian captivity. "What!" said he. "Bitch of a Galilean, isn't it enough to have the Inquisitor? Must this scoundrel share with me too?"

So saying, he drew a long dagger which he always carried and, thinking that his adversary was unarmed, threw himself upon Candide; but our good Westphalian had received an excellent sword from the old woman along with his suit of clothes. He drew his sword, and although he had a most gentle character, laid the Israelite stone-dead on the floor at the feet of the fair Cunegonde.

"Holy Virgin!" she exclaimed, "what will become of us? A man killed in my house! If the police come we are lost."

"If Pangloss had not been hanged," said Candide, "he would have given us good advice in this extremity, for he was a great philosopher. In default of him, let us consult the old woman."

She was extremely prudent and was beginning to give her advice when another little door opened. It was an hour after midnight, and Sunday was beginning. This day belonged to My Lord the Inquisitor. He came in and saw the flogged Candide sword in hand, a corpse lying on the ground, Cunegonde in terror, and the old woman giving advice. At this moment, here is what happened in Candide's soul and the manner of his reasoning: "If this holy man calls for help, he will infallibly have me burned; he might do as much to Cunegonde; he had me pitilessly lashed; he is my rival; I am in the mood to kill, there is no room for hesitation."

His reasoning was clear and swift; and, without giving the Inquisitor time to recover from his surprise, he pierced him through and through and cast him beside the Jew.

"Here's another," said Cunegonde, "there is no chance of mercy; we are excommunicated, our last hour has come. How does it happen that you, who were born so mild, should kill a Jew and a prelate in two minutes?"

"My dear young lady," replied Candide, "when a man is in love, jealous, and has been flogged by the Inquisition, he is beside himself."

The old woman than spoke up and said: "In the stable are three Andalusian horses, with their saddles and bridles; let the brave Candide prepare them; mademoiselle has moidores[42] and diamonds; let us mount quickly, although I can only sit on one buttock, and go to Cadiz;[43] the weather is beautifully fine, and it is most pleasant to travel in the coolness of the night."

Candide immediately saddled the three horses. Cunegonde, the old woman and he rode thirty miles without stopping. While they were riding away, the Holy Hermandad[44] arrived at the house; My Lord was buried in a splendid church and Issachar was thrown into a sewer.

Candide, Cunegonde and the old woman had already reached the little town of Aracena in the midst of the mountains of the Sierra Morena; and they talked in their inn as follows.

CHAPTER X

How Candide, Cunegonde and the Old Woman Arrived at Cadiz in Great Distress, and How They Embarked

"Who can have stolen my pistoles[45] and my diamonds?" said Cunegonde, weeping. "How shall we live? What shall we do? Where shall we find Inquisitors and Jews to give me others?"

"Alas!" said the old woman, "I strongly suspect a reverend Franciscan father who slept in the same inn at Badajoz with us; Heaven forbid that I should judge rashly! But he twice came into our room and left long before we did."

"Alas!" said Candide, "the good Pangloss often proved to me that this world's goods are common to all men and that every one has an equal right to them. According to these principles the monk should have left us enough to continue our journey. Have you nothing left then, my fair Cunegonde?"

"Not a maravedi,"[46] said she. "What are we to do?" said Candide.

"Sell one of the horses," said the old woman. "I will ride postillion behind Mademoiselle Cunegonde, although I can only sit on one buttock, and we will get to Cadiz."

In the same hotel there was a Benedictine prior. He bought the horse very cheap. Candide, Cunegonde and the old woman passed through Lucena, Chillas,

---

[42] Portuguese coins.

[43] A city in southwestern Spain about two hundred miles from Lisbon, Cadiz served as Spain's main port of departure for the New World (where, unfortunately for our travelers, the Inquisition functioned with the same intensity as it did in Europe).

[44] The Holy Brotherhood, a religious order with police powers, very active in eighteenth-century Spain.

[45] Spanish gold coins.

[46] Spanish copper coins of very little value.

Lebrixa, and at last reached Cadiz. A fleet was there being equipped and troops were being raised to bring to reason the reverend Jesuit fathers of Paraguay, who were accused of causing the revolt of one of their tribes against the kings of Spain and Portugal near the town of Sacramento.[47] Candide, having served with the Bulgarians, went through the Bulgarian drill before the general of the little army with so much grace, celerity, skill, pride and agility, that he was given the command of an infantry company. He was now a captain; he embarked with Mademoiselle Cunegonde, the old woman, two servants, and the two Andalusian horses which had belonged to the Grand Inquisitor of Portugal.

During the voyage they had many discussions about the philosophy of poor Pangloss. "We are going to a new world," said Candide, "and no doubt it is there that everything is for the best; for it must be admitted that one might lament a little over the physical and moral happenings in our own world."

"I love you with all my heart," said Cunegonde, "but my soul is still shocked by what I have seen and undergone."

"All will be well," replied Candide; "the sea in this new world already is better than the seas of our Europe; it is calmer and the winds are more constant. It is certainly the new world which is the best of all possible worlds."

"God grant it!" said Cunegonde, "but I have been so horribly unhappy in mine that my heart is nearly closed to hope."

"You complain," said the old woman to them. "Alas! you have not endured such misfortunes as mine."

Cunegonde almost laughed and thought it most amusing of the old woman to assert that she was more unfortunate. "Alas! my dear," said she, "unless you have been raped by two Bulgarians, stabbed twice in the belly, have had two castles destroyed, two fathers and mothers murdered before your eyes, and have seen two of your lovers flogged in an *auto-da-fé,* I do not see how you can surpass me; moreover, I was born a Baroness with seventy-two quarterings and I have been a kitchen wench."

"You do not know my birth," said the old woman, "and if I showed you my backside you would not talk as you do and you would suspend your judgment."

This speech aroused intense curiosity in the minds of Cunegonde and Candide. And the old woman spoke as follows.

CHAPTER XI
The Old Woman's Story

"My eyes were not always bloodshot and red-rimmed; my nose did not always touch my chin and I was not always a servant. I am the daughter of Pope Urban X

---

[47] The Society of Jesus (Jesuits), a Catholic order founded in sixteenth-century Spain (see Selection 21), caused the local natives to rise in revolt (1756) to prevent a transfer of the South American city of San Sacramento from Spanish to Portuguese control.

and the Princess of Palestrina.[48] Until I was fourteen I was brought up in a palace to which all the castles of your German Barons would not have served as stables; and one of my dresses cost more than all the magnificence of Westphalia. I increased in beauty, in grace, in talents, among pleasures, respect and hopes; already I inspired love, my breasts were forming; and what breasts! White, firm, carved like those of the Venus de' Medici. And what eyes! What eyelids! What black eyebrows! What fire shone from my two eyeballs, and dimmed the glitter of the stars, as the local poets pointed out to me. The women who dressed and undressed me fell into ecstasy when they beheld me in front and behind; and all the men would have liked to be in their place.

"I was betrothed to a ruling prince of Massa-Carrara.[49] What a prince! As beautiful as I was, formed of gentleness and charms, brilliantly witty and burning with love; I loved him with a first love, idolatrously and extravagantly. The marriage ceremonies were arranged with unheard of pomp and magnificence; there were continual fêtes, revels and comic operas; all Italy wrote sonnets for me and not a good one among them.

"I touched the moment of my happiness when an old marchioness who had been my prince's mistress invited him to take chocolate with her; less than two hours afterwards he died in horrible convulsions; but that is only a trifle. My mother was in despair, though less distressed than I, and wished to absent herself for a time from a place so disastrous. She had a most beautiful estate near Gaeta;[50] we embarked on a galley, gilded like the altar of St. Peter's at Rome. A Salle[51] pirate swooped down and boarded us; our soldiers defended us like soldiers of the Pope; they threw down their arms, fell on their knees and asked the pirates for absolution *in articulo mortis*.[52]

"They were immediately stripped as naked as monkeys and my mother, our ladies of honor and myself as well. The diligence with which these gentlemen strip people is truly admirable; but I was still more surprised by their inserting a finger in a place belonging to all of us where we women usually only allow the end of a syringe. This appeared to me a very strange ceremony; but that is how we judge everything when we leave our own country. I soon learned that it was to find out if we had hidden any diamonds there; 'tis a custom established from time immemorial among the civilised nations who roam the seas. I have learned

---

[48] Voltaire left an ironic comment on this passage, not published until 1829: "Note the extreme discretion of the author; hitherto there has never been a pope named Urban X; he avoided attributing a bastard to a known pope. What circumspection! What an exquisite conscience!"

[49] Small Italian duchy, northwest of Pisa.

[50] Italian town north of Naples.

[51] A Moroccan port, known as a haven for pirates.

[52] Latin: "at the moment of death." (Absolution administered by Muslim pirates during the act of murder seems of dubious Christian validity.)

that the religious Knights of Malta[53] never fail in it when they capture Turks and Turkish women; this is an international law which has never been broken.

"I will not tell you how hard it is for a young princess to be taken with her mother as a slave to Morocco; you will also guess all we had to endure in the pirates' ship. My mother was still very beautiful; our ladies of honor, even our waiting maids possessed more charms than could be found in all Africa; and I was ravishing, I was beauty, grace itself, and I was a virgin; I did not remain so long; the flower which had been reserved for the handsome prince of Massa-Carrara was ravished from me by a pirate captain; he was an abominable negro who thought he was doing me a great honor. The Princess of Palestrina and I must indeed have been strong to bear up against all we endured before our arrival in Morocco! But let that pass; these things are so common that they are not worth mentioning.

"Morocco was swimming in blood when we arrived. The fifty sons of the Emperor Muley Ismael had each a faction; and this produced fifty civil wars, of blacks against blacks, browns against browns, mulattoes against mulattoes.[54] There was continual carnage throughout the whole extent of the empire.

Scarcely had we landed when blacks of a party hostile to that of my pirate arrived with the purpose of depriving him of his booty. After the diamonds and the gold, we were the most valuable possessions. I witnessed a fight such as is never seen in your European climates. The blood of the northern peoples is not sufficiently ardent; their madness for women does not reach the point which is common in Africa. The Europeans seem to have milk in their veins; but vitriol and fire flow in the veins of the inhabitants of Mount Atlas[55] and the neighboring countries. They fought with the fury of the lions, tigers and serpents of the country to determine who should have us. A Moor grasped my mother by the right arm, my captain's lieutenant held her by the left arm; a Moorish soldier held one leg and one of our pirates seized the other. In a moment nearly all our women were seized in the same way by four soldiers. My captain kept me hidden behind him; he had a scimitar in his hand and killed everybody who opposed his fury. I saw my mother and all our Italian women torn in pieces, gashed, massacred by the monsters who disputed them. The prisoners, my companions, those who had captured them, soldiers, sailors, blacks, browns, whites, mulattoes, and finally my captain were all killed and I remained expiring on a heap of corpses. As every one knows, such scenes go on in an area of more than three hundred square leagues, and yet no one ever fails to recite the five daily prayers ordered by Mahomet.

"With great difficulty I extricated myself from the bloody heaps of corpses and dragged myself to the foot of a large orange tree on the bank of a stream;

---

[53] A medieval order of Christian knights.

[54] Mawlay Isma'il, the Sultan of Morocco from 1673 to 1727, left five hundred male children, all of whom possessed the right to rule. This situation led to extreme political instability.

[55] A mountain range in North Africa, extending through Morocco, Algeria, and Tunisia.

there I fell down with terror, weariness, horror, despair and hunger. Soon afterwards, my exhausted senses fell into a sleep which was more like a swoon than repose. I was in this state of weakness and insensibility between life and death when I felt myself oppressed by something which moved on my body. I opened my eyes and saw a white man of good appearance who was sighing and muttering between his teeth: *O che sciagura d'essere senza coglioni!*[56]

CHAPTER XII
Continuation of the Old Woman's Misfortunes

"Amazed and delighted to hear my native language, and not less surprised at the words spoken by this man, I replied that there were greater misfortunes than that of which he complained. In a few words I informed him of the horrors I had undergone and then swooned again. He carried me to a neighboring house, had me put to bed, gave me food, waited on me, consoled me, flattered me, told me he had never seen anyone so beautiful as I, and that he had never so much regretted that which no one could give back to him.

"'I was born at Naples,' he said, 'and every year they make two or three thousand children there into capons;[57] some die of it, others acquire voices more beautiful than women's, and others become the governors of States.[58] This operation was performed upon me with very great success and I was a musician in the chapel of the Princess of Palestrina.

"'Of my mother,' I exclaimed.

"'Of your mother!' cried he, weeping. 'What! Are you that young princess I brought up to the age of six and who even then gave promise of being as beautiful as you are?'

"'I am! my mother is four hundred yards from here, cut into quarters under a heap of corpses . . .'

"I related all that had happened to me; he also told me his adventures and informed me how he had been sent to the King of Morocco by a Christian power

---

[56] Italian: "Oh, what a misfortune to be without testicles!"

[57] A capon is actually a rooster that has been castrated so that it will become fatter and more tender for eating. The reference here is to the practice, especially among poor Italian families, of castrating trained male singers just before puberty in order to continue the use of their soprano or contralto voices. This unfortunate practice was first introduced in the late Middle Ages when women were banned from church choirs. It continued through the eighteenth century when, especially in Italian opera, the majority of male singers were *castrati*. Over two hundred of them sang in Catholic churches in Rome alone. (The roles created for them are now sung by women and countertenors.)

[58] An allusion to the famous male soprano Farinelli (1705–1782) who, after a successful musical career, served and considerably influenced two Spanish kings, Philip V and Ferdinand VI.

to make a treaty with that monarch whereby he was supplied with powder, cannons and ships to help to exterminate the commerce of other Christians. 'My mission is accomplished,' said this honest eunuch, 'I am about to embark at Ceuta[59] and I will take you back to Italy. *Ma che sciagura d'essere senza coglioni!*'

"I thanked him with tears of gratitude; and instead of taking me back to Italy he conducted me to Algiers and sold me to the Dey.[60] I had scarcely been sold when the plague which had gone through Africa, Asia and Europe, broke out furiously in Algiers. You have seen earthquakes; but have you ever seen the plague?"

"Never," replied the Baroness.

"If you had," replied the old woman, "you would admit that it is much worse than an earthquake. It is very common in Africa; I caught it. Imagine the situation of a Pope's daughter aged fifteen, who in three months had undergone poverty and slavery, had been raped nearly every day, had seen her mother cut into four pieces, had undergone hunger and war, and was now dying of the plague in Algiers. However, I did not die; but my eunuch and the Dey and almost all the seraglio of Algiers perished.

"When the first ravages of this frightful plague were over, the Dey's slaves were sold. A merchant bought me and carried me to Tunis; he sold me to another merchant who re-sold me at Tripoli; from Tripoli I was resold to Alexandria, from Alexandria re-sold to Smyrna, from Smyrna to Constantinople.[61] I was finally bought by an Aga of the Janizaries,[62] who was soon ordered to defend Azov against the Russians who were besieging it.[63]

"The Aga, who was a man of great gallantry, took his whole seraglio with him, and lodged us in a little fort on the Islands of Palus-Maeotis,[64] guarded by two black eunuchs and twenty soldiers. He killed a prodigious number of Russians but they returned the compliment as well. Azov was given up to fire and blood, neither sex nor age was pardoned; only our little fort remained; and the enemy tried to reduce it by starving us. The twenty Janizaries had sworn never to surrender us. The extremities of hunger to which they were reduced forced them to eat our two eunuchs for fear of breaking their oath. Some days later they resolved to eat the women. We had with us a most pious and compassionate Imam[65] who delivered a

---

[59] A city at the northwestern tip of Africa, opposite Gibraltar.

[60] The title for the Turkish governor of a North African province.

[61] In Voltaire's day Constantinople (modern Istanbul) was the capital of the Ottoman (Turkish) Empire.

[62] The Janizaries (or Janissaries) led by officers known as Agas, were elite units of Turkish infantry that included former slaves and sons of captured Christians. The latter were pressed into service when young and turned into fanatical converts to Islam.

[63] The Russians besieged the Turkish settlement at Azov in southern Russia in 1695–1696.

[64] Ancient Roman name for the Sea of Azov.

[65] Muslim religious official.

fine sermon to them by which he persuaded them not to kill us altogether. 'Cut,' said he, 'only one buttock from each of these ladies and you will make very good cheer; if you have to return, there will still be as much left in a few days; Heaven will be pleased at so charitable an action and you will be saved.'

"He was very eloquent and persuaded them. This horrible operation was performed upon us; the Imam anointed us with the same balm that is used for children who have just been circumcised; we were all at the point of death.

"Scarcely had the Janizaries finished the meal we had supplied when the Russians arrived in flat-bottomed boats; not a Janizary escaped. The Russians paid no attention to the state we were in. There are French doctors everywhere; one of them who was very skilful, took care of us; he healed us and I shall remember all my life that, when my wounds were cured, he made propositions to me. For the rest, he told us all to cheer up; he told us that the same thing had happened in several sieges and that it was a law of war.

"As soon as my companions could walk they were sent to Moscow. I fell to the lot of a Boyar[66] who made me his gardener and gave me twenty lashes a day. But at the end of two years this lord was broken on the wheel with thirty other Boyars owing to some court disturbance,[67] and I profited by this adventure; I fled; I crossed all Russia; for a long time I was servant in an inn at Riga, then at Rostock, at Wismar, at Leipzig, at Cassel, at Utecht, at Leyden, at the Hague, at Rotterdam; I have grown old in misery and in shame, with only half a backside, always remembering that I was the daughter of a Pope; a hundred times I wanted to kill myself but I still loved life. This ridiculous weakness is perhaps the most disastrous of our inclinations; for is there anything sillier than to desire to bear continually a burden one always wishes to throw on the ground; to look upon oneself with horror and yet to cling to oneself; in short, to caress the serpent which devours us until he has eaten our heart?

"In the countries it has been my fate to traverse and in the inns where I have served I have seen a prodigious number of people who hated their lives; but I have only seen twelve who voluntarily put an end to their misery: three negroes, four Englishmen, four Genevans and a German professor named Robeck.[68] I ended up as servant to the Jew, Don Issachar; he placed me in your service, my fair young lady; I attached myself to your fate and have been more occupied with your adventures than with my own. I should never even have spoken of my misfortunes, if you had not piqued me a little and if it had not been the custom on board ship to tell stories to pass the time. In short, Mademoiselle, I have had

---

[66] A Russian nobleman.

[67] An allusion to an ineffectual uprising in 1698 against Czar Peter the Great, which provoked a massive and atrocious program of reprisals.

[68] Johann Robeck maintained that the love of life was a ridiculous notion, wrote a treatise in defense of suicide, and drowned himself in 1739 at the age of sixty-seven.

experience, I know the world; provide yourself with an entertainment, make each passenger tell you his story; and if there is one who has not often cursed his life, who has not often said to himself that he was the most unfortunate of men, throw me headfirst into the sea."

• • •

[*Editor's summary of the events in chapters XIII–XXVIII:* After the extraordinary narration by the old woman, the group sails on to Buenos Aires, where its governor displays a strong desire for Cunegonde. When a pursuing ship from Spain arrives in the harbor, Candide flees for the jungles of Paraguay, along with a loyal mixed-breed valet, Cacambo, whom he had hired in Cadiz. There, he finds Cunegonde's brother, as astonishingly alive as his sister, now the Baron of Thunder-ten-tronckh, who has become commander of the Jesuit armies which in Paraguay "make war on the Kings of Spain and Portugal and in Europe act as their confessors." When, on the basis of social rank, the Baron objects violently to Candide's intention to marry his sister, Candide runs him through with a sword and escapes into the jungle. Everywhere that Candide and Cacambo wander, both in South America and later back in Europe, they meet with further adventures proving the stupidity, cruelty, and greed of humanity. There is only one exception to this principle: the land of El Dorado in a very remote area of South America. There, everyone lives happily according to reason in a sort of deistic utopia without priests, monks, churches, prisons, or courts of justice. Not having the good sense to remain in El Dorado, Candide returns to Europe, wealthy with the gold that forms the ground of El Dorado, giving some of it to Cacambo, whom he orders back to Buenos Aires with lots of bribery money in order to regain Cunegonde. On the journey back to Europe Candide employs a disillusioned pessimist, Martin, as a companion. Martin is the philosophical foil to Pangloss. Reuniting with Cacambo after many more distressing episodes, the two journey to Constantinople in the continuing quest for Cunegonde. Nowhere can Candide find a truly happy person among all those whom he meets. Arriving in Constantinople, they buy two galley slaves to free them from their misery. The two turn out to be Pangloss, who had survived a hanging and dissection in Lisbon, and Cunegonde's brother, cured of the wound inflicted by Candide in South America. The following two chapters conclude the narrative.]

CHAPTER XXIX

How Candide Found Cunegonde and the Old Woman Again

While Candide, the Baron, Pangloss, Martin and Cacambo were relating their adventures, reasoning upon contingent or non-contingent events of the universe,[69] arguing about effects and causes, moral and physical evil, free will and necessity, and the consolation to be found in the Turkish galleys, they came to the house of the Transylvanian prince on the shores of Propontis.

The first objects which met their sight were Cunegonde and the old woman hanging out towels to dry on the line. At this sight the Baron grew pale. Candide, that tender lover, seeing his fair Cunegonde sunburned, blear-eyed, flat-breasted, with wrinkles round her eyes and red, chapped arms, recoiled three paces in horror, and then advanced from mere politeness. She embraced Candide and her brother. They embraced the old woman; Candide bought them both.

In the neighborhood was a little farm; the old woman suggested that Candide should buy it, until some better fate befell the group. Cunegonde did not know that she had become ugly, for nobody had told her so; she reminded Candide of his promises in so peremptory a tone that the good Candide dared not refuse her. He therefore informed the Baron that he was about to marry his sister.

"Never," said the Baron, "will I endure such baseness on her part and such insolence on yours; nobody shall ever reproach me with this infamy; my sister's children could never enter the chapters[70] of Germany. No, my sister shall never marry anyone but a Baron of the Empire."

Cunegonde threw herself at his feet and bathed them in tears; but he was inflexible.

"Madman," said Candide, "I rescued you from the galleys, I paid your ransom and your sister's; she was washing dishes here, she is ugly; I am so kind as to make her my wife, and you pretend to oppose me! I should re-kill you if I listened to my anger."

"You may kill me again," said the Baron, "but you shall never marry my sister while I am alive."

CHAPTER XXX

Conclusion

At the bottom of his heart Candide had not the least wish to marry Cunegonde. But the Baron's extreme impertinence determined him to complete the marriage, and Cunegonde urged it so warmly that he could not retract. He consulted Pangloss, Martin and the faithful Cacambo. Pangloss wrote an excellent memorandum by which he proved that the Baron had no rights over his sister and that by all the laws of the empire she could make a left-handed marriage[71]

---

[69] A contingent event is a possible but not inevitable happening; a noncontingent event is inevitable.

[70] Assemblies of German knights.

[71] A marriage between persons of unequal rank in which the lower-ranking spouse and the children could make no claim on the other spouse's rank or property.

with Candide. Martin advised that the Baron should be thrown into the sea; Cacambo decided that he should be returned to the Levantine captain and sent back to the galleys, after which he would be returned by the first ship to the Vicar-General at Rome. This was thought to be very good advice; the old woman approved it; they said nothing to the sister; the plan was carried out with the aid of a little money and they had the pleasure of duping a Jesuit and punishing the pride of a German Baron.

It would be natural to suppose that when, after so many disasters, Candide was married to his mistress, and living with the philosopher Pangloss, the philosopher Martin, the prudent Cacambo and the old woman, having brought back so many diamonds from the country of the ancient Incas, he would lead the most pleasant life imaginable. But he was so cheated by the Jews that he had nothing left but his little farm;[72] his wife, growing uglier every day, became shrewish and unendurable; the old woman was ailing and even more bad tempered than Cunegonde. Cacambo, who worked in the garden and then went to Constantinople to sell vegetables, was overworked and cursed his fate. Pangloss was in despair because he did not shine in some German university.

As for Martin, he was firmly convinced that people are equally uncomfortable everywhere; he accepted things patiently. Candide, Martin and Pangloss sometimes argued about metaphysics and morals. From the windows of the farm they often watched the ships going by, filled with effendis, pashas, and cadis, who were being exiled to Lemnos, to Mitylene and Erzerum. They saw other cadis, other pashas and other effendis coming back to take the place of the exiles and to be exiled in their turn. They saw the neatly impaled heads which were taken to the Sublime Porte.[73] These sights redoubled their discussions; and when they were not arguing, the boredom was so excessive that one day the old woman dared to say to them: "I should like to know which is worse, to be raped a hundred times by negro pirates, to have a buttock cut off, to run the gauntlet among the Bulgarians, to be whipped and flogged in an *auto-da-fé,* to be dissected, to row in a galley, in short, to endure all the miseries through which we have passed, or to remain here doing nothing?"

"'Tis a great question," said Candide.

These remarks led to new reflections, and Martin especially concluded that man was born to live in the convulsions of distress or in the lethargy of boredom. Candide did not agree, but he asserted nothing. Pangloss confessed that he had always suffered horribly; but, having once maintained that everything was for the best, he had continued to maintain it without believing it.

---

[72] Voltaire had suffered financial losses due to the bankruptcies of some Jewish bankers; this purely personal experience was the basis for his anti-Semitic remark here.

[73] The main gate of the sultan's palace in Constantinople where the heads of those who had been executed were often displayed as a gruesome deterrent to others.

One thing confirmed Martin in his destestable principles, made Candide hesitate more than ever, and embarrassed Pangloss. And it was this. One day there came to their farm Paquette and Friar Giroflée, who were in the most extreme misery; they had soon wasted their three thousand piastres, had left each other, made it up, quarrelled again, been put in prison, escaped, and finally Friar Giroflée had turned Turk. Paquette continued her occupation everywhere and now earned nothing by it.[74]

"I foresaw," said Martin to Candide, "that your gifts would soon be wasted and would only make them the more miserable. You and Cacambo were once bloated with millions of piastres and you are no happier than Friar Giroflée and Paquette."

"Ah! Ha!" said Pangloss to Paquette, "so Heaven brings you back to us, my dear child? Do you know that you cost me the end of my nose, an eye and an ear! What a plight you are in! Ah! What a world this is!"

This new occurrence caused them to philosophise more than ever. In the neighborhood there lived a very famous Dervish,[75] who was supposed to be the best philosopher in Turkey; they went to consult him; Pangloss was the spokesman and said: "Master, we have come to beg you to tell us why so strange an animal as man was ever created."

"What has it to do with you?" said the Dervish. "Is it your business?"

"But, reverend father," said Candide, "there is a horrible amount of evil in the world."

"What does it matter," said the Dervish, "whether there is evil or good? When his highness sends a ship to Egypt, does he worry about the comfort or discomfort of the rats in the ship?"[76]

"Then what should we do?" said Pangloss.

"Hold your tongue," said the Dervish.

"I flattered myself," said Pangloss, "that I should discuss with you effects and causes, this best of all possible worlds, the origin of evil, the nature of the soul and pre-established harmony."

At these words the Dervish slammed the door in their faces.

During this conversation the news went round that at Constantinople two viziers and the mufti[77] had been strangled and several of their friends impaled.

---

[74] Paquette was the maid of the opening chapter who gave "a lesson in experimental physics," as well as a syphilitic infection, to Doctor Pangloss. She had become a prostitute; Friar Giroflée was her unhappy companion. Candide, on his journey through Europe to Constantinople, had given them a gift of a large sum of money.

[75] A member of a Muslim religious order, some of whom practice ecstatic whirling and dancing.

[76] This pessimistic allegorical passage severely limits the extent of divine Providence.

[77] Intimate advisers of the sultan.

This catastrophe made a prodigious noise everywhere for several hours. As Pangloss, Candide and Martin were returning to their little farm, they came upon an old man who was taking the air under a bower of orange trees at his door. Pangloss, who was as curious as he was argumentative, asked him what was the name of the mufti who had just been strangled.

"I do not know," replied the old man. "I have never known the name of any mufti or of any vizier. I am entirely ignorant of the occurrence you mention; I presume that in general those who meddle with public affairs sometimes perish miserably and that they deserve it; but I never inquire what is going on in Constantinople; I content myself with sending there for sale the produce of the garden I cultivate."

Having spoken thus, he took the strangers into his house. His two daughters and his two sons presented them with several kinds of sherbert which they made themselves, caymac[78] flavored with candied citron peel, oranges, lemons, limes, pineapples, dates, pistachios and Mocha coffee which had not been mixed with the bad coffee of Batavia and the Isles. After which this good Muslim's two daughters perfumed the beards of Candide, Pangloss and Martin.

"You must have a vast and magnificent estate?" said Candide to the Turk.

"I have only twenty acres," replied the Turk. "I cultivate them with my children; and work keeps at bay three great evils: boredom, vice and need."

As Candide returned to his farm he reflected deeply on the Turk's remarks. He said to Pangloss and Martin: "That good old man seems to me to have chosen an existence preferable by far to that of the six kings with whom we had the honor to sup."

"Exalted rank," said Pangloss, "is very dangerous, according to the testimony of all philosophers; for Eglon, King of the Moabites, was murdered by Ehud; Absalom was hanged by the hair and pierced by three darts; King Nadab, son of Jeroboam, was killed by Baasha; King Elah by Zimri; Ahaziah by Jehu; Athaliah by Jehoiada; the Kings Jehoiakim, Jeconiah and Zedekiah were made slaves. You know in what manner died Crœsus, Astyages, Darius, Denys of Syracuse, Pyrrhus, Perseus, Hannibal, Jugurtha, Ariovistus, Cæsar, Pompey, Nero, Otho, Vitellius, Domitian, Richard II of England, Edward II, Henry VI, Richard III, Mary Stuart, Charles I, the three Henrys of France, the Emperor Henry IV. You know . . ."[79]

"I also know," said Candide, "that we should cultivate our gardens."

"You are right," said Pangloss, "for, when man was placed in the Garden of Eden, he was placed there *ut operaretur eum,* to dress it and to keep it; which proves that man was not born for idleness."

---

[78] Turkish word for cream.

[79] Pangloss's need to recite this catalog of powerful men who died violent deaths exemplifies Voltaire's satirical view of such self-inflated pedants.

"Let us work without theorizing," said Martin; "'tis the only way to make life endurable."

The whole small fraternity entered into this praiseworthy plan, and each started to make use of his talents. The little farm yielded well. Cunegonde was indeed very ugly, but she became an excellent pastry cook; Paquette embroidered; the old woman took care of the linen. Even Friar Giroflée performed some service; he was a very good carpenter and even became a man of honor; and Pangloss sometimes said to Candide: "All events are linked up in this best of all possible worlds; for, if you had not been expelled from the noble castle, by hard kicks in your backside for love of Mademoiselle Cunegonde, if you had not been clapped into the Inquisition, if you had not wandered about America on foot, if you had not stuck your sword in the Baron, if you had not lost all your sheep from the land of Eldorado, you would not be eating candied citrons and pistachios here."[80]

"'Tis well said," replied Candide, "but we must cultivate our gardens."

---

[80] The final reduction to absurdity of Pangloss's philosophy.

31

꒰

Olaudah Equiano

THE INTERESTING NARRATIVE

One of the major categories of African, African-American, and African-British writing is the slave narrative. Of the many accounts that have been published, that of Olaudah Equiano is the best known. Equiano was born around 1745 in southern Nigeria, apparently in the region of the Igbo people. He was captured around the age of eleven, so that facts he recounts about his childhood are not known to be completely certain. We cannot identify, for example, the location of the place he names as his hometown. However, the details he provides of life in Africa before being captured by African slave traders offer a compelling portrait of eighteenth-century Igbo culture. The story of his capture, and his transportation through West Africa and across the ocean, provides an unforgettable description of the horrors of slavery.

Equiano's life was strikingly rich. After crossing the Atlantic to Barbados in the Caribbean, he was sent to Virginia. He soon was purchased by a naval officer who renamed him Gustavus Vassa, and began working on slave ships that traveled between the Caribbean and England. He traveled widely with Captain Pascal, serving during the campaigns of General Wolfe in Canada and in the Mediterranean during the Seven Years War. Returning to England, he stayed with various families where he acquired an education and mastered the English language, preparing him for his later work as a shipping clerk and amateur navigator. At the age of twenty-one he was able to buy his own freedom using his own savings. He subsequently visited the Mediterranean, traveled to the Mosquito Coast of Central America in order to establish a plantation, traded between the islands of the Caribbean and the American colonies, and even participated in an expedition to the Arctic. In 1775, he was baptized into the Anglican Church and remained a Christian as well as a British subject, even after he became a fervent spokesman for the abolition of slavery.

Freedom was no guarantee of security for ex-slaves. Equiano experienced continual acts of discrimination and exploitation as a result of his race. The act of writing his autobiography marked his commitment to work for the cause of abolition. Indeed, he was acquainted with the leading lights of the abolition move-

ment in England, including Granville Sharp, and he was appointed Commissary of Stores for the Black Poor, that is, the freed slaves returning to Sierra Leone. He reported an incident to Granville Sharp in which 132 sick slaves aboard the slave ship Zong *were deliberately drowned so that the owners could collect insurance payments. As a result of his action the matter came before the British Parliament in their debate over the slave trade.*

Equiano married an Englishwoman, Susanna Cullen, in 1792. Gustavus and Susanna Vassa had two daughters, although only one child outlived him. Unlike most Britons of the time, he was wealthy enough to need a will for his sole heir. He may have become the only African-Briton in the eighteenth century in that secure a position, bequeathing his daughter a substantial sum.

Most significantly, in 1789 he published The Interesting Narrative of the Life of Olaudah Equiano, or Gustavus Vassa, the African, *so as to bear witness to the trials of slavery. Soon an immense success,* Equiano's Travels *ran into seventeen editions in England and the United States in the forty years following its publication, and was translated into Dutch, German, and Russian. After the publication of his book, he traveled throughout England making speeches against the slave trade, incurring considerable opposition and personal attacks from those who profited from it.*

In the selection from his Narrative *that follows, taken from the first American printing in 1791, Equiano recounts the unhappy moments of his capture, his transport down to the coast, and the hardship of the middle passage.*

❧

To the Lords Spiritual and Temporal, and the Commons of the Parliament of Great Britain

My Lords and Gentlemen,

Permit me, with the greatest deference and respect, to lay at your feet the following genuine narrative; the chief design of which is to excite in your august assemblies a sense of compassion for the miseries which the Slave-Trade has entailed on my unfortunate countrymen. By the horrors of that trade I was first torn away from all the tender connections that were naturally dear to my heart; but these, through the mysterious ways of Providence, I ought to regard as infinitely more than compensated by the introduction I have thence obtained to the knowledge of the Christian religion, and of a nation which, by its liberal sentiments, its humanity, the glorious freedom of its government, and its proficiency in arts and sciences, has exalted the dignity of human nature.

Olaudah Equiano, *The Interesting Narrative of the Life of Olaudah Equiano, or Gustavus Vassa, The African.* New York: W. Durell, 1791. Adapted from the Preface and Chapter 2.

I am sensible I ought to entreat your pardon for addressing to you a work wholly devoid of literary merit; but, as the production of an unlettered African, who is actuated by the hope of becoming an instrument towards the relief of his suffering countrymen, I trust that *such a man,* pleading in *such a cause,* will be acquitted of boldness and presumption.

May the God of Heaven inspire your hearts with peculiar benevolence on that important day when the question of Abolition is to be discussed, when thousands, in consequence of your determination, are to look for Happiness or Misery!

I am, My Lords and Gentlemen,
Your most obedient,
And devoted humble servant,

OLAUDAH EQUIANO,
or
GUSTAVUS VASSA[1]

• • •

CHAPTER 2

The author's birth and parentage—His being kidnapped with his sister—Their separation—Surprise at meeting again—Are finally separated—Account of the different places and incidents the author met with till his arrival on the coast—The effect the sight of a slave-ship had on him—He sails for the West Indies—Horrors of a slave-ship—Arrives at Barbadoes, where the cargo is sold and dispersed.

I hope the reader will not think I have trespassed on his patience in introducing myself to him with some account of the manners and customs of my country. They had been implanted in me with great care, and made an impression on my mind, which time could not erase, and which all the adversity and variety of fortune I have since experienced, served only to rivet and record: for, whether the love of one's country be real or imaginary, or a lesson of reason, or an instinct of nature, I still look back with pleasure on the first scenes of my life, though that pleasure has been for the most part mingled with sorrow.

I have already acquainted the reader with the time and place of my birth. My father, besides many slaves,[2] had a numerous family, of which seven lived to grow up, including myself and a sister, who was the only daughter. As I was the youngest of the sons, I became, of course, the greatest favorite with my mother,

---

[1] In attempting to influence the parliamentary debates on the regulation and abolition of slavery, Equiano adopts an appropriately humble and respectful tone. By "unlettered," he means lacking formal education—especially in the Greek and Latin languages. His "suffering countrymen" are his fellow Africans, still subject to slavery; his political countrymen are now, like him, British subjects who can petition Parliament.

[2] Slavery was to be found among some African peoples, often as a result of warfare or punishment for a crime. Securing slaves by kidnapping was far less common.

and was always with her; and she used to take particular pains to form my mind. I was trained up from my earliest years in the art of war: my daily exercise was shooting and throwing javelins, and my mother adorned me with emblems,[3] after the manner of our greatest warriors. In this way I grew up till I had turned the age of eleven, when an end was put to my happiness in the following manner: Generally, when the grown people in the neighborhood were gone far in the fields to labor, the children assembled together in some of the neighboring premises to play; and commonly some of us used to get up a tree to look out for any assailant, or kidnapper, that might come upon us—for they sometimes took those opportunities of our parents' absence, to attack and carry off as many as they could seize. One day as I was watching at the top of a tree in our yard, I saw one of those people come into the yard of our next neighbor but one, to kidnap, there being many stout young people in it. Immediately on this I gave the alarm of the rogue, and he was surrounded by the stoutest of them, who entangled him with cords, so that he could not escape, till some of the grown people came and secured him. But, alas! ere long it was my fate to be thus attacked, and to be carried off, when none of the grown people were near.

One day, when all our people were gone out to their works as usual, and only I and my dear sister were left to mind the house, two men and a woman got over our walls, and in a moment seized us both, and, without giving us time to cry out, or make resistance, they stopped our mouths, and ran off with us into the nearest wood. Here they tied our hands, and continued to carry us as far as they could, till night came on, when we reached a small house, where the robbers halted for refreshment, and spent the night. We were then unbound, but were unable to take any food; and, being quite overpowered by fatigue and grief, our only relief was some sleep, which allayed our misfortune for a short time. The next morning we left the house, and continued travelling all the day. For a long time we had kept the woods, but at last we came into a road which I believed I knew. I had now some hopes of being delivered; for we had advanced but a little way before I discovered some people at a distance, on which I began to cry out for their assistance; but my cries had no other effect than to make them tie me faster and stop my mouth, and then they put me into a large sack. They also stopped my sister's mouth, and tied her hands; and in this manner we proceeded till we were out of sight of these people. When we went to rest the following night, they offered us some victuals, but we refused it; and the only comfort we had was in being in one another's arms all that night, and bathing each other with our tears. But alas! we were soon deprived of even the small comfort of weeping together.

The next day proved a day of greater sorrow than I had yet experienced; for my sister and I were then separated, while we lay clasped in each other's arms. It was in vain that we besought them not to part us; she was torn from me, and

---

[3] Emblems here might denote dye used to decorate the body.

immediately carried away, while I was left in a state of distraction not to be described. I cried and grieved continually; and for several days did not eat anything but what they forced into my mouth. At length, after many days' travelling, during which I had often changed masters, I got into the hands of a chieftain, in a very pleasant country. This man had two wives and some children, and they all used me extremely well, and did all they could do to comfort me; particularly the first wife, who was something like my mother. Although I was a great many days' journey from my father's house, yet these people spoke exactly the same language with us. This first master of mine, as I may call him, was a smith, and my principal employment was working his bellows, which were the same kind as I had seen in my vicinity. They were in some respects not unlike the stoves here[4] in gentlemen's kitchens, and were covered over with leather; and in the middle of that leather a stick was fixed, and a person stood up, and worked it in the same manner as is done to pump water out of a cask with a hand pump. I believe it was gold he worked, for it was of a lovely bright yellow color, and was worn by the women on their wrists and ankles.

I was there I suppose about a month, and they at last used to trust me some little distance from the house. This liberty I used in embracing every opportunity to inquire the way to my own home; and I also sometimes, for the same purpose, went with the maidens, in the cool of the evenings, to bring pitchers of water from the springs for the use of the house. I had also remarked where the sun rose in the morning, and set in the evening, as I had travelled along; and I had observed that my father's house was towards the rising of the sun. I therefore determined to seize the first opportunity of making my escape, and to shape my course for that quarter; for I was quite oppressed and weighed down by grief after my mother and friends; and my love of liberty, ever great, was strengthened by the mortifying circumstance of not daring to eat with the free-born children, although I was mostly their companion.

While I was projecting my escape, one day an unlucky event happened, which quite disconcerted my plan, and put an end to my hopes. I used to be sometimes employed in assisting an elderly slave to cook and take care of the poultry; and one morning, while I was feeding some chickens, I happened to toss a small pebble at one of them, which hit it on the middle, and directly killed it. The old slave, having soon after missed the chicken, inquired after it; and on my relating the accident (for I told her the truth, for my mother would never suffer me to tell a lie), she flew into a violent passion, and threatened that I should suffer for it; and, my master being out, she immediately went and told her mistress what I had done. This alarmed me very much, and I expected an instant flogging, which to me was uncommonly dreadful, for I had seldom been beaten at home. I therefore resolved to fly; and accordingly I ran into a thicket that was hard by, and hid myself in the bushes. Soon afterwards my mistress and the slave returned, and,

---

[4] That is, England.

not seeing me, they searched all the house, but not finding me, and I not making answer when they called to me, they thought I had run away, and the whole neighborhood was raised in the pursuit of me.

In that part of the country, as in ours, the houses and villages were skirted with woods, or shrubberies, and the bushes were so thick that a man could readily conceal himself in them, so as to elude the strictest search. The neighbors continued the whole day looking for me, and several times many of them came within a few yards of the place where I lay hid. I expected every moment, when I heard a rustling among the trees, to be found out, and punished by my master; but they never discovered me, though they were often so near that I even heard their conjectures as they were looking about for me; and I now learned from them that any attempts to return home would be hopeless. Most of them supposed I had fled towards home; but the distance was so great, and the way so intricate, that they thought I could never reach it, and that I should be lost in the woods. When I heard this I was seized with a violent panic, and abandoned myself to despair. Night, too, began to approach, and aggravated all my fears. I had before entertained hopes of getting home, and had determined when it should be dark to make the attempt; but I was now convinced it was fruitless, and began to consider that, if possibly I could escape all other animals, I could not those of the human kind; and that, not knowing the way, I must perish in the woods. Thus was I like the hunted deer—

——Every leaf and every whisp'ring breath,
Convey'd a foe, and every foe a death.[5]

I heard frequent rustlings among the leaves, and being pretty sure they were snakes, I expected every instant to be stung by them. This increased my anguish, and the horror of my situation became now quite insupportable. I at length quitted the thicket, very faint and hungry, for I had not eaten or drank anything all the day, and crept to my master's kitchen, from whence I set out at first, which was an open shed, and laid myself down in the ashes with an anxious wish for death, to relieve me from all my pains. I was scarcely awake in the morning, when the old woman slave, who was the first up, came to light the fire, and saw me in the fireplace. She was very much surprised to see me, and could scarcely believe her own eyes. She now promised to intercede for me, and went for her master, who soon after came, and, having slightly reprimanded me, ordered me to be taken care of, and not ill treated.

Soon after this, my master's only daughter, and child by his first wife, sickened and died, which affected him so much that for sometime he was almost frantic, and really would have killed himself, had he not been watched and prevented. However, in a short time afterwards he recovered, and I was again sold. I was now

---

[5] Lines adapted by Equiano from Sir John Denham's famous topographical poem, *Cooper's Hill* (1642).

carried to the left of the sun's rising,[6] through many dreary wastes and dismal woods, amidst the hideous roarings of wild beasts. The people I was sold to used to carry me very often, when I was tired, either on their shoulders or on their backs. I saw many convenient well-built sheds along the road, at proper distances, to accommodate the merchants and travellers, who lay in those buildings along with their wives, who often accompany them; and they always go well armed.

From the time I left my own nation, I always found somebody that understood me till I came to the sea coast. The languages of different nations did not totally differ, nor were they so copious as those of the Europeans, particularly the English. They were therefore easily learned; and, while I was journeying thus through Africa, I acquired two or three different tongues. In this manner I had been travelling for a considerable time, when, one evening, to my great surprise, whom should I see brought to the house where I was but my dear sister! As soon as she saw me, she gave a loud shriek, and ran into my arms — I was quite overpowered; neither of us could speak, but, for a considerable time, clung to each other in mutual embraces, unable to do anything but weep. Our meeting affected all who saw us; and, indeed, I must acknowledge, in honor of those sable destroyers of human rights, that I never met with any ill treatment, or saw any offered to their slaves, except tying them, when necessary, to keep them from running away.

When these people knew we were brother and sister, they indulged us to be together; and the man, to whom I supposed we belonged, lay with us, he in the middle, while she and I held one another by the hands across his breast all night; and thus for a while we forgot our misfortunes, in the joy of being together; but even this small comfort was soon to have an end; for scarcely had the fatal morning appeared when she was again torn from me forever! I was now more miserable, if possible, than before. The small relief which her presence gave me from pain, was gone, and the wretchedness of my situation was redoubled by my anxiety after her fate, and my apprehensions lest her sufferings should be greater than mine, when I could not be with her to alleviate them. Yes, thou dear partner of all my childish sports! thou sharer of my joys and sorrows! happy should I have ever esteemed myself to encounter every misery for you and to procure your freedom by the sacrifice of my own. Though you were early forced from my arms, your image has been always riveted in my heart, from which neither time nor fortune have been able to remove it; so that, while the thoughts of your sufferings have damped my prosperity, they have mingled with adversity and increased its bitterness. To that Heaven which protects the weak from the strong, I commit the care of your innocence and virtues, if they have not already received their full reward, and if your youth and delicacy have not long since fallen victims to the

---

[6] It has proved impossible to locate precisely Equiano's itinerary or even his home of origin, although he was certainly an Igbo and apparently lived in the eastern part of southern Nigeria. His reference to a large river most likely alludes to the Niger or one of the rivers in its delta region.

violence of the African trader, the pestilential stench of a Guinea ship, the seasoning in the European colonies, or the lash and lust of a brutal and unrelenting overseer.[7]

I did not long remain after my sister. I was again sold, and carried through a number of places, till after travelling a considerable time, I came to a town called Tinmah, in the most beautiful country I had yet seen in Africa. It was extremely rich, and there were many rivulets which flowed through it, and supplied a large pond in the centre of the town, where the people washed. Here I saw for the first time cocoanuts, which I thought superior to any nuts I had ever tasted before; and the trees, which were loaded, were also interspersed among the houses, which had commodious shades adjoining, and were in the same manner as ours, the insides being neatly plastered and whitewashed. Here I also saw and tasted for the first time, sugar-cane. Their money consisted of little white shells, the size of the finger nail. I was sold here for one hundred and seventy-two of them,[8] by a merchant who lived and brought me there.

I had been about two or three days at his house, when a wealthy widow, a neighbor of his, came there one evening, and brought with her an only son, a young gentleman about my own age and size. Here they saw me; and, having taken a fancy to me, I was bought of the merchant, and went home with them. Her house and premises were situated close to one of those rivulets I have mentioned, and were the finest I ever saw in Africa: they were very extensive, and she had a number of slaves to attend her. The next day I was washed and perfumed, and when meal time came, I was led into the presence of my mistress, and ate and drank before her with her son. This filled me with astonishment; and I could scarce help expressing my surprise that the young gentleman should suffer me, who was bound, to eat with him who was free; and not only so, but that he would not at any time either eat or drink till I had taken first, because I was the eldest, which was agreeable to our custom. Indeed, every thing here, and all their treatment of me, made me forget that I was a slave. The language of these people resembled ours so nearly, that we understood each other perfectly. They had also the very same customs as we. There were likewise slaves daily to attend us, while my young master and I, with other boys, sported with our darts and bows and arrows, as I had been used to do at home. In this resemblance to my former happy state, I passed about two months; and I now began to think I was to be adopted into the family, and was beginning to be reconciled to my situation, and to forget by degrees my misfortunes, when all at once the delusion vanished; for, without

---

[7] In this sentence, Equiano lists the stages of the African slave trade: capture in Africa and transportation to the coast; the infamous "middle passage" across the Atlantic; the introduction to forced labor in the New World, primarily in the Caribbean and Brazil.

[8] Cowrie shells were a common form of currency throughout West Africa. It is more likely that instead of 172 cowrie shells he was sold for 28–30 British pounds sterling.

the least previous knowledge, one morning early, while my dear master and companion was still asleep, I was awakened out of my reverie to fresh sorrow, and hurried away even amongst the uncircumcised.[9]

Thus, at the very moment I dreamed of the greatest happiness, I found myself most miserable; and it seemed as if fortune wished to give me this taste of joy only to render the reverse more poignant. The change I now experienced was as painful as it was sudden and unexpected. It was a change indeed, from a state of bliss to a scene which is inexpressible by me, as it discovered to me an element I had never before beheld, and till then had no idea of, and wherein such instances of hardship and cruelty continually occurred, as I can never reflect on but with horror.

All the nations and people I had hitherto passed through, resembled our own in their manners, customs, and language; but I came at length to a country, the inhabitants of which differed from us in all those particulars.[10] I was very much struck with this difference, especially when I came among a people who did not circumcise, and ate without washing their hands. They cooked also in iron pots, and had European cutlasses and cross bows, which were unknown to us, and fought with their fists among themselves. Their women were not so modest as ours, for they ate, and drank, and slept with their men. But above all, I was amazed to see no sacrifices or offerings among them. In some of those places the people ornamented themselves with scars, and likewise filed their teeth very sharp. They wanted sometimes to ornament me in the same manner, but I would not suffer them; hoping that I might some time be among a people who did not thus disfigure themselves, as I thought they did. At last I came to the banks of a large river which was covered with canoes, in which the people appeared to live with their household utensils, and provisions of all kinds. I was beyond measure astonished at this, as I had never before seen any water larger than a pond or a rivulet; and my surprise was mingled with no small fear when I was put into one of these canoes, and we began to paddle and move along the river. We continued going on thus till night, and when we came to land, and made fires on the banks, each family by themselves; some dragged their canoes on shore, others stayed and cooked in theirs, and laid in them all night. Those on the land had mats, of which they made tents, some in the shape of little houses; in these we slept; and after the morning meal, we embarked again and proceeded as before. I was often very much astonished to see some of the women, as well as the men, jump into the water, dive to the bottom, come up again, and swim about.

---

[9] In this African context, Equiano uses "uncircumcised" as a term of contempt. He frequently draws analogies between the Igbos of his childhood memory and the Jews of the Old Testament. In Chapter One, he states, "We practised circumcision like the Jews, and made offerings and feasts on that occasion."

[10] Possibly the Ibibio people who lived north of Bonny, the Nigerian port through which much of the slave trade of the region passed.

Thus I continued to travel, sometimes by land, sometimes by water, through different countries and various nations, till, at the end of six or seven months after I had been kidnapped, I arrived at the sea coast. It would be tedious and uninteresting to relate all the incidents which befell me during this journey, and which I have not yet forgotten; of the various hands I passed through, and the manners and customs of all the different people among whom I lived—I shall therefore only observe, that in all the places where I was, the soil was exceedingly rich; the pumpkins, eadas, plantains, yams, &c. &c., were in great abundance, and of incredible size. There were also vast quantities of different gums, though not used for any purpose, and everywhere a great deal of tobacco. The cotton even grew quite wild, and there was plenty of red-wood. I saw no mechanics whatever in all the way, except such as I have mentioned. The chief employment in all these countries was agriculture, and both the males and females, as with us, were brought up to it, and trained in the arts of war.

The first object which saluted my eyes when I arrived on the coast, was the sea, and a slave ship, which was then riding at anchor, and waiting for its cargo. These filled me with astonishment, which was soon converted into terror, when I was carried on board. I was immediately handled, and tossed up to see if I were sound, by some of the crew; and I was now persuaded that I had gotten into a world of bad spirits, and that they were going to kill me. Their complexions, too, differing so much from ours, their long hair, and the language they spoke (which was very different from any I had ever heard), united to confirm me in this belief.[11] Indeed, such were the horrors of my views and fears at the moment, that, if ten thousand worlds had been my own, I would have freely parted with them all to have exchanged my condition with that of the meanest slave in my own country. When I looked round the ship too, and saw a large furnance of copper boiling, and a multitude of black people of every description chained together, every one of their countenances expressing dejection and sorrow, I no longer doubted of my fate; and, quite overpowered with horror and anguish, I fell motionless on the deck and fainted. When I recovered a little, I found some black people about me, who I believed were some of those who had brought me on board, and had been receiving their pay; they talked to me in order to cheer me, but all in vain. I asked them if we were not to be eaten by those white men with horrible looks, red faces, and long hair. They told me I was not, and one of the crew brought me a small portion of spirituous liquor in a wine glass; but being afraid of him, I would not take it out of his hand. One of the blacks therefore took it from him and gave it to me, and I took a little down my palate, which, instead of reviving me, as they thought it would, threw me into the greatest consternation at the strange feeling it produced, having never tasted any such liquor before. Soon after this, the blacks who brought me on board went off, and left me abandoned to despair.

---

[11] His arrival on the coast provides Equiano with his first sight of Europeans, although he has been experiencing various forms of African slavery since his kidnapping.

I now saw myself deprived of all chance of returning to my native country, or even the least glimpse of hope of gaining the shore, which I now considered as friendly; and I even wished for my former slavery in preference to my present situation, which was filled with horrors of every kind, still heightened by my ignorance of what I was to undergo. I was not long suffered to indulge my grief; I was soon put down under the decks, and there I received such a salutation in my nostrils as I had never experienced in my life: so that, with the loathsomeness of the stench, and crying together, I became so sick and low that I was not able to eat, nor had I the least desire to taste anything. I now wished for the last friend, death, to relieve me; but soon, to my grief, two of the white men offered me eatables; and, on my refusing to eat, one of them held me fast by the hands, and laid me across, I think, the windlass, and tied my feet, while the other flogged me severely. I had never experienced anything of this kind before, and, although not being used to the water, I naturally feared that element the first time I saw it, yet, nevertheless, could I have got over the nettings, I would have jumped over the side, but I could not; and besides, the crew used to watch us very closely who were not chained down to the decks, lest we should leap into the water; and I have seen some of these poor African prisoners most severely cut, for attempting to do so, and hourly whipped for not eating. This indeed was often the case with myself.

In a little time after, amongst the poor chained men, I found some of my own nation, which in a small degree gave ease to my mind. I inquired of these what was to be done with us? They gave me to understand, we were to be carried to these white people's country to work for them. I then was a little revived, and thought, if it were no worse than working, my situation was not so desperate; but still I feared I should be put to death, the white people looked and acted, as I thought, in so savage a manner; for I had never seen among any people such instances of brutal cruelty; and this not only shown towards us blacks, but also to some of the whites themselves. One white man in particular I saw, when we were permitted to be on deck, flogged so unmercifully with a large rope near the foremast, that he died in consequence of it; and they tossed him over the side as they would have done a brute. This made me fear these people the more; and I expected nothing less than to be treated in the same manner. I could not help expressing my fears and apprehensions to some of my countrymen; I asked them if these people had no country, but lived in this hollow place the ship? They told me they did not, but came from a distant one. "Then," said I, "how comes it in all our country we never heard of them?" They told me because they lived so very far off. I then asked where were their women? had they any like themselves? I was told they had. "And why," said I, "do we not see them?" They answered, because they were left behind. I asked how the vessel could go? They told me they could not tell; but that there was cloth put upon the masts by the help of the ropes I saw, and then the vessel went on; and the white men had some spell or magic they put in the water when they liked, in order to stop the vessel. I was exceedingly amazed at this account, and really thought they were spirits. I therefore wished much to be from amongst them, for I expected they would sacrifice me;

but my wishes were vain—for we were so quartered that it was impossible for any of us to make our escape.

While we stayed on the coast I was mostly on deck; and one day, to my great astonishment, I saw one of these vessels coming in with the sails up. As soon as the whites saw it, they gave a great shout, at which we were amazed; and the more so, as the vessel appeared larger by approaching nearer. At last, she came to an anchor in my sight, and when the anchor was let go, I and my countrymen who saw it, were lost in astonishment to observe the vessel stop—and were now convinced it was done by magic. Soon after this the other ship got her boats out, and they came on board of us, and the people of both ships seemed very glad to see each other. Several of the strangers also shook hands with us black people, and made motions with their hands, signifying I suppose, we were to go to their country, but we did not understand them.

At last, when the ship we were in had got in all her cargo, they made ready with many fearful noises, and we were all put under deck, so that we could not see how they managed the vessel. But this disappointment was the least of my sorrow. The stench of the hold while we were on the coast was so intolerably loathsome, that it was dangerous to remain there for any time, and some of us had been permitted to stay on the deck for the fresh air; but now that the whole ship's cargo were confined together, it became absolutely pestilential. The closeness of the place, and the heat of the climate, added to the number in the ship, which was so crowded that each had scarcely room to turn himself, almost suffocated us. This produced copious perspirations, so that the air soon became unfit for respiration, from a variety of loathsome smells, and brought on a sickness among the slaves, of which many died—thus falling victims to the improvident avarice, as I may call it, of their purchasers. This wretched situation was again aggravated by the galling of the chains, now became insupportable, and the filth of the necessary tubs,[12] into which the children often fell, and were almost suffocated. The shrieks of the women, and the groans of the dying, rendered the whole a scene of horror almost inconceivable. Happily perhaps, for myself, I was soon reduced so low here that it was thought necessary to keep me almost always on deck; and from my extreme youth I was not put in fetters. In this situation I expected every hour to share the fate of my companions, some of whom were almost daily brought upon deck at the point of death, which I began to hope would soon put an end to my miseries. Often did I think many of the inhabitants of the deep much more happy than myself. I envied them the freedom they enjoyed, and as often wished I could change my condition for theirs. Every circumstance I met with, served only to render my state more painful, and heightened my apprehensions, and my opinion of the cruelty of the whites.

One day they had taken a number of fishes; and when they had killed and satisfied themselves with as many as they thought fit, to our astonishment who

---

[12] Latrines.

were on deck, rather than give any of them to us to eat, as we expected, they tossed the remaining fish into the sea again, although we begged and prayed for some as well as we could, but in vain; and some of my countrymen, being pressed by hunger, took an opportunity, when they thought no one saw them, of trying to get a little privately; but they were discovered, and the attempt procured them some very severe floggings.

One day, when we had a smooth sea and moderate wind, two of my wearied countrymen who were chained together (I was near them at the time), preferring death to such a life of misery, somehow made through the nettings and jumped into the sea; immediately, another quite dejected fellow, who, on account of his illness, was suffered to be out of irons, also followed their example; and I believe many more would very soon have done the same, if they had not been prevented by the ship's crew, who were instantly alarmed. Those of us that were the most active, were in a moment put down under the deck; and there was such a noise and confusion amongst the people of the ship as I never heard before, to stop her, and get the boat out to go after the slaves. However, two of the wretches were drowned, but they got the other, and afterwards flogged him unmercifully, for thus attempting to prefer death to slavery. In this manner we continued to undergo more hardships than I can now relate, hardships which are inseparable from this accursed trade. Many a time we were near suffocation from the want of fresh air, which we were often without for whole days together. This, and the stench of the necessary tubs, carried off many.

During our passage, I first saw flying fishes, which surprised me very much; they used frequently to fly across the ship, and many of them fell on the deck. I also now first saw the use of the quadrant;[13] I had often with astonishment seen the mariners make observations with it, and I could not think what it meant. They at last took notice of my surprise; and one of them, willing to increase it, as well as to gratify my curiosity, made me one day look through it. The clouds appeared to me to be land, which disappeared as they passed along. This heightened my wonder; and I was now more persuaded than ever, that I was in another world, and that every thing about me was magic.

At last we came in sight of the island of Barbadoes,[14] at which the whites on board gave a great shout, and made many signs of joy to us. We did not know what to think of this; but as the vessel drew nearer, we plainly saw the harbor, and other ships of different kinds and sizes, and we soon anchored amongst them, off Bridgetown. Many merchants and planters now came on board, though it was in the evening. They put us in separate parcels,[15] and examined us attentively. They also made us jump, and pointed to the land, signifying we were to go

---

[13] A navigational instrument used for determining one's location.

[14] In the Caribbean, off the coast of present-day Venezuela.

[15] Groups.

there. We thought by this, we should be eaten by these ugly men, as they appeared to us; and, when soon after we were all put down under the deck again, there was much dread and trembling among us, and nothing but bitter cries to be heard all the night from these apprehensions, insomuch, that at last the white people got some old slaves from the land to pacify us. They told us we were not to be eaten, but to work, and were soon to go on land, where we should see many of our country people. This report eased us much. And sure enough, soon after we were landed, there came to us Africans of all languages.

We were conducted immediately to the merchant's yard, where we were all pent up together, like so many sheep in a fold, without regard to sex or age. As every object was new to me, everything I saw filled me with surprise. What struck me first was that the houses were built with bricks and stories, and in every other respect different from those I had seen in Africa; but I was still more astonished on seeing people on horseback. I did not know what this could mean; and, indeed, I thought these people were full of nothing but magical arts. While I was in this astonishment, one of my fellow prisoners spoke to a countryman of his about the horses, who said they were the same kind they had in their country. I understood them, though they were from a distant part of Africa; and I thought it odd I had not seen any horses there; but afterwards, when I came to converse with different Africans, I found they had many horses amongst them, and much larger than those I then saw.

We were not many days in the merchant's custody, before we were sold after their usual manner, which is this: On a signal given (as the beat of a drum), the buyers rush at once into the yard where the slaves are confined, and make choice of that parcel they like best. The noise and clamor with which this is attended, and the eagerness visible in the countenances of the buyers, serve not a little to increase the apprehension of terrified Africans, who may well be supposed to consider them as the ministers of that destruction to which they think themselves devoted. In this manner, without scruple, are relations and friends separated, most of them never to see each other again.

I remember, in the vessel in which I was brought over, in the men's apartment, there were several brothers, who, in the sale, were sold in different lots; and it was very moving on this occasion, to see and hear their cries at parting. O, ye nominal Christians! might not an African ask you — Learned you this from your God, who says unto you, Do unto all men as you would men should do unto you? Is it not enough that we are torn from our country and friends, to toil for your luxury and lust of gain? Must ever tender feeling be likewise sacrificed to your avarice? Are the dearest friends and relations, now rendered more dear by their separation from their kindred, still to be parted from each other, and thus prevented from cheering the gloom of slavery, with the small comfort of being together, and mingling their sufferings and sorrows? Why are parents to lose their children, brothers their sisters, or husbands their wives? Surely, this is a new refinement in cruelty, which, while it has no advantage to atone for it, thus aggravates distress, and adds fresh horrors even to the wretchedness of slavery.

32

❧

Cirilo Villaverde

CECILIA VALDÉS

C irilo Villaverde (1812–1894), the author of one of the greatest Spanish
  American novels of the nineteenth century, Cecilia Valdés (1882), was born
on a sugar plantation in the region of Vuelta Abajo in western Cuba. His father
was a medical doctor who cared for the more than three hundred slaves who
worked on the plantation, and Villaverde was thus able to witness from an early
age the evils of the slavery system. At the age of eleven, Villaverde moved to Havana, where he would continue his education until he earned a law degree in
1834. Disenchanted by the corruption he found among lawyers and judges,
Villaverde gave up the practice of law and became a high school teacher. Meanwhile, he began to develop a literary career, publishing short novels and stories in
Cuban literary journals and popular magazines.

   During the 1830s and 1840s, Villaverde was a member of the literary circle
gathered at the Havana home of the aristocratic cultural promoter Domingo del
Monte. The gathering at del Monte's house was also a center for the spread of antislavery ideas in Cuba. At the time, Cuba was a Spanish colony, and would continue to be one until the Spanish-American War of 1898. The island's economy
was based on sugar plantations, which depended almost exclusively on slave labor.
The plantations were enormously profitable to a small but influential group of
Cuban landowners as well as to the Spanish nation, and thus public debate and
criticism of the slave system were expressly forbidden. From the del Monte group,
however, the first Cuban antislavery novels would emerge, a genre that circulated
clandestinely in Cuba almost until its abolition of slavery in 1886. Villaverde's
masterpiece, Cecilia Valdés, belongs in part to this genre, although it also transcends it by offering a panoramic view and analysis of the whole of nineteenth-
century Cuban society.

   The writing of Cecilia Valdés went through several stages: Initially, it was a
two-part short story, which in turn became a short novel (both published in Havana in 1839), until, forty-three years later, the third and definitive version of the

442

novel was published in New York. In those intervening years, Villaverde, who had become committed to Cuba's separation from Spain, worked as a journalist, was involved in several political conspiracies against Spanish rule, and in 1849, following a failed uprising against the Spanish colonial government, went into exile in the United States. In his political views, Villaverde originally favored the annexation of Cuba by the United States, but by 1868, at the outset of the Ten Years' War (1868–1878, the first of two insurrections that would culminate in Cuba's independence at the end of the nineteenth century), he became a supporter of independence. In New York, where he lived for the rest of his life, Villaverde founded various Spanish-language newspapers and magazines. Returning to teaching in 1874, he opened a school in Weehawken, New Jersey. He made only two brief trips back to Cuba, one between 1858 and 1860 and the second in 1888. He died in 1894, having witnessed the great success of the last version of Cecilia Valdés.

With an energetic and panoramic style reminiscent of works by the French writers Honoré de Balzac and Victor Hugo, Villaverde narrates in Cecilia Valdés *the story of the white, wealthy, young Leonardo Gamboa's love relationship with the beautiful but poor mulatto girl Cecilia Valdés, who is, as readers learn early in the novel, Leonardo's half-sister on their father's side. Leonardo does not know this, of course, since Don Cándido Gamboa, Leonardo's and Cecilia's father, has kept Cecilia's existence a secret to the rest of his family. In the course of the novel he desperately but covertly seeks to avert any sexual liaison between his two children, a liaison that would not have included marriage in any case—since marriage between two people of such different social classes and different races was out of the question in Cuba then. Rather than marriage, a sexual relationship between the two children would probably have repeated the sort of concubinage that gave birth to Cecilia herself.*

Within this tale of incest averted, of the sexual exploitation of black women, and of the strict separation between the classes and races in nineteenth-century Cuba, Villaverde includes an enormous cast of characters that ranges from the Governor-General of the colony to the black slave María de Regla, who is the wet nurse of both Cecilia and of Leonardo's sister, Adela. The novel also describes in considerable detail the structure, functioning, and consequences of the slavery system in Cuba, both for its beneficiaries, like Don Cándido Gamboa, and for the slaves who suffer it. Readers thus witness the cold machinations and calculated cruelty of the Havana slave traders like Gamboa, the abuses and punishments to which the slaves were subjected on the sugar plantations, and the often-failed attempts by the free blacks and mulattoes to rise above their low social station in colonial Cuba. Simultaneously, however, the novel reminds its readers of the close-knit—but not openly acknowledged—personal and cultural relationships that, despite the slavery system, existed between blacks and whites on the island, and that eventually gave rise to the modern Cuban people.

In the following selection, Chapters 5 and 6 of the First Part of Cecilia Valdés, *Villaverde portrays the colorful environment of the popular dances held by the*

free blacks and mulattoes of Havana, to which many upper-class young white
men (referred to as Creoles in the novel), like Leonardo, went in search of liaisons
with mulatto women. Readers also witness the dramatic impact that Cecilia
Valdés's beauty has on everyone around her, as she makes her entrance to the ball
followed by the admiring cry of "la virgencita de bronce" *("the little bronze vir-*
gin") directed at her by the crowd. Also introduced in this selection is the mulatto
musician José Dolores Pimienta, Cecilia's long-suffering admirer, who will mur-
der Leonardo Gamboa at the novel's end.

❧

"Have you, in all your life, seen such a sprightly female?"
"No; Nor has ever a more silky creature trod the village green."

Mañanas de Abril y Mayo — Calderón de la Barca

5

Commissioner Cantalapiedra, after strolling about the dance floor for a few moments, started to make the rounds of the house. As he stepped into the bedroom,
he caught sight of the mistress of the house leaning over the bed to lay down a
wrap belonging to a friend who had just arrived. As a joke, he stepped up behind
her and put his hands over her eyes. Now Mercedes Ayala, the woman in question, was a lively mulatto, and full of fun notwithstanding her 30 and some years,
plump, petite, and not a bit bad-looking. Even when nabbed suddenly from behind she lost none of her self-possession. With a perfectly natural movement she
grasped the commissioner's hands with her own and, without a second's hesitation, said:
"This couldn't be anybody but Cantalapiedra."
"How did you know it was me, mulata?" He asked.
"Very naturally," she replied. "By the sense of touch, of course."
"Whose touch? — yours or mine?"
"Both, Señor, so neither need be offended."
Then the commissioner put his right arm around her waist and gently drew
her close to him, whispering something into her ear which set her laughing; but
she replied, as she pushed him away with both hands: "Stop it, you flatterer. The
one who will really make you sit up and take notice is just getting out now. Yes,
yes, I — judge for yourself."
At that very instant two young women were stepping out of a luxurious carriage which had drawn up before the door, an event manifested by a general

---

From *Cecilia Valdés* by Cirilo Villaverde, copyright 1962 by Sydney G. Gest, translator.
New York: Vantage Press, 1962, pp. 53–72.

movement of heads and craning of necks inside and outside the house. If the Ayala woman was referring to one of these young women, there is not the slightest doubt that her opinion was well founded. There never could have existed a more lovely woman, nor one better calculated to drive a susceptible man out of his senses. She was the taller and more striking of the two and took the lead in stepping out of the carriage, as well as in entering the ballroom, which she did on the arm of a mulatto, who had gone out to receive her at the carriage door. With her regular features and graceful figure, her narrow waist contrasting with the comparative breadth of her bare shoulders, the adorable expression of her face, as well as the delicately bronzed tint of her skin, she could well have passed for the Afro-Caucasian Venus. She was clothed in sheer black lace over a white satin dress, short sleeves with two holes, which allowed little circles of skin to show, a band of wide, flesh-coloured ribbon across the breast, long silk gloves to the elbow, three strings of corals at the throat, and a white Marabou plume in combination with real flowers which, with the hair tied in a low rowel behind, and a row of curls from one side of the head to the other, back of the temples, gave her head the appearance of an old-fashioned black velvet bonnet, an illusion which she or her hairdresser had obviously tried to capture. Her companion's dress and coiffure were more or less in the same general style but, not being half so tall and beautiful, she did not excite the same attention.

The women stood on tiptoe to get a look at her, the men cleared a path to let her pass, addressing flattering remarks to her, not all of them too decorous in tone. Suddenly there was a cry of: "*La virgencita de bronce*," the little bronze virgin, "*la virgencita de bronce*," which was taken up and resounded from one end of the house to the other. The fact that the queen of the ball arrived at a moment when the orchestra was not playing made it all the more easy for the excitement and enthusiasm to spread everywhere. As she passed Pimienta, the clarinetist, she tapped him on the arm with her fan and smiled, which was a signal for the musician, who seemed to have been awaiting that very moment, to draw from his instrument the most melodious and appealing notes, as if the muse of his platonic dreams had descended to earth, in the form of a woman, solely to inspire him. In short, one might say that the touch of the fan affected the musician like an electric discharge, whose sensation, if one may so express it, could be read not only in his face but in his whole body from head to foot. Not a word passed between them, naturally, nor did it seem necessary, either, at least insofar as he was concerned, for the language of his eyes and his music was the most eloquent any human being could use to express the fervour of his passionate love.

The companion of the *virgencita de bronce* also smiled at Pimienta and touched him with her fan, but the least observant spectator could not fail to notice that her touch and smile did not have the same magic effect upon him. On the contrary, their eyes met in a natural and quiet manner, from which it was easy to surmise that there was an understanding between them but that it was an understanding based upon friendship or kinship rather than love. Be all this as it may, Pimienta followed the two girls with his eyes, insofar as the crowd of people permitted, until they entered the first room through the dining room door; then he ceased playing and stopped the music.

The young white men, headed by Cantalapiedra, had at length stationed themselves in the dining room, near the communicating door, so as to keep an eye on the women as they came in from the street and also observe those who left the salon for the ballroom. The young Creole[1] whom they called Leonardo, as soon as he noticed the approach of the carriage, made his way with some difficulty through the crowd to the street, walked directly to the coachman and said something to him in a low voice. The latter, lifting his hat as a sign of respect, and leaning down from his seat in the saddle in order better to hear him said, "*Sí, Señor,*" and made off quickly with the carriage, rounding the corner of the hospital of the Paulist nuns.

As the two girls walked from the dining room into the bedroom, the prettier of the two asked her friend in a tone of voice clearly audible to people standing near-by: "Did you see him?"

"Has love made you blind, 'Cilia?" answered her companion with another question.

"That isn't it; it's just that I didn't see him. Why should I have?"

"Because he shot right by you like an arrow as we were coming in."

On hearing this, the other began to search the crowd of heads already turned in her direction in an effort to find the right one and to attract his attention. But she was doubtless unable to catch his eye, for she frowned and turned away in disgust. Cantalapiedra, however, overhearing what she had just said and observing her look of disappointment, called out: "What? Don't you see me? Here I am, angel."

The young woman made a pleasant gesture and said nothing. But Nemesia, who was not given to beating about the bush, replied with more vigour than politeness: "You can keep on standing there for the rest of your life so far as we're concerned. No one asked about you."

"I wasn't talking to you, either, nitwit."

"Nor is it necessary, my friend."

"What a tongue, what a tongue," repeated the commissioner. All this was over in an instant, with scarcely a turn of the head on the part of the girls, and without a pause in their conversation, while the men were clearing a path for them to pass through the crowd.

At the door of the bedroom, Señora Ayala received them with open arms and much demonstration of affection. Whether it was meant as a mere compliment or an expression of her true feelings, she almost shouted at the girls: "We were

---

[1] Throughout the novel, the term "Creole" (*criollo*) is used to refer to the Cubans of Spanish descent. The term "mulatto" refers to a person who is partly of African ancestry. Cecilia herself is a mulatta, although one whose physical appearance allows her to "pass" for white.

waiting for you to open the ball. How is Chepilla?" she continued, addressing the younger of the girls. "Didn't she come? I was beginning to think something had happened."

"I very nearly didn't come, myself," the girl answered. "Chepilla didn't feel a bit well and then she got so cross. The gig waited for us a half hour, at least."

"It was better for her not to come," continued Mercedes, "because this thing will go on till morning and she couldn't have stood it. Give me your cloaks."

It was high time for the party to begin. At about that moment, a tall, bald, and no longer young but robust mulatto entered the room where the elderly women were gathered and planted himself in front of Mercedes Ayala. Raising his arms he addressed her in a deep voice: "I've come for the most beautiful and charming lady to open the ball."

"But, my friend, she's not here. Try the other door," replied Señora Ayala with a loud laugh.

"Now don't try any of those excuses on me, *Señora,* because I'm too stubborn. And then, too, only the hostess has the honour of opening the ball, and especially when its her birthday."

"That might be so if there were not, in this select gathering, pretty girls to whom the power and the glory rightfully belongs everywhere in the world."

"Yes, that's true," answered the bald man. "There's no lack of pretty girls tonight in this select gathering, but that qualification, which also holds good in the case of the hostess, does not give them the right to open the ball. Today is your saint's day, Mercedes. You are the lady of the house, where we are holding this happy celebration, and you symbolize the beauty and charm of the world. Have I not expressed the sentiments of all?" he concluded, looking at the faces of the people standing nearby for signs of approval.

Since everyone, either verbally or tacitly expressed his acquiescence, Señora Ayala had no option but to rise and follow her partner to the ballroom. The men had already cleared the floor, leaving a fair amount of space in the center free for dancing. The bald man took Mercedes by the hand and they formed a square in front of the orchestra to whom he gave the command, in an imperious voice, to play a minuet. This formal and ceremonious dance had fallen into disuse in the era of which we are speaking. Being a dance favoured principally by the aristocracy, it was reserved by the coloured people for the opening number at their balls.

Mercedes danced the old-fashioned air with considerable grace, and was enthusiastically applauded by the bystanders; but the man made a grotesque spectacle of himself. After the minuet, the ball, that is to say the Cuban dances, began. They differ so radically from Spanish dances that one can scarcely detect their origin. One of the many men present was bold enough to request a dance of the young women of the white feather or, as we might say, the muse of the party, and she, without raising any objection or waiting to be urged, accepted immediately. As she was leaving the salon for the ballroom to take her place in the line of dancers, one of the women was heard to exclaim:

"What a perfectly beautiful girl! May God keep her and bless her."

"The image of her mother, may she have found peace in heaven," added another.

"What! Is that child's mother dead?" asked a third with astonishment.

"Why, of course! Is that just now dawning upon you?" replied the one who had spoken second. "Why, didn't you hear everyone say she had died as a result of having lost her child a few days after it was born?"

"I don't understand how she lost the child if she is still alive."

"You haven't let me finish, Señá Caridad. She lost her child a few days after it was born because they took it away from her when she least expected it. Some say that the grandmother did it so that she could be put in the Royal Cradle House,[2] where she might pass for a white child; others say it was not the grandmother but the little girl's father, who was a gentleman of wealth and position, who had repented of his conduct and wished to evade his obligations respecting the mother. The latter lost her reason when they took the child away from her and, later, when they gave the daughter back to her, on the advice of the doctors, it was too late. Her reason returned, though some doubt it, but she never recovered her health and died in Paula."[3]

"You have told quite a story, Señá Trinidad," said Señora Ayala, softly, when the mulatto had concluded, and her smile betrayed considerable doubt as to its accuracy.

"My dear," replied Trinidad in a loud voice, "I'm telling it to you as they told it to me. I haven't added a jot or tittle on my own account."

"Well, according to the story, which I believe was quite authentic," continued Señora Ayala, "you or the person who told you the story did add a lot to it. I say this because it isn't known for sure whether the child's mother is alive or dead; the only thing that is absolutely certain is that the grandmother is keeping the granddaughter in ignorance regarding the identity of her father. But anybody would have to be blind not to know who he is. He is probably walking by the windows right now, keeping an eye on the daughter, for he does not let her get out of his sight for an instant. It seems that this heartless and inhuman fellow, suffering remorse because of the way he treated Rosarito Alarcón, can find no way to atone for his guilt but to follow her from pillar to post, trying to protect her from the perils of the world. Make no mistake about it; his efforts are futile. Just imagine trying to cut the bird's wings after it has once learned to fly."

"But, may I ask," inquired the one they called Caridad, "who is this important personage you're talking about? I'm one person who doesn't know him, and I don't consider myself blind or deaf, either."

---

[2] The Royal Cradle House (*La Real Casa-Cuna*) was an orphanage and refuge for illegitimate children in nineteenth-century Havana. Originally endowed by a wealthy Creole landowner whose surname was Valdés, all the children placed in that institution bore the surname Valdés.

[3] "Paula" is a reference of the Hospital de Santa Paula, another landmark of old Havana.

"I know what it is to suffer from unsatisfied curiosity, Señá Caridad, so I'm going to tell you," said Señora Ayala, drawing her chair closer, "I feel that I'm talking to a woman who knows how to keep a secret, so I'm going to tell you the whole business from beginning to end. There is no reason, now, why I should keep it from you. The man's name is"—and, putting both hands on her friend's shoulders, she whispered into her ear. Then Señora Ayala added aloud: "Do you know him now?"

"Why, of course, I do," replied Señora Caridad, "as well as I know my own name; to think that I thought I knew him so well. But I did hear that—but, be still my tongue."

At about ten o'clock the ball was in full swing. They danced with fury; we say "fury" because we can find no expression to so vividly describe that incessant movement of feet, shuffling smoothly, in harmony with the body, and in perfect time with the music; that revolving and pressing and squeezing, in the midst of a dense crowd of dancers and spectators, and that rise and fall of the dance without rest or respite. Above the sound of the orchestra, with its deafening kettledrums, could be heard, in perfect time with the music, the monotonous and continual shuffling of feet, without which requisite the coloured people think they cannot keep perfect time to the Creole music.

In the era to which we are referring, the square dance was in vogue; some of the figures were difficult and complex, so much so that the principles had to be mastered before attempting to execute them. If a player made a mistake he exposed himself to ridicule. If he made a slip they would say he got "lost" or "lost himself." The leader placed himself at the head of the group, executed the figure, and the rest of the couples either followed him exactly or dropped out. They generally had a leader at all *cuna* balls; he was selected or he took it upon himself to outline the figure, and when he came round to the head again he had the right to change it to suit his fancy. The one who devised the strangest and most complicated figures gained the reputation of being the best dancer, and the women considered it a great honour to be his partner. In addition to the distinction of being the best dancer, the leader avoided the possibility of "losing himself" and being under the painful necessity of sitting down without having participated in the dance.

On the night in question, the leader was dancing with Nemesia, who was the close friend of the young woman of the white feather. He had danced a great number of unusual figures, leaving the most difficult and complicated for the last. The second, third, fourth, and fifth couples passed the test successfully, executing the figures with the same linking and unlinking, and the same attitudes and postures as the leader. The *virgencita de bronce* and her partner were the sixth couple in the dance, which gave them the advantage of seeing the figures danced by five couples. But the young man could not get it into his head and, as his turn approached, his anxiety increased and he looked, with an expression of supplication, in the direction of the musicians, hoping that they would divine his predicament and stop the music. The girl very soon caught his feeling of concern, for she realized that she was about to suffer the ignominy of having to take a seat at the most lively and interesting part of the dance. Fear took complete possession of her, and she looked pale and nervous. What was going on in the minds of the couple very soon became apparent to the other dancers and to many of the spectators.

The very idea that the queen of the *cuna* might be compelled to drop out filled the other girls with a cruel and invidious satisfaction. For they had been dreadfully mortified at the preference shown her, and the eulogistic remarks made about her, by the men from the moment of her arrival. In these critical circumstances, Pimienta, who did not let his fantastic gyrations and the tumult of the dance prevent his keeping the *virgencita de bronce* under close observation, took in the situation at a glance and, without warning, brought the music to a sudden stop. The young man heaved a sigh of relief, and his partner repaid the leader for his well-timed succour with a celestial smile.

> In all the maddening crowd
> Which, burning, churning,
> Whirls upon its way,
> Not one was heard to say:
> "He who, in silence, ever doth adore thee
> Is looking, listening, standing there, before thee."

15 de Agosto — Ramón Palma

6

The discerning reader will already have gathered that the *virgencita de bronce* was none other than Cecilia Valdés, the little street waif, whom we described at the beginning of this true story. She was now in full flower of youth and beauty and had begun to receive the idolatrous worship always rendered liberally to those twin goddesses by a sensual and corrupt people. When one takes into consideration her lack of proper upbringing and adds to this the ungallant manner in which men treated her because she belonged to a mixed race, regarded as inferior, he may form an approximate idea of her pride and vanity, secret keys to her rebellious character. So it was that, without shame or hesitation, she often showed a preference for men of the white and dominant race, for it was from them that she could expect privileges and pleasures, for which reason she used to say, quite openly, that all one could expect from a mulatto was a silk shawl and, from a Negro, eyes and hair.

It is obvious that an opinion so bluntly expressed, and so unflattering to the men of the last two classes mentioned, did not create the best of feeling among them; in spite of all this, possibly because they did not believe she meant what she said, or, perhaps, because they hoped she might make an exception in their case, or merely because she was so pretty they could not help falling in love with her, the fact is that more than one mulatto lost his head over her, especially Pimienta, the musician, as we are already well aware. The latter enjoyed the no small advantage over the other suitors of being the brother of Cecilia's best friend, whom she had known since childhood. This circumstance made it possible for him to see her frequently and treat her on a plane of intimacy, make himself indispensable to her, and perhaps win her rebellious heart by devotion and loyalty. Who, at some time in his life, has not cherished hopes more ephemeral? In any event, he always bore in mind that popular song of the Spanish poets, which begins: "Water, without being hard, will wear away the hardest marble." In strict fairness, it must be said that Cecilia regarded him highly among the men of his class who came to pay her court, even though such distinction had not, up to the present, passed beyond an occasional pleasantry with a man who, nevertheless, was very kind, courteous, and attentive to women.

The dance over, they returned to the salon, which they soon filled to overflowing; the men formed groups around various women, chosen for their beauty, gracious manner, or coquettish disposition. But in the midst of the apparent confusion which reigned in the house anyone could observe that, at least among the men of colour and the Creoles, there was a dividing line, tacitly and to all appearances unconsciously established, which both classes respected. The truth is that some of them entered into the pleasures of the moment with such enthusiasm that they seemed, momentarily, to forget their mutual jealousies and antagonisms. Moreover, the white men did not abandon the dining room and the principal living room, to which repaired the coloured women with whom they were on terms of friendship, or other relations, actual or anticipated. There was nothing new or surprising about this, granting the marked predilection of the two races for each other. Cecilia and Nemesia, for one or another of these motives, or because of their close friendship with the mistress of the house, went into the salon, immediately following the dance, and sat down behind the elderly women on the side next to the dining room. A group of young Creoles formed around them immediately, for they were the belles of the ball. The police commissioner, Cantalapiedra, Diego Meneses and his chum, the young Creole whom they called Leonardo, were easily the most conspicuous of the group. He was resting his hand on the back of Cecilia's chair and, whether unknowingly or on purpose, she leaned back, pressing his fingers against the chair.

"Is that the way you treat your friends?" said Leonardo, without taking his hand away, although it hurt him considerably.

Cecilia merely looked at him sidewise and her expression showed she was provoked, as if to say that the word "friend" sounded odd, coming from one who should have known that he was being treated as an enemy.

"This little girl is acting very haughty, today," said Cantalapiedra, who had observed the incident and the look she gave Leonardo.

"And why shouldn't she?" answered Nemesia, without turning her face.

"Nobody has handed you a candle for you to take part in this funeral procession," the commissioner replied.

"And you, *señor*, who has authorized you to butt in?"

"Authorized me? — Leonardo."

"And me? — Cecilia, of course."

"Don't pay any attention to him, Nemesia," said Cecilia.

"If it weren't for — I'd make you as smooth and pliable as a glove," added Cantalapiedra, looking straight at Cecilia.

"The man who can put a yoke around my neck hasn't been born yet," she replied.

"You're not being very polite tonight," said Leonardo at that point, leaning down and speaking almost directly into her ear.

"You owe me an apology and I'm making you pay," replied Cecilia like lightning, in the same tone of voice.

"'The honest borrower has no fear of giving security,' my father often says."

"I don't know anything about that," replied Cecilia. "I only know that you have offended me tonight."

"I? Why, darling—"

At that very moment Pimienta walked into the room, greeting a number of the women to right and left. When he was within reach of Cecilia, she touched him on the arm with unaccustomed familiarity and said in a glib tone and manner: "Listen! How well a certain man keeps his promise."

"Young lady," he said solemnly, and it was apparent that he was taking the situation too seriously. "José Dolores Pimienta always keeps his word."

"Nevertheless, the number you promised to play hasn't been played."

"It will be played, *virgencita,* it will be played; because you must remember that grapes ripen at the proper season."

"I was expecting it to be the first number."

"You shouldn't have. Musical numbers which are dedicated to some one are never played first; they are always played in the second dance, and mine will be played according to the rules."

"What are you going to call it?" asked Cecilia.

"I'm calling it by the name which the girl to whom it is dedicated deserves to have it called: *Caramelo Vendo.*"[4]

"Well, it's not me, that's a sure thing," said the young woman, somewhat abashed.

"Who knows, little girl? You got here very late," he added, turning to his sister Nemesia.

"Don't blame me, José Dolores," she replied. "It was only by the grace of God that we were able to convince Chepilla to let us come alone; of course she wasn't able to come with us. She finally gave her consent because we were coming in a carriage. And even so" (as she spoke she looked inquiringly at Cecilia), "if we hadn't got right into the gig she would have stopped us from going. Chepilla was mad as a hornet when she came to the door as we drove away and recognized — ."

"Chepilla didn't get mad because of anything of the kind," interrupted Cecilia, vehemently. "She didn't want us to come because it was a bad night to go out to a ball. And she was perfectly right, only I'd promised we'd be here."

---

[4]"I Sell Caramels."

From motives of prudence, or otherwise, Pimienta left them without waiting to hear further explanations. But Cantalapiedra, who was an inquisitive soul, if ever there was one, remained, and with a malicious smile said to Nemesia: "May I ask why Chepilla got mad when she recognized the gig in which you came to the ball?"

"As I'm nobody's baggage," replied Nemesia promptly, "I'll tell you the truth" (at which Cecilia gave her a pinch, but she finished the phrase). "It was because she recognized the gig as belonging to Leonardo, of course."

The gaze of all within earshot of Nemesia centered upon the young Creole. Thereupon Cantalapiedra, placing his hand upon Leonardo's shoulder, said: "Come, come, now, don't blush; lending one's carriage to a couple of pretty girls on such a bad night is no reason why anyone should suspect any improper motive on the part of a gentleman."

"The carriage, as well as the heart of its owner," replied Leonardo, with no sign of embarrassment, "are ever at the service of the fair."

This remark happened to be overheard by Pimienta as he was coming out of the dining room, and he rightly inferred that it was Leonardo's gig which had brought Cecilia and his sister Nemesia to the ball. The realization of this fact hurt him to the quick, and he cast a sad glance in the direction of the white men as he walked rapidly by them on his way to the ballroom. Picking up his clarinet, he blew a few notes as a signal to his companions that it was time for them to take their places in the orchestra. They tuned their instruments and immediately started playing a new Cuban dance. They had not played more than a few measures when it was apparent that the music was exciting great interest. Then came a salvo of applause, not merely because the music was good, but also because the audience were true connoisseurs. This statement will easily be believed by anyone who knows how talented the coloured people are in the field of music. The announcement, "*Caramelo Vendo,* dedicated to the *Virgencita de Bronce,*" brought forth another round of applause. We may add, in passing, that the success of this Cuban dance melody surpassed that of any other Creole composition of its day. The tune was played at every ball for the rest of that year and the winter of the next, after which it became a popular song among all classes of Cuban society.

It seems fair to say with respect to this new Cuban dance melody, conducted in person by its own composer, and played with the greatest sentiment and skill, that the dancers did the rest, in the sense that they carried the tune with body and feet, intoning, as it were, the piece as played by the orchestra. One could hear the silvery notes of the clarinet distinctly saying, "*Caramelo vendo, vendo caramelo.*" At the same time the violins and the bass viol repeated the words in a different tone, and the kettledrums beat their clamorous chorus to the sad voice of the vendor of sugar candy. But who was the author of the piece which caused such a sensation? In the excitement of the dance was there one who remembered his name? Alas! not one.

As the night advanced with no signs of fair weather, the curious crowd began to desert the door and the windows from which they had been watching the ball, and by 11 the white people had gone home and only an occasional coloured face was seen. The young Creoles who, as we said, were of the better Havana families, took advantage of this circumstance to dance with the mulatto women, with less likelihood that their censurable behaviour would be reported to their families. Cantalapiedra selected the hostess, Mercedes Ayala, as his partner. Diego Meneses took Nemesia, and Leonardo, Cecilia; and partly to maintain as far as possible a line of demarcation, partly due to the remnants of that same dormant scruple, they went into the dining room, notwithstanding its narrowness and untidy condition.

One may well imagine the agony which this move caused to the soul of Pimienta. He beheld the muse of his inspiration, the woman he adored, in the arms of a young white man, in all probability her heart's choice, for she was not one to hide her feelings, given over entirely to the ecstasy of the dance, while he, Pimienta, stood bound to the orchestra, as to a rock, a witness and a contributor to her enjoyment. Even this was not enough to mar his perfect direction of the orchestra or impair his skill in the playing of his favourite instrument. On the contrary, his anxiety and his passion seemed to find a source of relief in the keys of his instrument, which exhaled, if one may so express it, the exotic and melodious notes he imparted to them, disseminating charm and animation among the dancers. As the saying goes, not a puppet was left with his head on in the living room, the dining room, the main bedroom or the open patio of the house. To whom among the crowd of gay participants did it ever occur that the creator and soul of all that feasting and merriment, José Dolores Pimienta, composer of the new Cuban melody, was suffering the tortures born of love and jealousy?

It was past midnight when the music stopped again, and in a little while the people who were not intimate friends of the hostess began to take their leave, for supper had not yet been announced. To speed the parting guests Mercedes took two of her intimate friends by the arm and practically dragged then to the far end of the patio where, as we said, a table laden with all sorts of food awaited them. They were followed by the other women and by the men, among the latter, Pimienta and Brindis, the musicians, Cantalapiedra and his inseparable Man Friday, he of the long, black side-burns, Leonardo and his friend Diego Meneses. As there were only enough chairs for the women, the men remained standing, each behind the lady of his choice. Mercedes sat at the head of the table with Cantalapiedra at her side, whether a coincidence or a means of showing honour to the police commissioner and his rank, we cannot say.

It was quite obvious that the exercise on the dance-floor had sharpened the appetites of the guests of both sexes; some attacked the ham, others the fish, olives and other dishes, and in a few moments all were busy eating and soon had relieved the table of a fair portion of its weight. The inner man being satisfied, the guests turned to conversation; there were signs of gallantry and lovemaking, which in all countries are the keys to determine the cultural level of the persons concerned. The historical characters, whose lineaments we are here sketching briefly, were generally speaking not even of the middle class, much less of the class which in Cuba receives the best education, and so it is not difficult to understand why the examples of gallantry and lovemaking had nothing particularly delicate or refined about them.

"Speech from Cantalapiedra," cried one of the men.

"Cantalapiedra doesn't talk when he's eating," replied that individual as he gnawed a turkey drumstick.

"Well, let him stop eating so he can talk," burst out another.

"It can't be done, my friend, for I shall eat and I shall talk until the day of judgment. But, anyway, how do you expect me to speak until I wet my whistle?"

"Take my glass! Here, take mine! Take this one!" exclaimed at least ten voices, and the same number of arms reached out over the table in the direction of the commissioner, who downed one glass after another, each one full of a different wine, the whole quickly blending in his interior with no evidence of effect other than a rosy glow and a slight watering of the eyes. He then filled his own glass with a choice champagne, cleared his throat, threw out his chest and in a resounding but somewhat harsh voice said:

"Your attention, please! On this very happy birthday of my friend, Mercedes Ayala, a little poem in her honour:

> Merceditas, you're the apple of my eye.
> Have compassion I implore you on a sad one;
> For your glance contains a thorn,
> And by it my heart is torn.
> Your compassion will transform me to a glad one.
> I'm one who sighs for your eyes,
> And who dies for your eyes,
> And who lies for your eyes,
> And who, without your eyes,
> Could not endure life in this vale of tears.

Though crude and in bad taste, this extemporaneous effort was greeted by resounding *vivas* and prolonged applause with boisterous drumming on plates with spoons. As a reward for his poetic labours he received from one female an olive impaled on the same fork with which she had just conveyed food to her mouth, from another a slice of ham, from a third a bit of turkey, from a fourth a caramel, and from her neighbour a candied egg yolk, until finally Señora Ayala put a stop to this torrent of gifts as she rose and passed her glass, full of sherry, to Leonardo so that he, too, might extemporize as had done the obliging commissioner. Taking advantage of the respite thus given him to leave the table, Cantalapiedra went immediately but by a roundabout way to avoid detection to the well in the patio, stuck two fingers down his throat, threw up everything he had eaten and drunk (no small amount) and, feeling refreshed and as good as new, returned to the table. Thanks to such a simple yet efficacious remedy he was able to go on eating and drinking as though he had not eaten a bite nor drunk a drop during the whole evening.

Very few of the other men who had drunk to excess and who were unfamiliar with Cantalapiedra's method were able to keep a steady head, not excepting the young Creole, Leonardo, himself.

To this lamentable circumstance must be attributed the fact that such a refined and well-mannered young man should lead himself to versifying and to paying tribute to the belle of the ball. Although they were poor poems he recited them anyway and was no less applauded and rewarded than the other rhymester. It was noticeable, however, that Cecilia Valdés did not applaud his poetic efforts as did the others; instead she kept silent and appeared visibly ashamed. Nor did Nemesia join the others in praising his verses, but for a very different reason, namely because she was engaged in a rapid and private dialogue with her brother, José Dolores Pimienta.

"Well, but isn't the luggage rack behind the seat empty?" he repeated.

"Perhaps not," she answered.

"And how do you know whether it is or it isn't?"

"The same way I know a lot of things. Do you think I'm still at the age when I have to be fed with a spoon?"

"Yes, but you don't explain yourself."

"Because there isn't time, now."

"There's time to spare, sister."

"Also, walls have ears."

"Nonsense, they do if you shout."

"Come, come, now, don't be pigheaded. I'm telling you not to do it."

"I'm not going to miss the chance."

"You'll have a bad time of it."

"What do I care, if it's what I want to do."

"I'm telling you again, José Dolores, don't bite off more than you can chew. Don't be so stubborn. You're getting so obstinate you make me feel like wanting to stop helping you. I understand all this better than you do. I'm keeping an eye on it."

Before the uproar of voices, hand-clapping, beating on plates and pounding on the table had died down, Leonardo whispered something to Cecilia and hurried out of the house, dragging Meneses along with him by the arm, without saying "Good night" to anyone—taking French leave, as Cantalapiedra expressed it when he missed him a few moments later. Once outside the two lads walked arm in arm along the Calle de la Habana in the direction of the center of the city. It was drizzling, but they continued on foot. At the first corner, where the street crosses the Calle San Isidro, Meneses walked straight on and Leonardo turned off at the corner of the Paula hospital.

Light chiaroscuro clouds, broken up into little particles by a cool wind from the northeast, were passing, one by one, in regular procession in front of a waning moon which had already passed the zenith and which, every so often, sent down beams of whitish light. Leonardo continued along the narrow and tortuous cross street, unable to see his way clearly until he reached the little plaza in front of the hospital. Occasionally he could see a little of the road along the left side of the street, but the right side was completely dark, for the high, sombre walls of the Church of Santa Paula cast a double shadow over a wide area. He was barely able to distinguish his carriage, drawn up alongside the wall; the horses, looking very dejected, carried their heads and ears low in an effort to avoid the wind and rain which came at them from the front. The hood of the carriage was up and the rider was nowhere to be seen, neither in his usual place in the saddle, nor on the luggage rack, nor in the wide doorway of the church, which might have served him as a shelter. A second glance showed Leonardo where he was. He was seated on the floor of the coach, his dangling legs encased in field boots. He was leaning over on his side, his head and arms resting on the soft, Moroccan leather cushions. His quirt lay on the ground where it had fallen out of his hand as he dropped off to sleep. Leonardo snatched it up, raised the hood slightly, and with all his might gave him two or three strokes on the back with the rawhide lash.

"*Señor!*" cried the driver in pain and alarm as he started to get up.

One could see that he was a young mulatto, well built, broad-shouldered, taller and with a stronger face than the man who had just given him the thrashing. Dressed like those of his calling in Cuba, he wore a dark jacket, trimmed in braid, piqué waistcoat, shirt open at the neck, sailor fashion, linen trousers, enormous field boots resembling leggings, and a round, black hat trimmed with gold. As a rule these drivers, who always rode the horse that drew the carriage or one of them if a pair were used, wore heavy, silver spurs, but the mulatto we are describing was not wearing his spurs at the time.

"Hey! Get up!" cried his master, who was none other than our young Creole, Leonardo. "You were sound asleep while the horses were standing unhitched. Eh? What might have happened had something frightened them and they had started running through the streets of Barrabas?"

"I wasn't asleep, *niño*,"[5] the driver ventured to observe.

"So you weren't asleep, eh? Aponte, Aponte, either you don't know me or you think I'm still at the thumb-sucking age. Now look, get on your horse. We'll go into this later. Drive the carriage to the *cuna*, get the girls you brought to the ball, and take them home. I'll be waiting for you along the wall of the Santa Clara Convent at the corner of the Calle de la Habana. Don't let anyone ride on the luggage rack. D'you understand?"

"*Sí, señor,*" answered Aponte, and he drove off in the direction of the San José sentry box.

At the door of the house where the ball was being held Aponte did not dismount. Seeing a stranger about to enter, he called to him:

"Would you do me the favour of telling the *niña* Cecilia that the carriage is here?"

In spite of his use of the word *niña*, which is customarily reserved in Cuba to describe a child or young person of the white race, the stranger delivered the

---

[5] Cuban slaves always referred to the sons of their masters as "*niño*" ("child").

message without question or mistake. And she rose at once from the table and went to get her shawl, followed by Nemesia and Mercedes Ayala. The latter accompanied them to the front door, where a few men who had not yet departed were gathered. Then, with her arm still around Cecilia's waist in token of friendship and affection, she said: "Have no faith in men, darling, they will be your undoing."

"And do you think I have shown faith in any man tonight, Merceditas?" replied Cecilia with surprise.

"Yes, I know, but that carriage has an owner, and nobody gives away timber, gratis. A word to the wise; I think you understand what I mean."

Thereupon she and Nemesia stepped into the carriage, assisted by Pimienta, while Cantalapiedra, who was a droll fellow, caused much laughter by pretending to weep at Cecilia's departure. This brought the party to a close.

It was now about one in the morning. The wind had not abated, and every now and again a few drops of rain fell from the fleeting clouds upon a dark and slumbering city. The darkness, as the common expression goes, was like the mouth of a wolf. But the young musician did not on this account lose the trail of the carriage in which his sister and her friend were riding; first he followed the sound of the horses' hoofs on the stony surface of the streets, and then the sound of splashing as the carriage drove through puddles of rainwater. He started at a fast walk and then broke into a dogtrot, until he caught up with them at the Calle de Acosta, when he started to run. Grasping the luggage rack behind the seat, he was able, due to the speed at which he was going, to vault lightly onto the rack, where he sat like a woman riding a side saddle. The driver felt the jar and immediately stopped.

"Get down," said Nemesia through an opening in the little window at the back of the carriage.

"You shouldn't do this," said Cecilia.

"I'm acting as your rear guard," said Pimienta.

"Get down," said Aponte as he jumped off his horse.

"Didn't I tell you?" added Nemesia to her brother.

"These girls are my sister and my lady friend," said the musician, addressing himself to the driver.

"That may be all very true," was the reply, "but I don't allow riders on the luggage rack of my gig. It will ruin it." And he added the word "comrade" rather than "*señor*" when he saw that he was dealing with a mulatto like himself.

"Get down," insisted Nemesia, once more.

José Dolores obeyed after what appeared to be a severe, silent struggle within himself in which prudence triumphed. Although he admitted defeat at that juncture, he did not give up his determination to follow the carriage. The driver remounted and the carriage drove straight on to where the street runs into the Calle de Luz, whence the driver turned to the left and continued in the direction of the Calle de la Habana. There is a cannon at the corner, and a man stood nearby, sheltered from the wind and a drizzling rain by the high mud walls of the patio belonging to the convent of the Santa Clara nuns. Aponte reined in his horses and brought the gig to a stop. The man climbed aboard the luggage rack and in a low but audible voice said: "Drive on!"

The gig thereupon started off at full speed, but not soon enough to prevent the musician from recognizing the person who had taken his place on the rack as the same young white man, Leonardo, who had so aroused his jealousy at the *cuna* ball.

33

⚜

Karl Marx and Friedrich Engels

THE COMMUNIST MANIFESTO

Although, in the early twenty-first century after the dissolution of the Soviet Union, Communism may appear to be everywhere in decline, nevertheless, its doctrines have had a far-reaching influence on other modern economic and intellectual systems. In the words of the distinguished historian of ideas Isaiah Berlin, "No thinker in the nineteenth century has had so direct, deliberate and powerful an influence upon mankind as Karl Marx." In the early nineteenth century with the ever-intensifying development of the Industrial Revolution, the dehumanizing exploitation of the growing number of factory laborers—both men and women—occasioned many passionate criticisms of the prevailing system of early capitalism.

The most systematic and influential attack upon the new industrial capitalism was mounted by two young Germans, Karl Marx (1818–1883) and Friedrich Engels (1820–1895). Marx, an outstanding student of philosophy, studied at the universities of Bonn and Berlin, where he came strongly under the influence of Hegelian philosophers. He completed his doctorate at the University of Jena in 1842, then found work as a newspaper editor. When his liberal newspaper was suppressed in 1843, Marx moved around Western Europe developing his socialist theories into a more revolutionary communism. In that same year, he married Jennie von Westphalen, the daughter of a Prussian aristocrat, and met a wealthy manufacturer's son, Friedrich Engels, who became his lifelong friend, collaborator, and financial supporter. After Marx's death Engels edited and published his manuscripts. The two dedicated their lives to the replacement of capitalist society by a new economic and political order they labeled communism or "scientific socialism"—to distinguish their version from the nonrevolutionary theories they labeled as "utopian socialism." Their general method and ideology ultimately came to be known as Marxism—a combination of philosophical, economic, and historical theory and revolutionary practice. With its dogma of inevitable revolutionary victory, Marxism soon became the theoretical basis for the *leading socialist parties around the world and eventually for the Bolsheviks who took power in Russia in 1917, less than a half-century after Marx's death.*

The underlying philosophy of Marxism was dialectical materialism, a system that inverted the dialectical idealism of the influential German thinker Georg Wilhelm Friedrich Hegel (1770–1831). Marxism followed Hegel in asserting that all existence was a process that evolved in a rational pattern according to the dialectic, the real "laws of motion" of nature, society, and thought; however, Marxism rejected Hegel's idealist perspective that "ideas" (Spirit) are superior to "matters." Marxism rather held matter to be the ultimate stuff of all reality. It embodied a theory of history that saw all social change as basically determined by economic-technological forces ("the modes of production") and as moving inevitably through conflicts of opposites (dialectic) to the resolution of all contradictions in the final historical synthesis of communism.

Marx and Engels were interested in ideas mainly as a means of influencing the course of events. They were not satisfied, like Hegel, with understanding the world; rather, they wished to change it. Thus it was that Marx, while living in Brussels, was commissioned by the London Congress of the Communist League in December 1847 to compose a definitive statement of its aims and beliefs. In February, 1848, with both Marx and Engels collaborating on its composition, the first edition of the Manifest der Kommunistischen Partei *was printed in London. Within a few years translations in most of the modern languages were published around the world. (The English translation excerpted here is the standard version of 1888 by Samuel Moore with revisions by Engels himself.) With liberal and radical uprisings occurring in Western Europe throughout 1848, the distribution of the* Manifesto *was frequently cited at the time as a major cause of urban riots; copies were seized by the police in various cities. Clearly unwelcome on the continent—in fact, officially expelled from Belgium and Prussia—Marx went into permanent exile in London where he continued his research and writing, his family saved from extreme poverty by the generosity of Engels who eventually supported the family entirely.*

The Communist Manifesto *was not only a statement of social and economic theory by Marx and Engels; as a radical organization's platform it was also a call to arms. Its revolutionary appeal was stated in the context of an outline of European history. Tracing the development of socio-political systems in the past, Marx and Engels projected this evolution into the future. For them, all historical change was characterized by the struggle of economic classes. This class conflict was always caused by private ownership which was the source of all evil in society by producing class distinctions, class interests, and ultimately class struggle. The instrument for the last violent transformation of society was the proletariat, the class of industrial wage earners. Once the proletariat achieved full consciousness of its role, it would organize economically and politically to overthrow the capitalist system and inevitably make all other classes and all national states obsolete in a world communist system—thereby, eliminating the possibility of future class struggle. Certainly, Marx was prescient in his vision of "the world market," with its "freedom of commerce" and "uniformity in the mode of production" that the "development of the bourgeoisie" made possible. One shortcoming in the* Mani-festo's *economic analysis is that its examples of capitalist oppression of the prole-tariat are based on the most extreme examples of the unregulated factory system, abuses which were already being corrected in Marx's time. Another shortcoming of Marxism is its insistence that all motivations are ultimately economic. ("The mode of production of material life determines the social, political and intellec-tual life process in general. It is not the consciousness of men that determines their existence, but rather it is their social existence that determines their consciousness" [from Marx's* Critique of Political Economy, *1859].) The Marxist materialist view of human nature is a narrow one, only partial, not consistent with the rich varieties of observable behavior. Even though communism has clearly fallen far short in its predictive accuracy, the* Manifesto, *as well as Marxism generally, has demonstrated wide appeal, especially in relatively undeveloped societies that, iron-ically, have no significant proletarian class. Its appeal rests in the perceptiveness of its historical analysis, its almost religious sense of certainty about the dissolution of the current class structures of society, and its assurances of inevitable success.*

૨૧

A specter is haunting Europe — the specter of communism. All the powers of old Europe have entered into a holy alliance to exorcise this specter: Pope and Czar, Metternich[1] and Guizot,[2] French Radicals[3] and German police spies.

Where is the party in opposition that has not been decried as communistic by its opponents in power? Where the Opposition that has not hurled back the branding reproach of communism, against the more advanced opposition par-ties, as well as against its reactionary adversaries?

Two things result from this fact:

I. Communism is already acknowledged by all European powers to be itself a power.

From *Manifesto of the Communist Party* by Karl Marx and Friedrich Engels, trans. Samuel Moore (New York: Socialist Labor Party, 1888), 7–21, 28.

[1]Prince von Metternich (1773–1859) was chancellor of the Austrian Empire when Marx and Engels were working on the German original of the *Manifesto* in 1847 and early 1848. Metternich had been largely responsible for the reactionary European balance of powers that followed Napolean's defeat in 1815. In March, 1848, a rebellious Vienna mob forced Metternich to resign.

[2]François Pierre Guizot (1787–1874), French statesman and historian, was prime minis-ter at the time of the uprisings of 1848 and, like Metternich, was then overthrown.

[3]Radicals who wanted to replace the French monarchy with a republic.

II. It is high time that Communists should openly, in the face of the whole world, publish their views, their aims, their tendencies, and meet this nursery tale of the specter of communism with a manifesto of the party itself.

To this end, Communists of various nationalities have assembled in London, and sketched the following manifesto, to be published in the English, French, German, Italian, Flemish, and Danish languages.

I

Bourgeois and Proletarians[4]

The history of all hitherto existing society is the history of class struggles.

Freeman and slave, patrician and plebian, lord and serf, guildmaster and journeyman,[5] in a word, oppressor and oppressed, stood in constant opposition to one another, carried on an uninterrupted, now hidden, now open fight, a fight that each time ended, either in a revolutionary reconstitution of society at large, or in the common ruin of the contending classes.

In the earlier epochs of history, we find almost everywhere a complicated arrangement of society into various orders, a manifold gradation of social rank. In ancient Rome we have patricians, knights, plebians, slaves; in the Middle Ages, feudal lords, vassals,[6] guild-masters, journeymen, apprentices, serfs; in almost all of these classes, again, subordinate gradations.

The modern bourgeois society that has sprouted from the ruins of feudal society, has not done away with class antagonisms. It has but established new classes, new conditions of oppression, new forms of struggle in place of the old ones.

Our epoch, the epoch of the bourgeoisie, possesses, however, this distinctive feature: It has simplified the class antagonisms. Society as a whole is more and more splitting up into two great hostile camps, into two great classes directly facing each other—bourgeoisie and proletariat.[7]

---

[4] Terms that Marx adapted from older usages: In French *bourgeois* originally meant a citizen of a town or city; in Latin *proletarius* meant a person whose only wealth was his offspring.

[5] In ancient Rome a patrician was a member of the hereditary aristocracy, a plebian a person of the lowest class of freemen. In the feudal European Middle Ages a lord was the aristocratic proprietor of a manorial estate, a serf a peasant on a manor, involuntarily bound to that property. In medieval towns a guildmaster was a full member of a medieval trade or craft guild, the proprietor of his own business; a journeyman was a skilled worker employed by the day by a guildmaster.

[6] Medieval lords and the vassals who owed them allegiance comprised the ruling feudal military and land-holding aristocracy.

[7] By *bourgeoisie* Marx means, specifically, that class of entrepreneurs and capitalists, relatively few in the early nineteenth century, who own and control the means of production. By *proletariat* he means the large and constantly increasing number of wage-earning laborers who neither own nor control the means of production.

From the serfs of the Middle Ages sprang the chartered burghers of the earliest towns. From these burgesses the first elements of the bourgeoisie were developed.

The discovery of America, the rounding of the Cape,[8] opened up fresh ground for the rising bourgeoisie. The East-Indian and Chinese markets, the colonization of America, trade with the colonies, the increase in the means of exchange and in commodities generally, gave to commerce, to navigation, to industry, an impulse never before known, and thereby, to the revolutionary element in the tottering feudal society, a rapid development.

The feudal system of industry, in which industrial production was monopolized by closed guilds,[9] now no longer sufficed for the growing wants of the new markets. The manufacturing system took its place. The guild-masters were pushed aside by the manufacturing middle class; division of labor between the different corporate guilds vanished in the face of division of labor in each single workshop.

Meantime the markets kept ever growing, the demand ever rising. Even manufacture no longer sufficed.[10] Thereupon, steam and machinery revolutionized industrial production. The place of manufacture was taken by the giant, modern industry, the place of the industrial middle class, by industrial millionaires — the leaders of whole industrial armies, the modern bourgeois.

Modern industry has established the world market, for which the discovery of America paved the way. This market has given an immense development to commerce, to navigation, to communication by land. This development has, in its turn, reacted on the extension of industry; and in proportion as industry, commerce, navigation, railways extended, in the same proportion the bourgeoisie developed, increased its capital, and pushed into the background every class handed down from the Middle Ages.

We see, therefore, how the modern bourgeoisie is itself the product of a long course of development, of a series of revolutions in the modes of production and of exchange.

Each step in the development of the bourgeoisie was accompanied by a corresponding political advance of that class. An oppressed class under the sway of the feudal nobility, it became an armed and self-governing association in the medieval commune; here independent urban republic (as in Italy and Germany), there taxable "third estate" of the monarchy (as in France); afterwards, in the period of manufacture proper, serving either the semifeudal or the absolute

---

[8] The Cape of Good Hope at the southern tip of Africa.

[9] The medieval guilds that controlled the economic life of the towns were associations of skilled craftsmen or tradesmen who owned their own businesses; they limited their own numbers and regulated their prices.

[10] By *manufacture* Marx means the system of production that came after the guild system but still relied mainly upon direct human labor for power. Marx distinguishes *manufacture* from modern industry which arose when water- and steam-driven machinery was introduced.

monarchy as a counterpoise against the nobility, and, in fact, cornerstone of the great monarchies in general — the bourgeoisie has at last, since the establishment of modern industry and of the world market, conquered for itself, in the modern representative state, exclusive political sway. The executive of the modern state is but a committee for managing the common affairs of the whole bourgeoisie.

The bourgeoisie has played a most revolutionary role in history.

The bourgeoisie, wherever it has got the upper hand, has put an end to all feudal, patriarchal, idyllic relations. It has pitilessly torn asunder the motley feudal ties that bound man to his "natural superiors," and has left no other bond between man and man than naked self-interest, than callous "cash payment." It has drowned the most heavenly ecstasies of religious fervor, of chivalrous enthusiasm, of philistine sentimentalism, in the icy water of egotistical calculation. It has resolved personal worth into exchange value, and in place of the numberless indefeasible chartered freedoms, has set up that single, unconscionable freedom — Free Trade. In one word, for exploitation, veiled by religious and political illusions, it has substituted naked, shameless, direct, brutal exploitation.

The bourgeoisie has stripped of its halo every occupation hitherto honored and looked up to with reverent awe. It has converted the physician, the lawyer, the priest, the poet, the man of science, into its paid wage-laborers.

The bourgeoisie has torn away from the family its sentimental veil, and has reduced the family relation to a mere money relation.

The bourgeoisie has disclosed how it came to pass that the brutal display of vigor in the Middle Ages, which reactionaries so much admire, found its fitting complement in the most slothful indolence. It has been the first to show what man's activity can bring about. It has accomplished wonders far surpassing Egyptian pyramids, Roman aqueducts, and Gothic cathedrals; it has conducted expeditions that put in the shade all former migrations of nations and crusades.

The bourgeoisie cannot exist without constantly revolutionizing the instruments of production, and thereby the relations of production, and with them the whole relations of society. Conservation of the old modes of production in unaltered form, was, on the contrary, the first condition of existence for all earlier industrial classes. Constant revolutionizing of production, uninterrupted disturbance of all social conditions, everlasting uncertainty and agitation distinguish the bourgeois epoch from all earlier ones. All fixed, fast-frozen relations, with their train of ancient and venerable prejudices and opinions, are swept away, all new-formed ones become antiquated before they can ossify. All that is solid melts into air, all that is holy is profaned, and man is at last compelled to face with sober senses his real conditions of life and his relations with his kind.

The need of a constantly expanding market for its products chases the bourgeoisie over the whole surface of the globe. It must nestle everywhere, settle everywhere, establish connections everywhere.

The bourgeoisie has through its exploitation of the world market given a cosmopolitan character to production and consumption in every country. To the great chagrin of reactionaries, it has drawn from under the feet of industry the national ground on which it stood. All old-established national industries have been destroyed or are daily being destroyed. They are dislodged by new industries, whose introduction becomes a life and death question for all civilized nations, by industries that no longer work up indigenous raw material, but raw material drawn from the remotest zones; industries whose products are consumed, not only at home, but in every quarter of the globe. In place of the old wants, satisfied by the production of the country, we find new wants, requiring for their satisfaction the products of distant lands and climes. In place of the old local and national seclusion and self-sufficiency, we have intercourse in every direction, universal interdependence of nations. And as in material, so also in intellectual production. The intellectual creations of individual nations become common property. National one-sidedness and narrow-mindedness become more and more impossible, and from the numerous national and local literatures there arises a world literature.

The bourgeoisie, by the rapid improvement of all instruments of production, by the immensely facilitated means of communication, draws all nations, even the most barbarian, into civilization. The cheap prices of its commodities are the heavy artillery with which it batters down all Chinese walls, with which it forces the barbarians' intensely obstinate hatred of foreigners to capitulate. It compels all nations, on pain of extinction, to adopt the bourgeois mode of production; it compels them to introduce what it calls civilization into their midst; *i.e.,* to become bourgeois themselves. In a word, it creates a world after its own image.

The bourgeoisie has subjected the country to the rule of the towns. It has created enormous cities, has greatly increased the urban population as compared with the rural, and has thus rescued a considerable part of the population from the idiocy of rural life. Just as it has made the country dependent on the towns, so it has made barbarian and semibarbarian countries dependent on the civilized ones, nations of peasants on nations of bourgeois, the East on the West.

More and more the bourgeoisie keeps doing away with the scattered state of the population, of the means of production, and of property. It has agglomerated population, centralized means of production, and has concentrated property in a few hands. The necessary consequence of this was political centralization. Independent, or but loosely connected provinces, with separate interests, laws, governments and systems of taxation, became lumped together into one nation, with one government, one code of laws, one national class interest, one frontier and one customs tariff.

The bourgeoisie, during its rule of scarce one hundred years, has created more massive and more colossal productive forces than have all preceding generations together. Subjection of nature's forces to man, machinery, application of chemistry to industry and agriculture, steam-navigation, railways, electric telegraphs, clearing of whole continents for cultivation, canalization of rivers, whole populations conjured out of the ground—what earlier century had even a presentiment that such productive forces slumbered in the lap of social labor?

We see then that the means of production and of exchange, which served as the foundation for the growth of the bourgeoisie, were generated in feudal society. At a certain stage in the development of these means of production and of exchange, the conditions under which feudal society produced and exchanged, the feudal organization of agriculture and manufacturing industry, in a word, the feudal relations of property became no longer compatible with the already developed productive forces; they became so many fetters. They had to be burst asunder; they were burst asunder.

Into their place stepped free competition, accompanied by a social and political constitution adapted to it, and by the economic and political sway of the bourgeois class.

A similar movement is going on before our own eyes. Modern bourgeois society with its relations of production, of exchange and of property, a society that has conjured up such gigantic means of production and of exchange, is like the sorcerer who is no longer able to control the powers of the nether world whom he has called up by his spells. For many a decade past the history of industry and commerce is but the history of the revolt of modern productive forces against modern conditions of production, against the property relations that are the conditions for the existence of the bourgeoisie and of its rule. It is enough to mention the commercial crises that by their periodical return put the existence of the entire bourgeois society on trial, each time more threateningly. In these crises a great part not only of the existing products, but also of the previously created productive forces, are periodically destroyed. In these crises there breaks out an epidemic that, in all earlier epochs, would have seemed an absurdity—the epidemic of overproduction. Society suddenly finds itself put back into a state of momentary barbarism; it appears as if a famine, a universal war of devastation had cut off the supply of every means of subsistence; industry and commerce seem to be destroyed. And why? Because there is too much civilization, too much means of subsistence, too much industry, too much commerce. The productive forces at the disposal of society no longer tend to further the development of the conditions of bourgeois property; on the contrary, they have become too powerful for these conditions, by which they are fettered, and no sooner do they overcome these fetters than they bring disorder into the whole of bourgeois society, endanger the existence of bourgeois property. The conditions of bourgeois society are too narrow to comprise the wealth created by them. And how does the bourgeoisie get over these crises? On the one hand by enforced destruction of a mass of productive forces; on the other, by the conquest of new markets, and by the more thorough exploitation of the old ones. That is to say, by paving the way for more extensive and more destructive crises, and by diminishing the means whereby crises are prevented.

The weapons with which the bourgeoisie felled feudalism to the ground are now turned against the bourgeoisie itself.

But not only has the bourgeoisie forged the weapons that bring death to itself; it has also called into existence the men who are to wield those weapons—the modern working class—the proletarians.

In proportion as the bourgeoisie, *i.e.,* capital, is developed, in the same proportion is the proletariat, the modern working class, developed—a class of laborers, who live only so long as they find work, and who find work only so long as their labor increases capital. These laborers, who must sell themselves piecemeal, are a commodity, like every other article of commerce, and are consequently exposed to all the vicissitudes of competition, to all the fluctuations of the market.

Owing to the extensive use of machinery and to division of labor, the work of the proletarians has lost all individual character, and, consequently, all charm for the workman. He becomes an appendage of the machine, and it is only the most simple, most monotonous, and most easily acquired knack, that is required of him. Hence, the cost of production of a workman is restricted, almost entirely, to the means of subsistence that he requires for his maintenance, and for the propagation of his race. But the price of a commodity, and therefore also of labor, is equal to its cost of production. In proportion, therefore, as the repulsiveness of the work increases, the wage decreases. Nay more, in proportion as the use of machinery and division of labor increases, in the same proportion the burden of toil also increases, whether by prolongation of the working hours, by increase of the work exacted in a given time, or by increased speed of the machinery, etc.

Modern industry has converted the little workshop of the patriarchal master into the great factory of the industrial capitalist. Masses of laborers, crowded into the factory, are organized like soldiers. As privates of the industrial army they are placed under the command of a perfect hierarchy of officers and sergeants. Not only are they slaves of the bourgeois class, and of the bourgeois state; they are daily and hourly enslaved by the machine, by the overlooker, and, above all, by the individual bourgeois manufacturer himself. The more openly this despotism proclaims gain to be its end and aim, the more petty, the more hateful and the more embittering it is.

The less the skill and exertion of strength implied in manual labor, in other words, the more modern industry develops, the more is the labor of men superseded by that of women. Differences of age and sex have no longer any distinctive social validity for the working class. All are instruments of labor, more or less expensive to use, according to their age and sex.

No sooner has the laborer received his wages in cash, for the moment escaping exploitation by the manufacturer, than he is set upon by the other portions of the bourgeoisie, the landlord, the shopkeeper, the pawnbroker, etc.

The lower strata of the middle class—the small tradespeople, shopkeepers, and retired tradesmen generally, the handicraftsmen and peasants—all these sink gradually into the proletariat, partly because their diminutive capital does not suffice for the scale on which modern industry is carried on, and is swamped in the competition with the large capitalists, partly because their specialized skill is rendered worthless by new methods of production. Thus the proletariat is recruited from all classes of the population.

The proletariat goes through various stages of development. With its birth begins its struggle with the bourgeoisie. At first the contest is carried on by individual laborers, then by the work people in a factory, then by the operatives of one trade, in one locality, against the individual bourgeois who directly exploits them. They direct their attacks not against the bourgeois conditions of production, but against the instruments of production themselves; they destroy imported wares that compete with their labor, they smash machinery to pieces, they set factories ablaze, they seek to restore by force the vanished status of the workman of the Middle Ages.

At this stage the laborers still form an incoherent mass scattered over the whole country, and broken up by their mutual competition. If anywhere they unite to form more compact bodies, this is not yet the consequences of their own active union, but of the union of the bourgeoisie, which class, in order to attain its own political ends, is compelled to set the whole proletariat in motion, and is moreover still able to do so for a time. At this stage, therefore, the proletarians do not fight their enemies, but the enemies of their enemies, the remnants of absolute monarchy, the landowners, the nonindustrial bourgeoisie, the petty bourgeoisie. Thus the whole historical movement is concentrated in the hands of the bourgeoisie; every victory so obtained is a victory for the bourgeoisie.

But with the development of industry the proletariat not only increases in number; it becomes concentrated in greater masses, its strength grows, and it feels that strength more. The various interests and conditions of life within the ranks of the proletariat are more and more equalized, in proportion as machinery obliterates all distinctions of labor and nearly everywhere reduces wages to the same low level. The growing competition among the bourgeoisie, and the resulting commercial crisis, make the wages of the workers ever more fluctuating. The unceasing improvement of machinery, ever more rapidly developing, makes their livelihood more and more precarious; the collisions between individual workmen and individual bourgeois take more and more the character of collisions between two classes. Thereupon the workers begin to form combinations (trade unions) against the bourgeoisie; they club together in order to keep up the rate of wages; they found permanent associations in order to make provision beforehand for these occasional revolts. Here and there the contest breaks out into riots.

Now and then workers are victorious, but only for a time. The real fruit of their battles lies, not in the immediate results, but in the ever expanding union of the workers. This union is furthered by the improved means of communication which are created by modern industry, and which place the workers of different localities in contact with one another. It was just this contact that was needed to centralize the numerous local struggles, all of the same character, into one national struggle between classes. But every class struggle is a political struggle. And that union, to attain which the burghers of the Middle Ages, with their miserable highways, required centuries, the modern proletarians, thanks to railways, achieve in a few years.

This organization of the proletarians into a class, and consequently into a political party, is continually being upset again by the competition between the workers themselves. But it ever rises up again, stronger, firmer, mightier. It compels legislative recognition of particular interests of the workers, by taking advantage of the divisions among the bourgeoisie itself. Thus the ten-hour bill in England was carried.[11]

Altogether, collisions between the classes of the old society further the course of development of the proletariat in many ways. The bourgeoisie finds itself involved in a constant battle. At first with the aristocracy; later on, with those portions of the bourgeoisie itself whose interests have become antagonistic to the progress of industry; at all times with the bourgeoisie of foreign countries. In all these battles it sees itself compelled to appeal to the proletariat, to ask for its help, and thus, to drag it into the political arena. The bourgeoisie itself, therefore, supplies the proletariat with its own elements of political and general education, in other words, it furnishes the proletariat with weapons for fighting the bourgeoisie.

Further, as we have already seen, entire sections of the ruling classes are, by the advance of industry, precipitated into the proletariat, or are at least threatened in their conditions of existence. These also supply the proletariat with fresh elements of enlightenment and progress.

Finally, in times when the class struggle nears the decisive hour, the process of dissolution going on within the ruling class, in fact within the whole range of old society, assumes such a violent, glaring character, that a small section of the ruling class cuts itself adrift, and joins the revolutionary class, the class that holds the future in its hands. Just as, therefore, at an earlier period, a section of the nobility went over to the bourgeoisie, so now a portion of the bourgeoisie goes over to the proletariat, and in particular, a portion of the bourgeois ideologists, who have raised themselves to the level of comprehending theoretically the historical movement as a whole.

Of all the classes that stand face to face with the bourgeoisie today, the proletariat alone is a really revolutionary class. The other classes decay and finally disappear in the face of modern industry; the proletariat is its special and essential product.

The lower middle class, the small manufacturer, the shopkeeper, the artisan, the peasant, all these fight against the bourgeoisie, to save from extinction their existence as fractions of the middle class. They are therefore not revolutionary, but conservative. Nay more, they are reactionary, for they try to roll back the wheel of history. If by chance they are revolutionary, they are so only in view of their impending transfer into the proletariat; they thus defend not their present,

---

11 "The Ten Hours Act," passed by Parliament in 1847, limited the working day of all factory workers to ten hours.

but their future interests; they desert their own standpoint to adopt that of the proletariat.

The "dangerous class," the social scum (*Lumpenproletariat*),[12] that passively rotting mass thrown off by the lowest layers of old society, may, here and there, be swept into the movement by a proletarian revolution; its conditions of life, however, prepare it far more for the part of a bribed tool of reactionary intrigue.

The social conditions of the old society no longer exist for the proletariat. The proletariat is without property; his relation to his wife and children has no longer anything in common with bourgeois family relations; modern industrial labor, modern subjection to capital, the same in England as in France, in America as in Germany, has stripped him of every trace of national character. Law, morality, religion, are to him so many bourgeois prejudices, behind which lurk in ambush just as many bourgeois interests.

All the preceding classes that got the upper hand, sought to fortify their already acquired status by subjecting society at large to their conditions of appropriation. The proletarians cannot become masters of the productive forces of society, except by abolishing their own previous mode of appropriation, and thereby also every other previous mode of appropriation. They have nothing of their own to secure and to fortify; their mission is to destroy all previous securities for, and insurances of, individual property.

All previous historical movements were movements of minorities, or in the interest of minorities. The proletarian movement is the self-conscious, independent movement of the immense majority, in the interest of the immense majority. The proletariat, the lowest stratum of our present society, cannot stir, cannot raise itself up, without the whole superincumbent strata of official society being sprung into the air.

Though not in substance, yet in form, the struggle of the proletariat with the bourgeoisie is at first a national struggle. The proletariat of each country must, of course, first of all settle matters with its own bourgeoisie.

In depicting the most general phases of the development of the proletariat, we traced the more or less veiled civil war, raging within existing society, up to the point where that war breaks out into open revolution, and where the violent overthrow of the bourgeoisie lays the foundation for the sway of the proletariat.

Hitherto, every form of society has been based, as we have already seen, on the antagonism of oppressing and oppressed classes. But in order to oppress a class, certain conditions must be assured to it under which it can, at least, continue its slavish existence. The serf, in the period of serfdom, raised himself to membership in the commune, just as the petty bourgeois, under the yoke of feudal absolutism,

---

[12] By the *Lumpenproletariat* Marx means the castoffs created by the capitalist modes of production—for example, beggars, thieves, criminals, and drifters—all of whom he excludes from the properly defined proletariat, despite their poverty, because they lack the true proletarian relationship to the means of production: wage labor.

managed to develop into a bourgeois. The modern laborer, on the contrary, instead of rising with the progress of industry, sinks deeper and deeper below the conditions of existence of his own class. He becomes a pauper, and pauperism develops more rapidly than population and wealth. And here it becomes evident, that the bourgeoisie is unfit any longer to be the ruling class in society, and to impose its conditions of existence upon society as an overriding law. It is unfit to rule because it is incompetent to assure an existence to its slave within his slavery, because it cannot help letting him sink into such a state, that it has to feed him, instead of being fed by him. Society can no longer live under this bourgeoisie; in other words, its existence is no longer compatible with society.

The essential condition for the existence and sway of the bourgeois class, is the formation and augmentation of capital; the condition for capital is wage-labor. Wage-labor rests exclusively on competition between the laborers. The advance of industry, whose involuntary promoter is the bourgeoisie, replaces the isolation of the laborers, due to competition, by their revolutionary combination, due to association. The development of modern industry, therefore, cuts from under its feet the very foundation on which the bourgeoisie produces and appropriates products. What the bourgeoisie therefore produces, above all, are its own gravediggers. Its fall and the victory of the proletariat are equally inevitable.

II

Proletarians and Communists[13]

In what relation do the Communists stand to the proletarians as a whole?

The Communists do not form a separate party opposed to other working-class parties.

They have no interests separate and apart from those of the proletariat as a whole.

They do not set up any sectarian principles of their own, by which to shape and mold the proletarian movement.

The Communists are distinguished from the other working-class parties by this only: 1. In the national struggles of the proletarians of the different countries, they point out and bring to the front the common interests of the entire proletariat, independently of all nationality. 2. In the various stages of development which the struggle of the working class against the bourgeoisie has to pass through, they always and everywhere represent the interests of the movement as a whole.

The Communists, therefore, are on the one hand, practically, the most advanced and resolute section of the working-class parties of every country, that

---

[13] "Communists" here refers specifically to the Communist League for which the *Manifesto* was written, not to other communist groups or theories.

section which pushes forward all others; on the other hand, theoretically, they have over the great mass of the proletariat the advantage of clearly understanding the line of march, the conditions, and the ultimate general results of the proletarian movement.

The immediate aim of the Communists is the same as that of all the other proletarian parties: Formation of the proletariat into a class, overthrow of bourgeois supremacy, conquest of political power by the proletariat.

The theoretical conclusions of the Communists are in no way based on ideas or principles that have been invented, or discovered, by this or that would-be universal reformer.

They merely express, in general terms, actual relations springing from an existing class struggle, from a historical movement going on under our very eyes. The abolition of existing property relations is not at all a distinctive feature of communism.

All property relations in the past have continually been subject to historical change consequent upon the change in historical conditions.

The French Revolution, for example, abolished feudal property in favor of bourgeois property.

The distinguishing feature of communism is not the abolition of property generally, but the abolition of bourgeois property. But modern bourgeois private property is the final and most complete expression of the system of producing and appropriating products that is based on class antagonisms, on the exploitation of the many by the few.

In this sense, the theory of the Communists may be summed up in the single sentence: Abolition of private property.

We Communists have been reproached with the desire of abolishing the right of personally acquiring property as the fruit of a man's own labor, which property is alleged to be the groundwork of all personal freedom, activity and independence.

Hard-won, self-acquired, self-earned property! Do you mean the property of the petty artisan and of the small peasant, a form of property that preceded the bourgeois form? There is no need to abolish that; the development of industry has to a great extent already destroyed it, and is still destroying it daily.

Or do you mean modern bourgeois private property?

But does wage-labor create any property for the laborer? Not a bit. It creates capital, *i.e.,* that kind of property which exploits wage-labor, and which cannot increase except upon condition of begetting a new supply of wage-labor for fresh exploitation. Property, in its present form, is based on the antagonism of capital and wage-labor. Let us examine both sides of this antagonism.

To be a capitalist, is to have not only a purely personal, but a social *status* in production. Capital is a collective product, and only by the united action of many members, nay, in the last resort, only by the united action of all members of society, can it be set in motion.

Capital is therefore not a personal, it is a social, power.

When, therefore, capital is converted into common property, into the property of all members of society, personal property is not thereby transformed into social property. It is only the social character of the property that is changed. It loses its class character.

Let us now take wage-labor.

The average price of wage-labor is the minimum wage, *i.e.,* that quantum of the means of subsistence which is absolutely requisite to keep the laborer in bare existence as a laborer. What, therefore, the wage-laborer appropriates by means of his labor, merely suffices to prolong and reproduce a bare existence. We by no means intend to abolish this personal appropriation of the products of labor, an appropriation that is made for the maintenance and reproduction of human life, and that leaves no surplus wherewith to command the labor of others. All that we want to do away with is the miserable character of this appropriation, under which the laborer lives merely to increase capital, and is allowed to live only insofar as the interest of the ruling class requires it.

In bourgeois society, living labor is but a means to increase accumulated labor. In Communist society, accumulated labor is but a means to widen, to enrich, to promote the existence of the laborer.

In bourgeois society, therefore, the past dominates the present; in Communist society, the present dominates the past. In bourgeois society capital is independent and has individuality, while the living person is dependent and has no individuality.

And the abolition of this state of things is called by the bourgeoisie, abolition of individuality and freedom! And rightly so. The abolition of bourgeois individuality, bourgeois independence, and bourgeois freedom is undoubtedly aimed at.

By freedom is meant, under the present bourgeois conditions of production, free trade, free selling and buying.

But if selling and buying disappear, free selling and buying disappear also. This talk about free selling and buying, and all the other "brave words" of our bourgeoisie about freedom in general, have a meaning, if any, only in contrast with restricted selling and buying, with the fettered traders of the Middle Ages, but have no meaning when opposed to the Communist abolition of buying and selling, of the bourgeois conditions of production, and of the bourgeoisie itself.

You are horrified at our intending to do away with private property. But in your existing society, private property is already done away with for nine-tenths of the population; its existence for the few is solely due to its nonexistence in the hands of those nine-tenths. You reproach us, therefore, with intending to do away with a form of property, the necessary condition for whose existence is the nonexistence of any property for the immense majority of society.

In a word, you reproach us with intending to do away with your property. Precisely so; that is just what we intend.

From the moment when labor can no longer be converted into capital, money, or rent, into a social power capable of being monopolized, *i.e.,* from the moment when individual property can no longer be transformed into bourgeois property, into capital, from that moment, you say, individuality vanishes.

You must, therefore, confess that by "individual" you mean no other person than the bourgeois, than the middle-class owner of property. This person must, indeed, be swept out of the way, and made impossible.

Communism deprives no man of the power to appropriate the products of society; all that it does is to deprive him of the power to subjugate the labor of others by means of such appropriation.

It has been objected, that upon the abolition of private property all work will cease, and universal laziness will overtake us.

According to this, bourgeois society ought long ago to have gone to the dogs through sheer idleness; for those of its members who work, acquire nothing, and those who acquire anything, do not work. The whole of this objection is but another expression of the tautology: There can no longer be any wage-labor when there is no longer any capital.

All objections urged against the Communist mode of producing and appropriating material products, have, in the same way, been urged against the Communist modes of producing and appropriating intellectual products. Just as, to the bourgeois, the disappearance of class property is the disappearance of production itself, so the disappearance of class culture is to him identical with the disappearance of all culture.

That culture, the loss of which he laments, is, for the enormous majority, a mere training to act as a machine.

But don't wrangle with us so long as you apply, to our intended abolition of bourgeois property, the standard of your bourgeois notions of freedom, culture, law, etc. Your very ideas are but the outgrowth of the conditions of your bourgeois production and bourgeois property, just as your jurisprudence is but the will of your class made into a law for all, a will whose essential character and direction are determined by the economic conditions of existence of your class.

The selfish misconception that induces you to transform into eternal laws of nature and of reason, the social forms springing from your present mode of production and form of property — historical relations that rise and disappear in the progress of production — this misconception you share with every ruling class that has preceded you. What you see clearly in the case of ancient property, what you admit in the case of feudal property, you are of course forbidden to admit in the case of your own bourgeois form of property.

Abolition of the family! Even the most radical flare up at this infamous proposal of the Communists.

On what foundation is the present family, the bourgeois family, based? On capital, on private gain. In its completely developed form this family exists only among the bourgeoisie. But this state of things finds its complement in the practical absence of the family among the proletarians, and in public prostitution.

The bourgeois family will vanish as a matter of course when its complement vanishes, and both will vanish with the vanishing of capital.

Do you charge us with wanting to stop the exploitation of children by their parents? To this crime we plead guilty.

But, you will say, we destroy the most hallowed of relations, when we replace home education by social.

And your education! Is not that also social, and determined by the social conditions under which you educate, by the intervention of society, direct or indirect, by means of schools, etc.? The Communists have not invented the intervention of society in education; they do but seek to alter the character of that intervention, and to rescue education from the influence of the ruling class.

The bourgeois claptrap about the family and education, about the hallowed co-relation of parent and child, becomes all the more disgusting, the more, by the action of modern industry, all family ties among the proletarians are torn asunder, and their children transformed into simple articles of commerce and instruments of labor.

But you Communists would introduce community of women, screams the whole bourgeoisie in chorus.

The bourgeois sees in his wife a mere instrument of production. He hears that the instruments of production are to be exploited in common, and, naturally, can come to no other conclusion than that the lot of being common to all will likewise fall to the women.

He has not even a suspicion that the real point aimed at is to do away with the status of women as mere instruments of production.

For the rest, nothing is more ridiculous than the virtuous indignation of our bourgeois at the community of women which, they pretend, is to be openly and officially established by the Communists. The Communists have no need to introduce community of women; it has existed almost from time immemorial.

Our bourgeois, not content with having the wives and daughters of their proletarians at their disposal, not to speak of common prostitutes, take the greatest pleasure in seducing each other's wives.

Bourgeois marriage is in reality a system of wives in common and thus, at the most, what the Communists might possibly be reproached with is that they desire to introduce, in substitution for a hypocritically concealed, an openly legalized community of women. For the rest, it is self-evident, that the abolition of the present system of production must bring with it the abolition of the community of women springing from that system, *i.e.,* of prostitution both public and private.

The Communists are further reproached with desiring to abolish countries and nationality.

The workingmen have no country. We cannot take from them what they have not got. Since the proletariat must first of all acquire political supremacy, must rise to be the leading class of the nation, must constitute itself *the* nation, it is, so far, itself national, though not in the bourgeois sense of the word.

National differences and antagonisms between peoples are vanishing gradually from day to day, owing to the development of the bourgeoisie, to freedom of commerce, to the world market, to uniformity in the mode of production and in the conditions of life corresponding thereto.

The supremacy of the proletariat will cause them to vanish still faster. United action, of the leading civilized countries at least, is one of the first conditions for the emancipation of the proletariat.

In proportion as the exploitation of one individual by another is put an end to, the exploitation of one nation by another will also be put an end to. In proportion as the antagonism between classes within the nation vanishes, the hostility of one nation to another will come to an end.

The charges against communism made from a religious, a philosophical, and, generally, from an ideological standpoint, are not deserving of serious examination.

Does it require deep intuition to comprehend that man's ideas, views, and conceptions, in one word, man's consciousness, changes with every change in the conditions of his material existence, in his social relations and in his social life?

What else does the history of ideas prove, than that intellectual production changes its character in proportion as material production is changed? The ruling ideas of each age have ever been the ideas of its ruling class.

When people speak of ideas that revolutionize society, they do but express the fact that within the old society the elements of a new one have been created, and that the dissolution of the old ideas keeps even pace with the dissolution of the old conditions of existence.

When the ancient world was in its last throes, the ancient religions were overcome by Christianity. When Christian ideas succumbed in the eighteenth century to rationalist ideas, feudal society fought its death-battle with the then revolutionary bourgeoisie. The ideas of religious liberty and freedom of conscience, merely gave expression to the sway of free competition within the domain of knowledge.

"Undoubtedly," it will be said, "religion, moral, philosophical and juridical ideas have been modified in the course of historical development. But religion, morality, philosophy, political science, and law, constantly survived this change."

"There are, besides, eternal truths, such as Freedom, Justice, etc., that are common to all states of society. But communism abolishes eternal truths, it abolishes all religion, and all morality, instead of constituting them on a new basis; it therefore acts in contradiction to all past historical experience."

What does this accusation reduce itself to? The history of all past society has consisted in the development of class antagonisms, antagonisms that assumed different forms at different epochs.

But whatever form they may have taken, one fact is common to all past ages, *viz.,* the exploitation of one part of society by the other. No wonder, then, that the social consciousness of past ages, despite all the multiplicity and variety it displays, moves within certain common forms, or general ideas, which cannot completely vanish except with the total disappearance of class antagonisms.

The Communist revolution is the most radical rupture with traditional property relations; no wonder that its development involves the most radical rupture with traditional ideas.

But let us have done with the bourgeois objections to communism.

We have seen above, that the first step in the revolution by the working class, is to raise the proletariat to the position of ruling class, to establish democracy.

The proletariat will use its political supremacy to wrest, by degrees, all capital from the bourgeoisie, to centralize all instruments of production in the hands of the state, *i.e.,* of the proletariat organized as the ruling class; and to increase the total of productive forces as rapidly as possible.

Of course, in the beginning, this cannot be effected except by means of despotic inroads on the rights of property, and on the conditions of bourgeois production; by means of measures, therefore, which appear economically insufficient and untenable, but which, in the course of the movement, outstrip themselves, necessitate further inroads upon the old social order, and are unavoidable as a means of entirely revolutionizing the mode of production.

These measures will of course be different in different countries.

Nevertheless in the most advanced countries, the following will be pretty generally applicable.

1. Abolition of property in land and application of all rents of land to public purposes.
2. A heavy progressive or graduated income tax.
3. Abolition of all right of inheritance.
4. Confiscation of the property of all emigrants and rebels.
5. Centralization of credit in the hands of the state, by means of a national bank with state capital and an exclusive monopoly.
6. Centralization of the means of communication and transport in the hands of the state.
7. Extension of factories and instruments of production owned by the state; the bringing into cultivation of waste lands, and the improvement of the soil generally in accordance with a common plan.
8. Equal obligation of all to work. Establishment of industrial armies, especially for agriculture.
9. Combination of agriculture with manufacturing industries; gradual abolition of the distinction between town and country, by a more equable distribution of the population over the country.
10. Free education for all children in public schools. Abolition of child factory labor in its present form. Combination of education with industrial production, etc.

When, in the course of development, class distinctions have disappeared, and all production has been concentrated in the hands of a vast association of the whole nation, the public power will lose its political character. Political power, properly so called, is merely the organized power of one class for oppressing another. If the proletariat during its contest with the bourgeoisie is compelled, by the force of circumstances, to organize itself as a class; if, by means of a revolution, it makes itself the ruling class, and, as such sweeps away by force the old conditions of production, then it will, along with these conditions, have swept away the conditions for existence of class antagonisms, and of classes generally, and will thereby have abolished its own supremacy as a class.

In place of the old bourgeois society, with its classes and class antagonisms, we shall have an association, in which the free development of each is the condition for the free development of all.

• • •

IV

Position of the Communists in Relation to the Various Existing Opposition Parties

• • •

The Communists fight for the attainment of the immediate aims, for the enforcement of the momentary interests of the working class; but in the movement of the present, they also represent and take care of the future of that movement. In France the Communists ally themselves with the Social-Democrats, against the conservative and radical bourgeoisie, reserving, however, the right to take up a critical position in regard to phrases and illusions traditionally handed down from the great Revolution.[14]

• • •

In Germany they fight with the bourgeoisie whenever it acts in a revolutionary way, against the absolute monarchy, the feudal squirearchy,[15] and the petty bourgeoisie.[16]

But they never cease, for a single instant, to instill into the working class the clearest possible recognition of the hostile antagonism between bourgeoisie and proletariat, in order that the German workers may straightway use, as so many weapons against the bourgeoisie, the social and political conditions that the bourgeoisie must necessarily introduce along with its supremacy, and in order that, after the fall of the reactionary classes in Germany, the fight against the bourgeoisie itself may immediately begin.

---

[14] The French Revolution, 1789–1795.

[15] The landed gentry (small landowners).

[16] Small shopkeepers and independent craftsmen.

The Communists turn their attention chiefly to Germany, because that country is on the eve of a bourgeois revolution[17] that is bound to be carried out under more advanced conditions of European civilization and with a much more developed proletariat than what existed in England in the 17th and in France in the 18th century, and because the bourgeois revolution in Germany will be but the prelude to an immediately following proletarian revolution.

In short, the Communists everywhere support every revolutionary movement against the existing social and political order of things.

In all these movements they bring to the front, as the leading question in each case, the property question, no matter what its degree of development at the time.

Finally, they labor everywhere for the union and agreement of the democratic parties of all countries.

The Communists disdain to conceal their views and aims. They openly declare that their ends can be attained only by the forcible overthrow of all existing social conditions. Let the ruling classes tremble at a Communist revolution. The proletarians have nothing to lose but their chains. They have a world to win.

Workingmen of all countries, unite!

---

[17] There were unsuccessful liberal revolutions throughout much of Europe in 1848 and 1849.

34

❧

Benito Pérez Galdós

FORTUNATA AND JACINTA

The great master of novelistic realism in Spain, Benito Pérez Galdós *(1843–1920), was born in the Canary Islands (a Spanish possession off the coast of North Africa). After early studies in his native islands, he went to Madrid in 1862 to study law. He soon grew more interested in literature, and in the lively, politically charged atmosphere of the capital. Spanish literature of the time was still very much influenced by Romanticism's passionate rhetoric, while in the political sphere, a sometimes violent struggle was taking place between the monarchy and those who favored a republican form of government. Coups, countercoups, and armed rebellions (particularly in the northern regions of Spain) were the order of the day.*

After a brief trip to France in 1868, Galdós began his career as a journalist and novelist; his first novel, La fontana de oro *(The Golden Fountain) dates from that year. As his fame grew, his writings became more abundant. Working with rapid intensity, Galdós began publishing in 1873 a series of historical accounts called the* Episodios nacionales, *in which he retold, in a slightly fictionalized way, some of the turning points of nineteenth-century Spanish history. He would continue to write these* Episodios, *with some interruptions, until 1912, for a grand total of forty-six volumes.*

Almost at the same time, he was writing and publishing purely novelistic and fictional works. Between 1876 and 1885 he published a total of ten novels, of which the best known are Doña Perfecta (Madame Perfection, *1876*), La desheredada (The Disinherited One, *1881*), El amigo Manso (My Friend Manso, *1882*), and Lo prohibido (Forbidden Things, *1884–1885*). Along with his journalistic and novelistic work, Galdós occupied at various times the political position of* diputado *(congressman), not so much out of political conviction, but to supplement his often-meager income as a journalist. Between 1886 and 1892, he published another series of novels, chief among them his masterpiece,* Fortunata y Jacinta (Fortunata and Jacinta, *1886–1887*).

After 1892, Galdós devoted himself to writing for the theatre, with varying degrees of success. Many of his plays were adaptations of his novels to the theatre. In 1897, Galdós was elected a member of the prestigious Academia de la Lengua Española, one of the highest honors for a Spanish writer. Despite his prestige, the last years of Galdós's life were shadowed by blindness, poverty, and illness. He died in his beloved Madrid in 1920.

Like all realist writers, Galdós was concerned with representing people, objects, and events that his readers could recognize, using literary techniques that his readers could easily grasp. For him, therefore, as for the French writers—such as Honoré de Balzac, the Goncourt brothers, and Émile Zola—who were partly his models, language was chiefly a vehicle for conveying information about the psychology, appearance, customs, and environment of his fictional characters. Galdós in particular was not fond of stylistic flourishes; he wrote in a simple, direct, almost conversational Spanish. The effect of his work thus tends to be cumulative, growing out of the details with which Galdós describes the characters and their environment. Partly as a reaction to the intensely subjective writing style of the Romantics, the realists tried to present an "objective" view of people and their world. Realism was also often motivated by the writer's desire to promote social change by educating and informing readers about the major societal problems of the day. Many realist writers, including Galdós, regarded themselves primarily as analysts and commentators of their societies, rather than as artists.

Fortunata and Jacinta, if not Galdós's most perfect work, is certainly his most typical, and offers a synthesis of his novelistic style. As its subtitle (Two Stories of Married Women) announces, the novel tells the story of two women of Madrid, Jacinta, from the wealthy merchant class, and Fortunata, from the urban poor, who both fall in love with the same man, the egotistic Juanito Santa Cruz, scion of the wealthy Santa Cruz–Arnáiz family. The placid Jacinta's marriage to Juanito is overshadowed by her incapacity to give him the heir that he and his family so much desire. On the other hand, the passionate and beautiful Fortunata, whom Juanito meets while visiting the poorer sections of Madrid, is finally able to give him a son; but she is unable to keep his affections due to her lower-class background.

As befits its panoramic view of Madrid's society, the novel's cast of characters is large; there are more than fifteen characters who play important roles in the narration at different moments. One such character is Plácido Estupiñá, an old servant and friend of the Santa Cruz family, who lives in the poor quarter near the Plaza Mayor (Main Square) of Madrid. The following selection, from Chapter 3 of the novel's first part, begins with a detailed account of Estupiñá's life and personality and his relation to the Santa Cruz family. Written in a gently mocking tone, it culminates in the scene in which Juanito Santa Cruz, going to visit the ailing Estupiñá, accidentally meets Fortunata for the first time. The encounter takes place in the inauspicious environment of a poultry shop, and includes a now-celebrated scene in which Fortunata offers to share with Juanito the raw egg that she is eating.

ोर्

CHAPTER 3
Estupiñá

1

In the Arnáiz shop, next to the window with the grill that looks out over San Cristóbal Lane, there are three seats in curved Austrian wood. Many years ago they replaced a bench without a back, covered in black oil-cloth, and that bench had taken the place of a large chest or empty packing case. This was the sacred site where the renowned circle of friends centred on the shop would gather to gossip and argue. There was no shop without such a *tertulia*[1] any more than there was one without a counter or a patron saint. This was a supplementary service to society provided by the business fraternity at a time when casinos[2] did not exist, for although there were secret societies and clubs and cafés of a more or less patriotic nature, the majority of peace-loving citizens did not go to them, preferring to chat in the shops. Barbarita[3] even has vague memories of the *tertulia* of her childhood. A very thin friar called Father Alelí used to go; an extremely small man with spectacles who was Isabel's father, then there were several military men and other people whom she got thoroughly confused with the two mandarin dummies.

They did not talk only about politics and the civil war, but about business matters. Barbarita remembers having heard about the first matches to come on the market and even having seen them. You put the wax match into what looked like a small bottle and it came out burning. She also heard people talk about the first moquette carpets, the first spring mattresses and the first railways, which one of the circle of friends had seen abroad, since there was not a sign of them here. There was also something about a bank-note, for paper money was not common in Madrid until several years after this, and was only used then for major bank

---

From *Fortunata and Jacinta: Two Stories of Married Women* by Benito Pérez Galdós. Copyright 1973 by Lester Clark, translator. Pp. 73–89.

[1] A *"tertulia"* is a name given in Spanish to any informal gathering of friends and acquaintances who meet regularly to converse.

[2] *"Casinos"* were social clubs where members of the same social class could meet for *tertulias* as well as to play games of chance.

[3] Barbarita Arnáiz, the mother of Juanito Santa Cruz.

payments. Barbarita remembers having seen the first bank-note brought into the shop. It was a great curiosity and everyone agreed that coins were better. Gas came much later than all this.

The shop changed a great deal, but the *tertulia* remained the same throughout the years. Some people left the circle and others came. We do not know which era was under discussion in the odd sentences Barbarita, who was already married, would half overhear when she went into the shop to rest a little after having been for a walk or out shopping:

'The Third Fusiliers looked magnificent this morning with their new pompom decorations'—'The Duke went to mass today in the Calatravas Church. He went with Linaje and San Miguel'—'Do you know what they are saying now, Estupiñá? Well, it seems the English are planning to build ships made of *iron!*'

Estupiñá was indispensable at all the shop *tertulias,* for when he was not at the Arnáiz shop, everyone started asking questions: 'What has become of Plácido? Where is he?' When he did come in, people were overjoyed to see him, because with his presence alone he would always liven up the conversation. I knew this man in 1871. His boast was that he had seen all Spanish history in this century. He was born in 1803 and called himself a birthday brother of Mesonero Romanos,[4] for they were both born on 19 July 1803. One sentence of his will prove his immense knowledge of living history, learnt though his own eyes, 'I saw José I just as I see you now.' He seemed to lick his lips with delight when they asked him,

'Did you see the Duke of Angoulème, and Lord Wellington?'

'I should think I did.'

His reply was always the same, 'Just as I see you now.' He even used to get upset if anyone questioned him in a doubtful tone.

'Of course I saw María Cristina[5] enter the city! For heaven's sake, if it is anything to do with history . . .'

In order to complete his visual erudition, he used to talk about 'the way Madrid looked' on 1 September 1840, as if it were last week. He had seen Canterac die; Merino brought to justice, 'right on the very scaffold', for he was a brother of la Paz y Caridad; he had seen Chico killed—well not exactly seen, but he had heard the shots as he happened to be in the Calle de las Velas; he had seen Fernando VII on 7 July when he came out on to the balcony to tell the militia that they should trounce the Civil Guard; he had seen Rodil and Sergeant García haranguing the crowd from another balcony in 1836; he had seen O'Donnell

---

[4] Ramón de Mesonero Romanos (1803–1882) was a Spanish Romantic writer who specialized in descriptions of daily life in Madrid.

[5] María Cristina de Borbón, wife of King Fernando VII, was queen of Spain and occupied the regency (1833–1840) after the death of her husband, until her daughter Isabel II was of legal age to occupy the throne.

and Espartero embracing each other; Espartero alone, saluting the people, O'Donnell on his own, and all this on a balcony; and finally, about the same time, he had seen another public figure on a balcony shouting that the days of the monarchy were over. All the history Estupiñá knew was written on balconies.[6]

The man's biographical details as far as business is concerned are as curious as they are simple. He was a very young man when he entered Arnáiz's shop as an assistant. He served in the shop for many years and was always highly regarded by Arnáiz for his evident honesty and the deep interest he took in everything to do with the firm. Yet in spite of such qualities, Estupiñá was not a good employee. If he delivered goods, he would entertain the customers for far too long, and if he was sent to the customs house with a message or on an errand, he was so long coming back that Don Bonifacio often thought he had been officially detained. The strange fact that the owners of the shop could not do without Plácido, although he behaved in this strange way, is explained by the blind confidence he inspired, for when he was in charge of the shop and the till, Arnáiz and his family could go to sleep if they wanted to. His loyalty was as great as his humility, for they could rebuke him and shout angrily at him as much as they liked and he never got upset. For these reasons Don Bonifacio was very sorry that Plácido left the firm in 1837, when he was very keen to set up on his own with the money he had been left in a small legacy. His employer, who knew him well, made some very gloomy prophecies about Plácido's commercial future working for himself.

He gave promise of happily fulfilling those prophecies in the flannel and linen shop he established on the Plaza Mayor next to the Panadería. He did not have any employees because he did so little business he could not afford them, but his *tertulia* was the most lively and argumentative in the whole district. This was the reason he gave so little of himself to the business and the justification of Don Bonifacio's prophecies. Estupiñá had a chronic hereditary vice against which all other driving forces in his soul were powerless, a vice all the more enslaving for appearing to be so inoffensive. It was not drink, nor love, nor gambling, nor luxury; it was conversation. For the sake of a good talk, Estupiñá was capable of letting the most profitable sale in the world go to the devil. If he had launched enthusiastically into a conversation the sky could fall about his ears and his tongue would have to be cut out before the thread of his conversation could be broken. The most frenzied talkers used to go to his shop, because vice attracts vice. If someone came in to buy something at a particularly stimulating point in the conversation, Estupiñá would look daggers at the customer, and if what

---

[6] This paragraph alludes to a series of events in Spanish history that took place after Spain's War of Independence from France (1808–1814), during the restoration of King Fernando VII to the monarchy (1822–1833), and during the factional power struggles between Generals O'Donnell and Espartero after the death of King Fernando VII.

was wanted was on the counter, he would point it out with a swift gesture, wanting to get the interruption over quickly. If, however, the goods were high on the shelves, he would glance upwards wearily as if asking God to give him patience, saying, 'Yellow flannel? Just look at it! It seems to me there isn't enough for what you want.' On other occasions he doubted, or pretended to doubt, whether he had what was being asked for: 'Caps for a small boy? Do you want them with oilcloth peaks? I think there are some, but people don't wear them like that any more.'

If he was playing *tute* or *mus*,[7] the only games he knew, and he was an expert at them, the world would have to disintegrate around him before he could be distracted from the cards. His desire for conversation and social contact was so great, his body and soul craved it with such vehemence, that if people did not come to the shop to talk, he could not resist his longing for the vice. He would lock up, put the key in his pocket and go to another shop in search of the verbal liquor that intoxicated him. At Christmas, when the stalls in the main square began to be erected, the poor man had not the heart to remain cooped up in his dingy little shop. The sound of the human voice, the lights and the noise of the street were as necessary to his existence as the air he breathed. He would close up shop and go to gossip with the women stall-holders. He knew them all, and got to know all about what they were going to sell and what had happened in the family of each one. Estupiñá, then, belonged to that race of shopkeepers, of which there are very few left, whose role in the commercial world seems to be the prevention of all the harm done to the consumer by an unhealthy inclination to spend money.

'Don Plácido, have you got any blue velveteen?'

'Blue velveteen! How did you develop such luxurious tastes? I've got it, all right; but it's very expensive for the likes of you.'

'Show it to me and I'll see if I can manage it.'

Then Estupiñá would make a great effort, as if he were sacrificing his most cherished feelings and tastes to the demands of duty, and fetch down the piece of material.

'Well now, here's the velveteen. If you don't want to buy it and you're just bothering me, why do you ask to see it? Do you think I've got nothing better to do?'

'Haven't you got a better quality?'

'What did I say? These women would try the patience of a saint. Yes, señora, there is a better quality. Now do you want to buy it, yes or no? It's twenty-two *reales*, and no less.'

'But let me see it—what a man you are! Do you think I'm going to eat it or something?'

'It's twenty-two *reales*.'

'Oh forget it. You can go to the devil!'

'And the same to you, you ill-mannered, loud-mouthed old dragon!'

---

[7] *"Tute"* and *"mus"* were popular card games of the period.

He was very refined with ladies of a better class. His affability went something like this:

'Fine woollen cloth? Certainly we have some. Do you see the material up there? It seems to me, señora, that it is not at all what you are looking for; I say "it seems to me", for I would not for a moment suggest . . . These days it is fashionable to have fine stripes, and I have none with stripes. I am expecting a delivery next month. I saw your little girls yesterday, with Don Cándido. How they are growing! And how is Señor Mayor? I have not seen him since we both went to the shrine of San Ginés!'

With this system of selling, after four years of business you could count the number of people who crossed the threshold in a week. After six years not even the flies went into his shop. Estupiñá opened up every morning, swept and sprinkled water on the pavement, put on his green oversleeves and sat down behind the counter to read the *Diario de Avisos*.[8] Gradually his friends would start to arrive, those soul-mates who seemed to Plácido, in his solitude, rather like the dove that flew down on to Noah's Ark, but there was something more than an olive branch in this dove's beak: his friends brought him speech, the succulent fruit and flower of life, the alcohol of the soul that inflamed his vice. They spent the whole day telling stories, commenting on political events, talking in a very familiar way about Mendizábal, Calatrava,[9] María Cristina and even God; drawing out plans of campaign in extravagant tactical moves on the counter with one finger: demonstrating that Espartero really should move here and Villarreal ought to go there; they chatted about business matters and the arrival of this or that sort of merchandise; important matters relating to the Church, the militia, women, the Court, together with everything else within the scope of human prattle. Throughout all this, the till was not opened once and the yardstick for measuring the cloth, sunk deep in placid repose, would have needed very little to grow green and flower once more. Since months went by without the stock being renewed, and everything there was out-of-date and old, the final scandal was sensational and sudden. One day all his property was seized and Estupiñá, his sorrow as great as his dignity, left the shop.

2

The great philosopher did not submit to desperation. His friends noted that he was calm and resigned. In his bearing and the repose of his face, he was rather like Socrates, bearing in mind that Socrates was inclined to talk for seven hours on end. The important thing was that Plácido had come through with his honour untarnished, paying off all his debts from the stock in hand. He had been left with his dignity and nothing else. The only furniture he had left was his measuring

---

[8] *Diario de Avisos* was a Madrid newspaper.

[9] Juan Alvarez y Mendízabal (1790–1853) and José María Calatrava (1781–1846) were Spanish politicians who were household names at the time.

yard. It was essential, then, to find some way of earning a living. What should he dedicate himself to? In which branch of commerce should he employ his great gifts? Thinking about this, he came to realize that in the midst of all this poverty, he still had a source of capital that many would envy: the people he knew. He was acquainted with so many shopkeepers in Madrid; all doors would open to him, and everywhere people were well disposed towards him, because of his honesty, good manners and above all for the conversational gifts with which God had blessed him. His friends, and his particular abilities, led him to the idea of devoting himself to selling from within the trade. Don Baldomero Santa Cruz, plump Arnáiz, Bringas, Moreno, Labiano and others who sold drapery, cloth or specialized novelties, gave him samples so that he could show them from shop to shop. He would earn two percent commission on what he sold. Heavens above, could there be a more delightful life? How wise he was to follow such a line, because one could hardly imagine anything more suited to his temperament! Always being on the move, going into endless shops, greeting fifty people in the street and asking about their families, this was life to him, and anything else was death. Plácido was not born to manage a shop. His element was the street, the open air, discussion, business transaction, greeting people, coming and going, questioning, inquiring, passing lightly from serious matters to a joke. There was one morning when he had something to eat or drink in every place on the Calle de Toledo and the Concepción Jerónima, Átocha y Carretas.

Several years passed in this way. As his needs were very modest, since he had no family to maintain and no vices, for the expenditure of saliva was no longer a vice, the little money he earned was enough for him to live. Moreover, many rich merchants protected him. At best, one of them would give him a cloak; another, a suit of clothes; yet another might present him with a hat, or even things to eat and sweet delicacies. The haughtiest of business families would sit him at table with them, not only out of friendship but from egoism, because it was amusing to hear him talk about such varied matters with his enchanting picturesque accuracy and precise attention to detail. His diverting chatter had two main characteristics, and they were: that he never admitted to being ignorant on any subject, and that he never spoke ill of anyone. If by chance he did allow himself a critical word, it was against the Customs, but his accusations were never levelled against a particular person.

Now Estupiñá, as well as being a representative for various shops, was also a smuggler. The number of twenty-six-kilo bales of Hamburg cloth that slipped with cunning ingenuity through the Gil Imón Customs barrier could not be counted. There was no one like him for creeping along certain streets at dead of night with a bundle under his cloak, pretending that he looked like a beggar carrying a child on his back. No one else possessed the art of slipping a *duro* into the revenue officer's hand in moments of danger as he did, and he had reached such an understanding with the officials through this subterfuge that the leading firms used to turn to him to sort out their problems with the Treasury officials. There is no way of writing fiscal sins into the Ten Commandments. The public spirit rebelled, more in those days than now, against considering cheating the Treasury as a real sin and, conforming to this opinion, Estupiñá felt not the slightest twinge of conscience when he brought one of these undertakings to a successful conclusion. According to him, what the Treasury people considered theirs was not theirs at all, but belonged to the nation, that is, to the man in the street, and to trick the Treasury is to give back to the man in the street what rightly belongs to him. This idea, fervently sustained by the people, has had its heroes as well as its martyrs. Plácido subscribed to the faith with no less enthusiasm than any Andalusian horse bandit, except that he was in the infantry and did not kill anyone. His conscience, shrouded in horrifying mists over fiscal matters, was pure and shining as far as personal propriety was concerned. He was a man who would have remained silent for a month rather than keep a *peseta* that did not belong to him.

Barbarita was very fond of him. From the moment she could see and respond to things, he had been in her house. From her father's opinion and her own experience, she knew the accomplishments and the loyalty of this talkative man very well. When Barbarita was a little girl, Estupiñá used to take her to the school on the corner of the Calle Imperial, and at Christmas time she would go with him to see the nativity cribs and the stalls in Santa Cruz Square. When Don Bonifacio Arnáiz was on his death bed, Plácido did not leave him while he was ill and even after he was dead, until he was in his grave. He was always the most sincere participant in all the sorrows and joys of the house. His situation in that respected family was somewhere between friendship and service, for if Barbarita had him sitting with her at table on many occasions, most days of the year she employed him on errands and commissions, which he knew how to carry out to perfection. Sometimes he would be off to Cebada Square for fresh early vegetables, sometimes to the Cava Baja to get to know the carriers who were bringing in goods, or even to Maravillas where the firm's ironing woman and the lace-maker lived. Such was Barbarita's influence over that simple soul, and with such blind faith did he respect and obey her, that if she had said to him, 'Plácido, please throw yourself off the balcony into the street,' the unfortunate man would not have hesitated for one moment to do it.

After many years had gone by, when Estupiñá was already getting old and no longer sold goods or smuggled them, an extremely delicate item was delivered to the Santa Cruz establishment. As he was such a trustworthy person, and so blindly loyal to the family, Barbarita entrusted Juanito to him, so that the old man could take him and bring him home from the Massarnáu College, or take him for walks on Sundays and days of fiesta. Barbarita was quite certain that Plácido's vigilance would be just like that of a father, and she knew quite well that he would die a hundred times over before allowing anyone to harm a single hair on the head of the Delfín,[10] as he used to call Juanito. The boy was already growing up, and developing some of the airs of manhood, when Estupiñá took him to the

---

[10] Literally "dauphin," or the king's eldest son.

bullfight, initiating him into the mysteries of the art, which he prided himself on knowing like any good man of Madrid. The boy and the old man were equally enthusiastic about the barbarous and picturesque spectacle, and at the start of the fight, Plácido would relate his own bullfighting exploits, for he too, in his youth, had side-stepped the bull and made passes with the red cape; he even had a complete suit with spangles all over it, and he used to fight young bulls very skillfully without forgetting any of the rules. As Juanito was very keen to see the suit, Plácido had to tell him that many years ago, his sister the dressmaker (whom God preserve) had made it into a tunic for a Nazarene which is to be found in the church of Duganzo de Abajo.

Apart from chattering, Estupiñá had no vices at all, nor did he ever associate closely with vulgar or disreputable people. Only once in his life did he get mixed up with a rough group of people and that was at the christening of the son of a nephew of his who was married to a woman who ran a gambling den. On that occasion something happened to him that he remembered and felt ashamed of all his life. The stupid young nephew plotted with his friends and succeeded in getting him drunk by surreptitiously giving him a drink that would have made a stone move about. It was a stupid drunken bout, the first and last of his life; the memory of that night's degradation made him sad every time he thought of it. How disgraceful to play such a trick on one who was sobriety itself! They made him drink that disgusting stuff by barefaced deceit, and afterwards they did not hesitate to jeer at him with as much cruelty as vulgarity. They asked him to sing *la Pitita,* and there is reason to believe he did sing it, although he denies it to everyone. Even while his senses were befuddled, he was aware of the state they had made him reach, and decorum put the idea of running away into his mind. He got out of the area, thinking that the night air would clear his head; but although he did feel a little better, his faculties and senses continued to be subject to the most serious errors. On reaching the corner by the Cava de San Miguel he saw the night watchman, or more correctly what he saw was the watchman's lantern, as the man was walking towards the corner of the Calle de Cuchilleros. He thought it was the lantern preceding a priest on his way to administer the last rites; kneeling down and taking off his hat, he said a short prayer: 'May God grant whatever suits him best!' The louts who tricked him were following, and their guffaws brought him to his senses, and when he understood his mistake, he escaped into his house which was only a few paces away. He slept, and the following day behaved as if nothing had happened. He felt deep remorse, however, which made him sigh and remain sunk in thought for some time. Nothing afflicted his honourable heart so much as the idea that Barbarita should hear about the mistake over the priest's lantern. Fortunately, she did not know about it, or if she did, she never mentioned the matter.

3

When I knew this worthy son of Madrid personally, he was just on seventy but wearing very well. He was of less than average height, dumpy and he had rather a stoop. Those who would like to know what his face was like should look at a portrait of the elderly Rossini as it has come down to us in prints and photographs of the great musician, and they can say they have the admirable Estupiñá before them. The shape of the head, the smile, the profile, above all the hooked nose, the cavernous mouth, the roguish eyes, were all a perfect copy of that rather wickedly joking beauty which, accentuated by the lines of age, was rather like a portrait of Punch. Age was making Estupiñá's profile somewhat like that of a parrot.

Towards the end of his life, from 1870 onwards, he dressed with a certain originality, not from destitution, since the Santa Cruz family took care that he lacked nothing, but from a spirit of tradition and repugnance at introducing anything new into his wardrobe. He wore a flat hat with a very low crown and a smooth brim which belonged to an era that had already forgotten makers of the *sombrero,* and a cape of green material which only flowed from his shoulders between July and September. He had very little hair, one might almost say none at all, but he did not wear a wig. To protect his head from cold draughts in church, he carried a black cap in his pocket which he would press firmly on his head when he went inside. He was a great dawn riser, and in the chilly early hours he would go to the Santa Cruz church, then to Santo Tomás and finally to San Ginés. Having heard several masses in each church, his cap pulled down to his ears, and having had a little chat with the faithful or the sacristans, he would go from chapel to chapel saying different prayers in each. On leaving, he used to wave to the paintings, as one would greet a friend on a balcony, and then he would take his holy water, without his cap on, and so out into the street.

When they demolished the Santa Cruz church in 1869, Estupiñá went through a very bad period. Neither the bird whose nest is destroyed, nor the man who is driven from his birth-place could have looked more devastated than he did as he watched the chunks of rubble falling in clouds of dust. Because he was a man, he did not weep. Barbarita had been brought up in the shadow of that venerable tower and, if she did not cry to see such a sacrilegious spectacle, it was because she was furious and anger would not allow her to shed tears. Nor could she explain to herself why her husband said Don Nicolás Rivero[11] was a great person. When the temple disappeared, when it was razed to the ground and as the years passed a house was built on the sacred ground, Estupiñá would not accept it. He was not one of those accommodating people who recognize actions that have actually taken place. For him, the church was always there, and every time my friend went over the exact spot where the door had been, he would cross himself and take off his hat.

Plácido was a brother of la Paz y Caridad, a fraternity based in the most disreputable part of the town. He used to go to the chapel to help men under sentence of death and talk with them at this supremely vital time, telling them of the futility of this life, the goodness of God and the richness of the life they would experience in glory. What would become of the poor convicts if they had

---

[11] Nicolás María Rivero (1814–1878), Spanish politician and orator.

no one to provide some hollow comfort before they offered their necks to the executioner!

At ten in the morning Estupiñá would always conclude what we could call his religious day. After that hour in the morning, the solemn gravity he maintained in the church would disappear from his Rossinian face, and he used to become once more the affable, talkative, delightful man of the shop *tertulias*. He would have his lunch at the home of Santa Cruz or Villuendas or Arnáiz, and if Barbarita had no instructions for him, he used to undertake the task of 'looking after the youngsters', for he always played the role of one who worked like a black. His supposed job at that time was an employment agent, and he pretended that he found people jobs for a fee. There was some truth in this, but for the most part it was pure farce. When anyone asked him if business was going well, he used to reply in the tone of a shrewd merchant who does not wish to reveal his substantial earnings, 'My dear fellow, I'm not exactly struggling; can't complain . . . This month I've found positions for thirty lads . . . or it might have been forty.'

Plácido lived in the Cava de San Miguel. His house was one of those on the west side of the Plaza Mayor, and as the base of these houses is much lower than the level of the Plaza, that side is imposingly high and as formidable as a fortress. The floor he lived on was the fourth for the Plaza and the seventh for the Cava. There are no greater heights in Madrid, and to scale them you had to brave a hundred and twenty steps, *all stone,* as Plácido used to say proudly, for he could not imagine that it could be otherwise in his home. The fact that the steps are all stone from the Cava to the garrets gives the staircase a lugubrious and monumental air, like a legendary castle, and Estupiñá could not forget this fact, adding as it did a certain interest to the place. It is just not the same to climb up to your home on a staircase like those in the Escorial rather than mounting rough wooden steps like anyone else in the neighbourhood.

The pride of mounting those well-worn granite steps did not diminish the fatigue of getting up them, but my friend knew how to exploit his excellent relationships in order to shorten the labour. The owner of a shoe-shop on the Plaza called Dámaso Trujillo, whose sign read 'At the Branch of the Lilies', had a door on the Cava staircase, and by using this door Plácido could shed thirty steps.

The chatterer's home was a mystery to everyone, since no one had ever been to see him, for the simple reason that Don Plácido was only at home when he was asleep. He had never had an illness that prevented him from going out during the day. He was the healthiest man you can imagine. Old age, however, cannot be denied, and one day in December 1869 the wonderful old fellow was missed in the places he always visited. The rumour that he was ill spread quickly, and everyone who knew him was deeply concerned. Many shop-assistants toiled up those stone steps to get news of the well-loved patient, who was suffering from severe rheumatism in his right leg. Barbarita at once sent her doctor round and, not satisfied with this she ordered Juanito to visit him, which the Delfín did most willingly.

The Delfín's visit to the old servant and friend of the family must now be brought to light, because if Juanito Santa Cruz had not visited him, this story would not have been written. Another would have been written, that is certain, for wherever man may go, there is a novel within him; but it would not be this novel.

4

Juanito saw the number eleven on the door of a shop selling poultry and eggs. No doubt this is where he had to go, treading all over feathers and crushing egg-shells. He asked two women who were plucking hens and cockerels, and they replied with a gesture towards a partition door that that was the entrance to the staircase to number eleven. The entrance and the shop were one and the same thing in that building, which was characteristic of the older parts of Madrid. It was then that Juanito realized why Estupiñá often had various birds' feathers stuck to his boots. He picked them up on his way out, just as Juanito had, in spite of the care he had taken to avoid walking in the places where there were feathers and a certain amount of blood. It upset him to see the bodies of those poor birds, who had hardly been plucked when they were hung up by the head, retaining their tails like a sarcastic comment on their miserable destiny. To the left of the entrance the Delfín saw cases full of eggs, the harvest of this particular trade. Man's voracity knows no bounds, and he sacrifices to his appetite not only present but also future generations of chickens. To the right, further along that murky room, a blood-stained assassin was garrotting the birds. The murderer was twisting their necks with the swift elegance born of long practice, and hardly had one victim jumped up and been handed over in its death throes to be plucked when another was grasped and given a similar caress. There were enormous cages everywhere, full of birds sticking their red heads between the wicker canes, thirsty and exhausted, trying to breathe a little air, and even there the unfortunate prisoners were giving little pecks as if to say: 'if you stick your beak out further than mine . . . if they take me now for sticking my neck right out . . .'

Having observed this graceless spectacle, the smell of the poultry-yard that permeated everything and the noise of wings, the pecking and screeching of so many victims, Juanito took it all in his stride along with those famous granite steps, now black and worn. The effect was that of the approach to a castle or State prison. The wall-facing was plaster on brick and it was covered with marks and inscriptions that were either coarse or stupid. On the side nearer the street, strong iron grilles completed the feudal impression of the building. Passing close to the door of one of the rooms between floors, and seeing it was open, Juanito naturally looked in because his curiosity was greatly aroused by everything about the place. He did not expect to see anything, but he saw something that impressed him at once: a pretty, tall young woman. She seemed to be lurking there, as curious as Santa Cruz himself, longing to know who on earth could be climbing that infernal staircase at such an hour. The girl had a pale-blue scarf on her head, and a shawl on her shoulders, and as soon as she saw the Delfín, she flounced the shawl; what I mean to say is that she arched her arms and raised her shoulders in that characteristic way lower-class Madrid women snuggle into a shawl, a movement that makes them look rather like a chicken that puffs up its feathers and stretches upwards, then subsides to its normal size.

Seeing how pretty the girl was, and how attractive she looked in her little shoes, Juanito was far from shy and dearly wanted to get to know her.

'Does Señor Estupiñá live here?' he asked her.

'Don Plácido? Right at the very top,' replied the girl, moving out a few paces.

Juanito thought, 'You're coming out so that I can see your ankle. Very neat too . . .' As he was thinking this, he noticed that the girl moved one scarlet-mittened hand from under the shawl and up to her mouth. Brimming with confidence now, young Santa Cruz could not stop himself saying,

'What are you eating, child?'

'Can't you see?' she replied, showing it to him. 'An egg.'

'A raw egg!'

Very gracefully the girl raised the broken egg to her lips a second time and sipped at it again.

'I don't know how you can eat that raw slime,' said Santa Cruz, finding no better way of continuing the conversation.

'Better than stewed-up stuff. Want some?' she replied offering him what was left in the shell.

Glutinous transparent threads dripped between the girl's fingers. Juanito was tempted to accept her offer but he did not. He found raw eggs repulsive.

'Thank you, no.'

She then sucked out the rest and flung the shell away. It burst and spattered out against the wall of the stairs below. She was wiping her fingers on her scarf, and Juanito was wondering what to say next, when a terrible voice from below rang out, *'Fortunataaa!'* Then the girl leaned over the banisters and gave vent to an *'I'm coming'* in such a penetrating screech that Juanito thought his ear-drums would burst. It was like the harsh scream of steel against steel. Having let out a cry worthy of such an animal, the girl hurled herself down the stairs below with such speed that she seemed to be bouncing down them on wheels. Juanito saw her disappear, heard the noise of her skirts whipping against the steps and thought she was going to break her neck. At last everything was silent, and the young man started his laborious climb again. He met no one else on the stairs, not even a fly, and he heard no sound other than his own steps.

When Estupiñá saw him enter, he was so overjoyed that he was on the point of getting better at once from happiness alone. The talkative old man was not in bed, but in an armchair, because the bed wearied him, and the lower half of his body could not be seen because it was bound round like a mummy and wrapped in rugs and pieces of material. The black cap he used in church covered his head, including his ears. What bothered the patient far more than rheumatic pains was not having anyone to talk to, since the woman who looked after him, a certain Doña Brígida, who held the house keys, was not affable and a woman of very few words. Estupiñá did not possess a single book, for he did not need them for instruction. His library was society, and his texts the latest utterances of living people. His science was his religious faith, and he needed neither breviaries nor devotional books to pray, since he knew all his prayers by heart. Printed matter, to him, was rubbish: scrawling characters of no use to anyone. One of the men Plácido admired least was Gutenberg. The boredom of his illness, however, made him desire one of those mute talkers we call books. Search here and there as they might, there was nothing printed to be found. At last, in a dusty old chest, Doña Brígida found a vast tome belonging to a secularized monk who had lived in the same house back in 1840. Estupiñá opened it with great respect: and what was it? The eleventh volume of the *Ecclesiastical Bulletin of the Diocese of Lugo*. So he plunged into this because there was nothing else. He waded through it from end to end without missing a word, pronouncing each syllable correctly and murmuring in a low voice as if he were praying. No stumbling block interrupted his reading, for when he came across a lengthy and obscure Latin passage, he got his tongue round it without a moment's hesitation. Pastoral letters, comments from the bishop, papal bulls and other entertaining matters offered by the book, were the only relief in his solitude. The best thing about it was that he began to develop a taste for such insipid morsels, and he read through some paragraphs twice, chewing over the words with a smile, so he would have led any uninformed observer to believe that the massive volume was by Paul de Kock.[12]

'It's very fine,' said Estupiñá holding the book close to him as he saw that Juanito was laughing.

He was so happy that the Delfín should have visited him that he just looked at him. The young man's good looks, youth and elegance made him feel better. If Juanito had been his son he could not have gazed on him with greater love. He patted the boy on the knee and interrogated him at great length on all the members of the family, from Barbarita, who was number one, down to the cat. After satisfying his friend's curiosity, the Delfín asked questions in his turn about the neighbourhood of the house.

'They're good folk,' replied Estupiñá. 'There are just a few tenants who get rowdy at nights. The place belongs to Señor de Moreno-Isla, and you could say I'll run it from next year. He wants it that way. His mother has already spoken to me about it and I've told them I'm at their service. It's a fine building, with marvellous flint stone foundations . . . stone staircase, you'll have seen that already, only it's a bit long. When you come again, if you want to cut out thirty steps, go through 'The Branch of Lilies', the shoe-shop on the Plaza. You know Dámaso Trujillo. If you don't, just say, "I'm going to see Plácido," and he'll let you through.'

Estupiñá spent over a week more without leaving his room, and the Delfín went to see him every day. Every day! This made my friend happier than Christmas or Easter. Instead of going in through the shoe-shop Juanito, who was certainly not wearied by the stairs, always entered through the egg and poultry shop on the Cava.

---

[12] Paul de Kock (1794–1871), a popular French novelist.

PART
VI

GODS, HUMANS, AND NATURE

※

The rationalism of the Enlightenment, that attempted to organize society on a scientific basis, illustrated in Part V, caused many countermovements throughout major institutions: religious, political, and educational. In addition, personal reactions against the rationalist structuring of society and its stifling conventions were typical of the era's romantic literature. The central movement of nineteenth-century romanticism was the releasing of personal passions that societal institutions had restrained. Many of the selections of Part VI (Selections 35–48) illustrate this exaltation of the personal. For example, all of the poets of Selection 41—Wordsworth, Coleridge, Keats, and Whitman—focus on the intensity of their own feelings, beside which the traditional demands of society seem inhumanly unnatural.

In the world of politics, Edmund Burke's *Reflections on the Revolution in France* (Selection 40) is a classic statement of romantic conservatism. Burke finds any destruction of the natural inheritance as destructive of society. He distrusts any great single-shot plans for reform that do not evolve naturally from the historical context. To be unnatural, for Burke, is to be a rationalist who assumes his ideas are more valid than the naturally developing order of things. Romanticism, however, was more likely to be radical than conservative. Jean-Jacques Rousseau (Selection 39), for example, gives us an influential educational theory in *Emile* that puts the emotional development of the child ahead of the subjects to be studied. Similarly, Rousseau's politics finds the corruption of mankind to be caused by the artificiality of civilization, which has perverted man's innately noble nature.

The romantic belief in man's innately noble nature gave rise to much interest in the folk literature of preliterate people. In Europe, for example, the nineteenth-century Grimm brothers collected German folktales that had survived among the peasantry. Similarly, Selections 35–38 are examples of non-European literature, originally composed and transmitted orally, that gave sophisticated literary and scholarly audiences insight into the humanity they shared with groups that had formerly been strange to them.

The note of personal freedom, a constant romantic obsession, is also struck by Frederick Douglass's autobiographical account of racial slavery in the United States (Selection 45) and by Henry David Thoreau's assertion of the right of a just individual to stand up against the unjust policies of his own government. It was Thoreau's essay on *Civil Disobedience* (Selection 46) that informed the twentieth-century civil rights strategies of Mohandas K. Gandhi and Martin Luther King. On the other hand, the negative possibilities inherent in personal freedom, when the average man's nature actually craves authority and security, are explored by Dostoevsky (Selection 47). And unrestrained freedom only for the elite individuals, those superior individuals capable of going *Beyond Good and Evil,* is demanded by the German philosopher Friedrich Nietzsche (Selection 48).

Finally, another aspect of romanticism, as well as of eighteenth- and nineteenth-century politics generally, is the emergence of national movements and national literatures throughout the globe, as various peoples became conscious of their diverse heritages and began to identify with them, rather than with any abstract rationalist ideology. For example, in Selections 42–44 we see the development of significant national literatures, and concurrent nationalist consciousness, on the Indian subcontinent and in Vietnam. That awakening of nationalist spirit, fostered by literature, would ultimately have a great effect on world affairs in the twentieth century.

35

✿

NATIVE AMERICAN LITERATURE

The few strands collected here from the vast tapestry of Native American literature will help to give some idea of its extraordinary richness and variety. Unfortunately, only a small fraction of that literature has been transcribed, since much of it is oral, committed to memory over the generations. Even less has been translated into European languages. But what is available has still sufficed to occupy hundreds of scholars in North, Central, and South America, and will continue to do so for many years to come. Moreover, the literature produced in Native American languages continues to exist, to grow, and to develop in many countries and regions in the Western Hemisphere, including the Andean region (from Venezuela to Chile), Brazil, Canada, Mexico and Central America, and the United States.

Predominantly anonymous and often collective in origin, all of these poems and stories were composed after the coming of the Europeans, although much of their content is rooted in the pre-Columbian past of the Native Americans. In some cases, such as the powerful "Elegy on the Death of Atahuallpa," from the Quechua people of Peru, the poem itself is a testimony and a remembrance of the violence of the encounter between those labeled as Indians and Europeans. Other works, such as the liturgical poetry of the Navajo, as well as the tales of the Cherokee, Assiniboine, and Comanche of North America, still bear the stamp of ancestral myths and rituals.

Because of their oral origins and their ancestral content, the chronological ordering of these texts is highly problematical. In the case of written texts, they are ordered here on the basis of their probable dates of composition (as determined by scholars), while texts from the oral tradition are ordered in reference to the time when they were first written down. Thus, our first selection is the "Elegy on the Death of Atahuallpa," which has been dated to approximately the 1780s. The selections from the native peoples of North America are from the oral tradition, and most were collected in the last years of the nineteenth century and the early years of the twentieth.

The "Elegy of the Death of Atahuallpa" was found by a Peruvian anthropologist in the 1940s in a handwritten collection of folk poetry and songs from the *region of Cuzco, Peru. Since Quechua, the language of the Incas, had no writing (not even hieroglyphs), the "Elegy" had been transcribed by its anonymous author into our alphabet following conventions developed since the time of the Spanish conquest. Scholars believe this poem dates back to the late eighteenth century in Peru, when the Indian and peasant uprisings led by the guerilla leader Tupac Amaru II against Spanish rule were accompanied by a revival of interest in the literary uses of Quechua. Although its language and many of its images adhere to the ancient Quechua traditions, the form of poem is European, with its stanzas made up of long and short alternating verses (known as* pie quebrado *in Spanish).*

As its title suggests, "Elegy on the Death of Atahuallpa" is a lament on the death of the last ruler of the Inca Empire, Atahuallpa, who was imprisoned by Francisco de Pizarro in 1535 and was beheaded by his captors shortly thereafter. The poem uses a number of striking images from the Quechua tradition. Most notable is that of the "black rainbow" in the poem's first line, which alludes to the Quechua myth of pachakuti *(literally, "the world upside down"), in which a cosmic catastrophe threatens the order of nature. Scholars have also noted in this poem allusions to the* inkarrí, *a post-conquest Andean myth that foretold that the beheaded Atahuallpa's buried head would germinate like a seed and bring about the Lord Inca's return to rule over his people.*

The Cherokee, Assiniboine, and Comanche peoples of North America are represented in this section by a series of cosmogonic myths and stories, that is, stories about the creation of the world: "How the World Was Made," "What the Stars Are Like" (from the Cherokee); "The Boy Who Caught the Sun," and "Morning Star" (from the Assiniboine), and "Why the Bear Waddles When He Walks" (from the Comanche).

The Cherokee are an Iroquoian-speaking North American Indian nation that originally lived near the Great Lakes, but after a war with the Iroquois and Delaware nations, migrated to the Southeast, populating the mountains of the western Carolinas, northern Georgia, and eastern Tennessee. After the American Revolution (in which they sided with the British) the Cherokee adopted many white cultural practices of the time, such as plow agriculture, cotton and wool industries, and even slavery. In 1820, the Cherokee educator Sequoya invented a syllabic alphabet, and in 1827 the Cherokee established a constitutional form of government modeled after that of the United States. Throughout the nineteenth century, the Cherokees, like other Indian nations, were forcibly removed from their lands, and today the majority of full-blooded Cherokee live in eastern Oklahoma and parts of North Carolina.

The Assiniboine are a Dakota-speaking Indian nation from the Great Plains of North America. Calling themselves the Nakota ("the allies" or "the people"), they are a typical Plains warrior society, relying on the buffalo for food, shelter, and clothing, and upon the horse for mobility in hunting and warfare. Currently, the largest group of Assiniboine, known as Stoney Indians, resides in the Canadian province of Alberta, while other groups live in the state of Montana.

The Comanche peoples were originally from west of the Rockies, but by the 1700s they had moved into the southern plains, driving out various Apache groups. They speak a uto-Aztecan language, closely related to Shoshone. Their historic territory encompassed southeastern Colorado along the flanks of the Rockies south to the Pecos River in Texas and north through western Oklahoma and southwest Kansas. Expert horsemen and buffalo hunters, the warlike Comanches were able to prevent French and Spanish expansion into the southern plains during most of the eighteenth century. War waged against them by the U.S. government eventually restricted their territory to a portion of southwestern Oklahoma.

This selection closes with four poems from the Navajo: "Tsegihi: The House Made of Dawn," "The Beaver's Song," "The Bear's Song," and "The Owl's Song." The Navajo are currently the largest North American Indian nation in the United States. Their principal lands encompass parts of northeastern Arizona, northwestern New Mexico, and southeastern Utah. The Navajo (who originally called themselves Dinneh, "the people") are relative newcomers to the Southwest. They may have arrived in the region not more than five hundred years ago, after moving south from northwest Canada and interior Alaska. They speak a version of the Athabaskan language. Contact with other long-established southwestern peoples, such as the Pueblo, as well as adaptation to a radically different natural environment, led to significant changes in their culture. Originally nomadic, the Navajo learned techniques of farming from the Pueblo peoples. Livestock, particularly sheep, acquired from the Spanish in the early seventeenth century, also became a significant part of their economy. Currently, the Navajo are considered to have one of the best preserved Native American cultures in North America.

AN ELEGY ON THE DEATH OF ATAHUALLPA: TO THE OMNIPOTENT LORD ATAHUALLPA (*APU INCA ATAHUALLPAMAN*)

[Quechua]

What rainbow is this black rainbow that rises?
The horrible lightning of Cuzco's enemy flashes,[1]
and a sinister hailstorm all around strikes.

My heart forebode at every moment,
even in my dreams — restless, struck dumb — ,
the blue bottle-fly announcing death: Sorrow without end!

The sun turns pale, night falls
— another omen — , and shrouds Atahuallpa,
and in his name consecrates this death
in the blink of an eye.

They say that his beloved head has been cut
by atrocious enemies;
and that a river of blood flows ever forking, endlessly.
His gnashing teeth are broken to pieces.
Oh fierce sadness!

They say the sun-like eyes of the great Inca
are turning to lead;
that the noble heart of Atahuallpa is turning to ice;
they say that the Four Quarters mourn him,[2]
wailing without cease.

---

[1] Cuzco, in present-day Peru, was the capital of the Inca Empire. The phrase "Cuzco's enemy" alludes to the Spanish conquest.

[2] "Four Quarters" is the standard translation for the Quechua word *Tawantinsuyo,* the name the Incas gave to their empire.

They say that the clouds descend
bringing the night with them;
that the mother moon grows pale and wanes,
and that everything hides away, suffering.

They say that the earth refuses her womb
to her lord,
as if ashamed of wanting his body,
as if afraid of devouring her owner.

And the rock scream for their lord,
singing funeral chants;
the river also roars in pain,
swelling and mingling with the tears.

Is there a man who would not cry
for the one who loved him?
What son would not be sobbing for his father,
aching, his heart wounded and without love?

What dove would not be raving for her mate?
What wild deer would not cry tears of blood
for his love,
thus bereft of his happiness?

Bathing with the shining torrent of their tears
the noble body,
sheltering it tenderly in their laps,
caressing it tenderly with their ten hands,

shrouding him with the wings of their hearts,
covering him with their heartstrings,
screaming with the cry of grieving widows,

the princesses swirl around him like a black storm-cloud
and the great priest of the Sun
dresses in mourning.
All men march towards his tomb.

The Queen Mother, mortally wounded,
raves from pain;
torrents of tears flow from her;
a yellow corpse, her face and mouth rigid:

"Where are you going, disappearing from my sight,
leaving this world to my sorrow,
tearing yourself forever from my heart?"

Full the house of gold and silver,
the white enemies

—their horrible hearts hungering for power,
pushing each other,
with ever growing greediness,
enraged beasts—

killed you, after you surrendered everything.
You, and only you fulfilled all their desires,
and dying in Cajamarca, you perish.

The blood in your veins begins to coagulate;
the light in your eyes is dimmed
—your gaze that shines like the brightest star.

Your dove sobs, suffers, walks, runs;
—raving, delirious—
your beloved moans and cries,
her heart broken
by the wound of infinite separation.

The seat in your golden litter stolen,
all the golden vases distributed,
the cursed booty—in foreign hands—destroyed,

we cry, perplexed, without a past, alone,
seeing ourselves bereft;
with no one and no place to turn to, we rave.

Will your heart permit, oh powerful Inca,
that we may be completely lost, disunited,
dispersed, subjugated by others,
trampled on?

Come and open your sweet eyes
that shoot darts of light;
come and stretch your generous hands;
and comforted by that happiness, bid us farewell.

HOW THE WORLD WAS MADE
[Cherokee]

The earth is a great island floating in a sea of water, and suspended at each of the four cardinal points by a cord hanging down from the sky vault, which is of solid rock. When the world grows old and worn out, the people will die and the cords will break and let the earth sink down into the ocean, and all will be water again. The Indians are afraid of this.

When all was water, the animals were above in Galûñ´lati, beyond the arch; but it was very much crowded, and they were wanting more room. They wondered what was below the water, and at last Dâyuni´si, "Beaver's Grandchild," the little

Water-beetle, offered to go and see if it could learn. It darted in every direction over the surface of the water, but could find no firm place to rest. Then it dived to the bottom and came up with some soft mud, which began to grow and spread on every side until it became the island which we call the earth. It was afterward fastened to the sky with four cords, but no one remembers who did this.

At first the earth was flat and very soft and wet. The animals were anxious to get down, and sent out different birds to see if it was yet dry, but they found no place to alight and came back again to Galûñ´lati. At last it seemed to be time, and they sent out the Buzzard and told him to go and make ready for them. This was the Great Buzzard, the father of all the buzzards we see now. He flew all over the earth, low down near the ground, and it was still soft. When he reached the Cherokee country, he was very tired, and his wings began to flap and strike the ground, and wherever they struck the earth there was a valley, and where they turned up again there was a mountain. When the animals above saw this, they were afraid that the whole world would be mountains, so they called him back, but the Cherokee country remains full of mountains to this day.

When the earth was dry and the animals came down, it was still dark, so they got the sun and set it in a track to go every day across the island from east to west, just overhead. It was too hot this way, and Tsiska´gili, the Red Crawfish, had his shell scorched a bright red, so that his meat was spoiled; and the Cherokee do not eat it. The conjurers put the sun another hand-breadth higher in the air, but it was still too hot. They raised it another time, and another, until it was seven hand-breadths high and just under the sky arch. Then it was right, and they left it so. This is why the conjurers call the highest place Gûlkwâ´gine Di´galûñ´latiyûñ´, "the seventh height," because it is seven hand-breadths above the earth. Every day the sun goes along under this arch, and returns at night on the upper side to the starting place.

There is another world under this, and it is like ours in everything — animals, plants, and people — save that the seasons are different. The streams that come down from the mountains are the trails by which we reach this underworld, and the springs at their heads are the doorways by which we enter it, but to do this one must fast and go to water and have one of the underground people for a guide. We know that the seasons in the underworld are different from ours, because the water in the springs is always warmer in winter and cooler in summer than the outer air.

When the animals and plants were first made — we do not know by whom — they were told to watch and keep awake for seven nights, just as young men now fast and keep awake when they pray to their medicine. They tried to do this, and nearly all were awake through the first night, but the next night several dropped off to sleep, and the third night others were asleep, and then others, until, on the seventh night, of all the animals only the owl, the panther, and one or two more were still awake. To these were given the power to see and go about in the dark, and to make prey of the birds and animals which must sleep at night. Of the trees only the cedar, the pine, the spruce, the holly, and the laurel were awake to the end, and to them it was given to be always green and to be greatest for medicine, but to the others it was said: "Because you have not endured to the end you shall lose your hair every winter."

Men came after the animals and plants. At first there were only a brother and sister until he struck her with a fish and told her to multiply, and so it was. In seven days a child was born to her, and thereafter every seven days another, and they increased very fast until there was danger that the world could not keep them. Then it was made that a woman should have only one child in a year, and it has been so ever since.

WHAT THE STARS ARE LIKE

[Cherokee]

There are different opinions about the stars. Some say they are balls of light, others say they are human, but most people say they are living creatures covered with luminous fur or feathers.

One night a hunting party camping in the mountains noticed two lights like large stars moving along the top of a distant ridge. They wondered and watched until the light disappeared on the other side. The next night, and the next, they saw the lights again moving along the ridge, and after talking over the matter decided to go on the morrow and try to learn the cause. In the morning they started out and went until they came to the ridge, where, after searching for some time, they found two strange creatures about *so* large (making a circle with outstretched arms), with round bodies covered with fine fur or downy feathers, from which small heads stuck out like the heads of terrapins. As the breeze played upon these feathers showers of sparks flew out.

The hunters carried the strange creatures back to the camp, intending to take them home to the settlements on their return. They kept them several days and noticed that every night they would grow bright and shine like great stars, although by day they were only balls of gray fur, except when the wind stirred and made the sparks fly out. They kept very quiet, and no one thought of their trying to escape, when, on the seventh night, they suddenly rose from the ground like balls of fire and were soon above the tops of the trees. Higher and higher they went, while the wondering hunters watched, until as last they were only two bright points of light in the dark sky, and then the hunters knew that they were stars.

THE BOY WHO CAUGHT THE SUN

[Assiniboine]

An orphan boy and his sister were living together. The boy had a sinew string. During the daytime he was never home. "What do you do during the day?" his sister asked. "I am trying to ensnare the sun with my sinew." One day he caught him and there was no daylight. The girl asked, "What is the matter? Why is there no light?" "I have caught the sun." "You had better release him; if we don't see the daylight, we shall die." The boy approached the sun, but it got too hot for him. He returned to his sister, and said, "I cannot free him, he is too hot." At last, he sent a small mouse to gnaw up the sinew, The mouse went close. All its hair was burnt up, nevertheless it gnawed the sinew in two. Then the sun was free, and there was daylight once more.

MORNING-STAR
[Assiniboine]

A man and his wife were camping by themselves. She was pregnant. While her husband was away, another man would come and embrace her. Her lover wished to elope with her, but he did not like to take her with the baby in her womb. So he once entered her lodge and said, "I want to eat food from your belly." She asked, "How shall I sit?" "Lie down on your back, and place the dish on your belly." She obeyed. When he was done eating, he stuck a knife into her, and took out the child, which he left in the lodge.

Then the lovers fled underground, entering the earth under the fireplace. When the woman's husband returned, he found the child's body, and saw that his wife was gone. He split trees and dried up the creeks where he thought she might have fled. When the lovers came above ground again, he tracked them. They turned into snakes and crawled into a hollow tree. He followed in pursuit, and saw the snakes, but did not recognize them as the fugitives. He thought the lovers had gone up the tree. He climbed up, but could not find them. At last he climbed higher still, reached the sky, and became the Morning Star.

WHY THE BEAR WADDLES
WHEN HE WALKS
[Comanche]

In the beginning days, nobody knew what to do with the sun. It would come up and shine for a long time. Then it would go away for a long time, and everything would be dark.

The daytime animals naturally wanted the sun to shine all the time, so they could live their lives without being interrupted by the dark. The nighttime animals wanted the sun to go away forever, so they could live the way they wanted to.

At last they all got together, to talk things over.

Old Man Coyote said, "Let's see what we can do about that sun. One of us ought to have it, or the other side ought to get rid of it."

"How will we do that?" Scissor-tailed Flycatcher asked. "Nobody can tell the sun what to do. He's more powerful than anyone else in the world."

"Why don't we play hand game for it?" Bear asked. "The winning side can keep the sun or throw it away, depending on who wins and what they want to do with it."

So they got out the guessing bones to hide their hands, and they got out the crow-feathered wands for the guessers to point with, and they got out the twenty painted dogwood sticks for the umpires to keep score with. Coyote was the umpire for the day side, and nighttime umpire was Owl.

The umpires got a flat rock, like a table, and laid out their counting sticks on that. Then the two teams brought legs, and lined them up facing one another, with the umpires and their flat rock at one end, between the two teams.

That was a long hand game. The day side held the bones first, and they were so quick and skillful passing them from hand to hand behind their backs and waving them in the guessers' faces that it seemed surely they must win. Then Mole, who was guessing for the night side, caught both Scissor-tail and Hawk at the same time, and the bones went to the night side, and the day people began to guess.

Time and again the luck went back and forth, each team seeming to be about to beat the other. Time and again the luck changed, and the winning team became the losing one.

The game went on and on. Finally the sun, waiting on the other side of the world to find out what was going to happen to him, got tired of it all.

The game was so long that Bear got tired, too. He was playing on the night side. He got cramped sitting on the log, and his legs began to ache. Bear took off his moccasins to rest his feet, and still the game went on and on.

At last the sun was so bored that he decided to go and see for himself what was happening. He yawned and stretched and crawled out of his bed on the underneath side of the world. He started to climb up his notched log ladder to the top side, to find out what was happening.

As the sun climbed the light grew stronger, and the night people began to be afraid. The game was still even; nobody had won. But the sun was coming and coming, and the night animals had to run away. Bear jumped up in such a hurry that he put his right foot in his left moccasin, and his left foot in his right moccasin.

The sun was full up now, and all the other night animals were gone. Bear went after them as fast as he could in his wrong moccasins, rocking and waddling from side to side, and shouting, "Wait for me! Wait for me!"

But nobody stopped or waited, and Bear had to go waddling along, just the way he has done ever since.

And because nobody won the game, the day and night took turns from that time on. Everybody had the same time to come out and live his life the way he wanted to as everybody else.

TSEGIHI: THE HOUSE MADE OF DAWN

[Navajo]

In Tsegihi (oh you who dwell!)
In the house made of the dawn,
In the house made of the evening twilight,
In the house made of the dark cloud,
In the house made of the he-rain,
In the house made of the dark mist,
In the house made of the she-rain,
In the house made of pollen,
In the house made of grasshoppers,
Where the dark mist curtains the doorway,
The path to which is on the rainbow,
Where the zigzag lightning stands high on top,
Where the he-rain stands high on top,
Oh, male divinity!
With your moccasins of dark cloud, come to us.
With your leggings of dark cloud, come to us.
With your shirt of dark cloud, come to us.
With your headdress of dark cloud, come to us.
With your mind enveloped in dark cloud, come to us.
With the dark thunder above you, come to us soaring.
With the shapen cloud at your feet, come to us soaring.
With the far darkness made of the dark cloud over your head, come
        to us soaring.
With the far darkness made of the he-rain over your head, come
        to us soaring.
With the far darkness made of the dark mist over your head, come
        to us soaring.
With the far darkness made of the she-rain over your head, come
        to us soaring.
With the zigzag lightning flung out on high over your head, come
        to us soaring.
With the rainbow hanging high over your head, come to us soaring.
With the far darkness made of the dark cloud on the ends of your
        wings, come to us soaring.
With the far darkness made of the he-rain on the ends of your
        wings, come to us soaring.
With the far darkness made of the dark mist on the ends of your
        wings, come to us soaring.
With the far darkness made of the she-rain on the ends of your
        wings, come to us soaring.

With the zigzag lightning out on high on the ends of your wings,
    come to us soaring.
With the rainbow hanging high on the ends of your wings, come
    to us soaring.
With the near darkness made of the dark cloud, of the he-rain, of
    the dark mist, and of the she-rain, come to us.
With the darkness on the earth, come to us.
With these I wish the foam floating on the flowing water over the
    roots of the great corn.
I have made your sacrifice.
I have prepared a smoke for you.
My feet restore for me.
My limbs restore for me.
My body restore for me.
My mind restore for me.
My voice restore for me.
To-day, take out your spell for me.
To-day, take away your spell for me.
Away from me you have taken it.
Far off from me it is taken.
Far off you have done it.
Happily I recover.
Happily my interior becomes cool.
Happily my limbs regain their power.
Happily my head becomes cool.
Happily my limbs regain their power.
Happily I hear again.
Happily for me (the spell) is taken off.
Happily I walk.
Impervious to pain, I walk.
Feeling light within, I walk.
With lively feelings, I walk.
Happily (or in beauty) abundant dark clouds I desire.
Happily abundant dark mists I desire.
Happily abundant passing showers I desire.
Happily an abundance of vegetation I desire.
Happily an abundance of pollen I desire.
Happily abundant dew I desire.
Happily may fair white corn, to the ends of the earth, come with you.
Happily may fair yellow corn, to the ends of the earth, come with you.
Happily may fair blue corn, to the ends of the earth, come with you.
Happily may fair corn of all kinds, to the ends of the earth, come with you.
Happily may fair plants of all kinds, to the ends of the earth, come
    with you.

Happily may fair goods of all kinds, to the ends of the earth, come
    with you.
Happily may fair jewels of all kinds, to the ends of the earth, come
    with you.
With these before you, happily may they come with you.
With these behind you, happily may they come with you.
With these below you, happily may they come with you.
With these above you, happily may they come with you.
With these all around you, happily may they come with you.
Thus happily you accomplish your tasks.
Happily the old men will regard you.
Happily the old women will regard you.
Happily the young men will regard you.
Happily the young women will regard you.
Happily the boys will regard you.
Happily the girls will regard you.
Happily the children will regard you.
Happily the chiefs will regard you.
Happily, as they scatter in different directions, they will regard you.
Happily, as they approach their homes, they will regard you.
Happily may their roads home be on the trail of pollen (peace).
Happily may they all get back.
In beauty (happily) I walk.
With beauty before me, I walk.
With beauty behind me, I walk.
With beauty below me, I walk.
With beauty above me, I walk.
With beauty all around me, I walk.
It is finished (again) in beauty,
It is finished in beauty,
It is finished in beauty,
It is finished in beauty.

THE BEAVER'S SONG

[Navajo]

I follow the river
In quest of a young beaver.
Up the river I go
Through the cut willow path I go
In quest of a young beaver.

THE BEAR'S SONG
[Navajo]

A foot,
A foot with toes,
A foot with toes came.
He came with a foot with toes.
Aging as he came with a foot with toes.

THE OWL'S SONG
[Navajo]

I am the owl.
I sit on the spruce tree.
My coat is gray.
I have big eyes.
My head has two points.
The white smoke from my tobacco can be seen
As I sit on the spruce tree.
The little rabbit comes in sight,
Nearby where I sit on the spruce tree.
I think soon my claws will get into its back,
As I sit on the spruce tree.
Now it is dawn, now it is dawn.
The old man owl's head has two points.

36

❧

AFRICAN ORAL LITERATURE

In Africa, oral literature includes tales, riddles, proverbs, praise songs, epics, and much more. In fact, each of these categories tends to be broad. We cannot be very accurate in defining the kinds of narratives generally categorized under this heading in part because each particular ethnic group might have at its disposal its own special set of literary modes. Thus, "tales" might designate many different kinds of stories, clearly differentiated into specific types by a given culture, types for which no English terms exist. The efforts of scholars and researchers are opening the window onto the vast storehouse of African oral narratives that preceded or that continue to accompany written narratives. We cannot characterize that oral storehouse as ancient since the storytelling tradition continues into the present, but the tales, proverbs, and riddles that are repeated from generation to generation contain materials and forms that are inherited from earlier times. The storyteller, the griot, the performer of the tale, will often take received material and shape it into his or her own story. For Mervyn Hiskett, a specialist in Hausa oral literature, contemporary oral Hausa song may at times be closely associated with past forms, since popular songs dating to the eighteenth or nineteenth century resemble those of present times. "In default of earlier examples," he claims, "modern songs may be quoted in the reasonable belief that they are part of a tradition that has not changed in its essentials." To some extent we can apply the same statement to oral literature as a whole, while also recognizing that each performance affords the performer the opportunity to change the material, to place her or his special stamp on it, and to give it new life.

What is unique and special about oral literature is its relationship to the community in which it is created: It is an expression of the community, and it is recited to members of the community in such a way that we can assign the term "performance" to the typical recitation of oral narratives. For Roger Abrahams, noted specialist in African and African-American folktales, a group not only expresses itself through the tales, it defines itself by the traditional forms of performance and the items it shares. In Africa there are specific, well-defined qualities *that ordinarily emerge in many tales. For instance, we find that the relationship between the performer and group often takes a dynamic form, so that the listening audience interacts with the reciter, often overlapping their responses with the words of the reciter. This overlap echoes African musical forms which are often richly textured with polyphonic voices and multiple-metered rhythms. Abrahams interprets this relationship as one that brings opposition and multiplicity into cohesion, much as a group of competing voices finds harmony.*

In the past, oral literatures generally sprang out of village life, except perhaps for epics. Even now, the performer reacts to and shapes the village community by reinforcing traditional values, by providing the community with a means to evaluate and criticize the behavior of its members, and, in a more subtle sense, affirm the community's understanding of the world and the community's relationship to it. Rather than expressing these understandings by direct, unvarnished statements, oral narratives are indirect, subtle, and complex, arguing, according to Abrahams, by analogy, "not only with regard to how people should or should not act to be useful members of society, community and family, but also in regard to how such actions give meaning and power to the very being of all within the community." The resultant stories may accomplish these goals while simultaneously explaining how the world came to exist, how death entered into the world, how two friends, like Hare and Mosquito, fell out, how kings cannot rule without the wisdom of the elders to assist them, and so on. Tales of admonition might focus upon the behavior of those who are foolish and thus fail to control their emotions or their tongues, or of maidens who refuse reasonable suitors, only to be seduced and destroyed by handsome strangers, strangers who might actually be demonic beings in disguise. Tales of tricksters also abound, often entailing competitions of magical or intellectual powers between such creatures as Hare and Hornbill.

Perhaps what is most distinctive about the oral tradition is its attitude towards the word itself. Just as the group is defined by the oral performance, so too is the power of the word employed to create the community, its values and its life force. This unique strength of the word is seen in the nature of various verbal combats in tales and epics where mastery over the word is the condition for mastery over one's self as well as the community, and even over the forces that give substance to life and death. The griots, at times called "masters of the word," the women storytellers, the elders who skillfully manipulate proverbs, all testify to the nobility of a way of living and creating together that has gradually changed with the onset of colonialism, its demise, and the vast social and cultural transformations of our times.

Where known, the name of the ethnic group and its country of origin will be noted for each of the following selections.

HOW THE WORLD WAS CREATED
FROM A DROP OF MILK
[Fulani, from Mali]

At the beginning there was a huge drop of milk.
Then Doondari[1] came and he created the stone.
Then the stone created iron;
And iron created fire;
And fire created water;
And water created air.
Then Doondari descended the second time. And he took the five elements
And he shaped them into man.
But man was proud.
Then Doondari created blindness and blindness defeated man.
But when blindness became too proud,
Doondari created sleep, and sleep defeated blindness;
But when sleep became too proud,
Doondari created worry, and worry defeated sleep;
But when worry became too proud,
Doondari created death, and death defeated worry.
But when death became too proud,
Doondari descended for the third time,
And he came as Gueno, the eternal one,
And Gueno defeated death.

"How the World was created from a drop of milk," "The Woman who tried to change her fate," "A man's luck cannot be driven away—only delayed," from *The Origin of Life and Death*, edited by Ulli Beier, copyright 1974, pp. 1–2, 23–41, 54–55. Reprinted by permission of Heinemann Educational Publishers, a division of Reed Educational & Professional Publishing Ltd. "Life" from *Igbo Traditional Verse*, edited by Romanus Egudu and Donatus Nwaga, copyright 1973, pp. 31–32. "Eshu, God of Fate" from *Oral Poetry from Africa*, edited by Jack Mapanje and Londeg White, copyright 1983, p. 100. "What an old man can see sitting down—a young man can't see standing up" from *Not Even God Is Ripe Enough*, edited by Bakare Gbadamosi and Ulli Beier, copyright 1975, pp. 51–53. Reprinted by permission of Heinemann Educational Publishers, a division of Reed Educational & Professional Publishing Ltd. "Hare and Hornbill," "Hare and Mosquito," and "Labongo and Kapir" from *Hare and Hornbill*, edited by Okot p'Bitek, copyright 1978, pp. 1–2, 43–44, 71–74. Reprinted by permission of Heinemann Educational Publishers, a division of Reed Educational & Professional Publishing Ltd. Proverbs from *Things Fall Apart*, by Chinua Achebe, copyright 1972, pp. 6, 8, 10, 17–18, 19, 20. Reprinted by permission of Heinemann Educational Publishers, a division of Reed Educational & Professional Publishing Ltd. Proverbs and riddles from *African Oral Literature*, by Isadore Okpewho, copyright 1992, pp. 228, 233, 236, 237, 240, 241, 246, 247, 249. Reprinted by permission of Indiana University Press.

[1] Supreme being.

LIFE

[Igbo, from Nigeria]

God the Creator,
Sky and Earth,
Son of the Supreme Creator,
Our Ancestors:
It is life
And what it is supported with—
Wealth upon wealth—
These we ask of you.

ESHU, GOD OF FATE[2]

[Yoruba, from Nigeria]

Eshu turns right into wrong, wrong into right.
When he is angry, he hits a stone until it bleeds.
When he is angry, he sits on the skin of an ant.
When he is angry, he weeps tears of blood.
Eshu slept in the house—
But the house was too small for him:
Eshu slept on the verandah—
But the verandah was too small for him:
Eshu slept in a nut—
At last he could stretch himself!
Eshu walked through the groundnut farm.
The tuft of his hair was just visible:
If it had not been for his huge size,
He would not be visible at all.
Lying down, his head hits the roof:
Standing up, he cannot look into the cooking pot.
He throws a stone today
And kills a bird yesterday!

---

[2] Eshu is a Yoruba trickster god, as well as a god of fate.

THE WOMAN WHO TRIED
TO CHANGE HER FATE
[Ijaw, from Nigeria]

There was once a large field, and in this field stood an enormous Iroko tree with large buttresses. At the sides of the field appeared pairs of men and women, each woman holding a broom and each man a bag. As the women swept the field the men collected the dirt into their bags. And the dirt was manillas.[3] Some collected ten or more manillas, others none, and when the field was swept clean they disappeared back into the edges of the field, two by two. The sky darkened, and there descended on the field a large table, a large chair, and an immense "Creation Stone," and on the table was a large quantity of earth. Then there was lightning and thunder; and Woyengi (the Mother) descended. She seated herself on the chair and placed her feet on the "Creation Stone." Out of the earth on the table Woyengi moulded human beings. But they had no life and were neither man nor woman, and Woyengi, embracing them one by one, breathed her breath into them, and they became living beings. But they were still neither men nor women, and so Woyengi asked them one by one to choose to be man or woman, each according to his choice.

Next Woyengi asked them, one by one, what manner of life each should like to lead on earth. Some asked for riches, some for children, some for short lives, and all manner of things. And these Woyengi bestowed on them one by one, each according to his wish. Then Woyengi asked them one by one by what manner of death they would return to her. And out of the diseases that afflict the earth they chose each a disease. To all of these wishes Woyengi said, "So be it."

Among this group of newly created men and women were two women. One of them asked of Woyengi rich and famous children, and the other asked for only powers, mystic powers that would have no equal in the world—and this woman was Ogboinba. Both chose to be born in the same town.

Woyengi finally led these created men and women to two streams, streams flowing to the habitation of men. One was muddy and the other clean. Into the muddy steam she led all those who had asked her for riches, children, and all worldly possessions. Into the clear stream she lead all who had asked of her no material possessions.

And so Ogboinba and the other woman came to be born in the same town and became inseparable friends. They ate and played together, sharing all their secrets and grew up as children of the same parents. But Ogboinba was an extraordinary child. At an early age she could heal and cure and had second-sight. She understood the tongues of birds and beasts, trees, and even of the blades of grass. She prophesied and performed things strange and wonderful, and her name became a byword on every lip.

---

[3] Metal bracelets used as currency.

When Ogboinba and her friend came of age, each took to herself a husband. Soon Ogboinba's friend had her first child. But Ogboinba had no child and was not expecting one. Her powers, however, continued to increase. Her friend became pregnant the second time and soon delivered the child. Still Ogboinba had no child but her fame went far and wide and she became the most sought-after medicine-woman of all time. In spite of this, she was worried. She felt her life bare — she wanted a child. She wanted children and yearned for them.

Her friend had more and more children according to what she had asked of Woyengi, and Ogboinba loved them all and took care of them with her mystic powers as if they were her own. But this gave her no satisfaction. She wanted children of her own to care for. Her mystic powers, however, continued to increase just as she had asked of Woyengi. But there was no joy in her heart.

After a time, she could not bear it any longer and secretly resolved on a journey, a journey back to Woyengi to recreate herself. So one day she went into her medicine room, where she also kept her mystic powers, and asked them one by one if they would accompany her on the journey she had resolved to undertake. All of them showed signs of their willingness to accompany her. But out of them all she picked only the most mystic powers and the most powerful medicines and put them into a bag. She then went to her friend and told her she was going on a short journey. When her friend heard this, she was aggrieved, for, since they came to know each other as friends they had not parted, not even for a day. So the prospect of not seeing Ogboinba for a day and more made her very sad. Her children too would then have no more protection. But Ogboinba assured her that even though she would be away the children would still be under her protection and that nothing would harm them. With this, Ogboinba took leave of her and started her journey to Woyengi.

So along a wide road Ogboinba walked with her bag of mystic powers and medicines slung over her shoulder. A wide road that led to a large sea. Between her and the sea was a forest, a mangrove forest where lived Isembi, the king of the forest. As she walked along, day and night without food or rest, she soon heard the noise of the sea, the waves breaking on the shore. With each forward step the noise came nearer. But Ogboinba walked steadily along and soon reached the mangrove forest, the Kingdom of Isembi.

As she picked her way through the forest she heard a voice, a voice calling from behind. She turned, and it was Isembi.

"Are you not the Ogboinba I've heard so much about?" he asked, raising his voice.

Ogboinba replied, "There is only one Ogboinba in the world, and I am the one."

"If you are," Isembi replied, "You've not treated me well by not calling on me as the king of this place. We've all heard your fame and to find you here like this is an honour. Come with me to my house."

So Ogboinba went with Isembi to his house and there was well entertained to a sumptuous meal and palm wine. After the entertainment, Isembi asked Ogboinba where she was bound.

Ogboinba said, "I've not given birth to a child since I was married many years ago. So I'm going to Woyengi to ask her to recreate me."

"Turn back from here," said Isembi. "It's impossible to see Woyengi while you are yet alive. Your journey is in vain, so turn back from here."

But Ogboinba said her mind was made up and though she was yet alive, see Woyengi she must. And so she left Isembi and his wife to continue her journey to the sea. But she had only gone a little way when she turned and came back to Isembi and asked him if he would try her powers with his. Isembi said he would not fight a woman and asked Ogboinba to go on her way. Still Ogboinba insisted on the trial of powers, adding that though a woman she was challenging him. This enraged Isembi, and he said:

"Haven't you heard of my powers? I'm Isembi the king of the forest. How dare you, a woman, challenge me?"

With this he went to his medicine hut. There, all his pots of medicine[4] showed negative signs. But he was not to be daunted by such things where a woman was concerned. So, in spite of the warnings, he went out armed with such medicines and mystic powers that he required, to fight it out with Ogboinba.

Outside, he asked Ogboinba to try her powers on him first. But Ogboinba declined. She said that he, Isembi, being the elder of the two, should try her first with all he had. Isembi, being anxious to do away with Obgoinba without any further delay, repeated his incantations. Immediately Ogboinba's bag became empty of all her powers. Her mystic powers and the powerful medicines had all gone! She at once repeated her own incantations, circling round and round to counteract Isembi's powers. As she did so, her mystic powers and medicines returned to the bag, one by one. And then she came to the end of her incantations; they had all returned to the bag and she was once more herself.

Then she asked Isembi to try her with more of his powers. But Isembi had nothing more powerful than the powers he had already used on her, and asked her to try him with her powers if she had any. So Ogboinba started to repeat her incantations, circling round and round. As she did so, all the powers and medicines of Isembi entered her bag, one by one, and Isembi himself fell down dead. Then she slung her bag over her shoulder and proceeded on her journey. But as she was leaving Isembi's wife called her to come back and wake her husband for her. This touched Ogboinba's heart, as she herself had a husband. So Ogboinba went back and, after repeating some of her incantations Isembi woke. Then Isembi's wife pleaded for the return of her husband's powers and medicines. But that Ogboinba said she would not do, and left to continue her journey.

Soon, Ogboinba left the mangrove forest behind her and reached the town of Egbe by the seashore. As she passed by, someone hailed her from behind. She looked back, and it was Egbe.

---

[4] Medicine here refers to magical substances.

"Is that not the Ogboinba I've heard so much about?" asked Egbe.

Ogboinba said, "There is only one Ogboinba in the world, and I am the one."

"Your fame has been here before you," continued Egbe. "Come to my house. I'm the king of this town and you can't pass like an unheard-of person through my town. Come, I'll entertain you."

Ogboinba went with Egbe to his house and there was well entertained with plenty of food and palm wine. After the meal Egbe asked Ogboinba what the object of her journey was. Ogboinba replied, "I've been married many, many years, but have not had a child. I've not for once been pregnant; so I'm on my way to meet Woyengi to recreate myself."

Egbe was astonished on hearing this and counselled her, "Turn back from here. No person who is alive ever sees Woyengi."

But Ogboinba said that she had made up her mind to, slung the bag of powers over her shoulder and left to continue her journey. But presently she came back to Egbe and asked if he would like to try his powers with hers. Egbe was enraged on hearing this and choked with anger. When he found his voice again he said with contempt:

"Go your way, you are a woman."

But Ogboinba would not move and insisted on their trial of powers, their mystic powers.

Egbe had not been known to have refused a challenge from any living being and this, though from a woman, he would not now overlook since she insisted on it. So he said, "Come on, and let's see who's more powerful, you, a woman, or Egbe, the king of the town and the sea shore." With this he went into his medicine hut and armed himself with the most powerful medicines he had always used in overcoming all those who had come to challenge him. He came out and asked Ogboinba to try him first. But Ogboinba, as usual, refused and asked him to try her first with all he had. Egbe, not wishing to make this a long argument, at once repeated his long incantations. As he did so Ogboinba's bag became empty of all her powers. All her powers, plus those of Isembi she had acquired, had been scattered away in all directions by Egbe's mystic powers. On noticing this, she at once repeated her counteracting incantations moving round and round in a circle. As she did so, her own powers plus those of Isembi returned to the bag. When she found all the powers complete in her bag, she stopped her incantations and asked Egbe to try her once more with more of his powers. But Egbe had nothing more powerful than the powers he had already used and asked Ogboinba to try him with her own powers. So Ogboinba started her own incantations and before she had been half-way through, all the powers of Egbe had entered her bag and when she stopped, Egbe fell down dead. With Egbe on the ground she left to continue her journey to the sea with the bag containing her powers plus those of Isembi and now those of Egbe, slung over her shoulder. But Ogboinba had taken only a few steps when she heard Egbe's wife weeping and calling her to come back and wake her husband for her. Ogboinba taking pity on her went back and after repeating her incantations brought Egbe back to life. Egbe's wife again pleaded for the return of her husband's powers. But Ogboinba refused this request and resumed her journey to the sea.

And so Ogboinba came to the brink of a mighty sea. A sea that no living person had ever crossed. A sea with high waves breaking thunderously on the shore, a turbulent roaring sea. It struck terror into the heart of Ogboinba. But cross she must; there was no other way.

As she stood regarding the sea, it spoke! "I am the mighty Sea that no one ever crosses." Then Ogboinba with all the audacity at her command said, "I am Ogboinba, the only Ogboinba in the world, and am on my way to Woyengi. I must cross." The Sea replied, "I am the mighty Sea that no one ever crosses. I'll take you into my bowels if you dare." Ogboinba was terrified by what she heard. But she wanted a child and the only way to get it lay in her seeing Woyengi. Nothing would stop her.

Urged on by this resolve, she made for the sea and as her feet touched it, waves rolled towards her and submerging her feet, began to rise. Soon it was up to her ankles and then up to the knees. Fear gripped her, Ogboinba could not move herself, she was powerless, hopeless, and just stood there watching herself being swallowed up by the sea. It continued to rise and soon the sea was up to her waist. She raised her bag of powers above her head. Still the sea continued to rise and now it had come up to her chest. Still the sea rose until it came to Ogboinba's chin. Then she cried out in fear:

"O Sea, are you really the sea that no one crosses?" and repeated her incantations. As she did so, the sea immediately started to recede. Soon it had come down to her waist, then to the knees and then to her feet. So it continued to recede until the bed of the sea lay bare exposing the gods and spirits of the sea. Then Ogboinba, with her bag of powers, picked her way across. On the other side, she turned to the dry bed of the sea and commanding it back to its place continued her journey.

The next Kingdom that she came to was that of the Tortoise. Tortoise was the king and lived with his parents Alika and Arita and his wife Opoin. Tortoise saw Ogboinba as she walked along and calling her, wanted to know if she was not the Ogboinba he had heard so much about. Ogboinba gave her usual reply.

"There is only one Ogboinba in the world and I am the one."

"Come, let's go to my house," Tortoise said, "We've heard so much about you and we all want to know you. Please come."

So Ogboinba went with Tortoise to his house and there had food and palm wine with the family. After the meal Tortoise, always curious, asked Ogboinba:

"What has brought you over this side of the sea? No human beings live this side; pray, tell me, what has made you come like this?"

Ogboinba replied, "I have had a husband for many years but have not had a child, so I am on my way to see Woyengi and ask her to recreate me."

"Go back from here," Tortoise advised, "No one who is yet alive ever sees Woyengi."

But Ogboinba said her mind was set on seeing Woyengi and that she would not turn back. Then Tortoise warned her:

"Beyond me live the gods Ada and Yisa the great, the most powerful, who possesses two small 'creating stones.' Nobody ever goes that way. So end your journey here."

But Ogboinba said nothing would stop her and shouldering her bag, which had now become quite heavy with the powers she had acquired on the way, left to continue her journey.

After going a little way she came back to Tortoise and confronted him with her usual request for a trial of powers. Tortoise did not take it seriously and asked her to go on the journey she had set her heart on. But Ogboinba insisted on their contest of powers. Then Tortoise began to boast:

"Haven't you heard of me? My name has gone round the world for my mystic powers. If you really mean what you say I'm ready for you."

With this he went into his medicine hut and armed himself with his powerful medicines and mystic powers. When he came out Ogboinba asked him to try her first with his powers. But Tortoise said that could not be, for he was a man and besides he was the Tortoise. Still Ogboinba insisted on his starting the contest and so Tortoise began his incantations. As he repeated them Ogboinba's bag dropped from her hand to the ground and all the powers were dispersed to all the corners of the world.

Ogboinba at once repeated her own incantations to counteract the powers of Tortoise. First the bag returned, followed by the powers, one by one. When the powers had all returned Ogboinba asked Tortoise to try with more of his powers. But Tortoise had no more and asked her to do her worst if she could. So Ogboinba began her own incantations and before she had gone half-way, Tortoise had fallen down dead and all his powers had entered Ogboinba's bag. With Tortoise lying on the ground Ogboinba shouldered her bag and made to continue her journey. But before she could take a step she was stopped by the weeping voice of Opoin the wife of Tortoise. Opoin begged her to wake Tortoise, her husband, for her. Ogboinba took pity on her and waking Tortoise with her mystic powers resumed her journey.

On and on she walked day and night, with her bag of powers over her shoulder. Soon she reached the kingdom of the god Ada. Ada, on seeing her, asked her if she was not the Ogboinba he had heard so much about. Ogboinba gave her usual reply:

"There is only one Ogboinba in the world and I am the one." Ada said he would not allow her to pass on like that without entertaining her, she being such a famous person. So Ogboinba, as usual, went with Ada to his house and there was well entertained to a meal of yam, plantain and all other choice dishes that befitted a god and king to entertain a famous person. After the meal Ada asked Ogboinba:

"What has brought you here where only the gods dwell? This place is virgin to the feet of human beings. No human being has been here before you; tell me, why have you come?" On Ogboinba's giving the reason for her journey, Ada said: "Turn from here for no one ever sees Woyengi, not even me."

But Ogboinba would not turn, for her heart had been hardened by desire, desire for a child. So she told Ada she would not now turn and would continue her journey to Woyengi wherever she might be. With that Ogboinba shouldered her bag of powers and left to continue her journey. But she came back presently to Ada and asked him if he would try his powers with her own. Ada was surprised — a human being to seek contest of powers with a god! All he said was to ask Ogboinba if she really meant what he had heard her say. Ogboinba replied by repeating her request. Ada went into his medicine hut. But here, the contents of all his medicine pots had turned to blood! No, he said, I won't heed this; she is but a human being. So heedless of the warning his medicines gave him, he came out and asked Ogboinba to try him with her powers. But Ogboinba refused and asked him instead to try her first. Ada, moved with anger, at once directed his powers on Ogboinba. Ogboinba fell down apparently dead. But she regained her consciousness after a while and began her own incantations. As she did so all the powers of Ada left him and entered her bag, and in the end Ada fell down dead. Once more victorious, Ogboinba shouldered her bag of powers and continued her journey.

On and on she walked, a lone figure on a wide road, until she reached the kingdom of Yasi, the great and powerful god. Yasi had seen her and had watched her progress a long way away even before she came within range of human vision. So as she wandered along on his territory Yasi asked her if she was not the Ogboinba he had heard so much about. Ogboinba gave her customary reply.

"There is only one Ogboinba in the world and I am the one."

Yasi said, "I am the king of this place; come and I'll give your food and drink." So Ogboinba went with Yasi to his house and there again was well entertained to a meal of rare dishes and palm wine befitting for a king to entertain a famous guest. After the meal, Yasi asked Ogboinba why she had come on her journey. Ogboinba told him:

"I'm a woman as you see, and have been married many years, but I am without child; I've not even for once been pregnant. I am barren so am on my way to see Woyengi, and ask her to recreate me."

The Yasi said, "No living person ever sees Woyengi, so turn from here." But Ogboinba would not listen and said she would continue her journey. With that she shouldered her bag of powers and set forth. But she came back presently and made her usual request for a contest of powers. Yasi could not believe what he had heard and asked Ogboinba to repeat what she had said. Ogboinba repeated her request. Yasi then replied in anger:

"I am the greatest and the most powerful of all gods. How dare you, a human being, a woman, throw a challenge at me for a contest of powers! Go your way, you're no match for me."

But Ogboinba insisted on the contest. So Yasi in fury went to his medicine hut. But there the contents of his medicine pots had turned to blood! "This can't be," he whispered in surprise, "she's but a human being. She shall have the contest she wants," and taking the two small "creating stones" came out and asked Ogboinba to begin. But Ogboinda, as was her wont, refused and asked Yasi to begin. Yasi at once directed the force of his powers on her. Ogboinda's head was immediately severed and went up into the sky while her body remained standing, holding the bag of powers. Soon the head come down from the sky and rejoined the body and Ogboinba was once more whole and live. Ogboinba then asked Yasi to try her with more of his powers; but Yasi having none more powerful than the ones he had already used asked Ogboinba to try him with her powers. So Ogboinba started to repeat her own incantations, moving round and round in a circle. The force of her powers also severed the head of Yasi from the body and it went up high into the sky. But his body remained standing on the "creating stones" and Ogboinba noticing this, pushed it down on the ground. When Yasi's head came down from the sky there was no body for it to rejoin and it smashed itself on the ground. So Yasi the god was overcome and Ogboinba was once more victorious. But she would not move on without the "creating stones" and made for them. She tried to lift them but found that they could not be moved, small as they were. For a moment Ogboinba was at a loss what next to do. Then she repeated some of her incantations and immediately she was able to move them and lifted them on to her shoulder. She then moved on, bent double, with the weight of the "creating stones" and the bag of powers to the kingdom of Cock.

Cock on spying Ogboinba from the roof of his house flew down and asked if she was not the Ogboinba everybody, even the gods, had heard so much about. On Ogboinba giving her usual reply Cock said, "If you are the Ogboinba I've heard about, come into my house and I'll give you food and palm wine befitting me as king to entertain you." So Ogboinba, never refusing, went to Cock's house and there was well entertained to a meal of choice dishes and palm wine. After the meal Cock asked Ogboinba the reason for her journey and she said:

"I've been married many, many years but am without a child. I possess all the parts of a woman but I am barren. I am barren and so I'm on my way to see Woyengi face to face and ask her to recreate me."

"Journey no further," said Cock. "No one ever sees Woyengi alive. Mine is the last kingdom. Beyond me is void, so turn back from here," Cock advised.

But Ogboinba said she would journey on, and shouldering her bag of powers and the "creating stones" took to the road. Presently she came back and asked Cock for a trial of powers. But Cock liked nothing better than a show of powers and at once began to boast:

"My face has gone round the world for my powers. I am the ruler of the first and the last kingdom of things that die. Come, and I'll show you my powers; nothing pleases me more."

So boasting, Cock flew to the roof of his medicine hut and crew several times, summoning his powers. Then, flying back, he stood in front of Ogboinba and asked her to begin. But as was usual with her she refused and asked Cock to begin. Cock, not wishing to prolong matters, began with all he had at once.

Immediately Ogboinba became bare of all powers and Cock, noticing this, began boasting once more. "Mine's the first and the last kingdom of things that die. How can you stand my powers?" As he boasted thus, Ogboinba repeated her own incantations and got all her powers back. She asked Cock to try her with more of his powers. But Cock said he had used all the powers he had and if Ogboinba had any powers to match his, it was now her turn to use them on him. As Ogboinba repeated her incantations, Cock's town suddenly burst into flames and burned down to ashes.

Thus with more powers in her bag, Ogboinba journeyed beyond Cock's town and kingdom, the last kingdom of things that die, to the large field. The large field with the large Iroko tree with the large buttresses. There she hid herself in the buttresses of the Iroko tree and watched.

Soon, men and women appeared in pairs from the sides of the field. The women carried brooms and the men, bags. As the women swept the men collected the dirt into their bags. When the field had been swept clean they disappeared back into the sides of the field, pair by pair. As she waited, she saw the sky darken and a table descend on the field followed by a chair and a large "Creating Stone." Then there was lightning and thunder. Woyengi came down and sat on the chair and placed her feet on the "Creating Stone." Then on the table descended a quantity of earth and with it Woyengi went through her usual process of creation and led the men and women to the two streams, the streams that flowed to the habitation of man. Then Woyengi returned to the field and ordered up the table, the chair and then the "Creation Stone." These things went up one by one into the sky. When Woyengi was about to ascend, Ogboinba rushed out from her hiding place and challenged her to a contest of powers. Then Woyengi said:

"I know you were hiding in the buttresses of the Iroko tree. I saw you leave your town on your journey to find me. I saw you overcome all living things and gods on the way with the powers that I gave you which were your heart's desire. Now it's children you want, and for that you have come to see me and to challenge me to a contest of powers. You have come to challenge me, the source of your powers, strong-hearted Ogboinba. I now command all the powers you acquired on the way back to their owners."

Immediately Woyengi made this pronouncement, Isembi, Egbe, the Sea, Tortoise, the gods Ada and Yasi, and Cock, all had their powers back. And Ogboinba, overcome by fear, turned from the face of Woyengi and fled in panic to hide in the eyes of a pregnant woman she met on the way.

On seeing this Woyengi left Ogboinba alone, for a commandment she had given to men was that pregnant women should never be killed—and she would not now violate it because of Ogboinba. So Woyengi turned and went up to her abode. But Ogboinba remained in hiding and is still in hiding not only in the eyes of pregnant woman but in the eyes of men and children as well. So the person that looks out at you when you look into somebody's eyes is Ogboinba.

WHAT AN OLD MAN CAN SEE SITTING DOWN — A YOUNG MAN CAN'T SEE STANDING UP

[Yoruba, from Nigeria]

There was once a powerful king whose mad ambition was to rule without the advice of his elders.

After a man is cured he beats his doctor. The king did not realise that his strong position was due to the advice he had received from the elders so far. His irritation with them grew. "Why should I not act as I like, and when I like?" he said to himself. "Always I have to sit and listen to the idle talk of these old men."

Some people will scratch out an eye, because it itches. The king called some ambitious young men and told them: "You have the brains and the energy to rule my kingdom. Why should you have to sit aside and let your father talk? You are fit to hold all the important chieftaincy titles in this town. Go home — and let everybody kill his own father. It is time you should have your own share of the world."

The knife destroys its own house, and thinks it is only an old sheath. The young men actually went home and each one killed his father. Only one of them found himself unable to do it. As he got ready to kill his father, the old man said: "Spare my life. It is only in times of crises that you may know what use I can be to you. No one can appreciate the importance of his bottom, until it has a boil." The young man thought deeply over these words, and instead of killing his father he hid him in a remote farm hut.

Now the king kept his promise and he distributed the chieftaincy titles among the young. For a while he felt happy, but soon he realized that the young men were even more anxious to interfere with his rule than the old. When a year had passed, he got so irritated with them that he decided to get rid of them. He called them together one morning and announced that he had decided to add a new section to the palace as every king was supposed to do. He ordered everybody to start building the next day. But to distinguish this building from all other buildings it would have to be built from the top downwards, beginning with the highest point on the roof and ending up at ground level. He further announced that anybody who refused to participate in the building would be considered disloyal to the king and therefore had to be killed.

Then the young men got very frightened and they did not know what to do. But the son who had spared his father went to the farm in the night and asked his advice. When the old man had heard the story, he smiled and said: "What an old man can see sitting down, a young man can't see standing up." And then he instructed him what to do the following day.

On the next day they all appeared at the palace with trembling knees and watery bellies. But the young man whose father was alive stepped forward boldly and addressed the king: "Kabiyesi, we are ready to build your palace following your instructions. But according to the custom, it is you, as the landlord, who will have to lay the foundation stone."

Then the king was amazed at this answer and he asked the young man who had taught him such wisdom and the young man confessed that he had never killed his father. Then the king sent for the old man and he installed him as the Bashorun and he said to him: "Truly it is your wisdom that shall guide my kingdom from now on. Because what an old man sees sitting down, a young man can't see standing up."

A MAN'S LUCK CANNOT BE DRIVEN AWAY — ONLY DELAYED

[Yoruba, from Nigeria]

There were once two friends, one was blind and the other was lame. Each morning they went out begging together and in the evening they shared the money they had collected.

There came a time, however, when the harvest was bad and the people became reluctant to give alms. From morning to evening the two friends were waiting at the usual corner, but the people hurried by, pretending to look in another direction.

Then the blind man said to the lame man: "There is no hope left in our lives. Rather than die a slow death in this town and be left to lie in the streets to be eaten by the dogs, let us go and die quietly in the bush."

Then the blind man carried the lame man on his shoulders and the lame man told the blind man where to go. They wandered through the deep forest, looking for a quiet place to die.

Now you may think your end has come, but have you considered what God may do for you?

As they were stumbling along the lame man suddenly saw a dead elephant lying by the river. They stopped and made a fire and the lame man began to roast the elephant meat and eat it.

The blind man smelled the meat and said to the lame man: "What is this wonderful meat you are eating?" But the lame man was so greedy that he wanted to eat the entire elephant by himself. "Oh, it is only a toad," he said, "I will roast some for you too." He quickly killed a toad and roasted it and gave it to the blind man.

But this was the day when the god of fate turned good into evil and evil into good. When the blind man bit into the toad the burning juice squirted into his eye — and suddenly he could see again!

Then the blind man saw the elephant and he realized that his friend had deceived him. He got so angry that he picked up the lame man's crutch and he beat him so hard that it could have made a stone bleed. As he was beaten thus, the lame man suddenly felt that he could walk again.

Then the two friends fell on each other and beat each other so hard that the birds were scattering in the trees, and the fish felt cold with fear in the river.

In the end they both collapsed sweating and panting like dogs.

Then the blind man said to the lame man: "Why are you beating me? Is it not I who made you able to walk again?"

And the lame man said to the blind man: "Why are you beating me? Was it not I who made you able to see again?"

Then they embraced and they praised Eshu the god of fate saying:

"Eshu, confuser of men,

Eshu who turns right into wrong, wrong into right,

Having thrown a stone yesterday, you kill a bird today."

HARE AND HORNBILL

[Uganda]

Hare and Hornbill were great friends.

One day Hare said: "My friend, we have looked for girls all over this land, and there are none that are good enough for you and me. Let us go up to Sky-land, perhaps we will find some suitable ones."

Hornbill replied: "I know it is getting a bit late for us to get married, but you know my problem, you know I have this terrible thing!"

"You mean your chronic diarrhea? But that is nothing to worry about." Hare produced a cork of the right size and blocked up Hornbill's anus.

The two friends made preparations for the journey, and after saying good-bye to their families, Hare got on Hornbill's back and they flew up through the clouds into Skyland. There was a big marriage dance. Hare and Hornbill put on their dancing costumes and went straight into the arena. Hornbill danced gracefully, touching the ground lightly and moving his wings up and down to the rhythm of the drums. His neck swayed this way and that way, and his eyes sparkled with love. Hare danced as best he could, but he could not follow the rhythm of the dance, and sang out of tune; moreover, his big ears looked funny. Beautiful girls fought to dance before Hornbill, but none came anywhere near Hare; and when he approached the girls they ran away from him. That night Hornbill slept with a very pretty girl. Hare slept cold.

The next day Hornbill won two girls; Hare again slept cold. The next night when Hornbill was asleep, resting beside his fourth lover, Hare tip-toed into the house and unhooked the cork. Three days' accumulation of diarrhea spewed out and flooded the entire house. The stench rose like smoke and the dancers fled from the arena, and Hornbill woke up, and in great shame flew down through the clouds, leaving Hare behind.

There was much commotion as the Skylanders tried to find out what had happened. Hare denied all knowledge of the cause of the trouble.

"But where is your handsome friend?" they asked.

"I am also looking for him," said Hare, adding, "I must find him otherwise it will be a bit difficult to return to earth."

When they failed to find Hornbill the Skylanders decided to get rid of Hare by lowering him down to earth on a rope of plaited grass. The girls cut many heaps of grass. They made the rope and tied one end around Hare's waist and continued to plait the other end as Hare was lowered downwards. The Skylanders gave Hare a drum and told him, "As soon as you reach earth beat this drum very hard so that the girls may stop plaiting the rope." Hare thanked the Skylanders, said good-bye and began his homeward journey.

Hare descended slowly through the clouds, but on seeing the faint tips of the highest mountain he hit the drum very hard. The Skylanders stopped plaiting and dropped the rope. Hare came hurtling down like a falling stone. But just before hitting the ground he cried to the smallest black ants, "Collect me! Collect me! Collect . . ."

Hare hit the ground and broke up into many many very small pieces. The smallest black ants collected the pieces and put them together again, and Hare became alive. But today when Hare is running you hear his chest making crackling sounds, because the bones of his chest were not put together properly.

HARE AND MOSQUITO

[Uganda]

Hare and Mosquito were great friends. One day Hare said to Mosquito: "My friend, come and visit me tomorrow," and Mosquito agreed. The next day Mosquito came singing through the air. As he came nearer Hare's home he could smell the most delicious food being cooked. When he got there Hare welcomed him and took him into the boy's hut. Very soon Hare's mother called Hare to come and fetch the food. Hare went and returned with a dish of chicken. Mosquito's mouth watered.

They washed their hands and began to eat. Then Mosquito said to Hare: "My friend, you know I cannot break a piece of the chicken, my hands are not very strong. Can you help, please?"

"How weak can you be, my friend?" replied Hare. "My mother has cooked the chicken very well and it is as soft as it can be. Is it really all that difficult to tear it like this and put in your mouth like this?" Hare asked as he tore the leg off a chicken and ate it. Hare ate all that food himself. Mosquito only ate the millet bread and the soup.

When he was going back Mosquito said to Hare: "My friend, come and visit me tomorrow. My father collected a lot of honey recently, come and let us enjoy some." Now Hare was most fond of honey, so the next day Hare was at Mosquito's home very early in the morning. There was a strong scent of honey and Hare was dying to start eating it. Very soon Mosquito's mother called him to fetch the honey. Mosquito flew out and came back carrying a big earthen vase with a long thin neck. He put it on the ground, and after washing their hands they were ready to eat the honey. Mosquito dipped his hand into the vase and put the honey into his mouth and said: "Mm, how delicious!" The saliva from Hare's mouth could be seen dropping like rain. When Hare tried to put his hand into the vase it just stopped at the mouth and could not enter.

"My hand is too big my friend, can you not help me? This honey is too sweet."

Mosquito replied: "But Hare, is it so difficult to dip your hand into the vase like this and take the honey like this and eat it like this?" as he ate the honey. Hare jumped up and down and begged Mosquito to help him. But Mosquito ate all the honey himself. And that was the end of their friendship.

LABONGO AND KIPIR
[Uganda]

Luo, the first man, broke the surface of the ground from inside the earth. He had a son called Ipiti; and Ipiti's wife gave birth to a daughter who was named Kilak. One day Kilak went to collect firewood from the forest, but she did not come back home. An alarm was sounded and a search mounted, but Kilak could not be found anywhere.

After some months Kilak appeared in the homestead. She was pregnant. And when the time arrived, she gave birth to twins: Labongo and Kipir. The strange thing was that the boys were born with bells on their legs and feathers on their heads; and they were very fond of dancing. When they grew up their father gave them spears, and they became great hunters. Both of them got married and had some children.

One day an elephant came to eat the millet in the field. Labongo took a spear that was near at hand and speared the elephant and drove it away. But the beast did not die. It went away with the spear in its body. The spear actually belonged to Kipir who was not at home at that time.

When he returned from his journey, Kipir asked his wife where his spear was and his wife told him that Labongo had taken it. Kipir went to Labongo and said: "Where is my spear?" Labongo explained that he had used it to drive the elephant from the field and the elephant had gone off with it in its body. "I want my spear," Kipir said.

Labongo offered to give his brother another spear to replace his, but Kipir refused. Labongo offered a bull and told his brother: "Let me go to the smith and ask him to make a new spear," but Kipir would not listen.

He said: "This spear was given me by my father, and he blessed it. I do not want any other spear."

Labongo decided to look for his brother's spear and bring it to him. His wife made food for the journey, and after saying goodbye to his mother and children he set out with his dog. They followed the spoor of the wounded animal for a long long way until they entered a dark and thick forest. This was the home of elephants.

Labongo was met by a fierce and wiry mother of elephants who appeared in the form of a human being. She stormed at Labongo, shouting: "You are the people who kill my children. Today, you will be killed, torn to shreds."

Labongo replied: "We kill your children because they are thieves. Why have you not taught your children to be good people?"

The old elephant woman replied: "This is not true, my children are not thieves. You kill them because you want their tusks." The two argued for a long time, until the elephant woman was convinced of Labongo's innocence.

Then she brought Labongo into her home and asked him: "Why have you come to our home?"

Labongo told the woman how one of her children was eating the millet when he speared it to save the crop. "I did not kill it, but it came away with my spear in its body. I have come to get that very spear, because it is very important."

The woman brought a big bundle of spears. Labongo looked at each of the spears but could not find the one he wanted. Many other bundles were brought but the one he had come for was not among them. When the last bundle was brought Labongo picked out a spear and said: "This is my spear."

The mother of elephants gave him the spear and made some food for his journey. She fried some peas, and mixed some beads in with the beans. She told Labongo not to move about during the day so that the elephants might not see him. "They are very angry with human beings. If they see you they will certainly kill you," she warned.

That night Labongo set out for home with Kipir's spear in his hand. He walked and walked for days and days. When he was near home, he sent his dog to go and announce his approach. When the dog arrived, somone shouted that Labongo's dog was home. "Perhaps Labongo is coming back at last!" When Labongo's mother heard this she burst into tears, saying that people were laughing at her sorrow.

But Labongo walked into the homestead. He was stopped at the gate, and a small ceremony was conducted to welcome him among the living, because he had been away so long that most people believed he had been killed by the wild beasts. People gathered around Labongo and asked him many questions but he walked straight to his brother's house and said: "Kipir, here is your spear!" Kipir was very happy to see his spear; he was also relieved to see Labongo alive, as he was being blamed for his supposed death.

One morning Labongo sat in the compound and began to thread colourful beads. Kipir's wife came to admire the beads; and as they sat there her baby son took one of the beads and swallowed it. Labongo stopped threading and said: "I want my bead."

When the mother of the baby saw that he had swallowed the bead she said to Labongo: "O, wait until he has defecated then you will get your bead." But Labongo told her that he wanted the bead immediately, because that was the one he was going to thread next.

The woman ran to her husband. "Kipir, Kipir," she called, "come quickly."

"What is the matter?" Kipir asked.

"Your baby has swallowed Labongo's bead, and he wants it immediately," she told her husband.

Kipir went to his brother and said: "Labongo, my brother, can you not wait until the child defecates?"

Labongo looked at his brother and replied: "Did you accept another spear instead of yours?"

Kipir went to his house and picked up his hunting knife. He came to Labongo and threw the knife to him, saying: "If you want your bead immediately, take this knife and kill the baby and take it!"

Labongo replied: "All I want is my bead, and I want it now."

Kipir was very annoyed with himself, and ashamed. He took the knife and split open his son's belly, took the bead and gave it to his brother. Labongo took the bloody bead, blew away the blood and threaded it. And he continued to thread his beads until they were ready.

The two could no longer live together. So Kipir and his people moved towards the west; and when they reached the Kir river he threw an axe in the water, and the water parted, so that they crossed to the other side on dry ground.

AFRICAN PROVERBS

The following proverbs are located in Chinua Achebe's *Things Fall Apart,* a Nigerian novel in English, first published in 1958:[5]

> Proverbs are the palm oil with which words are eaten.
> If a child washed his hands, he could eat with kings.

---

[5] Chinua Achebe has asserted, in a conversation with the editor (Harrow), in September of 1993, that the proverbs that he employed in *Things Fall Apart* can be considered to date back to earlier than the twentieth century, and in some instances even earlier than the nineteenth century. Although dating is imprecise, it is reasonable to place it in this period that falls between the fifteenth and nineteenth centuries.

When the moon is shining the cripple becomes hungry for a walk.

Let the kite perch and let the eagle perch too. If one says no to the other, let his wing break.

An old woman is always uneasy when dry bones are mentioned in a proverb.

A toad does not run in the daytime for nothing.

Eneke the bird says that since men have learnt to shoot without missing, he has learnt to fly without perching.

The lizard that jumped from the high iroko tree said he could praise himself if no one else did. (Igbo, from Nigeria)

The following proverbs and riddles are cited in Isadore Okpewho's *African Oral Literature:*

A Bila spear killed the Bila.[6] (Nigeria)

Tomorrow, tomorrow did not kill the white man.[7] (Nigeria)

Water will not dry up.[8] (Sierra Leone)

Death may end the man; death doesn't end his name. (Mali)

Do not follow the vanquished into the bush.[9] (Kenya)

The earth does not get fat.[10] (Malawi)

Proverbs are the horses of speech—when the truth is elusive, it is proverbs that we use to discover it. (Nigeria)

African Riddles:

I wandered around from one village to another with my winnowing basket. (*Answer:* a river)

Water standing up. (*Answer:* sugar cane)

A mountain here and a mountain there and in between there is ululation. (*Answer:* the buttocks)

Something I threw over to the other side of the river. (*Answer:* eyes; i.e., desire that goes beyond what is possible)

---

[6] Refers to an eighteenth-century incident in which two royal Nigerian cousins argued, resulting in the killing of one by the other. "Spear" symbolically stands for their weapons which were actually cannons and guns, and the proverb itself warns against hostility between blood relations.

[7] Refers to an incident in 1830 in which two British explorers were captured and detained, and eventually ransomed by a king. Apparently one of the explorers was slated to be killed but was saved by the procrastination of one of the kings. The proverb thus concerns the effects of delaying decisions.

[8] Expresses the certainty that money and goods will not cease to be paid in bride-price (dowry paid to bride's parents) and marriages will continue to be contracted, just as the rivers and streams in Sierra Leone will continue to abound.

[9] Do not press one's victory too far.

[10] The earth has a limitless capacity to receive the dead.

A flame in the hill. (*Answer:* a leopard)

Black cattle that stay in a forest. (*Answer:* lice)

The sweet stalk of millet within the boundary—however sweet I shan't break it. (*Answer:* blood relationship; i.e., a warning to initiates against incest)

What dines with an oba [king] and leaves him to clear the dishes? (*Answer:* a fly)

A beautiful woman who is never married. (*Answer:* the moon)

A great packer of loads, king among divinities

He packs two hundred yams with a groundnut shell.

He sends people to tell those in his house,

That he is just learning how to pack loads. (*Answer:* a termite)

37

∂℞

AFRICAN POETRY

Prior to the twentieth century, most forms of literature in Africa were oral. Songs, epics, praise songs, prayers, chronicles, and many other genres were communicated, at times orally, at times in written form. There is no clear line between poetry and prose in much of the oral literature of the world, and in Africa one finds a multitude of literary forms that defy simple Western categories such as prose and poetry. Nonetheless, we can identify traditions of literature in which the basic traits of poetry are to be found, including regular metric patterns, rhyme schemes, stanza structures, and conventional patterns of wording—in short, elements of genre that characterize received poetic traditions.

The works presented here range over a wide gamut of genres. The selections start with the hunting-gathering San people of southern Africa whose prayers and hymns give us effective, pithy expressions: the "Prayer to the Hunting Star" presents the hunter's feelings of humility before the powerful glories of Canopus, the star. In the next selection, from the same region, the Khoikhoi, mostly cattle-herders in past centuries, sing their praises of the Supreme Being, Tsui-Xgoa, in terms that evoke the deity's role as all-giving father—a prayer that finds echoes in all parts of the continent.

Another widespread poetic form is praise singing. Though often associated with West African griots, professional bards, various types of praise singing, with or without bardic type performers, have been noted throughout much of Africa. Included are two of the more formal examples of the Hausa praise singers, both male and female, taken from a long-standing tradition in which both shorter praise epithets and longer praise songs are found. One such example of the latter is sung in praise of the king of the city of Gobir, Bawa Jangwarzo (d.1790). Other examples can be found dating back to the fourteenth century. A related Hausa poem, an elegy for a monarch killed in battle, Sarkin Rano, displays both the eulogizing function and the warriors' typically aggressive attitude. Next, two great African rulers are given fulsome praise in the formal tradition of praise singing: the eighteenth-century Sultan of Bornu, Nigeria, and the great nineteenth-century Zulu monarch, Shaka.

535

Born in the late eighteenth century, Shaka was the son of a Zulu chief, Sen-zangakhona, but he grew to maturity in the army of the greatest Zulu warrior of his day, Dingiswayo. Rivalries within the Zulu leadership had led to Shaka's exile, but with the support of Dingiswayo, Shaka was able to assume the Zulu chieftainship on the death of his father in 1816. By the time of Shaka's death twelve years later, he had forged the Zulu people into a nation, creating a power-ful militaristic state. His praise poem has been described as less personal and more national, reflecting his militarism and the enlarged status he acquired through his conquests. In these praise poems we find the majestic, formal repeti-tions of line and of structure typical of oral celebrations of royalty.

Next, Igbo praises, short and effective, like hot pepper, celebrate such virtues as stature, beauty, title, strength, ability, and wealth.

Short poems expressing feelings of love, abandonment, despair, admiration, and so on, are sung or recited on various occasions. One such poem from Uganda, "Last night I slept alone," expresses a wife's feelings of sexual frustration; it is sung while she pounds the mortar. Another Ugandan poem expresses the poet's sadness at her lover's inability to pay the necessary bride-price to acquire his beloved for a wife.

The next selections are from two of the most extensive poetic traditions in Africa. They are both located in East Africa—the Swahili East coast (extending from Kenya to Tanzania) and Somalia. Love and religious feeling often inform Swahili poetry. "Wedding Song," from Zanzibar, begins with an enumeration of the physical properties of the betrothed's beauty, and ends with her intellectual qualities. In the poem that follows on his first wife, Muyaka Bin Hajji gives voice in restrained terms to his feelings of sadness at her loss. Next comes a poem con-cerning his second wife in which he now addresses, with a candor previously un-known to much early African poetry, the disappointment he experiences in his marriage. Swahili poetry is often infused with heroic or religious sentiments. Thus the earliest verse sings of the story of the hero, Liongo (Volume II, Selection 13), while eighteenth- and nineteenth-century poems include Islamic exhorta-tions and laments. In "The Inkishafi," one of the great Swahili poets, Saiyid Ab-dallah, presents us with a powerful homily on the inevitability of death, the tran-sitoriness of wealth, and the dangers of damnation facing the human soul for those who disregard divine injunctions. Other Swahili poets deal with the beauty of their beloved, the joys of loving, and sorrows over failed love.

A number of the themes of Swahili poetry are echoed in Somali poetry, one example being Raage Ugaas's moving lament on the death of his wife. One of the great Somali poets of the last century was Mohammad Abdille Hasan, who cele-brates the defeat of the English forces led by Richard Corfield. This poem was central to one of Somalia's major twentieth-century novels, Close Sesame, *by Nuruddin Farah. Last, as with the Swahili love poetry, we have a Somali exam-ple of the lover's lament, Siraad Haad's "Lament for a Dead Lover," in which the stark landscape of the Horn of Africa provides the forceful imagery for the poet.*

Thus we find, throughout the continent, anonymous, devotional, conven-tional, and occasional poems, handed down from generation to generation, along with individual works of creation by poets whose fame and influence were wide-spread, and who worked within the confines of established poetic traditions.

PRAYER TO THE HUNTING STAR, CANOPUS, SAID BY X-NANNI[1]

San [Southern Africa]

Xkoagu,[2] give me your heart
that you sit with in plenty.
Take my heart, my heart
small and famished without hope
so that like you I too may be full
for I hunger.

San, "Prayer to the Hunting-Star, Canopus" and Khoikhoi, "Hymn to Tsui-Xgoa," transcribed and translated from Bushman (San) click language by W. H. I. Black and Lucy Lloyd (1860); this version by Jock Cope (1968). Reprinted in Michael Chapman and Achmat Dangor (eds.), *Voices from Within: Black Poetry from Southern Africa* (Johannesburg, Ad. Donker, 1982). Reprinted by permission of Michael Chapman, pp. 19, 21. Hausa Praise singing, "Bawa Jangwarzo" and "Sarkin Rano" from *A History of Hausa Islamic Verse,* by Mervyn Hiskett, copyright 1975, the School of Oriental and African Studies (London) pp. 3–4, 6. "The Sultan of Bornu," "Pounding Song," and "The Horn of My Love" from *Oral Poetry from Africa,* edited by Jack Mapanje and Landeb White, copyright 1983, pp. 8–9, 25–28, 59, 84. "Shaka," from *Izibongo: Zulu Praise-Poems,* edited by Trevor Cope, translated by Daniel Malcolm, collected by James Stuart (1968), © 1968 Oxford University Press, pp. 88, 96, 98, 100, 166. Reprinted by permission of Oxford University Press. "Praise of an Influential Man," "Praise of a Beautiful Lady," "Ozo Title Holder Praising Himself: Based on Farming," "Puberty Praise Song: Money" from *Igbo Traditional Verse,* edited by Romanus Egudu and Donatus Nwaga, copyright 1973, pp. 19–21, 27. "Wedding Song," "A Poem to His First Wife," "Poem about His Second Wife" from *Four Centuries of Swahili Verse,* by Jan Knappert, copyright 1979, pp. 80, 144, 146–147. Reprinted by permission of Heinemann Educational Publishers, a division of Reed Educational & Professional Publishing Ltd. "The Poem Inkishafi" from *Swahili Poetry,* by Lyndon Harries (1962), © 1962 Oxford University Press, pp. 91, 93, 95, 97, 99, 101, 103. Reprinted by permission of Oxford University Press. "Poet's Lament on the Death of His Wife," "The Death of Richard Corfield," and "Lament for a Dead Lover" from *Somali Poetry,* by B. W. Andrzejewski and I. M. Lewis, copyright 1964, pp. 64, 72, 74, 138. Reprinted by permission of I. M. Lewis.

[1] Recited by the San X-nanni to W.H.I. Bleek in 1885, and recorded and interpreted by Bleek.

[2] San name for the star.

You seem to me full-bellied, Xkoagu
and in my eyes not small
    but I am hungry.

Star, give to me your belly
that fills you with a good feeling,
and you shall take my stomach from me
so you as well can know its hunger.
Give me your right arm too
and you shall take my arm from me,
my arm that does not kill
    for I miss my aim.

Xkoagu, blind with your light
    the Springbok's eyes,
and you shall give me your arm
for my arm that hangs here
that makes me miss my mark.

HYMN TO TSUI-XGOA[3]

[Khoi-Khoi[4] from Southern Africa]

You, O Tsui-Xgoa
you, all-father
you, our father!
Let stream to earth the thundercloud,
give that our flocks may live,
give life to us.
I am so stricken with weakness
I thirst and I hunger.
Allow that I gather and eat the field fruits,
for are you not our first one
the father of fathers,
you, Tsui-Xgoa—
that we may sing to you in praise
that we may measure to you in return,
you, all-father
you, our maker
you, O Tsui-Xgoa.

---

[3] Supreme being.

[4] The pastoral Khoikhoi are thought to be related to the San, and have long inhabited
southern Africa.

HAUSA PRAISE SONGS
[Nígeria]
Bawa Jangwarzo[5]

Causer of terror, chief of iron ore,
Son of Alasan, owner of the drum,
Causer of terror, iron gate of the town,
Bawa, you kinsman of Magajin Gari,
His name is "Hate-flight",
His name is "Put-to-flight",
As for me, I do not decline to follow Bawa,
Here is my saddle, all laid out,
My bridle is here, laid out,
My spur is here, laid out,
My tethering peg is here, planted in the ground,
I lack only a horse,
It is not to talk of war that we came,
It is to console you in bereavement that we came,
Had we come to talk of war,
Wurno would not have lasted the day, let alone the night,
Shiki and Dole, the rebellious towns,
Are our little chicks,
Galadi yonder, and Tubali,
Are your full-grown hens,
Do not wake them up until the feast day!
Dan Taka'ida, leader of the town,
Uban Dawaki Salami,
He clashed with the young warriors of Jitau,
They unhorsed him at the foot of the mimosa tree
And to this day he has not risen up!
O men of Badarawa, stop beating your drums,
It is not on your account that Bawa comes.
Come, let us follow the leader of the town
So that we may obtain horses to mount.
When we sallied forth, we went by way of Gaya,
No single thorn as much as pricked us.
Bawa, son of Babari, the son of Alasan,
The forked pole that supports the roof,
Dan Taka'ida, fence of the town,
Bawa, it is you whom I follow, there is no nonsense about this.

---

[5] Bawa Jagwarzo was the ruler of the city of Gobir in Northern Nigeria. He died in 1790.

Come, follow him who gives you personal adornments,
That you may obtain glory from him.
As for me, that which I desire from you is that
Wherever you go, you take me with you,
As for me, I am your foster-child,
That I may obtain happiness.
Bawa, you it is who begins to conquer the town,
Son of Alasan, wealthy one.
My brethren, come, let us follow the wealthy one,
That we may obtain horses to mount.

Sarkin Rano[6]

Sarkin Rano is a beloved of God,
Since he fell in battle marriage has become unmanageable.
Sarkin Rano, at Ningi he made camp,
His foot soldiers camped in Bira country,
Halilu, see, here is porridge, but I do not eat it,
Halilu, here is gruel, but I do not drink,
Give me my quiver and give me my bow,
I must seize Dan Yaya and strangle him.
On the day of the clash with the Gudiya people,
The swordsman was hacking,
The spearman was thrusting,
And he with the dagger was stabbing,
He with the axe was hacking.

• • •

At the fight to the west of Rantam
We saw terrors there more than a thousand,
Joiner of marriage, joiner of relationship,
Since he fell, marriage has become unmanageable.

THE SULTAN OF BORNU[7]

[Hausa, from Northern Nigeria]

Carefully weave the acts of kingship:
Hear all and weave:

---

[6] Sarkin is an honorific title among the Hausa of northern Nigeria, and Rano is the name of the city ruled by the Sarkin of this poem which dates to approximately 1830. The poem is an elegy for the Sarkin killed in battle against non-Muslim warriors of Ningi. This song was apparently to be sung by a female, and it joins together the lament for the loss of the great ruler with regret over the destabilization of the institution of marriage.

Weave as your grandfather did,
Weave as your first ancestor did.
You are a match for even the wily men of the town of Dubura of
        the fig trees.
Dabaga of the large *Damsa* tree, the town of Dalla, is yours:
In Dubura a Kauwa Melemi, your ancestor, is buried:
In Tumbur a Kauwa Melemi, your ancestor, is buried:
In Gazajemi, Mai Biri Melemi, one of your ancestors, is buried,
And one in Biddum of the Rocks, seven worlds above it, seven
        rivers below.
May Allah preserve you in the same way as he does not allow friendship
        to grow old!
O King, your bounty is to us as the milk of a cow which never goes dry
        to the calf at it side:
From you we find our food in the evening, and water to drink in the
        morning.
May Allah grant that we may see you every day and rejoice!
May Allah grant the fulfilment of all your kingly plans!
Always you are the son of Aji,
Aji Duniana, you are the greatest chief on earth.
In your kingdom, men live in peace,
And of the chiefs in the tents you are the greatest:
Of those who wear turbans, and of those who wear only loincloths, you
        are the chief:
You are the ruler alike of men who have a leather loin-cloth tied between
        their legs and of those who ride on fine horses.
Of the prosperous land of Yamte, full of *Jujube* trees,
        you are the King.
Of the prosperous land of Yamte in which is the Crested Rock,
        you are the King.
Father, Sultan of Bornu,
The Kurata Arabs in the Kanem towns are your slaves:
You are the strength of Bornu,
The scourge of every pagan town you will remain.
O King, you are a man in the prime of his health, and your beasts of
        burden are all in good condition.
O King, yours is all the power, you have no equal.
The plans for every day are in your hands, Owner of Gagara Wunji,
Wunji, from which you sallied forth to take your captives, and cause

---

[7] Ruler of the ancient kingdom of Bornu in northern Nigeria. The poem was recorded in 1926, and it describes the Muslim Sultan Momadu Ajimi who reigned from 1737 to 1751. The ruler is praised for his prowess in battle, his generosity, and his extraordinary power, a power linked to his ancestors.

their relations to follow you with piteous entreaties.
O King, you are the bush fire which burns up the towns of the pagans:
You, son of Aji, can collect or disperse people at your will,
And turn again and make a town with those you have dispersed.
You are the scourge of Jillam, Dalla Darge and Dakkinam Dalla
      Damaram.
Some towns are founded during the cold season of the year,
But some of yours have been founded through your victories, Aji Gana
      the Intriguer.
O King, your reign is the equal of any:
You, son of Aji, have accomplished this!

SHAKA[8]

[Zulu, from South Africa]

Dlungwana son of Ndaba![9]
   Ferocious one of the Mbelebele brigade,
Who raged among the large kraals,[10]
So that until dawn the huts were being turned upside down.
   He who is famous without effort, son of Menzi,[11]
He who beats but is not beaten, unlike water,[12]
Axe that surpasses other axes in sharpness;
Shaka, I fear to say he is Shaka,
Shaka, he is the chief of the Mashobas.
He of the shrill whistle, the lion;
He who armed in the forest, who is like a madman,
The madman who is in full view of the men.[13]
He who trudged wearily the plain going to Mfene;
The voracious one of Senzangakhona,
Spear that is red even on the handle . . .[14]
   The attacker has been long attacking them:
He attacked Phungashe of the Buthelezi clan,
He attacked Sondaba of Mthanda as he sat in council,

---

[8] Shaka (1787–1828) was a Zulu ruler who established a large kingdom in southeastern
Africa. This *izibongo,* or praise song, was composed in Zulu.

[9] A praise name meaning "the rager" or "ferocious one."

[10] Enclosures for cattle and other domestic animals.

[11] Menzi is a praise name for Shaka's father.

[12] Water can be beaten, but to no effect; Shaka cannot be beaten at all.

[13] A reference to the story that Shaka, as a young man, had confronted and killed a madman who was terrorizing people.

He attacked Macingwane at Ngonyameni,
He attacked Mangcengeza of the Mbatha clan,
He attacked Dladlama of the Majolas,
He attacked Nxaba son of Mbhekane,
He attacked Gambushe in Pondoland,
He attacked Faku in Pondoland.[15]

The young viper grows as it sits,
Always in a great rage
With a shield on its knees.[16]

He who while devouring some devoured others
And as he devoured others he devoured some more;
He who while devouring some devoured others
And as he devoured others he devoured some more;
He who while devouring some devoured others
And as he devoured others he devoured some more;
He who while devouring some devoured others
And as he devoured others he devoured some more;
He who while devouring some devoured others
And as he devoured others he devoured some more.

Painful stabber, they will exhort one another,
Those who are with the enemy and those who are at home.[17]
He who is dark as the bile of a goat.

Butterfly of Phunga[18]
With colours in circles as if they had been painted on;
He who is hazy as the shadows of the mountains,
When it is dark the evil-doers move about.

The rival of Phunga and Mageba[19]
Which looked at me until I got accustomed to it.

Powerful limbs, calf of a beast,
The kicking of this beast puzzled me,
It kicked the milker and left the one holding it.[20]

Hawk that I saw descending from the hills of Mangcengaza,
And from those of Phungashe he disappeared;

---

[14] Red because of so much stabbing.

[15] This list of names includes the major rulers whom Shaka defeated in Natal, the region of South Africa in which he forged his kingdom.

[16] Shaka inherited this praise from his great-grandfather Ndaba who was always ready for a fight.

[17] Shaka inherits this praise from his father; its significance is obscure, but indicates a disturbance over a great distance.

[18] Famous ancestor.

[19] Famous ancestor.

They said, "Hawk, here he is, there he is,"
Whereas he was silent in the forests like the leopards and lions.[21]
    Shaka went and erected temporary huts
Between the Nsuze and the Thukela,[22]
In the country of Nyanya son of Manzawane;
He ate up Mantonodo son of Tayi,
He felt him tasteless and spat him out,
He devoured Shihayo.
    He who came dancing on the hillsides of the Phuthiles,
And overcame Msikazi among the Ndimoshes.[23]
    He met a long line of ibises
When he was going to raid the foolish Pondos;
Shaka did not raid herds of cattle,
He raided herds of buck.
    The one who gets stiff![24]
The one who was cooked in the deep pot of Ntombazi,[25]
He was cooked and got stiff.
    The one who goes along making fires and leaving behind conflagrations,
Who when he was rubbed flared up like a fire;
There was no longer a beast lowing at little Ntombazi's,
It was now lowing at our place at Bulawayo.[26]
    Our own bringer of poverty at Bulawayo,
Who made Zwide destitute by great strides.
    The sky that rumbled, the sky of Mageba,[27]
That thundered above Nomangci mountain,
It thundered behind the kraal at Kuqhobekeni and struck,
It took the shields of the Maphela and Mankayiya,[28]
And the head decorations of the Zimpaka were left in the bushes;
He devoured Nomahlanjana son of Zwide of the Maphelas,
He devoured Mphepha son of Zwide of the Maphelas,

---

[20] It takes two to milk a cow, one to hold its head and the other to milk it. This stanza suggests an attack that was an error in judgment.

[21] Mangcengeza and Phugashe were both badly defeated by Shaka, but they themselves escaped.

[22] In preparation for a campaign against the Nyuswas.

[23] It was sufficient for Shaka merely to show himself.

[24] The poet begins a long passage of nine stanzas dealing with the war against Zwide, one of Shaka's principal rivals.

[25] Shaka's mother, perhaps the chief inspiration for his conquests.

[26] Shaka's capital kraal.

[27] Shaka's famous ancestor.

He devoured Nombengula son of Zwide of the Maphelas,
He devoured Dayingubo son of Zwide of the Maphelas,
He devoured Sonsukwana son of Zwide of the Maphelas,
He devoured the chief's wife, daughter of Lubongo,
He devoured Mtimona[29] son of Gaqa of the Maphelas,
He devoured Mpondo-phumela-kwezinde of the Maphelas,
He devoured Ndengezi-mashumi of the Maphelas,
He devoured Sikloloba-singamabele of Zwide's people,
He devoured Sihla-mthini-munye of Zwide's people,
He devoured Nqwangube son of Lundiyane,
He belonged to our side, having turned round his shield.
   Return, Trickster, indeed you have finished this matter,
As for Zwide, you have made him into a homeless criminal,
And now today you have done the same to the son . . .[30]

   Young raging one of Ndaba!
He lives in a great rage,
And his shield he keeps on his knees;
He had not let them settle down, he keeps them in a state of excitement,
Those among the enemy and those at home.
   Mandla kaNgome![31]
He crossed over and founded the Ntontela regiment,
They said he would not found it and he founded it.
   He who attempted the ocean without crossing it,
It was crossed by swallows and white people.[32]
   He who sets out at midday, son of Ndaba, or even afternoon;
Pursuer of a person and he pursues him persistently,
For he pursued Mbemba born among the Gozas,
He pursued him until he put him at Silutshana . . .
   Axe of Senzangahona,
Which when it was chopping worked very energetically.
   He who saw the cattle right on top of the hill,
And brought them down by means of long spears and they came
     down . . .

---

[28] Here begins the sequence of conquests against Zwide's forces.

[29] People of Zwide's household. The hyphenated names that follow are praise names.

[30] Having defeated Zwide's forces, Shaka later defeats the remnants of Zwide's forces led by his son.

[31] A praise name that may mean "Mighty Power."

[32] Referring to Shaka's mission to King George, conducted by an English settler named King and a Zulu representative of Shaka. The mission embarked from Port Natal in South Africa, but only reached Algoa in present day Mozambique.

Little leopard that goes about preventing other little leopards at
　　　the fords.[33]
　　Finisher off! Black finisher off!

PRAISE OF AN INFLUENTIAL MAN[34]
[Igbo, from Nigeria]

The son of Ezenovo's son of the line of hill movers,
The brother of the *Ozo,* son of the hard Iron-King
The brother of the *Ozo,* who is the Knife that cuts bushes,
The son of Amadiwhe, who is the King that cuts through hills,
The brother of the *Ozo,* who eats accompanied with the music of
　　　the gong,
Shall I praise you once or twice?
By the right or by the left?
See him—one who though short is not a dwarf
For shortness is the natural compression of effect.

PRAISE OF A BEAUTIFUL LADY
[Igbo, from Nigeria]

Young lady, you are:
A mirror that must not go out in the sun
A child that must not be touched by dew
One that is dressed up in hair
A lamp with which people find their way
Moon that shines bright
An eagle feather[35] worn by a husband
A straight line drawn by God.

OZO[36] TITLE HOLDER PRAISING HIMSELF:
[Igbo, from Nigeria]
(a) Based on Farming

I am:
One who tills hills

---

[33] He is in full control of the country.

[34] This and the following short praise songs are from the Igbo people.

[35] In the Igbo tradition, the mirror and the eagle feather are symbols of beauty and nobility respectively.

One who with yams challenges soil
Knife that clears bushes
Barn that is wide
Bush that yields wealth
Bush that is colossal
Bush that is fearful
Hoe-User untouched by hunger.

(b) Based on Wine Tapping

I am:
Height that is fruitful
Climbing rope that makes king
Knife that harvests money
Wealth from height.

(c) Based on Hunting

I am:
Killer of tiger
Tiger that roams in wilderness
Bullet that give life
Tiger with claws
King of wilderness.

PUBERTY PRAISE SONG
(for a Female): MONEY
[Igbo, from Nigeria]

She was married with money
    Money   (Chorus)
One like her husband
    Money
Fertile egg
    Money
Eagle of surplus beauty
    Money
Husband's sweetheart
    Money
Breast that feeds a child
    Money

---

[36] Ozo is a title of nobility conferred on those who have made significant achievements in their lives.

Conduct that is highest valued
> Money
Woman is the joy of a home
> Money.

POUNDING SONG[37]

[Uganda]

Last night I slept alone.
My man was away, drinking,
He would not come home.
Mother, last night I slept alone.
My man was totally drunk,
He would not touch me.
My clansmen, last night I slept alone.
My man was drunk,
He turned his back to me.
My people, last night I slept alone.
My man was drunk,
He slept like a corpse.

THE HORN OF MY LOVE

[Uganda]

Where has my love blown his horn?
The tune of his horn is well known.
Young men of my clan,
Have you heard the horn of my love?

The long distance has ruined me, oh,
The distance between me and my companion.
Youths of my clan,
Have you heard the horn of my love?

The shortage of cattle has ruined my man!
The poverty of my love!
You men of my clan,
Listen to the horn of my love.

Where has my love blown his horn?
The tune of his horn is well known.
Young men of my clan,

---

[37] Sung while the woman pounds the mortar with her pestle.

Listen to the horn of my clan.

WEDDING SONG[38]
[Swahili, from Zanzibar]

A fine little mouth, like a rose stem,[39]
with a gap in the middle, that is her beauty;
that is our lady, your wife, full of love,
who shames the men in public.[40]
The pleasure of a husband is eating and fine clothes,
and kind words having a soothing effect,
and good tobacco that makes one a little intoxicated,
he wants betel and leaves.[41]

My girl[42] is not to be ordered around;
do not give her a hoe to go and cultivate;
I gave her a book to go and study,
so she could study science and the Koran.

A POEM TO HIS FIRST WIFE[43]
[Swahili, from East Africa]
Muyaka Bin Hajji

I would rather have the small boat,
my first little vessel,

---

[38] This Swahili song from Zanzibar was sung in response to the bridegroom's party's playful questions concerning the status of the bride's children. In return, the bride's party advertises her finer points.

[39] An ambiguous symbol of femininity, the rose stem "gives birth" to rosy progeny. A small round mouth, like the circular edge of a reed tube, is considered a sign of beauty.

[40] The wife with social standing and self-respect will not acknowledge inappropriate remarks made to her in public, and will know how to turn offensive remarks against their speakers.

[41] Wives are expected to serve their husbands tobacco and betel nuts in leaves for chewing.

[42] The poem's narrator is apparently the bride's parents, who conclude the poem by boasting of the fine education they gave her.

although it was unsteady and shaky,
the waves never rose above her head;
but she drowned near Ngozoa
on a dark night.
That is what I am thinking about today,
it makes me feel confused and numb.

My little boat, my seaworthy boat,
when I first made it float on the water,
it was full of playfulness,
and I was pleased and charmed by it;
I crossed over on it to the other shore,
and the waves did not rise about it.
That is why today I am thinking about her,
it makes me fell confused and numb.

POEM ABOUT HIS SECOND WIFE[44]
[Swahili, from East Africa]
Muyaka Bin Hajji

Do not talk to me about that time
when my mother and father were alive,
when my kinsmen filled the house
and I knew what to do with you.
Today I am alone, we have remained,
but the wise counsellors are no longer there.
That is what I have to say; are your thoughts the same,
or do you have something else on your mind?

You are a continuous source of bitterness to me.
and you add to my grief;
you don't permit my heart to rest

---

[43] A moving account by Muyaka Bin Hajji (1776–1837) of his love for his first wife who died one dark night in the past. As public emotion is considered unseemly for a Swahili, and God's will is not to be opposed, the poet takes for his wife the image of his first seaworthy vessel on which he made his maiden voyage as a captain.

[44] Muyaka's second marriage was apparently an unhappy one. Here Muyaka reveals a lyrical strain. Although it is not customary in Swahili society to air intimate matters in public, Muyaka succeeds in evoking the problems in his marriage, including his wife's abrasive ways and her boastfulness. He challenges his wife to speak, rather than peremptorily shutting her up or abusing her physically, as he might well have done at the time (around 1800).

with your constant abrasive remarks.
What is my fault,
what have I done wrong to you?
This is what I have to say; are your thoughts the same,
or do you have something else to say?

When you tell me that what you do is not shameful,
even for a noble, respectable person,
of impeccable virtue and righteousness,
one who is well versed in eloquence;
then don't do a thing that is not fitting,
and remove my distress.
This is what I have to say; are your thoughts the same,
or do you have something else to say?

If you have no more need for me,
do not give me just oblique hints;
I kept silence, I do not speak;
but with you I do not feel at ease,
I cannot set my tongue free,
I have no joy, I never laugh.
This is what I have to say; are your thoughts the same,
or do you have something else hidden away?

THE POEM INKISHAFI[45]
[Swahili, from East Africa]
Saiyid Abdallah

I put first "In the Name of God"   as I compose this poem   and I
     write "The merciful One"   and after that "The Benign
     One."[46]
I want to put praise first   lest the curious ask   saying, Have you
     deprived us of the praising   and so spread a wrong that
     has no like?
Praise having been offered   illuminating us like a lamp   prayers

---

[45] Written around 1810–1820, this is considered one of the great works of Swahili poetry.
The moral of the homily, a warning against the punishments to be faced for moral
turpitude, may owe some of its tone to the earlier downfall of the sultanate of Pate. The
Muslim sense of divine retribution and power infuses the poet's vision. The Swahili
term "Inkishafi" means, roughly, self-examination, in the sense conveyed by the poet's
quest into his own heart, and by his address to his heart and soul.

and peace follow on   let us pray for the Prophet Muhammad.

And for his kinsfolk of the clan Qinan   and for his four named Companions   let us pray for them all together   may prayer and compassion leave their mark on them.

O my Lord Allah, Granter of requests   let us pray for the Prophet who came   and who of Thy One-ness, O Lord of slaves taught us the meaning.

When the full measure is complete   of setting in order prayer and praise   let me make clear my treatise   which I purpose in my heart.

My inner intention   is to make a necklace, entwining it   shining with large pearls   and to put little pearls at the end.

I will make a clasp by correcting it   arranging the pearls on every side and let me call its name *Inkishafi*   so that the darkness of sins be withdrawn from me.

May the darkness of ignorance be effaced   and light and radiance give forth brightness   and whosoever reflects (on what I write) let it be pardon to him who repents.

My preface is now ended   I wish to give counsel to my heart which is overcome by the lusts of the world   with the wiles of Satan which deceive.

O my heart, why dost thou not awake?   but what is it that deceives thee?   Thou dost not explain to me for me to discern it if it have a countenance may I not reject it?

O my heart, why dost thou not explain it?   Let us say thou art clever to discriminate   but knowest thou not that the world is vanity?   Why dost thou follow its turmoiled paths?

This world is a raging sea   it has coral reefs and much insubordination   who rides it knows it is a tyrant   responsible for every loss.

It is like a well without a bottom   a place where the tossing bull who approaches it breaks his horns   without succeeding at all in drinking its water.

Or look at the dust in a ray of light   when the sun rises   if one gets near to grasp it   he sees nothing he can hold on to.

Or look at the mirage when it glistens   when the sun is at the meridian   the thirsty one says, There is water   and runs to take of it.

When he goes he finds only the sun's fire   not the water he wants, so

---

[46] Conventions of Muslim poetry call for setting forth the attributes of Allah, followed by praise for Muhammad and his companions.

he rends himself   gaining nothing but trouble   and so
  it is unceasing remorse for him.
All vices and hardships   the difficulties and troubles which you have
  had   they come from this world which you love   with
  its very base condition and its troubles.
The world is corrupt, cleave not unto it   it loves not man but only
  the infidel   How does it come about that you, so able to
  comprehend   should fight with dogs and be thus profaned? [47]
For me it possesses only what is evil   it abounds in much cunning
  it is very fierce at striking a glancing blow   dealing men a
  coup de grâce over and over again.
How many who have passed through this world   enjoying life after
  their fashion   and the world upset their apple-cart (lit.
  their deliberations)   and they fell only to gnaw the finger
  of repentance?
The noose of death met up with them   and they gnawed their fingers
  in remorse   and their world obliterated them   saying,
  Depart, keep away from me.
The world says, Get going, this is it   this is the end of further tarrying
  The merchandise of pride and arrogance   you have dealt
  in it, I can witness.
The arrow of death pierces them   death enters deep into their mortal
  flesh   Don't let the wide-mouthed be so aghast   saying, Who is it? what has happened?
Rendering up their lives   the depriver of pleasure (death) walks with
  them   without so much as a cougher who coughs   nor
  one who from the Journey can refrain.
How many alarums were alerted   You were warned but you were not
  ready   When will you stop this presumption?   Tell me
  the end of it and listen.
By this my beard, O heart   thou art not converted by my counsel
  thou dost barter thy future life to the world   by too much
  deception and you have chosen it.
Listen well to what I tell you   O soul, behold, a lantern in the wind
  nothing can prevent its being put out   at once you see it
  has been extinguished.
Or look at the roaring fire   in the forest-glade in the thickets   a
  cloud comes down in the hot season   and the fire is put
  right out and you cannot revive it.

---

[47] Dogs are often regarded as unclean in the Islamic world.

O heart, kneel prostrate before Him   Come then, please take heed
    lest the accursed Satan laugh at you   and tomorrow see
    you even as he is himself.

This world that thou desirest   what is its good that you so love   it
    has no eternal quality, it does not last   If thou hadst do-
    minion (over it) what wouldst thou do with it?

Was not the prophet Solomon[48]   ruler of men and of jinns   yet
    did not earth banish him and cheat him?   If it were an-
    other, what then would earth do to him?

How many children (of earth) have you seen   and been certain of
    their subsequent happiness   but now the houses of the
    earth (i.e. graves) enfold them   in the sepulchre which en-
    shrouds them?

How many rich men have you seen   who shone like the sun   who
    had control of the weapons of war   and stored up silver
    and gold?

All the world paid them homage   and their world was straight ahead
    for them   they walked with heads held disdainfully   and
    eyes closed in scorn.

Swinging their arms and arching their necks   while behind and in
    front crowds accompanied them   everywhere they live
    there are seats of honour   and troops of soldiers attend
    them.

Their lighted houses were aglow   with lamps of crystal and brass
    the nights were as the day   beauty and honour surrounded
    them.

They decorated their houses with choice porcelain   and every goblet
    was engraved   and in the midst they put crystal pitchers
    amongst the decorations that glittered.

The rails for the decorations to please the eye   I swear by God the
    All-Wealthy   were of teak and of ebony   placed rank
    upon rank in order to look fine.

The mens' halls hummed with chatter   and the harem chambers rang
    out with laughter   with noise of talk from slaves and ser-
    vants   merriment and shouts of joy waxed loud.

And while they lay down for rest   they had masseurs and fanners
    and gay-robed women, the minstrels   singing melodies
    ceaselessly.

---

[48] In the Islamic tradition, the biblical King Solomon is regarded as one of the major
prophets and the mightiest monarch who ever ruled in this world.

On lovely couches well-chosen   upon beds of padded cushions
    with pillows of green at head and foot   worked with
    braided skein.

Folded fabrics they arranged   above the divans to cover them   they
    were sprinkled with rose-water   attar and sandal-wood
    they anointed themselves with these.

Yet even though wealth has its boasting   they were taken on the great
    Journey   and descended to the mansions of the grave
    where the crumbling earth demolished them.

Now they lie in a town of finger's span   with no fine curtains nor
    cushions   and their bodies are destroyed   for the con-
    straint of the grave has come upon them.

Their perspiration is at an end   the pus and the blood oozes out of
    them   maggots pass down through noses and mouths
    the beauty and the countenances are transformed.

They have all become food for insects   who eat their bodies   the
    termites and the ants lay them waste   and the snake and
    the scorpion have them encoiled.

Their radiant faces are become dark-hued   the likeness of a bear or of
    a baboon   their skins are lacerated   their bones and
    flesh are shrivelled.

Their lighted mansions are uninhabited   the young of bats cling up
    above   you hear no whisperings nor shoutings   spiders
    crawl over the beds.

The wall-niches for porcelain in the houses   are now the resting-place
    for nestlings   owls hoot within the house   mannikin
    birds and ducks dwell within.

Young vultures perch on the rails   and young doves arch their necks
    and flap their wings in lazy fashion   wild pigeons and
    swallows have built there.

In the houses the cockroach rustles   the cricket calls in the mens' halls
    stilled is the hum in the ante-rooms   for silence and dark-
    ness encloses all.

The courtyards are overgrown with bush   with lots of weeds and liana
    people fear the outside doors   for silence and darkness
    cover them.

If you do not believe and say it is a lie   go to their houses and turn
    your neck   if you call you get no reply but an echo
    the voice of men has come to an end.

O heart, you have not yet understood   when alarums come, are you
    not perturbed?   yet you have ears to hear   I consider,
    for these matters which follow.

So now, my heart, for your part I will ask you also   explain to me entirely so that I can understand   Where are the parents who bore you?   tell me where they are, that I may greet them.

Where now is Ali b. Nasir[49]   and his brother-in-law Abu Bakr and Sharifs Aidarus[50] and Muhadhar?   where did they go yonder?   show me the way they went.

I tell you so listen to me   they have been made mock of in the darkest of mansions   where there is no light nor brightness   these are the resting-places to which they have descended.

Where is Kiungu and those who filled the halls?   and the good Shaikhs of Sarambi?[51]   they sleep in the mansions of the dust   the grave-boards strain hard upon them.

Where are the brave men of Pate sultanate   men of noble and shining mien?   they have been forced into the mansions of the eternal sands   sovereignty and might have been removed from them.

There were lords and viziers   who went with troops of soldiery wide-yawning graves opened up for them   the fetters of death enshackled them.

There were judges, dispensers of justice   students of books who proved things   leaders of people in the right paths   yet they were called and all have answered.

Ah me, where are the dove-like women[52]   balm for the eyes, soothers of passions?   they are all gone and departed   now they have gone and faded right away.

O heart, these things of men I state   the Pen of God has written their fate (lit. got them)   and you, for certain, will be even as they   unless you have your own belief, Islam, to which you hold fast.

O heart, beware, be not a firebrand   abandon false pride, hold to the right   your friends are saved, so be thou saved also   lest

---

[49] The poet's father.

[50] Aidarus (or Idarusi) was the first known poet who used Swahili for artistic expression (excluding the semilegendary Liongo); he lived a century and half before his descendant, Saiyid Abdallah who wrote this fierce meditation.

[51] The Swahili name of the meter of this poem, *kisarambe,* is also the name of the great hall in which the sultans of Pate used to give audience to their people — the same hall in which the poems in *kisarambe* meter were recited to royal listeners. The rulers, called "shaikh" (shah) in this strophe, claim descent from the Persians whose great epic by Firdowsi (see Volume II, Selection 12) is titled *Shahnama.* The *Shahnama* was written in a meter of eleven syllables per line, the same as this *kisarambe* meter.

[52] Sweethearts are conventionally associated with doves.

the fire of Hell take you.

Know that earth's day shall be changed   and the seven heavens will be
moved from their place   the moon will be stilled and the
sun   but fire and heat will not cease from us.

The day of the burning spleens inwardly   and people's roofs being
torn off,   where will you flee for succour?   show me a
refuge that I can depend on it as well.

Consider the day when the multitudes shall stand   for every deed to
be revealed   the time when the oppressed shall bend the
knee   saying, O Lord, judge between him and me.

Judge me, for this man has oppressed me   by your judgement which
is strict   and God the All-Powerful will judge   As he
did him ill, so shall he pay.

The recompense for them who are oppressed   is not the nugget-gold
nor washed gold   they take no money though they be
given it   in nought but virtue is their payment.

And he who has neither merit nor reward   is fastened by the jaw like
unto a horse   and is made to carry the sins of the oppressed   and is told, Come on, carry them for him.

O heart, take thought of Jahannam[53] with its chains and ropings
when the Judge doth proclaim to it   it says, I am here, let
me give forth answering cry.

Cometh the trumpet's fearsome blast   sounding like the voice of an
ass   the sinner cringes, with the face of an ape   the fire
and the flames engulf him.

Then there is Hawiya, listen hard   it is a fierce fire, it has no repose
when the rebel enters it he tastes conflict   he finds his
breath fail him.

The fire of Sairi, understand it well   it is a fierce fire in flames
there is much smoke and bubbling   serpents and pythons
dwell there.

And the fire of Ladha, also, listen   if cast in that fire at once you burn
you find that lumps of flesh come off   you see your joints
split apart.

Know again about this same Hutama   its glowing fire with its roaring
it breaks the bones, it rives the flesh   the brains and pus
gush out.

Now I will end, now I put the ending   he who follows and attends
these words   shall gain at length a good end   O Lord,
we pray Thee, grant us this.

---

[53] One of the degrees of the Muslim hell, as are references to Hawiya, Sairi, Ladha, and
Hutma mentioned later.

O Lord, bless him who is the composer of this poem   and he who has
  finished these verses is a humble bard   Prayer and peace
  be their safeguards who read them   O Lord, let thy favour
  come down to them.[54]

POET'S LAMENT ON THE DEATH
OF HIS WIFE
[Somali, from Somalia]
Raage Ugaas[55]

Like the *yu'ub*[56] wood bell tied to gelded camels that are running away,
Or like camels which are being separated from their young,
Or like people journeying while moving camp,
Or like a well which has broken its sides or a river which has overflowed
  its banks,
Or like an old woman whose only son was killed,
Or like the poor, dividing the scraps for their frugal meal,
Or like the bees entering their hive, or food crackling in the frying,
Yesterday my lamentations drove sleep from all the camps.
Have I been left bereft in my house and shelter?
Has the envy of others been miraculously fulfilled?

THE DEATH OF RICHARD CORFIELD[57]
[Somali, from Somalia]
Mohammad Abdille Hasan

You have died, Corfield, and are no longer in this world,
A merciless journey was your portion.
When, Hell-destined, you set out for the Other World
Those who have gone to Heaven will question you, if God is willing;
When you see the companions of the faithful and the jewels of Heaven,

---

[54] The last two verses are often considered later interpolations.

[55] A nineteenth-century Somali poet.

[56] A Somali tree.

Answer them how God tried you.

Say to them:[58] "From that day to this the Dervishes never ceased their assaults upon us.

The British were broken, the noise of battle engulfed us;

With fervour and faith the Dervishes attacked us."

Say: "They attacked us at mid-morning."

Say: "Yesterday in the holy war a bullet from one of their old rifles struck me.

And the bullet struck me in the arm."

Say: "In fury they fell upon us."

Report how savagely their swords tore you,

Show these past generations in how many places the daggers were plunged.

Say: "'Friend,' I called, 'have compassion and spare me!'"

Say: "As I looked fearfully from side to side my heart was plucked from its sheath."

Say: "My eyes stiffened as I watched with horror;

The mercy I implored was not granted."

Say: "Striking with spear-butts at my mouth they silenced my soft words;

My ears, straining for deliverance, found nothing;

The risk I took, the mistake I made, cost my life"

Say: "Like the war leaders of old, I cherished great plans for victory."

Say: "The schemes the djinns planted in me brought my ruin."

Say: "When pain racked me everywhere

Men lay sleepless at my shrieks."

Say: "Great shouts acclaimed the departing of my soul."

Say: "Beasts of prey have eaten my flesh and torn it apart for meat."

Say: "The sound of swallowing the flesh and the fat comes from the hyena."

Say: "The crows plucked out my veins and tendons."

Say: "If stubborn denials are to be abandoned, then my clansmen were defeated."

In the last stand of resistance there is always great slaughter.

Say: "The Dervishes are like the advancing thunderbolts of a storm, rumbling and roaring."

---

[57] Richard Corfield led a British force against the Somali "Dervishes," or clans opposed to British rule. He died in the battle of Dul Madoobe, struck in the head by a Dervish bullet. The poem was composed by Sheikh Mohammad Abdille Hasan shortly after the news of the battle was reported to him.

[58] The use of "Say" to begin this and the following echoes the style found in the *Koran*.

LAMENT FOR A DEAD LOVER
[Somali, from Somalia]
Siraad Haad

You are the fence standing between our land and the descendants of 'Ali,
Now in your departure you are the sky which gives no rain while mist
　　　shrouds the world,
The moon that shines no more,
The risen sun extinguished,
The dates on their way from Basra cut off by the seas.

38

ॐ

AFRICAN-AMERICAN TALES

From the seventeenth to the mid-nineteenth centuries the oral tradition in African-American culture provided one of the means for the original African traditions to be handed down, while at the same time undergoing transformation under the impress of slavery. As a result of the meeting of African and American cultures, the stories that emerged contained familiar African themes and faces, such as the trickster, now placed in a new context. We see characters like John (sometimes called Little John, or John de Conquer) outwitting stronger figures or masters, just as a trickster hare called Leuk outwitted lions or elephants in Wolof tales from Senegal. In one of our tales from Africa (Uganda), we see a similar version of Hare outwit the more handsome Hornbill (Selection 36). What is often different in African-American tales is that the trickster is ultimately portrayed as one who takes charge of his fate, overcoming not only gullible bullies but also Old Massa, the slave owner. The trickster in African tales, on the other hand, is not an underdog or a figure standing for an oppressed people; he (usually a male) more typically embodies cleverness and power joined together, at times represented by divine figures like the Yoruba God Eshu who determines the direction of people's lives (see Selection 36).

In addition to having clever plot twists, role reversals and empowering or liberating conclusions, these African-American tales also highlight the play of language, often expressed through exaggeration, verbal contests, and turns of speech that emphasize the uniqueness and difference of black English. The language itself is the strongest testimony to the creation of a new culture, often molded under the duress of struggle and anguish. Lying underneath that new culture, but still discernible, is to be found much of the African substratum, carrying on the values, the memories, and the worldviews of the past. We see this in the powerful short tale, "The Terrapin That Could Talk," in which the warning against the dangers of foolish or unreflective speech, has exact counterparts in African tales.

In the African-American stories that follow we see the most famous of tricksters, Br'er Rabbit, fooled by the tar baby in one, and teaching Br'er Bear a lesson in another. The Terrapin (turtle) story is a typical explanatory tale that not

561

only conveys communal values by exposing the selfishness of the turtle, and the stress of needing to have enough food, but provides the explanation for why the turtle's shell is striated. The tales about Africans flying contain a common folk motif, expressive of the yearning for power and homeland. Finally, many tales of spirits not included here evoke a dislocated African spirituality, marked by its original sense of awesome dread of the otherworldly realm, but without the signposts of familiar deities or rituals to regulate the intercourse between human and divine.

TAR BABY

Rabbit says to himself, "Gee, it's gittin' dry here; can't git any mo' water. Git a little in the mornin' but that ain't enough." So he goes along an' gits the gang to dig a well. So the Fox goes roun' an' calls all the animals together to dig this well. He gits Possum, Coon, Bear, an' all the animals an' they start to dig the well. So they come to Rabbit to help. Rabbit he sick. They say, "Come on, Brother Rabbit, help dig this well; we all need water." Rabbit say, "Oh the devil, I don't need no water; I kin drink dew." So he wouldn't go. So when the well was done Rabbit he was the first one to git some of the water. He went there at night an' git de water in jugs. The other animals see Rabbit's tracks from gittin' water in jugs. So all the animals git together an' see what they goin' to do about Brother Rabbit. So Bear say, "I tell you, I'll lay here an' watch for it. I'll ketch that Rabbit." So Bear watched but Rabbit was too fast for him. So Fox said, "I tell you, let's study a plan to git Brother Rabbit." So they all sit together an' study a plan. So they made a tar baby an' put it up by the well. So Brother Rabbit come along to git some water. He see the tar baby an' think it is Brother Bear. He say, "Can't git any water tonight; there's Brother Bear layin' for me." He looked some more, then he said, "No, that ain't Brother Bear, he's too little for Brother Bear." So he goes up to the tar baby an' say, "Whoo-oo-oo-oo." Tar Baby didn't move. So Rabbit got skeered. He sneaked up to it an' said, "Boo!" Tar Baby didn't move. Then Rabbit run all aroun' an' stood still to see did he move. But Tar Baby kept still. Then he moved

"Tar Baby," recorded by Elsie Clews Parson, *Journal of American Folklore* (1922:35), pp. 256–257; "Rabbit Teaches Bear a Song" and "T'appin (Terrapin)," The American Folklore Society, reprinted in *The Book of Negro Folklore*, eds. Langston Hughes and Arna Bontemps, published by Dodd, Mead and Company, 1958, pp. 3–4, 20–23. "The Terrapin That Could Talk," from the Slave Narrative Collection of the Federal Writers' Project, reprinted in *Lay My Burden Down*, edited by B. A. Botkin, University of Chicago Press. 1945, pp. 4–5, 7. "All God's Chillen Had Wings," in *The Doctor to the Dead*, collected and copyright by John Bennet, 1945, pp. 139–142, reprinted by permission of University of South Carolina Press.

his claw at him. Tar Baby stood still. Rabbit said, "That must be a chunk o' wood." He went up to see if it was a man. He said, "Hello, old man, hello, old man, what you doin' here?" The man didn't answer, He said again, "Hello, old man, hello, old man, what you doin' here?" The man didn't answer. Rabbit said, "Don't you hear me talkin' to you? I'll slap you in the face." The man ain't said nothin'. So Rabbit hauled off sure enough an' his paw stuck. Rabbit said, "Turn me loose, turn me loose or I'll hit you with the other paw." The man ain't said nothin'. So Rabbit hauled off with his other paw an' that one stuck too. Rabbit said, "You better turn me loose, I'll kick you if you don't turn me loose." Tar Baby didn't say anything. "Bup!" Rabbit kicked Tar Baby an' his paw stuck. So he hit him with the other an' that one got stuck. Rabbit said, "I know the things got blowed up now; I know if I butt you I'll kill you." So all the animals were hidin' in the grass watchin' all this. They all ran out an' hollered, "Aha, we knowed we was gonna ketch you, we knowed we was gonna ketch you." So Rabbit said, "Oh, I'm so sick." So the animals said, "Whut we gonna do?" So they has a great meetin' to see what they gonna do. So someone said, "Throw him in the fire." But others said, "No, that's too good; can't let him off that easy." So Rabbit pleaded an' pleaded, "Oh, please, please throw me into the fire." So someone said, "Hang him." They all said, "He's too light, he wouldn't break his own neck." So a resolution was drawed up to burn him up. So they all went to Brother Rabbit an' said, "Well, today you die. We gonna set you on fire." So Rabbit said, "Aw, you couldn't give me anything better." So they all say, "We better throw him in the briar patch." Rabbit cry out right away, "Oh, for God's sake, don't do dat. They tear me feet all up; they tear me behind all up; they tear me eyes out." So they pick him up an' throw him in the briar patch. Rabbit run off an' cry, "Whup-pee, my God, you couldn't throw me in a better place! There where my mammy born me, in the briar patch."

RABBIT TEACHES BEAR A SONG

Br'er Rabbit. . . . This rabbit an' Bear goin' to see a Miss Reyford's daughter. N'Br'er Rabbit been killin' Miss Reyford's hogs. Miss Reyford didn't know he was killin' her hogs. She said to him, "If you tell me who been killin' my hogs I'll give you my daughter." N' so he said he'd go an' find out. He went to Mr. Bear an' said, "They's some ladies down here an' they're givin' a social. Y'know, you have a wonderful voice, an' they want you to sing a bass solo." So Bear he felt real proud an' he said, "All right." So Rabbit said, "I'm gonna try to train your voice. Now you just listen to me an' do everything I tell you." So Bear said, "All right." So Rabbit said, "Now I'm gonna sing a song. Listen to me. When I say these lines:

> Who killed Mr. Reyford's hogs,
> Who killed Mr. Reyford's hogs?

you just sing back:

Nobody but me.

So Br'er Rabbit started singing:

> Who killed Mr. Reyford's hogs,
> Who killed Mr. Reyford's hogs?

Then Bear answered back:

> Nobody but me.

Rabbit said, "That's right, Br'er Bear, that's, fine. My, but you got one fine voice." So ol' Bear he felt real good, 'cause Rabbit flatterin' him, tellin' him that his voice was such a wonderful one. So they went up there to Miss Reyford's party an' pretty soon Rabbit an' Bear commence to sing. Rabbit sang:

> Who killed Mr. Reyford's hogs,
> Who killed Mr. Reyford's hogs?

an' Bear sang out:

> Nobody but me.

So Mr. Reyford shot Bear. Then Rabbit said to Miss Reyford, "I told you Mr. Bear killed your hogs." Bear said to Rabbit, "All right, I'll git you." Ol' Rabbit jes' grin. So later Bear caught him n' tol' him he was gonna kill him. So Rabbit said, "Please don't kill me, please don't kill me." So Rabbit said he'd show him some honey. So Rabbit carried Bear to some honey. He said, "Here's the honey." The bees started on Bear an' Bear started hollerin', but Rabbit he yelled, "Taint nothin' but the briars, 'taint nothin' but the briars." So Bear got killed by the bees.

T'APPIN (TERRAPIN)

It was famine time an' T'appin had six chillun. Eagle hide behin' cloud an' he went crossed de ocean an' go gittin' de palm oil; got de seed to feed his chillun wid it. T'appin see it, say, "hol' on, it har' time. Where you git all dat to feed your t'ree chillun? I got six chillun, can't you show me wha' you git all dat food?" Eagle say, "No, I had to fly 'cross de ocean to git dat." T'appin say, "Well, gimme some o' you wings an' I'll go wid you." Eagle say, "A' right. When shall we go?" T'appin say, "Morrow mornin' by de firs' cock crow." So 'morrow came but T'appin didn' wait till mornin'. T'ree 'clock in de mornin' T'appin come in fron' Eagle's house say, "Cuckoo—cuckoo—coo." Eagle say, "Oh, you go home. Lay down. 'Taint day yit." But he kep' on, "Cuckoo—cuckoo—coo." An bless de Lor' Eagle got out, say, "Wha' you do now?" T'appin say, "You put t'ree wings on this side an' t'ree on udda side." Eagle pull out six feathers an' put t'ree on one side an' t'ree on de udda. Say, "Fly, le's see." So T'appin commence to fly. One o' de wings fall out. But T'appin said, "Da's all right, I got de udda wings. Le's go."

So dey flew an' flew; but when dey got over de ocean all de eagle wings fell out. T'appin about to fall in de water. Eagle went out an' ketch him. Put him under his wings. T'appin say, "Gee it stink here." Eagle let him drop in ocean. So he went down, down, down to de underworl'. De king o' de underworl' meet him. He say, "Why you come here? Wha' you doin' here?" T'appin say, "King, we in te'bul condition on de earth. We can't git nothin' to eat. I got six chillun an' I can't git nothin' to eat for dem. Eagle he on'y got t'ree an' he go 'cross de ocean an' git all de food he need. Please gimme sumpin' so I kin feed my chillun." King say, "A' right, a' right," so he go an' give T'appin a dipper. He say to T'appin, "Take dis dipper. When you want food for your chillun say:

> Bakon coleh
> Bakon cawbey
> Bakon cawhubo lebe lebe."

So T'appin carry it home an' go to de chillun. He say to dem, "Come here." When dey all come he say:

> Bakon coleh
> Bakon cawbey
> Bakon cawhubo lebe lebe.

Gravy, meat, biscuit, ever'ting in de dipper. Chillun got plenty now. So one time he say to de chillun, "Come here. Dis will make my fortune. I'll sell dis to de King." So he showed de dipper to de King. He say:

> Bakon coleh
> Bakon cawbey
> Bakon cawhubo lebe lebe.

Dey got somet'ing. He feed ev'ryone. So de King went off, he call ev'ryboda. Pretty soon ev'ryboda eatin'. So dey ate an' ate, ev'ryt'ing, meats, fruits, all like dat. So he took his dipper an' went back home. He say, "Come, chillun." He try to feed his chillun; nothin' came. (You got a pencil dere, ain't you?) When it's out it's out. So T'appin say, "Aw right, I'm going back to de King an' git him to fixa dis up." So he went down to de underworl' an' say to de King, "King, wha' de matter? I can't feeda my chillun no mora." So de King say to him, "You take dis cow hide an' when you want somepin' you say:

> Sheet n oun
> n-jacko
> nou o quaako.

So T'appin went off an' he came to cross roads. Den he said de magic:

> Sheet n oun
> n-jacko
> nou o quaako.

De cowhide commence to beat um. It beat, beat. Cowhide said, "Drop, drop." So T'appin droup an' de cowhide stop beatin'. So he went home. He called his chillun in. He gim um de cowhide an' tell dem what to say, den he went out. De chillun say:

> Sheet n oun
> n-jacko
> nou o quaako.

De cowhide beat de chillun. It say, "Drop, drop." Two chillun dead an' de others sick. So T'appin say, "I will go to de King." He calls de King, he call all de people. All de people came. So before he have de cowhide beat, he has a mortar made an' gits in dere an' gits all covered up. Den de King say:

> Sheet n oun
> n-jacko
> nou o quaako.

So de cowhide beat, beat. It beat ev'ryboda, beat de King too. Dat cowhide beat, beat, beat right t'roo de mortar wha' was T'appin an' beat marks on his back, an' da's why you never fin' T'appin in a clean place, on'y under leaves or a log.

THE TERRAPIN THAT COULD TALK

This nigger went down to the spring and found a terrapin, and he say, "What brung you here?" Just imagine how he felt when it say to him, "Teeth and tongue bring me here, and teeth and tongue will bring you here." He run to the house and told his master that he found a terrapin that could talk. They went back, and he asked the terrapin what bring him here and it wouldn't say a word. Old Master didn't like it 'cause he went down there just to see a common ordinary terrapin, and he told the nigger he was going to get into trouble for telling him a lie. Next day the nigger seen the terrapin and it say the same thing again. Soon after that this nigger was lynched right close to the place he saw the terrapin.

ALL GOD'S CHILLEN HAD WINGS

Once all Africans could fly like birds; but owing to their many transgressions, their wings were taken away. There remained, here and there, in the sea islands and out-of-the-way places in the low country, some who had been overlooked, and had retained the power of flight, though they looked like other men.

There was a cruel master on one of the sea islands who worked his people till they died. When they died he bought others to take their places. These also he killed with overwork in the burning summer sun, through the middle hours of the day, although this was against the law.

One day, when all the worn-out Negroes were dead of overwork, he bought, of a broker in the town, a company of native Africans just brought into the country, and put them at once to work in the cottonfield.

He drove them hard. They went to work at sunrise and did not stop until dark. They were driven with unsparing harshness all day long, men, women, and children. There was no pause for rest during the unendurable heat of the midsummer noon, though trees were plenty and near. But through the hardest hours, when fair plantations gave their Negroes rest, this man's driver pushed the work along without a moment's stop for breath, until all grew weak with heat and thirst.

There was among them one young woman who had lately borne a child. It was her first; she had not fully recovered from bearing, and should not have been sent to the field until her strength had come back. She had her child with her, as the other women had, astraddle on her hip, or piggyback.

The baby cried. She spoke to quiet it. The driver could not understand her words. She took her breast with her hand and threw it over her shoulder that the child might suck and be content. Then she went back to chopping knot-grass; but being very weak, and sick with the great heat, she stumbled, slipped and fell.

The driver struck her with his lash until she rose and staggered on.

She spoke to an old man near her, the oldest man of them all, tall and strong, with a forked beard. He replied; but the driver could not understand what they said; their talk was strange to him.

She returned to work; but in a little while she fell again. Again the driver lashed her until she got to her feet. Again she spoke to the old man. But he said, "Not yet, daughter; not yet." So she went on working, though she was very ill.

Soon she stumbled and fell again. But when the driver came running with his lash to drive her on with her work, she turned to the old man and asked: "Is it time yet, daddy?" He answered: "Yes, daughter; the time has come. Go; and peace be with you!" . . . and stretched out his arms toward her . . . so.

With that she leaped straight into the air and was gone like a bird, flying over field and wood.

The driver and overseer ran after her as far as the edge of the field; but she was gone, high over their heads, over the fence, and over the top of the woods, gone, with her baby astraddle of her hip, sucking at her breast.

Then the driver hurried the rest to make up for her loss; and the sun was very hot indeed. So hot that soon a man fell down. The overseer himself lashed him to his feet. As he got up from where he had fallen the old man called to him in an unknown tongue. My grandfather told me the words that he said; but it was a long time ago, and I have forgotten them. But when he had spoken, the man turned and laughed at the overseer, and leaped up into the air, and was gone, like a gull, flying over field and wood.

Soon another man fell. The driver lashed him. He turned to the old man. The old man cried out to him, and stretched out his arms as he had done for the other two; and he, like them, leaped up, and was gone through the air, flying like a bird over field and wood.

Then the overseer cried to the driver, and the master cried to them both: "Beat the old devil! He is the doer!"

The overseer and the driver ran at the old man with lashes ready; and the master ran too, with a picket pulled from the fence, to beat the life out of the old man who had made those Negroes fly.

But the old man laughed in their faces, and said something loudly to all the Negroes in the field, the new Negroes and the old Negroes.

And as he spoke to them they all remembered what they had forgotten, and recalled the power which once had been theirs. Then all the Negroes, old and new, stood up together; the old man raised his hands; and they all leaped up into the air with a great shout; and in a moment were gone, flying, like a flock of crows, over the field, over the fence, and over the top of the wood; and behind them flew the old man.

The men went clapping their hands; and the women went singing; and those who had children gave them their breasts; and the children laughed and sucked as their mothers flew, and were not afraid.

The master, the overseer, and the driver looked after them as they flew, beyond the wood, beyond the river, miles on miles, until they passed beyond the last rim of the world and disappeared in the sky like a handful of leaves. They were never seen again.

Where they went I do not know; I never was told. Nor what it was that the old man said . . . that I have forgotten. But as he went over the last fence he made a sign in the master's face, and cried "Kuli-ba! Kuli-ba!" I don't know what that means.

But if I could only find the old wood sawyer, he could tell you more; for he was there at the time, and saw the Africans fly away with their women and children. He is an old, old man, over ninety years of age, and remembers a great many strange things.

As told by Caesar Grant, of John's Island, carter and laborer.

39

☙

Jean-Jacques Rousseau

ÉMILE

"*M*an *is born free, and everywhere he is in chains"—this celebrated epigram from Jean-Jacques Rousseau's* The Social Contract *(1762) has been repeated by reformers and revolutionaries for over two centuries. Indeed, Rousseau's influence on late eighteenth-century social thought, and on events such as the French Revolution and the romantic movement in literature, was profound and continues to this day.*

Rousseau (1712–1778) was born in Geneva, Switzerland. His mother died in childbirth, and he was raised by his father and by an aunt. At sixteen, he left Geneva and led an unsettled life until he arrived in the province of Savoy and come under the protection of Madame de Warens, a Swiss convert to Catholicism and a patroness of the arts. De Warens, who became his lover, also influenced Rousseau's conversion from the Calvinism of his family to Catholicism. The relationship with de Warens also developed Rousseau's latent talents in music, literature, and philosophy.

In 1742, Rousseau moved to Paris, where a new system of musical notation he had developed attracted the attention of Denis Diderot. Diderot invited him to contribute articles on music to the Encyclopédie. *The latter was not only the first modern encyclopedia, but also an organ for the politically radical and anticlerical opinions of the intellectuals who contributed to it, such as Voltaire (Selection 30) and d'Alembert. With his eloquent and forceful style, Rousseau soon became one of the* Encyclopédie's *leading lights. Rousseau also wrote music, and his opera* Le Devin du village (The Cunning Man or The Village Soothsayer, 1752) *was greatly admired at the court of the French monarch and even influenced the young Mozart. But Rousseau had scant interest in fame, and work for the theatre did not appeal to his growing sense of moralism and his rejection of worldly values.*

In 1745, Rousseau met an unlettered servant girl, Thérèse Levasseur, with whom he fathered a number of illegitimate children whom he abandoned to an orphanage. In 1745 he reconverted to Protestantism. He had recently published his first book, Discourse on the Sciences and the Arts *(1750), in which he argued that civilization had entered a period of decline due to an excess of refinement. He followed up on this idea in his* Discourse on the Origin of Inequality *(1755), where he developed the proposition that man was inherently good but had descended from primitive innocence to corrupt sophistication. That is, the growth of civilization had corrupted man's natural goodness.*

In 1762, he published two of his most influential books, The Social Contract *and* Émile, or On Education. *The first was concerned with the means whereby, after losing their freedom to coercive and unjust forms of social organization, men might recover their liberty through obedience to a self-imposed law in a republican system of government. In* Émile, *Rousseau set out to test how future citizens could be formed by means of the education of children. The book takes the form of a pedagogical novel in five parts, telling of the education of Émile, a solitary boy, by a wise tutor. The fifth part is devoted to the education of Sophie, Émile's future partner, who is brought up to play a secondary, supportive role. Rousseau's fundamental argument in this book is that vice and error are alien to a child's nature, and that educators must work with nature, and not against it, to further the child's natural inclination towards virtue. Rousseau's "progressive" theories of experiential "natural" education would exert great influence on such important educators as the Swiss Pestalozzi, the Italian Montessori, and the American Dewey.*

Throughout the 1750s and 1760s, Rousseau had moved from Paris to Geneva and back, and had even lived for a time in England under the protection of the English philosopher David Hume. Although his novel Julie, or The New Héloïse *(1761) had achieved considerable popularity and influence through its portrayal of emotions and feelings that were freely expressed by the characters, Rousseau's ideas on religion, which amounted to a generalized deism that rejected both biblical authority and rationalist ethics, brought him into conflict with the authorities as well as with some of his more radical philosopher friends. Thus, partly due to real persecution by the authorities in Paris and Geneva, Rousseau's personality began to show symptoms of what today would be classified as paranoia. He quarreled with his friends among the French intellectuals, fled England when he began to suspect that the English intellectuals were secretly mocking him, and finally, believing that she was the only person he could rely on, decided to marry Thérèse in 1768.*

Rousseau spent the last decade of his life under the protection of several French noblemen. He was occupied by his autobiographical writings, all of which were published posthumously, such as Rousseau, Judge of Jean-Jacques *(1780), and most importantly, his* Confessions *(1782–1789), in which he revealed his most intimate feelings. The* Confessions *were partly modeled on those of St. Augustine and have achieved nearly the same classic status. Rousseau died in 1778 in Ermenonville, France. The following selection begins Book One of* Émile, *in which Rousseau explains the natural, social, and psychological foundations of his educational program.*

Everything is good as it leaves the hands of the Author of things; everything degenerates in the hands of man. He forces one soil to nourish the products of another, one tree to bear the fruit of another. He mixes and confuses the climates, the elements, the seasons. He mutilates his dog, his horse, his slave. He turns everything upside down; he disfigures everything; he loves deformity, monsters. He wants nothing as nature made it, not even man; for him, man must be trained like a school horse; man must be fashioned in keeping with his fancy like a tree in his garden.

Were he not to do this, however, everything would go even worse, and our species does not admit of being formed halfway. In the present state of things a man abandoned to himself in the midst of other men from birth would be the most disfigured of all. Prejudices, authority, necessity, example, all the social institutions in which we find ourselves submerged would stifle nature in him and put nothing in its place. Nature there would be like a shrub that chance had caused to be born in the middle of a path and that the passers-by soon cause to perish by bumping into it from all sides and bending it in every direction.

It is you that I address myself, tender and foresighted mother,* who are capable of keeping the nascent shrub away from the highway and securing it from the

---

From *Émile, or On Education* by Jean-Jacques Rousseau, by Alan Bloom, translator. Pp. 37–53. Copyright © 1979 by Basic Books, Inc. Reprinted by permission of Basic Books, a member of Perseus Books, L.L.C.

* The first education is the most important, and this first education belongs incontestably to women; if the Author of nature had wanted it to belong to men, He would have given them milk with which to nurse the children. Always speak, then, preferably to women in your treatises on education; for, beyond the fact that they are in a position to watch over it more closely than are men and always have greater influence on it, they also have much more interest in its success, since most widows find themselves almost at the mercy of their children; then their children make mothers keenly aware, for good or ill, of the effect of the way they raised their children. The laws — always so occupied with property and so little with persons, because their object is peace not virtue — do not give enough authority to mothers. However, their status is more certain than that of fathers; their duties are more painful; their cares are more important for the good order of the family; generally they are more attached to the children. There are occasions on which a son who lacks respect for his father can in some way be excused. But if on any occasion whatsoever a child were unnatural enough to lack respect for his mother — for her who carried him in her womb, who nursed him with her milk, who for years forgot herself in favor of caring for him alone — one should hasten to strangle this wretch as a monster unworthy of seeing the light of day. Mothers, it is said, spoil their children. In that they are doubtless wrong — but less wrong than you perhaps who deprave them. The mother wants her child to be happy, happy now. In that she is right. When she is mistaken about the means, she must be enlightened. Fathers' ambition, avarice, tyranny, and false foresight, their negligence, their harsh insensitivity are a hundred times more disastrous for children than is the blind tenderness of mothers. Moreover, the sense I give to the name *mother* must be explained; and that is what will be done hereafter. *[Rousseau's note.]*

impact of human opinions! Cultivate and water the young plant before it dies. Its fruits will one day be your delights. Form an enclosure around your child's soul at an early date. Someone else can draw its circumference, but you alone must build the fence.

Plants are shaped by cultivation, and men by education. It man were born big and strong, his size and strength would be useless to him until he had learned to make use of them. They would be detrimental to him in that they would keep others from thinking of aiding him.* And, abandoned to himself, he would die of want before knowing his needs. And childhood is taken to be a pitiable state! It is not seen that the human race would have perished if man had not begun as a child.

We are born weak, we need strength; we are born totally unprovided, we need aid; we are born stupid, we need judgment. Everything we do not have at our birth and which we need when we are grown is given us by education.

This education comes to us from nature or from men or from things. The internal development of our faculties and our organs is the education of nature. The use that we are taught to make of this development is the education of men. And what we acquire from our own experience about the objects which affect us is the education of things.

Each of us is thus formed by three kinds of masters. The disciple in whom their various lessons are at odds with one another is badly raised and will never be in agreement with himself. He alone in whom they all coincide at the same points and tend to the same ends reaches his goal and lives consistently. He alone is well raised.

Now, of these three different educations, the one coming from nature is in no way in our control; that coming from things is in our control only in certain respects; that coming from men is the only one of which we are truly masters. Even of it we are the masters only by hypothesis. For who can hope entirely to direct the speeches and the deeds of all those surrounding a child?

Therefore, when education becomes an art, it is almost impossible for it to succeed, since the conjunction of the elements necessary to its success is in no one's control. All that one can do by dint of care is to come more or less close to the goal, but to reach it requires luck.

What is that goal? It is the very same as that of nature. This has just been proved. Since the conjunction of the three educations is necessary to their perfection, the two others must be directed toward the one over which we have no power. But perhaps this word *nature* has too vague a sense. An attempt must be made here to settle on its meaning.

---

*Similar to them on the outside and deprived of speech as well as of the ideas it expresses, he would not be in a condition to make them understand the need he had of their help, and nothing in him would manifest this need to them. *[Rousseau's note.]*

Nature, we are told, is only habit. What does that mean? Are there not habits contracted only by force which never do stifle nature? Such, for example, is the habit of the plants whose vertical direction is interfered with. The plant, set free, keeps the inclination it was forced to take. But the sap has not as a result changed its original direction; and if the plant continues to grow, its new growth resumes the vertical direction. The case is the same for men's inclinations. So long as one remains in the same condition, the inclinations which result from habit and are the least natural to us can be kept; but as soon as the situation changes, habit ceases and the natural returns. Education is certainly only habit. Now are there not people who forget and lose their education? Others who keep it? Where does this difference come from? If the name *nature* were limited to habits conformable to nature, we would spare ourselves this garble.

We are born with the use of our senses, and from our birth we are affected in various ways by the objects surrounding us. As soon as we have, so to speak, consciousness of our sensations, we are disposed to seek or avoid the objects which produce them, at first according to whether they are pleasant or unpleasant to us, then according to the conformity or lack of it that we find between us and these objects, and finally according to the judgments we make about them on the basis of the idea of happiness or of perfection given us by reason. These dispositions are extended and strengthened as we become more capable of using our senses and more enlightened; but constrained by our habits, they are more or less corrupted by our opinions. Before this corruption they are what I call in us *nature*.

It is, then, to these original dispositions that everything must be related; and that could be done if our three educations were only different from one another. But what is to be done when they are opposed? When, instead of raising a man for himself, one wants to raise him for others? Then their harmony is impossible. Forced to combat nature or the social institutions, one must choose between making a man or a citizen, for one cannot make both at the same time.

Every particular society, when it is narrow and unified, is estranged from the all-encompassing society. Every patriot is harsh to foreigners. They are only men. They are nothing in his eyes. This is a drawback, inevitable but not compelling. The essential thing is to be good to the people with whom one lives. Abroad, the Spartan was ambitious, avaricious, iniquitous. But disinterestedness, equity, and concord reigned within his walls. Distrust those cosmopolitans who go to great length in their books to discover duties they do not deign to fulfill around them. A philosopher loves the Tartars so as to be spared having to love his neighbors.

Natural man is entirely for himself. He is numerical unity, the absolute whole which is relative only to itself or its kind. Civil man is only a fractional unity dependent on the denominator; his value is determined by his relation to the whole, which is the social body. Good social institutions are those that best know how to denature man, to take his absolute existence from him in order to give him a relative one and transport the *I* into the common unity, with the result that each individual believes himself no longer one but a part of the unity and no longer feels except within the whole. A citizen of Rome was neither Caius nor Lucius; he was a Roman. He even loved the country exclusive of himself. Regulus claimed he was Carthaginian on the grounds that he had become the property of his masters. In his status of foreigner he refused to sit in the Roman senate; a Carthaginian had to order him to do so. He was indignant that they wanted to save his life. He conquered and returned triumphant to die by torture. This has little relation, it seems to me, to the men we know.[1]

The Lacedaemonian Pedaretus runs for the council of three hundred. He is defeated. He goes home delighted that there were three hundred men worthier than he to be found in Sparta. I take this display to be sincere, and there is reason to believe that it was. This is the citizen.[2]

A Spartan woman had five sons in the army and was awaiting news of the battle. A Helot arrives; trembling, she asks him for news. "Your five sons were killed." "Base slave, did I ask you that?" "We won the victory." The mother runs to the temple and gives thanks to the gods. This is the female citizen.[3]

He who in the civil order wants to preserve the primacy of the sentiments of nature does not know what he wants. Always in contradiction with himself, always floating between his inclinations and his duties, he will never be either man or citizen. He will be good neither for himself nor for others. He will be one of these men of our days: a Frenchman, an Englishman, a bourgeois. He will be nothing.

To be something, to be oneself and always one, a man must act as he speaks; he must always be decisive in making his choice, make it in a lofty style, and always stick to it. I am waiting to be shown this marvel so as to know whether he is a man or a citizen, or how he goes about being both at the same time.

From these necessarily opposed objects come two contrary forms of instruction—the one, public and common; the other, individual and domestic.

Do you want to get an idea of public education? Read Plato's *Republic*. It is not at all a political work, as think those who judge books only by their titles. It is the most beautiful educational treatise ever written.

---

[1] Marcus Atilius Regulus was a Roman general and statesman of the third century B.C. In 256 B.C. he defeated the Carthaginian army and navy, but the Carthaginians struck back and defeated and captured him the following year. Sent on parole to Rome to negotiate peace terms and a prisoner exchange, he is said to have convinced the Romans to reject the Carthaginian terms. He returned voluntarily to Carthage, where he died in prison, possibly from torture.

[2] The story of Pedaretus, a citizen of the ancient Greek city-state Sparta, is told in Plutarch's *Lycurgus*, Book 25.

[3] The anecdote of the Spartan mother and the slave messenger is from Plutarch's *Agesilaus*, Book 29.

When one wishes to refer to the land of chimeras, mention is made of Plato's institutions. If Lycurgus had set his down only in writing, I would find them far more chimerical. Plato only purified the heart of man; Lycurgus denatured it.[4]

Public instruction no longer exists and can no longer exist, because where there is no longer fatherland, there can no longer be citizens. These two words, *fatherland* and *citizen,* should be effaced from modern languages. I know well the reason why this is so, but I do not want to tell it. It has nothing to do with my subject.[5]

I do not envisage as a public education those laughable establishments called *colleges.** Nor do I count the education of society, because this education, tending to two contrary ends, fails to attain either. It is fit only for making double men, always appearing to relate everything to others and never relating anything except to themselves alone. Now since these displays are common to everyone, no one is taken in by them. They are so much wasted effort.

From these contradictions is born the one we constantly experience within ourselves. Swept along in contrary routes by nature and by men, forced to divide ourselves between these different impulses, we follow a composite impulse which leads us to neither one goal nor the other. Thus, in conflict and floating during the whole course of our life, we end it without having been able to put ourselves in harmony with ourselves and without having been good either for ourselves or for others.

There remains, finally, domestic education or the education of nature. But what will a man raised uniquely for himself become for others? If perchance the double object we set for ourselves could be joined in a single one by removing the contradictions of man, a great obstacle to his happiness would be removed. In order to judge this, he would have to be seen wholly formed: his inclinations would have to have been observed, his progress seen, his development followed. In a word, the natural man would have to be known. I believe that one will have made a few steps in these researches when one has read this writing.

To form this rare man, what do we have to do? Very much, doubtless. What must be done is to prevent anything from being done. When it is only a question

---

[4]Lycurgus is said to have been the founder of the constitution of Sparta, and the designer of that Greek city-state's rigid social and military structure. Plutarch states that he lived in the early eighth century B.C., although modern scholars doubt his existence.

[5]Rousseau develops his critique of the concepts of "fatherland" and "citizen" in *The Social Contract,* Book 4.

*There are in the academy of Geneva and the University of Paris professors whom I like very much and believe to be very capable of instructing the young well, if they were not forced to follow the established practice. I exhort one among them to publish the project of reform which he has conceived. Perhaps, when it is seen that the ill is not without remedy, there will be a temptation to cure it. [*Rousseau's note.*]

of going against the wind, one tacks. But if the sea is heavy and one wants to stand still, one must cast anchor. Take care, young pilot, for fear that your cable run or your anchor drag and that the vessel drift without your noticing.

In the social order where all positions are determined, each man ought to be raised for his. If an individual formed for his position leaves it, he is no longer fit for anything. Education is useful only insofar as fortune is in agreement with the parents' vocation. In any other case it is harmful to the student, if only by virtue of the prejudices it gives him. In Egypt where the son was obliged to embrace the station of his father, education at least had a sure goal. But among us where only the ranks remain and the men who compose them change constantly, no one knows whether in raising his son for his rank he is not working against him.

In the natural order, since men are all equal, their common calling is man's estate and whoever is well raised for that calling cannot fail to fulfill those callings related to it. Let my student be destined for the sword, the church, the bar. I do not care. Prior to the calling of his parents is nature's call to human life. Living is the job I want to teach him. On leaving my hands, he will, I admit, be neither magistrate nor soldier nor priest. He will, in the first place, be a man. All that a man should be, he will in case of need know how to be as well as anyone; and fortune may try as it may to make him change place, he will always be in his own place. *Occupavi te fortuna atque cepi omnesque aditus tous interclusi, ut ad me aspirare non posses.*[6]

Our true study is that of the human condition. He among us who best knows how to bear the goods and the ills of this life is to my taste the best raised: from which it follows that the true education consists less in precept than in practice. We begin to instruct ourselves when we begin to live. Our education begins with us. Our first preceptor is our nurse. Thus this word *education* had another meaning for the ancients which we no longer give to it. *Educit obsterix,* says Varro, *educat nutrix, instituit pedagogus, docet magister.*[7]

Thus education, instruction, and teaching are three things as different in their object as are the governess, the preceptor, and the master. But these distinctions are ill drawn; and, to be well led, the child should follow only a single guide.

We must, then, generalize our views and consider in our pupil abstract man, man exposed to all the accidents of human life. If men were born attached to a country's soil, if the same season lasted the whole year, if each man were fixed in his fortune in such a way as never to be able to change it—the established prac-

---

[6] "I have caught you, Fortune, and blocked all your means of access, so that you could not get near me." The quote is from Cicero's *Tusculan Disputations,* Book 5.

[7] "The midwife delivers, the nurse feeds, the pedagogue instructs, the master teaches." Varro (116–27 B.C.), was one of the greatest Roman scholars.

tice would be good in certain respects. The child raised for his station, never leaving it, could not be exposed to the disadvantages of another. But given the mobility of human things, given the unsettled and restless spirit of this age which upsets everything in each generation, can one conceive of a method more senseless than raising a child as though he never had to leave his room, as though he were going to be constantly surrounded by his servants? If the unfortunate makes a single step on the earth, if he goes down a single degree, he is lost. This is not teaching him to bear suffering; it is training him to feel it.

One thinks only of preserving one's child. That is not enough. One ought to teach him to preserve himself as a man, to bear the blows of fate, to brave opulence and poverty, to live, if he has to, in freezing Iceland or on Malta's burning rocks. You may very well take precautions against his dying. He will nevertheless have to die. And though his death were not the product of your efforts, still these efforts would be ill conceived. It is less a question of keeping him from dying than of making him live. To live is not to breathe; it is to act; it is to make use of our organs, our senses, our faculties, of all the parts of ourselves which give us the sentiment of our existence. The man who has lived the most is not he who has counted the most years but he who has most felt life. Men have been buried at one hundred who died at their birth. They would have gained from dying young; at least they would have lived up to that time.

All our wisdom consists in servile prejudices. All our practices are only subjection, impediment, and constraint. Civil man is born, lives, and dies in slavery. At his birth he is sewed in swaddling clothes; at his death he is nailed in a coffin. So long as he keeps his human shape, he is enchained by our institutions.

It is said that many midwives claim that by kneading newborn babies' heads, they give them a more suitable shape. And this is tolerated! Our heads are ill fashioned by the Author of our being! We need to have them fashioned on the outside by midwives and on the inside by philosophers. The Caribs[8] are twice as lucky as we are.

> Hardly has the baby emerged from the mother's womb, and hardly has he enjoyed the freedom to move and stretch his limbs before he is given new bonds. He is swaddled, laid out with the head secured and the legs stretched out, the arms hanging beside the body. He is surrounded with linens and trusses of every kind which do not permit him to change position, and he is lucky if he has not been squeezed to the point of being prevented from breathing and if care was taken to lay

---

[8]An American Indian people that originally inhabited parts of the Caribbean and South American coasts. Rousseau regarded them as happily uncorrupted by European civilization.

him on his side in order that the waters that should come out of his mouth can fall by themselves, for he would not have the freedom of turning his head to the side to facilitate the flow.[9]

The newborn baby needs to stretch and move its limbs in order to arouse them from the torpor in which, drawn up in a little ball, they have for so long remained. They are stretched out, it is true, but they are prevented from moving. Even the head is subjected to caps. It seems that we are afraid lest he appear to be alive.

Thus, the impulse of the internal parts of a body which tends to growth finds an insurmountable obstacle to the movements that impulse asks of the body. The baby constantly makes useless efforts which exhaust its forces or retard their progress. He was less cramped, less constrained, less compressed in the amnion than he is in his diapers. I do not see what he gained by being born.

The inaction, the constraint in which a baby's limbs are kept can only hinder the circulation of the blood, of the humors, prevent the baby from fortifying himself, from growing, and cause his constitution to degenerate. In the places where these extravagant precautions are not taken, men are all tall, strong, and well proportioned. The countries where children are swaddled teem with hunchbacks, cripples, men with stunted or withered limbs, men suffering from rickets, men misshapen in every way. For fear that bodies be deformed by free movements, we hurry to deform the children by putting them into a press. We would gladly cripple them to keep them from laming themselves.

Could not so cruel a constraint have an influence on their disposition as well as on their constitution? Their first sentiment is a sentiment of pain and suffering. They find only obstacles to all the movements which they need. Unhappier than a criminal in irons, they make vain efforts, they get irritable, they cry. Their first voices, you say, are tears. I can well believe it. You thwart them from their birth. The first gifts they receive from you are chains. The first treatment they experience is torment. Having nothing free but the voice, how would they not make use of it to complain? They cry because you are hurting them. Thus garroted, you would cry harder than they do.

Where does this unreasonable practice come from? From a denatured practice. Since mothers, despising their first duty, have no longer wanted to feed their children, it has been necessary to confide them to mercenary women who, thus finding themselves mothers of alien children on whose behalf nature tells them nothing, have sought only to save themselves effort. It would be necessary to be

---

[9] This quote is from Buffon's *Histoire naturelle*, Volume 4. George Louis Leclerc, Comte de Buffon (1707–1788) was a French naturalist, whose forty-four volume *Histoire naturelle* (*Natural History*) was one of the most widely read scientific works of the eighteenth century.

constantly watchful over a child in freedom. But when it is well bound, one throws it in a corner without being troubled by its cries. Provided that there be no proofs of negligence on the part of the nurse, provided that her charge does not break an arm or a leg, beyond that what difference does it make that he wastes away or remains infirm for the rest of his days? His limbs are preserved at the expense of his body, and whatever happens, the nurse is exonerated.

Do they know, these gentle mothers who, delivered from their children, devote themselves gaily to the entertainments of the city, what kind of treatment the swaddled child is getting in the meantime in the village? At the slightest trouble that arises he is hung from a nail like a sack of clothes, and while the nurse looks after her business without hurrying, the unfortunate stays thus crucified. All those found in this position had violet faces. The chest was powerfully compressed, blocking circulation, and the blood rose to the head. The sufferer was believed to be tranquil, because he did not have the strength to cry. I do not know how many hours a child can remain in this condition without losing its life, but I doubt that this can go on very long. This is, I think, one of the great advantages of swaddling.

It is claimed that children in freedom could assume bad positions and make movements capable of hurting the good conformation of their limbs. This is one of those vain reasonings of our false wisdom that has never been confirmed by any experience. Of that multitude of children who, among peoples more sensible than us, are reared with complete freedom of their limbs, not a single one is seen who wounds or cripples himself. They could not give their movements sufficient force to make them dangerous; and, when they take a strained position, the pain soon warns them to change it.

We have not yet taken it into our heads to swaddle little dogs or cats. Do we see that they have any problems as a result of this negligence? Children are heavier. Agreed. But they are also proportionately weaker. They can hardly move. How would they cripple themselves? If they were stretched out on their backs, they would die in this position, like the tortoise, without ever being able to turn themselves over.

Not satisfied with having given up nursing their children, women give up wanting to have them. The result is natural. As soon as the condition of motherhood becomes burdensome, the means to deliver oneself from it completely is soon found. They want to perform a useless act so as always to be able to start over again, and they turn to the prejudice of the species the attraction given for the sake of multiplying it. This practice, added to the other causes of depopulation, presages the impending fate of Europe. The sciences, the arts, the philosophy, and the morals that this practice engenders will not be long in making a desert of it. It will be peopled with ferocious beasts. The change of inhabitants will not be great.

I have sometimes seen the little trick of young women who feign to want to nurse their children. They know how to have pressure put on them to give up this whim. Husbands, doctors, especially mothers, are adroitly made to intervene. A husband who dared consent to his wife's nursing her baby would be a man lost.

He would be made into a murderer who wants to get rid of her. Prudent husbands, paternal love must be immolated for the sake of peace; you are fortunate that women more continent than yours can be found in the country, more fortunate yet if the time your wives save is not destined for others than you!

There is no question about the duty of women. But there is dispute as to whether, given the contempt they have for it, it makes any difference for the children to be nursed with the mother's milk or that of another. Let me take this question, of which the doctors are the judges, to be decided just as the women would like. For my part I, too, certainly think that it is preferable for a child to suck the milk of a healthy nurse than of a spoiled mother, if he had some new ill to fear from the same blood out of which he was formed.

But should the question be envisaged only from the physical side, and does the child have less need of a mother's care than of her breast? Other women, even beasts, will be able to give him the milk that she refuses him. There is no substitute for maternal solicitude. She who nurses another's child in place of her own is a bad mother. How will she be a good nurse? She could become one, but slowly; habit would have to change nature; and the child, ill cared for, will have the time to perish a hundred times before his nurse has gained a mother's tenderness for him.

From this very advantage results a drawback which alone should take from every sensitive woman the courage to have her child nursed by another. The drawback is that of sharing a mother's right, or rather of alienating it, of seeing her child love another woman as much as and more than her, of feeling that the tenderness that he preserves for his own mother is a favor and that the tenderness he has for his adoptive mother is a duty. Where I found a mother's care do not I owe a son's attachment?

Their way of remedying this drawback is to inspire contempt in the children for their nurses by treating them as veritable servants. When their service is complete, the child is taken back or the nurse dismissed. By dint of giving her a poor reception, she is discouraged from coming to see her charge. At the end of a few years he no longer sees her, no longer knows her. The mother who believes she replaces the nurse and makes up for her neglect by her cruelty is mistaken. Instead of making a tender son out of a denatured nursling, she trains him in ingratitude, she teaches him one day to despise her who gave him life as well as her who nursed him with her milk.

How I would insist on this point were it not so discouraging to keep raising useful subjects in vain! More depends on this one than is thought. Do you wish to bring everyone back to his first duties? Begin with mothers. You will be surprised by the changes you will produce. Everything follows successively from this first depravity. The whole moral order degenerates; naturalness is extinguished in all hearts; home life takes on a less lively aspect; the touching spectacle of a family aborning no longer attaches husbands, no longer imposes respect on outsiders; the mother whose children one does not see is less respected. One does not reside in one's family; habit does not strengthen the blood ties. There are no longer fathers, mothers, children, brothers, or sisters. They all hardly know each other. How could they love each other? Each thinks only of himself. When home is only a sad solitude, one must surely go elsewhere for gaiety.

But let mothers deign to nurse their children, morals will reform themselves, nature's sentiments will be awakened in every heart, the state will be repeopled. This first point, this point alone, will bring everything back together. The attraction of domestic life is the best counterpoison for bad morals. The bother of children, which is believed to be an importunity, becomes pleasant. It makes the father and mother more necessary, dearer to one another; it tightens the conjugal bond between them. When the family is lively and animated, the domestic cares constitute the dearest occupation of the wife and the sweetest enjoyment of the husband. Thus, from the correction of this single abuse would soon result a general reform; nature would soon have reclaimed all its rights. Let women once again become mothers, men will soon become fathers and husbands again.

Superfluous speeches! The very boredom of worldly pleasures never leads back to these. Women have stopped being mothers; they will no longer be; they no longer want to be. If they should want to be, they hardly could be. Today the contrary practice is established. Each one would have to combat the opposition of every woman who comes near her, all in league against an example that some did not give and the rest do not want to follow.

There are, nevertheless, still sometimes young persons of a good nature who on this point, daring to brave the empire of fashion and the clamors of their sex, fulfill with a virtuous intrepidity this duty so sweet imposed on them by nature. May their number increase as a result of the attraction of the goods destined for those who devote themselves to it! Founded on conclusions given by the simplest reasoning and on observations that I have never seen belied, I dare to promise these worthy mothers a solid and constant attachment on the part of their husbands, a truly filial tenderness on the part of their children, the esteem and respect of the public, easy deliveries without mishap and without aftermath, a firm and vigorous health; finally the pleasure of seeing themselves one day imitated by their own daughters and cited as examples to others' daughters.

No mother, no child. Between them the duties are reciprocal, and if they are ill fulfilled on one side, they will be neglected on the other. The child ought to love his mother before knowing that he ought to. If the voice of blood is not strengthened by habit and care, it is extinguished in the first years, and the heart dies, so to speak, before being born. Here we are, from the first steps, outside of nature.

One leaves it by an opposite route as well when, instead of neglecting a mother's care, a woman carries it to excess; when she makes an idol of her child; when she increases and nurses his weakness in order to prevent him from feeling it; and when, hoping to exempt him from the laws of nature, she keeps hard blows away from him. She preserves him for a moment from a few discomforts without thinking about how many mishaps and perils she is thereby accumulating for him to bear later, and how barbarous a precaution it is which adds childhood's weakness to mature men's toils. Thetis, to make her son invulnerable, plunged him, according to fable, in the water of the Styx.[10] This allegory is a lovely one, and it is clear. The cruel mothers of whom I speak do otherwise: by dint of plunging their children in softness, they prepare them for suffering; they open their pores to ills of every sort to which they will not fail to be prey when grown.

Observe nature and follow the path it maps out for you. It exercises children constantly; it hardens their temperament by tests of all sorts; it teaches them early what effort and pain are. Teething puts them in a fever; sharp colics give them convulsions; long coughs suffocate them; worms torment them; plethora corrupts their blood; various leavens ferment in it and cause perilous eruptions. Almost all the first age is sickness and danger. Half the children born perish before the eighth year. The tests passed, the child has gained strength; and as soon as he can make use of life, its principle becomes sounder.

That is nature's rule. Why do you oppose it? Do you not see that in thinking you correct it, you destroy its product, you impede the effect of its care? To do on the outside what nature does on the inside redoubles the danger, according to you; and, on the contrary, this diverts the danger and weakens it. Experience teaches that even more children raised delicately die than do others. Provided the limit of their strength is not exceeded, less is risked in employing that strength than in sparing it. Exercise them, then, against the attacks they will one day have to bear. Harden their bodies against the intemperance of season, climates, elements; against hunger, thirst, fatigue. Steep them in the water of the Styx. Before the body's habit is acquired, one can give it the habit one wants to give it without danger. But when it has once gained its consistency, every alteration becomes perilous for it. A child will bear changes that a man would not bear; the fibers of the former, soft and flexible, take without effort the turn that they are given; those of the man, more hardened, change only with violence the turn they have received. A child, then, can be made robust without exposing its life and its health; and if there were some risk, still one must not hesitate. Since these are risks inseparable from human life, can one do better than shift them to that part of its span when they are least disadvantageous?

A child becomes more precious as he advances in age. To the value of his person is joined that of the effort he has cost; to the loss of his life is joined in him the sentiment of death. It is, then, especially of the future that one must think in looking after his preservation. It is against the ills of youth that he must be armed

---

[10] In Greek myth the goddess Thetis dipped her only son, Achilles, in the waters of the Styx, a river of the Underworld, attempting to render him immortal.

before he reaches them; for if the value of life increases up to the age of making use of it, what folly is it not to spare childhood some ills while multiplying them for the age of reason? Are those the lessons of the master?

The fate of man is to suffer at all times. The very care of his preservation is connected with pain. Lucky to know only physical ills in his childhood—ills far less cruel, far less painful than are the other kinds of ills and which far more rarely make us renounce life than do the others! One does not kill oneself for the pains of gout. There are hardly any but those of the soul which produce despair. We pity the lot of childhood, and it is our own that should be pitied. Our greatest ills come to us from ourselves.

A child cries at birth; the first part of his childhood is spent crying. At one time we bustle about, we caress him in order to pacify him; at another, we threaten him, we strike him in order to make him keep quiet. Either we do what pleases him, or we exact from him what pleases us. Either we submit to his whims, or we submit him to ours. No middle ground; he must give orders or receive them. Thus his first ideas are those of domination and servitude. Before knowing how to speak, he commands; before being able to act, he obeys. And sometimes he is chastised before he is able to know his offenses or, rather, to commit any. It is thus that we fill up his young heart at the outset with the passions which later we impute to nature and that, after having taken efforts to make him wicked, we complain about finding him so.

A child spends six or seven years thus in the hands of women, victim of their caprice and of his own. And after having made him learn this and that—that is, after having burdened his memory either with words he cannot understand or with things that are good for nothing to him; after having stifled his nature by passions that one has caused to be born in him—this factitious being is put in the hands of a preceptor who completes the development of the artificial seeds that he finds already all formed and teaches him everything, except to know himself, except to take advantage of himself, except to know how to live and to make himself happy. Finally when this child, slave and tyrant, full of science and bereft of sense, frail in body and soul alike, is cast out into the world, showing there his ineptitude, his pride, and all his vices, he becomes the basis for our deploring human misery and perversity. This is a mistake. He is the man of our whims; the man of nature is differently constituted.

Do you, then, want him to keep his original form? Preserve it from the instant he comes into the world. As soon as he is born, take hold of him and leave him no more before he is a man. You will never succeed without that. As the true nurse is the mother, the true preceptor is the father. Let them be in agreement both about the order of their functions and about their system; let the child pass from the hands of the one into those of the other. He will be better raised by a judicious and limited father than the cleverest master in the world; for zeal will make up for talent better than talent for zeal.

But business, offices, duties . . . Ah, duties! Doubtless the least is that of father?* Let us not be surprised that a man whose wife did not deign to nurse the fruit of their union does not deign to raise him. There is no picture more charming than that of the family, but a single missing feature disfigures all the others. If the mother has too little health to be nurse, the father will have too much business to be preceptor. The children, sent away, dispersed in boarding schools, convents, colleges, will take the love belonging to the paternal home elsewhere, or to put it better, they will bring back to the paternal home the habit of having no attachments. Brothers and sisters will hardly know one another. When all are gathered together for ceremonial occasions, they will be able to be quite polite with one another. They will treat one another as strangers. As soon as there is no more intimacy between the parents, as soon as the society of the family no longer constitutes the sweetness of life, it is of course necessary to turn to bad morals to find a substitute. Where is the man stupid enough not to see the chain formed by all these links?

A father, when he engenders and feeds children, does with that only a third of his task. He owes to his species men; he owes to society sociable men; he owes to the state citizens. Every man who can pay this triple debt and does not do so is culpable, and more culpable perhaps when he pays it halfway. He who cannot fulfill the duties of a father has no right to become one. Neither poverty nor labors nor concern for public opinion exempts him from feeding his children and from raising them himself. Readers, you can believe me. I predict to whoever has vitals and neglects such holy duties that he will long shed bitter tears for his offense and will never find consolation for it.

But what does this rich man — this father of a family, so busy, and forced, according to him, to leave his children uncared for — do? He pays another man to take responsibility for these cares which are a burden to him. Venal soul! Do you believe that you are with money giving your son another father? Make no mistake about it; what you are giving him is not even a master but a valet. This first valet will soon make a second one out of your son.

We spend a lot of time trying to figure out the qualities of a good governor. The first quality I would exact of him, and this one alone presupposes many others, is that he not be a man for sale. There are callings so noble that one cannot follow them for money without proving oneself unworthy of following them.

---

*When one reads in Plutarch that Cato the Censor, who governed Rome so gloriously, himself raised his son from the cradle and with such care that he left everything to be present when the nurse — that is to say, the mother — changed and bathed him; when one reads in Suetonius that Augustus, master of the world that he had conquered and that he himself ruled, himself taught his grandsons to write, to swim, the elements of the sciences, and that he had them constantly around him — one cannot keep from laughing at the good little people of those times who enjoyed themselves in the like foolishness, doubtless too limited to know how to mind the great business of the great men of our days. *[Rousseau's note.]*

Such is that of the man of war; such is that of the teacher. "Who then will raise my child?" I already told you: you, yourself. "I cannot." You cannot! . . . Find yourself a friend then. I see no other solution.

A governor! O what a sublime soul . . . in truth, to make a man, one must be either a father or more than a man oneself. That is the function you calmly confide to mercenaries.

The more one thinks about it, the more one perceives new difficulties. It would be necessary that the governor had been raised for his pupil, that the pupil's domestics had been raised for their master, that all those who have contact with him had received the impressions that they ought to communicate to him. It would be necessary to go from education to education back to I know not where. How is it possible that a child be well raised by one who was not well raised himself?

Is this rare mortal not to be found? I do not know. In these degraded times who knows to what point of virtue a human soul can still attain? But let us suppose this marvel found. It is in considering what he ought to do that we shall see what he ought to be. What I believe I see in advance is that a father who sensed all the value of a good governor would decide to do without one, for he would expend more effort in acquiring him than in becoming one himself. Does he then want to find a friend? Let him raise his son to be one. Thus, he is spared seeking for him elsewhere, and nature has already done half the work.

Someone of whom I know only the rank had the proposal to raise his son conveyed to me. He doubtless did me a great deal of honor; but far from complaining about my refusal, he ought to congratulate himself on my discretion. If I had accepted his offer and my method were mistaken, the education would have been a failure. If I had succeeded, it would have been far worse. His son would have repudiated his title; he would no longer have wished to be a prince.

I am too impressed by the greatness of a preceptor's duties, I feel my incapacity too much ever to accept such employment from whatever quarter it might be offered to me, and the interest of friendship itself would be but a further motive for refusal. I believe that after having read this book, few people will be tempted to make me this offer, and I beg those who might be, not to make this useless effort any more. In the past I made a sufficient trial of this calling to be certain that I am not proper for it, and my condition would excuse me from it if my talents made me capable of it. I believed I owed this public declaration to those who appear not to accord me enough esteem to believe me sincere and well founded in my resolutions.

Not in a condition to fulfill the most useful task, I will dare at least to attempt the easier one; following the example of so many others, I shall put my hand not to the work but to the pen; and instead of doing what is necessary, I shall endeavor to say it.

I know that in undertakings like this one, an author — always comfortable with systems that he is not responsible for putting into practice — may insouciantly offer many fine precepts which are impossible to follow. And in the absence of details and examples, even the feasible things he says, if he has not shown their application, remain ineffectual.

I have hence chosen to give myself an imaginary pupil, to hypothesize that I have the age, health, kinds of knowledge, and all the talent suitable for working at his education, for conducting him from the moment of his birth up to the one when, become a grown man, he will no longer have need of any guide other than himself. This method appears to me useful to prevent an author who distrusts himself from getting lost in visions; for when he deviates from ordinary practice, he has only to make a test of his own practice on his pupil. He will soon sense, or the reader will sense for him, whether he follows the progress of childhood and the movement natural to the human heart.

This is what I have tried to do in all the difficulties which have arisen. In order not to fatten the book uselessly, I have been content with setting down the principles whose truth everyone should sense. But as for the rules which might need proofs, I have applied them all to my Emile or to other examples; and I have shown in very extensive detail how what I have established could be put into practice. Such at least is the plan that I have proposed to follow. It is up to the reader to judge if I have succeeded.

The result of this procedure is that at first I have spoken little of my Emile, because my first educational maxims, although contrary to those which are established, are so evident that it is difficult for any reasonable man to refuse his consent to them. But in the measure I advance, my pupil, differently conducted than yours, is no longer an ordinary child. He requires a way of life special to him. Then he appears more frequently on the scene, and toward the last times I no longer let him out of sight for a moment until, whatever he may say, he has no longer the least need of me.

I do not speak at all here of a good governor's qualities; I take them for granted, and I take for granted that I myself am endowed with all these qualities. In reading this work, one will see with what liberality I treat myself.

I shall only remark that, contrary to common opinion, a child's governor ought to be young and even as young as a wise man can be. I would want him to be a child himself if it were possible, to be able to become his pupil's companion and attract his confidence by sharing his enjoyments. There are not enough things in common between childhood and maturity for a really solid attachment ever to be formed at this distance. Children sometimes flatter old men, but they never love them.

One would wish that the governor had already educated someone. That is too much to wish for; the same man can only give one education. If two were required in order to succeed, by what right would one undertake the first?

With more experience one would know how to do better, but one would no longer be able to. Whoever has once fulfilled this function well enough to sense all its difficulties does not attempt to engage himself in it again; and if he has fulfilled it poorly the first time, that is an unfavorable augury for the second.

It is quite different, I agree, to follow a young man for four years than to lead him for twenty-five. You give a governor to your son after he is already all formed; as for me, I want him to have one before he is born. Your short-term man can change pupils; mine will have only one. You distinguish the preceptor from the governor: another folly! Do you distinguish the student from the pupil? There is only one science to teach to children. It is that of man's duties. This science is one, and whatever Xenophon says about the education of the Persians,[11] it is not divisible. Moreover, I call the master of this science *governor* rather than *preceptor* because his task is less to instruct than to lead. He ought to give no precepts at all; he ought to make them be discovered.

If the governor must be chosen with so much care, it is certainly permissible for him to choose his pupil as well, especially when what we are about is pro-pounding a model. This choice cannot be made on the basis of the child's genius or character, which can be known only at the end of the work, whereas I am adopting the child before his birth. If I could choose, I would take only a common mind, such as I assume my pupil to be. Only ordinary men need to be raised; their education ought to serve as an example only for that of their kind. The others raise themselves in spite of what one does.

Locale is not unimportant in the culture of men. They are all that they can be only in temperate climates. The disadvantage of extreme climates is obvious. A man is not planted like a tree in a country to remain there forever; and he who leaves one extreme to get to the other is forced to travel a road double the length of that traveled by him who leaves from the middle point for the same destination.

Let the inhabitant of a temperate country visit the two extremes one after the other. His advantage is still evident, for although he is affected as much as the one who goes from one extreme to the other, he is nevertheless only half as far from his natural constitution. A Frenchman can live in Guinea and in Lapland; but a Negro will not live likewise in Torne, nor a Samoyed in Benin. It appears, moreover, that the organization of the brain is less perfect in the two extremes. Neither the Negroes nor the Laplanders have the sense of the Europeans. If, then, I want my pupil to be able to be an inhabitant of the earth, I will get him in a temperate zone — in France, for example — rather than elsewhere.

In the north, men consume a lot of barren soil; in the south, they consume little on fertile soil. From this a new difference is born which makes the ones industrious and the others contemplative. Society presents us in a single place the image of these differences between the poor and the rich. The former inhabit the barren soil, and the latter the fertile country.

---

[11] Xenophon (c. 430 – c. 354 B.C.), was a Greek historian and soldier. A former follower of Socrates, he served as a mercenary in the army of the Persian Cyrus the Younger. Banished from his native Athens because of his pro-Spartan sympathies, Xenophon later served in the Spartan Army. Rousseau's allusion is to Xenophon's *Education of Cyrus.*

The poor man does not need to be educated. His station gives him a compulsory education. He could have no other. On the contrary, the education the rich man receives from his station is that which suits him least, from both his own point of view and that of society. Besides, the natural education ought to make a man fit for all human conditions. Now, it is less reasonable to raise a poor man to be rich than a rich man to be poor, for, in proportion to the number of those in the two stations, there are more men who fall than ones who rise. Let us, then, choose a rich man. We will at least be sure we have made one more man, while a poor person can become a man by himself.

For the same reason I will not be distressed if Emile is of noble birth. He will, in any event, be one victim snatched from prejudice.

Emile is an orphan. It makes no difference whether he has his father and mother. Charged with their duties, I inherit all their rights. He ought to honor his parents, but he ought to obey only me. That is my first or, rather, my sole condition.

I ought to add the following one, which is only a consequence of the other, that we never be taken from one another without our consent. This clause is essential, and I would even want the pupil and the governor to regard themselves as so inseparable that the lot of each in life is always a common object for them. As soon as they envisage from afar their separation, as soon as they foresee the moment which is going to make them strangers to one another, they are already strangers. Each sets up his own little separate system; and both, engrossed by the time when they will no longer be together, stay only reluctantly. The disciple regards the master only as the insignia and the plague of childhood; the master regards the disciple only as a heavy burden of which he is burning to be relieved. They agree in their longing for the moment when they will see themselves delivered from one another; and since there is never a true attachment between them, the one is not going to be very vigilant, the other not very docile.

But when they regard themselves as people who are going to spend their lives together, it is important for each to make himself loved by the other; and by that very fact they become dear to one another. The pupil does not blush at following in his childhood the friend he is going to have when he is grown. The governor takes an interest in concerns whose fruit he is going to harvest, and whatever merit he imparts to his pupil is an investment he makes for his old age.

This agreement made in advance assumes a satisfactory delivery, a child well formed, vigorous, and healthy. A father has no choice and ought to have no preferences in the family God gives him. All his children are equally his children; he owes to them all the same care and the same tenderness. Whether they are crippled or not, whether they are sickly or robust, each of them is a deposit of which he owes an account to the hand from which he receives it; and marriage is a contract made with nature as well as between the spouses.

But whoever imposes on himself a duty that nature has in no way imposed on him ought to be sure beforehand that he has the means of fulfilling it. Otherwise he makes himself accountable even for what he will have been unable to accomplish. He who takes charge of an infirm and valetudinary pupil changes his function from governor to male nurse. In caring for a useless life, he loses the time which he had intended to use for increasing its value. He exposes himself to facing an afflicted mother reproaching him one day for the death of a son whom he has preserved for her for a long time.

I would not take on a sickly and ill-constituted child, were he to live until eighty. I want no pupil always useless to himself and others, involved uniquely with preserving himself, whose body does damage to the education of his soul. What would I be doing in vainly lavishing my cares on him other than doubling society's loss and taking two men from it instead of one? Let another in my stead take charge of this invalid. I consent to it and approve his charity. But that is not my talent. I am not able to teach living to one who thinks of nothing but how to keep himself from dying.

40

❧

Edmund Burke

REFLECTIONS ON THE
REVOLUTION IN FRANCE

*W*ith its deliberate rejection of monarchy and of other established social, political, and religious traditions, the great French Revolution that began in
1789 created shock waves throughout Western civilization. Reflections on the
Revolution in France *(1790) by Edmund Burke (1729–1797) is the most famous and influential contemporaneous literary reaction to the disruptive events
of the Revolution. Born in Dublin, Ireland, Burke was the son of a Protestant attorney and his Catholic wife. Educated at a Quaker school in Ireland and at
Trinity College, Dublin, Burke's diverse religious background strongly influenced
him toward tolerance and human sympathy and away from abstract theories that
threatened to remake society or human nature in ways that Burke felt to be invariably destructive. Thus the satirical rationalism of Voltaire (Selection 30) and
the reliance on human passion of Jean-Jacques Rousseau (Selection 39) were
equally despised by Burke.*

*After graduating from Trinity College in 1748, Burke went to London to
study law but soon showed himself to be far more interested in literature, becoming a founding member of the Club, which also included such literary luminaries
as Samuel Johnson, Oliver Goldsmith, James Boswell, Adam Smith, and Joshua
Reynolds. In 1757 he married the daughter of an Irish Catholic doctor. Displaying a talent for the give and take of parliamentary politics Burke, representing
various constituencies, became one of the commanding figures in the House of
Commons from 1765 until his retirement in 1794. Most of his political career
was spent with the Whig opposition party as the valiant fighter for lost causes.
The Tory administration was making a mess of things in North America, attempting to reassert royal privileges, and Burke went to battle against their stupidity. Paradoxically, Burke, the conservative, saw the Whigs, the party of parliamentary liberalism, as an essential part of the English political inheritance. His*

famous speech On Conciliation with America *(1775) failed to secure the vote of parliament but it is certainly a masterpiece of classical rhetoric. In it Burke insists that, like their fellow Englishmen, the American colonists are entitled to representative parliamentary government which they inherited equally with their relations who remained in England. Burke closes his speech with a resounding tribute to common descent, common institutions, and common feelings as the strongest ties of empire. The speech was a courageous but futile attempt to avoid what Burke saw would ultimately be a catastrophe for England.*

Throughout Burke's long parliamentary and prolific literary life he devoted much of his effort to five great and honorable causes: (1) the freeing of the House of Commons from the control of King George III and his Tory supporters, (2) reconciliation with the American colonies and their ultimate liberation, (3) justice for Ireland and especially for its Roman Catholics, (4) the emancipation of India from the corrupt misgovernment of the British East India Company (a private profit-seeking organization forced to play a political role by the collapse of the Mughal Empire in India), and—exemplified in the following excerpt—(5) opposition to the atheistic radicalism of the French Revolution.

Burke saw the French Revolution, from its beginnings, as an attack on the whole social fabric of civilization. Written in the form of a long letter to "a very young gentleman at Paris," the Reflections *warns, with what would prove to be great accuracy, that the Revolution's radical policies would lead to bloody anarchy and military dictatorship. The* Reflections, *going through eleven printings in its first year, proved to be a powerful, though unsystematic, critique of the rationalist theories of the Enlightenment and, up to our own time, a valid statement of the basic principles of conservatism. In its religious mysticism and poetic rhetoric the* Reflections *reveals Burke's essentially romantic temperament. It is a conservative romanticism, however, that holds passionately on to the doctrine of natural inheritance, unlike the radical romanticism of Rousseau. Burke's conservative principles so outraged the radical Thomas Paine that he answered Burke with* The Rights of Man *in the following year (1791); and Burke's principles so pleased Louis XVI of France that he personally translated the volume into French. (Burke's warnings proved perceptive when Louis was beheaded by the revolutionaries in 1793. Burke also predicted the rise of a post-revolutionary military despot, a prediction that was validated by Napoleon's coup d'état just two years after Burke's death.) Nevertheless, if Burke had known the full extent of the French people's misery before the Revolution, he might have better understood the enthusiasm of its supporters.*

Burke saw society as a complex organism evolving slowly in the fixed channels of historical tradition. He rejected what he considered the unnatural abstractions of individual reason as the guide to social progress. Burke thought that humans, both individually and collectively, were not basically rational but really rather weak creatures of irrational impulses who needed to be restrained by a properly organized society. Religion, private property, custom, and "prejudices" (useful social myths) he asserted to be the social controls necessary to preserve a civilized order. Burke warned of the dangers of popular democracy when it was unrestrained by the responsible leadership of an hereditary aristocracy. The moral passion of the French Revolution was destroying the painfully evolved material and spiritual resources of society. Clearly, Burke was opposed to both the optimistic rationalism and the individualism of the eighteenth-century Enlightenment. In a sense Burke showed his flexible English qualities by accepting change, but for him social change must be evolutionary, never revolutionary. Society is not a machine to be tinkered with. An idea was sound for Burke only if it could be justly and judiciously effected. He detested abstract theories divorced from pragmatic continuity and social context. He asserted, "I do not like to see anything destroyed, any void produced in society, any ruin on the face of the land." A rare combination of practicing politician and political theorist, Burke, through his speeches and writings, became the touchstone of conservatism, a source of powerful arguments against radical reforms in any of the major institutions of society.

THE REVOLUTION SOCIETY[1]

I flatter myself that I love a manly, moral, regulated liberty as well as any gentleman of that society, be he who he will; and perhaps I have given as good proofs of my attachment to that cause in the whole course of my public conduct. . . . But I cannot stand forward and give praise or blame to anything which relates to human actions, and human concerns, on a simple view of the object, as it stands stripped of every relation, in all the nakedness and solitude of metaphysical abstraction. Circumstances (which with some gentlemen pass for nothing) give in reality to every political principle its distinguishing color and discrimination effect. The circumstances are what render every civil and political scheme beneficial or noxious to mankind. Abstractedly speaking, government, as

From Edmund Burke, *Reflections on the Revolution in France,* in *The Works of Edmund Burke* (Boston: Little, Brown, 1881), III, *passim.*

[1] The Revolution Society of London was formed to honor the Glorious Revolution of 1688–1689, in which the English Parliament had asserted its authority over the monarchy, causing the forced abdication of the Catholic James II and the succession of the Protestants William and Mary. In November 1789, when meeting for the festive centennial celebration of that bloodless revolution, the members of the Society drafted a document that congratulated the French revolutionaries, their contemporaries, on what they had so far achieved. Incurring Burke's total disapproval the members also expressed their hope for a similar democratization of the British Parliament. (The headings in this excerpt have been added by the editor to facilitate reading and discussion. Burke's original full text had no such headings.)

well as liberty, is good; yet could I, in common sense, ten years ago, have felicitated France on her enjoyment of a government (for she then had a government) without inquiry what the nature of that government was, or how it was administered? Can I now congratulate the same nation upon its freedom? Is it because liberty in the abstract may be classed amongst the blessings of mankind, that I am seriously to felicitate a madman, who has escaped from the protecting restraint and wholesome darkness of his cell, on his restoration to the enjoyment of light and liberty? Am I to congratulate a highwayman and murderer who has broke prison upon the recovery of his natural rights? This would be to act over again the scene of the criminals condemned to the galleys, and their heroic deliverer, the metaphysic knight of the sorrowful countenance.[2]

* * *

BRITISH LIBERTIES ARE CLOSELY LINKED WITH AN INHERITED AND STABLE MONARCHY

You will observe that from Magna Charta[3] to the Declaration of Right[4] it has been the uniform policy of our constitution to claim and assert our liberties as an entailed inheritance derived to us from our forefathers, and to be transmitted to our posterity — as an estate specially belonging to the people of this kingdom, without any reference whatever to any other more general or prior right. By this means our constitution preserves a unity in so great a diversity of its parts. We have an inheritable crown, an inheritable peerage, and a House of Commons and a people inheriting privileges, franchises, and liberties from a long line of ancestors.

This policy appears to me to be the result of profound reflection, or rather the happy effect of following nature, which is wisdom without reflection, and above it. A spirit of innovation is generally the result of a selfish temper and confined views. People will not look forward to posterity, who never look backward

---

[2] An allusion to the character of Don Quixote in Cervantes's 1605 novel (Selection 17) who foolishly freed violent criminals from their chains on the principle that every man has a right to liberty. The results were, of course, disastrous. Burke here is pointing out that the chivalric knight's actions were "abstract" or "metaphysical," that is, not related to the circumstances of the particular concrete situation.

[3] In 1215 the English nobility forced King John to accept the Magna Charta (Great Charter) in which, among other diminishments of his power, the king had to agree that he too was subject to the law.

[4] A document passed by Parliament in 1689; it guaranteed important political and civil rights both to Parliament and to the English people. (Burke saw this Declaration not as the gaining of new rights but rather as the preservation of the English inheritance of liberty and limited government.)

to their ancestors. Besides, the people of England well know that the idea of inheritance furnishes a sure principle of conservation and a sure principle of transmission, without at all excluding a principle of improvement. It leaves acquisition free, but it secures what it acquires. Whatever advantages are obtained by a state proceeding on these maxims are locked fast as in a sort of family settlement, grasped as in a kind of mortmain[5] forever. By a constitutional policy, working after the pattern of nature, we receive, we hold, we transmit our government and our privileges in the same manner in which we enjoy and transmit our property and our lives. The institutions of policy, the goods of fortune, the gifts of providence are handed down to us, and from us, in the same course and order. Our political system is placed in a just correspondence and symmetry with the order of the world and with the mode of existence decreed to a permanent body composed of transitory parts, wherein, by the disposition of a stupendous wisdom, moulding together the great mysterious incorporation of the human race, the whole, at one time, is never old or middle-aged or young, but, in a condition of unchangeable constancy, moves on through the varied tenor of perpetual decay, fall, renovation, and progression. Thus, by preserving the method of nature in the conduct of the state, in what we improve we are never wholly new; in what we retain we are never wholly obsolete. By adhering in this manner and on those principles to our forefathers, we are guided not by the superstition of antiquarians, but by the spirit of philosophic analogy. In this choice of inheritance we have given to our frame of polity the image of a relation in blood, binding up the constitution of our country with our dearest domestic ties, adopting our fundamental laws into the bosom of our family affections, keeping inseparable and cherishing with the warmth of all their combined and mutually reflected charities our state, our hearths, our sepulchres, and our altars.

Through the same plan of a conformity to nature in our artificial institutions, and by calling in the aid of her unerring and powerful instincts to fortify the fallible and feeble contrivances of our reason, we have derived several other, and those no small, benefits from considering our liberties in the light of an inheritance. Always acting as if in the presence of canonized forefathers, the spirit of freedom, leading in itself to misrule and excess, is tempered with an awful gravity. This idea of a liberal descent inspires us with a sense of habitual native dignity which prevents that upstart insolence almost inevitably adhering to and disgracing those who are the first acquirers of any distinction. By this means our liberty becomes a noble freedom. It carries an imposing and majestic aspect. It has a pedigree and illustrious ancestors. It has its bearing and its ensigns armorial.[6] It has its gallery of portraits, its monumental inscriptions, its records, evidences, and titles. We procure reverence to our civil institutions on the princi-

---

[5] Perpetual right to a property—a right that cannot be violated or transferred (literally, in French, a "dead hand").

[6] Coats of arms (symbolic designs) that identify the family's ancestors.

ple upon which nature teaches us to revere individual men: on account of their age, and on account of those from whom they are descended. . . .

. . .

LEVELING IS A FALSE PRINCIPLE OF EQUALITY AND WORKS AGAINST SOCIAL STABILITY

Believe me, Sir, those who attempt to level, never equalize. In all societies, consisting of various descriptions of citizens, some description must be uppermost. The levellers, therefore, only change and pervert the natural order of things; they load the edifice of society by setting up in the air what the solidity of the structure requires to be on the ground. The associations of tailors and carpenters, of which the republic (of Paris, for instance) is composed, cannot be equal to the situation into which by the worst of usurpations — and usurpation on the prerogatives of nature — you attempt to force them.

The Chancellor of France,[7] at the opening of the States,[8] said, in a tone of oratorical flourish, that all occupations were honorable. If he meant only that no honest employment was disgraceful, he would not have gone beyond the truth. But in asserting that anything is honorable, we imply some distinction in its favor. The occupation of a hairdresser or of a working candlemaker cannot be a matter of honor to any person — to say nothing of a number of other more servile employments. Such descriptions of men ought not to suffer oppression from the state; but the state suffers oppression if such as they, either individually or collectively, are permitted to rule. In this you think you are combating prejudice, but you are at war with nature.

. . .

The power of perpetuating our property in our families is one of the most valuable and interesting circumstances belonging to it, and that which tends the most to the perpetuation of society itself. It makes our weakness subservient to our virtue, it grafts benevolence even upon avarice. The possessors of family wealth, and of the distinction which attends hereditary possession (as most concerned in

---

[7] A high official of the king's administration.

[8] The Estates-General ("States") was the representative nationwide assembly of the three estates (social classes). The First Estate was the clergy, the Second the nobility, and the Third the commoners (including both urban bourgeoisie and rural peasants). This was the traditional tripartite structure required to pass new national taxes from the fourteenth century to the French Revolution of 1789.

it), are the natural securities for this transmission. With us the House of Peers[9] is formed upon this principle. It is wholly composed of hereditary property and hereditary distinction, and made, therefore, the third of the legislature[10] and, in the last event, the sole judge of all property in all its subdivisions. The House of Commons, too, though not necessarily, yet in fact, is always so composed, in the far greater part. Let those large proprietors be what they will—and they have their chance of being among the best—they are, at the very worst, the ballast in the vessel of the commonwealth. For though hereditary wealth and the rank which goes with it are too much idolized by creeping sycophants and the blind, abject admirers of power, they are too rashly slighted in shallow speculations of the petulant, assuming, shortsighted coxcombs of philosophy. Some decent, regulated preëminence, some preference (not exclusive appropriation) given to birth is neither unnatural, nor unjust, nor impolitic.

THE CALAMITOUS CONSEQUENCES FOR FRANCE BY ABANDONING TRUE PRINCIPLES

It is said that twenty-four millions ought to prevail over two hundred thousand. True; if the constitution of a kingdom be a problem of arithmetic. This sort of discourse does well enough with the lamppost for its second; to men who *may* reason calmly, it is ridiculous. The will of the many, and their interest must very often differ, and great will be the difference when they make an evil choice. A government of five hundred country attorneys and obscure curates is not good for twenty-four millions of men, though it were chosen by forty-eight millions, nor is it the better for being guided by a dozen of persons of quality who have betrayed their trust in order to obtain that power.[11] At present, you seem in everything to have strayed out of the high road of nature. The property of France does not govern it.

• • •

---

[9] The House of Lords ("Peers") is the upper house of Parliament. Membership in this assembly was restricted to hereditary nobles and high-ranking clergy. Not until 1999, was Parliamentary representation of the hereditary peerage greatly reduced in both power and number.

[10] The other thirds of the legislature are the king and the House of Commons.

[11] Burke is attacking those French noblemen, few in number, who had left their own peers to join the cause of the Third Estate.

THE ERRONEOUS CONCEPT
OF THE RIGHTS OF MEN

It is no wonder, therefore, that with these ideas of everything in their constitution and government at home, either in church or state, as illegitimate and usurped, or at best as a vain mockey, they[12] look abroad with an eager and passionate enthusiasm. Whilst they are possessed by these notions, it is vain to talk to them of the practice of their ancestors, the fundamental laws of their country, the fixed form of a constitution whose merits are confirmed by the solid test of long experience and an increasing public strength and national prosperity. They despise experience as the wisdom of unlettered men; and as for the rest, they have wrought underground a mine that will blow up, at one grand explosion, all examples of antiquity, all precedents, charters, and acts of parliament. They have "the rights of men." Against these there can be no prescription, against these no agreement is binding; these admit no temperament and no compromise; anything withheld from their full demand is so much of fraud and injustice. Against these their rights of men let no government look for security in the length of its continuance, or in the justice and lenity of its administration. The objections of these speculatists, if its forms do not quadrate with their theories, are as valid against such an old and beneficent government as against the most violent tyranny or the greenest usurpation. They are always at issue with governments, not on a question of abuse, but a question of competency and a question of title. . . .

THE TRUE CONCEPT
OF THE RIGHTS OF MEN

Far am I from denying in theory, full as far is my heart from withholding in practice (if I were of power to give or to withhold) the *real* rights of men. In denying their false claims of right, I do not mean to injure those which are real, and are such as their pretended rights would totally destroy. If civil society be made for the advantage of man, all the advantages for which it is made become his right. It is an institution of beneficence; and law itself is only beneficence acting by a rule. Men have a right to live by that rule; they have a right to do justice, as between their fellows, whether their fellows are in public function or in ordinary occupation. They have a right to the fruits of their industry and to the means of making their industry fruitful. They have a right to the acquisitions of their parents, to the nourishment and improvement of their offspring, to instruction in life and to consolation in death. Whatever each man can separately do, without trespassing upon others, he has a right to do for himself; and he has a right to a fair portion

---

[12] The Englishmen of the Revolution Society sympathetic to the French Revolution.

of all which society, with all its combinations of skill and force, can do in his favor. In this partnership all men have equal rights, but not to equal things. He that has but five shillings in the partnership has as good a right to it as he that has five hundred pounds has to his larger proportion. But he has not a right to an equal dividend in the product of the joint stock; and as to the share of power, authority, and direction which each individual ought to have in the management of the state, that I must deny to be among the direct original rights of man in civil society, for I have in my contemplation the civil social man, and no other. It is a thing to be settled by convention.

If civil society be the offspring of convention, that convention must be its law. That convention must limit and modify all the descriptions of constitution which are formed under it. Every sort of legislative, judicial, or executory power are its creatures. They can have no being in any other state of things; and how can any man claim, under the conventions of civil society, rights which do not so much as suppose its existence—rights which are absolutely repugnant to it? One of the first motives to civil society, and which becomes one of its fundamental rules, is, *that no man should be judge in his own cause.* By this each person has at once divested himself of the first fundamental right of uncovenanted man, that is, to judge for himself and to assert his own cause. He abdicates all right to be his own governor. He inclusively, in a great measure, abandons the right of self-defense, the first law of nature. Men cannot enjoy the rights of an uncivil and of a civil state together. That he may obtain justice, he gives up his right of determining what it is in points the most essential to him. That he may secure some liberty, he makes a surrender in trust of the whole of it.

THE TRUE NATURE OF GOVERNMENT

Government is not made in virtue of natural rights, which may and do exist in total independence of it, and exist in much greater clearness and in a much greater degree of abstract perfection; but their abstract perfection is their practical defect. By having a right to everything they want everything. Government is a contrivance of human wisdom to provide for human *wants.* Men have a right that these wants should be provided for by this wisdom. Among these wants is to be reckoned the want, out of civil society, of a sufficient restraint upon their passions. Society requires not only that the passions of individuals should be subjected, but that even in the mass and body, as well as in the individuals, the inclinations of men should frequently be thwarted, their will controlled, and their passions brought into subjection. This can only be done *by a power out of themselves,* and not, in the exercise of its function, subject to that will and to those passions which it is its office to bridle and subdue. In this sense the restraints on men, as well as their liberties, are to be reckoned among their rights. But as the liberties and the restrictions vary with times and circumstances and admit of infinite modifications, they cannot be settled upon any abstract rule; and nothing is so foolish as to discuss them upon that principle.

• • •

The science of constructing a commonwealth, or renovating it, or reforming it, is, like every other experimental science, not to be taught *a priori.*[13] Nor is it a short experience that can instruct us in that practical science, because the real effects of moral causes are not always immediate; but that which in the first instance is prejudicial may be excellent in its remoter operation, and its excellence may arise even from the ill effects it produces in the beginning. The reverse also happens: and very plausible schemes, with very pleasing commencements, have often shameful and lamentable conclusions. In states there are often some obscure and almost latent causes, things which appear at first view of little moment, on which a very great part of its prosperity or adversity may most essentially depend. The science of government being therefore so practical in itself and intended for such practical purposes—a matter which requires experience, and even more experience than any person can gain in his whole life, however sagacious and observing he may be—it is with infinite caution that any man ought to venture upon pulling down an edifice which has answered in any tolerable degree for ages the common purposes of society, or on building it up again without having models and patterns of approved utility before his eyes.

• • •

THE MOB RULES THE NATIONAL ASSEMBLY OF FRANCE

This, my dear Sir, was not the triumph of France. I must believe that, as a nation, it overwhelmed you with shame and horror. I must believe that the National Assembly find themselves in a state of the greatest humiliation in not being able to punish the authors of this triumph or the actors in it, and that they are in a situation in which any inquiry they may make upon the subject must be destitute even of the appearance of liberty or impartiality. The apology of that assembly is found in their situation; but when we approve what they *must* bear, it is in us the degenerate choice of a vitiated mind.

With a compelled appearance of deliberation, they vote under the dominion of a stern necessity. They sit in the heart, as it were, of a foreign republic: they have their residence in a city whose constitution has emanated neither from the charter of their king nor from their legislative power. There they are surrounded by an army not raised either by the authority of their crown or by their command, and which, if they should order to dissolve itself, would instantly dissolve them. There they sit, after a gang of assassins had driven away some hundreds of the members, whilst those who held the same moderate principles, with more patience or better hope, continued every day exposed to outrageous insults and murderous threats.

---

[13] Existing in the mind apart from any experience.

There a majority, sometimes real, sometimes pretended, captive itself, compels a captive king to issue as royal edicts, at third hand, the polluted nonsense of their most licentious and giddy coffeehouses. It is notorious that all their measures are decided before they are debated. It is beyond doubt that, under the terror of the bayonet and the lamppost and the torch to their houses, they are obliged to adopt all the crude and desperate measures suggested by clubs composed of a monstrous medley of all conditions, tongues, and nations.

• • •

ENGLISH DIFFERENT FROM FRENCH — DESPITE CLAIMS OF REVOLUTION SOCIETY

Thanks to our sullen resistance to innovation, thanks to the cold sluggishness of our national character, we still bear the stamp of our forefathers. We have not (as I conceive) lost the generosity and dignity of thinking of the fourteenth century,[14] nor as yet have we subtilized ourselves into savages. We are not the converts of Rousseau; we are not the disciples of Voltaire; Helvetius has made no progress among us.[15] Atheists are not our preachers; madmen are not our lawgivers. We know that *we* have made no discoveries, and we think that no discoveries are to be made, in morality, nor many in the great principles of government, nor in the ideas of liberty, which were understood long before we were born, altogether as well as they will be after the grave has heaped its mould upon our presumption and the silent tomb shall have imposed its law on our pert loquacity. In England we have not yet been completely embowelled of our natural entrails; we still feel within us, and we cherish and cultivate, those inbred sentiments which are the faithful guardians, the active monitors of our duty, the true supporters of all liberal and manly morals. We have not been drawn and trussed, in order that we may be filled, like stuffed birds in a museum, with chaff and rags and paltry blurred shreds of paper about the rights of man. We preserve the whole of our feelings still native and entire, unsophisticated by pedantry and infidelity. We have real hearts of flesh and blood beating in our bosoms. We fear God; we

---

[14] In 1356, the English defeated the king of France, John II, at Poitiers. John and his son Philip were taken prisoner by the English and held in England. They were, apparently, treated as if they were visiting royalty.

[15] Three eighteenth-century French philosophers: Rousseau (Selection 39) was a radical democrat who believed in the primacy of human feelings; Voltaire (Selection 30) was a satirical rationalist who fought against intolerance and censorship; Helvetius, an admirer of Voltaire, attempted a scientific account of human behavior and taught that humans are motivated by self-interest.

look up with awe to kings, with affection to parliaments, with duty to magistrates, with reverence to priests, and with respect to nobility. Why? Because when such ideas are brought before our minds, it is *natural* to be so affected; because all other feelings are false and spurious and tend to corrupt our minds, to vitiate our primary morals, to render us unfit for rational liberty, and, by teaching us a servile, licentious, and abandoned insolence, to be our low sport for a few holidays, to make us perfectly fit for, and justly deserving of, slavery through the whole course of our lives.

THROUGH JUSTIFIABLE PREJUDICE A MAN'S DUTY IS INTERNALIZED

You see, Sir, that in this enlightened age I am bold enough to confess that we are generally men of untaught feelings, that, instead of casting away all our old prejudices,[16] we cherish them to a very considerable degree, and, to take more shame to ourselves, we cherish them because they are prejudices; and the longer they have lasted and the more generally they have prevailed, the more we cherish them. We are afraid to put men to live and trade each on his own private stock of reason, because we suspect that the stock in each man is small, and that the individuals would do better to avail themselves of the general bank and capital of nations and of ages. Many of our men of speculation, instead of exploding general prejudices, employ their sagacity to discover the latent wisdom which prevails in them. If they find what they seek, and they seldom fail, they think it more wise to continue the prejudice, with the reason involved, than to cast away the coat of prejudice and to leave nothing but the naked reason; because prejudice, with its reason, has a motive to give action to that reason, and an affection which will give it permanence. Prejudice is of ready application in the emergency; it previously engages the mind in a steady course of wisdom and virtue and does not leave the man hesitating in the moment of decision skeptical, puzzled, and unresolved. Prejudice renders a man's virtue his habit, and not a series of unconnected acts. Through just prejudice, his duty becomes a part of his nature.

CONTEMPT FOR TRADITION IS TYPICAL OF THE ENLIGHTENMENT

Your literary men and your politicians, and so do the whole clan of the enlightened among us, essentially differ in these points. They have no respect for the wisdom of others, but they pay it off by a very full measure of confidence in their own. With them it is a sufficient motive to destroy an old scheme of things be-

---

[16] By "prejudices" Burke means traditional beliefs and customs.

cause it is an old one. As to the new, they are in no sort of fear with regard to the duration of a building run up in haste, because duration is no object to those who think little or nothing has been done before their time, and who place all their hopes in discovery. They conceive, very systematically, that all things which give perpetuity are mischievous, and therefore they are at inexpiable war with all establishments. They think that government may vary like modes of dress, and with as little ill effect; that there needs no principle of attachment, except a sense of present convenience, to any constitution of the state.

• • •

RELIGION IS THE BASIS OF CIVIL SOCIETY

We know, and what is better, we feel inwardly, that religion is the basis of civil society and the source of all good and of all comfort. In England we are so convinced of this, that there is no rust of superstition with which the accumulated absurdity of the human mind might have crusted it over in the course of ages, that ninety-nine in a hundred of the people of England would not prefer to impiety. We shall never be such fools as to call in an enemy to the substance of any system to remove its corruptions, to supply its defects, or to perfect its construction. If our religious tenets should ever want a further elucidation, we shall not call on atheism to explain them. We shall not light up our temple from that unhallowed fire. It will be illuminated with other lights. It will be perfumed with other incense than the infectious stuff which is imported by the smugglers of adulterated metaphysics. If our ecclesiastical establishment[17] should need a revision, it is not avarice or rapacity, public or private, that we shall employ for the audit, or receipt, or application of its consecrated revenue. . . .

We know, and it is our pride to know, that man is by his constitution a religious animal; that atheism is against, not only our reason, but our instincts; and that it cannot prevail long. But if, in the moment of riot and in a drunken delirium from the hot spirit drawn out of the alembic of hell, which in France is now so furiously boiling, we should uncover our nakedness by throwing off that Christian religion which has hitherto been our boast and comfort, and one great source of civilization among us, and among many other nations, we are apprehensive (being well aware that the mind will not endure a void) that some uncouth, pernicious, and degrading superstition might take place of it.

For that reason, before we take from our establishment the natural, human means of estimation and give it up to contempt, as you have done, and in doing it have incurred the penalties you well deserve to suffer, we desire that some other may be presented to us in the place of it. We shall then form our judgment.

---

[17] The Church of England.

On these ideas, instead of quarrelling with establishments, as some do who have made a philosophy and a religion of their hostility to such institutions, we cleave closely to them. We are resolved to keep an established church, an established monarchy, an established aristocracy, and an established democracy, each in the degree it exists, and in no greater.

• • •

TRADITION COULD AVOID SOCIAL EVILS

To avoid, therefore, the evils of inconstancy and versatility, ten thousand times worse than those of obstinacy and the blindest prejudice, we have consecrated the state that no man should approach to look into its defects or corruptions but with due caution, that he should never dream of beginning its reformation by its subversion, that he should approach to the faults of the state as to the wounds of a father, with pious awe and trembling solicitude. By this wise prejudice we are taught to look with horror on those children of their country who are prompt rashly to hack that aged parent in pieces and put him into the kettle of magicians, in hopes that by their poisonous weeds and wild incantations they may regenerate the paternal constitution and renovate their father's life.[18]

SOCIETY IS A PERMANENT CONTRACT

Society is indeed a contract. Subordinate contracts for objects of mere occasional interest may be dissolved at pleasure—but the state ought not to be considered as nothing better than a partnership agreement in a trade of pepper and coffee, calico or tobacco, or some other such low concern, to be taken up for a little temporary interest, and to be dissolved by the fancy of the parties. It is to be looked on with other reverence, because it is not a partnership in things subservient only to the gross animal existence of a temporary and perishable nature. It is a partnership in all science; a partnership in all art; a partnership in every virtue and in all perfection. As the ends of such a partnership cannot be obtained in many generations, it becomes a partnership not only between those who are living, but between those who are living, those who are dead, and those who are to be born. Each contract of each particular state is but a clause in the great primeval contract of eternal society, linking the lower with the higher natures, connecting the visible and invisible world, according to a fixed compact

---

[18] The ancient Greek legend of Medea, a sorceress, who, for the benefit of her lover, Jason, deceitfully persuaded the daughters of King Pelias to hack their father to pieces and boil the pieces in a cauldron in order to rejuvenate him. The experiment did not work.

sanctioned by the inviolable oath which holds all physical and all moral natures, each in their appointed place. This law is not subject to the will of those who, by an obligation above them, and infinitely superior, are bound to submit their will to that law.

• • •

THE POLICY OF THE NATIONAL ASSEMBLY IS DESTRUCTIVE

It is this inability to wrestle with difficulty which has obliged the arbitrary Assembly of France to commence their schemes of reform with abolition and total destruction.[19] But is it in destroying and pulling down that skill is displayed? Your mob can do this as well at least as your assemblies. The shallowest understanding, the rudest hand is more than equal to that task. Rage and frenzy will pull down more in half an hour than prudence, deliberation, and foresight can build up in a hundred years. The errors and defects of old establishments are visible and palpable. It calls for little ability to point them out; and where absolute power is given, it requires but a word wholly to abolish the vice and the establishment together. The same lazy, but restless disposition which loves sloth and hates quiet directs these politicians when they come to work for supplying the place of what they have destroyed. To make everything the reverse of what they have seen is quite as easy as to destroy. No difficulties occur in what has never been tried. Criticism is almost baffled in discovering the defects of what has not existed; and eager enthusiasm and cheating hope have all the wide field of imagination in which they may expatiate with little or no opposition.

SOCIAL REFORMS NEED TIME, MODERATION, AND SYMPATHETIC UNDERSTANDING, AND MUST BE GUIDED BY A RULING PRINCIPLE

At once to preserve and to reform is quite another thing. When the useful parts of an old establishment are kept, and what is superadded is to be fitted to what is retained, a vigorous mind, steady, persevering attention, various powers of comparison and combination, and the resources of an understanding fruitful in expedients are to be exercised; they are to be exercised in a continued conflict with

---

[19] In a proclamation of June 17, 1789, grown mainly out of the enthusiasm of the representatives of the Third Estate, the self-proclaimed National Assembly (1789–1791) assumed the right to exercise sovereign power in the name of the people of France. This was the first truly revolutionary act, since it was supported by no existing statute or custom.

the combined force of opposite vices, with the obstinacy that rejects all improvement and the levity that is fatigued and disgusted with everything of which it is in possession. But you may object—"A process of this kind is slow. It is not fit for an assembly which glories in performing in a few months the work of ages. Such a mode of reforming, possibly, might take up many years." Without question it might; and it ought. It is one of the excellences of a method in which time is among the assistants, that its operation is slow and in some cases almost imperceptible. . . . The true lawgiver ought to have a heart full of sensibility. He ought to love and respect his kind, and to fear himself. It may be allowed to his temperament to catch his ultimate object with an intuitive glance, but his movements towards it ought to be deliberate. Political arrangement, as it is a work for social ends, is to be only wrought by social means. There, mind must conspire with mind. Time is required to produce that union of minds which alone can produce all the good we aim at. Our patience will achieve more than our force. If I might venture to appeal to what is so much out of fashion in Paris, I mean to experience, I should tell you that in my course I have known and, according to my measure, have cooperated with great men; and I have never yet seen any plan which has not been mended by the observations of those who were much inferior in understanding to the person who took the lead in the business. . . . Where the great interests of mankind are concerned through a long succession of generations, that succession ought to be admitted into some share in the councils which are so deeply to affect them. If justice requires this, the work itself requires the aid of more minds than one age can furnish. It is from this view of things that the best legislators have been often satisfied with the establishment of some sure, solid, and ruling principle in government—a power like that which some of the philosophers have called a plastic nature; and having fixed the principle, they have left it afterwards to its own operation.

· · ·

ABUSE OF THE LABEL OF "LIBERTY" CAUSES POLITICIANS TO FOLLOW POLICIES THEY KNOW TO BE UNWISE

The effects of the incapacity shown by the popular leaders in all the great members of the commonwealth are to be covered with the "all-atoning name" of liberty. In some people I see great liberty indeed; in many, if not in the most, an oppressive, degrading servitude. But what is liberty without wisdom and without

---

[20] Lucan (39–65) was an ancient Roman poet much concerned with the theme of liberty. Pierre Corneille (1606–1684) was the creator of French tragedy and much concerned with the actions of great men.

virtue? It is the greatest of all possible evils; for it is folly, vice, and madness, without tuition or restraint. Those who know what virtuous liberty is cannot bear to see it disgraced by incapable heads on account of their having high-sounding words in their mouths. Grand, swelling sentiments of liberty I am sure I do not despise. They warm the heart; they enlarge and liberalize our minds; they animate our courage in time of conflict. Old as I am, I read the fine raptures of Lucan and Corneille with pleasure.[20] Neither do I wholly condemn the little arts and devices of popularity. They facilitate the carrying of many points of moment; they keep the people together; they refresh the mind in its exertions; and they diffuse occasional gaiety over the severe brow of moral freedom. Every politician ought to sacrifice to the Graces,[21] and to join compliance with reason. But in such an undertaking as that in France all these subsidiary sentiments and artifices are of little avail. To make a government requires no great prudence. Settle the seat of power, teach obedience, and the work is done. To give freedom is still more easy. It is not necessary to guide; it only requires to let go the rein. But to form a *free government,* that is, to temper together these opposite elements of liberty and restraint in one consistent work, requires much thought, deep reflection, a sagacious, powerful, and combining mind. This I do not find in those who take the lead in the National Assembly. Perhaps they are not so miserably deficient as they appear. I rather believe it. It would put them below the common level of human understanding. But when the leaders choose to make themselves bidders at an auction of popularity, their talents, in the construction of the state, will be of no service. They will become flatterers instead of legislators, the instruments, not the guides, of the people. If any of them should happen to propose a scheme of liberty, soberly limited and defined with proper qualifications, he will be immediately outbid by his competitors who will produce something more splendidly popular. Suspicions will be raised of his fidelity to his cause. Moderation will be stigmatized as the virtue of cowards, and compromise as the prudence of traitors, until, in hopes of preserving the credit which may enable him to temper and moderate, on some occasions, the popular leader is obliged to become active in propagating doctrines and establishing powers that will afterwards defeat any sober purpose at which he ultimately might have aimed.

---

[21] In Greek mythology the Graces are three sister-goddesses, daughters of Zeus, who personify gracefulness, charm, and beauty.

THE IMPROVEMENTS OF THE NATIONAL ASSEMBLY ARE SUPERFICIAL, ITS ERRORS FUNDAMENTAL

But am I so unreasonable as to see nothing at all that deserves commendation in the indefatigable labors of this Assembly? I do not deny that, among an infinite number of acts of violence and folly, some good may have been done. They who destroy everything certainly will remove some grievance. They who make everything new have a chance that they may establish something beneficial. To give them credit for what they have done in virtue of the authority they have usurped, or which can excuse them in the crimes by which that authority has been acquired, it must appear that the same things could not have been accomplished without producing such a revolution. Most assuredly they might, because almost every one of the regulations made by them which is not very equivocal was either in the cession of the king, voluntarily made at the meeting of the states, or in the concurrent instructions to the orders. Some usages have been abolished on just grounds, but they were such that if they had stood as they were to all eternity, they would little detract from the happiness and prosperity of any state. The improvements of the National Assembly are superficial, their errors fundamental.

• • •

41

❧

ROMANTIC POETRY OF THE NINETEENTH CENTURY

R omanticism emerged as a powerful complex of ideas and passions that began
to flourish in the Western world in the late eighteenth century and persists
in varied forms to the present. It represented, in part, a reaction against the rationalism of the Enlightenment and its reliance on the universal power of reason,
exemplified in such authors as the satirist Voltaire (Selection 30). Instead, romantic writers like Rousseau (Selection 39) asserted the natural power of individual feelings. Romanticism was often associated with political liberalism or
radicalism, but it could also be conservative as in Burke (Selection 40) with his
emphasis on the legitimating power of natural inheritance.

The chief emphasis of romantic writers lay in their freedom of individual
self-expression. Sincerity, spontaneity, and originality replaced the careful imitation of rationally proportioned classical models. Rejecting the ordered rationality
of the Enlightenment as too mechanical, impersonal, and artificial, the romantics
turned to the emotional directness of personal experience and the infinite bound-
lessness of the individual imagination. Restrained balance was overturned in
favor of emotional intensity—often taken to extremes of rapture, nostalgia (for
childhood or the past), melancholy, sentimentality, or even horror. There was a
new interest in folk legends and superstitions. The significance of childhood for
all later creative and personal development can be seen here in poems by
Wordsworth and Whitman. The absolute necessity for mankind to relate to physical nature was also part of the romantic credo. The creative imagination occupied
the center of romantic views of art, replacing the "mechanical" rules of conventional form with an "organic" principle of natural growth and free development.

Lyric poetry was perhaps the greatest literary expression of romanticism, and
it has seldom been equaled in its color, sensuousness, and imaginative scope. For
the romantics, the poem was an organic whole, expressing more than any paraphrase, to be grasped only in terms of the unique world it created. The poem
sprang from the individual creator's personal experience. The poems reprinted
here are prime examples of romantic lyric poetry.

William Wordsworth (1770–1850) was one of the fathers of romantic poetry in England. Late in life he gained official recognition with his appointment as Poet Laureate in 1843. His influence remains with us, especially for those poets reacting against postmodern humanity's divorce from nature. The first poem, "The World Is Too Much with Us," first published in 1807, is a sonnet expressing Wordsworth's despair at the commercial materialism of the Industrial Revolution and his preference for the direct relationship of earlier men and earlier religions to the curative forces of nature. In the long ode "Intimations of Immortality from Recollections of Early Childhood," also published in 1807, Wordsworth opens with an insistence on personal loss ("The things which I have seen I now can see no more"). He feels that he is no longer in tune with the harmony of the natural world. In stanza nine he takes consolation from the memories of childhood that remain with him. However, in the concluding stanzas he comes to a new and higher form of consolation — nature has value not only as a catalyst for unrestrained childlike joy, but for the insights of "the human heart" into the suffering of his fellow humans that nature enables — "In the soothing thoughts that spring / Out of human suffering; / In the faith that looks through death, / In years that bring the philosophic mind." It is, thus, "the human heart by which we live" that ultimately allows the poet to experience the significance of a flower that spurs "Thoughts that do often lie too deep for tears." It is typical of the romantics to assume that the process of maturing involves giving up a kind of wisdom usually accessible only to children. Many readers also may identify with such feelings of necessary loss. We see in Wordsworth a fervent identification with the transcendent in nature and the corresponding good in mankind.

Samuel Taylor Coleridge (1772–1834), another progenitor of the romantic movement, was a close friend and collaborator of Wordsworth during Coleridge's most productive years. Besides being a poet, Coleridge was the foremost literary critic and theorist of his time. He wrote in spasms of intense effort separated by long periods of indolence. Many of his works were left unfinished, as, for example, "Kubla Khan," reprinted here. In his preface Coleridge states that he was remembering the words and images that came to him in an opium-induced dream when he was interrupted by a person from the nearby town of Porlock. As a memory of a dream-vision, the poem makes no claim to rational coherence but has nevertheless been the subject of much critical commentary. In "Kubla Khan" we can see the results of Coleridge's prodigious reading, as well as his addiction to opium (caused by the medical prescriptions of the time). Like his "Rime of the Ancient Mariner," a longer poem not reprinted here, "Kubla Khan" is a work of mystery and demonism.

John Keats (1795–1821), one of the essential figures in romantic poetry, experienced an extraordinarily brief and tragic life. Apprenticed to an apothecary and surgeon from the age of fifteen, in 1816 the high-spirited young man abandoned the practice of medicine, for which he had just been certified, for the practice of poetry. Not even undertaking to write poetry until he turned eighteen, suddenly at twenty-one his talent emerged with the sonnet, reprinted here, "On First Looking into Chapman's Homer." In 1819, a miraculous year, he wrote "The Eve of Saint Agnes" and all of his great odes. The scourge of tuberculosis that had already killed his mother, orphaning Keats at fourteen, also killed his beloved younger brother, Tom, in 1818. Keats succumbed to the disease at the age of twenty-six in Rome where friends had taken him in the hope of a cure, fulfilling his forebodings of an early death. When tuberculosis compelled him to stop writing at the age of twenty-four, he had clearly exceeded the literary achievements of Chaucer, Shakespeare, or Milton at the same age. Who knows what he might have achieved if fate had permitted?

In the first (1816) of Keats's two brief sonnets reprinted here we can see his excitement at being introduced to Chapman's translation of Homer's adventurous epics. What is also evident is the romantic nature of Keats's reaction: He projects his own awestruck emotions back onto the text and out into the world. In the second sonnet (1818) we see Keats's foreboding of an early death that will prevent him from gleaning all the words exploding in his "teeming brain" and that will prevent him from fulfilling the love he wishes to share.

The last poem is by Walt Whitman (1819–1892), a robust American man of the people and romantic rebel. His "free verse," without rhyme or regular metrical structure, has large and powerfully flowing rhythmical units, which capture well his emotional intensity. In "Out of the Cradle Endlessly Rocking" (first published in 1859 and continually revised until its final form of 1881, reprinted here) Whitman returns to a rural Long Island beach scene of his own childhood, in a way that Wordsworth would have approved. He remembers the bird's song that he had heard as a child on this same spot. This evocation of his intense childhood experience enables the poet to explore that moment when his own poetic vocation was revealed to him as he identified with the grieving bird's song. The poem concludes with the adult speaker meditating on the nature of his creative force in terms recalling the attraction of death to other romantic poets, especially Keats. The union of the demonic and the beautiful in his memory of the grieving bird's song inspires the now grown speaker. His own songs merge in his imagination with the "strong and delicious word" spoken by the sea, another aspect of nature traditionally associated with both birth and death. In his powerful rhythms and his searching through the mists of childhood memory for a watershed moment, Whitman reminds us once more of a great Romantic theme: the mystery of creativity.

WILLIAM WORDSWORTH
The World Is Too Much With Us

The world is too much with us; late and soon,
Getting and spending, we lay waste our powers:
Little we see in Nature that is ours;
We have given our hearts away, a sordid boon!
This Sea that bares her bosom to the moon;
The winds that will be howling at all hours,
And are up-gathered now like sleeping flowers;
For this, for every thing, we are out of tune;
It moves us not. — Great God! I'd rather be
A Pagan suckled in a creed outworn;
So might I, standing on this pleasant lea,
Have glimpses that would make me less forlorn;
Have sight of Proteus[1] rising from the sea;
Or hear old Triton[2] blow his wreathèd horn.

Ode

Intimations of Immortality from Recollections of Early Childhood

The Child is Father of the Man;
And I could wish my days to be
Bound each to each by natural piety.[3]

1

There was a time when meadow, grove, and stream,
The earth, and every common sight,
    To me did seem
    Apparelled in celestial light,
The glory and the freshness of a dream.

---

[1] In ancient Greek myth (Homer's *Odyssey,* Book 4) Proteus is a minor sea-god who knows all things and has the power to assume different shapes in order to escape answering questions.

[2] Also in Greek myth, a merman deity with a fish's tail from the waist down. He is commonly shown as blowing on a conch-shell trumpet.

[3] The concluding lines of Wordsworth's short lyric that begins, "My heart leaps up when I behold / A rainbow in the sky: . . ." That poem's theme of human continuity, in which "The Child is Father of the Man," makes it an appropriate epigraph for this ode.

It is not now as it hath been of yore; —
      Turn wheresoe'er I may,
        By night or day,
The things which I have seen I now can see no more.

2

      The Rainbow comes and goes,
      And lovely is the Rose,
      The Moon doth with delight
Look round her when the heavens are bare,
      Waters on a starry night
      Are beautiful and fair;
      The sunshine is a glorious birth;
      But yet I know, where'er I go,
That there hath past away a glory from the earth.

3

Now, while the birds thus sing a joyous song,
    And while the young lambs bound
      As to the tabor's sound,[4]
To me alone there came a thought of grief:
A timely utterance gave that thought relief,
    And I again am strong:
The cataracts blow their trumpets from the steep;
No more shall grief of mine the season wrong;
I hear the Echoes through the mountains throng,
The Winds come to me from the fields of sleep,[5]
    And all the earth is gay;
      Land and sea
    Give themselves up to jollity,
    And with the heart of May
    Doth every Beast keep holiday; —
      Thou Child of Joy,
Shout round me, let me hear thy shouts, thou happy
    Shepherd-boy!

4

Ye blessed Creatures, I have heard the call
    Ye to each other make; I see

---

[4] A tabor is a small drum often used to beat time for dancing.

[5] Wordsworth often associated a rising wind with the revival of his spirit and his poetic inspiration.

The heavens laugh with you in your jubilee;
    My heart is at your festival,
    My head hath its coronal,[6]
The fulness of your bliss, I feel—I feel it all.
    O evil day! if I were sullen
    While Earth herself is adorning,
      This sweet May-morning,
    And the Children are culling
      On every side,
    In a thousand valleys far and wide,
    Fresh flowers; while the sun shines warm,
And the Babe leaps up on his Mother's arm:—
    I hear, I hear, with joy I hear!
    —But there's a Tree, of many, one,
A single Field which I have looked upon,
Both of them speak of something that is gone:
    The Pansy at my feet
    Doth the same tale repeat:
Whither is fled the visionary gleam?
Where is it now, the glory and the dream?

5

Our birth is but a sleep and a forgetting:
The Soul that rises with us, our life's Star,[7]
    Hath had elsewhere its setting,
    And cometh from afar:
    Not in entire forgetfulness,
    And not in utter nakedness,
But trailing clouds of glory do we come
    From God, who is our home:
Heaven lies about us in our infancy!
Shades of the prison-house begin to close
    Upon the growing Boy,
But He beholds the light, and whence it flows,
    He sees it in his joy;
The Youth, who daily farther from the east
    Must travel, still is Nature's Priest,
    And by the vision splendid
    Is on his way attended;

---

[6] A little crown of flowers, with which shepherd boys in May decorated their hats.

[7] The sun, metaphor for the soul.

At length the Man perceives it die away,
And fade into the light of common day.

6

Earth fills her lap with pleasures of her own;
Yearnings she hath in her own natural kind,
And, even with something of a Mother's mind,
　　　And no unworthy aim,
　　　The homely[8] Nurse doth all she can
To make her Foster-child, her Inmate Man,
　　　Forget the glories he hath known,
And that imperial palace whence he came.

7

Behold the Child among his new-born blisses,
A six years' Darling of a pigmy size!
See, where 'mid work of his own hand he lies,
Fretted by sallies of his mother's kisses,
With light upon him from his father's eyes!
See, at his feet, some little plan or chart,
Some fragment from his dream of human life,
Shaped by himself with newly-learnèd art;
　　　A wedding or a festival,
　　　A mourning or a funeral;
　　　　And this hath now his heart,
　　　And unto this he frames his song:
　　　　Then will he fit his tongue
To dialogues of business, love, or strife;
　　　But it will not be long
　　　Ere this be thrown aside,
　　　And with new joy and pride
The little Actor cons[9] another part;
Filling from time to time his "humorous stage"[10]

---

[8] Simple, unpretentious, and friendly—an older usage of "homely."

[9] Memorizes.

[10] Probably, an allusion to Jaques's famous "seven ages" of man speech in Shakespeare's *As You Like It* (2.7.139–166). Jaques was addicted to the melancholic humor. Humors were the bodily fluids that, according to Renaissance medicine, caused the various characters and temperaments of humanity, which were often represented in drama ("humorous stage"). The quoted phrase itself comes from a 1599 sonnet by the English poet Samuel Daniel.

With all the Persons, down to palsied Age,
That Life brings with her in her equipage;
  As if his whole vocation
  Were endless imitation.

8

Thou, whose exterior semblance doth belie
  Thy Soul's immensity;
Thou best Philosopher, who yet dost keep
Thy heritage, thou Eye among the blind,
That, deaf and silent, read'st the eternal deep,
Haunted for ever by the eternal mind,—
  Mighty Prophet! Seer blest!
  On whom those truths do rest,
Which we are toiling all our lives to find,
In darkness lost, the darkness of the grave;
Thou, over whom thy Immortality
Broods like the Day, a Master o'er a Slave,
A Presence which is not to be put by;
Thou little Child, yet glorious in the might
Of heaven-born freedom on thy being's height,
Why with such earnest pains dost thou provoke
The years to bring the inevitable yoke,
Thus blindly with thy blessedness at strife?
Full soon thy Soul shall have her earthly freight,
And custom lie upon thee with a weight,
Heavy as frost, and deep almost as life!

9

  O joy! that in our embers
  Is something that doth live,
  That nature yet remembers
  What was so fugitive!
The thought of our past years in me doth breed
Perpetual benediction: not indeed
For that which is most worthy to be blest;
Delight and liberty, the simple creed
Of Childhood, whether busy or at rest,
With new-fledged hope still fluttering in his breast:—
  Not for these I raise
  The song of thanks and praise;
  But for those obstinate questionings
  Of sense and outward things,

Fallings from us, vanishings;
    Blank misgivings of a Creature
Moving about in worlds not realised,[11]
High instincts before which our mortal Nature
Did tremble like a guilty Thing surprised:[12]
      But for those first affections,
      Those shadowy recollections,
    Which, be they what they may,
Are yet the fountain light of all our day,
Are yet a master light of all our seeing;
    Uphold us, cherish, and have power to make
Our noisy years seem moments in the being
Of the eternal Silence: truths that wake,
    To perish never;
Which neither listlessness, nor mad endeavour,
    Nor Man nor Boy,
Nor all that is at enmity with joy,
Can utterly abolish or destroy!
  Hence in a season of calm weather
    Though inland far we be,
Our Souls have sight of that immortal sea
    Which brought us hither,
  Can in a moment travel thither,
And see the Children sport upon the shore,
And hear the mighty waters rolling evermore.

10

Then sing, ye Birds, sing, sing a joyous song!
    And let the young Lambs bound
    As to the tabor's sound!
We in thought will join your throng,
    Ye that pipe and ye that play,
    Ye that through your hearts to-day
    Feel the gladness of the May!
What though the radiance which was once so bright
Be now for ever taken from my sight,
    Though nothing can bring back the hour
Of splendour in the grass, of glory in the flower;

---

[11] Made real.

[12] That is, like a supernatural spirit taken by surprise. "Guilty thing" is a phrase taken from Shakespeare's *Hamlet* (1.1.148) referring to the ghost of Hamlet's father who has just been seen haunting the castle.

We will grieve not, rather find
Strength in what remains behind;
In the primal sympathy
Which having been must ever be;
In the soothing thoughts that spring
Out of human suffering;
In the faith that looks through death,
In years that bring the philosophic mind.

11

And O, ye Fountains, Meadows, Hills, and Groves,
Forebode not any severing of our loves!
Yet in my heart of hearts I feel your might;
I only have relinquished one delight
To live beneath your more habitual sway.
I love the Brooks which down their channels fret,
Even more than when I tripped lightly as they;
The innocent brightness of a new-born Day
      Is lovely yet;
The Clouds that gather round the setting sun
Do take a sober colouring from an eye
That hath kept watch o'er man's mortality;
Another race hath been, and other palms are won.
Thanks to the human heart by which we live,
Thanks to its tenderness, its joys, and fears,
To me the meanest flower that blows[13] can give
Thoughts that do often lie too deep for tears.

SAMUEL TAYLOR COLERIDGE
Kubla Khan or, A Vision in A Dream. A Fragment

The following fragment is here published at the request of a poet of great and deserved celebrity [Lord Byron], and, as far as the Author's own opinions are concerned, rather as a psychological curiosity, than on the ground of any supposed *poetic* merits.

    In the summer of the year 1797, the Author, then in ill health, had retired to a lonely farm-house between Porlock and Linton, on the Exmoor confines of Somerset and Devonshire. In consequence of a slight indisposition, an anodyne

---

[13] That is, the lowliest flower that blooms.

had been prescribed,[14] from the effects of which he fell asleep in his chair at the moment that he was reading the following sentence, or words of the same substance, in "Purchas's Pilgrimage"[15]. "Here the Khan Kubla commanded a palace to be built, and a stately garden thereunto. And thus ten miles of fertile ground were inclosed with a wall." The Author continued for about three hours in a profound sleep, at least of the external senses, during which time he has the most vivid confidence, that he could not have composed less than from two to three hundred lines; if that indeed can be called composition in which all the images rose up before him as *things,* with a parallel production of the correspondent expressions, without any sensation or consciousness of effort.[16] On awaking he appeared to himself to have a distinct recollection of the whole, and taking his pen, ink, and paper, instantly and eagerly wrote down the lines that are here preserved. At this moment he was unfortunately called out by a person on business from Porlock, and detained by him above an hour, and on his return to his room, found, to his no small surprise and mortification, that though he still retained some vague and dim recollection of the general purport of the vision, yet, with the exception of some eight or ten scattered lines and images, all the rest had passed away like the images on the surface of a stream into which a stone has been cast, but, alas! without the after restoration of the latter!

> Then all the charm
> Is broken—all that phantom-world so fair
> Vanishes, and a thousand circlets spread,
> And each mis-shape[s] the other. Stay awhile,
> Poor youth! who scarcely dar'st lift up thine eyes—
> The stream will soon renew its smoothness, soon
> The visions will return! And lo, he stays,
> And soon the fragments dim of lovely forms
> Come trembling back, unite, and now once more
> The pool becomes a mirror.[17]

---

[14] The "anodyne" was laudanum (opium dissolved in alcohol), a standard prescription for pain at that time. Coleridge soon recognized that the drug was a worse evil than such illnesses as his severe rheumatism (which, of course, the opium did not cure). He was to become an opium addict as a result of this common medical practice.

[15] A Renaissance travel book about exotic places, published by Samuel Purchas in London, 1613. The historical Kublai Khan founded the Mongol (Yuan) Dynasty in China in the thirteenth century and was visited by Marco Polo. (See Volume II, Selection 50.)

[16] Coleridge's account here that he dreamed the poem and later wrote down what he could remember has been challenged recently by medical commentators who doubt that opium produces dreams.

[17] From Coleridge's poem "The Picture; or, The Lover's Resolution," lines 91–100.

Yet from the still surviving recollections in his mind, the Author has frequently purposed to finish for himself what had been originally, as it were, given to him. . . . but the to-morrow is yet to come. . . .

In Xanadu did Kubla Khan
A stately pleasure-dome decree:
Where Alph,[18] the sacred river, ran
Through caverns measureless to man
 Down to a sunless sea.
So twice five miles of fertile ground
With walls and towers were girdled round:
And there were gardens bright with sinuous rills,
Where blossomed many an incense-bearing tree;
And here were forests ancient as the hills,
Enfolding sunny spots of greenery.

But oh! that deep romantic chasm which slanted
Down the green hill athwart a cedarn cover!
A savage place! as holy and enchanted
As e'er beneath a waning moon was haunted
By woman wailing for her demon-lover!
And from this chasm, with ceaseless turmoil seething,
As if this earth in fast thick pants were breathing,
A mighty fountain momently was forced:
Amid whose swift half-intermitted burst
Huge fragments vaulted like rebounding hail,
Or chaffy grain beneath the thresher's flail:
And 'mid these dancing rocks at once and ever
It flung up momently the sacred river.
Five miles meandering with a mazy motion
Through wood and dale the sacred river ran,
Then reached the caverns measureless to man,
And sank in tumult to a lifeless ocean:
And 'mid this tumult Kubla heard from far
Ancestral voices prophesying war!
 The shadow of the dome of pleasure
 Floated midway on the waves;
 Where was heard the mingled measure
 From the fountain and the caves.

---

[18] Perhaps in Coleridge's mind, derived from the Greek river Alpheus. The Roman poet Ovid in his *Metamorphoses* wrote that the god of this river pursued the nymph Arethusa until she was changed by the moon goddess, Artemis, into a fountain that rose again in Sicily.

It was a miracle of rare device,
A sunny pleasure-dome with caves of ice!
  A damsel with a dulcimer
  In a vision once I saw:
  It was an Abyssinian maid,
  And on her dulcimer she played,
  Singing of Mount Abora.[19]
  Could I revive within me
  Her symphony and song,
  To such a deep delight 'twould win me,
That with music loud and long,
I would build that dome in air,
That sunny dome! those caves of ice!
And all who heard should see them there,
And all should cry, Beware! Beware!
His flashing eyes, his floating hair!
Weave a circle round him thrice,[20]
And close your eyes with holy dread,
For he on honey-dew hath fed,
And drunk the milk of Paradise.[21]

---

[19] Probably derived from a passage mentioning "Mount Amara" in John Milton's *Paradise Lost* (IV, 280–283): ". . . where Abassin kings their issue guard, / Mount Amara, though this by some supposed / True Paradise, under the Ethiop line / by Nilus' head, enclosed with shining rock,". . . .

[20] A magical ritual to protect the divinely inspired poet from intrusion (like the interruption by the "person on business from Porlock" while Coleridge was writing down the lines that he remembered from his dream).

[21] Compare in the *Ion* of Plato, the ancient Greek philosopher, a description of the madness of inspired poets: "For all good poets, epic as well as lyric, compose their beautiful poems not by art, but because they are inspired and possessed. . . . The lyric poets are not in their right mind when they are composing their beautiful strains: but when falling under the power of music and meter they are inspired and possessed; like Bacchic maidens who draw milk and honey from the rivers when they are under the influence of Dionysus but not when they are in their right mind. . . . For they tell us that they bring songs from honeyed fountains. . . ." (Dionysus, also known as Bacchus, was a god associated with wine, with the release of communal ecstatic emotions, and with a fertility cult celebrated in mysteries of great secrecy.)

JOHN KEATS

On First Looking into Chapman's Homer[22]

Much have I travell'd in the realms of gold,
  And many goodly states and kingdoms seen;
  Round many western islands have I been
Which bards in fealty to Apollo hold.[23]
Oft of one wide expanse had I been told
  That deep-brow'd Homer ruled as his demesne;[24]
  Yet did I never breathe its pure serene[25]
Till I heard Chapman speak out loud and bold:
Then felt I like some watcher of the skies
  When a new planet swims into his ken;
Or like stout Cortez[26] when with eagle eyes
  He star'd at the Pacific—and all his men
Look'd at each other with a wild surmise—
  Silent, upon a peak in Darien.

When I have fears that I may cease to be

When I have fears that I may cease to be
  Before my pen has glean'd my teeming brain,
Before high piled books, in charactry,[27]
  Hold like rich garners the full ripen'd grain;
When I behold, upon the night's starr'd face,
  Huge cloudy symbols of a high romance,
And think that I may never live to trace
  Their shadows, with the magic hand of chance;

---

[22] Keats's friend and former teacher Charles Cowden Clarke had introduced the poet to George Chapman's robust Renaissance translations of Homer's *Iliad* (1611) and *Odyssey* (1616) the night before Keats wrote this sonnet. They read through the October night of 1816, and Clarke received the poem in that morning's 10:00 mail.

[23] "Fealty" is the allegiance of a feudal vassal to his lord. Apollo is the ancient Greek god of poetry and music—among his many attributes.

[24] Kingdom or feudal possession.

[25] Clear air.

[26] Actually, it was Balboa, not Cortez (Cortés), who was the first European explorer to view the Pacific from the heights of Darien in Panama (1513); but, perhaps, that matters more to history than to poetry.

[27] Characters: printed letters of the alphabet.

And when I feel, fair creature of an hour,
  That I shall never look upon thee more,
Never have relish in the fairy power
  Of unreflecting love;—then on the shore
Of the wide world I stand alone, and think
Till love and fame to nothingness do sink.

WALT WHITMAN
Out of the Cradle Endlessly Rocking

Out of the cradle endlessly rocking,
Out of the mocking-bird's throat, the musical shuttle,
Out of the Ninth-month[28] midnight,
Over the sterile sands and the fields beyond, where the child leaving
        his bed wander'd alone, bareheaded, barefoot,
Down from the shower'd halo,
Up from the mystic play of shadows twining and twisting as if they
        were alive,
Out from the patches of briers and blackberries,
From the memories of the bird that chanted to me,
From your memories sad brother, from the fitful risings and fallings
        I heard,
From under that yellow half-moon late-risen and swollen as if
        with tears,
From those beginning notes of yearning and love there in the mist,
From the thousand responses of my heart never to cease,
From the myriad thence-arous'd words,
From the word stronger and more delicious than any,
From such as now they start the scene revisiting,
As a flock, twittering, rising, or overhead passing,
Borne hither, ere all eludes me, hurriedly,
A man, yet by these tears a little boy again,
Throwing myself on the sand, confronting the waves,
I, chanter of pains and joys, uniter of here and hereafter,
Taking all hints to use them, but swiftly leaping beyond them,
A reminiscence sing.

Once Paumanok,[29]
When the lilac-scent was in the air and Fifth-month grass was growing,

---

[28] September.

[29] The Indian name for Long Island, New York, where Whitman grew up and which still
held strong childhood memories for him.

Up this seashore in some briers,
Two feather'd guests from Alabama, two together,
And their nest, and four light-green eggs spotted with brown,
And every day the he-bird to and fro near at hand,
And every day the she-bird crouch'd on her nest, silent, with
          bright eyes
And every day I, a curious boy, never too close, never
          disturbing them,
Cautiously peering, absorbing, translating.

Shine! shine! shine!
Pour down your warmth, great sun!
While we bask, we two together.

Two together!
Winds blow south, or winds blow north,
Day come white, or night come black,
Home, or rivers and mountains from home,
Singing all time, minding no time,
While we two keep together.

Till of a sudden,
May-be kill'd, unknown to her mate,
One forenoon the she-bird crouch'd not on the nest,
Nor return'd that afternoon, nor the next,
Nor ever appear'd again.

And thenceforward all summer in the sound of the sea,
And at night under the full of the moon in calmer weather,
Over the hoarse surging of the sea,
Or flitting from brier to brier by day,
I saw, I heard at intervals the remaining one, the he-bird,
The solitary guest from Alabama.

Blow! blow! blow!
Blow up sea-winds along Paumanok's shore;
I wait and I wait till you blow my mate to me.

Yes, when the stars glisten'd,
All night long on the prong of a moss-scallop'd stake,
Down almost amid the slapping waves,
Sat the lone singer wonderful causing tears.

He call'd on his mate,
He pour'd forth the meanings which I of all men know.

Yes my brother I know,
The rest might not, but I have treasur'd every note,
For more than once dimly down to the beach gliding,

Silent, avoiding the moonbeams, blending myself with the shadows,
Recalling now the obscure shapes, the echoes, the sounds and sights after
        their sorts,
The white arms out in the breakers tirelessly tossing,
I, with bare feet, a child, the wind wafting my hair,
Listen'd long and long.

Listen'd to keep, to sing, now translating the notes,
Following you my brother.

Soothe! soothe! soothe!
Close on its wave soothes the wave behind,
And again another behind embracing and lapping, every one close,
But my love soothes not me, not me.

Low hangs the moon, it rose late,
It is lagging—O I think it is heavy with love, with love.
O madly the sea pushes upon the land,
With love, with love.

O night! do I not see my love fluttering out among the breakers?
What is that little black thing I see there in the white?

Loud! loud! loud!
Loud I call to you, my love!
High and clear I shoot my voice over the waves,
Surely you must know who is here, is here,
You must know who I am, my love.

Low-hanging moon!
What is that dusky spot in your brown yellow?
O it is the shape, the shape of my mate!
O moon do not keep her from me any longer.

Land! land! O land!
Whichever way I turn, O I think you could give me my mate back again if
        you only would,
For I am almost sure I see her dimly whichever way I look.

O rising stars!
Perhaps the one I want so much will rise, will rise with some of you.

O throat! O trembling throat!
Sound clearer through the atmosphere!
Pierce the woods, the earth,
Somewhere listening to catch you must be the one I want.

Shake out carols!
Solitary here, the night's carols!
Carols of lonesome love! death's carols!

Carols under that lagging, yellow, waning moon!
O under that moon where she droops almost down into the sea!
O reckless despairing carols.

But soft! sink low!
Soft! let me just murmur,
And do you wait a moment you husky-nois'd sea,
For somewhere I believe I heard my mate responding to me,
So faint, I must be still, be still to listen,
But not altogether still, for then she might not come immediately to me.

Hither my love!
Here I am! here!
With this just-sustain'd note I announce myself to you,
This gentle call is for you my love, for you.

Do not be decoy'd elsewhere,
That is the whistle of the wind, it is not my voice,
That is the fluttering, the fluttering of the spray,
Those are the shadows of leaves.

O darkness! O in vain!
O I am very sick and sorrowful.

O brown halo in the sky near the moon, drooping upon the sea!
O troubled reflection in the sea!
O throat! O throbbing heart!
And I singing uselessly, uselessly all the night.

O past! O happy life! O songs of joy!
In the air, in the woods, over fields,
Loved! loved! loved! loved! loved!
But my mate no more, no more with me!
We two together no more.

The aria sinking,
All else continuing, the stars shining,
The winds blowing, the notes of the bird continuous echoing,
With angry moans the fierce old mother incessantly moaning,
On the sands of Paumanok's shore gray and rustling,
The yellow half-moon enlarged, sagging down, drooping, the face of the
      sea almost touching,
The boy ecstatic, with his bare feet the waves, with his hair the
      atmosphere dallying,
The love in the heart long pent, now loose, now at last tumultuously
      bursting,
The aria's meaning, the ears, the soul, swiftly depositing,
The strange tears down the cheeks coursing,

The colloquy there, the trio, each uttering,
The undertone, the savage old mother incessantly crying,
To the boy's soul's questions sullenly timing, some drown'd
        secret hissing.
To the outsetting bard.

Demon or bird! (said the boy's soul),
Is it indeed toward your mate you sing? or is it really to me?
For I, that was a child, my tongue's use sleeping, now I have
        heard you,
Now in a moment I know what I am for, I awake,
And already a thousand singers, a thousand songs, clearer, louder
        and more sorrowful than yours,
A thousand warbling echoes have started to life within me, never
        to die.

O you singer solitary, singing by yourself, projecting me,
O solitary me listening, never more shall I cease perpetuating you,
Never more shall I escape, never more the reverberations,
Never more the cries of unsatisfied love be absent from me,
Never again leave me to be the peaceful child I was before what
        there in the night,
By the sea under the yellow and sagging moon,
The messenger there arous'd, the fire, the sweet hell within,
The unknown want, the destiny of me.

O give me the clew![30] (it lurks in the night here somewhere,)
O if I am to have so much, let me have more!

A word then, (for I will conquer it,)
The word final, superior to all,
Subtle, sent up—what is it?—I listen;
Are you whispering it, and have been all the time, you sea-waves?
Is that it from your liquid rims and wet sands?

Whereto answering, the sea,
Delaying not, hurrying not,
Whisper'd me through the night, and very plainly before daybreak,
Lisp'd to me the low and delicious word death,
And again death, death, death, death,
Hissing melodious, neither like the bird nor like my arous'd child's heart,
But edging near as privately for me rustling at my feet,

---

[30] Variant of "clue."

Creeping thence steadily up to my ears and laving[31] me softly
        all over,
Death, death, death, death, death.

Which I do not forget,
But fuse the song of my dusky demon and brother,
That he sang to me in the moonlight on Paumanok's gray beach,
With the thousand responsive songs at random,
My own songs awaked from that hour,
And with them the key, the word up from the waves,
The word of the sweetest song and all songs,
That strong and delicious word which, creeping to my feet,
(Or like some old crone rocking the cradle, swathed in sweet
        garments, bending aside,)
The sea whisper'd me.

---

[31] Bathing.

42

꙳

Varis Shah

HIR

An essential feature of the literature of the Indian subcontinent is its regional diversity. The subcontinent contains numerous geographic and cultural regions, most of them with their separate languages and long literary histories. The situation is analogous to that of Western Europe, an area approximately the same size as the Indian subcontinent and containing many different languages and literatures. As in Europe, so in India, the literatures of different languages, although they have distinctly separate identities, often follow similar patterns and share many common themes. Indian literature is thus predominantly a rich blend of many interrelated regional literatures rather than a single unified pan-Indian literature.

One of the finest works of Indian literature seen as a complex of regional literatures is the book-length poem Hir by Varis Shah (fl. mid-eighteenth century) from the region of the Punjab in northwestern India. It is considered to be the greatest literary classic of the Punjabi language. The poem belongs to the genre of the tales of romantic love popular over a large area, from the western edge of the Middle East to the eastern parts of the Indian subcontinent, from medieval to early modern times. It stands out among the tales of love for its superior poetic quality and for the epic scale on which it is written. Varis Shah was quite conscious of his poetic achievement and of having created a work of high literary order. Within the text of the poem, he says towards the conclusion, ". . . I composed my poem in the right manner. / Let other poets examine its quality, I have let my horse roam in the open pasture. / Other poets have wasted their energy on grinding grain on little hand-querns, I have ground my grain in the grand bullock-driven mill. / May the hearts of young men be filled with joy to read my poem, I have planted a flower for fragrance. . . . I have written verse filled with nuggets like a string of royal pearls. / I have written it giving full descriptions embellished with beauties of countless colors. / I have written it with metaphors, their beauty the beauty of a necklace of rubies. / One who reads it will receive immense pleasure, and all people will raise exclamations in its praise." Varis

Shah's hopes and assertions proved instantly prophetic. Since the very time of its writing, his Hir *has been known and loved throughout the Punjab. It is recited by bards and common people in country and in town, in public and in private, and, these days, also on the media. The Punjabis' love of* Hir *and Varis Shah is so great that they see them as the personifications of their land, just as the Greeks consider the* Iliad *and Homer as synonymous with Greece.*

Very little is known with certainty about Varis Shah's life. Only a few facts can be gleaned from Hir *itself. He was born at Jandiala Sher Khan, a village in the central Punjab in Sheikhupura district, sometime in the first half of the eighteenth century, probably a few years after 1730. His family were Sayyids, a high Muslim caste descended from the same clan as the prophet Muhammad's family. Varis Shah was always conscious of his social superiority as a Sayyid, particularly in comparison with the* jutts, *a racial caste, farmers and peasants by occupation, then and now economically and socially dominant in the rural Punjab. Varis Shah considered the jutts rustic and culturally inferior. As a community, the Sayyids were learned, its members serving a semi-priestly function in the Muslim religious establishment. Varis Shah studied for some time under a famous Sufi (Muslim mystic) of Kasur, near Lahore, the capital of the Punjab. Several eminent contemporaries of Varis Shah were also this teacher's pupils. Later Varis Shah went to Pakpatan, a town sacred to the memory of the famous medieval Sufi saint Farid Shakargunj of the Punjab. Here he seems to have fallen desperately in love with a woman, probably a jutti, of a neighboring village. The love proved unsuccessful, but it turned him into a poet. "The urge to write this tale arose in me when love appeared in my heart," says a verse in* Hir. *Varis Shah records the completion date of his poem. The date in the Muslim calendar translates into* A.D. *1766. He finished his poem at Hans Malikan, a village of the Kharal jutts, where he seems to have settled for the rest of his life after leaving Pakpatan.*

The story of Hir, often also known as the story of Hir and Ranjha, was treated by a number of other poets besides Varis Shah, not only in Punjabi but also in several contiguous languages, including Persian, Baluchi, Sindhi, and Urdu. In Punjabi, there already were at least three well-known versions of considerable literary merit and Varis Shah was indebted to the two more recent of these, even using some of the verses from them for his version. However, his poem is the most impressive; it is about three hundred pages long and written in baits, *a long meter made famous by Varis's use of it. Perhaps the story of Hir and Ranjha had a historical basis, but the historical facts, if they had ever existed, were long lost in the mists of time. The story was alive in the consciousness of people only because of its narration by different poets. Building on this consciousness and with the power of his genius, Varis Shah transformed the commonly known story into a monumental myth about love.*

A brief plot synopsis of Varis Shah's Hir *follows: Mistreated by his brothers and their wives, after the death of their father Mauju, the chief of the Ranjha clan of Takht Hazara, Dhido, the youngest, handsomest, and the most beloved of*

Mauju's eight sons, leaves home in desperation. He reaches the River Chenab, associated in Punjabi folklore with the tales of famous lovers. Crossing the river in a barge, he falls asleep in the boat on a couch which belongs to Hir, the daughter of Chuchak, the local chief of the Syals of Jhung. She is beside herself with rage to see a stranger on her couch. When Dhido awakens and greets her, they both instantly fall in love with each other. Hir has her father employ Dhido as the herder of their buffaloes. They meet daily in the wooded pastures. Her parents' kinsmen are displeased to see this. Most concerned is Kaido, who has pretensions of being a pious ascetic. He prevails upon Hir's parents to fire Dhido and send him away. However, the buffaloes refuse to move for any other herder. So Chuchak is compelled to bring Dhido back; but before returning, Dhido extracts from Maliki, Hir's mother, a tentative promise of Hir's hand in marriage.

The promise is not kept, because, under pressure from his kinsmen, Chuchak arranges to marry Hir to Saida, son of Aju, the chief of the Kheras of Rangpur. Hir proposes to Dhido that they elope, but he does not agree, for he wants a conventional marriage. As arranged, Hir is married to Saida and is taken to Rangpur with his wedding party. Ranjha (Dhido is now known mostly by this name, the name of his clan) gets to accompany them, because the buffaloes given in dowry by Hir's parents refuse to move for any other herdsman. On the way, Ranjha continues to meet with Hir. Getting suspicious the Kheras send him back to Jhung. Soon, however, he receives a message from Hir that she has refused to consummate the marriage with Saida and she wants him to come to Rangpur as a jogi *(Punjabi for yogi, a practitioner of yoga). Ranjha receives* jog *(the practice of yoga) from a famous guru, goes to Rangpur, setting up camp there as a holy man. Saida's sister, Sehti, who is also in love with a man not approved by her family, helps Hir to hatch a plan. Hir pretends that she has been bitten by a snake. Saida takes her to the* jogi, *Ranjha, for treatment which will require several days during which she is to stay in a hut with Ranjha accompanied only by one family member, Sehti. From there, both Hir and Sehti elope with their lovers. The Kheras pursue and capture Hir and Ranjha and bring them to the local ruler, known as "the Just." The ruler's magistrate, following religious law, rules that Hir go with Saida. As the Kheras leave, taking Hir with them, the ruler's capital begins to burn. Realizing that this is due to the unjust verdict given by the judge and the suffering of the lovers, he calls the Kheras and Hir back and grants Hir to Ranjha.*

Hir and Ranjha are now free to live their lives together. However, this time, Hir insists on a traditional marriage in the same manner as Ranjha had done earlier. They return to Jhung where Hir's parents make a show of welcoming them and agreeing to their marriage. Ranjha goes home to Takht Hazara to bring a wedding party of his kin to Jhung. While he is gone, Hir's parents and their kin treacherously poison Hir to death. Hearing the news of her death, at the poem's conclusion, Ranjha collapses with a cry of utter despair and dies.

What seems to be the secret of the phenomenal success and popularity of Varis Shah's Hir? *First of all, there is the obvious appeal of the tragic story of spontaneous love between young people in a society dominated by rigid social conven-*

tions and inhumane sex taboos. Varis's poignant evocation of the beautiful and exhilarating scenes of the lovers' meetings and of their grief in separation is a most prominent aspect of the poem. Another feature of central importance is the vivid and detailed portrayal of the vast panorama of life in the Punjab: its physical landscape, its flora and fauna, its seasons, the cycle of daily routine, and, above all, its social reality complete with the structure of society, religious practice, customs, manners, values, and mores. Varis Shah's outlook is essentially secular and free from sectarian bias, enabling him to provide a probing picture of his people. Often he exposes the corruption and hypocrisy hidden under conventional social and religious norms adhered to in individual and collective behavior. His exposé is charged with wit and irony, and frequently with trenchant satire. He makes countless generalizations distilled from keen observation and deep experience. Couched in smooth verse, these generalizations make Varis Shah's Hir *an inexhaustible mine of quotable sayings of proverbial wisdom. Following a traditional poetic convention, Varis Shah, sometimes speaking for himself and at other times in the voice of a character, addresses himself, concluding most of his verses with profound observations about one or another aspect of life. Punjabis therefore, find in* Hir *quotations suited for almost every occasion or subject. Hence the importance of the poem in their consciousness.*

The following excerpts are selected to exemplify some of the poem's main qualities.

HOMAGE

Let us begin with reciting the praise of God who brought forth the world
    out of love.
First Allah Himself fell in love and his beloved was His Messenger, the
    Prophet.[1]
Love marks the station of the saint and the sage; a loving man possesses
    unfathomed nobility.
Vast vistas of enlightenment open up in the hearts of those who have
    embraced love.
Next praise Allah's Prophet for whose sake He created all the heavens and
    earths.
Fashioning him out of dust, He yet placed him on high and purged him
    from all corruption.

Translated and adapted from the Punjabi by Surjit S. Dulai. Copyright 1999.

[1] Allah is the Arabic (and Islamic) word for God. The Prophet Muhammad, the founder of Islam, is, according to that religion, God's Messenger.

And he, though the lord of all the prophets, made himself dust before the almighty God.

Renouncing his own joys, he became care-worn to help the faithful on the Judgment Day.

Let us next whole-heartedly praise the Pir, even the humblest of whose servants become wise.[2]

But for this great sage there is no other true friend, though one search a hundred thousand times.

Those who are accepted in his grace have their houses filled with spiritual and with worldly gifts.

On the Judgment Day, the Pir's devotees will receive robes of honor from God's right hand.

Next praise the beloved son of Maudud, Shakargunj Masud,[3] full to brim with sweetness.

The perfect scion of the House of Chisht, the saint whose town, Patan, is most renowned.

The highest Pir of the twenty-two poles,[4] his humility and asceticism known all over,

Shakargunj occupies his holy seat in the Punjab and dispels the troubles and pains of the land.

GENESIS OF THE POEM

Friends gathered around me one day and made request, "Pray compose the tale of Hir afresh.

And narrate the whole story of her passionate love in sweet-tongued and beautiful poetic words.

Bring before the eye again the union of Hir and Ranjha with the magic of your marvelous verse,

So that hearing it in gatherings with friends, we may enjoy with full delight Hir's love of Ranjha."

Complying with this wish of friends, I pieced together this elegant tale of wondrous charm.

Composing and carefully perfecting each sentence, I plucked from the garden a fresh rose flower.

---

[2] This is a reference to a Muslim saint, Makhdum Jahania of the eighth century. He is one of the five Pirs, saints who are believed to have become immortal because of their piety. In the story they are the guardians of Ranjha.

[3] The Sufi saint, Sheikh Masud-ud-Din Farid (1173–1265) of the Chishti order, popularly known as Farid Shakargunj (Storehouse of Sugar), whose seat was Pakpatan in the Punjab.

[4] According to a Sufi belief, there are at any one time in the world twenty-two persons who serve as the highest reference points of the creed.

Through long travail and concentration of the mind, I have cut across
    the mountain like Farhad.[5]
In choicest verses, I have captured the beauty of the tale as perfume is
    distilled from the rose.

DHIDO LEAVES HIS VILLAGE, TAKHT HAZARA

How describe the beauty of Takht Hazara where the Ranjhas live in a
    whirl of joy and mirth![6]
Where the tall young men are happy and full of abandon, one more
    handsome than the other.
Rings on fingers and in ears, and flowing *lungis* around the waist,[7]
    splendors piled on splendors!
How may Varis describe the beauty of Hazara; it is as if paradise has
    descended to the earth!
Mauju Chaudhry has a say in the village and is recognized as superior
    and chief by his peers.
He is blessed with much wealth and a large family; he has eight sons
    and two daughters.
Held in high esteem and trust by his clan, he is well-known as an able
    arbitrator in their affairs.
Says Varis Shah, by God's will, Mauju bears the greatest love for his
    youngest son, Dhido.
The father loves him and the brothers hate. They are held back only by
    their fear of the father.
They berate him with subtle taunts. Their innuendoes sting his heart like
    a serpent's tooth.
Writhing in their helplessness, they hope to be rid of him by insinuations
    of countless kinds.
Varis Shah, so prevalent is the love of selfish gain that kinship is but a
    veneer without meaning.
As was the doing of fate, Mauju passed away and Dhido's brothers began
    to ride herd on him.
"You eat your fill and loaf, staring at women," from long-suppressed
    grudges, they pester him,

---

[5] Farhad was a legendary lover who cut though a mountain with just an adze because of
the promise of gaining his beloved, Shirin. When the promise was not fulfilled, he died
exhausted.

[6] Ranjha is the name of the clan to which the hero belongs. Dhido is his given name.

[7] A *lungi* is a sheetlike garment worn around the waist.

And daily tear afresh the heart's old wound with taunts as sharp-tongued
as the sharpest swords.

The brothers and sisters-in-law's talk is full of enmity, each is filled with
the tumult of this anger.

In the presence of elders brought before the *Qazi*,[8] the brothers had their
ancestral land divided.

By giving bribes, they had the finest land allotted to themselves and left
the sterile part to Ranjha.

Jumping with joy for having cheated, the brothers mock Dhido, for they
have made a fool of him.

Sisters-in-law added to the mockery; the villagers too talked and
laughed, but they also grieved.

Sisters-in-law say, "How can those, who shave the face and look in the
mirror, do the ploughing?

How will any woman want a lazy man who merely fattens his body and
carefully oils his hair?

The young man grumbles over his portion of land, he is never content
with whatever he is given.

He plays the flute and sings all day. Like the overstaying of a guest, his
days are numbered.

While we feed you pudding, you are filled with arrogance; you are
pampered by being well-fed.

The village wives all tease us, that we are fond of and enjoy the young
brother-in-law's love;

That we are one with Ranjha like sugar and butter and do not give away
the secret of our heart.

They say that the women fall for the handsome young lad as flies drop
and get stuck in honey.

On us alone you have fallen and lie like a curse; all other women live in
happiness and peace.

If you leave home, you will certainly starve to death. Then will you lose
all your waywardness.

Varis, when they meet those who are addicted to bad habits, all people
run far away from them."

"Your face looks hideous, O sister-in-law; why do you rake into fire the
moths already burnt?

What purpose do I have with you that I should let you shower me with
your sarcastic remarks?

Helping one on to the roof, you then remove all ladders of exit, such an
edifice of hate you build.

Says Varis, married into the Ranjha's clan, you are a lady, otherwise you
are of the lowest birth."

---

[8] A *Qazi* is an interpreter of the Muslim Law, frequently a judge.

"If you do not find our beauty to your taste and liking, go fetch Hir of
the Syals for your bride![9]

Playing your flute and casting the net of your love, bring as catch the
beautiful maiden of Syals.

You are known to have the knack of enticing women, go get Koklan
Rani down from her palace.[10]

If you cannot take her out by the front door by day, scale the back wall
at night to abduct her."

"I will bring the maiden of the Syals as my bride; put an end to this
mockery and these taunts.

She will sit reclining on a couch like a royal lady and the likes of you will
be her serving maids.

The foul-mouthed sisters-in-law like you deserve to be hurled into some
deep whirling waters.

Cease your chatter, sister-in-law, I am surfeited with the gifts with which
you have filled my lap."

"How infantile you are to make such a nasty row, taking issue with us as
only a co-wife would;

Make haste, do not let the freshness go to waste; the beauty of youth will
become stale and fade."

Ranjha beat his head in anger and said. "You cling to me like a cloth bug
gnawing at a garment.

You keep this home and the homeland too, I leave; let us end the
bickering, Bhabi, I am done."

Shoes in hand, a blanket over shoulders, Ranjha left home to wander and
be as Varis Shah. . . .[11]

Homeless and hunger-oppressed, after a whole day's walk, at night
Dhido arrived at a mosque.

In the middle of the night, he took up his flute to play and filled the air
with the joy of music.

Not a man or woman in the village was left but gathered around the
mosque to hear Dhido play.

Varis Shah *Mian,*[12] hearing the commotion, the mosque's *mullah,*[13] a
pack of quarrels, showed up.

---

[9] Syal is the name of the clan to which Hir belongs.

[10] Koklan Rani was a legendary queen, famous for her beauty.

[11] That is, Dhido Ranjha left to become a light traveler like the poet, Varis Shah.

[12] *Mian* is a term of address for a man somewhat similar to Mister.

[13] A *mullah* is a member of a quasi-clerical class in Islam and often the caretaker of a mosque.

Seeing Dhido's long locks,[14] at once the mullah cried, "Who are you the
    defier of Law? Be off.

There is no room here for scoundrels like you; abide by the Law, cut
    your curls to proper length.

Filled with pride, you act as if you were God; at last you too will perish
    as the heretic Mansur.[15]

Varis Shah, you cannot hide the smell of the spice, asafoetida, even if it is
    buried in camphor."[16]

"The beard of the *sheikh* and the deeds of the devil, O, how you villains
    entrap the passers-by!

Koran in hand, you mount on the *mimbar* and set the snares of your
    hypocritical pious looks.[17]

Are you trying to teach what is good and evil to us? We know the truth
    of Law better than you!

What filth you bring in to make us wallow in it! Thanks to God's bounty
    for saving us from it!"

"The mosques are the houses of God; we do not allow the lawless
    wretches entrance here.

Believers such as you, with long curls and with unshaved lip, we throw
    out of the mosque.

We tear up the lungi if it be too long and set fire to the moustaches of
    improper length.

If we run into a bad dog or a sinful *fakir,*[18] we tie them up and thrash
    them with thick clubs.

One who does not obey the rules of *fikah* deserves to be caught and
    hanged on the crucifix.[19]

Varis Shah, the enemies of God, no sooner seen, should be shooed away
    from afar, like dogs."

"What is your *namaz* made of;[20] from what was it created and by what
    processes did it develop?

---

[14] According to orthodox Islam, a Muslim man should not have hair, beard, or moustache
more than a specified length.

[15] Mansur is another name for Al-Hallaj (857–922), a Sufi who was executed for saying
that he was one with God, a heresy according to orthodox Islam.

[16] Asafoetida is a pungent spice used in cooking. The mullah means that scoundrels like
Ranjha stand out and cannot remain hidden.

[17] The *mimbar* is the podium in a mosque from which a leading Muslim gives a sermon.

[18] A man of renunciation, often a beggar.

[19] *Fikah* is Muslim jurisprudence.

[20] *Namaz* is the word for prayer in Islam. Here Ranjha makes fun of the ritual by describing the prayer as a woman.

How many ears and noses does she have; to be whose bane from the very
 beginning was it sent?

Is she tall or broad in stature and what would be her age; what does she
 wear to bedeck herself?

How many pegs has she with which, like the weavers' warp and woof,
 she holds herself intact?

You loudly fart in the house of God, shamelessly announcing when you
 are about to pass wind.

Idle as the blind, the lepers, the cripples, you sit and cast the *kurah* to
 prophesy on life and death.[21]

Smelling sweet puddings, keen on news of the dead, you kill the living
 with your medicaments.

You have made the Law a sheltering cover with which to shield and
 support the great who sin."

The *mullah* said, "O churlish jutt,[22] I will allow you to stay here and rest
 your arse for the night,

But you must wake up before the break of day and exit from here quietly,
 without obtrusion.

Do not raise contention with the house of God, avoid dire punishments
 for such diabolic deeds."

Varis Shah, to the houses of God the devilish *mullahs* cling like
 interminable cursed blights.

With the chirping of the sparrow, the travelers set out, and churns began
 to swirl in vats of milk.

When the true dawn arrived with its light, the eastern sky was dyed in
 different hues of rosy red.

The ploughmen took out their ploughs and oxen yokes to break the sod
 and prepare it for sowing.

The housewives were at the querns, grinding grain for flour to be
 kneaded into dough to cook.

Maidens got up to spin yarn on the spinning-wheels. The world was
 busy with the daily chores.

Those who had enjoyed their night in making love now rush to their
 bath to clean themselves.

Ranjha set out on his journey and arrived at the river to find the boat
 crammed with passengers.[23]

---

[21] Casting the *kurah* means predicting the future.

[22] Jutt refers to a racial ethnic group dominant in northwestern India. The jutts are land-
holding farmers.

[23] The river is the River Chenab, commonly associated by Punjabis with the stories of lovers.

Varis Shah, the head-boatman, Luddan, is a curmudgeon, looking like a
grocer's barrel of honey.

HIR AND RANJHA IN LOVE

The village buffalo herders reported, a handsome youth, arriving in the
boat, sits in it singing;

As he sings, flowers fall from his lips; he delivers long melodies worth
hundreds of thousands;

He adorns with his presence Hir's couch,[24] Luddan's two wives
accompanying him and serving.

Varis Shah, the maidens of Jhung are furies too.[25] What a storm they
will raise when they arrive!

Accompanied by her sixty maiden friends, Hir, drunk with pride of
youth and beauty, arrived.

Handfuls of pearls dangled from her ears; she resembled in magnificence
the houris[26] and fairies.

The red blouse clung to her breasts making one oblivious of all that
exists on earth or in the sky.

Her nose-ring shone like the pole star; she was bursting with the juice of
youth, a pent up storm.

You with heaps of ear rings, pause; on this earth many pitched their tents
before and are gone.

Varis Shah Mian, the *jutti* was full of pride, arrogance, and vanity and
relentlessly highhanded.

How may the poet do justice in rendering Hir's praise? Her brow shone
as the moon's splendor.

Killer tresses fell on her face as night around the moon; her face was of
the hue of ruddy wine.

She came in abandon with her friends, her body swaying like the
swaying of an eagle's wing.

Her narcissus eyes are the eyes of a fawn, her cheeks have the bloom of
the fresh petals of rose.

The eyebrows were like the arches of Lahore,[27] her beauty was beyond
measure and description.

---

[24] Hir keeps a couch on the river boat. Varis Shah often uses the word *saje* for it. However,
the saje is really the bedding on a couch, cot, or even the floor. The word has suggestions of luxury and a place for erotic enjoyment.

[25] Jhung is the village of the Syals.

[26] The beautiful virgins provided in Paradise to Muslims who have lived rightly.

[27] The ancient city of the Punjab, now in Pakistan. Throughout most of history, it has
been the capital of the Punjab. The arches refer to the arches in the impressive buildings
of the city.

Surma deep and dark lining her eyes looked like the hosts of Punjab invading the land of Hind.[28]

The features of her face were clean and sharp as the elegant letters of calligraphy in a book of art.

She stands out in the *trinjans,*[29] her inebriation with youth like the glory of the *nawab*'s elephant.[30]

Those who desire to meet Hir must have big brave hearts like the wide portals of large houses.

To see Hir is to visit the glorious night of the Prophet's birth; it is the means to win salvation. . . .

"You, sleeping on my *saje,* wake up! You lie inert like a wheat bug, oblivious of everything.

Did you spend a sleepless night that you are now drowned deeply in such sound sleepiness?

Seeing my *saje* vacant and unguarded, you, a slothful man of some place, have collapsed on it.

Do you have a fever, or are possessed by a ghost or jinn, or has an ogress swallowed your soul?

Varis Shah, is he alive and just asleep or has his life come to an end and he is dead in fact?"

Hir screamed and shrieked, a switch in hand. She was a fairy filled with terrible fury at a man.

Ranjha woke up and said, "Vah![31] O beautiful friend!" Hir smiled and was instantly soft and kind.

Flute under arm and rings in the ears and locks of disheveled hair scattering down his face;

Ranjha's curls are soft, his brow like the moon; *surma* in eyes starts battles in the field of looks.

Like Taimus's daughter on seeing Joseph,[32] Hir was amazed at the sight of Ranjha's handsomeness.

His wild eyes pierced deep into her heart like the thrust of a long, sharp-pointed warrior's spear.

---

[28] Through the ages, *surma* has been a common cosmetic black powder, both for men and women, applied to the edges of the eyes to beautify them. Hind is another name for India.

[29] A traditional rural institution of the Punjab. In a *trinjan* young, mostly unmarried women, get together in a group to spin cotton.

[30] The title of *nawab* refers to an aristocrat, often a governor of a province or a regional ruler. It is the root of the English "nabob."

[31] An exclamation expressing wonder and joy.

[32] Taimus's daughter refers to Zuleikha, the same as Potiphar's wife in the story about Joseph in the Bible (Genesis 39).

Seeing the *jutt's* beauty, Hir woke up as if from sleep, amazed and lost in
  devotion to Ranjha.

She sat down on the *saje,* nestling beside Ranjha like a bow in its cover,
  sweetly speaking to him:

"Thank God, I did not strike you or did anything that might have in any
  other way insulted you."

Varis Shah, there is not at all an exit for escape when four eyes meet on
  the battlefield of love.

"With folded hands, I vow to always be your bond-slave along with all
  my friends of the *trinjans.*

Our love will ever bloom in fast colors of eternal springs in the wooded
  pasture, with friends.

God has brought me the gift of union with the *chak,*[33] I leave behind
  the loves of my greener days.

By day you will enjoy the woods with me, at night I will go home to
  frolic in the *havelis.*"[34]

"At the spinning-wheel among your spinning friends, you will sit, the
  mistress of provisions, Hir.

I will come and stand waiting in the yard like dirt; no one will deign to
  pay heed to me, O Hir.

With a handout of bread, you will oust me from the yard; trick me not
  with fake promises, O Hir.

If you seriously intend to stay in love to the end, give a solemn oath,
  your word is true, O Hir."

"I swear by my *Babal,*[35] O Ranjha, may my Mother perish if I ever turn
  my face from your love.

Without you, to eat will be a sin to me; I will never glance at or touch in
  love another man.

I swear an oath on this seat of Khizr that I may be born as a sow if I ever
  breach the rite of love.[36]

May I go blind and die a leper if, Varis Shah, I ever long for another man
  to love than my Ranjha.

Hir gives her life for your name, gives away all the possessions that
  belong to her in this place.

In this dicing game of life, I put down my head as stake and you have
  won while I have lost."

---

[33] The word *chak* literally means servant. Since Ranjha is a servant of the Syals, Chak becomes an alternative name for him.

[34] Mansions.

[35] A term of address for a father used only by daughters. It has special connotations of
filial affection.

[36] Khizr is the lord and guardian of water in middle-eastern and Islamic tradition.

Ranjha becoming trustful, and confident in heart, went to meet the
Chief, Chuchak Khan.[37]

Hir led the way as his sponsor. Ushering him into her father's presence,
she herself stood by.

Smiling, the father asked, "Who is the lad, where has he come from and
from which quarter?

His skin is so delicate that it stains to touch; he is not suited for the work
of grazing buffaloes."

"Smart and clever, he is also very wise," pleaded Hir. "He grazes cattle
with the greatest care,

Driving them only with loving commands, without ever hitting them on
the horns with his stick.

He treats the cattle as his own, brings them home carefully, not seeing
his work as a serf's chore.

The light of Allah shines in his face and his lips keep on reciting God's
name without stopping."

"I gladly agree to your request. Entrust to his charge all the herds of
buffalo that belong to us.

Tell him to keep alert as he stands guard among cattle; the woods are
fraught with dangers.

He should not mingle with the thieves, he lacks the experience of having
grazed buffaloes before.

He must not be distracted by games lest thieves lift the buffaloes and
disgrace us in the village."

Hir said to Ranjha, "Eat butter, sugar, and *prauthay;*[38] let the buffaloes
out, invoking God's help!

Spend your days in enjoyment, lacking nothing when you are content to
live on a bowl of milk."

"God is your provider," Hir went on. "Do not pay any heed if people
laugh at you in mockery.

With my sixty maiden friends, I will keep constant watch to protect your
life at every moment.

Always staying with you in thought and deed, I will guard you and keep
you safe at every step.

Drive the buffalo into the thick of woods and you sit aside, enjoying
yourself in peace and quiet.

Varis, God has arranged things perfectly for us, but life is like a painting
drawn on a sugar-puff."[39]

---

[37] Hir's father.

[38] A type of bread fried on the griddle and richly soaked in butter.

[39] A Punjabi sugar-puff is of small size, spherical on top and flat on the bottom. It quickly
dissolves when put in water or in the mouth.

Reciting God's name, Ranjha entered the pasture; the sun's grueling heat
   utterly wore him down.

But it was the moment of his good fortune; he met the five *Pirs* who
   happened to be passing by.

"Son, eat *churi*,[40] milk the brown buffalo, thrive on its milk, and be not
   sad of heart!" they said.

Ranjha requested, "Grant me the gift of a beautiful lass; you are sharers
   of the power of God!"

"We grant you Hir from the court of God; remember us for help in the
   hour of dire trouble!" . . .

Hir brings the morning meal—sugar, milk pudding, and butter—to
   Ranjha in the grazing woods.

"I am worn searching you all over the pasture-land," she sobs and tells
   the story of her woes.

Kaido the Lame follows spying on her,[41] sniffing *churi* in the woods as
   Hir serves it to Ranjha.

Varis Shah Mian, see what satanic mischief the Lame Leg schemes to
   hatch and bring about!

Hir went to the river to fetch water. Kaido revealed himself to Ranjha,
   begging alms of him,

"I am starved and faint with hunger; in God's name, pray spare for me a
   morsel of your meal!"

Ranjha doled out to him a two-handed scoop; grabbing it, Kaido
   instantly took off for the village.

Ranjha asked Hir on her return, "Who was the lame fakir-like man?
   Where did he come from?"

Varis, Kaido is like one who makes fresh abrasions in the wound and
   rubs salt into the cuts.

Hir said to Ranjha, "You made a grievous error; we are beset by enemies
   of several kinds.

This man spies on us and carries tales to do us harm; day and night, he is
   busy in his evil work.

He machinates to separate lover from lover and schemes to disrupt and
   undo pledges of love.

He will malign us before my father and mother and fill my sisters-in-law's
   ears with his tales."

Half the *churi* spilled, half was left; collecting it to his best, Kaido carried
   it to the village kin.

Saying, "You utterly refused to believe me," he unwrapped the *churi* and
   showed it to them.

---

[40] A preparation made by kneading bread in butter and mixed with sugar.

[41] Kaido, a distant and poor kinsman of Hir, has set himself up as a guardian of tradition.

"No one seems to admonish Chuchak that he should beat some sense
into his daughter's head.

She roams unchaperoned in the woods with Chak; sooner or later, she
will cause us disgrace.

Varis Shah, we rue the day when Chak arrived; it was an evil day as it
brought us dishonor." . . .

As Hir came back home after her day in the woods, her parents called
the Qazi to their house.

They sat side by side along with the Qazi and asked Hir to come and sit
across in front of them.

"Be seated, child," said they in sweetest tones, "so that we may give you
some words of advice.

You should not be familiar with servants; they are low-class laborers of
some nowhere place.

Wise maidens stay at home with friends gathered to spin and entertain
themselves with song.

Spinning on the red wheels,[42] they have friendly contests and sing
beautiful songs of the Chenab!

You know well, Hir, that Chuchak Syal is the Chief of the clan and elder
leader of the village.

You must be mindful of your parents' honor; they are the highest of the
highest among the jutts.

It behooves not young maidens to roam about; messengers will carry
marriage proposals soon.

Wedding plans are all complete and set; the Kheras are busy readying
themselves for the rite.[43]

Varis Shah Mian, gathering together a wedding party, they will be here in
a just few more days." . . .

"A dreadful catastrophe has befallen us," Hir told Ranjha. "To save ourselves, we must flee.

Let us together take to the road and go far away; to live we need no
possessions or this land.

Once I am taken to the Khera's house, never will they permit me to leave
or come back to visit.

When my parents have packed me off in marriage, I will have no say or
freedom of action left.

We joined the lists on the battlefield of love; it is bad form for the
warrior to flee from the field.

Varis Shah, when love is replaced by separation, who can stand the
unbearable pangs it brings?"

---

[42] Red here means colorful. The spinning-wheels can be often very colorful and beautiful.

[43] Khera is the name of the clan into which Hir will be married.

"O Hir, there is utterly no joy in love that is obtained only by stealth and
by resort to eloping.

Leaving home leads to much trouble; whole hosts perished because of
women who eloped.

I clearly see the consequences of your advice; acting on it will bring us
both much disgrace.

You dissuade me from bravely staking head and life; who ever saw the
elopers' offspring thrive?

You and your mother tricked me into grazing herds, such are women's
devious, cunning ways.

Varis Shah, goldsmiths know well how to detect if someone tries to pass
counterfeited money."

Said Hir, "You did an awful thing; you made us let our time go to waste
in heedless neglect;

I kept trying to prevail upon you day and night. Amidst troubles, we let
our time together end.

A wretch that I am, I fell in love to find comfort, but received the
reverse, crises and troubles.

But, Varis Shah, I will not stay with the Kheras." Hir proclaimed her
resolve clearly and aloud. . . .

"O Ranjha, I tried my best to stop the marriage, but matters were finally
out of my control.

The Qazi, parents, and brothers married me off by force. They turned
our friendship into ashes.

I am resolved not to settle in the Kheras' house; I have declared a
permanent war against them.

God willing, if we stay alive, we will meet; for now, though, our
companionship has to end.

From the Kheras' house, I shall write to you about myself; you will soon
come there as a *fakir*.

You will become the disciple of a *jogi*;[44] have your ears torn open and
smear ashes on the body.[45]

Dissolving all distinctions of caste and creed, you will have your head
shaved completely clean.

Come give me a glimpse of your face while we live; I will not be let out
of Kheras' place alive.

---

[44] Punjabi equivalent of yogi.

[45] Torn ears for large rings, smearing ashes on the body, and a clean-shaved head are the
external requirements for jogis.

RANJHA BECOMES A *JOGI*

[*Editor's note.* At Hir's suggestion, Ranjha goes to *jogi* Bal Nath,[46] beseeching him to make him a *jogi*. The Nath grants Ranjha's request and advises him to live the ascetic's life, but Ranjha refuses and compels him to grant him Hir, for he became *jogi* for her sake, not for renunciation. Ranjha then goes to Rangpur, the Kheras' village, setting up camp in the local park. Colluding with her husband's sister, Sehti, who also has a lover, Hir pretends that she is bitten by a snake. She and Sehti stay with the disguised Ranjha in a hut for treatment. From there, they elope, Hir with Ranjha and Sehti with Murad, her lover. The Kheras capture Hir and Ranjha and take them to the local raja, the Just, who grants Hir to Ranjha. Free to live together, they return to Jhung Syal, because Hir wants a regular wedding, arranged by her parents. The parents make a show of agreeing and tell Ranjha to bring a wedding party from Takht Hazara. When he is gone, they deceitfully poison Hir to death. Hearing of her death, Ranjha utters a cry and falls down dead.]

CONCLUSION

Said the Nath, "Ranjha, pay heed, you have taken on a heavy moral
    burden in becoming a *jogi*.
Go blow your horn, proclaiming God's name and accept the piece of
    humble bread in alms.
Seeing an older woman, treat her as your mother and consider the
    younger ones your sisters.
Remain pure and celibate and humble; keep your loin cloth clean and
    free from the dirt of sex."
"If my loin cloth were to stay intact, listen, O Nath, why would I have
    given up home and hearth?
Were I to keep my tongue from expressing love, why would I engage in
    such demanding strife?
Could I keep my self subdued and tamed, why would I have entertained
    such ambitious plans?
Could I sit alone, content in the wilderness, why would have I agreed to
    herd the Syals' buffaloes?
Why would I have had my head shaved and ears torn, if I could control
    my pride, my ego kill?
Had I known that you would tear my ears, I would not have accepted
    these rings even to burn.
Had I known that you would forbid me love, I would not have so much
    as pissed on your retreat.

---

[46] Nath, the second name of the most accomplished jogis, also becomes their designation.

You either make my ears whole again or I will have to take recourse to
    intervention by the courts.

Varis Shah, it is not in me to pledge myself to being a *fakir,* I only need
    to have the garb of one."

The Nath sat in prayer. As he opened his eyes, he said to Ranjha, "Go,
    Son, your wish is granted.

The plant, the seed of which you had sown in the land of heaven, has
    come to bear its blossoms.

The true Almighty has granted Hir to you; the pearl is strung with the
    ruby on the same thread.

March, you will vanquish the Kheras; and afterwards you will sleep in
    peace and comfort."

Girding his loins for the journey, Ranjha was ready to set out quickly
    without wasting any time.

With folded hands, he stood before the Nath and implored, "Pray, be
    pleased to send me off!"

Varis Shah, as soon as the Nath saw him off, Ranjha flew from the
    mount like a leaf in the wind. . . .

After killing Hir, the Syals sent a man with a letter to Dhido, saying,
    God's will is unalterable.

Asking directions, the messenger arrived at Dhido's house and, sobbing,
    handed him the letter.

Ranja asked, "What news have you brought? What is the reason that you
    bear such a sad look?

Is everything well with my jewels?[47] For what reason do you keep on
    sighing and sobbing so?"

"Your jewel has been robbed by such a robber that no one is able to
    bring it back from him.

Hir has been dead for eight watches now; the Syals have sent me to
    convey this message to you.

The world is like children playing at watering fields; in the end, dust
    shall mingle with dust."

Ranjha uttered an anguished cry like Farhad; life passed out of his body
    and vanished into air.

Both Hir and Ranjha remained steadfast in *mijazi* love and kept their
    pledge of love until the end.[48]

Varis Shah, in this *serai* of dreams,[49] many came and blew their
    trumpets, and inevitably left.

---

[47] By jewels, Ranjha means the cattle that used to be in his charge.

[48] *Mijazi* love means true love in human terms, as distinguished from love of the divine.

[49] *Serai* means an inn.

43

ༀ

Ghalib

DIWAN

The name of Ghalib (1797–1869) is a household word in the Indian subcontinent. He is important not only because he is the best poet of the Urdu language, but also because he exemplifies the final phase of the traditional cultures of the East as they became overwhelmed by European colonialism. His poetry is permeated by the deep sadness of an age coming to an end: "Burnt by the flame of the night's bright revel, /A guttering candle sole remains, but that too is still." Yet, faced with a cultural dead end, the power of his literary heritage and personal experience gathered such force in Ghalib's poetic genius that in his poetry the fire of traditional Urdu poetry burned with a final, unprecedented brilliance.

Mirza Asadullah Khan Ghalib was born in Agra which had earlier been the capital of the Mughals, the powerful Muslim dynasty that had ruled India since the sixteenth century. The honorific "Mirza" signified that Ghalib was himself a Mughal. Ghalib ("conqueror") was his pen name which seems to show the poet's pride in his martial heritage. His ancestors were professional soldiers of Turkish descent like the Mughals. His grandfather had moved from Samarkand in Central Asia to India where he and his sons found high positions as army officers. Ghalib's father was killed in action when Ghalib was barely five years old. Therefore, his father's brother, Nasrullah Khan, a cavalry officer under the British East India Company, took over the care of the orphaned nephew. Just four years later, Nasrullah Khan was also killed. The East India Company, the de facto ruler of most of India by this time, conferred on Nasrullah Khan's family, including Ghalib and his brother, a pension to be disbursed by Nasrullah Khan's brother-in-law who, however, paid Ghalib only a fraction of his due share.

This deprivation did not affect Ghalib immediately, because he lived sumptuously in Agra with his mother's wealthy family, spending his time playing chess, flying kites, and socializing with friends. He had the freedom and the money to indulge in youthful excesses and the fashionable vices of the day. He acquired expensive aristocratic habits which were to prove painful in later life when his

647

resources became extremely curtailed. In the meantime, besides enjoying himself, he received the education typical of the cultured nobility, studying theology, astronomy, logic, philosophy, medicine, and literature under some of the best teachers of the day. The appreciation and writing of poetry were considered necessary parts of aristocratic education. Ghalib started writing poetry at the age of ten. He particularly mentions as his teacher a scholar from Persia, a Zoroastrian convert to Islam named Hurmuz. The poet attributes his mastery of the Persian language to Hurmuz's instruction. After moving to Delhi, Ghalib built on the foundation of his early education by extensive self-study.

When Ghalib was thirteen, his marriage was arranged. It was not a happy marriage. He described it as a "life sentence" and his wife as "a chain . . . tied round my feet." He and his wife were totally incompatible, she being devout and puritanic and he a worldly and passionate man. Yet the marriage remained stable. Although Ghalib was an admirer of beautiful women, it seems that he had only one passionate love affair, that with a courtesan. It ended sadly, for the courtesan committed suicide. Ghalib and his wife had seven children, but none of them lived longer than fifteen months. They adopted the wife's nephew. He too died while still a young man.

When Ghalib moved permanently to Delhi where his wife's family lived, the days of the Mughal glory had long been over. The East India Company was the supreme power of India and the Mughal emperor its pensioner. Still there was much literary activity at the Mughal court and in the city. Ghalib's father-in-law, himself a poet, had many literary friends. Contact with them tempered Ghalib's extravagant ways and inspired literary ambition in him. By his mid-twenties he became an accomplished poet noted for his strikingly different poetic manner.

About this time Ghalib began to feel the pinch of financial stringency. Without his mother's support and living in an aristocratic style, he found his pension far too meager. He began to incur debts and felt the urgency for the restoration of the full pension to which he thought he was entitled. He struggled vainly in that cause for sixteen years. The struggle included travel on horseback to Calcutta to put his case before the governor-general of the East India Company. Treated with respect by the British and exhilarated by the modernity and glamour of the city, he stayed there for eighteen months. As the case lingered, he returned to Delhi to pursue it from there, but eventually his petition was turned down. Further appeal to the company's directors in London and his effort to reach Queen Victoria for redress also ended in failure. In the process Ghalib incurred heavy debts. The fear of debtor's prison hung over him perpetually.

Ghalib now made desperate efforts to seek preferment at the Mughal court, but the emperor, Bahadur Shah Zafar, himself a poet, was not favorably disposed towards him. Ghalib was already fifty-three when the emperor finally conferred a title on him and gave him a small stipend to write a Persian prose history of the Timurid Dynasty, including the Mughals. After his court poet laureate's death, the emperor also made Ghalib his poetic mentor, and two imperial princes became his pupils as well. This modest good fortune, however, ended soon with the Mutiny of

1857. The mutiny was a rebellion of the East India Company's Indian troops. It quickly grew into a countrywide revolt. After the suppression of the revolt, the emperor, accused of complicity with the rebels, was deposed by the British and the Mughal Dynasty was terminated. Ghalib's pension stopped. For a while he survived by selling his household effects. Two years later, a friendly ruler, the nawab of Rampur, bestowed a stipend on him. Soon after, the company pension was restored. The poet's last days passed in relative freedom from financial worries.

Ghalib's cherished ambition was to achieve renown as a writer of Persian, but by an irony of the course of literary history which saw Urdu increasingly replacing Persian and the nature of his genius, Ghalib became famous for his Urdu ghazals which are far fewer in volume than his Persian writings. The publication during his lifetime of several successive editions of the Diwan-i-Ghalib (Collected Poems of Ghalib), *which consists almost entirely of his Urdu ghazals, shows that they were popular from the beginning. They have remained the most popular of his works to the present day.*

As a poetic genre, the ghazal had its origin in the customary erotic prelude of the pre-Islamic odes of Arabia (Volume II, Selection 8). Separating itself from the ode, the prelude became an independent lyric about love. Under the influence of Persian singers and later transported to Persia (Iran), the love lyric gradually developed into the ghazal proper. In the hands of the great Persian poets of the thirteenth and the fourteenth century, particularly Hafiz (Volume II, Selection 38), the ghazal achieved perfection. From Persian it spread to other languages of the Islamic world, most notably Urdu, a language which evolved around the courts of Muslim rulers from a mixture of Hindustani, the main vernacular of Northern India, with Persian, Turkish, and Arabic, the languages that the Muslims brought to India with them. Written in Persian script, Urdu is one of the major languages of India and the state language of Pakistan.

The ghazal possesses qualities unique in the world's literature. It functions within the confines of extremely strict conventions. Although during its history the ghazal has been used to address a countless variety of subjects, from human or divine love to social and political issues, technically it is a love poem in the sense that it is written in the language of love. A most perplexing feature of the ghazal for those unfamiliar with it is a complete lack of continuity or unity of theme or idea. It is by definition fragmentary and for that reason is sometimes described as "unstrung pearls." Each verse couplet in it makes an independent statement unconnected with the other verses. The only unities here are those of mood and form. Written in two-line units (couplets), the ghazal must contain at least five such units. There is no upper limit on length, but few ghazals are longer than ten or twelve couplets. The two lines of the first couplet rhyme with each other at the end, and the same end-ryhme is carried throughout the poem in the second line of each couplet: aa, ba, ca, da, and so on. The last couplet mentions the poet's name usually with an expression of the poet's pride. The language, imagery, similes and metaphors, characters, allusions—in short, all the poetic elements of the ghazal—are highly stereotypical, derived from literary convention rather than from direct experience of life. However, they are not devoid of beauty. On the contrary, they shine with a gemlike beauty. The poets arrange and rearrange them into beautiful patterns like mosaics. The Urdu poets before Ghalib had mastered the art of weaving such patterns with dexterous fluency and simplicity, making the beauties of the ghazal *accessible to the common reader and listener. Ghalib was obsessed with his poetic superiority and originality. Often this obsession resulted in mere eccentricity and difference for its own sake, in the form of difficult language and artificially complicated imagery. However, Ghalib was a poet of introspection and of genuine experience of the inner processes of the self. He needed an extraordinary language and a complex imagery to express this inner experience. When the experience and its expression fully matched, his poetry, despite, or because of, the complexity of its language and imagery, became utterly transparent and fluent. It also stood apart from the poetry of his contemporaries and predecessors.*

The underlying sentiment of Ghalib's poetry is an essentially pagan desire for enjoyment of life. His outlook centers on the value of human existence and its enjoyment as fundamental goods. Evil for him consists of obstacles to personal happiness. He had intensely experienced both happiness and suffering. His poetry moves between the two poles of joy and grief. His desire for happiness is no mere quest for easy self-indulgence. It is accompanied by a keen and rigorous intellect with which he looks objectively at truth and reality. Although he always remained formally a Muslim, he clearly saw through the fallacies of rigid religious belief and conventional morality. He did not categorically subscribe to any one religion, dogma, or philosophy, but rather kept an open mind, seeing good where he found it. He strongly criticized the society in which he lived for its life-denying values. He called it a prison, but he lacked the means for a constructive vision of a social order different from the one around him. He was highly impressed by the marvels of Western civilization, but he did not have the knowledge to understand the true nature of its positive and negative qualities. The cruelties of the Mutiny of 1857, perpetrated both by the Indians and the British, shook Ghalib to the depth of his being. The experience penetrated through the thick sheath of his aristocratic prejudice, and for the first time in his life, he felt for the helpless masses. However, he could not understand the causes of the Mutiny or its implications for the future. He was a product of the past, able to function only within the confines of the past. Endowed with love of life and an extraordinarily sharp intellect, he used the resources available to him to mould his experience into the last glorious outburst of traditional Urdu poetry.

The following selection contains eleven of the ghazals *from Ghalib's* Diwan. *The translation provides a rendering as literally close to the original and as closely replicating the form of the* ghazal *as sensitivity to poetic content and the differences between Urdu and English permit.*

1

Of whose impudent pen does the work of art complain?[1]
Each picture-perfect beauty a suppliant in paper dress appears.[2]

Ah, the hard labor of the lonely nights; about it do not ask!
To reach morning through the night, to cut in rock a stream of milk
　　　　appears.[3]

The passion beyond control of execution, you should see!
The sword's razor edge to leap beyond the sword's edge appears.

Howsoever far knowing may throw its listening net,
The meaning of my words a bird still beyond the net appears.

Though in prison, Ghalib, I yet carry flames beneath my feet;
The loop of my chain a hair curled before the fire's heat appears.

2

None besides Qais known brave in the battlefield of love had been,
But then his desert narrow due to the rivals' narrow eyes had been.[4]

My bursting out as a flower removed the black stain of the heart,
Which proves its substance nothing but the smoke of sighs had been.

In dreams, I dealt with debit and credit in my account of love with you,
When I woke up, I saw that in love neither gain nor loss had been.

I am as yet imbibing lessons at the school of heart's grief,
But so far have learned only the meaning of "gone" and "has been."

The shroud covered my vice's naked stain, of all virtue my being bereft,
Or I, in any other dress, a disgrace to the whole world had been.

The mountain-cutter could not die, Asad, without the adze's help;
His madness nothing but intoxication with rules and rites had been.

Translated from Urdu by Surjit S. Dulai. Copyright © Surjit S. Dulai, 1998.

[1] The poet here alludes to the creative act of God, who brings into being beautiful creatures, but gives them too short a life. Hence the creatures' complaint.

[2] In the olden days in Iran, it was customery for petitioners to appear in court dressed in paper.

[3] A reference to the story of Shirin and Farhad. In love with Shirin, Farhad was assigned by her father the ordeal of digging a channel through a mountain and filling it with milk to win Shirin's hand. The only implement that Farhad had for cutting through the mountain was an adze.

[4] Qais was the real name of Majnun (meaning "mad") from the love story of Laila and Majnun, well known in Arabic, Persian, and many other languages of the Islamic world. Unable to marry Laila, Qais went mad and wandered in the desert. Hence constancy in love, madness, the desert, and the wilderness are all associated with his name.

3

You say you will not give it back, if my heart lying around you found;
But where is the heart to lose, if in its loss, I have my purpose found?

When it found love, the heart the joy of existence found;
It found the remedy for pain and a pain beyond remedy found.

It is the enemy's friend, I know which way my heart leans;
I have found my sighs to be without effect and my cries futile found.

Naivete here is cunningness, unawareness being alert,
Beauty in its unconcern was trying the lovers' mettle found.

The bud has begun to bloom again. Today, the heart
That had been massacred and lost, have I once again found.

The condition of my heart I do not know, excepting that
Countless times I searched for it and you countless times found.

The admonishing of the advising man sprinkled salt on my wound;
Someone please should ask him this: what joy in doing this he found?

4

With a hidden searing my heat unstoppably burned down;
As a silently smouldering fire, it quietly burned down.

Not even a wish to meet or a remembrance of love in the heart remains,
Such a fire swept through this house, all there was in it burned down.

I am now gone still beyond the afterworld; or you would know how
Touched by my flaming sighs, the eagle's wing burned down?

Tell me who can bear the heat of thought's full power;
I had but thought of going wild, the wilderness burned down.[5]

The heart is no more, or I would show the blossoming of its scars;
What can I say of their shining light, the lighter of lights burned down?

Here I am, and a wish to be filled with sadness, Ghalib. For the heart,
Seeing the style of welcome of the dwellers of the world, burned down.

5

Every kind of love a rival of world's wherewithal turned out;
Even when veiled by his picture, Qais stark naked turned out.

The wound did not accommodate itself to the hearts's narrow space,
Even the shaft of her eyes out of the gashed breast fluttering turned out.

---

[5] Another reference to Majnun.

The scent of flowers, the heart's cry, smoke from the gathering's lamp,
Whatever came from your presence, all scattered turned out.

The yearning heart was the dining sheet for enjoying the food of pain,
The joy of this food to match the strength of lips and teeth turned out.

Courage, fond of hard pursuits, has newly begun to learn self-extinction;
Great hardship it is that this task too to be too easy turned out.

Again the urge to weep has raised commotion in the heart, Ghalib;
Ah, what had not come out a drop, to be a deluge turned out.

6

Fate did not grant that a meeting with my love should have been;
If I had lived on longer, the same lonely waiting would have been.

That I continued to live sustained by your promise, do not believe!
Had I believed you, don't you see that dead with joy I would have been?

I found out, the frailty of your promise came with your tenderness;
You could never break the promise, if any stronger it had been.

Only my heart can tell the effect of your eyes' half-pulled shaft;
Had it gone through the heart, how the sweet ache would have been?

What friendship is this that friends have turned advisers?
O someone a giver of comfort and a sharer of grief could have been!

The stone's veins would drip such blood as once started wouldn't stop,
If what you consider grief, instead, a spark in stone could have been.

Though grief grinds life in pain, once mustn't be a child, it is the heart;
Had there been no grief of love, grief of livelihood would have been.

Whom can I tell what it is; a terrible evil is the night of grief.
Why would I find death so bad, if only once it could have been?

If the infamy of death I had to bear, why didn't I drown in a river?
There would have been no funeral, nor a burial place would have been.

Who could bear to see Him, for he is unique and the only One existent;
Had one thought there are two, an encounter with Him would have been.

Such flights into divine truth and such beauty of expression, Ghalib!
We would have counted you a prophet, if you a drinker had not been.

7

It is hard indeed for any task easy to be;
It's not even given to humankind human to be.

My tears of grief are intent on the ruin of my house;
Doors and walls drip with portents of the wilderness-to-be.

Woe, the madness of love, my constantly going
To her on my own and unasked in trouble be.

As her showing herself demands being seen with admiration,
Even the power of the mirror strives simply an eye to be.

You who have desire, of the joy of being executed, do not ask;
A festival for the eyes it is for the executioner's sword naked to be.

I took into the ground with me the scar of my desire for joy, now
You can have the garden in any of a hundred hues you wish it to be!

The comfort of the disturbed heart is to be wounded with desire,
The joy of the heart's wound is in the salt cellar buried to be.

After having murdered me, she forswore cruelty;
O that easily distraught one's being distraught see!

8

Thus in every gesture, she signals a meaning of another kind;
I love her, but she suspects motives of an altogether other kind.

O God, she has neither understood, nor will understand my words,
Give her another heart, if you won't give me a tongue of another kind.

What connection does that proud glance have with the eyebrows?
The arrow is fixed, but it shoots from a bow of quite another kind.

While you are in town, there is no reason that I should worry;
If robbed, I will go and buy from the bazaar a heart of another kind.

Although I have become adept at breaking a few of the world's idols,
While I live, there still lie on the way heavy stones of another kind.

The heart's blood is in spate. I would have wept my heart's fill, if I,
For tears of blood, besides these two, had many eyes of another kind.

I die to hear her voice, it matters not if my head is struck off, provided
She keeps on telling the executioner to deal strokes of yet other kind!

People are deceived that the sun has come out to light the world;
Each day I reveal a hidden scar of the heart of still another kind.

When streams do not find a path in their flow, they overflow;
When stopped, my spirit moves faster with a force of another kind.

Although other fine poets in the world there also be,
They say, Ghalib's poetic manner is of an altogether other kind.

9

Life is over before sighs bear fruit, one has to wait till then.
The winning of your tress? Who ever lives to win till then?

Every wave a net, hundreds of crocodile mouths loops in every net;
The drop would one day be a pearl; let's see what it goes thru till then.

Love demands patience and desire is filled with impatience;
The heart will one day burst red, what color should I give it till then.

I grant that you will not be neglectful towards me, but
By the time you care to see, I will have turned to dust by then?

From the sight of the sun's face, the dew learns to cease to be;
I also wait for a kind glance from you. I am only till then.

For the twinkling of an eye is the time to live, O you who do not know!
The revel's life, a dancing spark, instantly ends. It lasts only till then.

What can cure the grief of life, Asad,[6] but death?
The candle burns in all shades till the morning, resting only then.

10

Any hope to fruition does not come;
Any answer to my condition does not come.

The day death will come is predetermined;
Why all night, a wink of slumber does not come?

Once I used to laugh at my heart's condition;
Now for any reason, laughter does not come.

The good of piety and penance I do know,
But the heart to this direction does not come.

There is a certain reason why I do not speak,
Or the ability to speak within my power does not come?

Why should I not scream, for she misses me
When the sound of my crying into her ear does not come.

If the wound of my heart, doctor, you cannot see,
Even the smell of its festering does not come?

I am there wherefrom even to myself
Any news of my own condition does not come.

I am dying with the desire to die,
Death comes, yet it does not come.

With what face, Ghalib, will you to the *Kaaba* go?[7]
But then the sense of shame in your mind does not come.

---

[6] The poet's first name which he often used as a pen name alternating it with Ghalib.

[7] The *Kaaba* is the holiest shrine of Islam. It is located in Mecca in Saudi Arabia. Muslims face towards the *Kaaba* while praying.

11

A playpen of children is the world before my eyes;
The play goes on night and day before my eyes.

In my eyes, the throne of Solomon is but a toy.
The miracles of Jesus are a tale before my eyes.

I do not accept the world's appearance except in name,
The existence of things is but an illusion before my eyes?

Before me the desert disappears into dust,
The river rubs its brow on the earth before my eyes.

Ask not how I fare after you have left,
Just see in what color you shine before my eyes!

'Tis true I am self-absorbed, self-bedecked; why shouldn't I be?
My beloved sits here shining like a mirror before my eyes.

Then see the way flowers scatter from my speech,
When someone sets a goblet of wine before my eyes.

I overcame jealousy to avoid the impression of my lack of love;
How can I tell my rival not to say her name before my eyes.

Faith pulls me back when I am drawn to *kufr*,[8]
The *Kaaba* is at my back, the holy church before my eyes.

I am a lover, but deluding the beloved is my trade,
So even Laila speaks ill of Majnun before my eyes.

Lovers are happy in union, but do not die in the joy of it as I do;
Wishing death in a night of separation has come before my eyes.

An ocean of blood surges in full force, may this be the limit!
We will see what other things are yet to come before my eyes.

Though the hand can move no more, the eyes still have life;
Let the cup and the flask yet stay before my eyes.

He is my companion in work, in temper and in trust;
Why speak ill of Ghalib, he is good before my eyes.

---

[8] *Kufr* means apostasy. Here it implies love of beauty. In the second line of the couplet, the love of a beautiful beloved is equated with the Christian church, an emblem of apostasy for Muslims.

44

ꝫ

Nguyen Du

THE TALE OF KIEU

Truyen Kieu (The Tale of Kieu) *is Vietnam's greatest and best loved epic. There's irony in the fact that this story, often read as a metaphor for the integrity and endurance of the Vietnamese people under foreign oppression, is in its origin a story out of China—Vietnam's oldest and longest foreign occupier. However, by the early nineteenth century when Nguyen Du finished recasting a rather mediocre sixteenth-century Chinese novel into a narrative poem of 1,627 couplets in the Vietnamese language, its title character, Kieu, had been shaped into an unforgettable Vietnamese woman who achieves moral survival under the weight of seemingly endless betrayal and ill fortune.*

Vietnam itself has had a troubled history. The country was invaded by the Chinese in 211 B.C. By A.D. 111, under the Han Dynasty, it was fully incorporated as a province of the Chinese state. It remained so until the political weakness of China after the fall of the T'ang Dynasty permitted establishment of Vietnamese independence in 939. Although there were brief periods of Chinese reconquest and the standard status of a tribute relationship to the Middle Kingdom, Vietnam largely retained its political identity until its conquest by the French in 1884. Through these two thousand years of Chinese presence, Chinese ideas and institutions had become the dominant elements in the Vietnamese cultural mix, resulting in a written language incorporating many Chinese characters, a government staffed by Confucian scholar-bureaucrats, a general acceptance of the Chinese version of Mahayana Buddhism, even a capital city, Hue, modeled on China's Ch'ang-an. Nguyen Du (1765–1820) was, therefore, a scholar-bureaucrat steeped in the Confucian tradition, and although The Tale of Kieu *is the classic expression of Vietnamese character, it nevertheless makes liberal use of Chinese philosophical, religious, and literary allusions.*

Nguyen Du himself lived through a particularly vexed period of his country's history. His family had long served the rulers of the later Le Dynasty (1428–1789), but in 1771 a peasant uprising, the Tay-son Rebellion, broke out in the

south. It was led by three brothers, one of whom became the model in The Tale of
Kieu *for the heroic rebel warrior Tu Hai. By 1788 one of the Tay-son brothers
had established a new dynasty, which Nguyen Du tried to serve despite its anti-
Chinese bias. By 1802, however, the Tay-son were in turn overthrown by a more
traditional Vietnamese dynasty, the Nguyen (no relation to the author) and once
again Nguyen Du was forced to find his career footing in a new regime. We do
not know exactly when he composed* The Tale of Kieu, *but do know it was circulated in manuscript among his friends, was published a short time after his death,
was soon recognized as the masterpiece of Vietnamese literature, and it continues
in that preeminent status.*

*The poem is set forth in six parts. In the first the virtuous and beautiful hero-
ine, Thuy Kieu, meets, falls in love and is betrothed to the talented and equally
virtuous scholar Kim Trong. In the second, excerpted here, disaster strikes this
idyllic scene of love and family. Kim is called away by his uncle's death; Kieu's father and brother are arrested on trumped-up charges; and Kieu, with a combination of Confucian filial devotion and Buddhist fatalism, sees it as her duty to sell
herself to raise money for her father's and brother's release. The excerpt, among
other things, reveals the difficult position of women in a patriarchal society. In
part three the uncouth "scholar" whom she thinks she has married turns out to be
a procurer for a brothel, where Kieu suffers the humiliation of learning "the trade
of love." She is briefly rescued in part four by a handsome and cultivated patron
who steals her away from the brothel, only to expose her to the wrath of his first
wife, who treats her as a slave. In part five, after briefly being betrayed into
brothel life again, she meets the rebel captain Tu Hai, certainly the most heroic
male figure of the story. Kieu loves him and lives with him for five years, until he
is treacherously murdered by an imperial general. Captured by the general and
about to be violated by him, Kieu seeks death by throwing herself into a river. In
the last segment, Kieu is rescued and revived by a pious Buddhist nun. Her family and her first love, Kim, learn of her whereabouts and bring her home. She
agrees to marry Kim, but believing that her body has been sullied beyond redemption, insists on a nonsexual relationship.*

*So her story has, in a sense, a happy ending, but not a wholly satisfactory one.
Kieu has undergone terrible spiritual and physical abuse, has been degraded and
betrayed, and her musings on* karma, *the Buddhist belief that fate is shaped by
one's actions, do not convince her or the reader that she has deserved any of this
mistreatment. Her heroism lies in the fact that she has maintained her integrity,
has submitted to her fate without being crushed by it. Her strength of spirit becomes the strength of the poem, and the secret of its lasting appeal to generations
of Vietnamese through nearly two centuries of national tribulation.*

FROM PART II

The brushwood gate unbolted, there came in
a houseboy with a missive fresh from home.
It said Kim's uncle while abroad had died,
whose poor remains were now to be brought back.
To far Liao-yang, beyond the hills and streams,
he'd go and lead the cortege, Father bade.
    What he'd just learned astounded Kim—at once
he hurried to her house and broke the news.
In full detail he told her how a death,
striking his clan, would send him far away:
"We've scarcely seen each other—now we part.
We've had no chance to tie the marriage tie.
But it's still there, the moon we swore by:
not face to face, we shall stay heart to heart.
A day will last three winters far from you:
my tangled knot of grief won't soon unknit.
Care for yourself, my gold and jade, that I,
at the world's ends, may know some peace of mind."
    She heard him speak, her feelings in a snarl.
With broken words, she uttered what she thought:
"Why does he hate us so who spins silk threads?
Before we've joined in joy we part in grief.
Together we did swear a sacred oath:
my hair shall gray and wither, not my love.
What matter if I must wait months and years?
I'll think of my wayfaring man and grieve.
We've pledged to wed our hearts—I'll never leave
and play my lute aboard another's boat.
As long as hills and streams endure, come back,
remembering her who is with you today."
    They lingered hand in hand and could not part,
but now the sun stood plumb above the roof.
Step by slow step he tore himself away—
at each farewell their tears would fall in streams.
Horse saddled and bags tied in haste, he left:
they split their grief in half and parted ways.

•   •   •

There she remained, her back against the porch,
her feelings snarled like raveled skeins of silk.
Through window bars she gazed at mists beyond—
a washed-out rose, a willow gaunt and pale.

Distraught, she tarried walking back and forth
when from the birthday feast her folks returned.
Before they could trade news of health and such,
in burst a mob of bailiffs on all sides.
With cudgels under arm and swords in hand,
those fiends and monsters rushed around, berserk.
They cangued[1] them both, the old man, his young son—
one cruel rope trussed two dear beings up.
Then, like bluebottles buzzing through the house,
they smashed workbaskets, shattered looms to bits.
They grabbed all jewels, fineries, personal things,
scooping the household clean to fill greed's bag.

From nowhere woe had struck—who'd caused it all?
Who'd somehow set the snare and sprung the trap?
Upon inquiry it was later learned
some knave who sold raw silk had brought a charge.
Fear gripped the household—cries of innocence
shook up the earth, injustice dimmed the clouds.
All day they groveled, begged, and prayed—deaf ears
would hear no plea, harsh hands would spare no blow.
A rope hung each from girders, by his heels—
rocks would have broken, let alone mere men.
Their faces spoke sheer pain and fright—this wrong
could they appeal to Heaven far away?
Lawmen behaved that day as is their wont,
wreaking dire havoc just for money's sake.[2]

By what means could she save her flesh and blood?
When evil strikes, you bow to circumstance,

---

[1] The cangue was a structure of heavy boards with a circular hole in the middle. It was fastened about a prisoner's neck, while his hands were often shackled to the sides of the device as well. Common in traditional China, it served both to prevent escape and to humiliate the prisoner, much in the manner of the stocks in England and the American colonies. Unlike the stocks, however, the cangue permitted a prisoner to be moved from place to place—painfully and shamefully.

[2] The vicious bailiffs in this passage are the hired agents of the mandarin (the government bureaucrat). In Chinese and Vietnamese literature they are often portrayed as venal and violent, doing the "dirty work" with which the Confucian magistrate would not soil his hands.

As you must weigh and choose between your love
and filial duty, which will turn the scale?
She put aside all vows of love and troth—
a child first pays the debts of birth and care.
Resolved on what to do, she said: "Hands off—
I'll sell myself and Father I'll redeem."

    There was an elderly scrivener surnamed Chung,
a bureaucrat who somehow had a heart.
He witnessed how a daughter proved her love
and felt some secret pity for her plight.
Planning to pave this way and clear that path,
he reckoned they would need three hundred *liang*.
He'd have her kinsmen freed for now, bade her
provide the sum within two days or three.

    Pity the child, so young and so naive—
misfortune, like a storm, swooped down on her.
To part from Kim meant sorrow, death in life—
would she still care for life, much less for love?
A raindrop does not brood on its poor fate;
a leaf of grass repays three months of spring.

    Matchmakers were advised of her intent—
brisk rumor spread the tidings near and far.
There lived a woman in that neighborhood,
who brought a suitor, one from out of town.
When asked, he gave his name as Scholar Ma
and claimed his home to be "Lin-ch'ing, near here."
Past forty, far beyond the bloom of youth,
he wore a smooth-shaved face and smart attire.
Master and men behind came bustling in—
the marriage broker ushered him upstairs.
He grabbed the best of seats and sat in state
while went the broker bidding Kieu come out.

    Crushed by her kinsfolk's woe and her own grief,
she crossed the sill, tears flowing at each step.
She felt the chill of winds and dews, ashamed
to look at flowers or see her mirrored face.
The broker smoothed her hair and stroked her hand,
coaxing a wilted mum, a gaunt plum branch.

    He pondered looks, gauged skills—he made her play
the moon-shaped lute, write verses on a fan.
Of her lush charms he relished each and all:
well pleased, he set to bargaining a deal.

    He said: "For jade I've come to this Blue Bridge:
tell me how much the bridal gift will cost."

The broker said: "She's worth her weight in gold!
But in distress they'll look to your big heart."
They haggled hard and long, then struck a deal:
the price for her, four hundred and some *liang*.
All was smooth paddling once they gave their word—
as pledges they swapped horoscopic cards
and set the day when, full paid for, she'd wed.
When cash is ready, what cannot be fixed?
Old Chung was asked to help—at his request
old Virong could on probation go back home.
    Pity the father facing his young child.
Looking at her, he bled and died within:
"You raise a daughter wishing she might find
a fitting match, might wed a worthy mate.
O Heaven, why inflict such woes on us?
Who slandered us to tear our home apart?
I would not mind the ax for these old bones,
but how can I endure my child's ordeal?
Death now or later only happens once—
I'd rather pass away than suffer so."
    After he'd said those words he shed more tears
and made to knock his head against a wall.
They rushed to stop him, then she softly spoke
and with some words of comfort calmed him down:
"What is she worth, a stripling of a girl
who's not repaid one whit a daughter's debts?
Ying once shamed me, petitioning the throne—
could I fall short of Li who sold herself?[3]
As it grows old, the cedar is a tree
that singly shoulders up so many boughs.
If moved by love you won't let go of me,
I fear a storm will blow and blast our home.
You'd better sacrifice just me—one flower
will turn to shreds, but green will stay the leaves.
Whatever lot befalls me I accept—
think me a blossom nipped when budding green.
Let no wild notions run around your head

---

[3] The references are to two stories out of Han Dynasty China. Ying was the daughter of a man with no son who was condemned to death. The girl offered her life instead, whereupon the emperor pardoned her father. Li sold herself as human sacrifice to a snake demon to save her impoverished parents. She killed the demon and so impressed a ruler that he sought her as his queen.

or you shall wreck our home and hurt yourself."
Words of good sense sank smoothly in his ear—
they stared at one another, pouring tears.
   Outside, that Scholar Ma appeared again—
they signed the contract, silver then changed hands.
A wanton god, the Old Man of the Moon,
at random tying couples with his threads!
When money's held in hand it's no great trick
swaying men's hearts and turning black to white.
Old Chung did all he could and gave all help:
gifts once presented, charges were dismissed.

   Her family's woes were settled for a time,
but now the bridal hour drew on apace.
Alone, she huddled by the midnight lamp,
with tear-soaked gown and sorrow-withered hair:
"No matter what fate deals me, I will grieve
for him who steadfast kept the vow he swore.
How much he toiled and strove to win my love!
But grown attached to me, he's marred his life.
The cup we both drank from has barely dried
when I now break my oath and play him false.
In far-away Liao-yang how can he guess
our union's torn asunder by my hand?
So many vows of love we traded once!
Oh, what will they amount to in this life?
But haunted by troth-incense we once burned,
I'll be reborn a beast and make amends.
Till I've paid off my debt of love to him,
my heart will stay a crystal down below."
Her secret thoughts kept spinning round and round—
as lamp oil burned away, tears drenched her scarf.
   Thuy Van,[4] who just awoke from some sweet dream,
stopped by the lamp and with concern inquired:
"In Heaven's complex scheme of flux and change,
you're left to bear the family's woes alone.
Is that why you've stayed up the livelong night?
Or with some secret are you still beset?"
   Kieu said: "My heart's near bursting, for it's caught
in love's own webs and tangles yet unsnarled.
I feel ashamed to part my lips and tell,

---

[4] Kieu's younger sister. She will marry Kim, as Kieu here asks her to do.

but if I hid it I would wrong his love.
Should you agree I'll ask you . . . Please sit down
and let me bow to you before I speak.
Midway my bonds of love with him have snapped—
let me trust you to mend and splice what's left.
Since I met Kim I gave my fan in pledge—
we drank of the same cup and swore our troth.
Then out of nowhere broke a storm on us—
how could both love and duty be fulfilled?
You have long days of spring ahead—please heed
the call of blood, redeem my pledge for me.
Though flesh and bones will then have turned to dust,
I'll breathe your happiness and smile down there.
Bracelets and pledge on paper decked with clouds:
preserve this troth, these things are jointly ours.
When bound as man and wife, you two will mourn
a star-crossed girl and nurse her in your hearts.
I shall have vanished leaving few remains:
a lute, troth-incense burned in days gone by.
Sometime, if ever you will tune this lute
or light that incense vessel, look outdoors:
among the grass and leaves you'll see a breeze
waft back and forth—you'll know that I've come home.
My soul, still haunted by the oath, will try
to keep my pledge though I'll have turned to naught.
The world of night will hide my face, my voice—
yet, please shed tears for someone wronged by fate.
Ah, now the pin has snapped, the vase has crashed:
past all expression, how I cherish him!
Through you I'll send my humblest bows to him:
the tie of love between us is cut short.
Why have I drawn a lot as gray as dirt?
The flower's doomed to drift along the stream.
O Kim, my dearest Kim! This is the end:
as of today I'll have betrayed your trust."

• • •

How to express her grief, while on the tower
a watchman tolled and tolled the hours of night?
A carriage, flower-decked, arrived outside
with flutes and lutes to bid dear kin part ways.
She grieved to go, they grieved to stay behind:
tears soaked stone steps as parting tugged their hearts.
Across a twilit sky dragged sullen clouds—

grasses and branches drooped, all drenched with dew.
He led her to an inn and left her there
within four walls, a maiden in her spring.
The girl felt torn between dire dread and shame—
she'd sadly brood, her heart would ache and ache.
A rose divine lay fallen in vile hands,
once kept from sun or rain for someone's sake:
"If only I had known I'd sink so low,
I should have let my true love pluck my bud.
Because I fenced it well from the east wind,
I failed him then and make him suffer now.
When we're to meet again, what will be left
of my poor body here to give much hope?
If I indeed was born to float and drift,
how can a woman live with such a fate?"
      Upon the table lay a knife at hand—
she grabbed it, hid it wrapped inside her scarf:
"Yes, if and when the flood should reach my feet,
this knife may later help decide my life."
      The autumn night wore on, hour after hour—
alone, she mused, half wakeful, half asleep.
She did not know that Scholar Ma, the rogue,
had always patronized the haunts of lust.
The rake had hit a run of blackest luck:
in whoredom our whoremaster sought his bread.
      Now, in a brothel, languished one Dame Tu
whose wealth of charms was taxed by creeping age.
Mere hazard, undesigned, can bring things off:
sawdust and bitter melon met and merged.
They pooled resources, opening a shop
to sell their painted dolls through all the year.
Country and town they scoured for "concubines"
whom they would teach the trade of play and love.
      With Heaven lies your fortune, good or ill,
and woe will pick you if you're marked for woe.
Pity a small, frail bit of womankind,
a flower sold to board a peddler's boat.
She now was caught in all his bag of tricks:
a paltry bridal gift, some slapdash rites.
      He crowed within: "The flag has come to hand!
I view rare jade—it stirs my heart of gold!
The kingdom's queen of beauty! Heaven's scent!
One smile of hers is worth pure gold—it's true.
When she gets there, to pluck the maiden's bud

princes and gentlefolk will push and shove.
She'll bring at least three hundred *liang,* about
what I have paid—net profit after that.
A morsel dangles at my mouth—what God
serves up I crave, yet money hate to lose.
A heavenly peach within a mortal's grasp:
I'll bend the branch, pick it, and quench my thirst.
How many flower-fanciers on earth
can really tell one flower from the next?
Juice from pomegranate skin and cockscomb blood
will heal it up and lend the virgin look.
In dim half-light some yokel will be fooled:
she'll fetch that much, and not one penny less.
If my old broad finds out and makes a scene,
I'll take it like a man, down on my knees!
Besides, it's still a long, long way from home:
if I don't touch her, later she'll suspect."

   Oh, shame! A pure camellia had to let
the bee explore and probe all ins and outs.
A storm of lust broke forth—it would not spare
the flawless jade, respect the pristine scent.
All this spring night was one bad dream—she woke
to lie alone beneath the nuptial torch.
Her tears of silent grief poured down like rain—
she hated him, she loathed herself as much:
"What breed is he, a creature foul and vile?
My body's now a blot on womanhood.
What hope is left to cherish after this?
A life that's come to this is life no more."

   By turns she cursed her fate, she moaned her lot.
She grabbed the knife and thought to kill herself.
She mulled it over: "If I were alone,
it wouldn't matter—I've two loved ones, though.
If trouble should develop afterwards,
an inquest might ensue and work their doom.
Perhaps my plight will ease with passing time.
Sooner or later, I'm to die just once."

   While she kept tossing reasons back and forth,
a rooster shrilly crowed outside the wall.
The watchtower horn soon blared through morning mists,
so Ma gave orders, making haste to leave.
Oh, how it rends the heart, the parting hour,
when horse begins to trot and wheels to jolt!

Ten miles beyond the city, at a post,
the father gave a feast to bid farewell.
While host and guests were making cheer outside,
mother and Kieu were huddling now indoors.

As they gazed at each other through hot tears.
Kieu whispered all her doubts in mother's ear:
"I'm just a girl, so helpless, to my shame—
when could I ever pay a daughter's debts?
Lost here where water's mud and dust's soil-free,
I'll leave with you my heart from now, for life.
To judge by what I've noticed these past days,
I fear a scoundrel's hands are holding me.
When we got there, he left me all alone.
He tarried coming in, but out he dashed.
He halts and stammers often when he talks.
His men make light of him, treat him with scorn.
He lacks the ease and grace of gentlefolk,
seeming just like some merchant on close watch.
What else to say? Your daughter's doomed to live
on foreign land and sleep in alien soil."
At all those words, Dame Virong let out a shriek
that would pierce heaven, crying for redress.

Before they had drunk dry the parting cup,
Ma rushed outside and urged the coach to leave.
Mourning his daughter in his heavy heart,
old Virong stood by the saddle begging Ma:
"Because fate struck her family, this frail girl
is now reduced to serving you as slave.
Henceforth, beyond the sea, at heaven's edge,
she'll live lone days with strangers, rain or shine.
On you, her lofty oak, she will depend,
a vine you'll shelter from cold frosts and snows."
Whereat the bridegroom said: "Our feet are bound
by that mysterious thread of crimson silk.
The sun's my witness—if I should break faith,
may all the demons strike me with their swords!"

By stormwinds hurtled under rolling clouds,
the coach roared off in swirls of ocher dust.
Wiping their tears, they followed with their eyes:
on that horizon, day and night, they'd gaze.

45

🎋

Frederick Douglass

MY BONDAGE AND MY FREEDOM

*S*lave narratives illustrate varied historical moments but comparable emotional dynamics. For example, in Olaudah Equiano's **Interesting Narrative** *(Selection 31) we read an eighteenth-century account of a young boy's kidnaping in Africa by other Africans, his transfer to a slave ship, his servitude in the colonial world of the Western Hemisphere, and his eventual purchase of his own freedom and achievement of prosperity in England.*

In My Bondage and My Freedom *(1855) by Frederick Douglass (1817?–1895) we see a detailed description of a childhood on a slave plantation written by an African-American adult who had escaped his bondage in 1838 and wished the world to know of these inhumane conditions. Virtually everything that is known of Douglass's early life comes from his own account. Because his earliest slave narrative endangered its author who feared being forcefully returned to Maryland as a fugitive slave, he left a free man's employment in maritime Massachusetts and went to Great Britain for two years of successful lecture appearances mainly before abolitionist societies.*

At the end of 1846 two Quaker Englishwomen purchased his freedom for £150 from his old master, Hugh Auld, and Douglass returned to the United States in March 1847. He then began a journalistic career, writing and publishing a number of short-lived newspapers, making himself a leader of his people, documenting and proclaiming the injustices to which black slaves were subject. Late in his life he held a number of U.S. government posts, including Recorder of Deeds in Washington D.C. and Minister Resident and Consul-General to Haiti. As a grief-stricken widower he married a prominent white woman, an ironic turnabout for one whose father was assumed to be a white slaveholder. Just after addressing a meeting of the National Council of Women with Susan B. Anthony he collapsed and died of heart failure in the presence of his wife. After a Washington memorial service attended by Supreme Court justices and U.S. senators, he was buried beside his first wife and his daughter in Rochester, New York, where many years earlier he had bought a house that he used as a station to assist escaping slaves in their journey to Canada.

Douglass casts his three autobiographies as voyages of self-discovery. At the beginning he does not know his own age, his birthday, or his paternity. Although he meets his mother he is able to spend almost no time with her; she is able to visit him only in the dark. His only identity, initially, is that of slave. The narrative is thus constructed by a fully literate grown man who has finally constructed his own selfhood. Indeed, his first autobiography ends with its author claiming his name: "I subscribe myself, FREDERICK DOUGLASS," neither his father's nor his mother's family name but rather the invented name of his freedom—taken from a Scottish literary source, Sir Walter Scott's "Lady of the Lake" (1810).

Frederick Douglass wrote three autobiographies: The Narrative of the Life of Frederick Douglass, An American Slave *(1845),* My Bondage and My Freedom *(1855), and two different editions of* Life and Times of Frederick Douglass *(1881, 1892). Reprinted below are chapters 1–3 and 5 of the second version (1855) which is the most detailed on his life as a slave. The excerpt is not only a painfully authentic recounting of Douglass's early childhood but a penetrating sociological analysis of the complex interrelatedness of blacks and whites in the plantation economy and the systematic degradation of blacks in the racial slavery system, especially in terms of the destruction of family bonds.*

LIFE AS A SLAVE
Chapter 1
The Author's Childhood

PLACE OF BIRTH—CHARACTER OF THE DISTRICT—TUCKAHOE—ORIGIN OF THE NAME—CHOPTANK RIVER—TIME OF BIRTH—GENEALOGICAL TREES— MODE OF COUNTING TIME—NAMES OF GRANDPARENTS—THEIR POSITION— GRANDMOTHER ESPECIALLY ESTEEMED—"BORN TO GOOD LUCK"—SWEET POTATOES—SUPERSTITION—THE LOG CABIN—ITS CHARMS—SEPARATING CHILDREN—AUTHOR'S AUNTS—THEIR NAMES—FIRST KNOWLEDGE OF BEING A SLAVE—"OLD MASTER"—GRIEFS AND JOYS OF CHILDHOOD—COMPARATIVE HAPPINESS OF THE SLAVE-BOY AND THE SON OF A SLAVEHOLDER

From Frederick Douglass. *My Bondage and My Freedom.* New York and Auburn: Miller, Orton & Mulligan, 1855. Chapters 1–3, 5.

In Talbot country, Eastern Shore, Maryland, near Easton, the county town of that county, there is a small district of country, thinly populated, and remarkable for nothing that I know of more than for the worn-out, sandy, desert-like appearance of its soil, the general dilapidation of its farms and fences, the indigent and spiritless character of its inhabitants, and the prevalence of ague and fever.

The name of this singularly unpromising and truly famine stricken district is Tuckahoe, a name well known to all Marylanders, black and white. It was given to this section of country probably, at the first, merely in derision; or it may possibly have been applied to it, as I have heard, because some one of its earlier inhabitants had been guilty of the petty meanness of stealing a hoe — or taking a hoe — that did not belong to him. Eastern Shore men usually pronounce the word *took*, as *tuck*; *Took-a-hoe*, therefore, is, in Maryland parlance, *Tuckahoe*. But, whatever may have been its origin — and about this I will not be positive—that name has stuck to the district in question; and it is seldom mentioned but with contempt and derision, on account of the barrenness of its soil, and the ignorance, indolence, and poverty of its people. Decay and ruin are everywhere visible, and the thin population of the place would have quitted it long ago, but for the Choptank river, which runs through it, from which they take abundance of shad and herring, and plenty of ague and fever.

It was in this dull, flat, and unthrifty district, or neighborhood, surrounded by a white population of the lowest order, indolent and drunken to a proverb, and among slaves, who seemed to ask, *"Oh! what's the use?"* every time they lifted a hoe, that I — without any fault of mine — was born, and spent the first years of my childhood.

The reader will pardon so much about the place of my birth, on the score that it is always a fact of some importance to know where a man is born, if, indeed, it be important to know anything about him. In regard to the *time* of my birth, I cannot be as definite as I have been respecting the *place*. Nor, indeed, can I impart much knowledge concerning my parents. Genealogical trees do not flourish among slaves. A person of some consequence here in the north, sometimes designated *father*, is literally abolished in slave law and slave practice. It is only once in a while that an exception is found to this statement. I never met with a slave who could tell me how old he was. Few slave-mothers know anything of the months of the year, nor of the days of the month. They keep no family records, with marriages, births, and deaths. They measure the age of their children by spring time, winter time, harvest time, planting time, and the like; but these soon become undistinguishable and forgotten. Like other slaves, I cannot tell how old I am. This destitution was among my earliest troubles. I learned when I grew up, that my master — and this is the case with masters generally — allowed no questions to be put to him, by which a slave might learn his age. Such questions are deemed evidence of impatience, and even of impudent curiosity. From certain events, however, the dates of which I have since learned, I suppose myself to have been born about the year 1817.

The first experience of life with me that I now remember—and I remember it but hazily—began in the family of my grandmother and grandfather, Betsy and Isaac Baily. They were quite advanced in life, and had long lived on the spot where they then resided. They were considered old settlers in the neighborhood, and, from certain circumstances, I infer that my grandmother, especially, was held in high esteem, far higher than is the lot of most colored persons in the slave states. She was a good nurse, and a capital hand at making nets for catching shad and herring; and these nets were in great demand, not only in Tuckahoe, but at Denton and Hillsboro, neighboring villages. She was not only good at making the nets, but was also somewhat famous for her good fortune in taking the fishes referred to. I have known her to be in the water half the day. Grandmother was likewise more provident than most of her neighbors in the preservation of seedling sweet potatoes, and it happened to her—as it will happen to any careful and thrifty person residing in an ignorant and improvident community—to enjoy the reputation of having been born to "good luck." Her "good luck" was owing to the exceeding care which she took in preventing the succulent root from getting bruised in the digging, and in placing it beyond the reach of frost, by actually burying it under the hearth of her cabin during the winter months. In the time of planting sweet potatoes, "Grandmother Betty," as she was familiarly called, was sent for in all directions, simply to place the seedling potatoes in the hills; for superstition had it, that if "Grandmamma Betty but touches them at planting, they will be sure to grow and flourish." This high reputation was full of advantage to her, and to the children around her. Though Tuckahoe had but a few of the good things of life, yet of such as it did possess grandmother got a full share, in the way of presents. If good potato crops came after her planting, she was not forgotten by those for whom she planted; and as she was remembered by others, so she remembered the hungry ones around her.

The dwelling of my grandmother and grandfather had few pretensions. It was a log hut, or cabin, built of clay, wood, and straw. At a distance it resembled—though it was much smaller, less commodious and less substantial—the cabins erected in the western states by the first settlers. To my child's eye, however, it was a noble structure, admirably adapted to promote the comforts and conveniences of its inmates. A few rough, Virginia fence-rails, flung loosely over the rafters above, answered the triple purpose of floors, ceilings and bedsteads. To be sure, this upper apartment was reached only by a ladder—but what in the world for climbing could be better than a ladder? To me, this ladder was really a high invention, and possessed a sort of charm as I played with delight upon the rounds of it. In this little hut there was a large family of children: I dare not say how many. My grandmother—whether because too old for field service, or because she had so faithfully discharged the duties of her station in early life, I know not—enjoyed the high privilege of living in a cabin, separate from the quarter, with no other burden than her own support, and the necessary care of the little children, imposed. She evidently esteemed it a great fortune to live so. The children were not her own, but her grandchildren—the children of her daughters. She took delight in having them around her, and in attending to their few wants. The practice of separating children from their mothers, and hiring the latter out at distances too great to admit of their meeting, except at long intervals, is a marked feature of the cruelty and barbarity of the slave system. But it is in harmony with the grand aim of slavery, which, always and everywhere, is to reduce man to a level with the brute. It is a successful method of obliterating from the mind and heart of the slave, all just ideas of the sacredness of *the family*, as an institution.

Most of the children, however, in this instance, being the children of my grandmother's daughters, the notions of family, and the reciprocal duties and benefits of the relation, had a better chance of being understood than where children are placed—as they often are—in the hands of strangers, who have no care for them, apart from the wishes of their masters. The daughters of my grandmother were five in number. Their names were JENNY, ESTHER, MILLY, PRISCILLA, and HARRIET. The daughter last named was my mother, of whom the reader shall learn more by-and-by.

Living here, with my dear old grandmother and grandfather, it was a long time before I knew myself to be *a slave*. I knew many other things before I knew that. Grandmother and grandfather were the greatest people in the world to me; and being with them so snugly in their own little cabin—I supposed it be their own—knowing no higher authority over me or the other children than the authority of grandmamma, for a time there was nothing to disturb me; but, as I grew larger and older, I learned by degrees the sad fact, that the "little hut," and the lot on which it stood, belonged not to my dear old grandparents, but to some person who lived a great distance off, and who was called, by grandmother, "OLD MASTER." I further learned the sadder fact, that not only the house and lot, but that grandmother herself, (grandfather was free,) and all the little children around her, belonged to this mysterious personage, called by grandmother, with every mark of reverence, "Old Master." Thus early did clouds and shadows begin to fall upon my path. Once on the track—troubles never come singly—I was not long in finding out another fact, still more grievous to my childish heart. I was told that this "old master," whose name seemed ever to be mentioned with fear and shuddering, only allowed the children to live with grandmother for a limited time, and that in fact as soon as they were big enough, they were promptly taken away, to live with the said "old master." These were distressing revelations indeed; and though I was quite too young to comprehend the full import of the intelligence, and mostly spent my childhood days in gleesome sports with the other children, a shade of disquiet rested upon me.

The absolute power of this distant "old master" had touched my young spirit with but the point of its cold, cruel iron, and left me something to brood over after the play and in moments of repose. Grandmammy was, indeed, at that time, all the world to me; and the thought of being separated from her, in any considerable time, was more than an unwelcome intruder. It was intolerable.

Children have their sorrows as well as men and women; and it would be well to remember this in our dealings with them. SLAVE-children *are* children, and prove no exceptions to the general rule. The liability to be separated from my grandmother, seldom or never to see her again, haunted me. I dreaded the thought of going to live with that mysterious "old master," whose name I never heard mentioned with affection, but always with fear. I look back to this as among the heaviest of my childhood's sorrows. My grandmother! my grandmother! and the little hut, and the joyous circle under her care, but especially *she,* who made us sorry when she left us but for an hour, and glad on her return,— how could I leave her and the good old home?

But the sorrows of childhood, like the pleasures of after life, are transient. It is not even within the power of slavery to write *indelible* sorrow, at a single dash, over the heart of a child.

> The tear down childhood's cheek that flows,
> Is like the dew-drop on the rose, —
> When next the summer breeze comes by,
> And waves the bush — the flower is dry.
> [from Sir Walter Scott, *Rokeby,* 1813]

There is, after all, but little difference in the measure of contentment felt by the slave-child neglected and the slave-holder's child cared for and petted. The spirit of the All Just mercifully holds the balance for the young.

The slaveholder, having nothing to fear from impotent childhood, easily affords to refrain from cruel inflictions; and if cold and hunger do not pierce the tender frame, the first seven or eight years of the slave-boy's life are about as full of sweet content as those of the most favored and petted *white* children of the slaveholder. The slave-boy escapes many troubles which befall and vex his white brother. He seldom has to listen to lectures on propriety of behavior, or on anything else. He is never chided for handling his little knife and fork improperly or awkwardly, for he uses none. He is never reprimanded for soiling the table-cloth, for he takes his meals on the clay floor. He never has the misfortune, in his games or sports, of soiling or tearing his clothes, for he has almost none to soil or tear. He is never expected to act like a nice little gentleman, for he is only a rude little slave. Thus, freed from all restraint, the slave-boy can be, in his life and conduct, a genuine boy, doing whatever his boyish nature suggests; enacting, by turns, all the strange antics and freaks of horses, dogs, pigs, and barn-door fowls, without in any manner compromising his dignity, or incurring reproach of any sort. He literally runs wild; has no pretty little verses to learn in the nursery; no nice little speeches to make for aunts, uncles, or cousins, to show how smart he is; and, if he can only manage to keep out of the way of the heavy feet and fists of the older slave boys, he may trot on, in his joyous and roguish tricks, as happy as any little heathen under the palm trees of Africa. To be sure, he is occasionally reminded, when he stumbles in the path of his master — and this he early learns to avoid — that he is eating his *"white bread,"* and that he will be made to *"see sights"* by-and-by. The threat is soon forgotten; the shadow soon passes, and our sable boy continues to roll in the dust, or play in the mud, as bests suits him, and in the veriest freedom. If he feels uncomfortable, from mud or from dust, the coast is clear; he can plunge into the river or the pond, without the ceremony of undressing, or the fear of wetting his clothes; his little tow-linen shirt—for that is all he has on—is easily dried; and it needed ablution as much as did his skin. His food is of the coarsest kind, consisting for the most part of corn-meal mush, which often finds its way from the wooden tray to his mouth in an oyster shell. His days, when the weather is warm, are spent in the pure, open air, and in the bright sunshine. He always sleeps in airy apartments; he seldom has to take powders, or to be paid to swallow pretty little sugar-coated pills, to cleanse his blood, or to quicken his appetite. He eats no candies; gets no lumps of loaf sugar; always relishes his food; cries but little, for nobody cares for his crying; learns to esteem his bruises but slight, because others so esteem them. In a word, he is, for the most part of the first eight years of his life, a spirited, joyous, uproarious, and happy boy, upon whom troubles fall only like water on a duck's back. And such a boy, so far as I can now remember, was the boy whose life in slavery I am now narrating.

Chapter II
The Author Removed from His First Home

THE NAME "OLD MASTER" A TERROR—COLONEL LLOYD'S PLANTATION—WYE RIVER—WHENCE ITS NAME—POSITION OF THE LLOYDS—HOME ATTRACTION—MEET OFFERING—JOURNEY FROM TUCKAHOE TO WYE RIVER—SCENE ON REACHING OLD MASTER'S—DEPARTURE OF GRANDMOTHER—STRANGE MEETING OF SISTERS AND BROTHERS—REFUSAL TO BE COMFORTED—SWEET SLEEP

That mysterious individual referred to in the first chapter as an object of terror among the inhabitants of our little cabin, under the ominous title of "old master," was really a man of some consequence. He owned several farms in Tuckahoe; was the chief clerk and butler on the home plantation of Col. Edward Lloyd; had overseers on his own farms; and gave directions to overseers on the farms belonging to Col. Lloyd. This plantation is situated on Wye river—the river receiving its name, doubtless, from Wales, where the Lloyds originated. They (the Lloyds) are an old and honored family in Maryland, exceedingly wealthy. The home plantation, where they have resided, perhaps for a century or more, is one of the largest, most fertile, and best appointed, in the state.

About this plantation, and about that queer old master—who must be something more than a man, and something worse than an angel—the reader will easily imagine that I was not only curious, but eager, to know all that could be known. Unhappily for me, however, all the information I could get concerning him but increased my great dread of being carried thither — of being separated from and deprived of the protection of my grandmother and grandfather. It was, evidently, a great thing to go to Col. Lloyd's; and I was not without a little curiosity to see the place; but no amount of coaxing could induce in me the wish to remain there. The fact is, such was my dread of leaving the little cabin, that I wished to remain little forever, for I knew the taller I grew the shorter my stay. The old cabin, with its rail floor and rail bedsteads up stairs, and its clay floor down stairs, and its dirt chimney, and windowless sides, and that most curious piece of workmanship of all the rest, the ladder stairway, and the hole curiously dug in front of the fire-place, beneath which grandmammy placed the sweet potatoes to keep them from the frost, was MY HOME — the only home I ever had; and I loved it, and all connected with it. The old fences around it, and the stumps in the edge of the woods near it, and the squirrels that ran, skipped, and played upon them, were objects of interest and affection. There, too, right at the side of the hut, stood the old well, with its stately and skyward-pointing beam, so aptly placed between the limbs of what had once been a tree, and so nicely balanced that I could move it up and down with only one hand, and could get a drink myself without calling for help. Where else in the world could such a well be found, and where could such another home be met with? Nor were these all the attractions of the place. Down in a little valley, not far from grandmammy's cabin, stood Mr. Lee's mill, where the people came often in large numbers to get their corn ground. It was a water-mill; and I never shall be able to tell the many things thought and felt, while I sat on the bank and watched that mill, and the turning of that ponderous wheel. The mill-pond, too, had its charms; and with my pin-hook, and thread line, I could get *nibbles,* if I could catch no fish. But, in all my sports and plays, and in spite of them, there would, occasionally, come the painful foreboding that I was not long to remain there, and that I must soon be called away to the home of old master.

I was A SLAVE — born a slave — and though the fact was incomprehensible to me, it conveyed to my mind a sense of my entire dependence on the will of *somebody* I had never seen; and, from some cause or other, I had been made to fear this somebody above all else on earth. Born for another's benefit, as the *firstling* of the cabin flock I was soon to be selected as a meet offering to the fearful and inexorable *demi-god,* whose huge image on so many occasions haunted my childhood's imagination. When the time of my departure was decided upon, my grandmother, knowing my fears, and in pity for them, kindly kept me ignorant of the dreaded event about to transpire. Up to the morning (a beautiful summer morning) when we were to start, and, indeed, during the whole journey — a journey which, child as I was, I remember as well as if it were yesterday — she kept the sad fact hidden from me. This reserve was necessary; for, could I have known all, I should have given grandmother some trouble in getting me started. As it was, I was helpless, and she

—dear woman!—led me along by the hand, resisting, with the reserve and solemnity of a priestess, all my inquiring looks to the last.

The distance from Tuckahoe to Wye river—where my old master lived—was full twelve miles, and the walk was quite a severe test of the endurance of my young legs. The journey would have proved too severe for me, but that my dear old grandmother—blessings on her memory!—afforded occasional relief by "toting" me (as Marylanders have it) on her shoulder. My grandmother, though advanced in years—as was evident from more than one gray hair, which peeped from between the ample and graceful folds of her newly-ironed bandana turban—was yet a woman of power and spirit. She was marvelously straight in figure, elastic, and muscular. I seemed hardly to be a burden to her. She would have "toted" me farther, but that I felt myself too much of a man to allow it, and insisted on walking. Releasing dear grandmamma from carrying me, did not make me altogether independent of her, when we happened to pass through portions of the somber woods which lay between Tuckahoe and Wye river. She often found me increasing the energy of my grip, and holding her clothing, lest something should come out of the woods and eat me up. Several old logs and stumps imposed upon me, and got themselves taken for wild beasts. I could see their legs, eyes, and ears, or I could see something like eyes, legs, and ears, till I got close enough to them to see that the eyes were knots, washed white with rain, and the legs were broken limbs, and the ears, only ears owing to the point from which they were seen. Thus early I learned that the point from which a thing is viewed is of some importance.

As the day advanced the heat increased; and it was not until the afternoon that we reached the much dreaded end of the journey. I found myself in the midst of a group of children of many colors; black, brown, copper colored, and nearly white. I had not seen so many children before. Great houses loomed up in different directions, and a great many men and women were at work in the fields. All this hurry, noise, and singing was very different from the stillness of Tuckahoe. As a new comer, I was an object of special interest; and, after laughing and yelling around me, and playing all sorts of wild tricks, they (the children) asked me to go out and play with them. This I refused to do, preferring to stay with grandmamma. I could not help feeling that our being there boded no good to me. Grandmamma looked sad. She was soon to lose another object of affection, as she had lost many before. I knew she was unhappy, and the shadow fell from her brow on me, though I knew not the cause.

All suspense, however, must have an end; and the end of mine, in this instance, was at hand. Affectionately patting me on the head, and exhorting me to be a good boy, grandmamma told me to go and play with the little children. "They are kin to you," said she; "go and play with them." Among a number of cousins were Phil, Tom, Steve, and Jerry, Nance and Betty.

Grandmother pointed out my brother PERRY, my sister SARAH, and my sister ELIZA, who stood in the group. I had never seen my brother nor my sisters before; and, though I had sometimes heard of them, and felt a curious interest in them, I really did not understand what they were to me, or I to them. We were brothers and sisters, but what of that? Why should they be attached to me, or I to them? Brothers and sisters we were by blood; but *slavery* had made us strangers. I heard the words brother and sisters, and knew they must mean something; but slavery had robbed these terms of their true meaning. The experience through which I was passing, they had passed through before. They had already been initiated into the mysteries of old master's domicile, and they seemed to look upon me with a certain degree of compassion; but my heart clave to my grandmother. Think it not strange, dear reader, that so little sympathy of feeling existed between us. The conditions of brotherly and sisterly feeling were wanting — we had never nestled and played together. My poor mother, like many other slave-women, had *many children,* but NO FAMILY! The domestic hearth, with its holy lessons and precious endearments, is abolished in the case of a slave-mother and her children. "Little children, love one another," are words seldom heard in a slave cabin.

I really wanted to play with my brother and sisters, but they were strangers to me, and I was full of fear that grandmother might leave without taking me with her. Entreated to do so, however, and that, too, by my dear grandmother, I went to the back part of the house, to play with them and the other children. *Play,* however, I did not, but stood with my back against the wall, witnessing the playing of the others. At last, while standing there, one of the children, who had been in the kitchen, ran up to me, in a sort of roguish glee, exclaiming, "Fed, Fed! grandmammy gone! grandmammy gone!" I could not believe it; yet, fearing the worst, I ran into the kitchen, to see for myself, and found it even so. Grandmammy had indeed gone, and was now far away, "clean" out of sight. I need not tell all that happened now. Almost heartbroken at the discovery, I fell upon the ground, and wept a boy's bitter tears, refusing to be comforted. My brother and sisters came around me, and said, "Don't cry," and gave me peaches and pears, but I flung them away, and refused all their kindly advances. I had never been deceived before; and I felt not only grieved at parting — as I supposed forever — with my grandmother, but indignant that a trick had been played upon me in a matter so serious.

It was now late in the afternoon. The day had been an exciting and wearisome one, and I knew not how or where, but I suppose I sobbed myself to sleep. There is a healing in the angel wing of sleep, even for the slave-boy; and its balm was never more welcome to any wounded soul than it was to mine, the first night I spent at the domicile of old master. The reader may be surprised that I narrate so minutely an incident apparently so trivial, and which must have occurred when I was not more than seven years old; but as I wish to give a faithful history of my experience in slavery, I cannot withhold a circumstance which, at the time, affected me so deeply. Besides, this was, in fact, my first introduction to the realities of slavery.

Chapter III

The Author's Parentage

AUTHOR'S FATHER SHROUDED IN MYSTERY—AUTHOR'S MOTHER—HER PERSONAL APPEARANCE—INTERFERENCE OF SLAVERY WITH THE NATURAL AFFECTIONS OF MOTHER AND CHILDREN—SITUATION OF AUTHOR'S MOTHER—HER NIGHTLY VISITS TO HER BOY—STRIKING INCIDENT—HER DEATH—HER PLACE OF BURIAL

If the reader will now be kind enough to allow me time to grow bigger, and afford me an opportunity for my experience to become greater, I will tell him something, by-and-by, of slave life, as I saw, felt, and heard it, on Col. Edward Lloyd's plantation, and at the house of old master, where I had now, despite of myself, most suddenly, but not unexpectedly, been dropped. Meanwhile, I will redeem my promise to say something more of my dear mother.

I say nothing of *father*, for he is shrouded in a mystery I have never been able to penetrate. Slavery does away with fathers, as it does away with families. Slavery has no use for either fathers or families, and its laws do not recognize their existence in the social arrangements of the plantation. When they *do* exist, they are not the outgrowths of slavery, but are antagonistic to that system. The order of civilization is reversed here. The name of the child is not expected to be that of its father, and his condition does not necessarily affect that of the child. He may be the slave of Mr. Tilgman; and his child, when born, may be the slave of Mr. Gross. He may be a *freeman;* and yet his child may be a *chattel.* He may be white, glorying in the purity of his Anglo-Saxon blood; and his child may be ranked with the blackest slaves. Indeed, he *may* be, and often *is,* master and father to the same child. He can be father without being a husband, and may sell his child without incurring reproach, if the child be by a woman in whose veins courses one thirty-second part of African blood. My father was a white man, or nearly white. It was sometimes whispered that my master was my father.

But to return, or rather, to begin. My knowledge of my mother is very scanty, but very distinct. Her personal appearance and bearing are ineffaceably stamped upon my memory. She was tall, and finely proportioned; of deep black, glossy complexion; had regular features, and, among the other slaves, was remarkably sedate in her manners. There is in *Prichard's Natural History of Man,* the head of a figure—on page 157—the features of which so resemble those of my mother, that I often recur to it with something of the feeling which I suppose others experience when looking upon the pictures of dear departed ones.

Yet I cannot say that I was very deeply attached to my mother; certainly not so deeply as I should have been had our relations in childhood been different. We were separated, according to the common custom, when I was but an infant, and, of course, before I knew my mother from any one else.

The germs of affection with which the Almighty, in his wisdom and mercy, arms the helpless infant against the ills and vicissitudes of his lot, had been directed in their growth toward that loving old grandmother, whose gentle hand and kind deportment it was the first effort of my infantile understanding to comprehend and appreciate. Accordingly, the tenderest affection which a beneficent Father allows, as a partial compensation to the mother for the pains and lacerations of her heart, incident to the maternal relation, was, in my case, diverted from its true and natural object, by the envious, greedy, and treacherous hand of slavery. The slave-mother can be spared long enough from the field to endure all the bitterness of a mother's anguish, when it adds another name to a master's ledger, but *not* long enough to receive the joyous reward afforded by the intelligent smiles of her child. I never think of this terrible interference of slavery with my infantile affections, and its diverting them from their natural course, without feelings to which I can give no adequate expression.

I do not remember to have seen my mother at my grandmother's at any time. I remember her only in her visits to me at Col. Lloyd's plantation, and in the kitchen of my old master. Her visits to me there were few in number, brief in duration, and mostly made in the night. The pains she took, and the toil she endured, to see me, tells me that a true mother's heart was hers, and that slavery had difficulty in paralyzing it with unmotherly indifference.

My mother was hired out to a Mr. Stewart, who lived about twelve miles from old master's, and, being a field hand, she seldom had leisure, by day, for the performance of the journey. The nights and the distance were both obstacles to her visits. She was obliged to walk, unless chance flung into her way an opportunity to ride; and the latter was sometimes her good luck. But she always had to walk one way or the other. It was a greater luxury than slavery could afford, to allow a black slave-mother a horse or a mule, upon which to travel twenty-four miles, when she could walk the distance. Besides, it is deemed a foolish whim for a slave-mother to manifest concern to see her children, and, in one point of view, the case is made out — she can do nothing for them. She has no control over them; the master is even more than the mother, in all matters touching the fate of her child. Why, then, should she give herself any concern? She has no responsibility. Such is the reasoning, and such the practice. The iron rule of the plantation, always passionately and violently enforced in that neighborhood, makes flogging the penalty of failing to be in the field before sunrise in the morning, unless special permission be given to the absenting slave. "I went to see my child," is no excuse to the ear or heart of the overseer.

One of the visits of my mother to me, while at Col. Lloyd's, I remember very vividly, as affording a bright gleam of a mother's love, and the earnestness of a mother's care.

I had on that day offended "Aunt Katy," (called "Aunt" by way of respect,) the cook of old master's establishment. I do not now remember the nature of my offense in this instance, for my offenses were numerous in that quarter, greatly depending, however, upon the mood of Aunt Katy, as to their heinousness; but she had adopted, that day, her favorite mode of punishing me, namely, making me go without food all day — that is, from after breakfast. The first hour or two after dinner, I succeeded pretty well in keeping up my spirits; but though I made an excellent stand against the foe, and fought bravely during the afternoon, I knew I must be conquered at last, unless I got the accustomed reënforcement of a slice of corn bread, at sundown. Sundown came, but *no bread,* and, in its stead, there came the threat, with a scowl well suited to its terrible import, that she "meant to *starve the life out of me!*" Brandishing her knife, she chopped off the heavy slices for the other children, and put the loaf away, muttering, all the while, her savage designs upon myself. Against this disappointment, for I was expecting that her heart would relent at last, I made an extra effort to maintain my dignity; but when I saw all the other children around me with merry and satisfied faces, I could stand it no longer. I went out behind the house, and cried like a fine fellow! When tired of this, I returned to the kitchen, sat by the fire, and brooded over my hard lot. I was too hungry to sleep. While I sat in the corner, I caught sight of an ear of Indian corn on an upper shelf of the kitchen. I watched my chance, and got it, and, shelling off a few grains, I put it back again. The grains in my hand, I quickly put in some ashes, and covered them with embers, to roast them. All this I did at the risk of getting a brutal thumping, for Aunt Katy could beat, as well as starve me. My corn was not long in roasting, and, with my keen appetite, it did not matter even if the grains were not exactly done. I eagerly pulled them out, and placed them on my stool, in a clever little pile. Just as I began to help myself to my very dry meal, in came my dear mother. And now, dear reader, a scene occurred which was altogether worth beholding, and to me it was instructive as well as interesting. The friendless and hungry boy, in his extremest need — and when he did not dare to look for succor — found himself in the strong, protecting arms of a mother; a mother who was, at the moment (being endowed with high powers of manner as well as matter) more than a match for all his enemies. I shall never forget the indescribable expression of her countenance, when I told her that I had had no food since morning; and that Aunt Katy said she "meant to starve the life out of me." There was pity in her glance at me, and a fiery indignation at Aunt Katy at the same time; and, while she took the corn from me, and gave me a large ginger cake, in its stead, she read Aunt Katy a lecture which she never forgot. My mother threatened her with complaining to old master in my behalf; for the latter, though harsh and cruel himself, at times, did not sanction the meanness, injustice, partiality and oppressions enacted by Aunt Katy in the kitchen. That night I learned the fact, that I was not only a child, but *somebody's* child. The "sweet cake" my mother gave me was in the shape of a heart, with a rich, dark ring glazed upon the edge of it. I was victorious, and well off for the moment; prouder, on my mother's knee, than a king upon his throne. But my triumph was short. I dropped off to sleep, and waked in the morning only to find my mother gone, and myself left at the mercy of the sable virago, dominant in my old master's kitchen, whose fiery wrath was my constant dread.

I do not remember to have seen my mother after this occurrence. Death soon ended the little communication that had existed between us; and with it, I believe, a life—judging from her weary, sad, downcast countenance and mute demeanor—full of heart-felt sorrow. I was not allowed to visit her during any part of her long illness; nor did I see her for a long time before she was taken ill and died. The heartless and ghastly form of *slavery* rises between mother and child, even at the bed of death. The mother, at the verge of the grave, may not gather her children, to impart to them her holy admonitions, and invoke for them her dying benediction. The bondwoman lives as a slave, and is left to die as a beast; often with fewer attentions than are paid to a favorite horse. Scenes of sacred tenderness, around the death-bed, never forgotten, and which often arrest the vicious and confirm the virtuous during life, must be looked for among the free, though they sometimes occur among the slaves. It has been a life-long, standing grief to me, that I knew so little of my mother; and that I was so early separated from her. The counsels of her love must have been beneficial to me. The side view of her face is imaged on my memory, and I take few steps in life, without feeling her presence; but the image is mute, and I have no striking words of her's treasured up.

I learned, after my mother's death, that she could read, and that she was the *only* one of all the slaves and colored people in Tuckahoe who enjoyed that advantage. How she acquired this knowledge, I know not, for Tuckahoe is the last place in the world where she would be apt to find facilities for learning. I can, therefore, fondly and proudly ascribe to her an earnest love of knowledge. That a "field hand" should learn to read, in any slave state, is remarkable; but the achievement of my mother, considering the place, was very extraordinary; and, in view of that fact, I am quite willing, and even happy, to attribute any love of letters I possess, and for which I have got—despite of prejudices—only too much credit, *not* to my admitted Anglo-Saxon paternity, but to the native genius of my sable, unprotected, and uncultivated *mother*—a woman, who belonged to a race whose mental endowments it is, at present, fashionable to hold in disparagement and contempt.

Summoned away to her account, with the impassable gulf of slavery between us during her entire illness, my mother died without leaving me a single intimation of *who* my father was. There was a whisper, that my master was my father; yet it was only a whisper, and I cannot say that I ever gave it credence. Indeed, I now have reason to think he was not; nevertheless, the fact remains, in all its glaring odiousness, that, by the laws of slavery, children, in all cases, are reduced to the condition of their mothers. This arrangement admits of the greatest license to brutal slaveholders, and their profligate sons, brothers, relations and friends, and gives to the pleasure of sin, the additional attraction of profit. A whole volume might be written on this single feature of slavery, as I have observed it.

One might imagine, that the children of such connections, would fare better, in the hands of their masters, than other slaves. The rule is quite the other way;

and a very little reflection will satisfy the reader that such is the case. A man who will enslave his own blood, may not be safely relied on for magnanimity. Men do not love those who remind them of their sins—unless they have a mind to repent—and the mulatto child's face is a standing accusation against him who is master and father to the child. What is still worse, perhaps, such a child is a constant offense to the wife. She hates its very presence, and when a slaveholding woman hates, she wants not means to give that hate telling effect. Women—white women, I mean—are IDOLS at the south, not WIVES, for the slave women are preferred in many instances; and if these *idols* but nod, or lift a finger, woe to the poor victim: kicks, cuffs and stripes are sure to follow. Masters are frequently compelled to sell this class of their slaves, out of deference to the feelings of their white wives; and shocking and scandalous as it may seem for a man to sell his own blood to the traffickers in human flesh, it is often an act of humanity toward the slave-child to be thus removed from his merciless tormentors.

It is not within the scope of the design of my simple story, to comment upon every phase of slavery not within my experience as a slave.

But, I may remark, that, if the lineal descendants of Ham are only to be enslaved, according to the scriptures,[1] slavery in this country will soon become an unscriptural institution; for thousands are ushered into the world, annually, who—like myself—owe their existence to white fathers, and, most frequently, to their masters, and master's sons. The slave-woman is at the mercy of the fathers, sons or brothers of her master. The thoughtful know the rest.

After what I have now said of the circumstances of my mother, and my relations to her, the reader will not be surprised, nor be disposed to censure me, when I tell but the simple truth, viz: that I received the tidings of her death with no strong emotions of sorrow for her, and with very little regret for myself on account of her loss. I had to learn the value of my mother long after her death, and by witnessing the devotion of other mothers to their children.

There is not, beneath the sky, an enemy to filial affection so destructive as slavery. It had made my brothers and sisters strangers to me; it converted the mother that bore me, into a myth; it shrouded my father in mystery, and left me without an intelligible beginning in the world.

My mother died when I could not have been more than eight or nine years old, on one of old master's farms in Tuckahoe, in the neighborhood of Hillsborough. Her grave is, as the grave of the dead at sea, unmarked, without stone or stake.

• • •

---

[1] In Genesis 9 and 10, Ham, one of the three sons of Noah, was disrespectful to his father. Noah therefore, cursed Ham's son, Canaan. Ham's descendants included, among others, the peoples of Africa. The "curse on Ham" has been interpreted in periods of racial slavery as black skin color and Negroid features, in order to legitimate the slavery and oppression of people of African origin.

Chapter V
Gradual Initiation into the Mysteries of Slavery

GROWING ACQUAINTANCE WITH OLD MASTER—HIS CHARACTER—EVILS OF
UNRESTRAINED PASSION—APPARENT TENDERNESS—OLD MASTER A MAN OF
TROUBLE—CUSTOM OF MUTTERING TO HIMSELF—NECESSITY OF BEING AWARE
OF HIS WORDS—THE SUPPOSED OBTUSENESS OF SLAVE-CHILDREN—BRUTAL
OUTRAGE—DRUNKEN OVERSEER—SLAVEHOLDERS' IMPATIENCE—WISDOM OF
APPEALING TO SUPERIORS—THE SLAVEHOLDER'S WRATH BAD AS THAT OF THE
OVERSEER—A BASE AND SELFISH ATTEMPT TO BREAK UP A COURTSHIP—A HAR-
ROWING SCENE

Although my old master—Capt. Anthony—gave me at first, very little attention, and although that little was of a remarkably mild and gentle description, a
few months only were sufficient to convince me that mildness and gentleness
were not the prevailing or governing traits of his character. These excellent qualities were displayed only occasionally. He could, when it suited him, appear to be
literally insensible to the claims of humanity, when appealed to by the helpless
against an aggressor, and he could himself commit outrages, deep, dark and name-
less. Yet he was not by nature worse than other men. Had he been brought up in
a free state, surrounded by the just restraints of free society—restraints which are
necessary to the freedom of all its members, alike and equally—Capt. Anthony
might have been as humane a man, and every way as respectable, as many who
now oppose the slave system; certainly as humane and respectable as are members
of society generally. The slaveholder, as well as the slave, is the victim of the slave
system. A man's character greatly takes its hue and shape from the form and color
of things about him. Under the whole heavens there is no relation more unfavorable to the development of honorable character, than that sustained by the slaveholder to the slave. Reason is imprisoned here, and passions run wild. Like the
fires of the prairie, once lighted, they are at the mercy of every wind, and must
burn till they have consumed all that is combustible within their remorseless
grasp. Capt. Anthony could be kind, and, at times, he even showed an affectionate disposition. Could the reader have seen him gently leading me by the hand—
as he sometimes did—patting me on the head, speaking to me in soft, caressing
tones and calling me his "little Indian boy," he would have deemed him a kind
old man, and, really, almost fatherly. But the pleasant moods of a slaveholder are
remarkably brittle; they are easily snapped; they neither come often, nor remain
long. His temper is subjected to perpetual trials; but, since these trials are never
born, patiently, they add nothing to his natural stock of patience.

Old master very early impressed me with the idea that he was an unhappy
man. Even to my child's eye, he wore a troubled, and at times, a haggard aspect.

His strange movements excited my curiosity, and awakened my compassion. He seldom walked alone without muttering to himself; and he occasionally stormed about, as if defying an army of invisible foes. "He would do this, that, and the other; he'd be d—d if he did not,"—was the usual form of his threats. Most of his leisure was spent in walking, cursing and gesticulating, like one possessed by a demon. Most evidently, he was a wretched man, at war with his own soul, and with all the world around him. To be overheard by the children, disturbed him very little. He made no more of *our* presence, than of that of the ducks and geese which he met on the green. He little thought that the little black urchins around him, could see, through those vocal crevices, the very secrets of his heart. Slaveholders ever underrate the intelligence with which they have to grapple. I really understood the old man's mutterings, attitudes and gestures, about as well as he did himself. But slaveholders never encourage that kind of communication, with the slaves, by which they might learn to measure the depths of his knowledge. Ignorance is a high virtue in a human chattel; and as the master studies to keep the slave ignorant, the slave is cunning enough to make the master think he succeeds. The slave fully appreciates the saying, "where ignorance is bliss, 'tis folly to be wise." When old master's gestures were violent, ending with a threatening shake of the head, and a sharp snap of his middle finger and thumb, I deemed it wise to keep at a respectable distance from him; for, at such times, trifling faults stood, in his eyes, as momentous offenses; and, having both the power and the disposition, the victim had only to be near him to catch the punishment, deserved or undeserved.

One of the first circumstances that opened my eyes to the cruelty and wickedness of slavery, and the heartlessness of my old master, was the refusal of the latter to interpose his authority, to protect and shield a young woman, who had been most cruelly abused and beaten by his overseer in Tuckahoe. This overseer—a Mr. Plummer—was a man like most of his class, little better than a human brute; and, in addition to his general profligacy and repulsive coarseness, the creature was a miserable drunkard. He was, probably, employed by my old master, less on account of the excellence of his services, than for the cheap rate at which they could be obtained. He was not fit to have the management of a drove of mules. In a fit of drunken madness, he committed the outrage which brought the young woman in question down to my old master's for protection. This young woman was the daughter of Milly, an own aunt of mine. The poor girl, on arriving at our house, presented a pitiable appearance. She had left in haste, and without preparation; and, probably, without the knowledge of Mr. Plummer. She had traveled twelve miles, bare-footed, bare-necked and bare-headed. Her neck and shoulders were covered with scars, newly made; and, not content with marring her neck and shoulders, with the cowhide, the cowardly brute had dealt her a blow on the head with a hickory club, which cut a horrible gash, and left her face literally covered with blood. In this condition, the poor young woman came down, to implore protection at the hands of my old master. I expected to see him boil over with rage at the revolting deed, and to hear him fill the air with curses upon the brutal

Plummer; but I was disappointed. He sternly told her, in an angry tone, he "believed she deserved every bit of it," and, if she did not go home instantly, he would himself take the remaining skin from her neck and back. Thus was the poor girl compelled to return, without redress, and perhaps to receive an additional flogging for daring to appeal to old master against the overseer.

Old master seemed furious at the thought of being troubled by such complaints. I did not, at that time, understand the philosophy of his treatment of my cousin. It was stern, unnatural, violent. Had the man no bowels of compassion? Was he dead to all sense of humanity? No. I think I now understand it. This treatment is a part of the system, rather than a part of the man. Were slaveholders to listen to complaints of this sort against the overseers, the luxury of owning large numbers of slaves would be impossible. It would do away with the office of overseer, entirely; or, in other words, it would convert the master himself into an overseer. It would occasion great loss of time and labor, leaving the overseer in fetters, and without the necessary power to secure obedience to his orders. A privilege so dangerous as that of appeal, is, therefore, strictly prohibited; and any one exercising it runs a fearful hazard. Nevertheless, when a slave has nerve enough to exercise it and boldly approaches his master, with a well-founded complaint against an overseer, though he may be repulsed, and may even have that of which he complains repeated at the time, and, though he may be beaten by his master, as well as by the overseer, for his temerity, in the end the policy of complaining is, generally, vindicated by the relaxed rigor of the overseer's treatment. The latter becomes more careful, and less disposed to use the lash upon such slaves thereafter. It is with this final result in view, rather than with any expectation of immediate good, that the outraged slave is induced to meet his master with a complaint. The overseer very naturally dislikes to have the ear of the master disturbed by complaints; and, either upon this consideration, or upon advice and warning privately given him by his employers, he generally modifies the rigor of his rule, after an outbreak of the kind to which I have been referring.

Howsoever the slaveholder may allow himself to act toward his slave, and, whatever cruelty he may deem it wise, for example's sake, or for the gratification of his humor, to inflict, he cannot, in the absence of all provocation, look with pleasure upon the bleeding wounds of a defenseless slave-woman. When he drives her from his presence without redress, or the hope of redress, he acts, generally, from motives of policy, rather than from a hardened nature, or from innate brutality. Yet, let but his own temper be stirred, his own passions get loose, and the slave-owner will go *far beyond* the overseer in cruelty. He will convince the slave that his wrath is far more terrible and boundless, and vastly more to be dreaded, than that of the underling overseer. What may have been mechanically and heartlessly done by the overseer, is now done with a will. The man who now wields the lash is irresponsible. He may, if he pleases, cripple or kill, without fear of consequences; except in so far as it may concern profit or loss. To a man of violent temper—as my old master was—this was but a very slender and inefficient restraint; I have seen him in a tempest of passion, such as I have just described—a passion into which entered all the bitter ingredients of pride, hatred, envy, jealousy, and the thirst for revenge.

The circumstances which I am about to narrate, and which gave rise to this fearful tempest of passion, are not singular nor isolated in slave life, but are common in every slaveholding community in which I have lived. They are incidental to the relation of master and slave, and exist in all sections of slaveholding countries.

The reader will have noticed that, in enumerating the names of the slaves who lived with my old master, *Esther* is mentioned. This was a young woman who possessed that which is ever a curse to the slave-girl; namely, — personal beauty. She was tall, well formed, and made a fine appearance. The daughters of Col. Lloyd could scarcely surpass her in personal charms. Esther was courted by Ned Roberts, and he was as fine looking a young man, as she was a woman. He was the son of a favorite slave of Col. Lloyd. Some slaveholders would have been glad to promote the marriage of two such persons; but, for some reason or other, my old master took it upon him to break up the growing intimacy between Esther and Edward. He strictly ordered her to quit the company of said Roberts, telling her that he would punish her severely if he ever found her again in Edward's company. This unnatural and heartless order was, of course, broken. A woman's love is not to be annihilated by the peremptory command of any one, whose breath is in his nostrils. It was impossible to keep Edward and Esther apart. Meet they would, and meet they did. Had old master been a man of honor and purity, his motives, in this matter, might have been viewed more favorably. As it was, his motives were as abhorrent, as his methods were foolish and contemptible. It was too evident that he was not concerned for the girl's welfare. It is one of the damning characteristics of the slave system, that it robs its victims of every earthly incentive to a holy life. The fear of God, and the hope of heaven, are found sufficient to sustain many slave-women, amidst the snares and dangers of their strange lot; but, this side of God and heaven, a slave-woman is at the mercy of the power, caprice and passion of her owner. Slavery provides no means for the honorable continuance of the race. Marriage—as imposing obligations on the parties to it —has no existence here, except in such hearts as are purer and higher than the standard morality around them. It is one of the consolations of my life, that I know of many honorable instances of persons who maintained their honor, where all around was corrupt.

Esther was evidently much attached to Edward, and abhorred—as she had reason to do—the tyrannical and base behavior of old master. Edward was young, and fine looking, and he loved and courted her. He might have been her husband, in the high sense just alluded to; but WHO and WHAT was this old master? His attentions were plainly brutal and selfish, and it was as natural that Esther should loathe him, as that she should love Edward. Abhorred and circumvented as he was, old master, having the power, very easily took revenge. I hap-

pened to see this exhibition of his rage and cruelty toward Esther. The time selected was singular. It was early in the morning, when all besides was still, and
before any of the family, in the house or kitchen, had left their beds. I saw but
few of the shocking preliminaries, for the cruel work had begun before I awoke. I
was probably awakened by the shrieks and piteous cries of poor Esther. My sleeping place was on the floor of a little, rough closet, which opened into the kitchen;
and through the cracks of its unplaned boards, I could distinctly see and hear
what was going on, without being seen by old master. Esther's wrists were firmly
tied, and the twisted rope was fastened to a strong staple in a heavy wooden joist
above, near the fire-place. Here she stood, on a bench, her arms tightly drawn
over her breast. Her back and shoulders were bare to the waist. Behind her stood
old master, with cowskin in hand, preparing his barbarous work with all manner
of harsh, coarse, and tantalizing epithets. The screams of his victim were most
piercing. He was cruelly deliberate, and protracted the torture, as one who was
delighted with the scene. Again and again he drew the hateful whip through his
hand, adjusting it with a view of dealing the most pain-giving blow. Poor Esther
had never yet been severely whipped, and her shoulders were plump and tender.
Each blow, vigorously laid on, brought screams as well as blood. *"Have mercy; Oh!
have mercy,"* she cried; *"I won't do so no more;"* but her piercing cries seemed only
to increase his fury. His answers to them are too coarse and blasphemous to be
produced here. The whole scene, with all its attendants, was revolting and shocking, to the last degree; and when the motives of this brutal castigation are considered, language has no power to convey a just sense of its awful criminality. After
laying on some thirty or forty stripes, old master untied his suffering victim, and
let her get down. She could scarcely stand, when untied. From my heart I pitied
her, and — child though I was — the outrage kindled in me a feeling far from
peaceful; but I was hushed, terrified, stunned, and could do nothing, and the fate
of Esther might be mine next. The scene here described was often repeated in the
case of poor Esther, and her life, as I knew it, was one of wretchedness.

46

꙾

Henry David Thoreau

CIVIL DISOBEDIENCE

T*he thought and writing of Henry David Thoreau (1817–1862) have had a tremendous influence upon both twentieth-century America and the rest of the world. Influential statesmen and human rights leaders, for example, Martin Luther King Jr., in the United States and Mohandas K. Gandhi, who established the independence of the modern Indian nation, acknowledged their central debt to Thoreau's ideas on civil disobedience. Similarly, twentieth-century conservationists and ecologists have claimed him as one of their forerunners because of his views on the necessity of natural wilderness for man's spiritual survival. However, the fame and popularity accorded to Thoreau's work in our time were virtually absent in his lifetime. He had simply hoped to make a modest living as a writer so that he could live his life according to his own desires.*

Had Thoreau been a conventional man, he would have taken advantage of what a kindly fate offered him as a youth. His father owned a small pencil-manufacturing business in Concord, Massachusetts, the town where Thoreau was to spend most of his life. After preparation at Concord Academy, Thoreau, assisted by a scholarship, studied at Harvard College, graduating as an average student in 1837. Rejecting the conventional career that a Harvard degree enabled, he preferred to remain around Concord: teaching at a local school (until he refused to administer corporal punishment), giving occasional public lectures, working as Ralph Waldo Emerson's handyman and helping Emerson edit his journal, The Dial. *Thoreau also served as surveyor for the town of Concord and assisted his father in pencil making. His major business, however, was constant writing, poetry (mostly undistinguished) and superb prose (most of it in his* Journal *awaiting posthumous publication). Thoreau knew that income from writing was usually meager; however, he cared little about the material goods that the marketplace had to offer. He sought quality, the intrinsic value, the genuine — in his writing and in his life.*

In order to discover what he was looking for at that time in his life (age twenty-eight), Thoreau, on July 4, 1845, withdrew to the shore of Walden Pond, wilderness land belonging to his friend Ralph Waldo Emerson. The location, less than two miles from the center of Concord, suggests that he wished to live in solitude but not as a total recluse. In fact, while living there and building his cabin, he was often visited by family and friends, many of whom disapproved of a life which seemed to them one of mere contemplative idleness. Thoreau, on the other hand, rejected the life of "quiet desperation" that he believed was led by "the mass of men." In his artful account of his sojourn by the pond, Walden, *or* Life in the Woods *(1854), Thoreau says: "I went to the woods because I wished to live deliberately, to face only the essential facts of life, and see if I could learn what it had to teach, and not, when I came to die, discover that I had not lived." He was to live over two years, until September 6, 1847, in the cabin he built near Walden Pond, although in* Walden *he transformed the experience into the passage of a single year. His formula was to simplify life down to its essentials so that he could discover his soul without it being obscured by the debris of civilization. He wished to live his life rather than waste it, as he saw it, in earning a conventional living.*

It was perhaps inevitable that at some critical moment Thoreau, with his keen perceptions and moral conscience, would come into collision with government. (He strongly disapproved of the coercion of any individual by organized society.) The immediate cause for his confrontation was the fact that Thoreau had not paid his local poll tax (a fee charged for the right to vote). Finally, in July 1846, while in the middle of his Walden Pond experience, he was taken to the jail in Concord. (Thoreau's arrest at that moment was due to a complex of local political factors, including the fact that Sam Staples — the town's tax collector, jailer, and Thoreau's friendly neighbor — would have had to pay the tax himself had he not collected it.) The moment had apparently arrived when Thoreau could make his moral point publicly. However, someone, probably his Aunt Maria who resided in Concord, quietly and without his knowledge paid the tax for Thoreau — thus depriving him of the chance to stand up to "unjust" government.

To pay his poll tax without protest was unacceptable to Thoreau because that would have made him a willing accomplice to government policies of which he wholly disapproved: an invasion of Mexico by the United States and, especially, the institution of slavery which, in 1846, was still legal in some of the states. (He became so well known as a speaker on the need to abolish slavery that once he was summoned to fill in for Frederick Douglass [Selection 45] at an abolitionist convention in Boston.) He demanded that governmental legislation and action be as anchored in morality as are the actions of a moral individual, like Thoreau. Most citizens submit to the demands of government because they are opportunistic or fear the consequences of refusal. Therefore, it is up to an individual to resist. Eventually, the individual's inner strength comes from the belief that the morality of one just person will triumph over a general condition of immorality. (He became a public champion of John Brown after the radical abolitionist's violent attack in 1859 on the federal arsenal at Harper's Ferry.) The effects of this Thoreauvian doctrine have been astonishing throughout the world. Although Walden *may be better known within the United States, elsewhere in the twentieth century it has often been* Civil Disobedience *that represents the highest American ideals of individual freedom.*

Thoreau lectured twice in 1848 on the topic of the individual's relation to government. (Ironically, he developed his concept of extreme individual liberty in the same year that Marx and Engels published the Communist Manifesto, *an assertion of extreme collectivism.) The lecture was first printed in 1849 as* Resistance to Civil Government *in Elizabeth Peabody's short-lived experimental magazine,* Aesthetic Papers. *(Peabody was Nathaniel Hawthorne's sister-in-law.) Thoreau's lecture did not acquire its present famous title until publication in a posthumous collection of 1866. When Thoreau died in Concord on May 6, 1862, little known outside the town, he had published only two separate books,* A Week on the Concord and Merrimack Rivers *and* Walden, *both of which were out of print.*

I heartily accept the motto,— "That government is best which governs least;"[1] and I should like to see it acted up to more rapidly and systematically. Carried out, it finally amounts to this, which also I believe— "That government is best which governs not at all;" and when men are prepared for it, that will be the kind of government which they will have. Government is at best but an expedient; but most governments are usually, and all governments are sometimes, inexpedient. The objections which have been brought against a standing army, and they are many and weighty, and deserve to prevail, may also at last be brought against a standing government. The standing army is only an arm of the standing government. The government itself, which is only the mode which the people have chosen to execute their will, is equally liable to be abused and perverted before the people can act through it. Witness the present Mexican war, the work of comparatively few individuals using the standing government as their tool; for, in the outset, the people would not have consented to this measure.[2]

This American government—what is it but a tradition, though a recent one, endeavoring to transmit itself unimpaired to posterity, but each instant losing

---

[1] A traditional political statement associated with Thomas Jefferson, these words appeared on the masthead of the *Democratic Review,* a New York political magazine that in 1843 had published two minor early Thoreau writings—a familiar essay and a book review.

[2] The Mexican War (April, 1846–February, 1848) began hostilities prior to a congressional declaration of war. Although the war ended in early 1848, Thoreau let his January 1848 lecture go to print in 1849 in its present form including the out-of-date reference.

some of its integrity? It has not the vitality and force of a single living man; for a single man can bend it to his will. It is a sort of wooden gun to the people themselves. But it is not the less necessary for this; for the people must have some complicated machinery or other, and hear its din, to satisfy that idea of government which they have. Governments show thus how successfully men can be imposed on, even impose on themselves, for their own advantage. It is excellent, we must all allow. Yet this government never of itself furthered any enterprise, but by the alacrity with which it got out of its way. *It* does not keep the country free. *It* does not settle the West. *It* does not educate. The character inherent in the American people has done all that has been accomplished; and it would have done somewhat more, if the government had not sometimes got in its way. For government is an expedient by which men would fain[3] succeed in letting one another alone; and, as has been said, when it is most expedient, the governed are most let alone by it. Trade and commerce, if they were not made of India-rubber, would never manage to bounce over the obstacles which legislators are continually putting in their way; and, if one were to judge these men wholly by the effects of their actions and not partly by their intentions, they would deserve to be classed and punished with those mischievous persons who put obstructions on the railroads.

But, to speak practically and as a citizen, unlike those who call themselves no-government men, I ask for, not at once no government, but *at once* a better government. Let every man make known what kind of government would command his respect, and that will be one step toward obtaining it.

After all, the practical reason why, when the power is once in the hands of the people, a majority are permitted, and for a long period continue, to rule is not because they are most likely to be in the right, nor because this seems fairest to the minority, but because they are physically the strongest. But a government in which the majority rule in all cases cannot be based on justice, even as far as men understand it. Can there not be a government in which majorities do not virtually decide right and wrong, but conscience?— in which majorities decide only those questions to which the rule of expediency is applicable? Must the citizen ever for a moment, or in the least degree, resign his conscience to the legislator? Why has every man a conscience, then? I think that we should be men first, and subjects afterward. It is not desirable to cultivate a respect for the law, so much as for the right. The only obligation which I have a right to assume is to do at any time what I think right. It is truly enough said, that a corporation has no conscience; but a corporation of conscientious men is a corporation *with* a conscience. Law never made men a whit more just; and, by means of their respect for it, even the well-disposed are daily made the agents of injustice. A common and natural result of an undue respect for law is, that you may see a file of soldiers,

---

[3] Preferably.

colonel, captain, corporal, privates, powder-monkeys,[4] and all, marching in admirable order over hill and dale to the wars, against their wills, indeed, against
their common sense and consciences which makes it very steep marching indeed,
and produces a palpitation of the heart. They have no doubt that it is a damnable
business in which they are concerned; they are all peaceably inclined. Now, what
are they? Men at all? or small movable forts and magazines, at the service of some
unscrupulous man in power? Visit the Navy Yard, and behold a marine, such a
man as an American government can make, or such as it can make a man with its
black arts—a mere shadow and reminiscence of humanity, a man laid out alive
and standing, and already, as one may say, buried under arms. . . .

The mass of men serve the state thus, not as men mainly, but as machines,
with their bodies. They are the standing army, and the militia, jailors, constables,
Posse comitatus,[5] etc. In most cases there is no free exercise whatever of the judgment or of the moral sense; but they put themselves on a level with wood and
earth and stones; and wooden men can perhaps be manufactured that will serve
the purpose as well. Such command no more respect than men of straw or a lump
of dirt. They have the same sort of worth only as horses and dogs. Yet such as
these even are commonly esteemed good citizens. Others—as most legislators,
politicians, lawyers, ministers, and office-holders—serve the state chiefly with
their heads; and, as they rarely make any moral distinctions, they are as likely to
serve the Devil, without *intending* it, as God. A very few, as heroes, patriots, martyrs, reformers in the great sense, and *men,* serve the state with their consciences
also, and so necessarily resist it for the most part; and they are commonly treated
as enemies by it. A wise man will only be useful as a man, and will not submit to
be "clay," and "stop a hole to keep the wind away". . . :[6]

I am too high-born to be propertied,
To be a secondary at control,
Or useful serving-man and instrument
To any sovereign state throughout the world.[7]

He who gives himself entirely to his fellow men appears to them useless and
selfish; but he who gives himself partially to them is pronounced a benefactor
and philanthropist.

How does it become a man to behave toward this American government
today? I answer, that he cannot without disgrace be associated with it. I cannot

[4] The men in charge of the explosives; in this case the men who transport the gunpowder
from storage areas to the artillery.

[5] Sheriff's posse (Latin).

[6] From Shakespeare's *Hamlet* 5.1.213–14, when Hamlet contemplates the inevitable fate
of even Caesar's corpse.

[7] From Shakespeare's *King John* 5.2.79–82, when Louis, the dauphin of France, refuses to
back down from his invasion of England.

for an instant recognize that political organization as *my* government which is the *slave's* government also.[8]

All men recognize the right of revolution; that is, the right to refuse allegiance to, and to resist, the government, when its tyranny or its inefficiency are great and unendurable. But almost all say that such is not the case now. But such was the case, they think, in the Revolution of 1775. If one were to tell me that this was a bad government because it taxed certain foreign commodities brought to its ports, it is most probable that I should not make an ado about it, for I can do without them. All machines have their friction; and possibly this does enough good to counterbalance the evil. At any rate, it is a great evil to make a stir about it. But when the friction comes to have its machine, and oppression and robbery are organized, I say, let us not have such a machine any longer. In other words, when a sixth of the population of a nation which has undertaken to be the refuge of liberty are slaves, and a whole country is unjustly overrun and conquered by a foreign army, and subjected to military law, I think that it is not too soon for honest men to rebel and revolutionize. What makes this duty the more urgent is the fact that the country so overrun is not our own, but ours is the invading army.[9]

• • •

. . .This people must cease to hold slaves, and to make war on Mexico, though it cost them their existence as a people. . . .

It is not a man's duty, as a matter of course, to devote himself to the eradication of any, even the most enormous wrong; he may still properly have other concerns to engage him; but it is his duty, at least, to wash his hands of it, and, if he gives it thought no longer, not to give it practically his support. If I devote myself to other pursuits and contemplations, I must first see, at least, that I do not pursue them sitting upon another man's shoulders. I must get off him first, that he may pursue his contemplations too. See what gross inconsistency is tolerated. I have heard some of my townsmen say, "I should like to have them order me out to help put down an insurrection of the slaves, or to march to Mexico; — see if I would go;" and yet these very men have each, directly by their allegiance, and so indirectly, at least, by their money, furnished a substitute.[10] The soldier is applauded who refuses to serve in an unjust war by those who do not refuse to support the unjust government which makes the war; he is applauded by those whose own act and authority he disregards and sets at naught. . . . Thus, under the name of Order and Civil Government, we are all made at last to pay homage

---

[8] In 1849 black slavery was still legal in those states that chose it. The Emancipation Proclamation, a strategic political act of the Civil War, was not signed by President Lincoln until January, 1863.

[9] Thoreau is referring here to the U.S. invasion of Mexico.

[10] Paying for a substitute soldier was a common method of avoiding military service.

to and support our own meanness. After the first blush of sin comes its indifference; and from immoral it becomes, as it were, *un*moral, and not quite unnecessary to that life which we have made. . . .

How can a man be satisfied to entertain an opinion merely, and enjoy *it*? Is there any enjoyment in it, if his opinion is that he is aggrieved? If you are cheated out of a single dollar by your neighbor, you do not rest satisfied with knowing that you are cheated, or with saying that you are cheated, or even with petitioning him to pay you your due; but you take effectual steps at once to obtain the full amount, and see that you are never cheated again. Action from principle, the perception and the performance of right, changes things and relations; it is essentially revolutionary. . . . It not only divides states and churches, it divides families; yes, it divides the *individual,* separating the diabolical in him from the divine.

Unjust laws exist: shall we be content to obey them, or shall we endeavor to amend them, and obey them until we have succeeded, or shall we transgress them at once? Men generally, under such a government as this, think that they ought to wait until they have persuaded the majority to alter them. They think that, if they should resist, the remedy would be worse than the evil. But it is the fault of the government itself that the remedy *is* worse than the evil. *It* makes it worse. Why is it not more apt to anticipate and provide for reform? Why does it not cherish its wise minority? Why does it cry and resist before it is hurt? Why does it not encourage its citizens to be on the alert to point out its faults, and *do* better than it would have them? Why does it always crucify Christ, and excommunicate Copernicus and Luther,[11] and pronounce Washington and Franklin rebels? . . .

If the injustice is part of the necessary friction of the machine of government, let it go, let it go: perchance it will wear smooth — certainly the machine will wear out. If the injustice has a spring, or a pulley, or a rope, or a crank, exclusively for itself, then perhaps you may consider whether the remedy will not be worse than the evil; but if it is of such a nature that it requires you to be the agent of injustice to another, then, I say, break the law. Let your life be a counter friction to stop the machine. What I have to do is to see, at any rate, that I do not lend myself to the wrong which I condemn.

As for adopting the ways which the state has provided for remedying the evil, I know not of such ways. They take too much time, and a man's life will be gone. I have other affairs to attend to. I came into this world, not chiefly to make this a good place to live in, but to live in it, be it good or bad. A man has not everything to do, but something; and because he cannot do *everything,* it is not necessary that he should do *something* wrong. It is not my business to be petitioning the Governor or the Legislature any more than it is theirs to petition me; and if they

---

[11] Thoreau uses, among others, Nicholas Copernicus (1473–1543), the Polish astronomer whose heliocentric astronomical system was condemned by the Catholic Church, and Martin Luther (1483–1546), the German leader of the Protestant Reformation who was excommunicated (Selection 20), as examples of courageous proclaimers of new truths.

should not hear my petition, what should I do then? But in this case the state has provided no way: its very Constitution is the evil. This may seem to be harsh and stubborn and unconciliatory; but it is to treat with the utmost kindness and consideration the only spirit that can appreciate or deserves it. So is all change for the better, like birth and death, which convulse the body.

I do not hesitate to say, that those who call themselves Abolitionists should at once withdraw their support, both in person and property, from the government of Massachusetts and not wait till they constitute a majority of one. . . . I think that it is enough if they have God on their side, without waiting for that other one. Moreover, any man more right than his neighbors constitutes a majority of one already.

I meet this American government, or its representative, the state government, directly, and face to face, once a year — no more — in the person of its tax-gatherer. This is the only way in which a man situated as I am necessarily meets it; and it then says distinctly, Recognize me; and the simplest and most effective, and, in the present posture of affairs, the most indispensable way of treating it is to deny it then. My civil neighbor, the tax-gatherer,[12] is the very man I have to deal with — for it is, after all, with men and not with parchment that I quarrel — and he has voluntarily chosen to be an agent of the government. How shall he ever know well what he is and does as an officer of the government, or as a man, until he is obliged to consider whether he shall treat me, his neighbor, for whom he has respect, as a neighbor and well-disposed man, or as a maniac and disturber of the peace. . . . I know this well, that if one thousand, if one hundred, if ten men whom I could name — if ten *honest* men only — yes, if *one* HONEST man, in this State of Massachusetts, *ceasing to hold slaves,* were actually to withdraw from this copartnership, and be locked up in the county jail therefor, it would be the abolition of slavery in America. For it matters not how small the beginning may seem to be: what is once well done is done forever. . . .

Under a government which imprisons any unjustly, the true place for a just man is also a prison. The proper place today, the only place which Massachusetts has provided for her freer and less desponding spirits, is in her prisons, to be put out and locked out of the State by her own act, as they have already put themselves out by their principles. It is there that the fugitive slave, and the Mexican prisoner on parole, and the Indian come to plead the wrongs of his race should find them; on that separate, but more free and honorable ground, where the State places those who are not *with* her, but *against* her — the only house in a slave State in which a free man can live with honor. If any think that their influence would be lost there, and their voices no longer afflict the ear of the State, that they would not be as an enemy within its walls, they do not know by how much truth is stronger than error, nor how much more eloquently and effectively he can combat injustice who has experienced a little in his own person. Cast your

---

[12] Sam Staples, who also sometimes assisted Thoreau in his jobs as a surveyor.

whole vote, not a strip of paper merely, but your whole influence. A minority is powerless while it conforms to the majority; it is not even a minority then; but it is irresistible when it clogs by its whole weight. If the alternative is to keep all just men in prison, or give up war and slavery, the State will not hesitate which to choose. If a thousand men were not to pay their tax-bills this year, that would not be a violent and bloody measure, as it would be to pay them, and enable the State to commit violence and shed innocent blood. This is, in fact, the definition of a peaceable revolution, if any such is possible. If the tax-gatherer, or any other public officer, asks me, as one has done, "But what shall I do?" my answer is, "If you really wish to do anything, resign your office." When the subject has refused allegiance, and the officer has resigned his office, then the revolution is accomplished. But even suppose blood should flow. Is there not a sort of blood shed when the conscience is wounded? Through this wound a man's real manhood and immortality flow out, and he bleeds to an everlasting death. I see this blood flowing now. . . .

When I converse with the freest of my neighbors, I perceive that whatever they may say about the magnitude and seriousness of the question, and their regard for the public tranquillity, the long and the short of the matter is, that they cannot spare the protection of the existing government, and they dread the consequences to their property and families of disobedience to it. For my own part, I should not like to think that I ever rely on the protection of the State. But, if I deny the authority of the State when it presents its tax-bill, it will soon take and waste all my property, and so harass me and my children without end. This is hard. This makes it impossible for a man to live honestly, and at the same time comfortably, in outward respects. It will not be worth the while to accumulate property; that would be sure to go again. You must hire or squat somewhere, and raise but a small crop, and eat that soon. You must live within yourself, and depend upon yourself always tucked up and ready for a start, and not have many interests. A man may grow rich in Turkey even, if he will be in all respects a good subject of the Turkish government. Confucius said: "If a state is governed by the principles of reason, poverty and misery are subjects of shame; if a state is not governed by the principles of reason, riches and honors are the subjects of shame." No: until I want the protection of Massachusetts to be extended to me in some distant Southern port, where my liberty is endangered, or until I am bent solely on building up an estate at home by peaceful enterprise, I can afford to refuse allegiance to Massachusetts, and her right to my property and life. It costs me less in every sense to incur the penalty of disobedience to the State than it would to obey. I should feel as if I were worth less in that case.

• • •

Some years ago, the State met me in behalf of the church, and commanded me to pay a certain sum toward the support of a clergyman whose preaching my father attended, but never I myself. "Pay it," it said, "or be locked up in the jail." I declined to pay. But, unfortunately, another man saw fit to pay it. I did not see why the schoolmaster should be taxed to support the priest, and not the priest the schoolmaster; for I was not the State's schoolmaster, but I supported myself by voluntary subscription. I did not see why the lyceum should not present its tax-bill, and have the State to back its demand, as well as the church. However, at the request of the selectmen, I condescended to make some such statement as this in writing:— "Know all men by these presents, that I, Henry Thoreau, do not wish to be regarded as a member of any incorporated society which I have not joined." This I gave to the town-clerk; and he has it. The State, having thus learned that I did not wish to be regarded as a member of that church, has never made a like demand on me since; though it said that it must adhere to its original presumption that time. If I had known how to name them, I should then have signed off in detail from all the societies which I never signed on to; but I did not know where to find a complete list.

I have paid no poll-tax for six years.[13] I was put into jail once on this account, for one night;[14] and, as I stood considering the walls of solid stone, two or three feet thick, the door of wood and iron, a foot thick, and the iron grating which strained the light, I could not help being struck with the foolishness of that institution which treated me as if I were mere flesh and blood and bones, to be locked up. I wondered that it should have concluded at length that this was the best use it could put me to, and had never thought to avail itself of my services in some way. I saw that, if there was a wall of stone between me and my townsmen, there was a still more difficult one to climb or break through before they could get to be as free as I was. I did not for a moment feel confined, and the walls seemed a great waste of stone and mortar. I felt as if I alone of all my townsmen had paid my tax. They plainly did not know how to treat me, but behaved like persons who are underbred. In every threat and in every compliment there was a blunder; for they thought that my chief desire was to stand the other side of that stone wall. I could not but smile to see how industriously they locked the door on my thoughts, which followed them out again without hindrance, and *they* were really all that was dangerous. As they could not reach me, they had resolved to punish my body; just as boys, if they cannot come at some person against whom they have a spite, will abuse his dog. I saw that the State was half-witted, that it was timid as a lone woman with her silver spoons, and that it did not know its friends from its foes, and I lost all my remaining respect for it, and pitied it.

Thus the State never intentionally confronts a man's sense, intellectual or moral, but only his body, his senses. It is not armed with superior wit or honesty, but with superior physical strength. I was not born to be forced. I will breathe after my own fashion. Let us see who is the strongest. What force has a multitude?

---

[13] A poll tax is a tax required for the right to vote (prohibited since 1964 by Amendment XXIV of the U.S. Constitution).

[14] The Middlesex County jail in Concord, a large three-story building.

They only can force me who obey a higher law than I. They force me to become like themselves. I do not hear of *men* being *forced* to live this way or that by masses of men. What sort of life were that to live? When I meet a government which says to me, "Your money or your life," why should I be in haste to give it my money? It may be in a great strait, and not know what to do: I cannot help that. It must help itself; do as I do. It is not worth the while to snivel about it. I am not responsible for the successful working of the machinery of society. I am not the son of the engineer. I perceive that, when an acorn and a chestnut fall side by side, the one does not remain inert to make way for the other, but both obey their own laws, and spring and grow and flourish as best they can, till one, perchance, overshadows and destroys the other. If a plant cannot live according to its nature, it dies; and so a man. . . .

When I came out of prison—for some one interfered, and paid that tax—I did not see that great changes had taken place in the town such as observed by one who went in a youth and emerged a tottering and gray-headed man; and yet a change had to my eyes come over the scene—the town, and State, and country—greater than any that mere time could bring about. I saw yet more distinctly the State in which I lived. I saw to what extent the people among whom I lived could be trusted as good neighbors and friends; that their friendship was for summer weather only; that they did not greatly propose to do right; that they were a distinct race from me by their prejudices and superstitions; . . . that in their sacrifices to humanity they ran no risks, not even to their property. . . . This may be to judge my neighbors harshly; for I believe that many of them are not aware that they have such an institution as the jail in their village. . . .

I have never declined paying the highway tax, because I am as desirous of being a good neighbor as I am of being a bad subject; and as for supporting schools, I am doing my part to educate my fellow-countrymen now. It is for no particular item in the tax-bill that I refuse to pay it. I simply wish to refuse allegiance to the State, to withdraw and stand aloof from it effectively. I do not care to trace the course of my dollar, if I could, till it buys a man or a musket to shoot with—the dollar is innocent—but I am concerned to trace the effects of my allegiance. In fact, I quietly declare war on the State, after my fashion, though I will still make what use and get what advantage of her I can, as is usual in such cases.

If others pay the tax which is demanded of me, from a sympathy with the State, they do but what they have already done in their own case, or rather they abet injustice to a greater extent than the State requires. If they pay the tax from a mistaken interest in the individual taxed, to save his property, or prevent his going to jail, it is because they have not considered wisely how far they let their private feelings interfere with the public good.

This, then, is my position at present. But one cannot be too much on his guard in such a case, lest his action be biased by obstinacy or an undue regard for the opinions of men. Let him see that he does only what belongs to himself and to the hour.

I think sometimes, Why, this people mean well, they are only ignorant; they would do better if they knew how: why give your neighbors this pain to treat you as they are not inclined to? But I think again, This is no reason why I should do as they do, or permit others to suffer much greater pain of a different kind. Again, I sometimes say to myself, When many millions of men, without heat, without ill will, without personal feeling of any kind, demand of you a few shillings only, without the possibility, such is their constitution, of retracting or altering their present demand, and without the possibility, on your side, of appeal to any other millions, why expose yourself to this overwhelming brute force? You do not resist cold and hunger, the winds and the waves, thus obstinately; you quietly submit to a thousand similar necessities. You do not put your head into the fire. But just in proportion as I regard this as not wholly a brute force, but partly a human force, and consider that I have relations to those millions as to so many millions of men, and not of mere brute or inanimate things, I see that appeal is possible, first and instantaneously, from them to the Maker of them, and, secondly, from them to themselves. But if I put my head deliberately into the fire, there is no appeal to fire or to the Maker of fire, and I have only myself to blame. If I could convince myself that I have any right to be satisfied with men as they are, and to treat them accordingly, and not according, in some respects, to my requisitions and expectations of what they and I ought to be, then, like a . . . fatalist, I should endeavor to be satisfied with things as they are, and say it is the will of God. And, above all, there is this difference between resisting this and a purely brute or natural force, that I can resist this with some effect; but I cannot expect, like Orpheus, to change the nature of the rocks and trees and beasts.[15]

I do not wish to quarrel with any man or nation. I do not wish to split hairs, to make fine distinctions, or set myself up as better than my neighbors. I seek rather, I may say, even an excuse for conforming to the laws of the land. I am but too ready to conform to them. Indeed, I have reason to suspect myself on this head; and each year, as the tax-gatherer comes round, I find myself disposed to review the acts and position of the general and State governments, and the spirit of the people, to discover a pretext for conformity. . . .

No man with a genius for legislation has appeared in America. They are rare in the history of the world. There are orators, politicians, and eloquent men, by the thousand; but the speaker has not yet opened his mouth to speak who is capable of settling the much-vexed questions of the day. We love eloquence for its own sake, and not for any truth which it may utter, or any heroism it may inspire. Our legislators have not yet learned the comparative value of free-trade and of freedom, of union, and of rectitude, to a nation. They have no genius or talent for comparatively humble questions of taxation and finance, commerce and

---

[15] In ancient Greek legend Orpheus was a pre-Homeric poet, so marvelous a player on the lyre that he could charm wild beasts and make even trees and rocks move to his music.

manufactures, and agriculture. If we were left solely to the wordy wit of legislators in Congress for our guidance, uncorrected by the seasonable experience and the effective complaints of the people, America would not long retain her rank among the nations. For eighteen hundred years, though perchance I have no right to say it, the New Testament has been written; yet where is the legislator who has wisdom and practical talent enough to avail himself of the light which it sheds on the science of legislation?

The authority of government, even such as I am willing to submit to — for I will cheerfully obey those who know and can do better than I . . . — is still an impure one: to be strictly just, it must have the sanction and consent of the governed. It can have no pure right over my person and property but what I concede to it. The progress from an absolute to a limited monarchy, from a limited monarchy to a democracy, is a progress toward a true respect for the individual. Even the Chinese philosopher[16] was wise enough to regard the individual as the basis of the empire. Is a democracy, such as we know it, the last improvement possible in government? Is it not possible to take a step further toward recognizing and organizing the rights of man? There will never be a really free and enlightened State until the State comes to recognize the individual as a higher and independent power, from which all its own power and authority are derived, and treats him accordingly. I please myself with imagining a State at last which can afford to be just to all men, and to treat the individual with respect as a neighbor; which even would not think it inconsistent with its own repose if a few were to live aloof from it, not meddling with it, nor embraced by it, who fulfilled all the duties of neighbors and fellow-men. A State which bore this kind of fruit, and suffered it to drop off as fast as it ripened, would prepare the way for a still more perfect and glorious State, which also I have imagined, but not yet anywhere seen.

---

[16] Confucius (6th–5th centuries B.C.) See Volume I, Selection 26.

47

ஃ

Fyodor Dostoevsky

THE BROTHERS KARAMAZOV: THE GRAND INQUISITOR

Modern psychology, with its concerns for the irrational, unconscious springs of human behavior and its doubts about the certainties of the old religious and social values, is sometimes said to have begun in the last half of the nineteenth century with Fyodor Mikhailovich Dostoevsky (1821–1881). Certainly, both Nietzsche (Selection 48) and Freud (in Volume IV) cited his writings as a significant influence upon their own analyses of humanity. Dostoevsky, a Russian, was among the first to lay bare the chaos at the center of people's souls, thus anticipating the intellectual confusion of much of the twentieth century.

Dostoevsky's literary art is inseparable from his ideas. In his novels he cast these ideas in artistic form, and his characters, for all their human particularity, are symbols of universal truths. Although he wrote in a clear direct style, the novels have an intricate, agitated quality that can involve the reader in a disturbing emotional reaction. Dostoevsky was a literary realist, with little romantic idealization of human nature; but he probed beneath the surfaces of realistic details into the tortured psyches of his characters. His work often focused on the most painfully upsetting aspects of human feelings and behavior: evil deeds and the suffering they caused. Dostoevsky saw humans as simultaneously both corrupt and capable of nobility. Human salvation, he believed, lies in faith in God and in following Jesus's example of suffering, forgiveness, and love. Dostoevsky was, however, no simple uncritical believer. His faith arose from his own agonizing doubts and was shaped by his sense of man's tragically unending quest for certain truth.

Dostoevsky's novels reflected the painful course of his own life and the torments of his restless mind and passionate nature. Beginning in his childhood, death, disease, and suffering were constant. His earliest memories, for example, were of growing up on the grounds of a Moscow charity hospital where his father was a resident physician. His mother was a weak and submissive woman who *died when Fyodor was sixteen. His father was a violent, abusive alcoholic. While Dostoevsky was away at a military engineering school in Saint Petersburg, his father was brutally mutilated and killed by his own servants who resented his cruelty. Archetypes of both his father and mother appear throughout his novels. Almost for the rest of his life, Dostoevsky blamed himself for his father's fate, feeling guilty for the antagonism he had frequently displayed toward his father.*

After graduating from the military engineering school in 1843 he almost immediately resigned his commission in order to pursue a career as a writer. After the initial success of his first novel, Poor Folk *(1846), Dostoevsky's literary star sank into a relative eclipse. Seeking new ideas he joined a political discussion group, "the Petrashevsky Circle," which discussed new ideas from the West, especially utopian socialism. The group soon came under the scrutiny of the tsarist police and in 1849 all were arrested. Although Dostoevsky's role had been merely that of a curious and interested onlooker, after eight months of imprisonment in Saint Petersburg he was one of the twenty-one members of the group sentenced to death. The jailers went through the cruel joke of bringing the twenty-one young men to the execution wall, tying the first three to the posts, and then announcing that their sentences had been commuted to imprisonment. Dostoevsky was to blame the seizures from which he later suffered on the psychic trauma of that event.*

He was sentenced to eight years imprisonment, four in a Siberian prison and four in the Russian army in Siberia. In December of 1849, Dostoevsky left Saint Petersburg, not to return for ten years. The experiences of his four prison years are recorded in the thinly veiled autobiography, Memoirs from the House of the Dead. *He returned to Saint Petersburg in 1859, married to the widow of a Siberian civil servant and greatly changed in political, philosophical, and religious outlook. He no longer believed in the value of political agitation that attempted to change external conditions; he was now interested only in the changes within the human heart. Dostoevsky had become a conservative, a mystical Russian nationalist, a firm upholder of the rule of the tsar and the Russian Orthodox faith. (This conversionary experience was to be repeated in the twentieth-century Stalinist labor camps by Aleksandr Solzhenitsyn, who would write about it in* The Gulag Archipelago, *excerpted in Volume IV.)*

From 1861 to 1863 Dostoevsky worked with his beloved brother Mikhail on a journal they had founded; but, as a result of bungled government censorship of one issue, the publishing venture eventually failed. Dostoevsky's financial difficulties, a problem through much of his life, were further compounded by the death of his wife and brother in 1865. Threatened with prison for failure to pay debts, he went to the West to flee from his creditors and to regain his failing health; there he promptly lost what little money he had at the gambling tables of Wiesbaden. He retained an obsessive and self-destructive passion for gambling for the rest of his life. Paradoxically, it was during this difficult period when he almost starved to death in a German boarding house that Dostoevsky's greatness began to show itself. In 1864 he wrote the great precursor to his major novels, Notes from the Underground, *which anticipates the neurotic urban intellectual antiheroes of much contemporary literature. In 1866 appeared the first of his major novels,* Crime and Punishment, *the story of Raskolnikov, an intellectual nihilist who murders an old pawnbroker to whom he feels superior, is sent to prison, and is redeemed through the self-sacrificing love of Sonia, a spiritually pure prostitute. (The German philosopher Nietzsche, Selection 48, developed his idea of the superman after reading Dostoevsky's novel.)*

From this point on his affairs improved. In order to fulfil his contractual obligation to an unscrupulous publisher who threatened to seize the rights to all his works, Dostoevsky had hired a young stenographer, Anna Grigorievna Snitkina, to whom in twenty-six intense days he dictated the text of The Gambler, *clearly an autobiographical novel of his own addiction. Anna was not only very efficient in her work but also very sympathetic to this extraordinary man. They married in 1867 and, thereafter, his practical affairs were managed to perfection. After his death she would work carefully to organize and preserve his manuscripts and to defend his literary reputation.*

After the triumph of Crime and Punishment *Dostoevsky's work showed no diminution of talent. Among the extraordinary works he wrote were* The Idiot *(1869), the tale of a Christlike figure who is completely virtuous but unable to save those around him;* The Possessed *or* The Devils *(1871–1872), a violent denunciation of nihilists and revolutionaries whose main character is possessed by "devils" which make him destroy others as well as himself; and perhaps his greatest novel,* The Brothers Karamazov *(1880). Dostoevsky died in January 1881 at the height of his fame. His funeral was the scene of great mourning, both official and among the general populace. His reputation endured even through the period of Soviet authority which criticized his deeply religious position, but his works were already too deeply ingrained in the Russian soul to be forgotten.*

The following selection is taken from The Brothers Karamazov, *which is a tragic tale of a middle-class Russian family. Its theme is the search for faith through struggle against evil. "The Grand Inquisitor" is the title of one chapter in the vast novel and refers to a tale that Ivan Karamazov, a rationalist and unbeliever, tells to his brother Alyosha, a saintly man living in a monastery. Essentially, it is an allegory of man's tragic predicament, in which he strives for true freedom but usually ends by rejecting it in favor of the happiness and security of obedience to authority. The story has also been read as a prophetic attack on authoritarian ideologies and systems which would deprive individuals of their moral choice and substitute their own ready rational answers to all human problems. (Ivan's story may reflect an anti–Roman Catholic bias on the author's part that hearkens back to the mutual excommunication of Eastern and Western Churches in 1054, a breach not officially healed until 1965, and may also reflect his general rejection of Western ideologies.)*

In the preceding chapter, "Rebellion," Ivan and Alyosha are seated at a table in a tavern. Ivan, as part of his explanation of why he rejects religious faith, proceeds to give a number of examples of the suffering of the innocent, focusing especially on the torture of little children by their parents. He points out that "too

*high a price has been placed on harmony," if the price of the ticket of faith in-
cludes accepting the suffering of innocent children as part of the divine plan.
"And therefore I hasten to return my ticket of admission." When Alyosha, the
seminarian, points out that Christ has the right to forgive everyone, "because he
gave his innocent blood for all," Ivan says that he has written a poem called "The
Grand Inquisitor."*

"Even this must have a preface—that is, a literary preface," laughed Ivan, "and I
am a poor hand at making one. You see, my action takes place in the sixteenth
century, and at that time, as you probably learned at school, it was customary in
poetry to bring down heavenly powers on earth. Not to speak of Dante,[1] in
France clerks, as well as the monks in the monasteries, used to give regular performances in which the Madonna,[2] the saints, the angels, Christ, and God Himself were brought on the stage. In those days it was done in all simplicity. In
Victor Hugo's[3] 'Notre Dame de Paris' an edifying and gratuitous spectacle was
provided for the people in the Hotel de Ville[4] of Paris in the reign of Louis XI[5]
in honor of the birth of the dauphin.[6] It was called *Le bon jugement de la très
sainte et gracieuse Vierge Marie,*[7] and she appears herself on the stage and pro-
nounces her *bon jugement.* Similar plays, chiefly from the Old Testament, were
occasionally performed in Moscow, too, up to the times of Peter the Great.[8] But
besides plays there were all sorts of legends and ballads scattered about the world,
in which the saints and angels and all the powers of Heaven took part when

---

From Fyodor Dostoevsky, *The Brothers Karamazov,* translated by Constance Garnett,
1912. Part Two, Book Five, chapter 5: "The Grand Inquisitor".

[1]Dante Alighieri (1265–1321), Italian poet who wrote *The Divine Comedy,* an epic poem
  in three parts that tells of Dante's journey through Hell, Purgatory, and Paradise.

[2]In Christian tradition, the human mother of Jesus.

[3]Victor-Marie Hugo (1802–1885) dominated nineteenth-century French literature with a
  prodigious flow of poetry, drama, and fiction. His novel *Notre Dame de Paris* (1831) was
  set in fifteenth-century Paris. Its descriptions of the medieval cathedral of Notre Dame
  caused the creation of a government commission to save France's historic buildings.

[4]City Hall.

[5]Louis XI ruled France from 1461 to 1483.

[6]Traditional title of the French king's eldest son.

[7]French: "The good judgment of the very holy and gracious Virgin Mary."

[8]Tsar (ruler) of Russia from 1682 to 1725.

required. In our monasteries the monks busied themselves in translating, copying, and even composing such poems—and even under the Tartars.[9] There is, for instance, one such poem (of course, from the Greek), 'The Wanderings of Our Lady Through Hell,' with descriptions as bold as Dante's. Our Lady[10] visits Hell, and the Archangel Michael leads her through the torments. She sees the sinners and their punishment. There she sees among others one noteworthy set of sinners in a burning lake; some of them sink to the bottom of the lake so that they can't swim out, and 'these God forgets'— an expression of extraordinary depth and force. And so Our Lady, shocked and weeping, falls before the throne of God and begs for mercy for all in Hell—for all she has seen there, indiscriminately. Her conversation with God is immensely interesting. She beseeches Him, she will not desist, and when God points to the hands and feet of her Son, nailed to the Cross, and asks, 'How can I forgive His tormentors?' she bids all the saints, all the martyrs, all the angels and archangels to fall down with her and pray for mercy on all without distinction. It ends by her winning from God a respite of suffering every year from Good Friday till Trinity day,[11] and the sinners at once raise a cry of thankfulness from Hell, chanting, 'Thou art just, O Lord, in this judgment.' Well, my poem would have been of that kind if it had appeared at that time. He comes on the scene in my poem, but He says nothing, only appears and passes on. Fifteen centuries have passed since He promised to come in His glory, fifteen centuries since His prophet wrote, 'Behold, I come quickly'; 'Of that day and that hour knoweth no man, neither the Son, but the Father,' as He Himself predicted on earth.[12] But humanity awaits him with the same faith and with the same love. Oh, with greater faith, for it is fifteen centuries since man has ceased to see signs from Heaven.

> No signs from Heaven come today
> To add to what the heart doth say.

There was nothing left but faith in what the heart doth say. It is true there were many miracles in those days. There were saints who performed miraculous cures; some holy people, according to their biographies, were visited by the Queen of Heaven[13] herself. But the devil did not slumber, and doubts were already arising among men of the truth of these miracles. And just then there appeared in the north of Germany a terrible new heresy. 'A huge star like to a torch' (that is,

---

[9] Nomadic Mongols who ruled much of Russia for centuries after the thirteenth-century invasion of Genghis Kahn.

[10] The Virgin Mary.

[11] Trinity Sunday (the eighth Sunday after Easter).

[12] Jesus's prophecy concerning his second coming (Matthew 24:36 and Mark 13:32).

[13] The Virgin Mary.

to a church) 'fell on the sources of the waters and they became bitter.'[14] These heretics began blasphemously denying miracles. But those who remained faithful were all the more ardent in their faith. The tears of humanity rose up to Him as before, awaiting His coming, loved Him, hoped for Him, yearned to suffer and die for Him as before. And so many ages mankind had prayed with faith and fervor. 'O Lord our God, hasten Thy coming,' so many ages called upon Him, that in His infinite mercy He deigned to come down to His servants. Before that day He had come down, He had visited some holy men, martyrs, and hermits, as is written in their, 'Lives.'[15] Among us, Tyutchev,[16] with absolute faith in the truth of his words, bore witness that

> Bearing the Cross, in slavish dress,
> Weary and worn, the Heavenly King
> Our mother, Russia, came to bless,
> And through our land went wandering.

And that certainly was so, I assure you.

"And behold, He deigned to appear for a moment to the people, to the tortured, suffering people, sunk in iniquity, but loving Him like children. My story is laid in Spain, in Seville, in the most terrible time of the Inquisition,[17] when fires were lighted every day to the glory of God, and 'in the splendid *auto-da-fé*[18] the wicked heretics were burned.' Oh, of course, this was not the coming in which He[19] will appear according to His promise at the end of time in all His heavenly glory, and which will be sudden 'as lightning flashing from east to west.' No, He visited His children only for a moment, and there where the flames were crackling round the heretics. In His infinite mercy He came once more among men in that human shape in which He walked among men for three years fifteen centuries ago.

---

[14] Revelation 8:10–11. (The reference to the "terrible new heresy" is to Martin Luther's Protestant Reformation in northern Germany about fifteen centuries after the New Testament period.)

[15] Biographies.

[16] Fyodor Tyutchev or Tiutchev (1803–1873), Russian romantic poet.

[17] The Inquisition, or the Congregation of the Holy Office (the official name of this Roman Catholic institution) was charged with seeking out heresy (false religious beliefs) and punishing heretics. (The Inquisition was founded in the early thirteenth century and abolished in 1834. In the fifteenth and sixteenth centuries—the setting of Ivan's "poem"—it raged most furiously in Spain, Portugal, and South America.)

[18] Portuguese: "act of faith." The phrase refers to the public sentencing and public punishment of convicted heretics. Frequently, since blood could not be shed by the Church, the death sentence consisted of the victims being burned at the stake. (See chapter 6 in Voltaire's *Candide*, Selection 30.)

[19] Jesus.

"He came down to the 'hot pavement' of the southern town in which on the day before almost a hundred heretics had, *ad majorem gloriam Dei,*[20] been burned by the cardinal, the Grand Inquisitor,[21] in a magnificent *auto-da-fé,* in the presence of the king, the court, the knights, the cardinals, the most charming ladies of the court, and the whole population of Seville.

"He came softly, unobserved, and yet, strange to say, every one recognized Him. That might be one of the best passages in the poem. I mean, why they recognized Him. The people are irresistibly drawn to Him, they surround Him, they flock about Him, follow Him. He moves silently in their midst with a gentle smile of infinite compassion. The sun of love burns in His heart, light and power shine from His eyes, and their radiance, shed on the people, stirs their hearts with responsive love. He holds out His hands to them, blesses them, and a healing virtue comes from contact with Him, even with His garments. An old man in the crowd, blind from childhood, cries out, 'O Lord, heal me and I shall see Thee!' and, as it were, scales fall from his eyes and the blind man sees Him. The crowd weeps and kisses the earth under His feet. Children throw flowers before Him, sing, and cry hosannah.[22] 'It is He—it is He!' all repeat. 'It must be He, it can be no one but Him!' He stops at the steps of the Seville cathedral at the moment when the weeping mourners are bringing in a little open white coffin. In it lies a child of seven, the only daughter of a prominent citizen. The dead child lies hidden in flowers. 'He will raise your child,' the crowd shouts to the weeping mother. The priest, coming to meet the coffin, looks perplexed and frowns, but the mother of the dead child throws herself at His feet with a wail. 'If it is Thou, raise my child!' she cries, holding out her hands to Him. The procession halts, the coffin is laid on the steps at His feet. He looks with compassion, and His lips once more softly pronounce, 'Maiden, arise!' and the maiden arises. The little girl sits up in the coffin and looks round, smiling with wide-open wondering eyes, holding a bunch of white roses they had put in her hand.

"There are cries, sobs, confusion among the people, and at that moment the cardinal himself, the Grand Inquisitor, passes by the cathedral. He is an old man, almost ninety, tall and erect, with a withered face and sunken eyes, in which there is still a gleam of light. He is not dressed in his gorgeous cardinal's robes, as he was the day before, when he was burning the enemies of the Roman Church[23]—at that moment he was wearing his coarse, old, monk's cassock. At a distance behind him come his gloomy assistants and slaves and the 'holy guard.'[24] He stops at the sight of the crowd and watches it from a distance. He sees everything; he sees them

---

[20] Latin: "to the greater glory of God."

[21] The high-ranking priest in charge of the Inquisition within a particular territory.

[22] A traditional cry of praise to God: "Save, we pray!"

[23] Roman Catholic Church.

[24] Bodyguard.

set the coffin down at His feet, sees the child rise up, and his face darkens. He knits his thick grey brows and his eyes gleam with a sinister fire. He holds out his finger and bids the guards take Him. And such is his power, so completely are the people cowed into submission and trembling obedience to him, that the crowd immediately makes way for the guards, and in the midst of death-like silence they lay hands on Him and lead Him away. The crowd instantly bows down to the earth, like one man, before the old inquisitor. He blesses the people in silence and passes on. The guards lead their prisoner to the close, gloomy, vaulted prison in the ancient palace of the Holy Inquisition and shut Him in it. The day passes and is followed by the dark, burning 'breathless' night of Seville. The air is 'fragrant with laurel and lemon.' In the pitch darkness the iron door of the prison is suddenly opened and the Grand Inquisitor himself comes in with a light in his hand. He is alone; the door is closed at once behind him. He stands in the doorway and for a minute or two gazes into His face. At last he goes up slowly, sets the light on the table and speaks. 'Is it Thou? Thou?' but receiving no answer, he adds at once, 'Don't answer, be silent. What canst Thou say, indeed? I know too well what Thou wouldst say. And Thou hast no right to add anything to what Thou hadst said of old. Why, then, art Thou come to hinder us? For Thou hast come to hinder us, and Thou knowest that. But dost Thou know what will be tomorrow? I know not who Thou art and care not to know whether it is Thou or only a semblance of Him, but tomorrow I shall condemn Thee and burn Thee at the stake as the worst of heretics. And the very people who have today kissed Thy feet, tomorrow at the faintest sign from me will rush to heap up the embers of Thy fire. Knowest Thou that? Yes, maybe Thou knowest it,' he added with thoughtful penetration, never for a moment taking his eyes off the Prisoner."

"I don't quite understand, Ivan. What does it mean?" Alyosha, who had been listening in silence, said with a smile. "Is it simply a wild fantasy, or a mistake on the part of the old man—some impossible *quid pro quo?*"[25]

"Take it as the last," said Ivan, laughing, "if you are so corrupted by modern realism and can't stand anything fantastic. If you like it to be a case of mistaken identity, let it be so. It is true," he went on, laughing, "the old man was ninety, and he might well be crazy over his set idea. He might have been struck by the appearance of the Prisoner. It might, in fact, be simply his ravings, the delusion of an old man of ninety, over-excited by the *auto-da-fé* of a hundred heretics the day before. But does it matter to us after all whether it was a mistake of identity or a wild fantasy? All that matters is that the old man should speak out, should speak openly of what he has thought in silence for ninety years."

"And the Prisoner too is silent? Does He look at him and not say a word?"

"That's inevitable in any case," Ivan laughed again. "The old man has told Him He hasn't the right to add anything to what He has said of old. One may say it is the most fundamental feature of Roman Catholicism, in my opinion at least. 'All has

---

[25] Latin: "something for something," one thing in return for another, a trade-off.

been given by Thee to the Pope,' they say, 'and all, therefore, is still in the Pope's hands, and there is no need for Thee to come now at all. Thou must not meddle for the time, at least.' That's how they speak and write, too—the Jesuits,[26] at any rate. I have read it myself in the works of their theologians. 'Hast Thou the right to reveal to us one of the mysteries of that world from which Thou hast come?' my old man asks Him, and answers the question for Him. 'No, Thou hast not; that Thou mayest not add to what has been said of old, and mayest not take from men the freedom which Thou didst exalt when Thou wast on earth. Whatsover Thou revealest anew will encroach on men's freedom of faith; for it will be manifest as a miracle, and the freedom of their faith was dearer to Thee than anything in those days fifteen hundred years ago. Didst Thou not often say then, "I will make you free"? But now Thou hast seen these "free" men,' the old man adds suddenly, with a pensive smile. 'Yes, we've paid dearly for it,' he goes on, looking sternly at Him, 'but at last we have completed that work in Thy name. For fifteen centuries we have been wrestling with Thy freedom, but now it is ended and over for good. Dost Thou not believe that it's over for good? Thou lookest meekly at me and deignest not even to be wroth with me. But let me tell Thee that now, today, people are more persuaded than ever that they have perfect freedom, yet they have brought their freedom to us and laid it humbly at our feet. But that has been our doing. Was this what Thou didst? Was this Thy freedom?'"

"I don't understand again," Alyosha broke in. "Is he ironical, is he jesting?"

"Not a bit of it! He claims it as a merit for himself and his Church that at last they have vanquished freedom and have done so to make men happy. 'For now' (he is speaking of the Inquisition, of course) 'for the first time it has become possible to think of the happiness of men. Man was created a rebel; and how can rebels be happy? Thou wast warned,' he says to Him. 'Thou hast had no lack of admonitions, and warnings, but Thou didst not listen to those warnings; Thou didst reject the only way by which men might be made happy. But, fortunately, departing Thou didst hand on the work to us. Thou hast promised, Thou hast established by Thy word, Thou hast given to us the right to bind and to unbind, and now, of course, Thou canst not think of taking it away. Why, then, hast Thou come to hinder us?'"

"And what's the meaning of 'no lack of admonitions and warnings'?" asked Alyosha.

"Why, that's the chief part of what the old man must say."

"'The wise and dread Spirit,[27] the spirit of self-destruction and nonexistence,' the old man goes on, 'the great spirit talked with Thee in the wilderness, and we are told in the books that he "tempted" Thee. Is that so? And could anything truer be

---

[26] Members of the Society of Jesus, which was viewed as the most aggressive and militant order of the Roman Catholic Church. (See Selection 21 for the *Spiritual Exercises* of its founder, Saint Ignatius of Loyola.)

[27] The devil.

said than what he revealed to Thee in three questions and what Thou didst reject, and what in the books is called "the temptation"?[28] And yet if there has ever been on earth a real stupendous miracle, it took place on that day, on the day of the three temptations. The statement of those three questions was itself the miracle. If it were possible to imagine simply for the sake of argument that those three questions of the dread spirit had perished utterly from the books, and that we had to restore them and to invent them anew, and to do so had gathered together all the wise men of the earth—rulers, chief priests, learned men, philosophers, poets— and had set them the task to invent three questions, such as would not only fit the occasion, but express in three words, three human phrases, the whole future history of the world and of humanity—doest Thou believe that all the wisdom of the earth united could have invented anything in depth and force equal to the three questions which were actually put to Thee then by the wise and mighty spirit in the wilderness? From those questions alone, from the miracle of their statement, we can see that we have here to do not with the fleeting human intelligence, but with the absolute and eternal. For in those three questions the whole subsequent history of mankind is, as it were, brought together into one whole, and foretold, and in them are united all the unsolved historical contradictions of human nature. At the time it could not be so clear, since the future was unknown; but now that fifteen hundred years have passed, we see that everything in those three questions was so justly divined and foretold, and has been so truly fulfilled, that nothing can be added to them or taken from them.

"'Judge Thyself who was right—Thou or he who questioned Thee then? Remember the first question; its meaning, in other words, was this: "Thou wouldst go into the world, and art going with empty hands, with some promise of freedom which men in their simplicity and their natural unruliness cannot even understand, which they fear and dread—for nothing has ever been more insupportable for a man and a human society than freedom. But seest Thou these stones in this parched and barren wilderness? Turn them into bread, and mankind will run after Thee like a flock of sheep, grateful and obedient, though forever trembling, lest Thou withdraw Thy hand and deny them Thy bread." But Thou wouldst not deprive man of freedom and didst reject the offer, thinking, what is that freedom worth, if obedience is bought with bread? Thou didst reply that man lives not by bread alone. But dost Thou know that for the sake of that earthly bread the spirit of the earth will rise up against Thee and will strive with Thee and overcome Thee, and all will follow him, crying, "Who can compare with this beast? He has given us fire from heaven!" Dost Thou know that the ages will pass, and human-

---

[28] The devil's three temptations of Jesus as related in the Gospels: Matthew 4:1–11, Luke 4:1–13, Mark 1:12–13. After Jesus had fasted in the desert forty days, the devil unsuccessfully tempted him to turn stones into bread (to relieve his hunger), to throw himself off a pinnacle of the Temple in Jerusalem (to demonstrate God's protection), and to gain all the kingdoms of the world.

ity will proclaim by the lips of their sages that there is no crime, and therefore no sin; there is only hunger? "Feed men, and then ask of them virtue!" that's what they'll write on the banner which they will raise against Thee, and with which they will destroy Thy temple. Where Thy temple stood will rise a new building; the terrible tower of Babel[29] will be built again, and though, like the one of old, it will not be finished, yet Thou mightest have prevented that new tower and have cut short the sufferings of men for a thousand years; for they will come back to us after a thousand years of agony with their tower. They will seek us again, hidden underground in the catacombs, for we shall be again persecuted and tortured. They will find us and cry to us, "Feed us, for those who have promised us fire from heaven haven't given it!" And then we shall finish building their tower, for he finishes the building who feeds them. And we alone shall feed them in Thy name, declaring falsely that it is in Thy name. Oh, never, never can they feed themselves without us! No science will give them bread so long as they remain free. In the end they will lay their freedom at our feet, and say to us, "Make us your slaves, but feed us." They will understand themselves, at last, that freedom and bread enough for all are inconceivable together, for never, never will they be able to share between them! They will be convinced, too, that they can never be free, for they are weak, vicious, worthless and rebellious. Thou didst promise them the bread of Heaven, but, I repeat again, can it compare with earthly bread in the eyes of the weak, ever-sinful and ignoble race of man? And if for the sake of the bread of Heaven thousands and tens of thousands shall follow Thee, what is to become of the millions and tens of thousands of millions of creatures who will not have the strength to forgo the earthly bread for the sake of the heavenly? Or dost Thou care only for the tens of thousands of the great and strong, while the millions, numerous as the sands of the sea, who are weak but love Thee, must exist only for the sake of the great and strong? No, we care for the weak, too. They are sinful and rebellious, but in the end they too will become obedient. They will marvel at us and look on us as gods, because we are ready to endure the freedom which they have found so dreadful and to rule over them—so awful it will seem to them to be free. But we shall tell them that we are Thy servants and rule them in Thy name. We shall deceive them again, for we will not let Thee come to us again. That deception will be our suffering, for we shall be forced to lie.

"'This is the significance of the first question in the wilderness, and this is what Thou hast rejected for the sake of that freedom which Thou hast exalted above everything. Yet in this question lies hidden the great secret of this world. Choosing "bread," Thou wouldst have satisfied the universal and everlasting craving of

---

[29] A tower (and city) built in the plain of Shinar (Genesis 11:1–9). The tower was intended by its builders to be so tall that it would reach into heaven. However, God punished the builders for their pride by replacing their single language with many diverse tongues. As a result the builders were unable to understand one another and so abandoned their project.

humanity—to find someone to worship. So long as man remains free he strives for nothing so incessantly and so painfully as to find someone to worship. But man seeks to worship what is established beyond dispute, so that all men would agree at once to worship it. For these pitiful creatures are concerned not only to find what one or the other can worship, but to find something that all would believe in and worship; what is essential is that all may be *together* in it. This craving for *community* of worship is the chief misery of every man individually and of all humanity from the beginning of time. For the sake of common worship they've slain each other with the sword. They have set up gods and challenged one another, "Put away your gods and come and worship ours, or we will kill you and your gods!" And so it will be to the end of the world, even when gods disappear from the earth; they will fall down before idols just the same. Thou didst know, Thou couldst not but have known, this fundamental secret of human nature, but Thou didst reject the one infallible banner which was offered Thee to make all men bow down to Thee alone—the banner of earthly bread; and Thou hast rejected it for the sake of freedom and the bread of Heaven. Behold what Thou didst further. And all again in the name of freedom! I tell Thee that man is tormented by no greater anxiety than to find someone quickly to whom he can hand over the gift of freedom with which the ill-fated creature is born. But only one who can appease their conscience can take over their freedom. In bread there was offered Thee an invincible banner; give bread, and man will worship Thee, for nothing is more certain than bread. But if someone else gains possession of his conscience—oh! then he will cast away Thy bread and follow after him who has ensnared his conscience. In that Thou wast right. For the secret of man's being is not only to live but to have something to live for. Without a stable conception of the object of life, man would not consent to go on living, and would rather destroy himself than remain on earth, though he had bread in abundance. That is true. But what happened? Instead of taking men's freedom from them, Thou didst make it greater than ever! Didst Thou forget that man prefers peace, and even death, to freedom of choice in the knowledge of good and evil? Nothing is more seductive for man than his freedom of conscience, but nothing is a greater cause of suffering. And behold, instead of giving a firm foundation for setting the conscience of man at rest forever, Thou didst choose all that is exceptional, vague and enigmatic; Thou didst choose what was utterly beyond the strength of men, acting as though Thou didst not love them at all—Thou who didst come to give Thy life for them! Instead of taking possession of man's freedom, Thou didst increase it, and burdened the spiritual kingdom of mankind with it sufferings forever. Thou didst desire man's free love, that he should follow Thee freely, enticed and taken captive by Thee. In place of the rigid, ancient law, man must hereafter with free heart decide for himself what is good and what is evil, having only Thy image before him as his guide. But didst Thou not know he would at last reject even Thy image and Thy truth, if he is weighed down with the fearful burden of free choice? They will cry aloud at last that the truth is not in Thee, for they could not have been left in greater confusion and suffering than Thou hast caused, laying upon them so many cares and unanswerable problems.

"'So that, in truth, Thou didst Thyself lay the foundation for the destruction of Thy kingdom, and no one is more to blame for it. Yet what was offered Thee? There are three powers, three powers alone, able to conquer and to hold captive forever the conscience of these impotent rebels for their happiness—those forces are miracle, mystery and authority. Thou hast rejected all three and hast set the example for doing so. When the wise and dread spirit set Thee on the pinnacle of the temple and said to Thee, "If Thou wouldst know whether Thou art the son of God then cast Thyself down, for it is written: the angels shall hold him up lest he fall and bruise himself, and Thou shalt know then whether Thou art the Son of God and shalt prove then how great is Thy faith in Thy Father." But Thou didst refuse and wouldst not cast Thyself down. Oh! of course, Thou didst proudly and well like God; but the weak, unruly race of men, are they gods? Oh, Thou didst know then that in taking one step, in making one movement to cast Thyself down, Thou wouldst be tempting God and have lost all Thy faith in Him, and wouldst have been dashed to pieces against that earth which Thou didst come to save. And the wise spirit that tempted Thee would have rejoiced. But I ask again, are there many like Thee? And couldst Thou believe for one moment that men, too, could face such a temptation? Is the nature of men such that they can reject miracle, and at the great moments of their life, the moments of their deepest, most agonizing spiritual difficulties, cling only to the free verdict of the heart? Oh, Thou didst know that Thy deed would be recorded in books, would be handed down to remote times and the utmost ends of the earth, and Thou didst hope that man, following Thee, would cling to God and not ask for a miracle. But Thou didst not know that when man rejects miracles he rejects God too; for man seeks not so much God as the miraculous. And as man cannot bear to be without the miraculous, he will create new miracles of his own for himself, and will worship deeds of sorcery and witchcraft, though he might be a hundred times over a rebel, heretic and infidel. Thou didst not come down from the Cross when they shouted to Thee, mocking and reviling Thee, "Come down from the Cross and we will believe that Thou art He." Thou didst not come down, for again Thou wouldst not enslave man by a miracle, and didst crave faith given freely, not based on miracle. Thou didst crave for free love and not the base raptures of the slave before the might that has overawed him forever. But Thou didst think too highly of men therein, for they are slaves, of course, though rebellious by nature. Look round and judge; fifteen centuries have passed; look upon them. Whom hast Thou raised up to Thyself? I swear, man is weaker and baser by nature than Thou hast believed him! Can he, can he do what Thou didst? By showing him so much respect, Thou didst, as it were, cease to feel for him, for Thou didst ask far too much from him—Thou who hast loved him more than Thyself! Respecting him less, Thou wouldst have asked less of him. That would have been more like love, for his burden would have been lighter. He is weak and vile. What though he is everywhere now rebelling against our power, and proud of his re-bellion? It is the pride of a child and a schoolboy. They are little children rioting and barring out the teacher at school. But their childish delight will end; it will cost them dear. They will cast down temples and drench the earth with blood. But they will see at last, the foolish children, that, though they are rebels, they are impotent rebels, unable to keep up their own rebellion. Bathed in their foolish tears, they will recognize at last that He who created them rebels must have meant to mock at them. They will say this in despair, and their utterance will be a blasphemy which will make them more unhappy still, for man's nature cannot bear blasphemy, and in the end always avenges it on itself. And so unrest, confusion and unhappiness—that is the present lot of man after Thou didst bear so much for their freedom! Thy great prophet tells in vision and in image that he saw all those who took part in the first resurrection and that there were of each tribe twelve thousand.[30] But if there were so many of them, they must have been not men but gods. They had borne Thy cross, they had endured scores of years in the barren, hungry wilderness, living upon locusts and roots—and Thou mayest indeed point with pride at those children of freedom, of free love, of free and splendid sacrifice for Thy name. But remember that they were only some thousands; and what of the rest? And how are the other weak ones to blame, because they could not endure what the strong have endured? How is the weak soul to blame that it is unable to receive such terrible gifts? Canst Thou have simply come to the elect and for the elect? But if so, it is a mystery and we cannot understand it. And if it is a mystery, we too have a right to preach a mystery, and to teach them that it's not the free judgment of their hearts, not love, that matters, but a mystery which they must follow blindly, even against their conscience. So we have done. We have corrected Thy work and have founded it upon *miracle, mystery* and *authority.* And men rejoiced that they were again led like sheep, and that the terrible gift that had brought them such suffering was, at last, lifted from their hearts. Were we right teaching them this? Speak! Did we not love mankind, so meekly acknowledging their feebleness, lovingly lightening their burden, and permitting their weak nature even sin with our sanction? Why hast Thou come now to hinder us? And why dost Thou look silently and searchingly at me with Thy mild eyes? Be angry. I don't want Thy love, for I love Thee not. And what use is it for me to hide anything from Thee? Don't I know to Whom I am speaking? All that I can say is known to Thee already. And is it for me to conceal from Thee our mystery? Perhaps it is Thy will to hear it from my lips. Listen, then. We are not working with Thee, but with *him*—that is our mystery. It's long—eight centuries—since we have been on *his* side and not on Thine. Just eight centuries ago, we took from him what Thou didst reject with scorn, that last gift he offered Thee, showing Thee all the kingdoms of the earth. We took from him Rome and the sword of Caesar, and proclaimed ourselves sole rulers of the earth,[31] though hitherto we have not been able to complete our work. But whose fault is that? Oh, the work is only

---

[30] In Revelation 7:4–8, twelve thousand from each of the twelve tribes of Israel will be saved from destruction on the Day of Judgment.

[31] In 381, Christianity became the official religion of the Roman Empire; and in 401, Pope Innocent I claimed authority over the entire Roman Church, thus replacing the empire as the only "universal" authority, since the empire had been officially divided into eastern and western portions since 395.

beginning, but it has begun. It has long to await completion and the earth has yet much to suffer, but we shall triumph and shall be Caesars, and then we shall plan the universal happiness of man. But Thou mightest have taken even then the sword of Caesar. Why didst Thou reject that last gift? Hadst Thou accepted that last counsel of the mighty spirit, Thou wouldst have accomplished all that man seeks on earth—that is, someone to worship, someone to keep his conscience, and some means of uniting all in one unanimous and harmonious ant heap, for the craving for universal unity is the third and last anguish of men. Mankind as a whole has always striven to organize a universal state. There have been many great nations with great histories, but the more highly they were developed the more unhappy they were, for they felt more acutely than other people the craving for world-wide union. The great conquerors, Timours and Genghis Khans,[32] whirled like hurricanes over the face of the earth, striving to subdue its people, and they too were but the unconscious expression of the same craving for universal unity. Hadst Thou taken the world and Caesar's purple,[33] Thou wouldst have founded the universal state and have given universal peace. For who can rule men if not he who holds their conscience and their bread in his hands? We have taken the sword of Caesar, and in taking it, of course, have rejected Thee and followed *him*. Oh, ages are yet to come of the confusion of free thought, of their science and cannibalism. For having begun to build their tower of Babel without us, they will end, of course, with cannibalism. But then the beast will crawl to us and lick our feet and spatter them with tears of blood. And we shall sit upon the beast and raise the cup, and on it will be written, "Mystery." But then, and only then, the reign of peace and happiness will come for men. Thou art proud of Thine elect, but Thou hast only the elect, while we give rest to all. And besides, how many of those elect, those mighty ones who could become elect, have grown weary waiting for Thee, and have transferred and will transfer the powers of their spirit and the warmth of their heart to the other camp, and end by raising their *free* banner against Thee. Thou didst Thyself lift up that banner. But with us all will be happy and will no more rebel, nor destroy one another as under Thy freedom. Oh, we shall persuade them that they will only become free when they renounce their freedom to us and submit to us. And shall we be right or shall we be lying? They will be convinced that we are right, for they will remember the horrors of slavery and confusion to which Thy freedom brought them. Freedom, free thought and science, will lead them into such straits and will bring them face to face with such marvels and insoluble mysteries that some of them, the fierce and rebellious, will destroy themselves; others, rebellious but weak, will destroy

---

[32] Timour or Timur or Tamerlane (c. 1336–1405) was a Mongol conqueror who led armies throughout central Asia and into Persia, Russia, India, Syria, and Asia Minor. Genghis Khan (1162–1227) was a Mongol conqueror whose hordes overran northern China, Korea, northern India, Persia, and parts of Russia. (See footnote 9.)

[33] Purple stripes decorated the togas of ancient Roman magistrates; thus, the color became a symbol of imperial power.

one another, while the rest, weak and unhappy, will crawl fawning to our feet and whine to us: "Yes, you were right, you alone possess His mystery, and we come back to you, save us from ourselves!"

"'Receiving bread from us, they will see clearly that we take the bread made by their hands from them, to give it to them, without any miracle. They will see that we do not change the stones to bread, but in truth they will be more thankful for taking it from our hands than for the bread itself! For they will remember only too well that in the old days, without our help, even the bread they made turned to stones in their hands, while since they have come back to us, the very stones have turned to bread in their hands. Too, too well they know the value of complete submission! And until men know that, they will be unhappy. Who is most to blame for their not knowing it, speak? Who scattered the flock and sent it astray on unknown paths? But the flock will come together again and will submit once more, and then it will be once for all. Then we shall give them the quiet humble happiness of weak creatures such as they are by nature. Oh, we shall persuade them at last not to be proud, for Thou didst lift them up and thereby taught them to be proud. We shall show them that they are weak, that they are only pitiful children, but that childlike happiness is the sweetest of all. They will become timid and will look to us and huddle close to us in fear, as chicks to the hen. They will marvel at us and will be awe-stricken before us, and will be proud at our being so powerful and clever, that we have been able to subdue such a turbulent flock of thousands of millions. They will tremble impotently before our wrath, their minds will grow fearful, they will be quick to shed tears like women and children, but they will be just as ready at a sign from us to pass to laughter and rejoicing, to happy mirth and childish song. Yes, we shall set them to work, but in their leisure hours we shall make their life like a child's game, with children's songs and innocent dance. Oh, we shall allow them even sin; they are weak and helpless, and they will love us like children because we allow them to sin. We shall tell them that every sin will be expiated, if it is done with our permission, that we allow them to sin because we love them, and the punishment for these sins we take upon ourselves. And we shall take it upon ourselves, and they will adore us as their saviors who have taken on themselves their sins before God. And they will have no secrets from us. We shall allow or forbid them to live with their wives and mistresses, to have or not to have children—according to whether they have been obedient or disobedient—and they will submit to us gladly and cheerfully. The most painful secrets of their conscience, all, all they will bring to us, and we shall have an answer for all. And they will be glad to believe our answer, for it will save them from the great anxiety and terrible agony they endure at present in making a free decision for themselves. And all will be happy, all the millions of creatures, except the hundred thousand who rule over them. For only we, we who guard the mystery, shall be unhappy. There will be thousands of millions of happy babes, and a hundred thousand sufferers who have taken upon themselves the curse of the knowledge of good and evil. Peacefully they will die, peacefully they will expire in Thy name, and beyond the grave they will find nothing but death. But we shall keep the secret, and for their happiness we shall allure them with the reward of heaven and eternity. Though if there were anything in the other world, it certainly would not be for such as they. It is prophesied that Thou wilt come again in victory, Thou wilt come with Thy chosen, the proud and strong, but we will say that they have only saved themselves, but we have saved all. We are told that the harlot who sits upon the beast, and holds in her hands the *mystery,* shall be put to shame, that the weak will rise up again, and will rend her royal purple and will strip naked her loathsome body. But then I will stand up and point out to Thee the thousand millions of happy children who have known no sin. And we who have taken their sins upon us for their happiness will stand up before Thee and say: "Judge us if Thou canst and darest." Know that I fear Thee not. Know that I too have been in the wilderness, I too have lived on roots and locusts, I too prized the freedom with which Thou hast blessed men, and I too was striving to stand among Thy elect, among the strong and powerful, thirsting "to make up the number." But I awakened and would not serve madness. I turned back and joined the ranks of those *who have corrected Thy work.* I left the proud and went back to the humble, for the happiness of the humble. What I say to Thee will come to pass, and our dominion will be built up. I repeat, tomorrow Thou shalt see that obedient flock who at a sign from me will hasten to heap up the hot cinders about the pile on which I shall burn Thee for coming to hinder us. For it anyone has ever deserved our fires, it is Thou. Tomorrow I shall burn Thee. *Dixi.*'" [34]

Ivan stopped. He was carried away as he talked and spoke with excitement; when he had finished, he suddenly smiled.

Alyosha had listened in silence; toward the end he was greatly moved and seemed several times on the point of interrupting, but restrained himself. Now his words came with a rush.

"But . . . that's absurd!" he cried, flushing. "Your poem is in praise of Jesus, not in blame of Him — as you meant it to be. And who will believe you about freedom? Is that the way to understand it? That's not the idea of it in the Orthodox Church.[35] . . . That's Rome, and not even the whole of Rome, it's false—those are the worst of the Catholics, the Inquisitors, the Jesuits! . . . And there could not be such a fantastic creature as your Inquisitor. What are these sins of mankind they take on themselves? Who are these keepers of the mystery who have taken some curse upon themselves for the happiness of mankind? When have they been seen? We know the Jesuits, they are spoken ill of, but surely they are not what you

---

[34] Latin: "I have spoken" (the closing phrase of a Church pronouncement).

[35] The Russian Orthodox Church, the national church of tsarist and present-day Russia. (After the division of the ancient Roman Empire, Christianity, too, split into two main branches: Roman Catholicism in the Latin West and the Orthodox churches in the dominantly Greek East. In 1054, the two branches excommunicated each other, a state of ill will which was not lifted officially by both sides until 1965.)

describe? They are not that at all, not at all. . . . They are simply the Romish army for the earthly sovereignty of the world in the future, with the Pontiff [36] of Rome for Emperor . . . that's their ideal, but there's no sort of mystery or lofty melancholy about it. . . . It's simple lust of power, of filthy earthly gain, of domination—something like a universal serfdom with them as masters—that's all they stand for. They don't even believe in God, perhaps. Your suffering Inquisitor is a mere fantasy."

"Stay, stay," laughed Ivan, "how hot you are! A fantasy you say, let it be so! Of course it's a fantasy. But allow me to say: do you really think that the Roman Catholic movement of the last centuries is actually nothing but the lust of power, of filthy earthly gain? Is that Father Paissy's teaching?" [37]

"No, no, on the contrary, Father Paissy did once say something rather the same as you . . . but of course it's not the same, not a bit the same," Alyosha hastily corrected himself.

"A precious admission, in spite of your 'not a bit the same.' I ask you why your Jesuits and Inquisitors have united simply for vile material gain? Why can there not be among them one martyr oppressed by great sorrow and loving humanity? You see, only suppose that there was one such man among all those who desire nothing but filthy material gain—if there's only one like my old Inquisitor, who had himself eaten roots in the desert and made frenzied efforts to subdue his flesh to make himself free and perfect. But yet all his life he loved humanity, and suddenly his eyes were opened, and he saw that it is no great moral blessedness to attain perfection and freedom, if at the same time one gains the conviction that millions of God's creatures have been created as a mockery, that they will never be capable of using their freedom, that these poor rebels can never turn into giants to complete the tower, that it was not for such geese that the great idealist dreamt his dream of harmony. Seeing all that, he turned back and joined—the clever people. Surely that could have happened?"

"Joined whom, what clever people?" cried Alyosha, completely carried away. "They have no such great cleverness and no mysteries and secrets . . . Perhaps nothing but atheism, [38] that's all their secret. Your Inquisitor does not believe in God, that's his secret!"

"What if it is so! At last you have guessed it. It's perfectly true that that's the whole secret, but isn't that suffering, at least for a man like that, who has wasted his whole life in the desert and yet could not shake off his incurable love of humanity? In his old age he reached the clear conviction that nothing but the advice of the great dread spirit could build up any tolerable sort of life for the feeble, unruly, 'incomplete, empirical creatures created in jest.' And so, convinced of this, he sees that he must follow the counsel of the wise spirit, the dread spirit of death

---

[36] The pope.

[37] Father Paissy, a learned Russian Orthodox monk.

[38] Denial of God's existence.

and destruction, and therefore accept lying and deception, and lead men consciously to death and destruction, and yet deceive them all the way so that they may not notice where they are being led, that the poor, blind creatures may at least on the way think themselves happy. And note, the deception is in the name of Him in Whose ideal the old man had so fervently believed all his life long. Is not that tragic? And if only one such stood at the head of the whole army 'filled with the lust of power only for the sake of filthy gain'—would not one such be enough to make a tragedy? More than that, one such standing at the head is enough to create the actual leading idea of the Roman Church with all its armies and Jesuits, its highest idea. I tell you frankly that I firmly believe that there has always been such a man among those who stood at the head of the movement. Who knows, there may have been some such even among the Roman Popes. Who knows, perhaps the spirit of that accursed old man who loves mankind so obstinately in his own way is to be found even now in a whole multitude of such old men, existing not by chance but by agreement, as a secret league formed long ago for the guarding of the mystery, to guard it from the weak and the unhappy, so as to make them happy. No doubt it is so, and so it must be indeed. I fancy that even among the Masons[39] there's something of the same mystery at the bottom, and that that's why the Catholics so detest the Masons as their rivals breaking up the unity of the idea, while it is so essential that there should be one flock and one shepherd. . . . But from the way I defend my idea I might be an author impatient of your criticism. Enough of it."

"You are perhaps a Mason yourself?" broke suddenly from Alyosha. "You don't believe in God," he added, speaking this time very sorrowfully. He fancied besides that his brother was looking at him ironically. "How does your poem end?" he asked, suddenly looking down. "Or was it the end?"

"I meant it to end like this: When the Inquisitor ceased speaking, he waited some time for his Prisoner to answer him. His silence weighed down upon him. He saw the Prisoner had listened intently all the time, looking gently in his face and evidently not wishing to reply. The old man longed for Him to say something, however bitter and terrible. But He suddenly approached the old man in silence and softly kissed him on his bloodless, aged lips. That was all His answer. The old man shuddered. His lips moved. He went to the door, opened it, and said to Him, 'Go, and come no more. . . . Come not at all, never, never!' And he let Him out into the dark alleys of the town. The Prisoner went away."

"And the old man?"

---

[39] The Freemasons constitute the world's largest secret society. Originating in medieval stonemason's guilds, by the eighteenth century it had grown to serve the present organization's fraternal (and partly religious) purposes. The Freemasons were condemned in Dostoevsky's day by both Roman Catholic and Orthodox churches.

"The kiss glows in his heart, but the old man adheres to his idea."

"And you with him, you too?" cried Alyosha, mournfully.

Ivan laughed.

"Why, it's all nonsense, Alyosha. It's only a senseless poem of a senseless student, who could never write two lines of verse. Why do you take it so seriously? Surely you don't suppose I am going straight off to the Jesuits, to join the men who are correcting His work? Good Lord, it's no business of mine. I told you, all I want is to live on to thirty, and then . . . dash the cup to the ground!"[40]

"But the little sticky leaves, and the precious tombs, and the blue sky, and the woman you love! How will you live, how will you love them?" Alyosha cried sorrowfully. "With such a hell in your heart and your head, how can you? No, that's just what you are going away for, to join them . . . if not, you will kill yourself, you can't endure it!"

"There is a strength to endure everything," Ivan said with a cold smile.

"What strength?"

"The strength of the Karamazovs—the strength of the Karamazov baseness."

"To sink into debauchery, to stifle your soul with corruption, yes?"

"Possibly even that . . . only perhaps till I am thirty I shall escape it, and then—"

"How will you escape it? By what will you escape it? That's impossible with your ideas."

"In the Karamazov way, again."

"'Everything is lawful,' you mean? Everything is lawful, is that it?"

Ivan scowled, and all at once turned strangely pale.

"Ah, you've caught up yesterday's phrase, which so offended Miusov [41]—and which Dmitri [42] pounced upon so naively and paraphrased!" he smiled queerly. "Yes, if you like, 'everything is lawful' since the word has been said. I won't deny it. And Mitya's version isn't bad." [43]

Alyosha looked at him in silence.

"I thought that going away from here I have you at least," Ivan said suddenly, with unexpected feeling; "but now I see that there is no place for me even in your heart, my dear hermit. The formula, 'all is lawful,' I won't renounce—will you renounce me for that, yes?"

Alyosha got up, went to him and softly kissed him on the lips.

"That's plagiarism," cried Ivan, highly delighted. "You stole that from my poem. Thank you, though. Get up, Alyosha, it's time we were going, both of us."

---

[40] A metaphorical phrase, meaning to end one's life.

[41] Peter Miusov, a relative of Ivan and Alyosha, a man of enlightened ideas.

[42] Half-brother of Ivan and Alyosha.

[43] Mitya is a variant name of Dmitri.

They went out, but stopped when they reached the entrance of the tavern.

"Listen, Alyosha," Ivan began in a resolute voice, "if I am really able to care for the sticky little leaves, I shall only love them remembering you. It's enough for me that you are somewhere here, and I shan't lose my desire for life yet. Is that enough for you? Take it as a declaration of love if you like. And now you go to the right and I to the left. And it's enough, do you hear—enough! I mean even if I don't go away tomorrow (I think I certainly shall go) and we meet again, don't say a word more on these subjects. I beg that particularly. And about Dmitri, too, I ask you especially never speak to me again," he added, with sudden irritation; "it's all exhausted, it has all been said over and over again, hasn't it? And I'll make you one promise in return for it. When, at thirty, I want to 'dash the cup to the ground,' wherever I may be I'll come to have one more talk with you, even though it were from America—you may be sure of that. I'll come on purpose. It will be very interesting to have a look at you, to see what you'll be by that time. It's rather a solemn promise, you see. And we really may be parting for seven years or ten. Come, go now to your Pater Seraphicus,[44] he is dying. If he dies without you, you will be angry with me for having kept you. Good-bye, kiss me once more; that's right, now go." . . .

---

[44] "Angelic Father" (said mockingly by Ivan), a reference to Father Zossima, the beloved and renowned elder at the monastery, who was a great influence upon Alyosha.

48

❦

Friedrich Nietzsche

BEYOND GOOD AND EVIL

The writings of Friedrich Wilhelm Nietzsche (1844–1900), more than those of any other philosopher, foreshadow the massive intellectual and spiritual dislocations of the twentieth century. More psychologically than rationalistically attuned, Nietzsche said that the Russian novelist Dostoevsky (Selection 47) was the only one who had taught him anything about human nature. In the twentieth century this German philosopher and poet became a seminal influence on a whole class of existential philosophers and fiction writers, such as Sartre and Camus, as well as on many theologians grappling with the problem of human choices in a world that often seemed godless, as well as on the whole school of psychoanalysis led by Freud. (See Volume IV.) There are even those who claim the twentieth-century Nazi doctrine of race as a manifestation of Nietzsche's "will to power," but that is clearly a distortion of Nietzsche's view; he would have regarded Nazi racism as an example of the "slave morality" of the "herd." He believed that only superior* individuals achieved superior values. Today, Nietzsche is accorded a place as a genuinely original thinker, one of the first to recognize the absurdity of human existence as the necessary basis for creative life and to stress the importance of irrational and illusional factors in shaping human behavior.*

Nietzsche was the son of a Lutheran minister who died when the boy was only five years old, a traumatic event for the youngster who thereafter grew up in a household dominated by older women. (His male desire to free himself from that female domination may perhaps be seen in the following selection.) Beset by doubts about religion, Nietzsche chose not to follow his father's pastoral vocation. A brilliant student, he was appointed as professor of classical philology at the distinguished University of Basel in Switzerland at the extraordinarily young age of twenty-four, a position he held for ten years until failing health forced his resignation. For most of his Basel years he was a close friend of Richard Wagner, the German composer, although he was later to break with Wagner, rejecting what he came to consider a decadent late romanticism.

Nietzsche's first important work, The Birth of Tragedy: Out of the Spirit of Music *(1872) took issue with what was then the conventional view of ancient Greek civilization as the embodiment of calm rationality and noble grandeur. He saw rather the dark irrationality essential to the tragic drama, and pointed out its two polarities—the passionate mysteries of Dionysus (god of wine and ecstasy) as well as the serene clarity of Apollo (god of prophecy, light, and reason). Insightful as it was, the book was attacked by philological scholars for its lack of conventional scholarship and even labeled as Wagnerian propaganda. Certainly, the book's thesis is typical of Nietzsche's desire to get under the surfaces of conventional ideas in a search for the motivating psychological forces that he believed ultimately generate all great historical and aesthetic movements.*

Nietzsche's constantly deteriorating health forced him to give up his professorial duties and become a wanderer through Switzerland, Italy, and southern France, writing constantly but beset by increasing solitude. Nietzsche's most popular work among the general population was Thus Spake Zarathustra *(1883–1885). The ancient Persian prophet, Zarathustra or Zoroaster, is the poetic incarnation of Nietzsche himself and at the same time the imaginary companion of his solitude. The book appealed to many readers for its prophetic, almost biblical, cadences and its memorably startling phrases, asserting Nietzsche's most deeply felt values in non-philosophical language: "Man is a rope stretched between the animal and the Superman—a rope over an abyss. . . . And it is the great noontide, when man is in the middle of his course between animal and Superman. . . . Dead are all the Gods: now do we desire the Superman to live.—Let this be our final will at the great noontide! . . . Only where there is life, is there also will: not, however, Will to Life, but—so teach I thee—Will to Power!"*

Nietzsche's failing health and his own temperament prevented him from carrying out the systematic exposition of his thoughts that he intended in a huge work to be titled Der Wille zur Macht *(The Will to Power); instead he frequently wrote aphorisms and poetry. In* The Genealogy of Morals *(1887) he traces the origins of Christian morality to a slave revolt against everything superior, and he advocates the return to an aristocratic "master morality." Nietzsche's mental breakdown came in Turin, Italy, in 1889. He wrote raving notes to his friends signed "Dionysus" and "The Crucified One." He lived on in Germany in increasing madness until 1900, mainly under the care of his mother and sister. There are those who have seen his fate at the dawn of the twentieth century as a foreshadowing of its various extreme ideologies, but this seems unfair to Nietzsche's varied individualistic perceptions. If he had a fault it was in the rhetorical extremism he sometimes adopted to make his points and the dialectical writing techniques he employed as a technique of argumentation, developing his ideas through stating conflicting opposites, which made them easy prey for those looking for isolated quotations only to buttress their own ideas.*

Nietzsche did not build a grand philosophical system. His ideas are often too unsystematic and elusive. His supercharged sayings do not always make for clarity, but they do allow him to strike off original insights into the conditions and nature of humanity. Like Dostoevsky, Nietzsche hated the ugliness and bourgeois materialism of European society in the late nineteenth century. He rejected all its "certainties"—democracy, Christianity, science, the life of reason—as diminutions of man's higher nature. Europe could be saved only by a "transvaluation" of all the traditional values, only by understanding the deepest feelings of humanity and harnessing them by an act of will *to creative ends. Nietzsche's affirmative values were those of the determined individuals (Übermenschen, "overmen" or "supermen") who, through disciplined struggle and suffering, would make their lives significant and for whom the good life was rooted in the very mystery of existence. His attacks on bourgeois civilization and his advocacy of relentless struggle against the "herd" who accepted its values served to inspire Social Darwinists, Fascists, and National Socialists (Nazis). However the groups that loved to quote Nietzsche often distorted his ideas. He clearly expressed his disgust with racism, nationalism, and all such collective perspectives. His individualistic point of view was the antithesis of any totalitarian doctrine. Of enduring value in Nietzsche's thought is his hatred of conventional falsehoods and false roles, of mediocrity and mass vulgarity, along with his insight into the irrational wellsprings of human creativity and his fierce sincerity. He disapproved of academic philosophy: the only true philosophy is that which one* lives.

Beyond Good and Evil: Prelude to a Philosophy of the Future (1886), from which the following selection is taken, is among the clearest statements of Nietzsche's philosophy. It shows his distrust of reason and his rejection of the values of a Christian democratic culture. Although his views cannot always be clearly understood or accepted, they do represent significant currents in human nature that should not be ignored.

PART ONE: PREJUDICES OF PILOSOPHERS

• • •

2

"*How could* anything originate out of its opposite? For example, truth out of error? or the Will to Truth out of the will to deception? or the generous deed out of selfishness? or the pure sun-bright vision of the wise man out of covetousness? Such genesis is impossible; whoever dreams of it is a fool, nay, worse than a fool; things of the highest value must have a different origin, an origin of *their own*—in this

---

From Friedrich Nietzsche, *Beyond Good and Evil*, trans. Helen Zimmern, 1907.

transitory, seductive, illusory, paltry world, in this turmoil of delusion and cupidity, they cannot have their source. But rather in the lap of Being, in the intransitory, in the concealed God, in the 'Thing-in-itself'—*there* must be their source and nowhere else!"—This mode of reasoning discloses the typical prejudice by which metaphysicians of all times can be recognized, this mode of valuation is at the back of all their logical procedure; through this "belief" of theirs, they exert themselves for their "knowledge," for something that is in the end solemnly christened "the Truth." The fundamental belief of metaphysicians is *the belief in antitheses of values.* It never occurred even to the wariest of them to doubt here on the very threshold (where doubt, however, was most necessary); though they had made a solemn vow, "*de omnibus dubitandum.*"[1] For it may be doubted, firstly, whether antitheses exist at all; and secondly, whether the popular valuations and antitheses of value upon which metaphysicians have set their seal, are not perhaps merely superficial estimates, merely provisional perspectives besides being probably made from some corner, perhaps from below—"frog perspectives," as it were, to borrow an expression current among painters. In spite of all the value which may belong to the true, the positive, and the unselfish, it might be possible that a higher and more fundamental value for life generally should be assigned to pretence, to the will to delusion, to selfishness, and cupidity. It might even be possible that *what* constitutes the value of those good and respected things, consists precisely in their being insidiously related, knotted, and crocheted to these evil and apparently opposed things—perhaps even in being essentially identical with them. Perhaps! But who wishes to concern himself with such dangerous "Perhapses"! For that investigation one must await the advent of a new order of philosophers, such as will have other tastes and inclinations, the reverse of those hitherto prevalent—philosophers of the dangerous "Perhaps" in every sense of the term. And to speak in all seriousness, I see such new philosophers beginning to appear.

• • •

4

The falseness of an opinion is not for us any objection to it: it is here, perhaps, that our new language sounds most strangely. The question is, how far an opinion is life-furthering, life-preserving, species-preserving, perhaps species-rearing; and we are fundamentally inclined to maintain that the falsest opinions (to which the synthetic judgments *a priori*[2] belong) are the most indispensable to us; that without a recognition of logical fictions, without a comparison of reality with the purely *imagined* world of the absolute and immutable, without a constant counterfeiting

---

[1] Latin: "All is to be doubted"; from the French philosopher René Descartes (Selection 28).

[2] Judgments existing in the mind independent of and prior to experience.

of the world by means of numbers, man could not live—that the renunciation of false opinions would be a renunciation of life, a negation of life. *To recognize untruth as a condition of life:* that is certainly to impugn the traditional ideas of value in a dangerous manner, and a philosophy which ventures to do so, has thereby alone placed itself beyond good and evil.

• • •

13

Psychologists should bethink themselves before putting down the instinct of self-preservation as the cardinal instinct of an organic being. A living thing seeks above all to *discharge* its strength—life itself is *Will to Power;* self-preservation is only one of the indirect and most frequent *results* thereof. In short, here, as everywhere else, let us beware of *superfluous* teleological principles!—one of which is the instinct of self-preservation (we owe it to Spinoza's inconsistency).[3] It is thus, in effect, that method ordains, which must be essentially economy of principles.

• • •

23

All psychology hitherto has run aground on moral prejudices and timidities, it has not dared to launch out into the depths. In so far as it is allowable to recognize in that which has hitherto been written, evidence of that which has hitherto been kept silent, it seems as if nobody had yet harboured the notion of psychology as the Morphology and *Development-doctrine of the Will to Power,* as I conceive of it. The power of moral prejudices has penetrated deeply into the most intellectual world, the world apparently most indifferent and unprejudiced, and has obviously operated in an injurious, obstructive, blinding, and distorting manner. A proper physiopsychology has to contend with unconscious antagonism in the heart of the investigator, it has "the heart" against it: even a doctrine of the reciprocal conditionalness of the "good" and the "bad" impulses, causes (as refined immorality) distress and aversion in a still strong and manly conscience—still more so, a doctrine of the derivation of all good impulses from bad ones. If, however, a person should regard even the emotions of hatred, envy, covetousness, and imperiousness as life-conditioning emotions, as factors which must be present, fundamentally and essentially, in the general economy of life (which must, therefore, be further developed if life is to be further developed), he will suffer from such a view of things as from sea-sickness. And yet this hypothesis is far from being the strangest and most painful in this immense and almost new domain of dangerous knowledge; and there are in fact a hundred good reasons why

---

[3] Teleology is the study of the evidence for design or purpose in nature. Nietzsche admired the seventeenth-century philosopher Spinoza for, among other things, his critique of teleology.

every one should keep away from it who *can* do so! On the other hand, if one has once drifted higher with one's bark, well! very good! now let us set our teeth firmly! let us open our eyes and keep our hand fast on the helm! We sail away right *over* morality, we crush out, we destroy perhaps the remains of our own morality by daring to make our voyage thither—but what do *we* matter! Never yet did a *profounder* world of insight reveal itself to daring travellers and adventurers, and the psychologist who thus "makes a sacrifice"—it is *not* the *sacrifizio dell' intelletto*,[4] on the contrary!—will at least be entitled to demand in return that psychology shall once more be recognised as the queen of the sciences, for whose service and equipment the other sciences exist. For psychology is once more the path to the fundamental problems.

PART TWO: THE FREE SPIRIT

. . .

29

It is the business of the very few to be independent; it is a privilege of the strong. And whoever attempts it, even with the best right, but without being *obliged* to do so, proves that he is probably not only strong, but also daring beyond measure. He enters into a labyrinth, he multiplies a thousandfold the dangers which life in itself already brings with it; not the least of which is that no one can see how and where he loses his way, becomes isolated, and is torn piecemeal by some minotaur of conscience. Supposing such a one comes to grief, it is so far from the comprehension of men that they neither feel it, nor sympathise with it. And he cannot any longer go back! He cannot even go back again to the sympathy of men!

. . .

32

Throughout the longest period of human history—one calls it the prehistoric period—the value or non-value of an action was inferred from its *consequences;* the action in itself was not taken into consideration, any more than its origin; but pretty much as in China at present, where the distinction or disgrace of a child redounds to its parents, the retro-operating power of success or failure was what induced men to think well or ill of an action. Let us call this period the *premoral* period of mankind; the imperative, "know thyself!" was then still unknown—In the last ten thousand years, on the other hand, on certain large portions of the earth, one has gradually got so far, that one no longer lets the consequences of an action, but its origin, decide with regard to its worth: a great achievement as a whole, an important refinement of vision and of criterion, the

---

[4]Italian: "sacrifice of the intellect."

unconscious effect of the supremacy of aristocratic values and of the belief in "origin," the mark of a period which may be designated in the narrower sense as the *moral* one: the first attempt at self-knowledge is thereby made. Instead of the consequences, the origin—what an inversion of perspective! And assuredly an inversion effected only after long struggle and wavering! To be sure, an ominous new superstition, a peculiar narrowness of interpretation, attained supremacy precisely thereby: the origin of an action was interpreted in the most definite sense possible, as origin out of an *intention;* people were agreed in the belief that the value of an action lay in the value of its intention. The intention as the sole origin and antecedent history of an action: under the influence of this prejudice moral praise and blame have been bestowed, and men have judged and even philosophised almost up to the present day.—Is it not possible, however, that the necessity may now have arisen of again making up our minds with regard to the reversing and fundamental shifting of values, owing to a new self-consciousness and acuteness in man—is it not possible that we may be standing on the threshold of a period which to begin with, would be distinguished negatively as *ultra-moral:* nowadays when, at least amongst us immoralists, the suspicion arises that the decisive value of an action lies precisely in that which is *not intentional,* and that all its intentionalness, all that is seen, sensible, or "sensed" in it, belongs to its surface or skin—which, like every skin, betrays something, but *conceals* still more? In short, we believe that the intention is only a sign or symptom, which first requires an explanation—a sign, moreover, which has too many interpretations, and consequently hardly any meaning in itself alone: that morality, in the sense in which it has been understood hitherto, as intention-morality, has been a prejudice, perhaps a prematureness or preliminariness, probably something of the same rank as astrology and alchemy, but in any case something which must be surmounted. The surmounting of morality, in a certain sense even the self-mounting of morality—let that be the name for the long secret labour which has been reserved for the most refined, the most upright, and also the most wicked consciences of today, as the living touchstones of the soul.

33

It cannot be helped: the sentiment of surrender, of sacrifice for one's neighbour, and all self-renunciation-morality, must be mercilessly called to account, and brought to judgment; just as the aesthetics of "disinterested contemplation," under which the emasculation of art nowadays seeks insidiously enough to create itself a good conscience. There is far too much witchery and sugar in the sentiments "for others" and "*not* for myself," for one not needing to be doubly distrustful here, and for one asking promptly: "Are they not perhaps—*deceptions?*"—That they *please*—him who has them, and him who enjoys their fruit, and also the mere spectator—that is still no argument in their *favour,* but just calls for caution. Let us therefore be cautious!

· · ·

41

One must subject oneself to one's own tests that one is destined for independence and command, and do so at the right time. One must not avoid one's tests, although they constitute perhaps the most dangerous game one can play, and are in the end tests made only before ourselves and before no other judge. Not to cleave to any person, be it even the dearest—every person is a prison and also a recess. Not to cleave to a fatherland, be it even the most suffering and necessitous—it is even less difficult to detach one's heart from a victorious fatherland. Not to cleave to a sympathy, be it even for higher men, into whose peculiar torture and helplessness chance has given us an insight. Not to cleave to a science, though it tempt one with the most valuable discoveries, apparently specially reserved for *us*. Not to cleave to one's own liberation, to the voluptuous distance and remoteness of a bird, which always flies further aloft in order always to see more under it—the danger of the flier. Not to cleave to our own virtues, nor become as whole a victim to any of our specialties, to our "hospitality" for instance, which is the danger of dangers for highly developed and wealthy souls, who deal prodigally, almost indifferently with themselves, and push the virtue of liberality so far that it becomes a vice. One must know how *to conserve oneself*—the best test of independence.

42

A new order of philosophers is appearing; I shall venture to baptize them by a name not without danger. As far as I understand them, as far as they allow themselves to be understood—for it is their nature to *wish* to remain something of a puzzle—these philosophers of the future might rightly, perhaps also wrongly, claim to be designated as *"tempters."* This name itself is after all only an attempt, or, if it be preferred, a temptation.

43

Will they be new friends of "truth," these coming philosophers? Very probably, for all philosophers hitherto have loved their truths. But assuredly they will not be dogmatists. It must be contrary to their pride, and also contrary to their taste, that their truth should still be truth for every one—that which has hitherto been the secret wish and ultimate purpose of all dogmatic efforts. "My opinion is *my* opinion: another person has not easily a right to it"—such a philosopher of the future will say, perhaps. One must renounce the bad taste of wishing to agree with many people. "Good" is no longer good when one's neighbour takes it into his mouth. And how could there be a "common good"! The expression contradicts itself; that which can be common is always of small value. In the end things must be as they are and have always been—the great things remain for the great, the abysses for the profound, the delicacies and thrills for the refined, and, to sum up shortly, everything rare for the rare.

. . .

PART SEVEN: OUR VIRTUES
238

To be mistaken in the fundamental problem of "man and woman," to deny here the profoundest antagonism and the necessity for an eternally hostile tension, to dream here perhaps of equal rights, equal training, equal claims and obligations: that is a *typical* sign of shallow-mindedness; and a thinker who has proved himself shallow at this dangerous spot—shallow in instinct!—may generally be regarded as suspicious, nay more, as betrayed, as discovered; he will probably prove too "short" for all fundamental questions of life, future as well as present, and will be unable to descend into *any* of the depths. On the other hand, a man who has depth of spirit as well as of desires, and has also the depth of benevolence which is capable of severity and harshness, and easily confounded with them, can only think of woman as *Orientals* do: he must conceive of her as a possession, as confinable property, as a being predestined for service and accomplishing her mission therein—he must take his stand in this matter upon the immense rationality of Asia, upon the superiority of the instinct of Asia, as the Greeks did formerly; those best heirs and scholars of Asia—who, as is well known, with their *increasing* culture and amplitude of power, from Homer to the time of Pericles,[5] became gradually *stricter* towards woman, in short, more oriental. *How* necessary, *how* logical, even *how* humanely desirable this was, let us consider for ourselves

. . .

PART NINE: WHAT IS NOBLE?
257

Every elevation of the type "man," has hitherto been the work of an aristocratic society and so it will always be—a society believing in a long scale of gradations of rank and differences of worth among human beings, and requiring slavery in some form or other. Without the *pathos of distance,* such as grows out of the incarnated differences of classes, out of the constant outlooking and downlooking of the ruling caste on subordinates and instruments, and out of their equally con-

---

[5] Homer (c. eighth century B.C.) was the greatest epic poet of ancient Greece; Pericles (fifth century B.C.) was the political leader of Athens during its Golden Age.

stant practice of obeying and commanding, of keeping down and keeping at a distance—that other more mysterious pathos could never have arisen, the longing for an ever new widening of distance within the soul itself, the formation of ever higher, rarer, further, more extended, more comprehensive states, in short, just the elevation of the type "man," the continued "self-surmounting of man," to use a moral formula in a supermoral sense. To be sure, one must not resign oneself to any humanitarian illusions about the history of the origin of an aristocratic society (that is to say, of the preliminary condition for the elevation of the type "man"): the truth is hard. Let us acknowledge unprejudicedly how every higher civilisation hitherto has *originated!* Men with a still natural nature, barbarians in every terrible sense of the word, men of prey, still in possession of unbroken strength of will and desire for power, threw themselves upon weaker, more moral, more peaceful races (perhaps trading or cattle-rearing communities), or upon old mellow civilisations in which the final vital force was flickering out in brilliant fireworks of wit and depravity. At the commencement, the noble caste was always the barbarian caste: their superiority did not consist first of all in their physical, but in their psychical power—they were more *complete* men (which at every point also implies the same as "more complete beasts").

· · ·

259

To refrain mutually from injury, form violence, from exploitation, and put one's will on a par with that of others: this may result in a certain rough sense in good conduct among individuals when the necessary conditions are given (namely, the actual similarity of the individuals in amount of force and degree of worth, and their co-relation within one organisation). As soon, however, as one wished to take this principle more generally, and if possible even as *the fundamental principle of society,* it would immediately disclose what it really is—namely, a Will to the *denial* of life, a principle of dissolution and decay. Here one must think profoundly to the very basis and resist all sentimental weakness: life itself is *essentially* appropriation, injury, conquest of the strange and weak, suppression, severity, obtrusion of peculiar forms, incorporation, and at the least, putting it mildest, exploitation;—but why should one for ever use precisely these words on which for ages a disparaging purpose has been stamped? Even the organisation within which, as was previously supposed, the individuals treat each other as equal—it takes place in every healthy aristocracy—must itself, if it be a living and not a dying organisation, do all that towards other bodies, which the individuals within it refrain from doing to each other: it will have to be the incarnated Will to Power, it will endeavour to grow, to gain ground, attract to itself and acquire ascendency—not owing to any morality or immorality, but because it *lives,* and because life *is* precisely Will to Power. On no point, however, is the ordinary consciousness of Europeans more unwilling to be corrected than on this matter;

people now rave everywhere, even under the guise of science, about coming conditions of society in which "the exploiting character" is to be absent:—that sounds to my ears as if they promised to invent a mode of life which should refrain from all organic functions. "Exploitation" does not belong to a depraved, or imperfect and primitive society: it belongs to the *nature* of the living being as a primary organic function; it is a consequence of the intrinsic Will to Power, which is precisely the Will to Life.—Granting that as a theory this is a novelty—as a reality it is the *fundamental fact* of all history: let us be so far honest towards ourselves!

260

In a tour through the many finer and coarser moralities which have hitherto prevailed or still prevail on the earth, I found certain traits recurring regularly together, and connected with one another, until finally two primary types revealed themselves to me, and a radical distinction was brought to light. There is *master-morality* and *slave-morality;*—I would at once add, however, that in all higher and mixed civilisations, there are also attempts at the reconciliation of the two moralities; but one finds still oftener the confusion and mutual misunderstanding of them, indeed, sometimes their close juxtaposition—even in the same man, within one soul. The distinctions of moral values have either originated in a ruling caste, pleasantly conscious of being different from the ruled—or among the ruled class, the slaves and dependents of all sorts. In the first case, when it is the rulers who determine the conception "good," it is the exalted, proud disposition which is regarded as the distinguishing feature, and that which determines the order of rank. The noble type of man separates from himself the beings in whom the opposite of this exalted, proud disposition displays itself: he despises them. Let it at once be noted that in this first kind of morality the antithesis "good" and "bad" means practically the same as "noble" and "despicable";—the antithesis "good" and *"evil"* is of a different origin. The cowardly, the timid, the insignificant, and those thinking merely of narrow utility are despised; moreover, also, the distrustful, with their constrained glances, the self-abasing, the dog-like kind of men who let themselves be abused, the mendicant flatterers, and above all the liars:—it is a fundamental belief of all aristocrats that the common people are untruthful. "We truthful ones"—the nobility in ancient Greece called themselves. It is obvious that everywhere the designations of moral value were at first applied to *men,* and were only derivatively and at a later period applied to *actions;* it is a gross mistake, therefore, when historians of morals start questions like, "Why have sympathetic actions been praised?" The noble type of man regards *himself* as a determiner of values; he does not require to be approved of; he passes the judgment: "What is injurious to me is injurious in itself"; he knows that it is he himself only who confers honour on things; he is a *creator of values.* He honours whatever he recognises in himself: such morality is self-glorification. In the foreground there is the feeling of plentitude, of power, which seeks to overflow, the happiness of high tension, the consciousness of a wealth which would fain give and bestow:—the noble man also helps the unfortunate, but not—or scarcely—out of pity, but rather from an impulse generated by the super-abundance of power. The noble man honours in himself the powerful one, him also who has power over himself, who knows how to speak and how to keep silence, who takes pleasure in subjecting himself to severity and hardness, and has reverence for all that is severe and hard. "Wotan placed a hard heart in my breast," says an old Scandinavian Saga: it is thus rightly expressed from the soul of a proud Viking. Such a type of man is even proud of *not* being made for sympathy; the hero of the Saga therefore adds warningly: "He who has not a hard heart when young, will never have one.". . . It is otherwise with the second type of morality, *slave-morality.* Supposing that the abused, the oppressed, the suffering, the unemancipated, the weary, and those uncertain of themselves, should moralise, what will be the common element in their moral estimates? Probably a pessimistic suspicion with regard to the entire situation of man will find expression, perhaps a condemnation of man, together with his situation. The slave has an unfavourable eye for the virtues of the powerful; he has a scepticism and distrust, a *refinement* of distrust of everything "good" that is there honoured—he would fain persuade himself that the very happiness there is not genuine. On the other hand, *those* qualities which serve to alleviate the existence of sufferers are brought into prominence and flooded with light; it is here that sympathy, the kind, helping hand, the warm heart, patience, diligence, humility, and friendliness attain to honour; for here these are the most useful qualities, and almost the only means of supporting the burden of existence. Slave-morality is essentially the morality of utility. Here is the seat of the origin of the famous antithesis "good" and "evil":—power and dangerousness are assumed to reside in the evil, a certain dreadfulness, subtlety, and strength, which do not admit of being despised. According to slave-morality, therefore, the "evil" man arouses fear; according to master-morality, it is precisely the "good" man who arouses fear and seeks to arouse it, while the bad man is regarded as the despicable being. The contrast attains its maximum when, in accordance with the logical consequences of slave-morality, a shade of depreciation—it may be slight and well-intentioned—at last attaches itself to the "good" man of this morality; because, according to the servile mode of thought, the good man must in any case be the *safe* man: he is good-natured, easily deceived, perhaps a little stupid, *un bonhomme.*[6] Everywhere that slave-morality gains the ascendency, language shows a tendency to approximate the significations of the words "good" and "stupid."—A last fundamental difference: the desire for *freedom,* the instinct for happiness and the refinements of the feeling of liberty belong as necessarily to slave-morals and morality, as artifice and enthusiasm in reverence and devotion are the regular symptoms of an aristocratic mode of thinking and estimating.

• • •

---

[6] French: literally, "a good man"; usually, refers to a simple, good-natured man, often a foolish or gullible person.

262

A *species* originates, and a type becomes established and strong in the long struggle with essentially constant *unfavourable* conditions. On the other hand, it is known by the experience of breeders that species which receive superabundant nourishment, and in general a surplus of protection and care, immediately tend in the most marked way to develop variations, and are fertile in prodigies and monstrosities (also in monstrous vices). Now look at an aristocratic commonwealth, say an ancient Greek *polis,* or Venice, as a voluntary or involuntary contrivance for the purpose of *rearing* human beings; there are there men beside one another, thrown upon their own resources, who want to make their species prevail, chiefly because they *must* prevail, or else run the terrible danger of being exterminated. The favour, the superabundance, the protection are there lacking under which variations are fostered; the species needs itself as species, as something which, precisely by virtue of its hardness, its uniformity, and simplicity of structure, can in general prevail and make itself permanent in constant struggle with its neighbours, or with rebellious or rebellion-threatening vassals. The most varied experience teaches it what are the qualities to which it principally owes the fact that it still exists, in spite of all gods and men, and has hitherto been victorious: these qualities it calls virtues, and these virtues alone it develops to maturity. It does so with severity, indeed it desires severity; every aristocratic morality is intolerant in the education of youth, in the control of women, in the marriage customs, in the relations of old and young, in the penal laws (which have an eye only for the degenerating): it counts intolerance itself among the virtues, under the name of "justice." A type with few, but very marked features, a species of severe, warlike, wisely silent, reserved and reticent men (and as such, with the most delicate sensibility for the charm and *nuances* of society) is thus established, unaffected by the vicissitudes of generations; the constant struggle with uniform *unfavourable* conditions is, as already remarked, the cause of a type becoming stable and hard. Finally, however, a happy state of things results, the enormous tension is relaxed; there are perhaps no more enemies among the neighbouring peoples, and the means of life, even of the enjoyment of life, are present in superabundance. With one stroke the bond and constraint of the old discipline severs: it is no longer regarded as necessary, as a condition of existence—if it would continue, it can only do so as a form of *luxury,* as an archaïsing *taste.* Variations, whether they be deviations (into the higher, finer, and rare), or deteriorations and monstrosities, appear suddenly on the scene in the greatest exuberance and splendour; the individual dares to be individual and detach himself. At this turning-point of history there manifest themselves, side by side, and often mixed and entangled together, a magnificent, manifold, virgin-forest-like up-growth and up-striving, a kind of *tropical tempo* in the rivalry of growth, and an extraordinary decay and self-destruction, owing to the savagely opposing and seemingly exploding egoisms, which strive with one another "for sun and light," and can no longer assign any limit, restraint, or forbearance for themselves by means of the hitherto existing morality. It was this morality itself which piled up the strength so enormously, which bent the bow in so threatening a manner:—it is now "out of date," it is getting "out of date." The dangerous and disquieting point has been reached when the greater, more manifold, more comprehensive life *is lived beyond* the old morality; the "individual" stands out, and is obliged to have recourse to his own lawgiving, his own arts and artifices for self-preservation, self-elevation, and self-deliverance. Nothing but new "Whys," nothing but new "Hows," no common formulas any longer, misunderstanding and disregard in league with each other, decay, deterioration, and the loftiest desires frightfully entangled, the genius of the race overflowing from all the cornucopias of good and bad, a portentous simultaneouness of Spring and Autumn, full of new charms and mysteries peculiar to the fresh, still inexhausted, still unwearied corruption. Danger is again present, the mother of morality, great danger; this time shifted into the individual, into the neighbour and friend, into the street, into their own child, into their own heart, into all the most personal and secret recesses of their desires and volitions. What will the moral philosophers who appear at this time have to preach? They discover, these sharp onlookers and loafers, that the end is quickly approaching, that everything around them decays and produces decay, that nothing will endure until the day after tomorrow, except one species of man, the incurably *mediocre.* The mediocre alone have a prospect of continuing and propagating themselves—they will be the men of the future, the sole survivors; "be like them! become mediocre!" is now the only morality which has still a significance, which still obtains a hearing.—But it is difficult to preach this morality of mediocrity! it can never avow what it is and what it desires! it has to talk of moderation and dignity and duty and brotherly love—it will have difficulty *in concealing its irony!*

263

There is an *instinct for rank,* which more than anything else is already the sign of a *high* rank; there is a *delight* in the *nuances* of reverence which leads one to infer noble origin and habits. The refinement, goodness, and loftiness of a soul are put to a perilous test when something passes by that is of the highest rank, but is not yet protected by the awe of authority from obtrusive touches and incivilities: something that goes its way like a living touchstone, undistinguished, undiscovered, and tentative, perhaps voluntarily veiled and disguised. He whose task and practice it is to investigate souls, will avail himself of many varieties of this very art to determine the ultimate value of a soul, the unalterable, innate order of rank to which it belongs: he will test it by its *instinct for reverence. Différence engendre haine:*[7] the vulgarity of many a nature spurts up suddenly like dirty water, when

---

[7]French: "Difference engenders hatred."

any holy vessel, any jewel from closed shrines, any book bearing the marks of great destiny, is brought before it; while on the other hand, there is an involuntary silence, a hesitation of the eye, a cessation of all gestures, by which it is indicated that a soul *feels* the nearness of what is worthiest of respect. The way in which, on the whole, the reverence for the *Bible* has hitherto been maintained in Europe, is perhaps the best example of discipline and refinement of manners which Europe owes to Christianity: books of such profoundness and supreme significance require for their protection an external tyranny of authority, in order to acquire the *period* of thousands of years which is necessary to exhaust and un-riddle them. Much has been achieved when the sentiment has been at last in-stilled into the masses (the shallow-pates and the boobies of every kind) that they are not allowed to touch everything, that there are holy experiences before which they must take off their shoes and keep away the unclean hand—it is almost their highest advance towards humanity. On the contrary, in the so-called cul-tured classes, the believers in "modern ideas," nothing is perhaps so repulsive as their lack of shame, the easy insolence of eye and hand with which they touch, taste, and finger everything; and it is possible that even yet there is more *relative* nobility of taste, and more tact for reverence among the people, among the lower classes of the people, especially among peasants, than among the newspaper-reading *demimonde*[8] of intellect, the cultured class.

· · ·

265

At the risk of displeasing innocent ears, I submit that egoism belongs to the essence of a noble soul, I mean the unalterable belief that to a being such as "we," other beings must naturally be in subjection, and have to sacrifice them-selves. The noble soul accepts the fact of his egoism without question, and also without consciousness of harshness, constraint, or arbitrariness therein, but rather as something that may have its basis in the primary law of things:—if he sought a designation for it he would say: "It is justice itself." He acknowledges under certain circumstances, which made him hesitate at first, that there are other equally privileged ones; as soon as he has settled this question of rank, he moves among those equals and equally privileged ones with the same assurance, as regards modesty and delicate respect, which he enjoys in intercourse with himself—in accordance with an innate heavenly mechanism which all the stars understand. It is an *additional* instance of his egoism, this artfulness and self-limitation in intercourse with his equals—every star is a similar egoist; he hon-ours *himself* in them, and in the rights which he concedes to them, he has no

---

[8] French: literally, "half world"; often used in reference to prostitutes or any group whose activities are ethically or legally questionable.

doubt that the exchange of honours and rights, as the *essence* of all intercourse, belongs also to the natural condition of things. The noble soul gives as he takes, prompted by the passionate and sensitive instinct of requital, which is at the root of his nature.

• • •

270

The intellectual haughtiness and loathing of every man who has suffered deeply—it almost determines the order of rank *how* deeply men can suffer—the chilling certainty, with which he is thoroughly imbued and coloured, that by virtue of his suffering he *knows more* than the shrewdest and wisest can ever know, that he has been familiar with, and "at home" in, many distant, dreadful worlds of which "*you* know nothing"!—this silent intellectual haughtiness of the sufferer, this pride of the elect of knowledge, of the "initiated," of the almost sacrificed, finds all forms of disguise necessary to protect itself from contact with officious and sympathising hands, and in general from all that is not its equal in suffering. Profound suffering makes noble: it separates.

• • •

287

—What is noble? What does the word "noble" still mean for us nowadays? How does the noble man betray himself, how is he recognised under this heavy overcast sky of the commencing plebeianism, by which everything is rendered opaque and leaden?—It is not his actions which establish his claim—actions are always ambiguous, always inscrutable; neither is it his "works." One finds nowadays among artists and scholars plenty of those who betray by their works that a profound longing for nobleness impels them; but this very *need of* nobleness is radically different from the needs of the noble soul itself, and is in fact the eloquent and dangerous sign of the lack thereof. It is not the works, but the *belief* which is here decisive and determines the order of rank—to employ once more an old religious formula with a new and deeper meaning,—it is some fundamental certainty which a noble soul has about itself, something which is not to be sought, is not to be found, and perhaps, also, is not to be lost.—*The noble soul has reverence for itself.*—

PART VII

CULTURAL ENCOUNTERS

❧

A ll the selections in this volume, in one way or another, exemplify the encounters, potential encounters, and even conflicts, of diverse cultures. The selections in Part VII, however, represent those encounters that have resulted in particularly massive cultural or historical or intellectual changes. In the modern age, with its increasingly faster modes of transportation and communication, those encounters have occurred with increasing frequency. The examples included in Selections 49–53 are of particular interest and significance.

Selection 49, "Columbus and His Spanish Successors" shows us both positive and negative aspects of the European expansion into the "New World." Its three excerpts show us many of the extremes of human nature: heroism, greed, cruelty, and kindness. First is Columbus's own account of his first landfall in what was erroneously labeled the "West Indies"—although the name still remains. Columbus's account is followed by a description of the Spaniards' cruelty that followed soon after the initial voyage of 1492; then comes an account of Cortés's daring march with a few hundred men into the great City of Mexico.

In Selection 50, we see the first detailed description of the vastness of China since Marco Polo's in the thirteenth century. Matteo Ricci, in the late Renaissance, was a member of the Jesuit order who admired the Confucian ideals of China and wrote an admiring description that shaped the West's concept of that civilization for centuries.

The next chapter, Selection 51, is unique in this volume. Rather than presenting a primary document, this chapter is an expert scholar's historical essay on the various cultural encounters in South and West Asia as Turks, Persians, Indians, English, and others met, fought, assimilated, and learned from each other in the years between 1500 and 1900.

Cultural encounters occur not only between different civilizations but *within* civilizations as members of diverse ethnic, racial, religious, and ideological groups experience the frictions, excitements, and strains of learning to live within the same borders. In Selection 52 we see an eighteenth-century Jew who has left an impoverished village in Poland to seek a wider world, more in keeping with his intellectual aspirations. He moves to Germany, becomes a distinguished philosopher but without a professorial appointment, and is never fully at home in Christian Europe.

This book's final selection, 53, shows a late nineteenth-century Cuban poet, journalist, and patriot who, while sojourning in New York City, described the attractions of Coney Island to his many Spanish-speaking readers south of the U.S.A. "Coney Island" is an appropriate selection to point us toward *The Twentieth Century,* the next volume in this *World Literature and Thought* series, since American cultural values played such a significant role in the twentieth century.

49

COLUMBUS AND HIS SPANISH SUCCESSORS

*C*hristopher Columbus's voyage of 1492 was not the first European "discovery" of the Western Hemisphere: Norse venturers sailing from Iceland had certainly touched the islands and, probably, the mainland of North America five centuries before. (See *The Greenland Saga, Volume II, Selection 47). Columbus's voyage, however, had far greater historical significance because it was followed by sustained programs of exploration, conquest, and colonization, first by the Spanish in Central and South America, and later by the Dutch, English, French, and Portuguese in both North and South America. Columbus's discoveries in the course of his four voyages were the first waves of one of the major sea changes in world history.*

The excerpts which follow touch upon three different but interconnected aspects of what the Spanish called the "Enterprise of the Indies"—the discovery and development of lands in the Caribbean, in Mexico, and in Central and South America. The first is an account in Columbus's own words of the first landfall in the West Indies. The second is an indictment of Spanish cruelty toward the native Americans they encountered in the early years of the Enterprise, written by a Spanish aristocrat named Bartolomé de las Casas, who became a priest in service to these same native Americans. The third and last excerpt is an account by Bernal Diaz del Castillo, an old soldier writing years after the event, of the march to Mexico City of Spanish conquistadors (soldiers and officers) under command of Hernando Cortés. Taken together, these excerpts suggest something of the broad range of human attributes and experiences—vision, heroism, religious faith, and rapacious greed, that characterized the Enterprise of the Indies.

CHRISTOPHER COLUMBUS
JOURNALS

The great irony of Columbus's work of exploration is that he died (in 1506) not even wanting to believe that he had discovered an immense new landmass, but rather believing, against mounting contrary evidence, that he had found a shorter route to Asia. Born in Genoa, Italy as Cristobal Colón in 1451, Columbus became a seaman and ultimately an officer aboard merchant vessels sailing the Mediterranean Sea and Atlantic Ocean as far as England, possibly as far as Iceland. His reading of Marco's Polo's *Description of the World* (Volume II, Selection 50) fired his imagination and provided the goal whose pursuit drove the remainder of his life. He developed a theory of world geography—quite mistaken as it turned out— such that the fabled lands of East Asia which Polo described could be reached by a comparatively short sail westward from Europe. For years he tried unsuccessfully to convince Portuguese, French, and English monarchs of the feasibility of his project. Finally he obtained the support he sought from the monarchs of a newly united Spain, Ferdinand and Isabella. In command of a squadron of three small ships, Columbus sailed from Palos, Spain, on August 3, 1492, and after a stop for repairs in the Canary Islands resumed his westward crossing, making landfall on one of the islands of the Bahamas chain on October 12.

The excerpt that follows comes from Columbus's *Diario,* or *Journal,* for that date. The *Journal* has not survived in its original form, but rather as an edited manuscript prepared sixty years later by Friar Bartolomé de Las Casas, author of the second excerpt in this sequence. Columbus tends to record the extraordinary new reality in European terms, seeing the similarities and not the differences. Despite Las Casas's paraphrases of Columbus, enough of the mind, will, and expansive vision of the great mariner come through this passage to give the reader, even half a millennium later, a sense of the high drama of that fateful day.

Thursday, 11 October

He navigated to the west-south-west; they had a rougher sea than they had experienced during the whole voyage. They saw sandpipers and a green branch near the ship. Those in the caravel *Pinta* saw a cane and a stick, and they secured another small stick, carved, as it appeared, with iron, and a piece of cane, and other vegetation which grows on land, and a small branch. Those in the caravel *Niña* also saw other indications of land and a small branch, covered with dog-roses. At these signs, all breathed again and rejoiced. On this day, to sunset,

From *The Voyages of Christopher Columbus,* translated and edited by Cecil Jane, N. Israel/Amsterdam, Da Capo Press/New York, copyright 1970, pp. 147–149.

they went twenty-seven leagues. After sunset, he steered his former course to the west; they made twelve miles an hour, and up to two hours before midnight they had made ninety miles, which are twenty-two leagues and a half. And since the caravel *Pinta* was swifter and went ahead of the admiral, she found land and made the signals which the admiral had commanded. This land, a sailor, who was called Rodrigo de Triana, first sighted, although the admiral, at ten o'clock in the night, being on the castle of the poop, saw a light. It was, however, so obscured that he would not affirm that it was land, but called Pero Gutierrez, a gentleman of the bedchamber to the king, and told him that there seemed to be a light, and that he should watch for it. He did so, and saw it. He said the same also to Rodrigo Sanchez de Segovia, whom the king and queen had sent in the fleet as *veedor*,[1] and he saw nothing, since he was not in a position from which it could be seen. After the admiral had so spoken, it was seen two or three times, and it was like a small wax candle, which was raised and lowered. Few thought that this was an indication of land, but the admiral was certain that it was on land. Accordingly, when they had said the *Salve*,[2] which all sailors are accustomed to say and to chant in their manner, and when they had all been gathered together, the admiral asked and urged them to keep a good look out from the forecastle and to watch carefully for land, and to him who should say first that he saw land, he would give at once a silk doublet, apart from the other rewards which the sovereigns had promised, which were ten thousand maravedis[3] annually to him who first sighted it. Two hours after midnight, land appeared, at a distance of two leagues from them. They shortened all sail, remaining with the mainsail, which is the great sail without bonnets, and lay to, waiting for day, a Friday, on which they reached a small island of the Lucayos, which is called in the language of the Indians "Guanahaní."[4] Immediately they saw naked people, and the admiral went ashore in the armed boat, and Martin Alonso Pinzón and Vicente Yañez, his brother, who was captain of the *Niña*. The admiral brought out the royal standard, and the captains went with two banners of the green cross, which the admiral flew on all the ships as a flag, with an F and a Y,[5] and over each letter their crown, one being on one side of the ☒ and the other on the other. When they had landed, they saw trees very green and much water and fruit of various kinds. The admiral called the two captains and the

---

[1] A *veedor* was a royal inspector.

[2] *Salve Regina* is a prayer to the Virgin Mary.

[3] *Maravedis* were ancient Castilian silver coins.

[4] The precise place of Columbus's first landfall is still a matter of controversy. Many modern scholars believe it was San Salvador in the Bahama Islands.

[5] For King Ferdinand and Queen Isabella, the spelling of whose name in Spanish would begin with the letter Y.

others who had landed, and Rodrigo de Escobedo, secretary of the whole fleet, and Rodrigo Sanchez de Segovia, and said that they should bear witness and testimony how he, before them all, took possession, as in fact he took, of the said island for the king and queen, his sovereigns, making the declarations which are required, as is contained more at length in the testimonies which were there made in writing. Soon much people of the island gathered there. This which follows is the actual words of the admiral, in his book of his first voyage and discovery of these Indies.

"I," he says, "in order that they might feel great amity towards us, because I knew that they were a people to be delivered and to be converted to our holy faith rather by love than by force, gave to some among them some red caps and some glass beads, which they hung round their necks, and many other things of little value. At this they were greatly pleased and became so entirely our friends that it was a wonder to see. Afterwards they came swimming to the ships' boats, where we were, and brought us parrots and cotton thread in balls, and spears and many other things, and we exchanged for them other things, such as small glass beads and hawks' bells, which we gave to them. In fact, they took all and gave all, such as they had, with good will, but it seemed to me that they were a people very deficient in everything. They all go naked as their mothers bore them, and the women also, although I saw only one very young girl. And all those whom I did see were youths, so that I did not see one who was over thirty years of age; they were very well built, with very handsome bodies and very good faces. Their hair is coarse and short, almost like the hairs of a horse's tail; they wear their hair down over their eyebrows, except for a few strands behind which they wear long and never cut. Some of them are painted black, and they are the colour of the people of the Canaries, neither black nor white, and some of them are painted white and some red and some in any colour that they find. Some of them paint their faces, some their whole bodies, some only the eyes, and some only the nose. They do not bear arms or know them, for I showed to them swords and they took them by the blade and cut themselves through ignorance. They have no iron. Their spears are certain reeds, without iron, and some of these have a fish tooth at the end, while others are pointed in various ways. They are all generally fairly tall, good looking and well proportioned. I saw some who bore marks of wounds on their bodies, and I made signs to them to ask how this came about, and they indicated to me that people had come from other islands, which are near, and wished to capture them, and they had defended themselves. And I believed and still believe that they came here from the mainland to take them for slaves. They should be good servants and of quick intelligence, since I see that they very soon say all that is said to them, and I believe that they would easily be made Christians, for it appeared to me that they had no creed. I, Our Lord willing, will carry away from here, at the time of my departure, six to your highnesses, that they may learn to talk. I saw no beast of any kind in this island, except parrots." All these are the words of the admiral.

FRIAR BARTOLOMÉ DE LAS CASAS
THE DEVASTATION OF THE INDIES

T*he Spanish exploration, conquest, and settlement of Central and South America in the wake of Columbus's discoveries soon came to be character-ized by a fourth term: exploitation. The imagination and genuine heroism which often characterized the Spanish of the Enterprise of the Indies became tragically tainted by rapacity and cruelty in their treatment of the indigenous peoples they encountered. Columbus's words in the preceding selection, in this account of the first meeting with these people, that "I knew that they were a people to be deliv-ered and to be converted to our holy faith rather by love than by force" came in retrospect to have a hollow sound.*

The first, and still one of the strongest, cries of protest against the degradation and destruction of the New World Indians came from a man who had seen it first hand and had even participated in it. Bartolomé de Las Casas (1474–1566) was born in Seville, migrated eighteen years later to the newly founded colony on His-paniola (the Caribbean island presently divided between Haiti and the Domini-can Republic). There for a time he was an encomendero, *a Spanish gentleman granted land and the forced labor of the Indians needed to work it. Revolted by the cruelty he saw in this system of virtual slavery and turning from a secular to a religious life, he took orders as a Dominican friar and priest in 1510, evidently the first person to receive holy orders in the New World. From then until his death he traveled widely through the expanding Spanish territories of the Caribbean, Mexico, and Central America, earning the name of "the apostle to the Indians," and returning frequently to Spain to argue his defense of the Indians at court.*

The Brevisima relación de la destructión de las Indias (The Devastation of the Indies: A Brief Account), *published in 1552, was written to inform the Span-ish monarchs of the horrors being committed by their agents and in their names, and to persuade them to take corrective action. The work was soon picked up and disseminated by the Dutch, who were struggling for independence from Spain, and became the basis for what would be called the "Black Legend" of Spanish imperial despotism (although Dutch, English, French, and Portuguese colonizers in time came to inscribe sufficiently black pages in their own histories in the New World). While Las Casas's pleas had little impact in the short run, some histori-ans see his forceful arguments in defense of the Indians and his questioning of the ethical and legal justification of colonialism as precursors of later theories of in-ternational law and human rights.*

※

The Indies were discovered in the year one thousand four hundred and ninety-two. In the following year a great many Spaniards went there with the intention of settling the land. Thus, forty-nine years have passed since the first settlers penetrated the land, the first so-claimed being the large and most happy isle called Hispaniola, which is six hundred leagues in circumference. Around it in all directions are many other islands, some very big, others very small, and all of them were, as we saw with our own eyes, densely populated with native peoples called Indians. This large island was perhaps the most densely populated place in the world. There must be close to two hundred leagues of land on this island, and the seacoast has been explored for more than ten thousand leagues, and each day more of it is being explored. And all the land so far discovered is a beehive of people; it is as though God had crowded into these lands the great majority of mankind.

And of all the infinite universe of humanity, these people are the most guile-less, the most devoid of wickedness and duplicity, the most obedient and faithful to their native masters and to the Spanish Christians whom they serve. They are by nature the most humble, patient, and peaceable, holding no grudges, free from embroilments, neither excitable nor quarrelsome. These people are the most de-void of rancors, hatreds, or desire for vengeance of any people in the world. And because they are so weak and complaisant, they are less able to endure heavy labor and soon die of no matter what malady. The sons of nobles among us, brought up in the enjoyments of life's refinements, are no more delicate than are these Indians, even those among them who are of the lowest rank of laborers. They are also poor people, for they not only possess little but have no desire to possess worldly goods. For this reason they are not arrogant, embittered, or greedy. . . .

Yet into this sheepfold, into this land of meek outcasts there came some Spaniards who immediately behaved like ravening wild beasts, wolves, tigers, or lions that had been starved for many days. And Spaniards have behaved in no other way during the past forty years, down to the present time, for they are still acting like ravening beasts, killing, terrorizing, afflicting, torturing, and destroy-ing the native peoples, doing all this with the strangest and most varied new meth-ods of cruelty, never seen or heard of before, and to such a degree that this Island of Hispaniola, once so populous (having a population that I estimated to be more than three millions), has now a population of barely two hundred persons.[6]

The island of Cuba is nearly as long as the distance between Valladolid and Rome: it is now almost completely depopulated. San Juan and Jamaica are two of the largest, most productive and attractive islands; both are now deserted and

---

[6] Las Casas's estimates of population are among the most controversial aspects of his book, and most scholars consider them considerably exaggerated, although there is no consen-sus as to the actual numbers of the pre-Columbian indigenous population of the Ameri-cas. Most historians believe the population of all the Caribbean islands at that time did not exceed three-quarters of a million, with the majority—about half a million—concentrated in Hispaniola.

devastated. On the northern side of Cuba and Hispaniola lie the neighboring Lucayos comprising more than sixty islands including those called *Gigantes*,[7] beside numerous other islands, some small some large. The least felicitous of them were more fertile and beautiful than the gardens of the King of Seville. They have the healthiest lands in the world, where lived more than five hundred thousand souls; they are now deserted, inhabited by not a single living creature. All the people were slain or died after being taken into captivity and brought to the Island of Hispaniola to be sold as slaves. When the Spaniards saw that some of these had escaped, they sent a ship to find them, and it voyaged for three years among the islands searching for those who had escaped being slaughtered, for a good Christian had helped them escape, taking pity on them and had won them over to Christ; of these there were eleven persons and these I saw.

More than thirty other islands in the vicinity of San Juan are for the most part and for the same reason depopulated, and the land laid waste. On these islands I estimate there are 2,100 leagues of land that have been ruined and depopulated, empty of people.

As for the vast mainland, which is ten times larger than all Spain, even including Aragon and Portugal, containing more land than the distance between Seville and Jerusalem, or more than two thousand leagues, we are sure that our Spaniards, with their cruel and abominable acts, have devastated the land and exterminated the rational people who fully inhabited it. We can estimate very surely and truthfully that in the forty years that have passed, with the infernal actions of the Christians, there have been unjustly slain more than twelve million men, women, and children. In truth, I believe without trying to deceive myself that the number of the slain is more like fifteen million.

The common ways mainly employed by the Spaniards who call themselves Christian and who have gone there to extirpate those pitiful nations and wipe them off the earth is by unjustly waging cruel and bloody wars. Then, when they have slain all those who fought for their lives or to escape the tortures they would have to endure, that is to say, when they have slain all the native rulers and young men (since the Spaniards usually spare only the women and children, who are subjected to the hardest and bitterest servitude ever suffered by man or beast), they enslave any survivors. With these infernal methods of tyranny they debase and weaken countless numbers of those pitiful Indian nations.

Their reason for killing and destroying such an infinite number of souls is that the Christians have an ultimate aim, which is to acquire gold, and to swell themselves with riches in a very brief time and thus rise to a high estate disproportionate to their merits. It should be kept in mind that their insatiable greed and ambition, the greatest ever seen in the world, is the cause of their villainies. And also, those lands are so rich and felicitous, the native peoples so meek and patient, so

---

[7] *Gigantes* means "giants" in Spanish. The Lucayos was an early Spanish name for the Bahama Islands.

easy to subject, that our Spaniards have no more consideration for them than beasts. And I say this from my own knowledge of the acts I witnessed. But I should not say "than beasts" for, thanks be to God, they have treated beasts with some respect; I should say instead like excrement on the public squares. And thus they have deprived the Indians of their lives and souls, for the millions I mentioned have died without the Faith and without the benefit of the sacraments. This is a well-known and proven fact which even the tyrant Governors, themselves killers, know and admit. And never have the Indians in all the Indies committed any act against the Spanish Christians, until those Christians have first and many times committed countless cruel aggressions against them or against neighboring nations. For in the beginning the Indians regarded the Spaniards as angels from Heaven. Only after the Spaniards had used violence against them, killing, robbing, torturing, did the Indians ever rise up against them.

BERNAL DIAZ DEL CASTILLO
THE DISCOVERY AND CONQUEST
OF MEXICO

If cruelty and destruction of human life were prominent aspects of the Spanish "Enterprise of the Indies," so too were acts of great daring. The expedition of a small band of conquistadors—fewer than four hundred in all—under Hernando Cortés in 1519, which resulted in the conquest of the great Aztec Empire in Mexico, was among the most amazing and terrible feats in the annals of empire building. The most detailed account of the Cortés campaign was set down nearly a half-century later by one of the foot soldiers of that small band, Bernal Diaz del Castillo (1492?–1584).

Bernal was born in Spain to parents of humble status and at the age of eighteen, like many young men of his day, sailed to seek his fortune in the new world. After brief service in several pre-Cortés expeditions, in one of which he was wounded by an Indian arrow, he enlisted under Cortés in 1519 and took part in the march to the Aztec capital, Tenochtitlan-Mexico (present Mexico City) and its eventual subjection and partial destruction. He wrote his account of the expedition, in part to counteract the tendency of the official court history of these events to glorify Cortés at the expense of the other participants, in part to establish a claim to a patent of nobility for himself or his descendants as a reward for his services to the Spanish crown. The excerpt which follows describes in vivid detail the

From Bernal Diaz del Castillo, *The Discovery and Conquest of Mexico,* 1517–1521, translated by A. P. Maudslay, Octagon Books, copyright 1956, pp. 191–194, 196. Reprinted by permission of the publisher, Farrar, Straus and Gixoux LLC.

Spaniards' approach to the city, the meeting with the Aztec ruler Montezuma, and his reception of the conquistadors.

Early next day we left Iztapalapa[8] with a large escort of those great Caciques[9] whom I have already mentioned. We proceeded along the Causeway[10] which is here eight paces in width and runs so straight to the City of Mexico that it does not seem to me to turn either much or little, but, broad as it is, it was so crowded with people that there was hardly room for them all, some of them going to and others returning from Mexico, besides those who had come out to see us, so that we were hardly able to pass by the crowds of them that came; and the towers and cues[11] were full of people as well as the canoes from all parts of the lake. It was not to be wondered at, for they had never before seen horses or men such as we are.

Gazing on such wonderful sights, we did not know what to say, or whether what appeared before us was real, for on one side, on the land, there were great cities, and in the lake ever so many more, and the lake itself was crowded with canoes, and in the Causeway were many bridges at intervals, and in front of us stood the great City of Mexico, and we—we did not even number four hundred soldiers! and we well remembered the words and warnings given us by the people of Huexotzingo and Tlaxcala, and the many other warnings that had been given that we should beware of entering Mexico, where they would kill us, as soon as they had us inside.

Let the curious readers consider whether there is not much to ponder over in this that I am writing. What men have there been in the world who have shown such daring? But let us get on, and march along the Causeway. When we arrived where another small causeway branches off [leading to Coyoacan, which is another city] where there were some buildings like towers, which are their oratories, many more chieftains and Caciques approached clad in very rich mantles, the brilliant liveries of one chieftain differing from those of another, and the causeways were crowded with them. The Great Montezuma had sent these great Caciques in advance to receive us and when they came before Cortés they bade us welcome in their language, and as a sign of peace, they touched their hands against the ground, and kissed the ground with the hand.

---

[8] Iztapalapa was a town on the outskirts of the Aztec capital, Tenochtitlan-Mexico.

[9] *Caciques* was an Aztec term for "chieftans."

[10] Tenochtitlan was built partially over water, on an island in the middle of Lake Texcoco. It was connected to the mainland by four long, broad stone causeways, one of the many marvels of Aztec engineering.

[11] *Cues* (pronounced "coo-es") is a Hispanicized version of the word *cu*, one of many Indian terms Bernal adopts. *Cu* was a generic Aztec term for "temple."

There we halted for a good while, and Cacamatzin, the Lord of Texcoco, and the Lord of Iztapalapa and the Lord of Tacuba and the Lord of Coyoacan went on in advance to meet the Great Montezuma, who was approaching in a rich litter accompanied by other great Lords and Caciques, who owned vassals. When we arrived near to Mexico, where there were some other small towers, the Great Montezuma got down from his litter, and those great Caciques supported him with their arms beneath a marvellously rich canopy of green coloured feathers with much gold and silver embroidery and with pearls and chalchihuites[12] suspended from a sort of bordering, which was wonderful to look at. The Great Montezuma was richly attired according to his usage, and he was shod with sandals, the soles were of gold and the upper part adorned with precious stones. The four Chieftains who supported his arms were also richly clothed according to their usage, in garments which were apparently held ready for them on the road to enable them to accompany their prince, for they did not appear in such attire when they came to receive us. Besides these four Chieftains, there were four other great Caciques who supported the canopy over their heads, and many other Lords who walked before the Great Montezuma, sweeping the ground where he would tread and spreading cloths on it, so that he should not tread on the earth. Not one of these Chieftains dared even to think of looking him in the face, but kept their eyes lowered with great reverence, except those four relations, his nephews, who supported him with their arms.

When Cortés was told that the Great Montezuma was approaching, and he saw him coming, he dismounted from his horse, and when he was near Montezuma, they simultaneously paid great reverence to one another. Montezuma bade him welcome and our Cortés replied through Doña Marina[13] wishing him very good health. And it seems to me that Cortés, through Doña Marina, offered him his right hand, and Montezuma did not wish to take it, but he did give his hand to Cortés and then Cortés brought out a necklace which he had ready at hand, made of glass stones, which I have already said are called Margaritas, which have within them many patterns of diverse colours, these were strung on a cord of gold and with musk so that it should have a sweet scent, and he placed it round the neck of the Great Montezuma and when he had so placed it he was going to embrace him, and those great Princes who accompanied Montezuma held back Cortés by the arm so that he should not embrace him, for they considered it an indignity.[14]

---

[12]An Aztec term for "emeralds."

[13]Doña Marina was the name Cortés gave to an Aztec woman, Malinche, whom he encountered in the Yucatan peninsula and took along on this expedition as interpreter, guide, and mistress.

[14]In Hispanic and Mediterranean cultures an embrace is a common form of greeting, but it was not so among the Aztecs. The Aztec ruler was not supposed even to be looked at, much less touched, by anybody. Cortés, of course, did not know this beforehand.

Then Cortés through the mouth of Doña Marina told him that now his heart rejoiced at having seen such a great Prince, and that he took it as a great honour that he had come in person to meet him and had frequently shown him such favour.

Then Montezuma spoke other words of politeness to him, and told two of his nephews who supported his arms, the Lord of Texcoco and the Lord of Coyoacan, to go with us and show us to our quarters, and Montezuma with his other two relations, the Lord of Cuitlahuac and the Lord of Tacuba who accompanied him, returned to the city, and all those grand companies of Caciques and chieftains who had come with him returned in his train. As they turned back after their Prince we stood watching them and observed how they all marched with their eyes fixed on the ground without looking at him, keeping close to the wall, following him with great reverence. Thus space was made for us to enter the streets of Mexico, without being so much crowded. But who could now count the multitude of men and women and boys who were in the streets and on the azoteas,[15] and in canoes on the canals, who had come out to see us. It was indeed wonderful, and, now that I am writing about it, it all comes before my eyes as though it had happened but yesterday. Coming to think it over it seems to be a great mercy that our Lord Jesus Christ was pleased to give us grace and courage to dare to enter into such a city; and for the many times He has saved me from danger of death, as will be seen later on, I give Him sincere thanks, and in that He has preserved me to write about it, although I cannot do it as fully as is fitting or the subject needs. Let us make no words about it, for deeds are the best witnesses to what I say here and elsewhere.

Let us return to our entry to Mexico. They took us to lodge in some large houses, where there were apartments for all of us, for they had belonged to the father of the Great Montezuma, who was named Axayaca, and at that time Montezuma kept there the great oratories for his idols, and a secret chamber where he kept bars and jewels of gold, which was the treasure that he had inherited from his father Axayaca, and he never disturbed it. They took us to lodge in that house, because they called called Teules,[16] and took us for such, so that we should be with the Idols or Teules which were kept there. However, for one reason or another, it was there they took us, where there were great halls and chambers canopied with the cloth of the country for our Captain, and for every one of us beds of matting with canopies above, and no better bed is given, however great the chief may be, for they are not used. And all these palaces were coated with shining cement and swept and garlanded.

As soon as we arrived and entered into the great court, the Great Montezuma took our Captain by the hand, for he was there awaiting him, and led him to the apartment and saloon where he was to lodge, which was very richly adorned according to their usage, and he had at hand a very rich necklace made of golden

---

[15] *Azoteas* is a Spanish word for "rooftops."

[16] *Teules* was an Aztec term for "gods."

crabs, a marvellous piece of work, and Montezuma himself placed it round the neck of our Captain Cortés, and greatly astonished his [own] Captains by the great honour that he was bestowing on him. When the necklace had been fastened, Cortés thanked Montezuma through our interpreters, and Montezuma replied—"Malinche,[17] you and your brethren are in your own house, rest awhile," and then he went to his palaces, which were not far away, and we divided our lodgings by companies, and placed the artillery pointing in a convenient direction, and the order which we had to keep was clearly explained to us, and that we were to be much on the alert, both the cavalry and all of us soldiers. A sumptuous dinner was provided for us according to their use and custom, and we ate it at once. So this was our lucky and daring entry into the great city of Tenochtitlan Mexico on the 8th day of November the year of our Saviour Jesus Christ, 1519.

Thanks to our Lord Jesus Christ for it all. And if I have not said anything that I ought to have said, may your honours pardon me, for I do not know now even at the present time how better to express it.

Let us leave this talk and go back to our story of what else happened to us, which I will go on to relate.

---

[17]See footnote 13. Evidently Montezuma mistakenly assumed that Malinche was Cortés's name.

50

Matteo Ricci

JOURNALS

Marco Polo's Travels, *written late in the thirteenth century (Volume II, Selection 50), was the basis for Europe's view of East Asia—and especially of China—for more than two hundred years. Although Polo's book was not the only, or even the first, account of China in a European language, his description of China's vastness, wealth, and cultural sophistication was etched into the Western image of the world. Polo's picture of China came to constitute part of the basic ground of that worldview, supplemented and modified by later reporters but never wholly eclipsed.*

Despite the lure to merchants and Christian missionaries that Polo's depiction of China held out, several major historical developments made it difficult to follow up immediately on these promises. Chief among these were the strengthened Muslim hold on the Middle East, the collapse in China of the Mongol Dynasty which Polo had so much admired, and the devastation caused by the Black Plague in the mid-fourteenth century. But in the fifteenth and sixteenth centuries, the first great age of European exploration and discovery, Portuguese navigators sailed around the southern tip of Africa and opened a sea route to South and East Asia which the Spanish, Dutch, and English soon followed.

While a strong impetus to finding and exploiting this sea route to the East was mercantile, development of this new avenue also coincided with the turmoil of the Protestant Reformation and Catholic Counter-Reformation. The latter, especially, produced a great surge of missionary activity. The older missionary orders of the Roman Catholic Church, the Franciscans and Dominicans, sent missionaries to East Asia, but it was a new order, the Jesuits, who contributed most to the stream of information about China and who did most to reshape Europe's image of the Middle Kingdom. The Jesuit order, the Society of Jesus, was established in 1534 by Saint Ignatius of Loyola (Selection 21) and soon became a major force in the Roman Catholic Church's effort to spread the faith and, if possible, to reverse the progress of Protestantism. Jesuit priests were men of learning as well as of faith, university trained, capable linguists, and as well equipped as any group of Europeans could have been to grasp the strength and subtlety of China's cultural tradition. Indeed, many of the Jesuits became long-term court intellectuals in China, contributing their valued knowledge in the realms of applied science and mathematics to the late Ming and Early Ch'ing Dynasty courts, all the while making converts among the scholar-government official class.

Matteo Ricci (1552–1610), who reached China in 1582, was not the first Jesuit on the scene, but his phenomenal command of the classical Chinese language and of the philosophical and literary traditions from Confucius onward and his acceptance as a peer by Chinese scholar-officials made him an ideal "inside" source for understanding China. The two volumes of his journal, edited and translated from Italian into Latin in 1615 by a fellow Jesuit, Nicholas Trigualt, soon became and for long remained the most important document since Polo's Travels in shaping the West's concept of China. Ricci admired the China he saw. Although he labored for its conversion to Catholicism, he saw great moral strength in the Confucian tradition and argued, both to the Chinese scholars and to his religious peers and superiors in Europe, that Christianity and Confucianism were basically compatible. At a time of bloody religious and political contention in Europe, Ricci praised the peace and good order of Chinese life, presided over by an emperor whom he saw as a philosopher king and administered by men of proven intellectual talent and moral worth. With Ricci and the other Jesuits who followed him in the seventeenth and early eighteenth centuries, nearly all of them respectful of China and its institutions, the Western picture of the Middle Kingdom took on new dimensions and a strongly favorable cast. China came to be seen as a model society, especially in the eyes of those who were increasingly critical of the faults of Europe. The following excerpts from Ricci's Journals reveal his high estimate of Confucius as a moral philosopher and of several aspects of Chinese government.

From *China in the Sixteenth Century* by Matthew Ricci, translated by Louis J. Gallagher, S. J. Copyright © 1942 and renewed 1970 by Louis J. Gallagher, S. J., pp. 30, 43, 44–45, 49, 54–56. Reprinted by permission of Random House, Inc.

BOOK ONE, 5

Concerning the Liberal Arts, the Sciences, and the Use of Academic Degrees Among the Chinese

The most renowned of all the Chinese philosophers was named Confucius. This great and learned man was born five hundred and fifty-one years before the beginning of the Christian era, lived more than seventy years, and spurred on his people to the pursuit of virtue not less by his own example than by his writings and conferences. His self-mastery and abstemious ways of life have led his countrymen to assert that he surpassed in holiness all those who in times past, in the various parts of the world, were considered to have excelled in virtue. Indeed, if we critically examine his actions and sayings as they are recorded in history, we shall be forced to admit that he was the equal of the pagan [i.e. Greek and Roman] philosophers and superior to most of them.[1] He is held in such high esteem by the learned Chinese that they do not dare to call into question any pronouncement of his and are ready to give full recognition to an oath sworn in his name. . . .

BOOK ONE, 6

The Administrations of the Chinese Commonwealth

There are no ancient laws in China under which the republic is governed in perpetuum, such as our Laws of the Twelve Tables and the Code of Caesar. Whoever succeeds in getting possession of the throne, regardless of his ancestry, makes new laws according to his own way of thinking. His successors on the throne are obliged to enforce the laws which he promulgated as founder of the dynasty, and these laws cannot be changed without good reason. The laws by which the Chinese are governed today are not older than Humvu [Hung-wu, founder of the Ming Dynasty in 1368], all of which he either formulated himself or accepted from his predecessors. His evident plan was to institute a code of comprehensive scope, admirably suited to ensure the peace of the realm and its long duration for himself and his descendants.

---

[1] Ricci's estimate of Confucius and Confucianism was widely, but not universally shared in Europe. Another Jesuit translated and published *The Analects* (Volume 1, Selection 26) in the mid-seventeenth century, making Confucian thought known to the Western world. But the Jesuit willingness to permit ceremonies of veneration for deceased ancestors among their Chinese converts led to the so-called "Rites Controversy," in the course of which missionary rivals of the Jesuits accused them of tolerating ancestor worship. The wrangling among Catholic factions grew so bitter and disruptive that in 1724, the Yung-cheng emperor banned Christian missionaries from China altogether.

The extent of their kingdom is so vast, its borders so distant, and their utter lack of knowledge of a transmaritime world is so complete that the Chinese imagine the whole world as included in their kingdom. Even now, as from time beyond recording, they call their Emperor . . . the Son of Heaven, and because they worship Heaven as the Supreme Being, the Son of Heaven and the Son of God are one and the same . . . .

Only such as have earned a doctor's degree[2] or that of licentiate are admitted to take part in the government of the kingdom, and due to the interest of the magistrates and of the King [i.e. the emperor] himself there is no lack of such candidates. Every public office is therefore fortified with and dependent upon the attested science, prudence, and diplomacy of the person assigned to it, whether he be taking office for the first time or is already experienced in the conduct of civil life. This integrity of life is prescribed by the law of Humvu, and for the most part it is lived up to, save in the case of such as are prone to violate the dictates of justice from human weakness and from lack of religious training among the gentiles. All magistrates, whether they belong to the military or to the civil . . . [branch], are called . . . commander or president, though their honorary or unofficial title . . . [signifies] lord or father. The Portuguese call the Chinese magistrates, mandarins, probably from . . . *mandare,* to order or command, and they are now generally known by this title in Europe. . . .

Besides the classes or orders of the magistrates already described [i.e. the six central bureaus] . . . there are two special orders never heard of among our people. These . . . [each consist] of sixty or more chosen philosophers, all prudent men and tried, who have already given exceptional proof of their fidelity to the King and to the realm. These two orders are reserved by the King for business of greater moment pertaining to the royal court or to the provinces, and by him they are entrusted with great responsibility, carrying with it both respect and authority. They correspond in some manner to what we would call keepers of the public conscience, inasmuch as they inform the King as often as they see fit, of any infraction of the law in any part of the entire kingdom. No one is spared from their scrutiny, even the highest magistrates, as they do not hesitate to speak, even though it concern the King himself or his household. . . . [T]hey do their duty so thoroughly that they are a source or wonder to outsiders and a good example for imitation. Neither King nor magistrates can escape their courage and frankness, and even when they arouse the royal wrath to such an extent that the King becomes severely angry with them, they will never desist from their admonitions and criticism until some remedy has been applied to the public evil against which they are inveighing. In fact, when the grievance is particularly acute, they

---

[2]Ricci here seeks for an equivalent in Western experience for the *chin shih* degree, the highest level of achievement in the fiercely competitive state-sponsored examination system. Most Western scholars still find this rough parallel useful.

are sure to put a sting into their complaints and to show no partiality where the crown or the courts are concerned. . . .

Before closing this chapter on Chinese public administration, it would seem to be quite worthwhile recording a few more things in which this people differ from Europeans. To begin with, it seems to be quite remarkable when we stop to consider it, that in a kingdom of almost limitless expanse and innumerable population, and abounding in copious supplies of every description, though they have a well-equipped army and navy that could easily conquer the neighboring nations, neither the King nor his people ever think of waging a war of aggression. They are quite content with what they have and are not ambitious of conquest. In this respect they are much different from the people of Europe, who are frequently discontent with their own governments and covetous of what others enjoy. While the nations of the West seem to be entirely consumed with the idea of supreme domination, they cannot even preserve what their ancestors have bequeathed them, as the Chinese have done through a period of thousands of years . . . .

Another remarkable fact and quite worthy of note as marking a difference from the West, is that the entire kingdom is administered by the Order of the Learned, commonly known as The Philosophers. The responsibility for the orderly management of the entire realm is completely committed to their charge and care. The army, both officers and soldiers, hold them in high respect and show them the promptest obedience and deference, and not infrequently the military are disciplined by them as a schoolboy might be punished by his master. Policies of war are formulated and military questions are decided by the Philosophers only, and their advice and counsel has more weight with the King than that of his military leaders. In fact very few of these, and only on rare occasions, are admitted to war consultations. Hence it follows that those who aspire to be cultured frown upon war and would prefer the lowest rank in the philosophical order to the highest in the military, realizing that the Philosophers far excel military leaders in the good will and respect of the people and in opportunities of acquiring wealth. What is still more surprising to strangers is that these same Philosophers . . . with respect to nobility of sentiment and in contempt of danger and earth, where fidelity to King and country is concerned, surpass even those whose particular profession is the defense of the fatherland. Perhaps this sentiment has its origin in the fact that the mind of man is ennobled by the study of letters. . . .

51

୬ᠺ

THE MOST SIGNIFICANT CULTURAL ENCOUNTERS IN SOUTH AND WEST ASIA: A HISTORICAL ESSAY

During our period, c. 1500–1900, South and West Asia fall into two broadly distinct cultural regions, the Indian subcontinent and the landmass west of India up to the Mediterranean Sea. South and West Asia's most important cultural phenomena in these four hundred years or so were, first, the continued impact of the Turks, who originally came from the steppes of Central Asia and had started their inroads into the Islamic world toward the end of the first millennium, and later, in the seventeenth to the nineteenth centuries, the rise of Europeans, especially the English. In western Asia, the rise of the Turks culminated in the establishment of two large empires, the Ottoman Empire, which actually had its center in Turkey and included significant areas in Europe besides its Asian possessions, and the Safavid Empire centered in Iran and the surrounding areas. The Turks had become Islamized, and Persianized in both empires, Persian being the preeminent language of high culture even in the Ottoman Empire, although Turkish was also used. Both empires were fairly homogeneous and stable and they endured for centuries without major problems.

The Turks also conquered the Indian subcontinent. However, their impact on the region did not lead to the creation of a homogeneous society free from major religious or social conflicts. Interaction between the conquerors and the earlier inhabitants remained a simmering issue for centuries. Consequently, the conflicts engendered by the cultural encounter of the people of the subcontinent with the Turks and with Islam were a uniquely Indian phenomenon and permanently so. Contrasted with western Asia, the impact of Western culture too was most significant in India, because, unlike India, the areas to its west were hardly ever actually occupied or ruled by a European power during our period. India, therefore, exemplifies most prominently the meeting and interaction between the native and foreign cultures in South and West Asia.

The period of Muslim rule over India falls into two phases: the Sultanate (1206–1526) and the Mughal rule (1526–1857). The kings (sultans) of the first phase were, at least theoretically, the deputies and representatives of the Muslim Caliphate, ruling over their territories by the formal approval of the Caliphs. They saw themselves as Muslim rulers ruling for the benefit of the Muslim community. Although they did have non-Muslim subjects and provided a fairly responsible government over them, they imposed certain disadvantages—such as payment of special taxes, sanctions against the building of religious places, and the like—on them. The non-Muslims were called the "tolerated" people. As Turks, the Sultans and the ruling class considered themselves racially superior not only to non-Muslims but also to native Indian converts to Islam; they tried to maintain their distinct and foreign identity. Indians were not given high-level positions in the government of the Sultanate for a long time. The years of the Sultanate were consequently ridden with much implicit or explicit social-political strife. However, despite the rulers' racism and policy of segregation, in the course of centuries the Turks inevitably became Indianized and began to mix with the natives. Their Indianization and a mutual cultural assimilation between the natives and the Turks, as well as between the other Muslims and the non-Muslims, began to manifest itself in a new cultural synthesis having both Indian and Muslim features.

Among the various manifestations of this synthesis, two were most prominent, one in language and literature and the other in religion. In the area of language and literature, several Muslim writers, such as Malik Muhasmmad Jayasi, the author of the famous romance in Hindi, *Padmini,* wrote in vernaculars on topics of Hindu life and lore. Another major Muslim poet of Hindi was Amir Khusrav. Conversely, many Hindu writers wrote in Persian and according to Muslim literary traditions. Naturally, since Persian was the language of culture of the rulers, this happened more frequently than Muslims writing in the vernacular languages. Besides this literary interaction, the most significant outcome of the meeting between Islam and India was the birth of a new language, Urdu, which during the Mughal rule became the common language of high culture in northern and central India. Urdu, literally meaning "camp or army," grew from a pidgin spoken around the Muslim courts and centers of political control which, to begin with, were the bases of the conquerors' military troops stationed in an alien land. The pidgin started out as a practical impromptu mixture of Indian languages with the languages the Turks brought with them. (Besides Turkish, they brought Arabic, the language of their religion, and Persian, the language of culture and literature assimilated from Iran.) Gradually, the pidgin grew in vocabulary and in grammatical structure, thus becoming a full-fledged language with Indian syntax and words of both Indian and foreign origin. Both the common and educated people used it. For writing, the language adopted the Persian script, itself derived from the Arabic. Before the end of the period of the Sultanate, Urdu was well on its way to becoming the language of courtly culture and the most common vernacular of northern India, used by Muslims and Hindus alike.

A still more profound Hindu-Muslim synthesis took place in religion in the form of numerous reformist religious sects cumulatively known as the *bhakti* (cults of devotion) movement. The origins of *bhakti* go back to the ancient Indian religion, but it was during the fifteenth to the seventeenth century that it became a widespread movement. The main feature of *bhakti* was the essential oneness of God, even though seen and worshiped in different forms with different names and associated with one religion or another. Other features were sincere love of God and God's creation, equality of all people, whatever their caste, creed, or sex. *Bhakti* attached no importance to externals and rituals of religion. It considered genuine inner devotion as the only requirement that religion needed. The affiliation of *bhakti* remained predominantly Hindu, but its characteristics were strongly eclectic. Its emphasis on the oneness of God and on the equality of all people most certainly reflected the assimilation in *bhakti* of two of the most important tenets of Islam. A particularly influential factor strengthening *bhakti* was Sufism, the mystical approach in the Muslim religion. Sufi teachers were the vanguard of Islam in its spread to new areas, such as India. The example of their piety and their concept of God as a loving being to be approached with love rather than a demanding taskmaster to be worshiped according to strict requirements of orthodox Islam had a popular appeal and reinforced the rise of *bhakti*. The movement expressed itself in religious terms, but its deeper impulse was social. It aimed to dissolve all distinctions of caste and creed and treat all people, Hindu or Muslim, equally as human beings. The teachers of *bhakti* addressed their teachings to the common people. Instead of the classical Hindu language, Sanskrit, or the Muslim classical languages, Persian or Arabic, they invariably used vernaculars.

Two of the most prominent examples of *bhakti* teachers late in the Sultanate period were Nanak (see Selection 24) and the pioneer Hindi poet of devotional verse, Kabir (1440–1518). Kabir was a low-caste weaver. He was probably born a Muslim, but his religious affiliation is not known with certainty and is, at any rate, irrelevant. He draws his themes from both Hindu and Muslim traditions. Rejection of all forms of idolatry and of caste are the hallmarks of his poetry. His poetry reflects strong Sufi influence. His verses are popular all over northern India. A short sample is given below.

> O brother, when I was forgetful, my true Guru showed me the way.
> Then I left all rites and ceremonies; I bathed no more in the holy waters.
> Then I learned that I alone was mad, and the whole world beside me was
>   sane; and I disturbed these wise people.
> From that time on I knew no more how to roll in the dust in obeisance.
> I do not ring the temple bell; I do not set the idol in its throne; I do not
>   worship the image with flowers.
> It is not the austerities that mortify the flesh which are pleasing to the Lord;
> When you leave off your clothes and kill your senses, you do not please
>   the Lord;

The man who is kind and who practices righteousness, who remains
    passive amidst the affairs of the world, who considers all creatures
    on earth as his own self,
He attains the Immortal being, the true God is ever with him.
Kabir says, "He attains the true Name whose words are pure, and who is
    free from pride and conceit." . . .
If God be within the mosque, then to whom does this world belong?
If Ram be within the image which you find upon your pilgrimage, then
    who is there to know what happens without?
Hari is in the East, Allah is in the West. Look within your heart, for
    there you will find both Karim and Ram;
All the men and women of the world are His living forms.
Kabir is the child of Allah and Ram; He is my Guru, He is my Pir.

[From Rabindranath Tagore, tr. *Songs of Kabir,* 1915.]

With few exceptions, the Mughal emperors actively fostered the Indo-Muslim synthesis that occurred during the Sultanate. The Mughals were highly cultured monarchs, most of them very liberal in outlook. They considered themselves to be professional rather than Muslim rulers. The emperor best known for his liberal policies was Akbar (1542–1605). He strove most assiduously to bring about a unity among Hindus and Muslims and his other subjects. He provided the opportunity for service in his government to Hindus on an equal basis with Muslims. Some of his best generals were Hindus; so was the ablest minister of finance. He gathered at his court learned men and artists, whatever their religion. He encouraged intermarriage between Hindus and Muslims, setting an example himself. His son, the next Mughal emperor, was born of a Hindu woman. Akbar built a place called the Hall of Worship as a forum of religious discussion to which he invited scholars of all religions and denominations, including the Jesuits from Goa, the Portuguese colony in India, and himself listened to the discussions regularly. He even instituted an eclectic religion of his own, *Din-i-Ilahi* (the Divine Faith), although the following remained small. Akbar thus gave a powerful impetus to a unified Indo-Muslim culture. This culture reached its acme in visual expression in the building of the Taj Mahal of Akbar's grandson, Shah Jahan (1592–1666). The mausoleum blends in a perfect form the voluptuousness of the Indian sensibility with the austerely rational esthetic of Islam.

Europeans had already arrived in India with the Portuguese Vasco da Gama reaching southwestern India by sea. The Portuguese did not have much inland influence in India, because their interest was in control of the Indian Ocean which they maintained from bases on the coast. By Akbar's time, mainly because of the emperor's interest in their religion, the Portuguese Jesuits had significant contacts with his court. When the British East India Company first arrived in India in 1604, the Portuguese schemed to upset their efforts to establish contacts with the Mughal court. It took a long time before the English received the formal permission from the Mughal government to establish trading factories on the Indian soil. For the next more than one hundred years, they maintained their stay and trade by earning the favor of the people and the officials they had to deal with. They also fortified their coastal bases and recruited Indian mercenaries for defense and protection. In the process they acquired knowledge about India and Indian culture. They were influenced by Indian culture and assimilated it in many ways.

The flow of cultural influence continued in that direction, from India to the English, until the last quarter of the eighteenth century, by which time the East India Company had become a major political power and the ruler of a very large portion of India. Important East India Company officials looked up to Indian culture and its institutions as valuable and superior. Warren Hastings (1732–1818), the East India Company's governor general from 1772 to 1788, actively supported the traditional system of Indian education and the study of the classics of Asian literature. He patronized scholars who studied or translated these classics. The best-known English scholar who went to India at this time was Sir William Jones. Jones was a prolific writer and a very able and sensitive translator. He was instrumental in the founding of the Asiatick Society (now the Asiatic Society of Bengal) and did the first translations of Asian classics into English, among them a translation of the ancient playwright Kalidasa's famous play, *Shakuntala* (Volume I, Selection 40).

By the beginning of the nineteenth century, the trend in cultural influence began to reverse itself. With the rise to political supremacy of the British East India Company, the Indian elite became interested in Western education and in learning English. To cater to their need, a Scotsman, along with some Englishmen interested in the education of Indians, helped found the Hindu College at Calcutta in 1816. The college began to influence Bengalis with modern Western ideas. They also learned to write English well for practical as well as literary purposes. Interestingly enough, the new ideas often made them patriotic. A well-known example was the Bengali Eurasian poet, Henry Louis Derozio (1809–1831) who was a professor at the Hindu College and wrote in English. Derozio, a contemporary of the English romantic poets, was, like Shelley, at England's Oxford University, charged with atheism and dismissed. He was so charged because of his criticism of the obsolescent orthodox Hindu beliefs. The best among Derozio's poems are sonnets in which he expresses his hope for a glorious future for India and Indian youth as in his "Sonnet to the Pupils of the Hindu College":

> Expanding like the petals of young flowers
> I watch the gentle opening of your minds,
> And the sweet loosening of the spell that binds
> Your intellectual energies and powers,
> That stretch (like young birds in soft summer hours)
> Their wings, to try their strength. O, how the winds
> Of circumstances, and freshening April showers

Of early knowledge, and unnumbered kinds
Of new perceptions shed their influence;
And how you worship truth's omnipotence.
What joyance rains upon me, when I see
Fame in the mirror of futurity,
Weaving the chaplets you have yet to gain,
Ah! Then I feel I have not lived in vain.

During the first quarter of the nineteenth century what type of education the East India Company should support became a hotly debated issue between the Orientalists, who argued the available money should be spent on the traditional Indian education, and the Anglicists, who argued that English and Western education would be more beneficial to Indians. The issue was settled with a decision by the president of the Committee on Public Instruction, Thomas Babington Macaulay, in 1834, to set up a Western system of education. He wrote in his "Minute of Education": "I have conversed both here and at home with men distinguished by their proficiency in the eastern tongues. I am quite ready to take the Oriental learning at the valuation of the Orientalists themselves. I have never found one among them who could deny that a single shelf of a good European library was worth the whole native literature of India and Arabia." Macaulay envisioned that Western education would produce "a class of persons, Indian in blood and color, but English in taste, in opinions, morals, and intellect." The leading native intellectual, Rammohun Roy, known as the Father of Indian Nationalism, also supported the introduction of Western education, not because he considered Indian classics inferior to the Western but rather because he thought that, added to the Eastern learning, the Western learning, especially in the sciences, would be most beneficial to Indians.

The introduction of Western education made a profound impact on the Indian mind. It created a strong intellectual ferment among the educated. Acquiring modern ways of thinking, they began to look afresh at their past and developed new aspirations for the future. The meeting between the old native traditions and the new ideas from the West gave rise to what came to be known as the Hindu Renascence. The educated Indians examined and reinterpreted their traditions in a new and rational light. As a result, several reformist sects arose. The Renascence functioned as a kind of intellectual and cultural nationalism. Political nationalism followed in another few decades. At first, the nationalist fervor was moderate, showing cooperation with the rulers and asking for better rights. A leading figure in this regard was Dadabhai Naoroji (1825–1917), the Grand Old Man of India. At the age of thirty he moved permanently to London to work for India's cause. The Indian National Congress which led India to independence was formed in 1885. Its politics remained moderate until the emergence of a more radical wing under the leadership of Bal Gangadhar Tilak who proclaimed that everything English was evil and proposed complete independence from the foreign rule.

He proposed and acted on methods such as the boycott of everything English, the setting up of a native system of education parallel to the English system, even resorting to terrorism. His approach produced a rift in the Congress which was eventually resolved by Mahatma Gandhi's (1869–1948) philosophy and practice of politics based on the use of nonviolent struggle for the right and true. It is interesting to point out that Gandhi derived his idea of nonviolent struggle for freedom from the English John Ruskin (1819–1900) and the American Henry David Thoreau (1817–1862).

—Surjit S. Dulai

52

꙰

Solomon Maimon

AUTOBIOGRAPHY

A mong the many "cultural encounters" exemplified in this volume are those which relate the "culture shock" experienced by those who were raised in traditional societies and then moved into the modern world. This is still happening throughout the globe. In Europe it was particularly evident during the eighteenth-century Enlightenment, when new ideas about human rights and universal literacy were widely promulgated, causing radical social changes—even revolutions. The French Revolution and the Napoleonic wars were to spread these ideas even into the most backward areas of Poland and Russia. Among the many European groups awakening to the new social, legal, and vocational possibilities were the Jews, who had long been separated from other ethnic and national groups in a Christian Europe, whether Catholic or Protestant.

Solomon ben Joshua Maimon (1753–1800), a particularly fascinating figure through the extraordinary force of his intellect and will, was able to bridge the gap from the poverty-stricken and despised Jewish settlements of Polish Lithuania to the intellectual elite of European, especially German, culture. From a very early age he combined a proficiency in the Hebrew language and an extensive familiarity with rabbinic learning with an intense desire to acquire the secular learning not available to him in his remote village. After acquiring a special reverence for the distinguished twelfth-century Spanish-Jewish philosopher Moses Maimonides, he took the philosopher's surname Maimon.

Married off by his father at the age of eleven (not unusual for that time and society) and a father himself at fourteen, Maimon said in his Autobiography: "My life in Poland from my marriage to my emigration was a series of miseries with a lack of all means for the promotion of culture." In 1770, at the age of seventeen, Maimon wrote an unorthodox and original commentary on Maimonides' theological classic Guide of the Perplexed. This earned him the hostility of his local fellow Jews. At the age of twenty-five he left Poland for German-speaking Prussia and wandered over Europe finding occasional employment as a tutor.

Eventually, with the help of members of both Jewish and Christian intellectual circles, he settled for a time in Berlin. Maimon's radical ideas, however, soon set him on the wanderer's path again. His material insecurity finally ended in 1790 when he was given patronage on the estate of a Prussian aristocrat who appreciated his intellectual gifts. During the next decade he wrote his major philosophical works, as well as his Lebensgeschichte (Autobiography), *1792. His acute skepticism caused him to be acknowledged by the leading German philosopher, Immanuel Kant, as his most perceptive critic. Kant said that Maimon understood his* Critique of Pure Reason *better than anyone else. By emphasizing the limits of pure thought in his several major philosophical works, Maimon helped to advance philosophical discussion of the connection between thought and experience and between knowledge and faith. In his view there was both religious and ethical value in the pursuit of truth, even though the ultimate goal was not completely attainable.*

In the following excerpts from his Autobiography, *translated form the German, we first see Maimon as a young boy struggling with the rigid limitations of his environment. In the last excerpt we see the man prepared to convert to what was probably the Lutheran branch of Protestant Christianity, simply in order to gain entrance to the intellectual professions of Europe denied to Jews. However, as always, the rationalist truthfulness of his intellect, as well as his skeptical nature, would not allow him to assert his belief in the supernatural mysteries of Christianity (or any other religion). We see here a particularly personal example of the rationalist European Enlightenment's cultural confrontation with the traditional systems of belief.*

My father had in his study a cupboard containing books. He had forbidden me indeed to read any books but the Talmud.[1] This, however, was of no avail: as he was occupied the most of his time with household affairs, I took advantage of the opportunity thus afforded. Under the impulse of curiosity I made a raid upon the cupboard and glanced over all the books. . . .

. . . [W]hat attracted me most powerfully was an astronomical work. In this work a new world was opened to me, and I gave myself up to the study with the greatest diligence. Think of a child about seven years of age, in my position, with an

From Salomon Maimon. *An Autobiography,* trans. J. Clark Murray. Boston, 1888. Pp. 27, 29, 32, 89–90, 253–257.

[1] A vast collection of Jewish laws, traditions, and commentaries, compiled by rabbis in Babylon and Palestine in the postbiblical period.

astronomical work thrown in his way, and exciting his interest. I had never seen or heard anything of the first elements of mathematics, and I had no one to give me any direction in the study: for it is needless to say, that to my father I dared not even let my curiosity in the matter be known, and, apart from that, he was not in a position to give me any information on the subject. How must the spirit of the child, thirsting for knowledge, have been inflamed by such a discovery! . . .

• • •

My brother Joseph and I were sent to Mir to school. My brother, who was about twelve years old, was put to board with a schoolmaster of some repute at that time, by name Jossel. This man was the terror of all young people, "the scourge of God"; he treated those in his charge with unheard of cruelty, flogged them till the blood came, even for the slightest offence, and not infrequently tore off their ears, or beat their eyes out. When the parents, of these unfortunates came to him, and brought him to task, he struck them with stones or whatever else came to hand, and drove them with his stick out of the house back to their own dwellings, without any respect of persons. All under his discipline became either blockheads or good scholars. I, who was then only seven years old, was sent to another schoolmaster.

• • •

By means of the instruction received from my father, but still more by my own industry, I had got on so well, that in my eleventh year I was able to pass as a full rabbi. Besides I possessed some disconnected knowledge in history, astronomy, and other mathematical sciences. I burned with desire to acquire more knowledge, but how was this to be accomplished in the lack of guidance, of scientific books, and of all other means for the purpose? I was obliged therefore to content myself with making use of any help that I could by chance obtain, without plan or method.

In order to gratify my desire of scientific knowledge, there were no means available but that of learning foreign languages. But how was I to begin? To learn Polish or Latin with a Catholic teacher was for me impossible, on the one hand because the prejudices of my own people prohibited to me all languages but Hebrew, and all sciences but the Talmud and the vast array of its commentators, on the other hand because the prejudices of Catholics would not allow them to give instruction in those matters to a Jew. Moreover I was in very low temporal circumstances. I was obliged to support a whole family by teaching, by correcting proofs of the Holy Scriptures, and by other work of a similar kind. For a long time therefore I had to sigh in vain for the satisfaction of my natural inclination.

At last a fortunate accident came to my help. I observed in some stout Hebrew volumes, that they contained several alphabets, and that the number of their sheets was indicated not merely by Hebrew letters, but that for this purpose the characters of a second and a third alphabet had also been employed, these being commonly Latin and German letters. Now, I had not the slightest idea of printing. I generally imagined that books were printed like linen, and that each page was an impression from a separate form. I presumed however that the characters, which stood in similar places, must represent one and the same letter, and as I had already heard something of the order of the alphabet in these languages, I supposed that, for example, *a,* standing in the same place as *aleph,* must likewise be an aleph in sound. In this way I gradually learnt the Latin and German characters.

• • •

I made a prosperous journey back to Hamburg, but here I fell into circumstances of the deepest distress. I lodged in a miserable house, had nothing to eat, and did not know what to do. I had received too much education to return to Poland, to spend my life in misery without rational occupation or society, and to sink back into the darkness of superstition and ignorance, from which I had hardly delivered myself with so much labour. On the other hand, to succeed in Germany was a result on which I could not calculate, owing to my ignorance of the language, as well as of the manners and customs of the people, to which I had never yet been able to adapt myself properly. I had learnt no particular profession, I had not distinguished myself in any special science, I was not even master of any language in which I could make myself perfectly intelligible. It occurred to me, therefore, that for me there was no alternative left, but to embrace the Christian religion, and get myself baptised in Hamburg. Accordingly I resolved to go to the first clergyman I should come upon, and inform him of my resolution, as well as of my motives for it, without any hypocrisy, in a truthful and honest fashion. But as I could not express myself well orally, I put my thoughts into writing in German with Hebrew characters, went to a schoolmaster, and got him to copy it in German characters. The purport of my letter was in brief as follows: —

"I am a native of Poland, belonging to the Jewish nation, destined by my education and studies to be a rabbi; but in the thickest darkness I have perceived some light. This induced me to search further after light and truth, and to free myself completely from the darkness of superstition and ignorance. In order to this end, which could be attained in my native place, I came to Berlin, where by the support of some enlightened men of our nation I studied for some years— not indeed after any plan, but merely to satisfy my thirst for knowledge. But as our nation is unable to use, not only such planless studies, but even those conducted on the most perfect plan, it cannot be blamed for becoming tired of them, and pronouncing their encouragement to be useless. I have therefore resolved, in order to secure temporal as well as eternal happiness, which depends on the attainment of perfection, and in order to become useful to myself as well as others, to embrace the Christian religion. The Jewish religion, it is true, comes, in its articles of faith, nearer to reason than Christianity. But in practical use the latter has an advantage over the former; and since morality, which consists not in opinions but in actions, is the aim of all religion in general, clearly the latter comes nearer than the former to this aim. Moreover, I hold the mysteries of the Christian religion for that which they are, that is, allegorical representations of the truths that are most important for man. By this means I make my faith in them harmonise with reason, but I cannot believe them according to their common meaning. I beg therefore most respectfully an answer to the question, whether after this confession I am worthy of the Christian religion or not. In the former case I am ready to carry my proposal into effect; but in the latter, I must give up all claim to a religion which enjoins me to lie, that is, to deliver a confession of faith which contradicts my reason."

The schoolmaster, to whom I dictated this, fell into astonishment at my audacity; never before had he listened to such a confession of faith. He shook his head with much concern, interrupted the writing several times, and became doubtful, whether the mere copying was not itself a sin. With great reluctance he copied it out, merely to get rid of the thing. I went then to a prominent clergyman, delivered my letter, and begged for a reply. He read it with great attention, fell likewise into astonishment, and on finishing entered into conversation with me.

"So," he said, "I see your intention is to embrace the Christian religion, merely in order to improve your temporal circumstances."

"Excuse me, Herr Pastor," I replied, "I think I have made it clear enough in my letter, that my object is the attainment of perfection. To this, it is true, the removal of all hindrances and the improvement of my external circumstances form an indispensable condition. But this condition is not the chief end."

"But," said the pastor, "do you not feel any inclination of the soul to the Christian religion without reference to any external motives?"

"I should be telling a lie, if I were to give you an affirmative answer."

"You are too much of a philosopher," replied the pastor, "to be able to become a Christian. Reason has taken the upper hand with you, and faith must accommodate itself to reason. You hold the mysteries of the Christian religion to be mere fables, and its commands to be mere laws of reason. For the present I cannot be satisfied with your confession of faith. You should therefore pray to God, that He may enlighten you with His grace, and endow you with the spirit of true Christianity; and then come to me again."

"If that is the case," I said, "then I must confess, Herr Pastor, that I am not qualified for Christianity. Whatever light I may receive, I shall always make it luminous with the light of reason. I shall never believe that I have fallen upon new truths, if it is impossible to see their connection with the truths already known to me. I must therefore remain what I am, —a stiffnecked Jew. My religion enjoins me to *believe* nothing, but to *think* the truth and to *practise* goodness. If I find any hindrance in this from external circumstances, it is not my fault. I do all that lies in my power."

With this I bade the pastor goodbye.

53

𢌛

José Martí

CONEY ISLAND

The revered architect of Cuba's independence and one of Spanish America's greatest poets, José Martí (1853–1895) was also a prolific journalist. Born in Havana to a Spanish father and a Cuban mother, in his early adolescence Martí became a fighter for Cuban independence from Spain. When he was only seventeen he was imprisoned in a forced labor camp by the colonial authorities and later banished to Spain. Because of his radical political beliefs and his willingness to speak out against injustice wherever he saw it, Martí was forced to lead a wandering life: At various times he lived in Spain, France, Mexico, and Venezuela. In 1881, he settled definitively in New York, where he worked as a foreign correspondent for many of the major newspapers in Spanish America and eventually reorganized and led the Cuban independence struggle. In 1892 he founded the Cuban Revolutionary party in Key West, Florida, and shortly afterwards he went with an expeditionary force to join the guerrillas already fighting the Spanish in the Cuban countryside. He was killed in a skirmish in Dos Ríos, Cuba, in 1895.

A highly cosmopolitan writer, Martí was a keen and often critical observer of life in the United States, in the tradition of the Frenchman Alexis de Tocqueville. His crónicas *(chronicles), short journalistic pieces on various subjects, which he sent every week from New York to dailies in Mexico, Venezuela, and Argentina, were hugely popular among readers in Spanish America. One of these articles, "Coney Island" (December, 1881), reflects Martí's ambivalent feelings about the United States, whose dynamism and democracy he admired even as he decried its materialism and its aggressions against its neighbors south of the border.*

𢌛

Human annals record nothing comparable to the marvelous prosperity of the United States. Do its roots go deep? Are the ties of common sacrifice and pain that hold other nations together more enduring than those of common interest? Does that colossal nation contain savage, uncontrollable forces? Does the absence of the feminine spirit, the source of the artistic sense and the complement of the national spirit, harden and corrupt the heart of that astounding country? These are questions which only time will answer.

What is apparent today is that there has never been a happier, more spirited, more comfortable, more integrated, more jovial and light-hearted people engaged in such useful pursuits in any land on earth, nor any that created and enjoyed greater wealth, covering its oceans and rivers with a greater number of gaily decorated steamers, or turning out with more bustling order and ingenuous happiness on sandy beaches, gigantic boardwalks, and brilliant, fantastic midways.

The North American newspapers are filled with extravagant descriptions of the unique beauties and singular attractions of one of these summer resorts, jammed with people, crowded with sumptuous hotels, traversed by an elevated railway, brightened by flower beds, with amusement stands, side shows, cafes, circuses, tents, legions of carriages, picturesque assemblages, portable bathhouses, barkers and splashing fountains. The echo of this fame is found in French papers.

From all parts of the United States, legions of intrepid ladies and Sunday-best farmers arrive to admire the splendid sights, the unexampled wealth, the dizzying variety, the herculean surge, the striking appearance of Coney Island, the now famous island, four years ago an abandoned sand bank, that today is a spacious amusement area providing relaxation and recreation for hundreds of thousands of New Yorkers who throng to its pleasant beaches every day.

There are four villages joined by drives, trolleys, and trains. One is called Manhattan Beach, where there is a hotel whose dining room can accommodate 4,000 persons comfortably at a sitting; another, which sprang full-blown like Minerva of helmet and lance, but armed instead with steamships, esplanades, boardwalks, murmuring orchestras, and hotels that are more akin to nations than to cities, is called Rockaway; Brighton, the least important, takes its name from an hotel of extraordinary size and ponderous construction. But what attracts the people from near and far is not distant Rockaway, monotonous Brighton, or aristocratic and sober Manhattan Beach. It is Cable Beach, with its soaring elevated which could overpass the spire of Trinity Church—twice as high as the spire of our cathedral—and from whose height one cannot look down without feeling dizzy. Cable Beach, with it two boardwalks ribbed with steel girders stretching three-quarters of a mile into the ocean on slender pillars; with its elegant palace at Sea Beach, which is only a hotel now, but was the famed Agricultural Building at the Philadelphia Centennial Exposition, from where it was transported to New

York and re-erected as if by magic on the beach at Coney Island in its original form, down to the last board. Cable Beach, with its museums at fifty cents admission, here human freaks are on display, exotic fishes, bearded ladies, melancholy dwarfs, and stunted elephants, blatantly advertised as the biggest elephants in the world. Cable Beach, with its hundred orchestras, gay dancing, endless rides for children, a gigantic cow that never runs dry although endlessly milked, fresh cider at twenty-five cents a glass, and innumerable couples of wandering lovers who bring to one's lip those tender verses of García Gutiérrez:

> Two and two
> In the meadows above
> The crested larks woo
> And the turtledoves.

Cable Beach, where entire families come to escape the foul, nauseous vapors of New York and fill their lungs with the healthy, invigorating salt air; where poor mothers, while they empty the contents of the huge hampers that contain the family lunch on the tables that are provided free in the spacious dining halls, press their wretched infants to their breasts. They seem devoured, sucked dry, consumed by the dreadful summer scourge that scythes children like a sickle wheat—infantile cholera. Steamers come and go; whistling, smoking trains, their serpent bellies swollen with families, arrive, disgorge their contents, and depart. The women rent bathing suits of blue flannel and sun hats of rough straw, which they tie with a ribbon under their chins. The men, in less cumbersome apparel, take them by the hand and enter the water. The children wait at the surf's edge for the hissing wave to lave their bare feet. But they scamper back, hiding their terror behind squeals and laughter, when it arrives, only to return in bands, as if better to defy the enemy, when it recedes. It is a game which the innocents, prostrated by the heat an hour before, never tire of playing. Or they flit in and out of the water like marine butterflies, and since each has his little pail and shovel, they amuse themselves by filling each other's bucket with the burning sand. After they have bathed, they throw themselves on the sand in imitation of their seniors of both sexes, who disregard the disapproving looks of those who think as we do in our lands, and allow themselves to be buried, pounded, and rolled in the fiery sand. This is regarded as healthy exercise and a wonderful opportunity to indulge in that superficial, vulgar, and noisy intimacy of which these prosperous people seem so fond.

But the amazing thing there is not this manner of bathing nor the cadaverous faces of the children, nor the whimsical bonnets and incredible attire of those young ladies, famed for the prodigality of their favors, careless ways, and exaggerated inclination to laughter; nor the murmurings of lovers, the bathhouses, and the operas sung from atop tables in the cafes by singers dressed as *Edgar* and *Romeo, Lucia* and *Juliet;* nor the grinning and shrieking of the Negro minstrels, who must be a far cry, alas, from the minstrels of Scotland, nor even the majestic beach, and the soft, still sunlight. The amazing thing there is the size, the quantity, the sudden tangible outcropping of human activity, that immense valve of pleasure opened to an immense nation, those dining rooms which, at a distance, seem the pitched camp of an army, those promenades that for a distance of two miles seem like carpets of heads, that daily overflow of a prodigious nation onto a prodigious beach, that mobility, that quality of advance, that purposefulness, constant change, feverish rivalry of wealth, that monumental aspect of the whole that makes that land of amusement worthy of measuring itself against the majesty of the nation which supports it, the ocean that caresses it and the sky that crowns it; that flowing tide, that overwhelming and irresistible expansiveness and the taking for granted of the marvelous: these are the things that amaze.

Other nations—ourselves among them—live devoured by a sublime demon within that drives us to the tireless pursuit of an ideal of love or glory. No sooner do we find within our grasp the ideal we pursue, with the pleasure with which one grapples an eagle, than a new desire seizes us, a new ambition spurs us on, a new aspiration sends us in pursuit of a new, burning ideal. From the captive eagle there emerges a rebellious butterfly, challenging pursuit and summoning us to follow its fitful flight.

Not so with those tranquil souls, stimulated only by a desire for gain. One scans those shimmering beaches; one strolls through these galleries as vast as plains; one ascends to the summit of those colossal structures, tall as mountains; one views the throngs seated in comfortable chairs along the seashore, filling their lungs with the fresh, invigorating air. But it is said that those from our lands who remain here long are overcome with melancholy; they seek and never find themselves. However much the first impressions gratify their senses, enamor their eyes, dazzle and bewitch their reason, the anguish of solitude overtakes them in the end, and a nostalgia for a superior spiritual world invades and oppresses them. They feel like lambs without ewe or shepherd, lost from the fold. Whether or not they rise to their eyes, bitter tears flood their souls because this great nation is void of spirit.